Cognitive Psychology

Cognitive Psychology

In and Out of the Laboratory

5e

Kathleen M. Galotti

Carleton College

$SAGE | TEXTS

Los Angeles | London | New Delhi
Singapore | Washington DC | Melbourne

Originally published in 2014 by

This South Asia adaptation published in 2015 by

SAGE Publications India Pvt Ltd
B1/I-1 Mohan Cooperative Industrial Area
Mathura Road
New Delhi 110 044, India

Published by Vivek Mehra for SAGE Publications India Pvt Ltd and printed at Saurabh Printers Pvt Ltd, Greater Noida.

Third Printing 2016

ISBN: 978-93-515-0277-7 (PB)

For Tim, for your challenges and your charm;
For Kimmie, for your energy and your enthusiasm;
and for Tandy, Bussey, Eskie, Flit, Tackle, Lizzy, and Tryker,
for keeping it real and keeping it interesting.

Thank you for choosing a SAGE product!
If you have any comment, observation or feedback,
I would like to personally hear from you.
Please write to me at **contactceo@sagepub.in**

Vivek Mehra, Managing Director and CEO,
SAGE Publications India Pvt Ltd, New Delhi

Bulk Sales

SAGE India offers special discounts
for bulk institutional purchases.

For queries/orders/inspection copy requests
write to **textbooksales@sagepub.in**

Publishing

Would you like to publish a textbook with SAGE?
Please send your proposal to **publishtextbook@sagepub.in**

Get to know more about SAGE

Be invited to SAGE events, get on our mailing list.
Write today to **marketing@sagepub.in**

This book is also available as an e-book.

BRIEF CONTENTS

Preface   XV

About the Author   XX

Chapter 1: Cognitive Psychology: History, Methods, and Paradigms   1

Chapter 2: The Brain: An Overview of Structure and Function   25

Chapter 3: Perception: Recognizing Patterns and Objects   39

Chapter 4: Attention: Deploying Cognitive Resources   66

Chapter 5: Working Memory: Forming and Using New Memory Traces   96

Chapter 6: Retrieving Memories from Long-Term Storage   119

Chapter 7: Knowledge Representation: Storing and Organizing
Information in Long-Term Memory   158

Chapter 8: Visual Imagery and Spatial Cognition   186

Chapter 9: Language   214

Chapter 10: Thinking and Problem Solving   250

Chapter 11: Reasoning and Decision Making   277

Chapter 12: Cognitive Development Through Adolescence   318

Chapter 13: Individual Differences in Cognition   347

Chapter 14: Cognition in Cross-Cultural Perspective   373

Glossary   G-1

Credits and Sources   C-1

References   R-1

Index   I-1

DETAILED CONTENTS

Preface   XV

About the Author   XX

CHAPTER 1 COGNITIVE PSYCHOLOGY: *History, Methods, and Paradigms*   1

Influences on the Study of Cognition   **4**
    Structuralism   5
    Functionalism   5
    Behaviorism   6
    Gestalt Psychology   8
    The Study of Individual Differences   9
    The "Cognitive Revolution" and the Birth of Cognitive Science   10
    General Points   13

Research Methods in Cognitive Psychology   **13**
    Experiments and Quasi-Experiments   13
    Naturalistic Observation   14
    Controlled Observation and Clinical Interviews   15
    Introspection   16
    Investigations of Neural Underpinnings   16
    General Points   16

Paradigms of Cognitive Psychology   **17**
    The Information-Processing Approach   17
    The Connectionist Approach   18
    The Evolutionary Approach   19
    The Ecological Approach   20
    General Points   21

CHAPTER 2 THE BRAIN: *An Overview of Structure and Function*   **25**

Structure of the Brain   **26**
    The Hindbrain and Midbrain   26
    The Forebrain   27

Localization of Function   **29**
    Faculty Psychology and Phrenology   29
    Studies of Aphasia and Other Mapping Techniques   30

Lateralization of Function   **31**
    Studies of Split-Brained Patients   32

Brain-Imaging Techniques   **33**
    CAT (CT) Scans   33
    Magnetic Resonance Imaging (MRI)   33

Positron Emission Tomography (PET)   43

Functional Magnetic Resonance Imaging (fMRI)   35

Other Brain-Recording Techniques   **36**

Electroencephalography (EEG)   36

Event-Related Potential (ERP)   36

Transcranial Magnetic Stimulation (TMS)   36

CHAPTER 3 PERCEPTION: *Recognizing Patterns and Objects*   **39**

Gestalt Approaches to Perception   **41**

Bottom-Up Processes   **45**

Template Matching   46

Featural Analysis   48

Prototype Matching   51

Top-Down Processes   **53**

Perceptual Learning   55

The Word Superiority Effect   56

A Connectionist Model of Word Perception   57

Direct Perception   **58**

Disruptions of Perception: Visual Agnosias   **61**

CHAPTER 4 ATTENTION: *Deploying Cognitive Resources*   **66**

Selective Attention   **68**

Bottleneck Theories   70

Spotlight Approaches   74

Schema Theory   75

Inattentional Blindness   76

Neural Underpinnings of Attention   **79**

Networks of Visual Attention   80

Event-Related Potentials and Selective Attention   80

Automaticity and the Effects of Practice   **82**

The Stroop Task   82

Automatic Versus Attentional (Controlled) Processing   83

Feature Integration Theory   86

Attentional Capture   88

Divided Attention   **89**

Dual-Task Performance   89

The Attention Hypothesis of Automatization   91

Divided Attention Outside the Laboratory: Cell Phone Usage While Driving   91

CHAPTER 5 WORKING MEMORY: *Forming and Using New Memory Traces*   **96**

Traditional Approaches to the Study of Memory   **98**
Sensory Memory   99
　　Iconic Memory   100
　　Echoic Memory   101
Short-Term Memory   103
　　Capacity and Coding   103
　　Retention Duration and Forgetting   104
　　Retrieval of Information   107

Working Memory   **108**

Executive Functioning   **113**

Neurological Studies of Memory Processes   **114**

CHAPTER 6 RETRIEVING MEMORIES FROM LONG-TERM STORAGE   **119**

Aspects of Long-Term Memory   **120**
Capacity   120
Coding   121
Retention Duration and Forgetting   121
Retrieval of Information   125
　　The Use of Mnemonics   125
　　Other Retrieval Principles   127
　　The Testing Effect   129

Subdivisions of Long-Term Memory   **129**
Semantic Versus Episodic Memory   129
Implicit Versus Explicit Memory   131
Declarative Versus Procedural Memory   134

The Levels-of-Processing View   **134**

The Reconstructive Nature of Memory   **137**
Autobiographical Memory   139
Flashbulb Memories   142
Eyewitness Memory   144
The Recovered/False Memory Debate   146

Amnesia   **149**
Anterograde Amnesia   150
Retrograde Amnesia   151

CHAPTER 7 KNOWLEDGE REPRESENTATION: *Storing and Organizing
Information in Long-Term Memory*   **158**

Organizing Knowledge   **159**
Network Models   160

ACT Models   164

Connectionist Models   166

Forming Concepts and Categorizing New Instances   **168**

The Classical View of Concepts and Categorization   169

The Prototype View of Concepts and Categorization   171

The Exemplar View of Concepts and Categorization   175

The Schemata/Scripts View of Concepts and Categorization   177

The Knowledge-Based View of Concepts and Categorization   180

CHAPTER 8 VISUAL IMAGERY AND SPATIAL COGNITION   **186**

Codes in Long-Term Memory   **188**

The Dual-Coding Hypothesis   188

The Relational-Organizational Hypothesis   189

Empirical Investigations of Imagery   **189**

Mental Rotation of Images   191

Scanning Images   194

The Nature of Mental Imagery   **198**

Principles of Visual Imagery   198

Implicit Encoding   198

Perceptual Equivalence   199

Spatial Equivalence   199

Transformational Equivalence   200

Structural Equivalence   200

Critiques of Mental Imagery Research and Theory   201

Tacit Knowledge and Demand Characteristics   201

The Picture Metaphor   202

Propositional Theory   205

Neuropsychological Findings   **206**

Spatial Cognition   **208**

CHAPTER 9 LANGUAGE   **214**

The Structure of Language   **216**

Phonology   218

Syntax   219

Semantics   222

Pragmatics   224

Language Comprehension and Production   **225**

Speech Perception   226

Speech Errors in Production   228

Sentence Comprehension   229

Comprehending Text Passages   232

Story Grammars   235

Gricean Maxims of Conversation   237

Language and Cognition   **240**

The Modularity Hypothesis   240

The Whorfian Hypothesis   241

Neuropsychological Views and Evidence   244

CHAPTER 10 THINKING AND PROBLEM SOLVING   **250**

Classic Problems and General Methods of Solution   **253**

Generate-and-Test Technique   253

Means–Ends Analysis   254

Working Backward   256

Backtracking   256

Reasoning by Analogy   258

Blocks to Problem Solving   **260**

Mental Set   261

Using Incomplete or Incorrect Representations   263

Lack of Problem-Specific Knowledge or Expertise   264

The Problem Space Hypothesis   **266**

Expert Systems   **269**

Finding Creative Solutions   **270**

Unconscious Processing and Incubation   271

Everyday Mechanisms   272

Critical Thinking   **273**

CHAPTER 11 REASONING AND DECISION MAKING   **277**

Reasoning   **278**

Types of Reasoning   **280**

Deductive Reasoning   281

Propositional Reasoning   281

Syllogistic Reasoning   285

Inductive Reasoning   288

Analogical Reasoning   289

Hypothesis Testing   290

Everyday Reasoning   291

Decision Making   **292**

Setting Goals   294

Gathering Information   294

Structuring the Decision   295

Making a Final Choice   295

Evaluating   295

Cognitive Illusions in Decision Making 295
  Availability 296
  Representativeness 299
  Framing Effects 301
  Anchoring 301
  Sunk Cost Effects 302
  Illusory Correlation 302
  Hindsight Bias 304
  Confirmation Bias 304
  Overconfidence 305

Utility Models of Decision Making 306
  Expected Utility Theory 307
  Multiattribute Utility Theory 309

Descriptive Models of Decision Making 312
  Image Theory 312
  Recognition-Primed Decision Making 313

Neuropsychological Evidence on Reasoning and Decision Making 313

CHAPTER 12 COGNITIVE DEVELOPMENT THROUGH ADOLESCENCE 318

Piagetian Theory 320
  General Principles 320
  Stages of Development 322
    The Sensorimotor Stage 322
    The Preoperational Stage 324
    The Concrete Operations Stage 326
    The Formal Operations Stage 327
  Reactions to Piaget's Theory 328

Non-Piagetian Approaches to Cognitive Development 329
  Perceptual Development in Infancy 330
  Toddlers' Acquisition of Syntax 331
  Preschoolers' Use of Memorial Strategies 334
  The Development of Reasoning Abilities in Middle and Late Childhood 335

Some Post-Piagetian Answers to the Question "What Develops?" 337
  Neurological Maturation 337
  Working-Memory Capacity and Processing Speed 338
  Attention and Perceptual Encoding 339
  The Knowledge Base and Knowledge Structures 341
  Strategies 342
  Metacognition 343

CHAPTER 13 INDIVIDUAL DIFFERENCES IN COGNITION 347

Individual Differences in Cognition 348
Ability Differences 348
Cognitive Styles 352
Learning Styles 354
Expert/Novice Differences 356
The Effects of Aging on Cognition 357

Gender Differences in Cognition 358
Gender Differences in Skills and Abilities 360
Verbal Abilities 361
Visuospatial Abilities 362
Quantitative and Reasoning Abilities 365
Gender Differences in Learning and Cognitive Styles 367
Motivation for Cognitive Tasks 368
Connected Learning 369

CHAPTER 14 COGNITION IN CROSS-CULTURAL PERSPECTIVE 373

Examples of Studies of Cross-Cultural Cognition 377
Cross-Cultural Studies of Perception 377
Picture Perception 378
Visual Illusions 381
Cross-Cultural Studies of Memory 382
Free Recall 383
Visuospatial Memory 384
Cross-Cultural Studies of Categorization 386
Cross-Cultural Studies of Reasoning 389
Cross-Cultural Studies of Counting 391

Effects of Schooling and Literacy 394

Situated Cognition in Everyday Settings 399

Glossary G-1

Credits and Sources C-1

References R-1

Index I-1

PREFACE

When I wrote the first edition of this book, more than 20 years ago, I had yet to become a mother and had just been tenured at Carleton College. I was still excited to get paid for doing a job that I loved enough to do for free. I still feel that way about what I do for a living—there is nothing better than teaching, and there are no better students than the Carleton kids I've grown so fond of. Many of them have influenced this and previous editions—in the examples I use to illustrate a concept, in their own independent projects that extend our understanding of those concepts, and in their feedback to me on previous editions. (They particularly enjoy finding my mistakes.)

Still, much has changed since 1992. I've birthed one son (now in college) and adopted an infant daughter from Vietnam (she's now 11). The students and campus have changed as well—we've all become much more adept with and dependent on technology, for example. And the field of cognitive psychology has changed a lot, placing much more emphasis both on neuroscience and situated cognition as well as making advances in the basic research that informs our understanding of how people acquire and use information. These changes certainly merit periodic revisions of the book, and voilà!—we have the fifth edition!

Undergraduate students studying psychology have different reactions to the field of cognitive psychology. Some find it exciting and elegant, covering topics essential to understanding the human mind. Cognitive psychology, after all, raises questions about how the mind works—how we perceive people, events, and things; how and what we remember; how we mentally organize information; how we call on our mental resources to make important decisions. Other students find the field of cognitive psychology technical and "geeky"—filled with complicated models of phenomena far removed from everyday life.

My goal throughout the writing of all editions of this book has been to bridge that gap—to try to reach out to students who are in the latter camp to show them what this field offers to be excited about. I think much of the problem is due to the disconnection of laboratory phenomena from everyday life. Too often, cognition texts focus exclusively on the laboratory research, without showing students how that work bears on important, real-world issues of consequence. I hope when students finish reading this book, they see why cognitive psychologists are so passionate about their topic and their research.

A textbook author can choose either to be comprehensive and strive for encyclopedic coverage or to be selective and omit many worthwhile topics and studies. I hope I've struck a balance between these extremes but must confess I prefer the latter. This reflects my own teaching goals; I like to supplement textbook chapters with primary literature from journals. I have tried to keep chapters relatively short in the hope instructors will supplement the text with other readings. My firm belief is that the best courses are those in which instructors are enthusiastic about the material; the relative brevity of the text is intended to encourage instructors to supplement and customize it with added coverage on topics they find especially interesting.

My further hope is to encourage instructors and students alike to consider cognitive phenomena as having contexts that both foster and constrain their occurrence. Universals assumed or generalized from the laboratory do not always translate to every person in every situation. Too often, topics in cognitive psychology are presented as absolute, unchanging aspects of everyone's experience. Recent work in developmental psychology, cross-cultural psychology, and individual differences strongly suggests that this presentation is, at best, oversimplification and, at worst, fiction. I hope newer work in cognitive psychology can retain its rigor and elegance but can frame questions and issues more inclusively, reflecting a recognition of the ways in which people and situations differ as well as share similarities.

ORGANIZATION OF THIS BOOK

Cognitive Psychology In and Out of the Laboratory is intended for a one-semester or one-term course for students who have already completed an introductory psychology course. We begin with a chapter that surveys the field and describes its research methods and paradigms. A chapter reviewing the structure and function of the brain comes next. These two introductory chapters are followed by chapters covering topics that would generally be regarded as core aspects of cognition: perception, attention, and memory. The emphasis in these chapters is to review both the "classic" studies that define the field and the newer approaches that challenge long-standing assumptions. Next come chapters on knowledge representation and organization. These chapters center on questions of how we mentally represent and store the vast amounts of information we acquire throughout our lives. The next few chapters, covering topics in "higher-order" cognition, include discussions of language, problem solving, reasoning, and decision making.

It is in the last three chapters where this book departs most from a "prototypical" cognitive psychology textbook. Chapter 12 gives an overview of the development of cognition from infancy through adolescence. The last two chapters, on individual differences and cross-cultural approaches, include material not often covered in cognitive psychology courses. I feel strongly that these topics belong in a thorough examination of cognitive phenomena. Although traditional cognitive psychologists don't always consider these issues in their work, I believe they ought to and, in the future, will.

All important material is integrated into the text rather than pulled out into boxes, asides, or extras that students might skip. This choice reflects my own experience as a student, as well as feedback from my students who say they find boxed material distracting and often treat it as optional. I hope that omitting these extras reinforces the message to students that their learning and mastery will be best enhanced through their own careful reading and note-taking rather than more superficial approaches such as highlighting or skimming.

NEW TO THIS EDITION

This is the most significant revision of the book to date. Not only has the book gone to a four-color presentation, but almost all of the photos, the entire interior design, and many of the figures are new. This gives the book a very new look and feel that help make it even more inviting to a diverse group of undergraduates.

Editorially, there has been much streamlining in this edition. Sections and chapters have been combined to improve the organization and to shorten the text. The 16 chapters of the fourth edition have been condensed into 14. The separate chapters on semantic memory and concepts and categorization have been integrated into one on knowledge representation. Similarly, the topics of reasoning and decision making, considered to be related examples of higher-order cognition, are now merged into a single chapter.

Throughout the book, discussion of recent work has been incorporated. To take just a few examples, there is now exposition of the configural superiority effect in Chapter 3 and the testing effect in Chapter 6 and coverage of the evaluation of work on learning styles in Chapter 13.

SUPPLEMENTS FOR INSTRUCTORS

INSTRUCTOR TEACHING SITE: www.sagepub.in/galotti_CP5e

A password-protected Instructor Teaching Site offers the following resources for each chapter:

- A **test bank** available in Microsoft Word offers a diverse set of test questions and answers to aid instructors in assessing students' progress and understanding.

- **PowerPoint presentations** designed to assist with reviews and lectures highlight essential content, features, and artwork from the book.

- **Classroom activities and discussion questions** are provided to reinforce active learning.

- A complete set of all colored images and tables used in the book for reference.

ACKNOWLEDGMENTS

The actual writing of the first edition of this book was a 5-year project. However, the groundwork for the book evolved over 15 years, stretching back to my own undergraduate and graduate education. I was fortunate to have benefited from the rigorous and dynamic teaching of Blythe Clinchy at Wellesley College and of Jonathan Baron, John Sabini, and Henry and Lila Gleitman at the University of Pennsylvania. My education and thinking about cognitive and developmental issues continued to profit from interactions with colleagues at Carleton College. Colleagues in Carleton's Cognitive Studies program—especially Roy Elveton and Susan Singer—as well as colleagues from other disciplines, including Deanna Haunsperger, Steven Kennedy, Marion Cass, Martha Paas, Steven Kozberg, and others, have sharpened my pedagogical philosophy and helped me maintain a sense of humor and balance about the craziness that periodically invades Carleton.

One of the real joys of working at Carleton has been the privilege of teaching some incredibly talented, motivated, and energetic students. Students in my Cognitive Processes courses over the past 25 years have been kind enough to give me feedback on which chapters worked well and which ones didn't, and I thank them for their candor. Other current and former Carleton students have helped me with the mundane but necessary tasks of checking references and writing for permissions throughout all of the editions; they include April Anderson, Stephanie Aubry, Julie Greene, Andy Hebrank, Simin Ho, Allison Logeman, Diane Mistele, Matt Maas, Kitty Nolan, Emily Snyder, Scott Staupe, Jennifer Tourjé, Elizabeth White, and James Whitney. My current and former administrative assistants, Marianne Elofson, Pamela Gaggioli, Ruby Hagberg, and Lorie Tuma, all have helped with one or more of these editions and just generally make the workplace much more inviting than it would otherwise be.

Several current and former students posed for some of the photographs in this edition, including Zoe Cohen, Zack Delpier, Jonathan Rowe, Jane Tandler, and Jessa Youso. Because my students have contributed so much to my thinking and professional development, it is special to me to be able to make them a tangible part of the book!

Carleton College has supported this book through various sabbaticals and faculty development grants. Then Dean of the College Roy Elveton enthusiastically endorsed and funded this endeavor from the start. A dean can really make a difference in a faculty member's professional development, and Roy often went above and beyond the call of duty for me and several of my talented colleagues at Carleton during his brief administrative tenure. His belief in my ability to write this book is something I will always be grateful for. As a colleague in our Cognitive Science Program and the Philosophy Department, Roy remains a most trusted mentor.

I owe a special debt to Vicki Knight, editor of the first and third editions. Her wise counsel, sharp sense of humor, love of animals, and excellent taste in restaurants made our collaboration a very engaging one. I never would have been able to finish the first book without her, and without the first book, there would not have been any subsequent ones! For the fourth edition, Michele Sordi took the reins, and I am again extremely fortunate to have her as editor for this edition (even though the book—and she—have migrated to a new publisher). As I've gotten to know Michele, I've been impressed by her good communication, her willingness to listen and negotiate, and her savvy knowledge of current trends in textbook publishing.

For this edition, I also enjoyed excellent collaboration with Eve Oettinger, Sarita Sarak, and Reid Hester. I can't say enough about how great they are to work with! They are on top of a myriad of details, they are patient as I try to learn a new system; they are fun to talk with on the phone, and they are so highly competent at their jobs it is almost frightening. Eve has been my go-to contact at Sage Publishing from the first set of reviews through production of this edition, and she's a real gem.

The cover designer, Scott Van Atta, worked with my plea to use the Robert Neffson painting, integrating text and elements beautifully. Paula Fleming is, no kidding, the best copy editor I've ever had, with eagle eyes and an attention to detail that never fails to astound. I like to believe her undergraduate experiences at Carleton have a lot to do with her excellence. I was told ahead of time that I would really enjoy working with Eric Garner, my production editor—and the prediction was spot on. I admire his ability to juggle multiple facets of a project, see the trees and the forest, and stay in a good mood throughout the process. Anthony Paular, the art director, has shown extraordinary patience with my complete lack of artistic ability and my lack of good vocabulary to describe the new figures I envision in my head.

Reviewers of past editions of the book, who have also made important contributions, include for the first edition Sharon Armstrong, Central College (Pella, Iowa); Terry Au, University of California, Los Angeles; Ira Fischler, University of Florida; John H. Flowers, University of Nebraska–Lincoln; Margery Lucas, Wellesley College; Robert Seibel; Steven M. Smith, Texas A&M University; and Margaret Thomas, University of Central Florida; and for the second edition Brenda J. Byers, Arkansas State University; Robert Campbell, Clemson University; L. Mark Carrier, Florida State University; David G. Elmes, Washington and Lee University; Ira Fischler, University of Florida; John H. Flowers, University of Nebraska–Lincoln; Nancy Franklin, SUNY–Stony Brook; Peter Graf, University of British Columbia; Morton A. Heller, Winston-Salem State University; Lorna Jarvis, Hope College–Peale Science Center; Douglas Johnson, Colgate University; James Juola, University of Kansas; Richard Metzger, University of Tennessee; John Pani, University of Louisville; Aimee M. Surprenant, Purdue University; Joseph Thompson, Washington and Lee University; and Lori R. Van Wallendael, University of North Carolina. For the third edition, I received many very constructive and helpful suggestions and insights for strengthening the book from Lisa Abrams, University of Florida; Nancy Alvarado, California State Polytechnic University, Pomona; Jeffrey Anastasi, Arizona State University; Krystine Batcho, Le Moyne College; Stephanie Buchert, Kent State University; Walt Chromiak, Dickinson College; John Flowers, University of Nebraska–Lincoln; Allen Keniston, University of Wisconsin–Eau Claire; Kristy Nielson, Marquette University; Evelyn Schaefer, University of Winnipeg; Elizabeth Spievak, Hanover College; Mark Stewart, Willamette University; Brian Sundermeier, University of Minnesota–Minneapolis; and Lori Van Wallendael, University of North Carolina–Charlotte.

Fourth edition reviewers are Sue Astley, Cornell College; Robert Boughner, Rogers State University; Laura Bowman, Central Connecticut State University; Myra Fernandes, University of Waterloo; Allen Keniston, University of Wisconsin; James MacDougall, Eckard College; Chuck Robertson, North Georgia College & State University; Linda Rueckert, Northeastern Illinois University; Dennis Shaffer, Ohio State University; Alycia Silman, Wake Forest University; Ami Spears, Mercer University; and Frank Yeatman, Stonehill College.

I have always benefitted from the wise comments of good reviewers, but I have to say that the set of prerevision reviews Sarita Sarak obtained for me this time were truly the best I've ever seen. The following reviewers all provided useful commentary and feedback on portions of this fifth edition at various stages: Michael Dodd, University of Nebraska–Lincoln; Rhiannon E. Hart, Rochester Institute of Technology; Kendall J. Eskine, Loyola University New Orleans; Conor T. McLennan, Cleveland State University; Stephen Dopkins, The George Washington University; Ruth Tincoff, Bucknell University; and Rolf Nelson, Wheaton College.

The remaining gaps and shortcomings in the book reflect my own stubbornness.

ABOUT THE AUTHOR

Kathleen M. Galotti holds a BA in psychology and economics from Wellesley College, as well as an MA and a PhD in psychology and an MSE in computer and information sciences from the University of Pennsylvania. At Carleton College she holds the title Professor of Cognitive Science and serves as the director of that interdisciplinary program, which she helped establish in 1989. She also is a former chair of the Psychology Department. She teaches courses in cognitive and developmental psychology and cognitive science and has also taught courses in statistics and introductory psychology.

Dr. Galotti's research centers on the development of reasoning and decision-making skills from the preschool period through adulthood and on the styles with which adolescents and adults plan for the future, make important life commitments, and learn new information. Her research has been funded through the National Science Foundation, the Spencer Foundation, and the National Institutes of Health. She is the author of *Making Decisions That Matter: How People Face Important Life Choices* (Erlbaum, 2002), as well as the textbook *Cognitive Development: Infancy Through Adolescence* (Sage, 2011). She has also authored or co-authored dozens of articles in peer-reviewed journals.

Dr. Galotti is the parent of two children, Timothy and Kimberlynn, and spends much of her time enjoying their youthful exuberance and energy. In her spare time, she raises and trains Bernese mountain dogs and shows them in competition in licensed obedience trials, and she is an approved obedience and rally judge for the American Kennel Club.

CHAPTER 1

COGNITIVE PSYCHOLOGY
History, Methods, and Paradigms

CHAPTER OUTLINE

Influences on the Study of Cognition
Structuralism
Functionalism
Behaviorism
Gestalt Psychology
The Study of Individual Differences
The "Cognitive Revolution" and the Birth of Cognitive Science
General Points
Research Methods in Cognitive Psychology
Experiments and Quasi-Experiments
Naturalistic Observation
Controlled Observation and Clinical Interviews
Introspection
Investigations of Neural Underpinnings
General Points
Paradigms of Cognitive Psychology
The Information-Processing Approach
The Connectionist Approach
The Evolutionary Approach
The Ecological Approach
General Points

This book is about cognitive psychology—that branch of psychology concerned with how people acquire, store, transform, use, and communicate information (Neisser,

1967). Put differently, cognitive psychology deals with our mental life: what goes on inside our heads when we perceive, attend, remember, think, categorize, reason, decide, and so forth.

To get a better feel for the domain of cognitive psychology, let's consider a few examples of cognitive activity.

> You're walking along a dark, unfamiliar city street. It's raining and foggy, and you are cold and a bit apprehensive. As you walk past a small alley, you catch some movement out of the corner of your eye. You turn to look down the alley and start to make out a shape coming toward you. As the shape draws nearer, you are able to make out more and more features, and you suddenly realize that it's . . .

What cognitive processes are going on in this admittedly melodramatic example? In general, this example illustrates the initial acquisition and processing of information. In particular, the cognitive processes depicted include **attention**, mentally focusing on some stimulus (the mysterious shape); **perception**, interpreting sensory information to yield meaningful information; and **pattern recognition**, classifying a stimulus into a known category. In recognizing the shape as something familiar, you no doubt called on **memory**, the storage facilities and retrieval processes of cognition. All this processing occurred rapidly, probably within a few seconds or less. Most of the cognitive processing in this example appears so effortless and automatic that we usually take it for granted.

Here's another example:

> You're in a crowded public place, such as a shopping mall during the holiday season. Throngs of people push past you, and you're hot and tired. You head for a nearby bench, aiming to combine some rest with some people watching. As you make your way, a young woman about your age jostles up against you. You both offer polite apologies ("Oh, excuse me!" "Sorry!"), glancing at each other as you do. She immediately exclaims, "Oh, it's you! How are you? I never thought I'd run into anyone I know here—can you believe it?" You immediately paste a friendly but vague smile on your face to cover your frantic mental search: Who is this woman? She looks familiar, but why? Is she a former classmate? Did you and she attend camp together? Is she saying anything that you can use as a clue to place her?

This example illustrates your use of memory processes, including **recognition** (you see the woman as familiar) and **recall** (you try to determine where you know her from). Other cognitive processes are involved here too, although they play a lesser role. For instance, you perceive the entity talking to you as a person, specifically a woman, more specifically a vaguely familiar woman. You pay attention to her. You may be using various strategies or techniques of **reasoning** and **problem solving** to try to figure out who she is. Your success or failure at this task may also depend on your mental organization of the knowledge you have accumulated in your lifetime—your **knowledge representation**. To communicate with her, you use **language** as well as nonverbal cues or signals. Eventually, you'll have to use **decision making** to determine how to deal with the situation: Will you admit your forgetfulness, or will you try to cover it up?

As these two examples demonstrate, our everyday lives involve a great deal of cognition. Furthermore, this everyday cognition is complex, often involving several cognitive processes. We tend to remain unaware of this complexity, however, because much of our cognitive processing occurs so often, so rapidly, and with so little effort that we may not even know it is taking place.

In both of the preceding examples, several cognitive processes were occurring either simultaneously or very closely in time. In fact, it is nearly impossible to specify, in either of these examples, exactly how many cognitive processes occurred or in what sequence. This uncertainty typifies everyday situations: So much is going on so quickly that we can't even be sure of what information is being received or used. How, then, can cognition be studied with any precision?

This kind of problem is one all scientists face: how to study a naturally occurring phenomenon with sufficient experimental rigor to draw firm conclusions. The answer, for many, is to try to isolate the phenomenon and bring it (or some stripped-down version of it) into the laboratory. With this approach, the challenge is to decide what is essential and what is inessential about the phenomenon under study.

For example, in studying how memory works, psychologists have often used experiments in which people are presented with lists of words or nonsense syllables. The experimenters then control or systematically vary variables such as the complexity, length, frequency, meaningfulness, relatedness, and rate of presentation of items on the list along with the state of alertness, expertise, practice, and interest of the research participants. The experimenters assume that factors that increase or decrease performance in the laboratory will also increase or decrease performance under less controlled conditions. Further, the researchers assume that although in everyday life people do not encounter material to be remembered in this manner, the processes of memory work in essentially the same ways in laboratory experiments as in everyday life. So if increasing the number of items to be remembered decreases memory performance in a laboratory, then we can expect that having to remember more information is more difficult than remembering less in an everyday situation.

The key challenge for all scientists, however, is to make sure the laboratory tasks they develop preserve the essential workings of the processes under study. The most rigorously controlled experiment is of, at best, limited value if the phenomenon being studied does not occur or occurs in significantly different ways outside the laboratory. Unfortunately, there is no simple or guaranteed way to ensure that laboratory tasks model everyday tasks. Therefore, students and other "consumers" of science must take a critical stance when considering how experimental situations apply to everyday ones. Throughout this book, we will be looking at how laboratory models do or don't accurately describe, explain, and predict cognitive processing in real life. We will also consider how situational and personal factors, such as people's level of development, personality variables, degree of expertise, gender, and cultural background, affect cognitive processing.

Before we discuss specific cognitive processes, however, an overview of the field of cognitive psychology will provide a useful framework within which to consider specific topics, experiments, and findings in the field. We will first examine the historical roots of cognitive psychology to see how the field has developed. Next, we'll look at traditional and common research methods used in cognitive psychology. Finally, we'll consider four paradigms, or schools of thought, that represent the current streams of thought in the field.

INFLUENCES ON THE STUDY OF COGNITION _____

A complete treatise on how modern cognitive psychology has evolved over the course of human history could fill several volumes and would obviously be beyond our scope. Worth noting, however, is that several ideas about certain mental abilities date back to at least the Greek philosophers Aristotle and Plato (Murray, 1988). For example, both of these philosophers wrote extensively on the nature of memory. Plato, for instance, likened storing something in memory to writing on a wax tablet. In other writings, he compared the mind to an aviary in which many birds are flying, and memory retrieval to trying to catch a specific bird: Sometimes you can, but at other times you can grab only a nearby bird. Similarly, when I try to recall the name of the girl who sat behind me in third grade, I have trouble latching onto exactly the right one (was it Joan? Joanne? Anne?), but my choices are probably pretty close.

Other historians of psychology trace the field's roots to the philosophers of the 17th to 19th centuries, including John Locke, David Hume, John Stuart Mill, René Descartes, George Berkeley, and Immanuel Kant. These philosophers also debated the nature of mind and knowledge, with Locke, Hume, Berkeley, and Mill following Aristotle and a more empiricist position and Descartes and Kant aligning with Plato and a nativist position.

Briefly, **empiricism** rests on the tenet that knowledge comes from an individual's own experience—that is, from the empirical information that people collect from their senses and experiences. Empiricists recognize individual differences in genetics but emphasize human nature's malleable, or changeable, aspects. Empiricists believe people are the way they are, and have the capabilities they have, largely because of previous learning. One mechanism by which such learning is thought to take place is through the mental **association** of two ideas. Locke (1690/1964) argued that two distinct ideas or experiences, having nothing to do with each other, could become joined in the mind simply because they happened to occur or to be presented to the individual at the same time. Empiricists accordingly believe the environment plays a powerful role in determining one's intellectual (and other) abilities.

Nativism, by contrast, emphasizes the role of constitutional factors—of native ability— over the role of learning in the acquisition of abilities and tendencies. Nativists attribute differences in individuals' abilities less to differences in learning than to differences in original, biologically endowed capacities and abilities. Nativism is an important idea in cognitive psychology, as we will see. Nativists often suggest that some cognitive functions come built in as part of our legacy as human beings. "Hard-wired" functions such as working memory, for example, are attributed to innate structures of the human mind that are present in at least rudimentary form at birth and are not learned, formed, or created as a result of experience.

Interestingly, only in the last 120 years have central cognitive issues such as the nature of mind and the nature of information in the mind been seen as amenable to scientific psychological investigation. Indeed, until the 1870s, no one really thought to ask whether actual data could help resolve any of these questions. When people began doing so, experimental psychology was born. However, the nativist–empiricist debate is still a controversial one in the 21st century (Pinker, 2002). We will look next at the different schools of experimental psychology that laid the foundations for cognitive psychology today.

STRUCTURALISM

Many students are surprised to find out that psychology as a formal discipline has been around for little more than a century. Historians often date the "founding" of the field of psychology back to 1879, when Wilhelm Wundt converted a laboratory into the first institute for research in experimental psychology (Fancher, 1979). Wundt wanted to establish a "science of mind" to discover the laws and principles that explained our immediate conscious experience. In particular, Wundt wanted to identify the simplest essential units of the mind. In essence, he wanted to create a table of "mental elements," much like a chemist's periodic chart. Once the set of elements was identified, Wundt believed, psychologists could determine how these units combine to produce complex mental phenomena. Wundt foresaw an entire field devoted to the study of how systematically varying stimuli would affect or produce different mental states; he described this field in a volume titled *Principles of Physiological Psychology* (Fancher).

Wundt and his students carried out hundreds of studies, many involving a technique of investigation called **introspection**. Although this term today connotes "soul searching," Wundt's technique was much more focused. It consisted of presenting highly trained observers (usually graduate students) with various stimuli and asking them to describe their conscious experiences. Wundt assumed that the raw materials of consciousness were sensory and thus "below" the level of meaning. In particular, Wundt thought any conscious thought or idea resulted from a combination of sensations that could be defined in terms of exactly four properties: *mode* (for example, visual, auditory, tactile, olfactory), *quality* (such as color, shape, texture), *intensity*, and *duration*.

Wundt's goal was to "cut through the learned categories and concepts that define our everyday experience of the world" (Fancher, 1979, p. 140). Wundt believed strongly that with proper training, people could detect and report the workings of their own minds. A student of Wundt, Edward B. Titchener, applied the term **structuralism** to his own endeavors as well as to Wundt's (Hillner, 1984). The term was meant to convey Wundt's focus on what the elemental components of the mind are rather than on the question of *why* the mind works as it does.

The method of introspection, unfortunately, proved problematic, as we'll see shortly. Nonetheless, modern cognitive psychologists owe Wundt more than a historical debt. A pioneer in the study of many cognitive phenomena, he was the first to approach cognitive questions scientifically and the first to design experiments to test cognitive theories.

FUNCTIONALISM

While Wundt was working in Leipzig, an American named William James was working to establish the new discipline of psychology in the United States. In many ways, Wundt and James were opposites. A prolific researcher who personally carried out or supervised hundreds of rigorous experiments, Wundt was not known for his interpersonal style. James (the brother of the writer Henry James), in contrast, carried out little original research but wrote eloquently about psychological findings and their relevance to everyday life (Fancher, 1979). His textbook *The Principles of Psychology* (1890/1983) is still highly regarded and widely cited today.

James regarded psychology's mission to be the explanation of our experience. Like Wundt, James was interested in conscious experience. Unlike Wundt, however, James was not interested in the elementary units of consciousness. Instead, he asked *why* the mind works the way it does. He assumed that the way the mind works has a great deal to do with its *function*—the purposes of its various operations. Hence, the term **functionalism** was applied to his approach.

James's writings, which introduced psychological questions to American academics, still offer food for thought to students and teachers of psychology, perhaps because they so directly address everyday life. Consider one of the best-known chapters in his textbook, on "habit." James saw habit as the "flywheel of society" (1890/1983, Vol. 1, p. 125), a mechanism basic to keeping our behavior within bounds. He saw habits as inevitable and powerful and drew from this a practical conclusion:

> Every smallest stroke of virtue or of vice leaves its ever so little scar. The drunken Rip Van Winkle, in Jefferson's play, excuses himself for every fresh dereliction by saying, "I won't count this time!" Well! he may not count it, and a kind Heaven may not count it; but it is being counted none the less. Down among his nerve-cells and fibres the molecules are counting it, registering and storing it up to be used against him when the next temptation comes. (James, Vol. 1, p. 131)

James's point, of course, is that people should take great care to avoid bad habits and establish good ones. He offered advice about how to do so, urging people to never allow an exception when trying to establish a good habit, to seize opportunities to act on resolutions, and to engage in a "little gratuitous effort" every day to keep the "faculty of effort" alive (James, 1890/1983, Vol. 1, p. 130). Other American psychologists shared James's assumptions and approaches. Fellow functionalists such as John Dewey and Edward L. Thorndike, for example, shared James's conviction that the most important thing the mind did was to let the individual adapt to her or his environment.

Functionalists drew heavily on Darwinian evolutionary theory and tried to extend biological conceptions of adaptation to psychological phenomena (Hillner, 1984). Structuralists and functionalists differed in their methods as well as their focus. The structuralists were convinced that the proper setting for experimental psychology was the laboratory, where experimental stimuli could be stripped of their everyday meanings to determine the true nature of mind. The functionalists disagreed sharply with this approach, attempting instead to study mental phenomena in real-life situations. Their basic belief was that psychologists should study whole organisms doing whole, real-life tasks (Hillner).

BEHAVIORISM

You probably learned the terms *classical conditioning* and *instrumental conditioning* in your introductory psychology class. The Russian psychologist Ivan Pavlov used the first, and psychologists such as Edward Thorndike used the second, to explain psychological phenomena strictly in terms of observable stimuli and responses.

In the United States, a school of psychology known as **behaviorism** took root in the 1930s and dominated academic psychology until well into the 1960s. Many regard it as a branch of functionalism (Amsel, 1989). One of the general doctrines of behaviorism is that references to unobservable, subjective mental states (such as consciousness), as well as to unobservable, subjective processes (such as expecting, believing, under-standing, remembering, hoping for, deciding, and perceiving), are to be banished from psychology proper, which behaviorists took to be the scientific study of behavior.

Behaviorists rejected such techniques of study as introspection, which they found in principle to be untestable. In an article published in 1913, John Watson most directly described his view of what psychology is and isn't:

> Psychology as the behaviorist views it is a purely objective natural science. Its theoretical goal is the prediction and control of behavior. Introspection forms no essential part of its methods, nor is the scien-tific value of its data dependent upon the readiness with which they lend themselves to interpretation in terms of consciousness. The behaviorist, in his efforts to get a unitary scheme of animal response, recognizes no dividing line between man and brute. The behavior of man, with all of its refinement and complexity, forms only a part of the behaviorist's total scheme of investigation. (p. 158)

Why did behaviorists so disdain the technique of introspection? Mainly because of its obviously subjective nature and its inability to resolve disagreements about theory. Suppose two observers are presented with the same stimulus and one reports an experience of "greenness" and the other an experience of "green-yellowness." Which one is correct? Is one misrepresenting or misinterpreting his or her experience? If no physiological cause (for example, color blindness) explains the different reports, then the scientist is left with an unresolvable dispute. Titchener restricted his research participants to graduate students trained to introspect "properly" (advising those who couldn't learn to do this to find another career). This, however, created more problems than it solved. The reasoning was circular: How do we know that a particular sensation is a true building block of cognition? Because trained observers report it to be so. How do we know the observers are trained? Because they consistently report that certain sensations and not others are the true elements of consciousness.

Watson, in fact, regarded all "mental" phenomena as reducible to behavioral and physi-ologic responses. Such things as "images" and "thoughts," he believed, resulted from low-level activity of glands or small muscles. In his first textbook, Watson cited evidence showing that when people report they are "thinking," muscles in the tongue and larynx are actually moving slightly. Thought, for Watson, simply amounted to perception of these muscle movements (Fancher, 1979).

Watson's contribution to cognitive psychology—banishing all "mental language" from use—was largely negative, insofar as he believed the scientific study of mental phe-nomena was simply not possible. Watson and his followers did, however, encourage psychologists to think in terms of measures and research methods that moved beyond subjective introspection, thereby challenging later psychologists to develop more rigor-ous and more testable hypotheses and theories, as well as stricter research protocols.

B. F. Skinner (1963/1984), psychology's best-known behaviorist, took a different tack with regard to mental events and the issue of mental representations. Skinner argued that such "mentalistic" entities as images, sensations, and thoughts should *not* be excluded simply because they are difficult to study. Skinner believed in the existence of images, thoughts, and the like and agreed they were proper objects of study, but he objected to treating mental events and activities as fundamentally different from behavioral events and activities. In particular, he objected to hypothesizing the exis-tence of **mental representations** (internal depictions of information), which he took to be internal copies of external stimuli. Skinner believed images and thoughts were likely to be no more or less than verbal labels for bodily processes. But even if mental events *were* real and separate entities, Skinner believed, they were triggered by external environmental stimuli and gave rise to behaviors. Therefore, he held, a simple functional analysis of the relationship between the stimuli and behaviors would avoid the well-known problems of studying mental events (Hergenhahn, 1986).

Other behaviorists were more accepting of the idea of mental representations. Edward Tolman, for example, believed that even rats have goals and expectations. As he explained it, a rat learning to run a maze must have the goal of attaining food and must acquire an internal representation—some cognitive map or other means of depicting information "in the head"—to locate the food at the maze's end. Tolman's work centered on demonstrating that animals had both expectations and internal representations that guided their behavior.

GESTALT PSYCHOLOGY

The school of **Gestalt psychology** began in 1911 in Frankfurt, Germany, in a meeting of three psychologists: Max Wertheimer, Kurt Koffka, and Wolfgang Köhler (Murray, 1988). As the name *Gestalt* (a German word that loosely translates to "configuration" or "shape") suggests, these psychologists' central assumption was that psychological phenomena could not be reduced to simple elements but rather had to be analyzed and studied in their entirety. Gestalt psychologists, who studied mainly perception and problem solving, believed an observer did not construct a coherent perception from simple, elementary sensory aspects of an experience but instead apprehended the total structure of an experience as a whole.

As a concrete example, consider Figure 1.1. Notice that (A), (B), and (C) contain the same elements— namely, eight equal line segments. However, most people experience the three arrays quite differently, seeing (A) as four pairs of line segments, (B) as eight line segments haphazardly

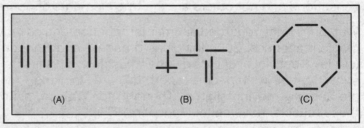

■ Figure 1.1: Examples of Gestalt figures. Although (A), (B), and (C) all contain eight equal lines, most people experience them differently, seeing (A) as four pairs of lines, (B) as eight unrelated lines, and (C) as a circle made up of eight line segments.

arranged, and (C) as a circle or, more precisely, an octagon made up of eight line segments. The arrangement of lines—that is, the relationships among the elements as a whole—plays an important role in determining our experience.

The Gestalt psychologists thus rejected structuralism, functionalism, and behaviorism as offering incomplete accounts of psychological and, in particular, cognitive experiences. They chose to study people's subjective experience of stimuli and to focus on how people use or impose structure and order on their experiences. They believed that the mind imposes its own structure and organization on stimuli and, in particular, organizes perceptions into *wholes* rather than discrete parts. These wholes tend to simplify stimuli. Thus, when we hear a melody, we experience not a collection of individual sounds but larger, more organized units: melodic lines.

THE STUDY OF INDIVIDUAL DIFFERENCES

Yet another strand of the history of psychology is important to mention here, even though no particular "school" is associated with it: the investigations into individual differences in human cognitive abilities by Sir Francis Galton and his followers. Galton, a half-cousin of Charles Darwin, inherited a substantial sum in his early 20s that afforded him the time and resources to pursue his interests. A child prodigy himself (he read and wrote by the age of 2½), Galton trained in medicine and mathematics at Cambridge University, England. Like many of his fellow students (and many of today's college students), Galton felt a great deal of academic pressure and competitiveness and "was constantly preoccupied with his standing relative to his fellow students" (Fancher, 1979, p. 257). This strong preoccupation (which may have contributed to a breakdown he suffered at Cambridge) developed into a lifelong interest in measuring intellectual ability.

Galton's interest in intellectual differences among people stemmed in part from his reading of his cousin Charles Darwin's writings on evolution. Darwin believed animals (including humans) evolved through a process he called natural selection, by which certain inherited traits are perpetuated because individuals possessing those traits are more likely to survive and reproduce. Galton wondered whether intellectual talents could also be inherited. Galton noticed "intelligence" or "smartness" or "eminence" seemed to run in families; that is, smart parents appeared to produce smart children. Of course, this could be explained in terms of either genetics or environment (for example, intelligent parents may have greater resources to spend on their children's education and/or greater interest or motivation to do so). Thus Galton's question of how large a role genetics plays in intelligence was difficult to answer. To address it, Galton put his mathematical training to use in analyzing data (usually family trees of "eminent" men) and, later, inventing statistical tests, some of which are still used today.

Galton (1883/1907) studied a variety of cognitive abilities, in each case focusing on ways of measuring the ability and then noting its variation among different individuals. Among the abilities he studied (in both laboratory and "naturalistic" settings) was mental imagery. He developed a questionnaire, instructing respondents to "think of some definite object—suppose it is your breakfast-table as you sat down this morning—and consider carefully the picture that rises before your mind's eye" (p. 58). He then asked, Is the image dim or clear? Are all of the objects in the image well defined? Does part of the image seem to be better defined? Are the colors of the objects in the image distinct and natural? Galton was surprised to discover much variability in this capacity: Some respondents reported almost no imagery; others experienced images so vividly they could hardly tell they *were* images.

Galton left a large legacy to psychology and to cognitive psychology in particular. His invention of tests and questionnaires to assess mental abilities inspired later cognitive psychologists to develop similar measures. His statistical analyses, later refined by other statisticians, allowed hypotheses to be rigorously tested. His work on mental imagery is still cited by current investigators. Most broadly, Galton's work challenged psychologists, both those who believed genetic influences are crucially important and those strongly opposed to the idea, to think about the nature of mental—that is, cognitive—abilities and capacities.

THE "COGNITIVE REVOLUTION" AND THE BIRTH OF COGNITIVE SCIENCE

Despite the early attempts to define and study mental life, psychology, especially American psychology, came to embrace the behaviorist tradition in the first five decades of the 1900s. A number of historical trends, both within and outside academia, came together in the years during and following World War II to produce what many psychologists think of as a "revolution" in the field of cognitive psychology. This **cognitive revolution**, a new series of psychological investigations, was mainly a rejection of the behaviorist assumption that mental events and states were beyond the realm of scientific study or that mental representations did not exist. In particular, the "revolutionaries" came to believe no complete explanation of a person's functioning could exist that did not refer to the person's mental representations of the world. This directly challenged the fundamental tenet of radical behaviorism, that concepts such as "mental representation" were not needed to explain behavior.

One of the first of these historical trends was a product of the war itself: the establishment of the field of **human factors engineering**. During the war, military personnel had to be trained to operate complicated pieces of equipment. Engineers quickly found they needed to design equipment (such as instrument operating panels, radar screens, and communication devices) to suit the capacities of the people operating it. Lachman, Lachman, and Butterfield (1979) offered an anecdote about why such problems were important to solve:

> One type of plane often crashed while landing. It turned out that the lever that the pilot had to use for braking was near the lever that retracted the landing gear. During landing, the pilot could not take his eyes off the runway: He had to work by touch alone. Sometimes pilots retracted their landing gear instead of putting on their brakes; they touched the ground with the belly of the plane at top speed. The best way to keep them from crashing was not to exhort them to be careful; they were already highly motivated to avoid crashing and getting killed. Improving training procedures was also an inefficient approach; pilots with many safe landings behind them committed this error as well as rookie pilots.
>
> The most reasonable approach was to redesign the craft's controls so that completely different arm movements were required for braking and for retracting the landing gear. (p. 57)

Psychologists and engineers thus developed the concept of the man–machine system, now more accurately referred to as the **person–machine system**: the idea that machinery operated by a person must be designed to interact with the operator's physical, cognitive, and motivational capacities and limitations.

Psychologists in World War II also borrowed concepts, terminology, and analogies from communications engineering. Engineers concerned with the design of such things as telephones and telegraph systems talked about the exchange of information through various "channels" (such as telegraph wires and telephone lines). Different kinds of channels differ in how much information they can transmit per unit of time and how accurately. Humans were quickly seen to be a particular kind of communication channel, sharing properties with better known, inanimate communications channels. Thus, people came to be described as **limited-capacity processors** of information.

What is a limited-capacity processor? As the name suggests, it means that people can do only so many things at once. When I'm typing, I find it difficult (actually, impossible) to simultaneously keep up my end of a conversation or read an editorial or follow a television news broadcast. Similarly, when I concentrate on balancing my checkbook,

I can't also recite multiplication tables or remember all the teachers I've had from kindergarten on. Although I can do some tasks at the same time (I can fold the laundry while I watch television), the number and kinds of things I can do at the same time are limited.

A classic paper focusing on capacity limitations was authored by George Miller, in 1956. This paper, entitled "The Magical Number Seven, Plus or Minus Two," observed that (a) the number of unrelated things we can perceive distinctly without counting, (b) the number of unrelated things on a list we can immediately remember, and (c) the number of stimuli we can make absolute discriminations among are for most normal adults between five and nine. Miller's work exemplified how the limits of people's cognitive capacities could be measured and tested.

At about the same time, developments in the field of **linguistics**, the study of language, made clear that people routinely process enormously complex information. Work by linguist Noam Chomsky revolutionized the field of linguistics, and both linguists and psychologists began to see the central importance of studying how people acquire, understand, and produce language.

In addition, Chomsky's early work (1957, 1959, 1965) showed that behaviorism cannot adequately explain language. Consider the question of how language is acquired. A behaviorist might explain language acquisition as the result of parents' reinforcing a child's grammatical utterances and punishing (or at least not reinforcing) ungrammatical utterances. However, both linguists and psychologists soon realized such an account had to be wrong. For one thing, psychologists and linguists who observed young children with their parents found that parents typically respond to the *content* rather than to the *form* of the child's language utterances (Brown & Hanlon, 1970). For another, even when parents (or teachers) explicitly tried to correct children's grammar, they could not. Children seemed simply not to "hear" the problems, as is evident in the following dialogue (McNeill, 1966, p. 69):

CHILD: Nobody don't like me.
MOTHER: No, say, "Nobody likes me." [eight repetitions of this dialogue]
MOTHER: No, now listen carefully; say, "Nobody likes me."
CHILD: Oh! Nobody don't likes me.

(Clearly, this mother was more focused on the child's linguistic than emotional development!)

Chomsky's work thus posed a fundamental challenge to psychologists: Here were human beings, already shown to be limited-capacity processors, quickly acquiring what seemed an enormously complicated body of knowledge—language—and using it easily. How could this be?

Reversing engineers' arguments that machines must be designed to fit people's capabilities, many linguists tried to describe structures complex enough to process language. Chomsky (1957, 1965) argued that underlying people's language abilities is an implicit system of rules, collectively known as a *generative grammar*. These rules allow speakers to construct, and listeners to understand, sentences that are "legal" in the language. For example, "Did you eat all the oat bran cereal?" is a legal, well-formed sentence, but "Bran the did all oat eat you cereal?" is not. Our generative grammar, a mentally represented system of rules, tells us so, because it can produce (generate) the first sentence but not the second.

Chomsky (1957, 1965) did not believe all the rules of a language are consciously accessible to speakers of that language. Instead, he believed the rules operate implicitly: We don't necessarily know exactly what all the rules are, but we use them rather easily to produce understandable sentences and to avoid producing gobbledygook.

Another strand of the cognitive revolution came from developments in **neuroscience**, the study of the brain-based underpinnings of psychological and behavioral functions. A major debate in the neuroscience community had been going on for centuries, all the way back to Descartes, over the issue of **localization of function**. To say a function is "localized" in a particular region is, roughly, to claim that the neural structures supporting that function reside in a specific brain area. In a major work published in 1929, a very influential neuroscientist, Karl Lashley, claimed there was no reason to believe that major functions (such as language and memory) are localized (H. Gardner, 1985).

However, research in the late 1940s and 1950s accumulated to challenge that view. Work by Donald Hebb (1949) suggested that some kinds of functions, such as visual perceptions, were constructed over time by the building of *cell assemblies*—connections of sets of cells in the brain. In the 1950s and 1960s, Nobel Prize–winning neurophysiologists David Hubel and Torsten Wiesel (1959) discovered that specific cells in the visual cortex of cats were in fact specialized to respond to specific kinds of stimuli (orientation of lines, particular shapes). Equally important, Hubel and Weisel demonstrated the importance of early experience on nervous system development. Kittens who were experimentally restricted to an environment with only horizontal lines would fail to develop the ability to perceive vertical lines. This work suggested that at least some functions are localized in the brain (H. Gardner, 1985).

There is yet one more thread to the cognitive revolution, also dating from about World War II: the development of computers and artificially intelligent systems. In 1936, a mathematician named Alan Turing wrote a paper describing "universal machines," mathematical entities that are simple in nature but capable in principle of solving logical or mathematical problems. This paper ultimately led to what some psychologists and computer scientists call the **computer metaphor**: the comparison of people's cognitive activities to an operating computer. Just as computers have to be fed data, people have to acquire information.

Both computers and people often store information and must therefore have structures and processes that allow such storage. People and computers often need to recode information—that is, to change the way it is recorded or presented. People and computers must also manipulate information in other ways—transform it, for example, by rearranging it, adding to or subtracting from it, deducing from it, and so on. Computer scientists working on the problem of **artificial intelligence** study how to program computers to solve the same kinds of problems humans can and to try to determine whether computers can use the same methods that people apparently use to solve such problems.

During the 1970s, researchers in different fields started to notice they were investigating common questions: the nature of mind and of cognition; how information is acquired, processed, stored, and transmitted; and how knowledge is represented. Scholars from fields such as cognitive psychology, computer science, philosophy, linguistics, neuroscience, and anthropology, recognizing their mutual interests, came together to found an interdisciplinary field known as **cognitive science**. H. Gardner (1985) even gave this field a birth date—September 11, 1956—when several founders of the field attended a symposium on information theory at the Massachusetts Institute of Technology.

H. Gardner (1985) pointed out that the field of cognitive science rests on certain common assumptions. Most important among these is the assumption that cognition must be analyzed at what is called the *level of representation*. This means cognitive scientists agree that cognitive theories incorporate such constructs as symbols, rules, images, or ideas—in Gardner's words, "the stuff . . . found between input and output" (p. 38). Thus, cognitive scientists focus on representations of information rather than on how nerve cells in the brain work or on historical or cultural influences.

GENERAL POINTS

Each school of psychology described so far has left a visible legacy to modern cognitive psychology. Structuralism asked the question, What are the elementary units and processes of the mind? Functionalists reminded psychologists to focus on the larger purposes and contexts that cognitive processes serve. Behaviorists challenged psychologists to develop testable hypotheses and to avoid unresolvable debates. The Gestalt psychologists pointed out that an understanding of individual units would not automatically lead to an understanding of whole processes and systems. Galton demonstrated that individuals can differ in their cognitive processing. Developments in engineering, computer science, linguistics, and neuroscience have uncovered processes by which information can be efficiently represented, stored, and transformed, providing analogies and metaphors for cognitive psychologists to use in constructing and testing models of cognition. As we take up particular topics, we will see more of how cognitive psychology's different roots have shaped the field.

Keep in mind that cognitive psychology shares in the discoveries made in other fields, just as other fields share in the discoveries made by cognitive psychology. This sharing and borrowing of research methods, terminology, and analyses gives many investigators a sense of common purpose. It also all but requires cognitive psychologists to keep abreast of new developments in fields related to cognition.

RESEARCH METHODS IN COGNITIVE PSYCHOLOGY

Throughout this book, we will be reviewing different empirical studies of cognition. Before we plunge into those studies, however, we will look at some of the different kinds of studies that cognitive psychologists conduct. The following descriptions do not exhaust all the studies a cognitive psychologist *could* conduct but should acquaint you with the major methodological approaches to cognitive psychology.

EXPERIMENTS AND QUASI-EXPERIMENTS

The most frequently adopted approach to cognitive investigations is the psychological experiment. A true **experiment** is one in which the experimenter manipulates one or more independent variables (the experimental conditions) and observes how the recorded measures (dependent variables) change as a result. A major distinction between experiments and observational methods (which we will examine in just a bit) is the investigator's degree of experimental control. Having experimental control means the experimenter can assign participants to different experimental conditions so as to minimize preexisting differences between them. Ideally, the experimenter can control all variables that might affect the performance of research participants *other than* the variables on which the study is focusing.

For example, an experiment in cognitive psychology might proceed as follows: An experimenter recruits a number of people for a study of memory; randomly assigns them to one of two groups; and presents each group with exactly the same stimuli, using exactly the same procedures and settings and varying only the instructions (the independent variable) for the two groups of participants. The experimenter then observes the overall performance of the participants on a later memory test (the dependent variable).

This example illustrates a **between-subjects design**, wherein different experimental participants are assigned to different experimental conditions and the researcher looks for differences in performance between the two groups. In contrast, a **within-subjects design** exposes the same experimental participants to more than one condition. For example, participants might perform several memory tasks but receive a different set of instructions for each task. The investigator then compares the performance of the participants in the first condition to the performance of the *same* participants in another condition.

Some independent variables preclude random assignment (that is, having the experimenter assign a research participant to a particular condition in an experiment). For example, experimenters cannot reassign participants to a different gender, ethnicity, age, or educational background. Studies that appear in other ways to be experiments but that have one or more of these factors as independent variables (or fail to be true experiments in other ways) are called **quasi-experiments** (D. T. Campbell & Stanley, 1963).

Scientists value experiments and quasi-experiments because they enable researchers to isolate causal factors and make better-supported claims about causality than is possible using observational methods alone. However, many experiments fail to fully capture real-world phenomena in the experimental task or research design. The laboratory setting or the artificiality or formality of the task may prevent research participants from behaving normally, for example. Further, the kinds of tasks amenable to experimental study may not be those most important or most common in everyday life. As a result, experimenters sometimes risk studying phenomena that relate only weakly to people's real-world experience.

NATURALISTIC OBSERVATION

As the name suggests, **naturalistic observation** consists of an observer watching people in familiar, everyday contexts going about their cognitive business. For example, an investigator might watch as people try to figure out how to work a new automated teller machine (ATM) at an airport. Ideally, the observer remains as unobtrusive as possible so as to disrupt or alter the behaviors being observed as little as possible. In this example, the investigator might stand nearby and surreptitiously note what people who use the ATM do and say. Being unobtrusive is much harder than it might sound. The observer needs to make sure the people being observed are comfortable and do not feel as though they are "under a microscope." At the same time, the observer wants to avoid causing the people being observed to "perform" for the observer. In any case, the observer can hardly fully assess his or her own effects on the observation: After all, how can one know what people would have done had they not been observed?

Observational studies have the advantage that the things studied occur in the real world and not just in an experimental laboratory. Psychologists call this property **ecological validity**. Furthermore, the observer has a chance to see just how cognitive processes work in natural settings: how flexible they are, how they are affected by environmental changes, how rich and complex actual behavior is. Naturalistic observation is relatively easy to do, doesn't typically require a lot of resources to carry out, and does not require other people to formally volunteer for study.

The disadvantage of naturalistic observation is a lack of **experimental control**. The observer has no means of isolating the causes of different behaviors or reactions. All he can do is collect observations and try to infer relationships among them. However plausible different hypotheses may seem, the observer has no way to verify them. Some psychologists believe that naturalistic observation is most appropriately used to identify problems, issues, or phenomena of interest to then be investigated with other research methods.

A second problem, which all scientists face, is that an observer's recordings are only as good as her initial plan for what is important to record. The settings and people she chooses to observe, the behaviors and reactions she chooses to record, the manner of recording, and the duration and frequency of observation all influence the results and conclusions she can later draw. Moreover, whatever biases the observer brings to the study (and, as we will see in Chapter 11, all of us are subject to a large number of biases) limit and possibly distort the recordings made.

CONTROLLED OBSERVATION AND CLINICAL INTERVIEWS

As the term **controlled observation** suggests, this method gives researchers some degree of influence over the setting in which observations are conducted. Investigators using this research method try to standardize the setting for all participants, in many cases manipulating specific conditions to see how participants will be affected. In the ATM machine example, for instance, the investigator might arrange for the ATM machine to display different instructions to different people. The study would still be observational (because the researcher would not control who used the machine or when), but the researcher would be trying to channel the observed behavior in certain ways.

In **clinical interviews**, the investigator tries to channel the process even more. The investigator begins by asking each participant a series of open-ended questions. The interviewer might ask the participant to think about a problem and describe his approaches to it. With the clinical interview method, however, instead of allowing the participant to respond freely, the interviewer follows up with another set of questions. Depending on the participant's responses, the interviewer may pursue one or another of many possible lines of questioning, trying to follow each participant's own thinking and experience while focusing on specific issues or questions.

INTROSPECTION

We have already seen one special kind of observation, dating back to the laboratory of Wilhelm Wundt. In the technique of introspection, the observer observes his or her own mental processes. For example, participants might be asked to solve complicated arithmetic problems without paper or pencil and to "think aloud" as they do so.

Introspection has all the benefits and drawbacks of other observational studies, plus a few more. One additional benefit is that observing one's own reactions and behavior may give one better insight into an experience and the factors that influenced it, thus yielding a richer, more complete picture than an outsider could observe. But observing yourself is a double-edged sword. Although perhaps a better observer in some ways than an outsider, you may also be more biased in regard to your own cognition. People observing their own mental processes may be more concerned with their level of performance and may be motivated to subtly and unconsciously distort their observations. They may try to make their mental processes appear more organized, logical, thorough, and so forth than they actually are, and they may be unwilling to admit when their cognitive processes seem flawed or random. Moreover, with some cognitive tasks (especially demanding ones), observers may have few resources left with which to observe and record while they work on the task.

INVESTIGATIONS OF NEURAL UNDERPINNINGS

Much work in cognitive neuroscience involves examining people's brains. Before the second half of the 20th century, this kind of examination could be conducted only after a patient died, during an autopsy. However, since the 1970s, various techniques of **brain imaging**, the construction of pictures of the anatomy and functioning of intact brains, have been developed. We will discuss many of these techniques in Chapter 2.

GENERAL POINTS

This brief outline of different research designs barely scratches the surface of all the important things we could look at. There are a few general points to note, however. First, cognitive psychologists use a variety of approaches to study cognitive phenomena. In part, these approaches reflect philosophical differences among psychologists over what is important to study and how tradeoffs should be made between certain drawbacks and benefits. In part, they reflect the intellectual framework or paradigms (examples to be discussed very shortly) within which researchers work. They may also reflect how amenable different areas of cognition are to different research approaches.

Second, no research design is perfect. Each has certain potential benefits and limitations that researchers must weigh in designing studies. Students, professors, and other researchers must also carefully think, both critically and appreciatively, about how the research design answers the research question posed. I hope you'll keep these thoughts in mind as you discover in the rest of this book examples of the wide variety of research studies that cognitive psychologists have carried out.

PARADIGMS OF COGNITIVE PSYCHOLOGY _____

Having looked at cognitive psychology's historical roots and research methods, we can now focus on modern cognitive psychology. In this section, we will examine the four major paradigms that cognitive psychologists use in planning and executing their research.

First of all, what is a **paradigm**? The word has several related meanings, but you can think of it as a body of knowledge structured according to what its proponents consider important and what they do not. Paradigms include the assumptions investigators make in studying a phenomenon. Paradigms also specify what kinds of experimental methods and measures are appropriate for an investigation. Paradigms are thus intellectual frameworks that guide investigators in studying and understanding phenomena.

In learning about each paradigm, ask yourself the following questions: What assumptions underlie the paradigm? What questions or issues does the paradigm emphasize? What analogies (such as the analogy between the computer and the mind) does the paradigm use? What research methods and measures does the paradigm favor?

THE INFORMATION-PROCESSING APPROACH

The **information-processing approach** dominated cognitive psychology in the 1960s and 1970s and remains influential today (Atkinson & Shiffrin, 1968). As its name implies, the information-processing approach draws an analogy between human cognition and computerized processing of information. Central to the information-processing approach is the idea that cognition can be thought of as information (what we see, hear, read about, think about) passing through a system (us or, more specifically, our minds).

Researchers following an information-processing approach often assume that information is processed (received, stored, recoded, transformed, retrieved, and transmitted) in stages and that it is stored in specific places while being processed. One goal within this framework, then, is to determine what these stages and storage places are and how they work.

Other assumptions underlie the information-processing approach as well. One is that people's cognitive abilities can be thought of as "systems" of interrelated capacities. We know different individuals have different cognitive capacities—different attention spans, memory capacities, and language skills, to name a few. Information-processing theorists try to find the relationships between these capacities to explain how individuals go about performing specific cognitive tasks.

In accordance with the computer metaphor, information-processing theorists assume that people, like computers, are general-purpose symbol manipulators. In other words, people, like computers, can perform astonishing cognitive feats by applying only a few mental operations to symbols (such as letters, numbers, propositions, or scenes). Information is then stored symbolically, and the way it is coded and stored greatly affects how easy it is to use it later (as when we want to recall information or manipulate it in some way).

A general-purpose information-processing system is shown in Figure 1.2. Note the various memory stores where information is held for possible later use and the different processes that operate on the information at different points or that transfer it from store to store. Certain processes, such as detection and recognition, are used at the beginning of information processing; others, such as recoding or retrieval, have to do with memory storage; still others, such as reasoning or concept formation, have to do with putting information together in new ways. In this model, boxes represent stores, and arrows represent

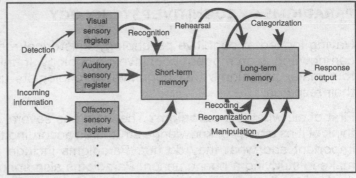

■ Figure 1.2: A typical information-processing model.

processes (leading some to refer to information-processing models as "boxes-and-arrows" models of cognition). Altogether, information-processing models are depicted best by something computer scientists call *flowcharts*, which illustrate the sequential flow of information through a system.

The information-processing tradition is rooted in structuralism, in that its followers attempt to identify the basic capacities and processes we use in cognition. The computer metaphor used in this approach also shows an indebtedness to the fields of engineering and communications. Psychologists working in the information-processing tradition are interested in relating individual and developmental differences to differences in basic capacities and processes. Typically, information-processing psychologists use experimental and quasi-experimental techniques in their investigations.

THE CONNECTIONIST APPROACH

Early in the 1980s, researchers from a variety of disciplines began to explore alternatives to the information-processing approach that could explain cognition. The framework they established is known as **connectionism** (sometimes also called *parallel-distributed processing,* or *PDP*). Its name is derived from models depicting cognition as a network of connections among simple (and usually numerous) processing units (McClelland, 1988). Because these units are sometimes compared to *neurons*, the cells that transmit electrical impulses and underlie all sensation and muscle movement, connectionist models are sometimes called **neural networks** (technically speaking, there are distinctions between connectionist and neural network models, but we will not review them here).

Each unit is connected to other units in a large network. Each unit has some level of activation at any particular moment in time. The exact level of activation depends on the input to that unit from both the environment and the other units to which it is connected. Connections between two units have weights, which can be positive or negative. A positively weighted connection causes one unit to excite, or raise the level of activation of units to which it is connected; a negatively weighted connection has the opposite effect, inhibiting or lowering the activation of connected units.

One major difference between the information-processing and the connectionist approaches is the manner in which cognitive processes are assumed to occur. In information-processing models, cognition is typically assumed to occur *serially*—that is, in discrete stages (first one process occurs, which feeds information into the next process, which feeds information into the next process, and so on). In contrast, most (but not all) connectionist models assume that cognitive processes occur in *parallel,* many at the same time.

The connectionist framework allows for a wide variety of models, which can vary in the number of units hypothesized, number and pattern of connections among units, and connection of units to the environment. All connectionist models share the assumption, however, that there is no need to hypothesize a central processor that directs the flow of information from one process or storage area to another. Instead, different patterns of activation account for the various cognitive processes (Dawson, 1998). Knowledge is not stored in various storehouses (such as the boxes depicted in Figure 1.2) but within connections between units. Learning occurs when new connective patterns are established that change the weights of connections between units.

Feldman and Ballard (1982), in an early description of connectionism, argue that this approach is more consistent with the way the brain functions than an information-processing approach. The brain, they argue, is made up of many neurons connected to one another in various complex ways. The authors assert that

> the fundamental premise of connectionism is that individual neurons *do not transmit large amounts of symbolic information.* Instead they compute by being *appropriately connected* to large numbers of similar units. This is in sharp contrast to the conventional computer model of intelligence prevalent in computer science and cognitive psychology. (p. 208)

Rumelhart (1989) puts the issue more simply: "Connectionism seeks to replace the computer metaphor of the information-processing framework with a brain metaphor" (p. 134).

Like the information-processing approach, connectionism draws from structuralism an interest in the elements of cognitive functioning. However, whereas information processors look to computer science, connectionists look to cognitive neuropsychology (the study of people with damaged or otherwise unusual brain structures) and cognitive neuroscience for information to help them construct their theories and models. Information-processing accounts of cognition try to provide explanations at a more abstract, symbolic level than do connectionist accounts. Connectionist models are more concerned with the "subsymbolic" level: how cognitive processes actually could be carried out by a brain. Connectionism, being much newer than information processing, is just beginning to map out explanations for individual and developmental differences. Most connectionist work seeks to replicate the findings of experimental and quasi-experimental research using computer programs based on a neural network model.

THE EVOLUTIONARY APPROACH

Some of our most remarkable cognitive abilities and achievements are ones we typically take for granted. Two that come immediately to mind are the ability to perceive three-dimensional objects correctly and the ability to understand and produce language. These abilities may seem rather trivial and mundane—after all, a 3-year-old can do quite a bit of both. However, researchers in the field of artificial intelligence quickly found that it is not easy to program computers to carry out even rudimentary versions of these tasks (Winston, 1992).

So why can young children do these tasks? In fact, how can a wide range of people, even people who don't seem particularly gifted intellectually, carry them out with seemingly little effort? Some psychologists search for an answer in evolutionary theory (Cosmides & Tooby, 2002; Richerson & Boyd, 2000). The argument goes something like this: Like other animal minds, the human mind is a biological system, one that has evolved over generations. Like other animal minds, it too is subject to the laws of natural selection. Therefore, the human mind has responded to evolutionary pressures to adapt in certain ways rather than others in response to the environments encountered by our predecessors. Evolutionary psychologist Leda Cosmides (1989) notes that the environments our ancestors experienced were not simply physical but ecological and social as well.

The idea here is that humans have specialized areas of competence produced by our evolutionary heritage. Cosmides and Tooby (2002) argue that people have "a large and heterogeneous set of evolved, reliably developing, dedicated problem-solving programs, each of which is specialized to solve a particular domain or class of adaptive problems (e.g., grammar acquisition, mate acquisition, food aversion, way-finding)" (p. 147). In other words, people have special-purpose mechanisms (including cognitive mechanisms) specific to a certain context or class of problems.

Cosmides and Tooby (2000, 2002) believe that some of the most significant issues our ancestors faced involved social issues, such as creating and enforcing social contracts. To do this, people must be especially good at reasoning about costs and benefits, and they must be able to detect cheating in a social exchange. Therefore, evolutionary psychologists predict that people's reasoning will be especially enhanced when they are reasoning about cheating, a topic we examine in much greater detail in Chapter 11.

In general, evolutionary psychologists believe we understand a system best if we understand the evolutionary pressures on our ancestors. Explaining how a system of reasoning works, they believe, is much easier if we understand how evolutionary forces shaped the system in certain directions rather than other, equally plausible ones.

THE ECOLOGICAL APPROACH

A fourth major approach to the study of cognition comes from both psychologists and anthropologists and overlaps much more with the evolutionary approach than it does with either the information-processing or connectionist approach. The central tenet of this approach is that cognition does not occur in isolation from larger cultural contexts; all cognitive activities are shaped by the culture and by the context in which they occur.

Jean Lave, a current theorist in this tradition, has conducted some fascinating work that illustrates the **ecological approach**. Lave (1988) describes the results of the Adult Math Project as "an observational and experimental investigation of everyday arithmetic practices" (p. 1). Lave, Murtaugh, and de la Rocha (1984) studied how people used arithmetic in their everyday lives. In one study, they followed people on grocery-shopping trips to analyze how and when people calculate "best buys." They found that people's methods of calculation varied with the context. This was somewhat surprising, because students in our culture are taught to use the same specified formulas on all problems of a given type to yield one definite numerical answer. To illustrate, compare a typical third-grade arithmetic problem presented by teachers to students—"Brandi had eight seashells. Nikki had five more. How many seashells did the two of them have together?"—with the following problem, posed and solved by one of the grocery shoppers, regarding the number of apples she should purchase for her family for the week:

> There's only about three or four [apples] at home, and I have four kids, so you figure at least two apiece in the next three days. These are the kinds of things I have to resupply. I only have a certain amount of storage space in the refrigerator, so I can't load it up totally.... Now that I'm home in the summertime, this is a good snack food. And I like an apple sometimes at lunchtime when I come home. (Murtaugh, 1985, p. 188)

Lave (1988) points out a number of contrasts between this arithmetic problem solving and the kind used in solving school problems. First, the second example has many possible answers (for example, 5, 6, 9), unlike the first problem, which has one (13). Second, the first problem is given to the problem solver to solve; the second is constructed by the problem solver herself. Third, the first problem is somewhat disconnected from personal experience, goals, and interests, whereas the second comes out of practical daily living.

Although there has been much recent interest in the ecological approach, the idea of studying cognition in everyday contexts actually arose several years earlier. A major proponent of this viewpoint was J. J. Gibson, whose work on perception we will discuss at length in Chapter 3. Ulric Neisser, a friend and colleague of Gibson, wrote a book in 1976 aimed at redirecting the field of psychology toward studying more "realistic" cognitive phenomena.

We can see the influences of both the functionalist and the Gestalt schools on the ecological approach. The functionalists focus on the purposes served by cognitive processes, certainly an ecological question. Gestalt psychology's emphasis on the context surrounding any experience is likewise compatible with the ecological approach. The ecological approach would deny the usefulness (and perhaps even the possibility) of studying cognitive phenomena in artificial circumstances divorced from larger contexts. Thus, this tradition relies less on laboratory experiments or computer simulations and more on naturalistic observation and field studies to explore cognition.

GENERAL POINTS

Each of these four paradigms makes an important contribution to cognitive psychology, and in some ways the four offer complementary perspectives on how the underlying principles of cognition ought to be investigated and understood. The information-processing paradigm, for example, focuses researchers on the functional aspects of cognition—what kinds of processes are used toward what ends. The connectionist approach, in contrast, focuses on the underlying "hardware"—how the global cognitive processes described by an information-processing model are implemented in the human brain. The evolutionary approach centers on questions of how a cognitive system or function has evolved over generations. The ecological approach stresses the need to consider the context of any cognitive process to understand more completely how that process functions in the real world.

Not all cognitive research fits neatly into one of these four paradigms. Some research incorporates parts of different paradigms; some fits no paradigm neatly. However, I hope these paradigms will provide a useful backdrop against which to consider individual studies.

This framework offers a sense of where we're headed in the rest of the book, as we take up specific cognitive topics in more detail. Throughout, you should examine how the research studies discussed bear on cognitive activities in your everyday life. Are the questions posed, and the research approaches used to answer them, appropriate? How do the theoretical assumptions shape the way the questions are posed? What do the research findings mean, and what new questions do they raise?

Cognitive psychology is my field. Not surprisingly, I've found it full of fascinating, deeply rooted questions; complex as well as elegant; and relevant to many real-world issues. I hope that you too, after reading this book, will find this field an important one—a field worth knowing about.

Summary

1. Cognition plays a large role in our everyday existence. We take much of our cognitive experience for granted because the ways in which we function cognitively are so routine we simply don't pay attention to them. Nonetheless, on closer inspection, we see that many cognitive activities are astonishingly complex.

2. We've examined different traditions in the study of cognition, tracing the history of the field back at least as far as Wundt's Leipzig laboratory. We've seen how major schools of thought—structuralism, functionalism, behaviorism, and Gestalt approaches—have framed cognitive questions.

3. Structuralism, a school of psychology associated with Wilhelm Wundt, seeks to discover the laws and principles that explain our immediate conscious experience. In particular, structuralists want to identify the simplest essential units of the mind and to determine how these units combine to produce complex mental phenomena.

4. Functionalism, a school of psychology associated with William James, takes as the basic aim of psychology understanding the function of the mind—the ways in which mental functions let individuals adapt to their environment.

5. Behaviorism, regarded by some as a branch of functionalism, takes as the central aim of psychology the scientific study of behavior, an observable consequence of psychological experience. Radical behaviorists insist that references to unobservable, subjective, mental states (such as consciousness) as well as to unobservable, subjective processes (such as expecting, believing, understanding, remembering, hoping for, deciding, perceiving) should be banished from psychology proper.

6. The school of Gestalt psychology holds as its central assumption that psychological phenomena cannot be reduced to simple elements but must be analyzed and studied in their entirety. Gestalt psychologists believe that observers do not construct a coherent perception from simple, elementary sensory aspects of an experience but instead apprehend the total structure of an experience as a whole.

7. Francis Galton emphasized the idea that individuals differ, even as adults, in their cognitive capacities, abilities, and preferences.

8. The present study of cognitive psychology grows out of, and contributes to, innovations in other fields, such as computer science, communications, engineering, linguistics, evolution, and anthropology.

9. Cognitive psychology draws upon many different research methods, including experiments, quasi-experiments, controlled observation, and naturalistic observation.

10. We've reviewed four paradigms, or intellectual frameworks of the study of cognition. Paradigms specify the assumptions, guiding questions, and research methods that investigators adopt.

11. The information-processing paradigm emphasizes stagelike processing of information and specific storage of that information during processing.

12. The connectionist approach depicts cognitive processing as a pattern of excitation and inhibition within a network of connections among simple (and usually numerous) processing units that operate in parallel.

13. The evolutionary paradigm examines how a cognitive process has been shaped by environmental pressure over long periods of time.

14. The ecological paradigm stresses the ways in which the environment and the context shape the way cognitive processing occurs.

Review Questions

1. What roles do laboratory experiments and naturalistic observation play in cognitive research?

2. What similarities and differences exist among the following three "schools" of psychology: structuralism, functionalism, behaviorism?

3. What is a mental representation, and how is this concept viewed by Gestalt psychologists, information-processing psychologists, behaviorist psychologists, and connectionists?

4. Describe how research on individual differences might bear on cognitive psychology.

5. What was the "cognitive revolution"? What resulted from it?

6. Describe and critique the major research methods of cognitive psychology.

7. Compare and contrast the four major paradigms of cognitive psychology reviewed in this chapter (information processing, connectionism, the evolutionary approach, the ecological approach).

Key Terms

artificial intelligence

association

attention

behaviorism

between-subjects design

brain imaging

clinical interview

cognitive revolution

cognitive science

computer metaphor

connectionism

controlled observation

decision making

ecological approach

ecological validity

empiricism

experiment

experimental control

functionalism

Gestalt psychology

human factors engineering

information-processing approach

introspection

knowledge representation

language

limited-capacity processor

linguistics

localization of function

memory

mental representation

nativism

naturalistic observation

neural network

neuroscience

paradigm

pattern recognition

perception

person–machine system

problem solving

quasi-experiment

reasoning

recall

recognition

structuralism

within-subjects design

CHAPTER OUTLINE

Structure of the Brain
  The Hindbrain and Midbrain
  The Forebrain
Localization of Function
  Faculty Psychology and Phrenology
  Studies of Aphasia and Other Mapping Techniques
Lateralization of Function
  Studies of Split-Brained Patients
Brain-Imaging Techniques
  CAT (CT) Scans
  Magnetic Resonance Imaging (MRI)
  Positron Emission Tomography (PET)
  Functional Magnetic Resonance Imaging (fMRI)
Other Brain-Recording Techniques
  Electroencephalography (EEG)
  Event-Related Potential (ERP)
  Transcranial Magnetic Stimulation (TMS)

When the field of cognitive psychology began (in the 1950s and '60s), cognitive psychologists found the workings of the brain to be quite interesting, but not necessarily relevant to their understanding of how cognitive processes worked. The idea was that description of cognitive processes and structures was best done at a level of abstraction above the neural level, which was thought to be too inordinately complicated. Many feared that a description of how each neuron in the brain worked would not yield a comprehensible explanation of, say, how your learning of French verb endings takes place. The level of detail of the neurons in your brain would simply not provide a very useful explanation, whereas one couched in terms of theoretical ideas such as memory storage areas (which might not physically exist) would. Theorists began to distinguish between different "levels" of explanation—a symbolic and abstract one for cognition as opposed to a neural level for the actual functioning of cognitive processes in real time.

There is still strong argument among psychologists, biologists, philosophers, and computer scientists over which level of explanation is most useful for different kinds of understanding. However, increasing numbers of cognitive psychologists have become interested in the functioning of the brain as an underpinning for cognitive activity. Although the question of which level provides the most useful explanation remains, many cognitive psychologists feel they cannot investigate cognition without a working knowledge of how the brain develops and functions.

Of course, the topic of brain functioning and its relationship to cognition is itself a vast and complex one, and only brief highlights are given here. The interested student is referred to other, in-depth treatments of the topic (e.g., Gazzaniga, 2009; Reuter-Lorenz, Baynes, Mangun, & Phelps, 2010). First, some growth statistics: The brain grows from 0 to 350 grams (about three-quarters of a pound) during the prenatal period, but this growth doesn't stop at birth. The maximum brain weight of 1,350 grams (about three pounds) is achieved when the individual is about 20 years old (Nowakowski & Hayes, 2002). Most postbirth growth takes place before the child's 4th birthday, but some changes continue through adulthood.

STRUCTURE OF THE BRAIN

There are obviously a lot of different structures to talk about when we talk about the brain. We'll need to discuss first the different divisions of the brain, and we'll begin with a phylogenetic division. Figure 2.1 shows various structures of the adult brain, including the midbrain. All of the structures above the midbrain are part of the forebrain (including the cerebral lobes, which we will discuss in detail momentarily). All of the structures below the midbrain are part of the hindbrain. In our brief discussion, we will focus specifically on the cerebral cortex, a part of the forebrain. However, it is worth talking briefly about the hindbrain and midbrain first.

THE HINDBRAIN AND MIDBRAIN

The **hindbrain** contains the pons, the medulla, and the cerebellum (B. Garrett, 2011). The **medulla** (sometimes called the *medulla oblongata*) transmits information from the spinal cord to the brain and regulates

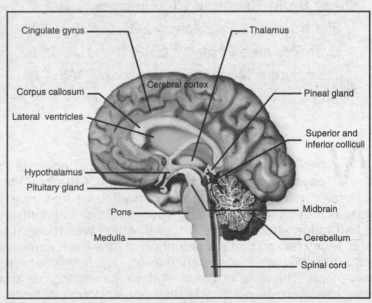

■ Figure 2.1: Lateral view of the interior features of the human brain.

life support functions such as respiration, blood pressure, coughing, sneezing, vomiting, and heart rate (Pritchard & Alloway, 1999). The **pons** (the name derives from the Latin word for *bridge*) also acts as a neural relay center, facilitating the "crossover" of information between the left side of the body and the right side of the brain and vice versa. It is also involved in balance, sleep, and arousal and in the processing of both visual and auditory information.

The **cerebellum** contains neurons that coordinate muscular activity (B. Garrett, 2011). It is one of the most primitive brain structures. It also governs balance and is involved in general motor behavior and coordination. Brain lesions in the cerebellum can cause irregular and jerky movements, tremors, and impairment of balance and of gait. The cerebellum has also been implicated in people's ability to shift attention between visual and auditory stimuli and deal with temporal stimuli such as rhythm (Akshoomoff & Courchesne, 1994).

The **midbrain** is located (unsurprisingly) in the middle of the brain. Many of the structures contained in the midbrain (such as the inferior and superior colliculi) are involved in relaying information between other brain regions, such as the cerebellum and forebrain. Another midbrain structure, the reticular formation, helps keep us awake and alert and is involved in arousal (B. Garrett, 2011).

THE FOREBRAIN

Because of our interest in cognitive issues, we will focus the remainder of our discussion of the brain on the **forebrain**. Some of the structures of the forebrain are also presented in Figure 2.1. The **thalamus,** for example, is yet another structure for relaying information, especially to the cerebral cortex (Pritchard & Alloway, 1999), which we will talk about shortly. The **hypothalamus** controls the

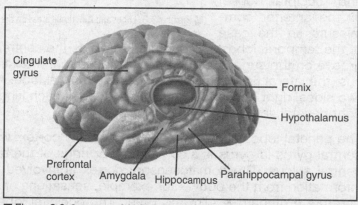

Cingulate gyrus

Fornix

Hypothalamus

Prefrontal cortex   Amygdala   Hippocampus   Parahippocampal gyrus

■ Figure 2.2: Structures of the limbic system.

pituitary gland by releasing hormones, specialized chemicals that help to regulate other glands in the body. The hypothalamus also controls so-called homeostatic behaviors, such as eating, drinking, temperature control, sleeping, sexual behaviors, and emotional reactions.

Other structures in the forebrain are shown in Figure 2.2. The **hippocampus**, involved in the formation of long-term memories, and the **amygdala**, which modulates the strength of emotional memories and is involved in emotional learning, are located in the forebrain (actually, inside the medial temporal lobes, which are described below), as are the basal ganglia, which are involved in the production of motor behavior.

We will discuss many of these structures, including the hippocampus and amygdala, in the chapters to come. For the present, we will focus on the cerebrum (from the

Latin word for *brain*), the largest structure in the brain. It consists of a layer called the **cerebral cortex**, consisting of about a half-dozen layers of neurons with white matter beneath, which carries information between the cortex and the thalamus or between different parts of the cortex.

Figure 2.3 presents a more detailed diagram of the cerebral cortex, which neurologists divide into four lobes: **frontal** (underneath the forehead), **parietal** (underneath the top rear part of the skull), **occipital** (at the back of the head), and **temporal** (on the side of the head). The left and right hemispheres are connected by either the corpus callosum (in the case of the frontal, parietal, and occiptal lobes) or the anterior commissure (in the case

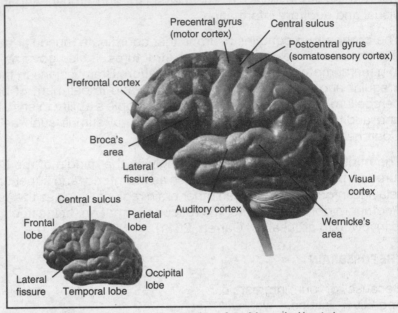

■ Figure 2.3: Lobes and functional areas on the surface of the cerebral hemispheres.

of the temporal lobes). A structure known as the central sulcus (a prominent, shallow groove on the surface of the brain) divides the frontal and parietal lobes; another sulcus, the lateral fissure, helps define the temporal lobe. Actually, since our heads have two sides, right and left, we have two lobes of each kind—the right frontal, left frontal, right parietal, left parietal, and so forth.

The parietal lobes contain the somatosensory cortex, which is contained in the postcentral gyrus (a gyrus is a convolution or ridge of the brain), the area just behind the central sulcus. The somatosensory cortex is involved in the processing of sensory information from the body— for example, sensations of pain, pressure, touch, or temperature (Pritchard & Alloway, 1999). The occipital lobes process visual information, and the temporal lobes process auditory information and enable the recognition of certain stimuli such as faces. Because the temporal lobes are just above structures such as the amygdala and hippocampus, both involved in memory, damage to the temporal lobes can result in memory disruption as well.

The frontal lobes have three separate regions. The **motor cortex** (located in the precentral gyrus) directs fine motor movement; the premotor cortex seems to be involved in planning such movements. The **prefrontal cortex** is involved with what neuroscientists call **executive functioning**—planning, making decisions, implementing strategies, inhibiting inappropriate behaviors, and using working memory to process information. Damage to certain parts of the prefrontal cortex can result in marked changes in personality, mood, affect, and the ability to control inappropriate behavior (Pritchard & Alloway, 1999).

The prefrontal cortex shows the longest period of maturation; it appears to be one of the last brain regions to mature (Casey, Giedd, & Thomas, 2000). Interestingly, this region may also be one of the "first to go" as aging affects the brain toward the end of life. It has been hypothesized that brain regions that show the most plasticity over the longest periods may be the most sensitive to environmental toxins or stressors.

LOCALIZATION OF FUNCTION

When I describe a particular brain region or structure as having a particular role to play (as in memory or attention), you may wonder what the basis of such a claim is. That is, how do neuroscientists *know* what brain region does what? The answer lies in studies of localization of function, a means of mapping the brain.

FACULTY PSYCHOLOGY AND PHRENOLOGY

The original idea of localization of function traces back to an Austrian anatomist named Franz Gall (1758–1828), who proposed an early localization theory. Gall believed in something called **faculty psychology**, a term that has nothing to do with why your college instructors are or are not crazy! Faculty psychology was the theory that different mental abilities, such as reading or computation, were independent and autonomous functions carried out in different parts of the brain (Fodor, 1983). Gall believed that different locations in the brain were associated with such faculties as parental love, combativeness, acquisitiveness, and secretiveness, to name a few. Later, Gall's student Johan Spurzheim carried on Gall's teachings, developing the study of **phrenology**, a now discredited idea that psychological strengths and weaknesses could be precisely correlated to the relative sizes of different brain areas. Photo 2.1 depicts a sculpture showing where the different faculties were supposedly located in the brain.

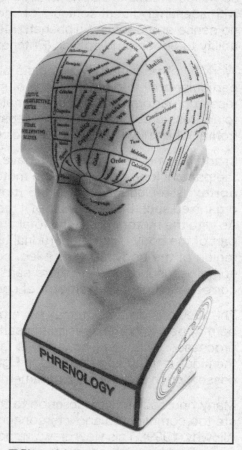

The major problem with phrenology is not the assumption that different parts of the brain control different functions but rather two subsidiary assumptions: (1) that the size of a portion of the brain corresponds to its relative power and (2) that different faculties are absolutely independent. We now know that different mental activities—for example, perception and attention—are not wholly distinct and independent but rather interact in many different ways. We also know that the overall size of a brain or brain area is not indicative of the functioning of that area. Therefore, having a different configuration

■ Photo 2.1: Phrenology head. Specific locations on the skull were thought to correspond to different specific abilities.

of bumps and indentations in a brain does not determine or even predict how an individual will function cognitively or socially.

STUDIES OF APHASIA AND OTHER MAPPING TECHNIQUES

More modern approaches to localizing function in the brain date back to Paul Broca (1824–1880), who in the early 1860s presented findings at a medical conference that injury to a particular part of the left frontal lobe (the posterior, inferior region shown in Figure 2.3) resulted in a particular kind of aphasia, or disruption of expressive language (Springer & Deutsch, 1998). This brain region has become known as Broca's area; injury to this area leads to a kind of aphasia known as Broca's or nonfluent aphasia, in which the person is unable to produce many words or to speak very fluently.

A decade after Broca's discovery, Carl Wernicke (1848–1904) announced the discovery of a second "language center" in the brain, this one thought to control language understanding (as opposed to language production). This region, which has come to be known as Wernicke's area, is located in the superior, posterior region of the temporal lobe, also typically in the left hemisphere, and is also shown in Figure 2.3. Patients with so-called Wernicke's aphasia (also called fluent aphasia) are able to produce speech with seemingly fluent contours of pitch and rhythm. However, the speech often makes no sense and contains gibberish. Moreover, these patients show impairments in their ability to understand speech (Pritchard & Alloway, 1999).

Work by other neuropsychologists began to establish connections between lesions in particular brain regions and loss of specific motor control or sensory reception. Using research performed either on animals or as part of neurosurgical procedures intended to address problems such as epilepsy, scientists began to "map out" the portion of the frontal lobe known as the motor cortex, as shown in Figure 2.3.

In addition, neuropsychologists have mapped out a second area of the brain, located in the parietal lobe just behind the motor cortex, known as the **primary somatosensory cortex** (see Figure 2.3). Like the motor cortex, the primary somatosensory cortex is organized such that each part of it receives information from a specific part of the body. As with the motor cortex, the total amount of "brain real estate" devoted to a particular part of the body is not proportional to the size of that body part. In other words, a large region of the body, such as a leg, corresponds to only a small portion of the primary somatosensory cortex. A more sensitive body part, such as the fingers or lips, has a correspondingly larger amount of cortex devoted to it.

The previous discussion may have given you the idea that every part of the brain can be mapped to some specific sensation, behavior, idea, thought, memory, or cognitive processes. This idea, however, is false. Although motor and sensory reception have the kinds of mapping depicted in Figure 2.3, most so-called higher-order cognitive processes, such as thinking and remembering, do not.

Many neuroscientists subscribe to the principle that higher-order cognitive processes are too complicated and interconnected to be localized to any one region (Pritchard & Alloway, 1999). This view drew support from the work of Karl Lashley (1890–1958), who performed several landmark studies in neuroscience measuring the effects of brain **ablation** (removal of parts of the brain) on the maze-running ability of rats. Lashley (1929) reported that impairment in maze running was related to the *total amount* of cortex removed, not to which specific area was removed.

Complicating this already involved picture is the notion of the **plasticity** of the brain (Black, 2004). Some brain regions can adapt to "take over" functions of damaged regions, depending on the injury and the function involved. In general, the younger the patient and the less extensive the injury, the better is the chance of regaining function.

LATERALIZATION OF FUNCTION

Paul Broca's report of a "language center" in his patients did more than argue for localization of function. Broca and many neuropsychologists since have been able to show that the two cerebral hemispheres seem to play different roles when it comes to some cognitive functions, especially language. We call this phenomenon **lateralization**.

Most individuals (around 95%) show a specialization for language in the left hemisphere. In these individuals, the left hemisphere is likely to be larger in size, especially in the areas where language is localized (Springer & Deutsch, 1998). We say that these individuals have a left-hemisphere dominance in language. A small percentage of people do not show such specialization, having language function in both hemispheres (these are called *bilateralized* individuals), and an even smaller percentage have language centers located in the right hemisphere.

If the left hemisphere is dominant for language, then what role does the right hemisphere play? Structurally, the right hemisphere often has larger parietal and temporal areas, and it is speculated that this leads to better integration of visual and auditory information and better spatial processing by the right than the left hemisphere. The right hemisphere is associated with working on geometric puzzles, navigation around familiar spaces, and even musical ability (Springer & Deutsch, 1998).

Some describe the difference in function between the two hemispheres by labeling the left hemisphere as the analytical one and the right hemisphere as the synthetic one (N. R. Carlson, 2013). The idea here is that the left hemisphere is particularly good at processing information serially—that is, information with events occurring one after another. If you think about processing a sentence, the events would be the individual words that are spoken or read in sequence. By contrast, the right hemisphere is thought to be more synthetic, putting individual elements together to make up a whole. Cognitive processes here might include constructing maps or other spatial structures, drawing sketches, and navigating through mazes.

Popular press articles have made much of the difference between the two cerebral hemispheres, going so far in some cases as to classify people as either right-brained or left-brained. It's very important to remember that this is a gross oversimplification. The vast majority of individuals have two quite functional cerebral hemispheres that continually interact to process information and carry out cognitive functions. The odds that only one hemisphere would be active in a normal person during any everyday task are remote. Moreover, the two hemispheres are connected by a large neural structure known as the **corpus callosum** (shown in Figure 2.1), which sends information from one hemisphere to another very quickly. (A second, smaller brain structure, known as the anterior commissure, also connects the two hemispheres; it is not depicted in Figure 2.3.)

STUDIES OF SPLIT-BRAINED PATIENTS

What happens when the corpus callosum is not able to transfer information from one hemisphere to another? As it turns out, scientists have some answers to this originally hypothetical question. Beginning in the late 1950s, researchers and neurologists were looking for ways of treating severe and intractable epilepsy in which seizures that began in one hemisphere of the brain spread to the other, often several times a day (N. R. Carlson, 2013). Surgeons took the dramatic step of severing the corpus callosum in these patients in an effort to stop the spread of the seizures. Neuropsychologists Roger Sperry, Michael Gazzaniga, and their associates began to study these patients to see what effects having a severed corpus callosum brought about (Gazzaniga & Sperry, 1967).

If you look carefully at Figure 2.1 again, focusing on the size of the corpus callosum, you might expect that severing it would have dramatic effects. But quite the opposite was true. As Gazzaniga and Sperry (1967) note, "The disruption of interhemispheric integration produces remarkably little disturbance in ordinary daily behavior, temperament, or intellect" (p. 131). Indeed, to detect any differences in cognition between so-called **split-brained patients** and those of us with an intact corpus callosum, the investigators had to resort to designing special tasks.

In one of these, depicted in Figure 2.4, the patient reached through a curtain to grasp a familiar object, in this case, a pair of sunglasses. It was already known from previous animal and human work that sensory information received from one side of the body projects to the *opposite* cerebral hemisphere (B. Garrett, 2011). Thus, in Figure 2.4, the patient grasps the sunglasses in his left hand, projecting the information to the right hemisphere. But, in most (especially right-handed) individuals, language centers are located in the left hemisphere. Thus, the patient would be unable to describe the object he was holding, even though if asked to "pick out" sunglasses from a set of familiar objects, he had no problem doing so. Further experiments showed that if special equipment (called a tachistoscope) was used, information could be (very briefly) projected to either the right or the left hemisphere of the patient. Gazzaniga and Sperry (1967) describe some of the results as follows:

■ Figure 2.4: A patient with severed corpus callosum identifying objects by touch.

The same sort of result was obtained in tasks that required intermodal integration going from vision to touch and vice versa. When a sample word such as pencil, tack, knife, sock, comb, etc., was presented in the left visual half field, the left hand, *but not the right,* could be used to search out the described correct matching object by touch from among an array of others, all shielded from vision. In such instances, when the stimulus and the matching answer were both presented exclusively to the right hemisphere, the subjects remained completely unaware of the given stimulus and response selection. . . . After making a correct manual response . . . they would commonly describe the selected object as some totally unrelated item that was obviously a pure guess. (pp. 139–140)

Clearly, the results from split-brained patients are intriguing and raise many more questions than they answer. The important point for now is to recognize that the two cerebral hemispheres appear to play very different roles for some cognitive processes, especially those concerning language.

BRAIN-IMAGING TECHNIQUES

In Broca's day, neurologists had to wait until a patient died to really investigate the structural features of his or her brain. In the early part of the 20th century, more information came from studies performed as patients underwent brain surgery—to remove a tumor or stop the spread of epilepsy, most commonly. Fortunately for people but unfortunately for science, ethical considerations precluded doing brain surgery on healthy people, which limited our understanding of how "normal" brains functioned.

However, in the last five decades, technology has advanced to the point where neurologists and neuropsychologists can examine the functioning of normal brains using noninvasive means. We will briefly review some of these methods, known collectively as brain-imaging techniques.

CAT (CT) SCANS

Some of these methods give us information about neuroanatomy—the structures of the brain. One of the earliest such brain-imaging techniques, developed in the 1970s, was X-ray computed tomography—also called X-ray CT, **computerized axial tomography**, or **CAT** scan—a technique in which a highly focused beam of X-rays is passed through the body from many different angles. Differing densities of body organs (including the brain) deflect the X-rays differently, allowing visualization of the organ. Photo 2.2 depicts a person undergoing a CAT scan.

Typically, CAT scans of a person's brain result in 9 to 12 different "slices" of the brain, each one taken at a different level of depth. CAT scans depend on the fact that structures of different density show up differently. Bone, for example, is denser than blood, which is denser than brain tissue, which is in turn denser than cerebrospinal fluid (Banich, 2004). Recent brain hemorrhages are typically indicated by the presence of blood; older brain damage, by areas of cerebrospinal fluid. Thus, clinicians and researchers can use CAT scans to pinpoint areas of brain damage and to make inferences about the relative age of the injury.

MAGNETIC RESONANCE IMAGING (MRI)

Although an important diagnostic tool in neuropsychology, CAT scans are used less often than a newer brain-imaging technique, **magnetic resonance imaging**, or **MRI**. Like CAT scans, MRI provides information about neuroanatomy. Unlike CAT scans, however, MRI requires no exposure to radiation and often permits clearer pictures. Photo 2.2 presents an MRI scan.

Someone undergoing an MRI typically lies inside a tunnel-like structure that surrounds the person with a strong magnetic field. Radio waves are directed at the head (or whatever body structure is being scanned), causing the centers of hydrogen atoms in those structures to align themselves in predictable ways. Computers collate information about how the atoms are aligning and produce a composite three-dimensional image from which any desired cross section can be examined further.

MRI scans are often the technique of choice, as they now produce some of the clearest images of a brain. However, not everyone can undergo an MRI scan. The magnetic fields generated in an MRI scan interfere with electrical fields, so people with pacemakers are not candidates for an MRI (pacemakers generate electric signals). Neither are people with metal in their bodies, such as a surgical clip on an artery or a metal shaving in the eye. The magnetic field could dislodge the metal in the body, causing trauma. (Metal anchored to hard surfaces, such as dental fillings, is not a problem). Because MRIs require people to lie very still in a tunnel-like machine that often leaves little room for arm movements, people with claustrophobia are also not good candidates for this technique.

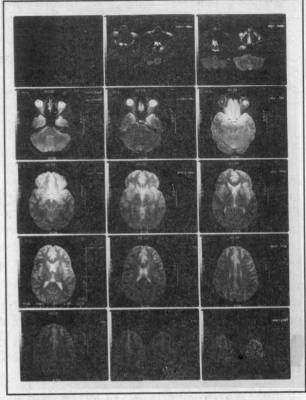

■ Photo 2.2: An MRI scan. The different images are of different "slices" through the brain.

As I've already mentioned, these two techniques provide pictures of brain structures, and investigators can use these pictures to pinpoint areas of damage or other abnormality. However, these scans provide relatively static pictures of the parts of a brain and do not give much information about how a brain functions—that is, what areas of the brain show activity when people perform different tasks. To answer such questions, different brain-imaging techniques are needed. Fortunately, recent developments have created techniques that fit the bill.

POSITRON EMISSION TOMOGRAPHY (PET)

A functional brain-imaging technique that also dates back to the 1970s is called **positron emission tomography**, or **PET**. This technique involves injecting a radioactively labeled compound (a radioisotope of carbon, nitrogen, oxygen, or fluorine, subatomic particles that rapidly emit gamma radiation, which can be detected by devices outside the head). PET scans measure the blood flow to different regions of the brain, allowing an electronic reconstruction of a picture of a brain that shows which areas are most active at a particular time (Posner & Raichle, 1994). A variation of the PET procedure involves measuring local metabolic changes instead of blood flow by using an injection of fluorodeoxyglucose, a radioisotope structurally similar to glucose.

PET scans rely on the fact that when an area of the brain is active, more blood flows to it, and its cells take up more glucose from the blood vessels that penetrate it (Frith & Friston, 1997; Kung, 1993). People undergoing a PET brain scan sit with their head in a ring of photocells. A radioactive tracer, typically 15O2 (oxygen with one electron removed), is injected into a vein as water (that is, as H215O). Within 30 seconds, the tracer starts to reach the brain. The tracer 15O accumulates in the brain in direct proportion to the amount of blood flowing to that brain region (Banich, 2004). Within the roughly 2 minutes before the radioactive tracer decays to its half-life, several scans can be made, showing the amount of blood flowing to that region (Frith & Friston, 1997).

Another technique to measure cerebral blood flow is known as single-photon emission computed tomography, or SPECT for short. The basic technique is similar to a PET scan, but it does not require some of the expensive equipment a PET scan does; thus, it is sometimes known as a "poor person's PET" (Zillmer & Spiers, 2001).

Like CAT scans, PET and SPECT scans use radiation. Moreover, PET scans show activity averaged over some amount of time, approximately between a minute and a half (for the tracer ^{15}O) to an hour, making it hard to pinpoint the time course of the brain activity. PET scans can also require very expensive equipment not widely available.

FUNCTIONAL MAGNETIC RESONANCE IMAGING (fMRI)

A newer technique offers a way out of these difficulties. **Functional magnetic resonance imaging**, or **fMRI**, relies on the fact that blood has magnetic properties. As blood is carried from the heart, it is maximally magnetic. As it passes through capillaries, it becomes less magnetic. Brain regions that show activity show a change in the ratio of oxygenated to deoxygenated blood (Banich, 2004). Such fMRI scans use existing MRI equipment but provide clinicians and investigators with a noninvasive, nonradioactive means of assessing blood flow to various brain regions. Figure 2.5 provides an example of an fMRI scan.

These techniques for studying the way the brain functions make possible new connections and new questions in cognitive psychology. Before the availability of these techniques, cognitive theories did not refer to the biological mechanisms that implement various cognitive processes. Now cognitive neuroscientists offer us findings from studies based on a new assumption: "The mapping

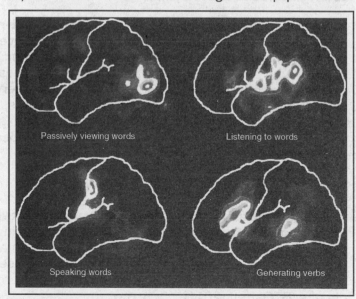

Passively viewing words

Listening to words

Speaking words

Generating verbs

■ Figure 2.5: An example of fMRI scans. More brightly colored regions of the brain scan indicate greater metabolic activity.

between physical activity in the brain and its functional state is such that when two experimental conditions are associated with different patterns of neural activity, it can be assumed that they have engaged distinct cognitive functions" (Rugg, 1997, p. 5). A review of 275 PET and fMRI studies (Cabeza & Nyberg, 2000), for example, showed different areas of activation for different cognitive functions: attention, perception, imagery, language, and memory.

OTHER BRAIN-RECORDING TECHNIQUES _____

Another "window on the brain" can be obtained through electrical recording methods. You may already know that when neurons in the brain (or anywhere else, for that matter) fire, they generate electrical activity. Some animal research has involved placing electrodes in individual neurons to detect when and how often those single cells fire. Such work is not done with humans. Instead, the sum total of electrical activity generated by a large number of neurons comprises the information gathered (Banich, 2004).

ELECTROENCEPHALOGRAPHY (EEG)

Electroencephalography (EEG) is used to detect different states of consciousness. Metal electrodes are positioned all over the scalp. The waveforms record changes in predictable ways when the person being recorded is awake and alert, drowsy, asleep, or in a coma. EEGs provide the clinician or researcher with a continuous measure of brain activity (Banich, 1997). A newer technique, **magnetoencephalography**, or **MEG**, measures changes in magnetic fields generated by electrical activities of neurons. It has been called the "magnetic equivalent" of EEG (Springer & Deutsch, 1998). MEG gives a more precise localization of brain region activity than does EEG.

EVENT-RELATED POTENTIAL (ERP)

Another electrical recording technique, called **event-related potential**, or **ERP**, measures an area of the brain's response to a specific event. Participants in an ERP study have electrodes attached to their scalp and are then presented with various external stimuli, such as sights or sounds. The recording measures brain activity from the time before the stimulus is presented until some time afterward. The brain waves recorded also have predictable parts, or components. That is, the shape of the waveform can vary depending on whether or not the participant expects the stimulus to occur or is attending to the location in which the stimulus appears and whether the stimulus is physically different from other recent stimuli.

TRANSCRANIAL MAGNETIC STIMULATION (TMS)

A newer noninvasive technique to study areas of activity in the brain is known as **transcranial magnetic stimulation**, or **TMS**, Briefly, an investigator places a magnetic coil close to a patient's scalp over a target area, say, an area in the primary motor cortex. Depending upon the rate at which the TMS is pulsed, that brain area will either be excited or inhibited. This allows the investigator to measure activity of specific brain circuits (B. Garrett, 2011).

Brain-imaging and recording techniques certainly include a lot of acronyms! How can the novice keep them all straight? One way to do so is to categorize the techniques according to the kind of information they provide. CAT and MRI scans yield neuroanatomical information. PET, SPECT, and fMRI provide dynamic information about how blood flows during various cognitive activities. MEG, EEG, ERP, and TMS all measure (or induce) electrical activity during cognitive activities. In the chapters to come, we will see examples of studies that have made use of each of these techniques to investigate the neural underpinnings of different cognitive activities.

We have covered a lot of ground in this chapter, and yet we have still only begun to grapple with the complexities of the human brain. The interested student should refer to a text on neuropsychology, physiology, or biological psychology for more detail on any of the topics introduced here (see, for example, Banich, 2004, and B. Garrett, 2011).

What is important to remember is that cognitive processes are implemented in human brains. Some researchers make an analogy between human minds and computers; in this view, the brain is the "hardware" ("wetware") and the cognitive processes the software. Although the two aspects of functioning can be distinguished, to really understand either we must have some familiarity with both and with how they interact. We'll return to this idea throughout the upcoming chapters.

Summary

1. The hindbrain, containing some of the most evolutionarily primitive structures, is responsible for transmitting information from the spinal cord to the brain, regulating life support functions, and helping to maintain balance.

2. The midbrain contains many "relay" centers to transfer information between different brain regions.

3. The forebrain contains the thalamus, hypothalamus, hippocampus, amygdala, and the cerebral cortex, structures that are most directly implicated in cognitive processes such as memory, language, planning, and reasoning.

4. The cerebral cortex has four lobes: frontal (involved with movement and planning), parietal (involving reception and integration of sensory information), occipital (processing visual information), and temporal (processing auditory information as well as information about taste and smell).

5. Although some specific brain areas have specific functions localized to them (for example, the motor cortex or the primary somatosensory cortex), most higher-order cognitive processes do not map to one specific neural area.

6. Aphasia, a disorder of language, has been traced to two areas of the brain, Broca's area and Wernicke's area, although other brain areas are likely involved as well.

7. Cerebral hemispheres have been shown to be lateralized in many individuals, with the left hemisphere usually processing analytical information and the right hemisphere synthesizing information. In normal operation, however, the two hemispheres communicate extensively.

8. A variety of modern techniques have been developed to measure the functioning of the brain during cognitive processing. Among the major techniques are CAT scans, MRI, PET scans, fMRI, EEG recordings, ERP recordings, and TMS.

Review Questions

1. Predict which brain areas are likely to be most involved with the cognitive processes of perception, attention, memory, language, and problem solving. Provide a rationale for your predictions.

2. Describe the functions of the four lobes of the cerebral cortex.

3. Explain how modern-day localization of brain function differs from phrenology.

4. What does it mean to say that the cerebral hemispheres show lateralization? What is the typical pattern of lateralization?

5. Compare and contrast the various brain-imaging and brain-recording techniques.

Key Terms

ablation

amygdala

cerebellum

cerebral cortex

computerized axial tomography (CAT)

corpus callosum

electroencephalography (EEG)

event-related potential (ERP)

executive functioning

faculty psychology

forebrain

frontal lobe

functional MRI (fMRI)

hindbrain

hippocampus

hypothalamus

lateralization

magnetic resonance imaging (MRI)

magnetoencephalography (MEG)

medulla

midbrain

motor cortex

occipital lobe

parietal lobe

phrenology

plasticity

pons

positron emission tomography (PET)

prefrontal cortex

primary somatosensory cortex

split-brained patient

temporal lobe

thalamus

transcranial magnetic stimulation (TMS)

3

PERCEPTION
Recognizing Patterns and Objects

CHAPTER OUTLINE

Gestalt Approaches to Perception

Bottom-Up Processes

Template Matching

Featural Analysis

Prototype Matching

Top-Down Processes

Perceptual Learning

The Word Superiority Effect

A Connectionist Model of Word Perception

Direct Perception

Disruptions of Perception: Visual Agnosias

Look across the room right now and notice the objects you see. If you are looking out a window, maybe you see some trees or bushes, perhaps a bicycle or car, a person walking or a group of children playing.

What you've just done, cognitively speaking, is an amazing achievement: You've taken sensory input and interpreted it meaningfully, in a process known as **perception**. In other words, you have perceived patterns, objects, people, and possibly events in your world. You may not consider this achievement at all remarkable—after all, you do it every day. However, computer scientists trying to create artificially intelligent systems have discovered just how complicated the process of perception is. Neuroscientists have estimated that the areas of our brain responsible for visual processing occupy up to half of the total cortex space (Tarr, 2000).

The central problem of perception is explaining how we attach meaning to the sensory information we receive. In the example just given, you received and somehow interpreted a great deal of sensory information: You "saw" certain objects as trees, people, and so forth. You recognized certain objects—that is, saw them as things you had seen before. The question for cognitive psychologists is how we manage to accomplish these feats so rapidly and (usually) without error.

The vast topic of perception can be subdivided into visual perception, auditory perception, olfactory perception, haptic (touch) perception, and gustatory (taste) perception. For the purposes of this chapter, we will concentrate on visual and auditory perception—in part to keep our discussion manageable and in part because those two are the kinds of perception psychologists study most. From time to time, however, we will also look at examples of other kinds of perception to illustrate different points.

Notice that when you look at an object, you acquire specific bits of information about it, including its location, shape, texture, size, and (for familiar objects) name. Some psychologists—namely, those working in the tradition of James Gibson (1979)—would argue that you also immediately acquire information about the object's function. Cognitive psychologists seek to describe how people acquire such information and what they then do to process it.

Several related questions suggest themselves. How much of the information we acquire through perception draws on past learning? How much of our perception do we infer, and how much do we receive directly? What specific cognitive processes enable us to perceive objects (and events, and states, and so on)? Where can the line be drawn between perception and sensation, which is the initial reception of information in a specific sensory modality—vision, hearing, olfaction? Where can the line be drawn between perception and other kinds of cognition, such as reasoning or categorization? Clearly, even defining perception so as to answer these questions is a challenge.

For the present, we will adopt what might be called the "classic" approach to defining perception. Figure 3.1 illustrates this approach for visual perception. Out in the real world are objects and events—things to be perceived—such as this book or, as in my earlier example, trees and shrubs. Each such object is a **distal stimulus**. For a living organism to process information about these stimuli, it must first

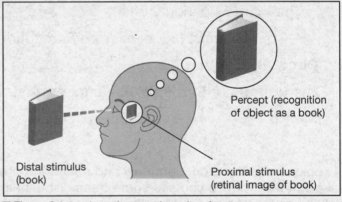

Percept (recognition of object as a book)

Distal stimulus (book)

Proximal stimulus (retinal image of book)

■ Figure 3.1: Distal stimuli, proximal stimuli, and percepts.

receive the information through one or more sensory systems—in this example, the visual system. The reception of information and its registration by a sense organ make up the **proximal stimulus**. In our earlier example, light waves reflect from the trees and cars to your eyes, in particular to a surface at the back of each eye known as the **retina**. There, an image of the trees and cars, called the **retinal image**, is formed. This image is two-dimensional, and its size depends on your distance from the window and the objects beyond (the closer you are, the larger the image). In addition, the image is upside down and is reversed with respect to left and right.

The meaningful interpretation of the proximal stimulus is the **percept**—your interpretation that the stimuli are trees, cars, people, and so forth. From the upside-down, backward, two-dimensional image, you quickly (almost instantaneously) "see" a set of objects you recognize. You also "recognize" that, say, the giant oak tree is closer to you than are the lilac shrubs, which appear to recede in depth away from you. This information is not part of the proximal stimulus; somehow, you must interpret the proximal stimulus to know this information.

Although researchers studying perception disagree about much, they agree that percepts are not the same things as proximal stimuli. Consider a simple demonstration of **size constancy**. Extend your arm away from your body and look at the back of your hand. Now, keeping the back of your hand facing you, slowly bring it toward you a few inches, then away from you. Does your hand seem to be changing size as it moves? Probably not, although the size of the hand in the retinal image is most certainly changing. The point here is that perception involves something other than the formation of retinal images.

Related to perception is a process called **pattern recognition**. This is the recognition of a particular object, event, and so on, as belonging to a class of objects, events, and so on. Your recognition of the object you are looking at as belonging to the class of things called "shrubs" is an instance of pattern recognition. Because the formation of most percepts involves some classification and recognition, most, if not all, instances of perception involve pattern recognition.

We will begin by considering proposals from the Gestalt school of psychology that perception involves the segmentation, or "parsing," of visual stimuli into objects and backgrounds (and just how complicated this seemingly easy process is). We will then turn to examine some (mostly) bottom-up models of perception. Then we will examine phenomena that have led many cognitive psychologists to argue that some top-down processes must occur in interaction with bottom-up processing. We will examine some neurological findings pertaining to object perception and will also consider a connectionist model of word perception.

We will also review a very different view: work inspired by J. J. Gibson (1979) on "direct perception." Gibson's view departs from most other theories of perception in that he claims perceivers actually do little "processing" of information, either bottom-up or top-down. Instead, he believes the information available in the world is sufficiently rich that all the perceiver needs to do is detect or "pick up on" that information. We will conclude by looking at some neuropsychological work on patients who have an inability to perceive (but have intact visual abilities) to illustrate just what the process of perception is all about.

GESTALT APPROACHES TO PERCEPTION

When stimuli occur close to one another in space and in time, they may group perceptually into coherent, salient patterns or wholes. Such Gestalts, as they are called, abound in our perceptual world, as when leaves and branches cluster into trees, and when trees merge into forests; when eyes, ears, noses and mouths configure into faces; when musical notes coalesce into chords and melodies; and when countless dots or pixels blend into a photograph.

The resulting wholes may have properties their component parts lack, such as the identity or expression on a face that is unrecognizable from any one part, or the key in which a melody is played that cannot be deduced from any single note. Understanding how parts combine into perceptual wholes was recognized as a central challenge in perceptual theory nearly 100 years ago . . .

—Pomerantz & Portillo, 2011, p. 1331

One of the most important aspects of visual perception has to do with how we interpret stimulus arrays as consisting of objects and backgrounds. Consider, for instance, Figure 3.2. This stimulus pattern can be seen in two distinct ways: as a landscape with two people standing in the lower right or as a baby framed by black lines. This segregation of the whole display into objects (also called the figure) and the background (also called the ground) is an important process known to cognitive psychologists as **figure-ground organization**.

■ Figure 3.2: Find the baby in the branches of this tree. This is a clever, modern illustration of a reversible figure: When you see the "baby," the branches become background; when you see the tree and people, the "baby" disappears into the background.

Reversible figures aren't just for perceptual psychologists, either! The artist Salvador Dali exploits the existence of reversible figures in his work *The Slave Market With Disappearing Bust of Voltaire,* shown in Figure 3.3.

■ Figure 3.3: Salvador Dali, *The Slave Market With Disappearing Bust of Voltaire*. The two nuns standing in the archway at left-center reverse to form a bust of Voltaire. The painting exploits the reversible figures phenomenon.

The segregation of figure from ground has many consequences. The part of the display seen as figure is seen as having a definite shape, as being some sort of "thing," and is better remembered than the part of the display interpreted as ground, which is seen as more shapeless, less formed, and farther away in space (Brown & Deffenbacher, 1979). Form perception is a cognitive task most of us perform quickly and easily and thus take for granted. We assume, intuitively, that we perceive objects and backgrounds because there really *are* objects and backgrounds and all we do is see them.

■ Figure 3.4: Subjective, or illusory, contours.

But consider Figure 3.4. Almost everyone sees this figure as consisting of two triangles, overlaid so as to form a six-pointed star. The corners of the top triangle are typically seen as resting on three colored circles. Now look closely at the figure, in particular at the top triangle. Recall that a triangle is defined as a closed geometric figure that has three sides. Notice that in the figure itself there are *no* sides. There is only white space that you, the viewer, interpret as a triangle. You, the viewer, are somehow adding the three sides or contours.

Gregory (1972), who studied this phenomenon (called *illusory* or **subjective contours**), believes that this relatively complex display is subject to a simplifying interpretation the perceiver makes without even being aware of making it: A triangle is lying on top of other parts of the figure and blocking them from view. The point here is that this perception is not completely determined by the stimulus display; it requires the perceiver's active participation.

A number of individuals in the early part of the 20th century—among them Max Wertheimer, Kurt Koffka, and Wolfgang Köhler—were deeply interested in how perceivers come to recognize objects or forms. As we saw in Chapter 1, these researchers, who formed the Gestalt school of psychology, were particularly concerned with how people apprehend *whole* objects, concepts, or units. The Gestalt psychologists believed that perceivers follow certain laws or principles of organization in coming to their interpretations.

They asserted that the whole, or *Gestalt,* is not the same as the sum of its parts. To put it another way, Gestalt psychologists rejected the claim that we recognize objects by identifying individual features or parts; instead, we see and recognize each object or unit as a whole.

What are the **Gestalt principles of perceptual organization** that allow us to see these wholes? The complete list is too long to explore here (see Koffka, 1935), so we will examine only five major principles. The first is the *principle of proximity,* or nearness. Look at Figure 3.5(A). Notice that you tend to perceive this as a set of rows rather than as a set of columns. This is because the elements within rows are closer than the elements within columns. Following the principle of proximity, we group together things that are nearer to each other.

Figure 3.5(B) illustrates the *principle of similarity.* Notice that you perceive this display as formed in columns (rather than rows), grouping together those elements that are similar.

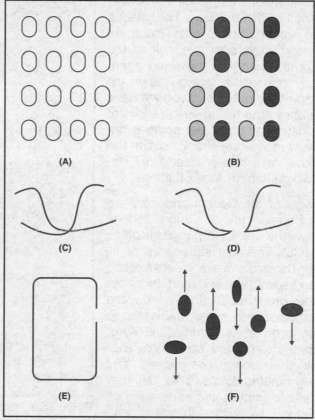

■ Figure 3.5: Gestalt principles of perceptual organization: (A) the principle of proximity; (B) the principle of similarity; (C) and (D) the principle of good continuation; (E) the principle of closure; and (F) the principle of common fate.

A third principle, the *principle of good continuation,* depicted in Figure 3.5(C), states that we group together objects whose contours form a continuous straight or curved line. Thus we typically perceive Figure 3.5(C) as two intersecting curved lines and not as other logically possible elements, such as those shown in Figure 3.5(D).

We encounter the fourth principle, the *principle of closure,* when we look at subjective contours in Figure 3.4. Figure 3.5(E) illustrates this principle more exactly. Note that we perceive this display as a rectangle, mentally filling in the gap to see a closed, complete, whole figure.

The fifth principle, the *principle of common fate,* is difficult to illustrate in a static drawing. The idea is that elements that move together will be grouped together, as depicted in Figure 3.5(F). You can construct a better demonstration of this principle yourself (Matlin, 1988). Take two pieces of transparent plastic (such as report covers cut in half). Glue some scraps of paper on each. Lay one sheet upside down on top of the other, and you will have a hard time telling which sheet of plastic any particular scrap is on. Now move one sheet, holding the other still. You will suddenly see two distinct groups of scraps.

Most of the Gestalt principles are subsumed under a more general law, the *law of Prägnanz* (Koffka, 1935). This law states that of all the possible ways of interpreting a display, we will tend to select the organization that yields the simplest and most stable shape or form. Thus, simple and symmetric forms are seen more easily than more complicated and asymmetric forms. This law may help to explain our experience of Figure 3.4 with subjective contours. Because the phantom "triangle" forms a simple, symmetric form, we "prefer" to interpret the pattern as if the triangle were there.

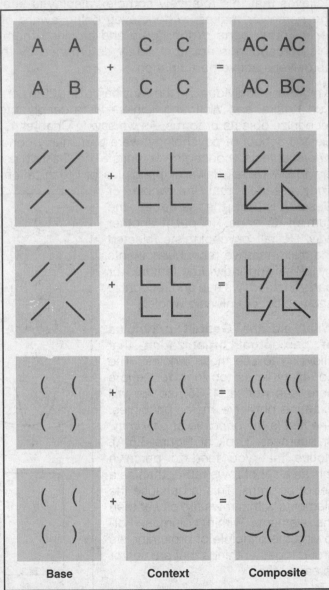

■ Figure 3.6: The odd-quadrant discrimination task. Top row shows a schematic odd-quadrant discrimination task. Participants only see base and composite displays, not context alone. A, B, and C are symbols standing for any stimulus component. The same base stimuli produces configural superiority effects (CSEs) in rows 2 and 4 but not in rows 3 or 5. This shows that emergent features depend on the context added.

In recent work, psychologists James Pomerantz and Mary Portillo (2011) are trying to dig deeper into the principles underlying what makes a Gestalt. They focus on the property of **emergence** in perception—the idea that "qualitative differences . . . [in a percept] appear as parts are added, such that wholes take on properties that are novel, unpredictable, even surprising" (p. 1331).

To demonstrate the property of emergence, Pomerantz and Potillo (2011) use an *odd-quadrant discrimination task,* depicted in Figure 3.6. Consider the top leftmost box (called the base display) containing four letters. The task of the research participant is to identify the stimulus that differs from the other three. In this case, it is the letter *B*. The second box in the row presents a contextual stimulus (in this case, the letter *C*), that is added to each stimulus in the base display to produce the stimuli in the composite display (the top rightmost box). Experimenters compare the length of time it takes a participant to correctly identify the "odd" stimulus (e.g., the *B* in the base display or the *BC* in the composite display) in the base to the length of time it takes in the composite display.

Although there are many good reasons to predict it will take longer with the composite displays (e.g., more information to process, more stimuli to distract attention), with some specific stimuli—the opposite result occurs. That is, perception of the "odd stimulus out" is *faster* in the composite stimulus display than in the base stimulus display (this is called a **configural superiority effect**, or **CSE**). In fact, the second and fourth rows of Figure 3.6 yield just such a pattern; the odd stimulus seems to "pop" out more dramatically in the composite display than it does in the base display. Pomerantz and Potillo (2011) believe that CSEs demonstrate Gestalt grouping principles, but in such a way as to make the strength of different principles measureable and comparable.

Many researchers of visual perception consider the Gestalt principles fundamental (Tarr, 2000; van den Berg, Kubovy, & Shirillo, 2011). Investigators have demonstrated the use of some Gestalt principles by infants as young as 3 to 6 months (Quinn, Bhatt, Brush, Grimes, & Sharpnack, 2002). Moreover, fMRI studies of the visual cortex activity during perception of CSEs are beginning to show neural correlates of the Gestalt grouping principles in action (Kubilius, Wagemans, & Op de Beeck, 2011).

BOTTOM-UP PROCESSES

Psychologists studying perception distinguish between **bottom-up** and **top-down processes**. The term *bottom-up* (or *data-driven*) essentially means that the perceiver starts with small bits of information from the environment and combines them in various ways to form a percept. A bottom-up model of perception and pattern recognition might describe your seeing edges, rectangular and other shapes, and certain lighted regions and putting this information together to "conclude" you are seeing the scene outside your window. That is, you would form a perception from only the information in the distal stimulus.

In *top-down* (also called *theory-driven* or *conceptually driven*) processing, the perceiver's expectations, theories, or concepts guide the selection and combination of the information in the pattern-recognition process. For example, a "top-down" description of the scene-outside-your-window example might go something like this: You knew you were in your dorm room and knew from past experience approximately how close to the window the various trees, shrubs, and other objects were. When you looked in that direction, you expected to see trees, shrubs, walkways with people on them, a street with cars going by, and so on. These expectations guided where you looked, what you looked at, and how you put the information together.

In this section, we will focus on bottom-up models. The idea here is that the system works in one direction, starting from the input and proceeding to a final interpretation. Whatever happens at a given point is unaffected by later processing; the system has no way of going back to an earlier point to make adjustments.

To picture bottom-up processing, imagine a row of students seated at desks. The student in the last seat of the row starts the process by writing a word on a piece of paper and handing the paper to the student in front of her. That student adds some information (maybe another word, maybe an illustration) and, in turn, hands the paper to the student in front of him, and so on, until the paper reaches the student at the front of the row. Students at the front of the row have no opportunity to ask students behind them for any clarification or additional information.

When psychologists speak of bottom-up perceptual processes, they typically have in mind something that takes information about a stimulus (by definition a "lower" level of processing) as input. Bottom-up processes are relatively uninfluenced by expectations or previous learning (the so-called higher-level processes). Posner and Raichle (1994) argue that bottom-up processes involve automatic, reflexive processing that takes place even when the perceiver is passively regarding the information. In this section, we will consider three distinct examples of bottom-up models of perception.

TEMPLATE MATCHING

Figure 3.7 shows a copy of a check. Notice the numbers at the bottom of the check. These numbers encode certain information about a checking account—the account number, the bank that manages it, and so forth. These numbers may look funny to you, but they wouldn't look at all funny to machines known as *check sorters,* such as those the Federal Reserve banks use to sort checks and deliver them to the correct banks for payment. These machines "read" the numbers and compare them to previously stored patterns, called **templates**. The machines "decide" which number is represented by comparing the

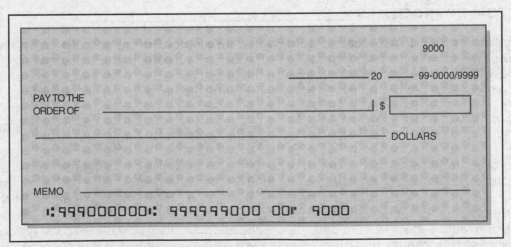

■ Figure 3.7: A sample bank check. Note the numbers at the bottom.

pattern to these templates, as shown in Figure 3.8. A tour of your local Federal Reserve bank would convince you that this system works most impressively.

You can think of a template as a kind of stencil—one of the art supplies you probably owned as a child. If you remember, those stencils let you trace as many copies as you

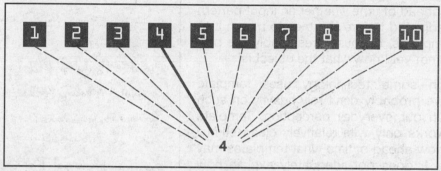

■ Figure 3.8: Illustration of template matching. The input "4" is compared either serially or simultaneously with all of the available templates. The match to "4" is the best.

wanted of the same thing. Templates work like stencils in reverse. An unknown incoming pattern is compared to all of the templates (stencils) on hand and identified by the template that best matches it.

As a model of perception, template matching works this way: Every object, event, or other stimulus that we encounter and want to derive meaning from is compared to some previously stored pattern, or template. The process of perception thus involves comparing incoming information to the templates we have stored and looking for a match. If a number of templates match or come close, we need to engage in further processing to sort out which template is most appropriate. Notice that this model implies that somewhere in our knowledge base we've stored millions of different templates—one for every distinct object or pattern we can recognize.

As may already be apparent to you, template-matching models cannot completely explain how perception works. First, for such a model to provide a complete explanation, we would need to have stored an impossibly large number of templates. Second, as technology develops and our experiences change, we become capable of recognizing new objects such as DVDs, laptop computers, and smartphones. Template-matching models thus have to explain how and when templates are created and how we keep track of an ever-growing number of templates.

A third problem is that people recognize many patterns as more or less the same thing, even when the stimulus patterns differ greatly. Figure 3.9 illustrates this point. I constructed this figure by having 14 people write the sentence "Cognitive psychology rocks!" in their own handwriting. You can read each sentence despite the wide variation in the size, shape, orientation, and spacing of letters.

How can a template-matching model explain your recognition that all 14 people have written the "same" sentence? In everyday life, much of the stimulus information we perceive is far from regular, whether because of deliberate alteration, degradation, or an unfamiliar orientation (compare an overturned cup or bicycle with one that is right side up). Is a separate template needed for each variation? And how is the perceiver to know whether an object should be rotated or otherwise adjusted before she tries to match it to a template? Remember, matching information to templates is supposed to tell the perceiver what the object is. The perceiver can't know ahead of time whether an input pattern should be adjusted before she tries to match it to different templates, because presumably the perceiver does not yet know what the object is!

So although some technology uses template matching, we probably don't rely heavily on such a process in our everyday perception. Template matching works only with relatively clean stimuli when we know ahead of time what templates may be relevant. It does not adequately explain how we perceive as effectively as we typically do the "noisy" patterns and objects—blurred or faint letters, partially blocked objects, sounds against a background of other sounds—that we encounter every day.

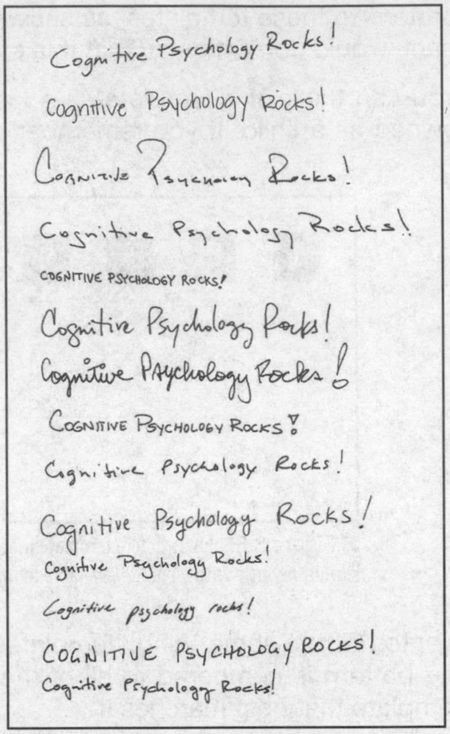

■ Figure 3.9: Handwriting samples.

FEATURAL ANALYSIS

As I write, I'm staring down at one of my dogs, curled up under the table. I'm able to recognize not only her but also certain parts of her: ears, muzzle, tail, back, paws, chest, and eyes to name just a few. Some psychologists believe such analysis of a whole into its parts underlies the basic processes used in perception. Instead of processing stimuli as whole units, we might instead break them down into their components, using our recognition of those parts to infer what the whole represents. The parts searched for and recognized are called **features**. Recognition of a whole object, in this model, thus depends on recognition of its features.

Such a model of perception—called *featural analysis*—fits nicely with some neurophysiologic evidence. Some studies of the retinas of frogs (Lettvin, Maturana, McCullogh, & Pitts, 1959) involved implanting microelectrodes in individual cells of the retina. Lettvin et al. found that specific kinds of stimuli could cause these cells to fire more frequently. Certain cells responded strongly to borders between light and dark and were called "edge detectors"—*edge* because they fired when stimulated by a visual boundary between light and dark, *detectors* because they indicated the presence of a certain type of visual stimulus. Others responded selectively to moving edges, and others, jokingly called "bug detectors," responded most vigorously when a small, dark dot (much like an insect) moved across the field of vision. Hubel and Wiesel (1962, 1968) later discovered fields in the visual cortexes of cats and monkeys that responded selectively to moving edges or contours in the visual field that had a particular orientation. In other words, they found evidence of separate "horizontal-line detectors" and "vertical-line detectors," as well as other distinct detectors.

How does this evidence support featural analysis? Certain detectors appear to scan input patterns, looking for a particular feature. If that feature is present, the detectors respond rapidly. If that feature is not present, the detectors do not respond as strongly. Each detector, then, appears designed to detect the presence of just one kind of feature in an input pattern. That such detectors exist, in the form of either retinal or cortical cells, confirms the applicability of the featural analysis model.

Irving Biederman (1987) proposes a theory of object perception that uses a type of featural analysis that is also consistent with some of the Gestalt principles of perceptual organization discussed earlier. Biederman suggests that

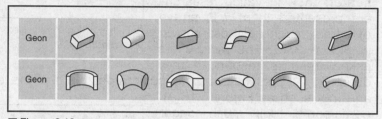

■ Figure 3.10: Some examples of geons.

when people view objects, they segment them into simple geometric components, called **geons**. Biederman posits a total of 36 such primitive components, some of which are pictured in Figure 3.10. From this base set of units, he believes, we can construct mental representations of a very large set of common objects. He makes an analogy between object and speech perception: From the 44 **phonemes**, or basic units of sound, in the English language, we can represent all the possible words in English (a number well into the hundreds of thousands). Likewise, Biederman argues, from the basic set of 36 geons, we can represent the thousands of common objects we can quickly recognize.

As evidence for his theory (called "recognition by components"), Biederman offers Figure 3.11, a line drawing of a fictional object probably none of us has ever seen. Nonetheless, we would all show surprising agreement over what the "parts" of the unknown object are: a central "box," a wavy thing at the lower left, a curved-handled thing on the lower right, and so on. Biederman believes the same perceptual processes we use to divide this unknown figure into parts are used for more familiar objects. We divide the whole into the parts, or geons (named for "geometrical ions"; Biederman, 1987, p. 118). We pay attention not just to *what* geons are present but also to the *arrangement* of geons. As Figure 3.12 shows, the same two geons combined in different ways can yield very different objects.

■ Figure 3.11: A fictional object.

It is worth noting that not all perception researchers accept the notion of geons as fundamental units of object perception. Tarr and Bülthoff (1995), for example, present a complex but interesting competing proposal.

Other research has provided additional evidence of featural processing in perception. For example, flashing letters on a computer screen for very brief intervals of time typically results in certain predictable errors. For example, people are much more likely to confuse a *G* with a *C* than with an *F*. Presumably this is because the letters *C* and *G* share certain features such as a curved line and an opening to the right.

Studies by Neisser (1963) confirmed that people use features to recognize letters. Neisser had participants perform a **visual search task** in which researchers presented them with arrays of letters, such as those shown in Figure 3.13. The researchers asked them to respond if they

■ Figure 3.12: Different objects containing the same geons in different arrangements.

detected the presence of a particular target, such as the letter Q or the letter Z. Shown an array such as Figure 3.13(A), participants took much longer to find a Z than they did to find a Q; the reverse was true for arrays similar to Figure 3.13(B). The nontarget letters in array (A) all share features like straight and angular lines, whereas those in array (B) share features such as roundness. Similarity between the target letter (Z or Q) and the non-target letters can make the search much harder.

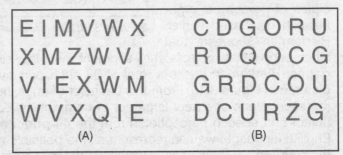

E I M V W X   C D G O R U
X M Z W V I   R D Q O C G
V I E X W M   G R D C O U
W V X Q I E   D C U R Z G
    (A)   (B)

■ Figure 3.13: Visual search stimuli. Notice how long it takes to find a Z or a Q in (A) and (B).

Similar findings have been reported for auditory perception of syllables that share many articulatory features. For example, *da* and *ta* are more likely to be confused than are two syllables that share fewer similarities, such as *da* and *sa* (G. A. Miller & Nicely, 1955). Examples of articulatory features (for consonants) include voicing, or vibration of the vocal cords (*b* is voiced, for example, but *p* is not); nasality, whether the air is directed into the nasal passages (*n*) or not (*l*); duration, how long the (consonant) sound lasts (compare *s* with *t*); and place of articulation, where in the mouth the sound is formed (compare *p* and *b,* formed in the front; *t* and *d,* formed in the middle; and *k* and *g,* formed in the back).

In fact, work on speech perception has demonstrated repeatedly that humans use **categorical perception** when they interpret speech sounds (Samuel, 2011). That is, we home in on the acoustic features, such as voicing or place of articulation, and use those features to group sounds into distinct categories. Lisker and Abramson (1970) demonstrated this phenomenon. They used a computer to generate artificial speech sounds consisting of a bilabial stop consonant (which sounds like either a \b\ or a \p\ sound) followed by an "ah" sound. The \b\ and \p\ sounds have the same consonantal features and differ only in the feature voice onset time. (Voice onset time, or VOT, has to do with how quickly after the consonant sound is released the vocal folds begin to vibrate; negative values of VOT indicate the vocal cords begin to vibrate *before* the sound is released.) Lisker and Abramson varied the VOT, by computer, from −0.15 second to +0.15 second, generating 31 syllables.

When they presented the syllables to listeners, the listeners "heard" only two sounds: a "ba" and a "pa." Any syllable with a VOT of +0.03 second or less was heard as a "ba," and any syllable with a VOT of more than +0.03 second was heard as a "pa." Participants did not report differences in the sounds of the syllables that were on the same side of the boundary. To them, a syllable with a VOT of –0.10 second was indistinguishable from a syllable with a VOT of –0.05 second. However, two syllables that were just as close in VOTs but fell on opposite sides of the boundary (such as 0.00 and +0.05) were identified by 100% of the participants as being different sounds: a "ba" sound and a "pa" sound, respectively.

Apparently, then, we pay attention to certain acoustic properties of speech (those that make a meaningful difference in our language) but ignore others. This might explain why we can understand the speech of a stranger (who speaks our language) quickly and effortlessly: We ignore the differences in his or her speech (pitch of voice, accent) that are not meaningful. Incidentally, categorical perception has also been demonstrated for some nonspeech sounds, such as tones, buzzes, and musical notes played on different instruments (Harnad, 1987). Moreover, studies of infants have shown that although very young infants can discriminate many, if not all, of the sound distinctions used in all the world's languages, that ability begins to narrow to just the phonemes in the infant's primary language when the infant is about 6 months of age (Eimas, 1985).

As a general model of perception, however, featural analysis models are not without problems. To begin with, there are at present no good definitions of what can be a feature and what cannot, except in very restricted domains, such as the perception of letters, the perception of line drawings of familiar objects, and the perception of speech. Consider the perception of a face. Are there general features for eyes, nose, and mouth? Are there specific features for right nostril, left eyebrow, and lower lip? Just how many features can there be? Do different kinds of objects have different sets of features? Then consider a vertical line. Although this feature is no doubt important for perceiving the letter *A,* how does it relate to perceiving a real human face? A beach ball? A wave crashing on shore? If there are different sets of features for different objects, how does the perceiver know which ones to use to perceive an object (remember, this must be decided *before* the perceiver knows what the object is)? If the same set of features applies to all objects, the list of possible features would appear huge. How then does the perceiver perceive objects so fast?

PROTOTYPE MATCHING

Another kind of perceptual model, one that attempts to correct some of the shortcomings of both template-matching and featural analysis models, is known as *prototype matching.* Such models explain perception in terms of matching an input to a stored representation of information, as do template models. In this case, however, the stored representation, instead of being a whole pattern that must be matched exactly or closely (as in template-matching models), is a **prototype**, an idealized representation of some class of objects or events—the letter *R,* a cup, a VCR, a collie, and so forth.

You can think of a prototype as an idealization of the thing it represents. The prototypical dog, for instance, would be a depiction of a very, very typical dog—the "doggiest" dog you could think of or imagine. There may or may not be in existence any particular dog that looks exactly like the prototype. Figure 3.14 shows variations of the letter *R.* If your intuitions agree with those of most people I've shown this figure to, you'll judge the letters toward the upper left and upper right of the figure to be more prototypical than those in the upper center.

Prototype-matching models describe perceptual processes as follows. When a sensory device registers a new stimulus, the device compares it with previously stored prototypes. An exact match is not required; in fact, only an approximate match is expected. Prototype-matching models thus allow for discrepancies between the input and the prototype, giving prototype models a lot more flexibility than template models. An object is "perceived" when a match is found.

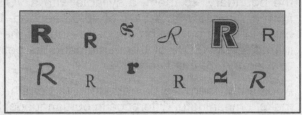

■ Figure 3.14: Examples of the letter R.

Prototype models differ from template and featural analysis models in that they do not require that an object contain any one specific feature or set of features to be recognized. Instead, the more features a particular object shares with a prototype, the higher the probability of a match. Moreover, prototype models take into account not only an object's features or parts but also the relationships among them.

Where, though, do prototypes come from? Posner and Keele (1968) demonstrated that people can form prototypes surprisingly quickly. These researchers created a series of dot patterns by arranging 9 dots in a 30-by-30 grid to form a letter, a triangle, or a random pattern. The dots were then moved to slightly different positions in the grid (Posner, Goldsmith, & Welton, 1967). The original patterns were designated *prototypes*, and the others (which were really variations on the same basic patterns), *distortions*. Some examples are shown in Figure 3.15.

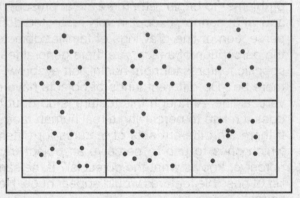

■ Figure 3.15: Stimuli used by Posner and Keele (1968). The top left-hand box shows the prototype; other boxes show distortions.

Participants viewed the various distortions but not the prototypes and were not told that the distortions were in fact distortions. Participants learned to classify the distortions into groups, based (unknown to the participants) on the original pattern from which the distortion was derived. After they could perform this classification without errors, participants were shown another series of dot patterns and asked to classify them in some way. The dot patterns shown in this part of the experiment were of three types: *old*—distortions participants had seen before; *new*—distortions participants had not previously encountered; and *prototypes*—also not previously seen. Participants correctly classified about 87% of the old stimuli, about 67% of new stimuli (still better than chance), and 85% of the prototypes than those in the upper center.

Given that participants had never seen the prototypes before, their accuracy in classifying them is surprising. How can it be explained? Posner and Keele (1968) argue that during the initial classification task, people formed some sort of mental representation of each class of items. These representations might be mental images or pictures. Some participants described verbal rules for where dots were clustered and in what kinds of configurations. In any event, they used these representations when classifying new patterns.

This work lends credence to the idea that we form and use prototypes in our everyday perception. And the effects are not simply a function of artificial stimuli such as dot patterns. Cabeza, Bruce, Kato, and Oda (1999) showed a similar "prototype effect" with photographs of faces altered by displacing features (for example, eyebrows, eyes, nose, and mouth) up or down by a certain number of pixels. Figure 3.16 shows examples of the stimuli used. Reporting findings similar to those of Posner and Keele (1968), Cabeza et al. found that research participants were more likely to "recognize" prototype faces they had never actually seen before than to recognize other, less prototypical new faces.

TOP-DOWN PROCESSES

All bottom-up models share a number of problems in explaining how viewers "make meaning" of the stimuli they perceive. Two of the biggest problems are **context effects** and expectation effects.

Consider the display in Figure 3.17. Notice that the second character of both words is identical. Despite this, you probably read the two words as "they bake," perceiving the character in question unambiguously as an *h* the first time and then, milliseconds later, as an *a*. The context surrounding the character, *t* and *ey* the first time and *b* and *ke* the second time, obviously influenced what you perceived. The context in which a pattern or object appears apparently sets up certain expectations in the perceiver as to what objects will occur.

Similar context effects have been demonstrated with perceivers looking to identify objects in real-world scenes: Both accuracy and the length of time needed to recognize objects vary with the context (Biederman, Glass, & Stacy, 1973; Palmer, 1975). For example, people recognize objects such as food or utensils faster in a scene depicting a kitchen than they do in the same scene jumbled up (see photos on the next page). These effects have led many psychologists to argue that any model of perception must incorporate context and expectations. We will look next at further demonstrations of the need to include top-down processes in theories and models of perception and pattern recognition.

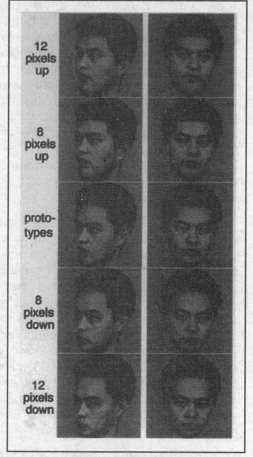

Figure 3.16: Stimuli used in the studies by Cabeza et al. (1999).

12 pixels up

8 pixels up

proto-types

8 pixels down

12 pixels down

Figure 3.17: An example of context effects in perception.

Top-down, or conceptually driven, processes are those directed by expectations derived from context or past learning or both. If someone were to tell you a fly is in the room you are in right now, where would you look? Notice how the direction of your glance would change if you were to look for a spider or a cockroach. Your past experience with such creatures guides where you look first—whether to the walls, the floor, or the ceiling. You can think of the processing you do when you look for different insects as being top-down, in that your expectations and knowledge guide where you look.

Top-down processes have to interact with bottom-up processes, of course. Otherwise, you would never be able to perceive anything you were not expecting, and you would always perceive what you expected to perceive—clearly not what actually happens. A well-known example of a largely perceptual model incorporating both bottom-up and top-down processes is that of David Marr (1982). Marr's model is quite technical and mathematically elegant, and the interested reader is referred to his full description of it. For our purposes here, I offer a very brief sketch.

Marr proposes that perception proceeds in terms of several different, special-purpose computational mechanisms, such as a module to analyze color, another to analyze motion, and so on. Each operates autonomously, without regard to the input from or output to any other module, and without regard to real-world knowledge. Thus, they are bottom-up processes.

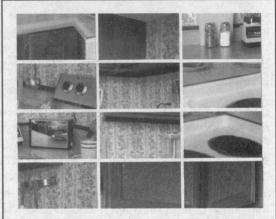

■ Photos 3.1 and 3.2: The context surrounding an object can make perceiving it easy or hard. If we were to measure reaction time, we might find that it took people longer to recognize the toaster in Photo 3.2 than in Photo 3.1. The coherent kitchen scene sets up a context that help us perceive the objects we expect to see in kitchens. The jumbled version of the scene destroys this context.

Marr believes that visual perception proceeds by constructing three different mental representations, or sketches. The first, called a *primal sketch,* depicts areas of relative brightness and darkness in a two-dimensional image as well as localized geometric structure. This allows the viewer to detect boundaries between areas but not to "know" what the visual information "means."

Once a primal sketch is created, the viewer uses it to create a more complex representation, called a 2½-D (two-and-a-half-dimensional) sketch. Using cues such as shading, texture, edges, and others, the viewer derives information about what the surfaces are and how they are positioned in depth relative to the viewer's own vantage point at that moment.

Marr proposes that both the primal sketch and the 2½-D sketch rely almost exclusively on bottom-up processes. Information from real-world knowledge or specific expectations (that is, top-down knowledge) is incorporated when the viewer constructs the final, 3-D sketch of the visual scene. This sketch involves both recognition of what the objects are and understanding of the "meaning" of the visual scene.

Marr's theory is not the only one to incorporate top-down processes. Other perceptual phenomena in which these processes seem to operate include perceptual learning and the word superiority effect, each of which we will cover in turn.

PERCEPTUAL LEARNING

That perception changes with practice has been well documented (E. J. Gibson, 1969); this phenomenon is called **perceptual learning**. A classic study by J. J. Gibson and E. J. Gibson (1955) illustrates this. Participants (both children and adults) were first shown the card in the very center of Figure 3.18, by itself, for about 5 seconds. Call this the *original*. Next, they were shown other cards, and randomly mixed in with these were four copies of the original. The participants' task was to identify any instances of the original in the deck. Participants received no feedback, but after seeing all the cards, they were shown the original card again for 5 seconds, then shown the full deck of cards in a new order. This procedure continued until each person correctly identified all and only the four copies of the original.

When J. J. Gibson and E. J. Gibson (1955) analyzed the errors participants made on this task, they found that the errors were not random. Rather, the number of errors seemed to depend most on the number of similarities a stimulus shared with the original. Participants were more likely to falsely recognize a stimulus that had the same number of coils and was oriented in the same direction as the original than to falsely recognize a stimulus that only had the same number of coils.

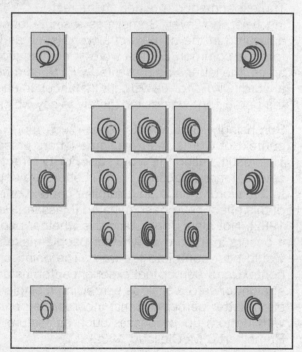

■ Figure 3.18: Stimuli used by Gibson and Gibson (1955).

Over time, participants seemed to notice more about the figures, responding to features of the stimuli they apparently had not noticed earlier. This explanation accords with other, everyday examples of perceptual learning. Take wine tasting as an example. Experienced wine tasters will tell you that one needs much practice to taste subtle differences. Novice wine tasters may be able to distinguish (by taste!) between a red and a white wine or even between a fruity and a dry white wine. Experts, by contrast, may be able to identify the vineyard that bottled a wine in a particular year. Novices simply miss this information—their taste buds may work exactly as do those of experts, but some information seems to be overlooked.

What exactly is going on? Apparently, perceptually practiced individuals learn what aspects of the stimulus to attend to and try harder to consciously distinguish between different kinds of stimuli. With regard to top-down processes, a perceiver's experience appears to help guide what aspects of the stimulus to focus on and to facilitate the "pickup" of more information (Gauthier & Tarr, 1997a, 1997b; Gauthier, Williams, Tarr, & Tanaka, 1998).

THE WORD SUPERIORITY EFFECT

A study by Reicher (1969) illustrates another top-down phenomenon—the effects of context on perception in practiced perceivers. The basic task was simple: Participants were asked to identify which of two letters (for instance, *D* or *K*) was briefly presented on a screen. Later, they were presented with two alternatives for what the letter might have been, displayed directly above the letter's original position. Figure 3.19 depicts the experimental procedure.

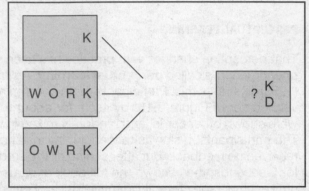

■ Figure 3.19: Stimulus displays and procedures used by Reicher (1969).

The experiment contained an interesting twist, however. Sometimes a single letter was presented. At other times, the letter appeared in the context of a word (such as *WORD* or *WORK;* notice that either *D* or *K* forms a common English word in combination with the same three letters). At still other times, the letter was presented with three other letters in a combination that did not form a word (*OWRD* or *OWRK,* for instance). In each case, the stimuli were then masked, and the participant was asked merely to say which letter, *D* or *K,* had been presented.

Surprisingly, participants could much more accurately identify letters presented in the context of words than the same letters presented alone or in the context of nonwords. This result, called the **word superiority effect** or the *word advantage,* has been replicated several times (Massaro, 1979). Letters are apparently easier to perceive in a familiar context (a word) than in an unfamiliar context or in no context at all. Theoretical explanations of this effect have been debated (Massaro; Paap, Newsome, McDonald, & Schvaneveldt, 1982). Not clear, for instance, is whether people detect more features in the letter when it occurs in a word or whether people make inferences about—guess at—the letter that would best complete the word. The point for our present purposes is that, once again, context and perceptual experience (for instance, with reading words) influence even as straightforward a task as perceiving a single letter. This insight has led to detailed models of letter perception that incorporate context-guided—that is, top-down—processes with bottom-up processes such as feature detection (McClelland & Rumelhart, 1981; Rumelhart & McClelland, 1982).

Interestingly, however, letter detection seems to operate very differently in a different context. When readers are asked to read a written text and cross out all the occurrences of a certain letter (say, *f*'s), they are very likely to miss the *f* in words like *of* or *for,* but to catch the *f*'s in words like *function* or *future,* a phenomenon known as the missing-letter effect (Greenberg, Healy, Koriat, & Kreiner, 2004). Presumably, as readers read connected text, they quickly divide the words into *content words* (which carry meaning) and *function words* (which structure the content words). They then focus their attention more on the moderately familiar content words and thus are likely to miss the letters in the highly familiar function words. The point for now is that the ability to detect letters is enhanced by word familiarity when words appear in isolation but is inhibited by increased familiarity or the word's role when a word appears within text.

A CONNECTIONIST MODEL OF WORD PERCEPTION

One detailed model is a connectionist model of letter and word perception presented by McClelland and Rumelhart (1981). Figure 3.20 illustrates some of the processing levels the model assumes. Note that the model assumes that input—whether written (visual), spoken (acoustic), or of a higher level, such as arising from the context or the observer's expectations—is processed at several levels, whether in terms of features, letters, phonemes (sounds), or words. Notice, too, the many arrows in the diagram. They manifest the assumption that the different levels of processing feed into one another. Each level of processing is assumed to form a representation of the information at a different level of abstraction, with features considered less abstract than letters and letters less abstract than words.

The model is presented in more detail in Figure 3.21. Each circle and oval in this figure depicts a node of processing in the model. The model assumes a different node for each distinct word, letter, and feature. Nodes have a certain level of activity at any given point in time. When a node reaches a given level of activity, we can say that its associated feature, letter, or word is perceived.

Note all the lines between nodes. These represent connections, which can be either excitatory or inhibitory. When an excitatory connection links two nodes, the two nodes suggest each other. Consider the nodes for the word *TRAP* and the letter *T,* for example. Imagine seeing a stimulus such as __*RAP* in a crossword puzzle in a family newspaper: four blanks, the last three of which are filled in with *R, A,* and *P.* If this pattern suggested the word *TRAP* to you, a connectionist would say your node for *TRAP* had been activated.

Once a node is activated, that activation spreads along that node's excitatory connections to other nodes. If the *TRAP* node has an excitatory connection to the *T* node, then the

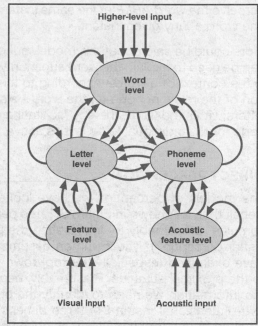

■ Figure 3.20: McClelland and Rumelhart's (1981) model of letter perception.

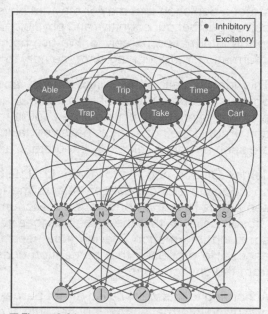

■ Figure 3.21: Nodes and connections in McClelland and Rumelhart's (1981) model of word perception.

T node will become more active when the *TRAP* node becomes more active, and vice versa. Excitatory connections are represented in Figure 3.21 by blue arrows ending with points. The brown lines ending in dots in Figure 3.21 indicate inhibitory connections, as in the line between the *TRAP* node and the *ABLE* node. Thus if the *TRAP* node is active, the *ABLE* node becomes less active. If you perceive the word *TRAP,* you are less likely to perceive the word *ABLE* at the same instant. The assumption is that you can perceive only one word at any given instant.

More could be said about this model, but our focus here is on how a connectionist model can be used to explain the word superiority effect. Why might a letter be easier to perceive in the context of a word? According to this model, perception of a word—that is, activation of the relevant node for the word—also activates the nodes corresponding to all the letters within the word, thereby facilitating their perception. Without the word context, the node for the individual letter is less active, so perception of the letter takes longer.

DIRECT PERCEPTION

The models of perception we have looked at so far all share a common assumption. Recall that, as shown in Figure 3.1, the perceiver must acquire information about a distal stimulus, presumably by interpreting the proximal stimuli (retinal images, in the case of visual perception). The common assumption underlying the models of perception we have examined (especially the top-down models) is that the perceiver does something to the proximal stimulus. Presumably, because the proximal stimulus doesn't contain all the information we need to identify the object (for instance, because retinal images are two-dimensional instead of three-dimensional or because objects might be blurred or blocked by other objects), we, as observers, must use our knowledge to fill in gaps.

To put it more simply, these models describe the act of perception as the construction of mental representations of objects. From the information we perceive, we somehow construct a depiction that may or may not physically resemble the object or event being perceived but that our cognitive and physiological processes can recognize as corresponding to the information perceived. We use both the information in the proximal stimulus and information from our long-term memory to construct these mental representations.

This idea is called the **constructivist approach to perception** (Hochberg, 1978), for obvious reasons. It describes people as adding to and distorting the information in the proximal stimulus to obtain a percept, a meaningful interpretation of incoming information. People are not seen as passively taking in all the available information; instead, they are seen as active selectors, integrators, and constructors of information.

James Gibson and his followers (J. J. Gibson, 1979; Michaels & Carello, 1981) adopt an opposite stance. Gibson rejects the idea that perceivers construct mental representations from memories of past encounters with similar objects and events. Instead, Gibson believes that the perceiver does very little work, mainly because the world offers so much information, leaving little need to construct representations and draw inferences. He proposes that perception consists of the direct acquisition of information from the environment.

According to this view, called **direct perception**, the light hitting the retina contains highly organized information that requires little or no interpretation. In the world we live in, certain aspects of stimuli remain invariant (or unchanging), despite changes over time or in our physical relationship to them. You may already be familiar with the idea of invariance. For example, consider a melody played on a piano in the key of C. Now, imagine that same melody transposed to the key of G. Although all the individual notes in the melody have been changed, the melody is still easily recognized. If sufficient time lapses between renditions, many listeners may not even recognize the key change. The elements (notes) have changed, but the relationships between the notes have remained constant, or invariant.

A visual example of perceptual invariance was demonstrated in a study by Johansson (1973). Researchers attached lightbulbs to the shoulders, elbows, wrists, hips, knees, and ankles of a model who wore black clothing and was photographed in the dark so only the lights could be seen (see Figure 3.22). Participants who were shown a still photograph of

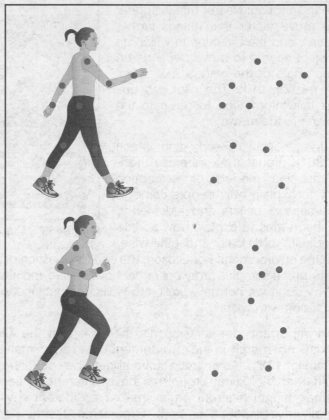

■ Figure 3.22: A depiction of Johanssons's (1973) experimental stimuli.

the model reported seeing only a random group of lights. Participants who saw a videotape of the model engaged in familiar activities—walking, dancing, climbing, and so forth—immediately recognized a person carrying out a particular activity.

Later work (Kozlowski & Cutting, 1977) even showed that observers could distinguish between a male and a female model just by the movement of the lights! Apparently, the motion of the lightbulbs relative to one another gave an observer enough information to perceive a human being in motion. Note that in this example, the observer did not see the person's shape or any individual features such as hair, eyes, hands, or feet. If a human form can be quickly recognized under these limited viewing conditions, imagine how much more information is available under normal circumstances. Recent work on this phenomenon, by the way, suggests many more amazing perceptual feats ordinary people can perform despite impoverished stimuli; it also examines the pattern of brain activity that accompanies this perception, typically in specific areas of the parietal or temporal lobes (Blake & Shiffrar, 2007).

J. J. Gibson (1950) became convinced that patterns of motion provide a great deal of information to the perceiver. His work with selecting and training pilots in World War II led him to think about the information available to pilots as they landed their planes. He developed the idea of optic flow, depicted in Figure 3.23 as the visual array presented to a pilot approaching a runway for landing. The arrows represent perceived movement—that is, the apparent movement of the ground, clouds, and other objects relative to the pilot. There is a texture to this motion: Nearer things appear to move faster than things farther away, and the direction in which an object seems to move depends on the angle of the plane's movement in relation to it. The pilot can use all this information to navigate the plane to the runway.

Turvey, Shaw, Reed, and Mace (1981) argue that whereas non-Gibsonian models of perception try to explain how people come to perceptual beliefs and judgments, Gibson tries to explain how people "adjust," physically and otherwise,

■ Figure 3.23: A depiction of optic flow.

to the environment. For Gibson, the central question of perception is not how we look at and interpret a stimulus array but rather how we see and navigate among real things in the world. Why don't we normally walk into walls, for instance, or flinch from a perceived impending collision with walls?

An important idea in Gibson's theory is that the information available to an organism exists not merely in the environment but in an animal–environment ecosystem (Michaels & Carello, 1981). As animals move about, they continuously experience their environments. Different biological organisms have different perceptual experiences because (among other things) different organisms have different environments, different relationships to their environments, or both. Organisms directly perceive not only shapes and whole objects but also each object's **affordances**—the "acts or behaviors permitted by objects, places, and events" (Michaels & Carello, p. 42)—in other words, the things offered by the environment to the organism. Thus, for human beings, chairs afford sitting, a handle or knob affords grasping, a glass window affords looking through. J. J. Gibson (1979) claims that affordances of an object are also directly perceived; that is, we "see" that a chair is for sitting just as easily as we "see" that a chair is 2 feet away or made of wood.

According to Gibson, then, we avoid crashing into walls and closed doors because such surfaces do *not* afford passing through and we perceive this as we move toward them. We sit on chairs or tables or floors but not on top of bodies of water, because the former afford sitting whereas the latter do not. By virtue of our activity with and around different objects, we pick up on these affordances and act accordingly. Perception and action, for Gibson, are intimately bound.

Gibsonian theory has been both staunchly admired and sharply criticized. Fodor and Pylyshyn (1981), for example, argue that Gibson's proposals, while intriguing, are not well defined. Without sharp definitions of what an affordance is, they claim, the theory is not helpful in explaining perception. They charge that Gibson failed to specify just what kinds of things are invariant and what kinds are not. Without this specification, the following kinds of circular explanations can result:

> How do people perceive that something is a shoe? There is a certain (invariant) property that all and only shoes have—namely, the property of being a shoe. Perceiving that something is a shoe consists in the pickup of this property. (Fodor & Pylyshyn, p. 142)

However the debate between supporters and critics of Gibson is eventually resolved, he has reminded everyone in cognitive psychology of the need to pay attention to the way cognition operates outside the laboratory and of the relationship between the way information is processed and the goals and needs of the organism doing the processing. We will return to these themes throughout the book.

DISRUPTIONS OF PERCEPTION: VISUAL AGNOSIAS_____

Earlier, I said that perception is a process by which we attach meaning to sensory information we receive. That definition distinguishes between sensation (for example, vision, hearing, olfaction), or the receiving of sensory information, and another process, perception, which makes sense of that sensory information.

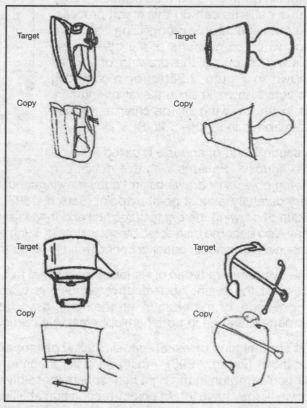

One of the best illustrations that sensation and perception are distinct processes comes from cognitive neuropsychological work on **visual agnosias,** impairments in the ability to *interpret* (although seeing) visual information (Banich, 1997). For example, consider Figure 3.24, which shows an agnosic patient's rendering of drawings of familiar objects. As you can see, this patient saw the original drawings clearly, and his renditions reproduce several details. But it is clear from the patient's copies that he has no idea

■ Figure 3.24: Drawings made by an agnosic patient of different target pictures.

what the depicted objects are. Rubens & Benson (1971) report on a similar case study in which their agnostic patient could not correctly name *any* of the objects he saw and drew, saying of a pig that it "could be a dog or any other animal" and of a bird that it "could be a beech stump" (p. 310).

Patients suffering from visual agnosia do not simply have a language problem, because they are similarly unable to use nonverbal means of recognizing familiar objects (such as pantomiming their usual uses). Nor do they have a memory problem, because they can tell you what a pig or a key is. Instead, the problem seems to lie in understanding what the visual pattern or object presented to them is (Farah, 1990). The deficit seems modality specific: Patients with visual agnosia can't recognize objects by sight but may be able to recognize them by sound, touch, or smell. Put in our earlier terms, the problem seems to lie in creating a percept from the proximal stimulus.

Researchers classify visual agnosias into different types. The first is called *apperceptive agnosia.* Patients with this disorder seem able to process a very limited amount of visual information. They can see the *contours,* or outlines, of a drawing or object but have a very difficult time matching one object to another or categorizing objects. Some cannot name objects at all, and at least one has been reported to be unable to distinguish printed *X*s from *O*s (Banich, 1997). Other patients can do this much processing but have trouble recognizing line drawings when some parts of the outlines are missing, such as the drawing of a chair shown in Figure 3.25(A), or recognizing objects shown in an unusual orientation, as in the drawing of the chair as viewed from above in Figure 3.25(B).

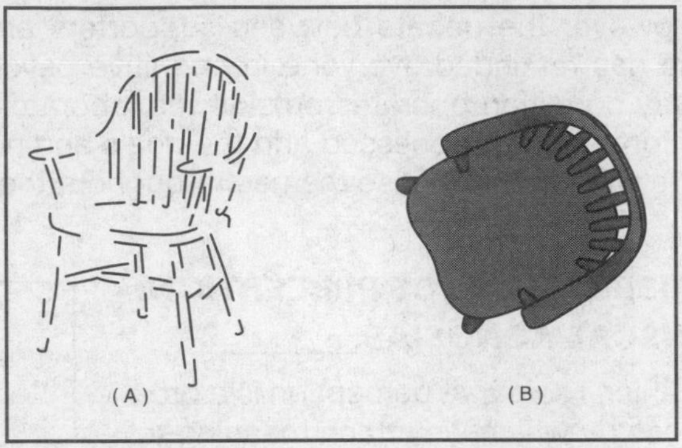

■ Figure 3.25: Examples of how contour information influences recognition in persons with apperceptive agnosia. (A) Patients with apperceptive agnosia have difficulty recognizing this object as a chair because they cannot interpolate the missing contours. (B) Patients with apperceptive agnosia have difficulty recognizing the chair when it is viewed from this unusual angle.

A second kind of agnosia is called *associative agnosia.* Patients with this deficit *can* match objects or drawings and copy drawings, but they tend to do so very slowly and very, very carefully, almost point by point (Banich, 1997), instead of using the more typical technique of drawing the big features first and then filling in details. Associative agnosic patients may also become distracted by small details, such as an extra dot or stray line on a drawing. Associative agnosic patients cannot readily name the objects they have seen and drawn.

The two different types of visual agnosia seem to be associated with injury to two different areas of the brain. Apperceptive agnosia is typically associated with one hemisphere, or one side, of the brain (often the right); associative agnosia is correlated with *bilateral* damage (damage in both hemispheres) to a particular region of the brain.

Yet another kind of visual agnosia, called **prosopagnosia**, is a very specific visual agnosia for faces (Farah, 1990). Prosopagnosic patients, who typically suffer from damage to a particular region in the right hemisphere (possibly with some left hemisphere involvement as well), may have intact object-recognition abilities but may be unable to recognize faces of their family members or political leaders or even photographs of their own faces. They can see details—a nose, an eyebrow, a mole—but can't seem to put the visual details together into a coherent percept. A book by Oliver Sacks (1985) gives vivid details of cases of prosopagnosia.

Visual agnosias are not the only kind of neurological deficit relevant to the cognitive processes of perception and pattern recognition. Another well-known impairment, known as *unilateral neglect* (sometimes also called hemineglect), comes about as a result of damage to the parietal cortex and causes the patient to virtually ignore stimuli on the opposite side (Mozer, 2002). For example, patients with right-hemisphere parietal damage may fail to wash the left side of their body, comb the hair on the left side of their face, or respond to stimuli that originate on the left side of the body.

This very brief review of neurological deficits in perception shows there is more to perception than simply receiving information. Seeing, whether or not it is believing, is certainly not perceiving!

Summary

Researchers have proposed a number of distinct approaches to the study of perception. Despite differences in the theoretical assumptions made and the experimental methods used in each approach, researchers agree on at least two general principles, given in points 1 and 2 in the following list.

1. Perception is more than the sum of static, individual sensory inputs. Perception clearly involves some integration and, perhaps, some interpretation of the sensations we receive. Perception is not a matter of simply taking in information from the world and creating from it a duplicate internal representation.

2. Perception sometimes involves "seeing" things that are not there (as in the case of subjective contours) or distorting things that are (as in the case of other context effects). Perception involves both bottom-up processes, which combine small bits of information obtained from the environment into larger pieces, and top-down processes, which are guided by the perceiver's expectations and theories about what the stimulus is.

3. One important perceptual task is the segregation of the figure from the background. Gestalt psychologists have offered many principles of how we accomplish this task, including the principles of proximity, similarity, good continuation, closure, and common fate. All of them follow the law of Prägnanz, which states that of all the possible interpretations a perceiver could make of a stimulus, he or she will select the one that yields the simplest, most stable form.

4. Various bottom-up models of perception include template matching, which holds that patterns are recognized when perceivers match them to stored mental representations; prototype matching, which posits that the stored mental representations are not exact copies of stimuli but rather idealizations; and featural analysis, which holds that we first recognize features or components of patterns and objects and then put information about those components together to form an integrated interpretation.

5. Top-down models of perception incorporate perceivers' expectations into the model of how we interpret sensory information. Research on the word superiority effect, for example, demonstrates that context changes our perception of stimuli.

6. The connectionist model of letter perception illustrates just how complex the task of recognizing single letters (all typewritten in a single, simple font) can be.

7. Perception involves a great deal of activity on the part of the perceiver. We do more than simply record the visual world around us; we are not cameras. In both the constructivist and the direct-perception approaches to perception, perception is assumed to be the result of activity, either mental or physical. We navigate the world, gathering information as we go and seeking more information about objects of interest as a matter of course. Any theory of perception must ultimately take into account our own activity in our everyday perception.

8. Disruptions of perception (as in visual agnosias, including prosopagnosia) involve not understanding or recognizing what is seen. Apperceptive agnosias involve intact recognition of contours but an inability to recognize what the object is. Associative agnosics can (sometimes, slowly) recognize the identity of objects but

focus intently on small details. Prosopagnosia is an inability to recognize faces, perhaps of relatives or of famous people, or even one's own reflection or photograph.

The topic of perception is fundamental to the study of cognition and relates to many topics discussed later in this book. Perception relates directly to attention, for example—the subject of Chapter 4—in that often our level of attention affects whether or not we perceive and remember something. When we talk about imagery, in Chapter 8, we will look again at how people process visual information. Moreover, what is perceived often constrains what else the perceiver can do with the information in terms of recording and storing it, thinking about it, and drawing inferences from it. We will thus continue to encounter perceptual issues in the chapters ahead.

Review Questions

1. Describe the differences in assumptions about perception made by researchers working in (a) the traditional information-processing paradigm, (b) the connectionist paradigm, and (c) the Gibsonian ecological paradigm.

2. Describe two of the Gestalt laws of perceptual organization, illustrating each with a specific example.

3. Distinguish between bottom-up and top-down perceptual processes.

4. In what ways are featural analysis and prototype-matching models an improvement over template-matching models? In what ways are they not?

5. Evaluate the fit between Gestalt theories of perceptual organization and Biederman's geon theory.

6. Describe some real-life examples of context effects in perception.

7. Consider McClelland and Rumelhart's connectionist model of letter perception. How might a Gestalt psychologist regard this model, and what would he or she see as the model's strengths and weaknesses? How might a cognitive neuropsychologist regard this model, and what would he or she see as its strengths and weaknesses?

8. Discuss the following: "Part of the reason that J. J. Gibson's supporters and detractors have such spirited debates is that they are talking past each other. Gibson doesn't just present a different model of perception—he redefines what the task of perception is."

9. What do the different visual agnosias tell us about perception? (More challenging: What are the limitations, both theoretical and empirical, of using case studies of brain-damaged individuals to inform theories of "normal" cognitive functions?)

Key Terms

affordance

bottom-up process

categorical perception

configural superiority effect (CSE)

constructivist approach to perception

context effects

direct perception

distal stimulus

emergence

feature

figure-ground organization

geon

Gestalt principles of perceptual organization

pattern recognition

percept

perception

perceptual learning

phoneme

prosopagnosia

prototype

proximal stimulus

retina

retinal image

size constancy

subjective contours

template

top-down process

visual agnosia

visual search task

word superiority effect

ATTENTION
Deploying Cognitive Resources

CHAPTER OUTLINE

Selective Attention
  Bottleneck Theories
  Spotlight Approaches
  Schema Theory
  Inattentional Blindness
Neural Underpinnings of Attention
  Networks of Visual Attention
  Event-Related Potentials and Selective Attention
Automaticity and the Effects of Practice
  The Stroop Task
  Automatic Versus Attentional (Controlled) Processing
  Feature Integration Theory
  Attentional Capture
Divided Attention
  Dual-Task Performance
  The Attention Hypothesis of Automatization
  Divided Attention Outside the Laboratory:
    Cell Phone Usage While Driving

Consider the task of driving a car. Besides involving many physical skills—such as steering, braking, and, if you're driving a car with a manual transmission, shifting—driving also involves many cognitive processes. Perception is obviously one of them: You need to quickly recognize relevant objects, such as stop signs, pedestrians, and oncoming cars. Driving also requires mental effort or concentration—what cognitive psychologists call *attention*. The amount of attention required at any given time depends partly on the complexity of the situation around you: Driving on wide side streets with no traffic is usually easier than driving during rush hour on crowded freeways. Your level of concentration also depends on your level of expertise at driving (Crundall, Underwood, & Chapman, 2002).

Recall your first driving experiences. Most people behind the wheel of a car for the first time wear a look of extreme concentration. Gripping the wheel tightly, eyes darting at the street or parking lot ahead, the novice driver has great difficulty carrying on a conversation, tuning the car radio to a favorite station, or eating a hamburger. Six months later, given both enough driving experience and normal conditions, the same driver may well be able to converse, fiddle with knobs, eat, and drive all at the same time.

Cognitive psychologists studying attention are concerned primarily with cognitive resources and their limitations. At any given time, they believe, people have only a certain amount of mental energy to devote to all the possible tasks and all the incoming information confronting them. If people devote some portion of those resources to one task, less is available for others. The more complex and unfamiliar the task, the more mental resources must be allocated to that task to perform it successfully.

Consider again the example of driving. The novice driver faces a complicated task indeed. She must learn to operate many mechanisms: gas pedal, brake, gear shift, clutch, lights, high-beam switch, turn signal, and so on. At the same time, while the car is in motion, the driver must scan ahead to see what is in front of the car (the road, trees, brick walls, and the like) and should also occasionally check the speedometer and the rearview mirrors. That's a lot to master, and, not surprisingly, it presents such a complicated set of demands that few cognitive resources are left for other kinds of tasks—talking, tuning the radio, fishing a stick of gum out of a purse or backpack, applying makeup.

However, with practice, the driver knows exactly where all the mechanisms are and how to operate them. An experienced driver can "find" the brake pedal with little effort, for example. The practiced driver has learned how to operate the car, scan the road, and check relevant instruments all more or less simultaneously. With many more cognitive resources available to devote to other tasks, experienced drivers do all sorts of other things while they drive—listen to the radio, talk on car phones, plan their day, rehearse speeches, and so on.

Anyone who has to operate complicated equipment or monitor many instruments simultaneously faces similar challenges. Air traffic controllers, commercial pilots, and medical personnel working in hospital intensive-care units or emergency rooms must all process a great deal of information from different monitors and instruments—much of it arriving simultaneously—and respond quickly and appropriately. Mistakes in any of these jobs can be costly. The following example, quoted in a study of the design of auditory warning sounds in airplane cockpits (Patterson, 1990), illustrates how too much incoming information can lead to a breakdown in task performance.

> I was flying in a Jetstream at night when my peaceful reverie was shattered by the stall audio warning, the stick shaker, and several warning lights. The effect was exactly what was not intended; I was frightened numb for several seconds and drawn off instruments trying to work out how to cancel the audio/visual assault rather than taking what should be instinctive actions. The combined assault is so loud and bright that it is impossible to talk to the other crew member, and action is invariably taken to cancel the cacophony before getting on with the actual problem. (p. 37)

Clearly, people who design equipment and instruments should know how people process large amounts of information and how much information we can process at one time. System designers often consult human factors psychologists, who study just these sorts of issues (Wickens, 1987).

My goal in this chapter is to explain what is going on, cognitively speaking, in the preceding examples. More specifically, we will examine the issue of mental resources and how they are assigned to various cognitive tasks. We'll first explore the notion of mental concentration. In particular, I will try to explain what "paying attention" to someone or something means. You will see that at least part of "paying attention" is concentrating—shutting out other activities or information to devote more mental resources to the object on which you want to focus.

We will next take a look at what some recent work in cognitive neuropsychology tells us about the brain mechanisms involved when people "pay attention." We will see that particular areas of the brain seem to become active when we pay attention or refocus our attention, and we'll see that information that is attended to elicits different responses in the brain from those elicited by unattended information.

We'll also examine how a person's concentration level changes with practice. For many tasks, extensive practice can result in the task's becoming so easy and effortless that performing it requires little attention. When this happens, performance is said to be automatic. This can mean, among other things, that attention is freed up for a person to do another task simultaneously with the automatic one. This topic, known as **divided attention**, has captured the interest of cognitive psychologists, and it will be explored toward the end of this chapter. Finally, we will examine some recent proposals about the relationship between attention and automatic processing.

Like many topics in psychology, attention captured the interest of William James in the late 1800s. James (1890/1983) anticipated the recent writings of investigators studying attention when he argued that only one system or process of conception can go on at a time very easily; to do two or more things at once, he believed, required that the processes be habitual. James's description of attention, as clear today as it was a hundred years ago, ably sums up the phenomenon psychologists study when they investigate attention:

> Everyone knows what attention is. It is the taking possession by the mind, in clear and vivid form, of one out of what seem several simultaneously possible objects or trains of thought. Focalization, concentration, of consciousness are of its essence. It implies withdrawal from some things in order to deal effectively with others, and is a condition which has a real opposite in the confused, dazed, scatterbrained state which in French is called distraction and Zerstreutheit in German. (pp. 381–382)

SELECTIVE ATTENTION

The term **selective attention** refers to the fact that we usually focus our attention on one or a few tasks or events rather than on many. To say we mentally focus our resources implies that we shut out (or at least process less information from) other, competing tasks. As attention researcher Hal Pashler (1998) puts it, "At any given moment, [people's] awareness encompasses only a tiny proportion of the stimuli impinging on their sensory systems" (p. 2).

Do your intuitions agree? Try this experiment. Stop and reflect: Can you hear noises in your environment? Probably, some or all of those noises were there just a second ago, when you read the preceding paragraph. But you weren't paying attention to those noises—they weren't "getting through." Ditto for other stimuli—can you feel your clothes or wristwatch or jewelry against your skin when you direct your attention to them? Probably, although you weren't aware of them a second ago. Presumably we process information differently depending on whether or not we have been actively focusing on a stimulus or not.

How do cognitive psychologists study what information people process about things to which they are not paying attention? If you think about it, this is a tough challenge: How do you present people with information while making sure they do *not* pay attention to it? Simply instructing them to not pay attention is almost guaranteed to have the opposite effect. (Try this: For the next 25 seconds, pay no attention to the feelings in your fingers.)

It turns out that a solution is well known to cognitive psychologists. Depicted in Figure 4.1, it is known as the **dichotic listening task**. It works like this: A person listens to an audiotape over a set of headphones. On the tape are different messages, recorded so as to be heard simultaneously in opposite **ears**. Participants in a dichotic listening task typically are played two or more different messages (often texts borrowed from literature,

■ Figure 4.1: Dichotic listening task. The listener hears two messages and is asked to repeat ("shadow") one of them.

newspaper stories, or speeches) and asked to "shadow"—that is, to repeat aloud—one of them. Information is typically presented at a rapid rate (150 words per minute), so the shadowing task is demanding. At the end of the task, participants are asked what information they remember from either message—the attended message or the unattended message. (Sometimes the tapes are recorded so that both messages are heard in both ears—called *binaural presentation*—and some researchers have used this technique in addition to dichotic listening tasks.)

The logic of this experimental setup is as follows: The person must concentrate on the message to be shadowed. Because the rate of presentation of information is so fast, the shadowing task is difficult and requires a great deal of mental resources. Therefore, fewer resources are available to process information from the nonshadowed, nonattended message.

Cherry (1953) demonstrated in a classic study that people can, with few errors, shadow a message spoken at a normal to rapid rate. When researchers later questioned these participants about the material in the unattended message, they could nearly always report accurately whether the message contained speech or noise and, if speech, whether the voice was that of a man or a woman. When the unattended message consisted of speech played backward, some participants reported noticing that some aspect of the message, which they assumed to be normal speech, was vaguely odd.

On the other hand, participants could not recall the content of the unattended message or the language in which it was spoken. In one variation of the procedure, the language of the unattended message was changed from English to German, but participants apparently did not notice the switch. Participants in another experiment (Moray, 1959) heard prose in the attended message and a short list of simple words in the unattended message. They failed to notice the occurrence of most words in the unattended message, even though the list was repeated 35 times!

BOTTLENECK THEORIES

To explain these findings, Broadbent (1958) proposed a **filter theory** of attention, which states that there are limits on how much information a person can attend to at any given time. Therefore, if the amount of information available at any given time exceeds capacity, the person uses an attentional filter to let some information through and block the rest. The filter is based on some physical (in this particular example, basic acoustic) aspect of the attended message: the location of its source or its typical pitch or loudness, for instance. Only material that gets past the filter can be analyzed later for meaning.

This theory explains why so little of the meaning of the unattended message can be recalled: The meaning from an unattended message is simply not processed. Put another way, Broadbent's filter theory maintains that the attentional filter is set to select which message to process early in the processing, typically before the meaning of the message is identified (Pashler, 1998).

Does this mean that people can never pay attention to two messages at once? Broadbent (1958) thought not, believing instead that what is limited is the amount of information we can process at any given time. Two messages that contain little information, or that present information slowly, can be processed simultaneously. For example, a participant may be able to attend simultaneously to more than one message if one message merely repeats the same word over and over again, because it would contain little information. In contrast, messages that present a great deal of information quickly take up more mental capacity, and fewer of them can be attended to at once. The filter thus protects us from "information overload" by shutting out messages when we hear too much information to process all at once.

Other investigators soon reported results that contradicted filter theory. Moray (1959) discovered one of the most famous, called the "cocktail party effect": Shadowing performance is disrupted when one's own name is embedded in either the attended or the unattended message. Moreover, the person hears and remembers hearing his name. You may have had a similar experience at a crowded social gathering: While engaged in conversation with one or more people, you hear someone behind you say your name. Until your name was spoken, you "heard" nothing that speaker was saying, but the sound of your name seemed to reach out and grab your attention.

Why does the cocktail party effect pose a problem for filter theory? Filter theory predicts that *all* unattended messages will be filtered out—that is, not processed for recognition or meaning—which is why participants in dichotic listening tasks can recall little information about such messages. The cocktail party effect shows something completely different: People sometimes *do* hear their own name in an unattended message or conversation, and hearing their name will cause them to switch their attention to the previously unattended message.

Moray (1959) concluded that only "important" material can penetrate the filter set up to block unattended messages. Presumably, messages such as those containing a person's name are important enough to get through the filter and be analyzed for meaning. Left unexplained, then, is how the filter "knows" which messages are important enough to let pass.

Note that participants did not *always* hear their name in the unattended channel: When not cued in advance to be vigilant, only 33% of the participants ever noticed their names (Pashler, 1998). Thus, an alternative explanation for the name recognition finding is that the shadowing task does not always take 100% of one's attention. Therefore, attention occasionally lapses and shifts to the unattended message. During these lapses, name recognition occurs.

Treisman (1960) discovered a phenomenon that argues against this alternative interpretation of the cocktail party effect. She played participants two messages, each presented to a different ear, and asked the participants to shadow one of them. At a certain point in the middle of the messages, the content of the first message and the second message was switched so that the second continued the first and vice versa. Immediately after the two messages "switched ears," many participants repeated one or two words from the "unattended ear." If participants processed the unattended message only when their attentional filter "lapsed," it would be very difficult to explain why these lapses always occurred at the point when the messages switched ears.

To explain this result, Treisman (1960) reasoned that participants must be basing their selection of which message to attend to at least in part on the meaning of the message—a possibility that filter theory does not allow for. Interestingly, most participants had no idea that the passages had been switched or that they had repeated words from the "wrong ear." Again, this poses a problem for filter theory, which would predict that information from the unattended channel would be shut out.

The issue of whether information from the unattended channel can be recognized was taken up by Wood and Cowan (1995). In one experiment, they had 168 undergraduate participants perform a dichotic listening task. Two of the groups shadowed an excerpt from the *Grapes of Wrath* (read very quickly, at a rate of 175 words per minute) in the attended channel (always presented to the right ear) and were also presented with an excerpt from *2001: A Space Odyssey* in the unattended channel, always presented to the left ear. Five minutes into the task, the speech in the unattended channel switched to backward speech for 30 seconds. Previous experiments had established that under these conditions, roughly half of the participants would notice the switch and half would not. The two groups differed only in how long the "normal" speech was presented after the backward speech: two and a half minutes for one group; one and a half minutes for the other. A third, control group of participants heard an unattended message with no backward speech.

Wood and Cowan (1995) first looked to see whether the people who noticed the backward speech in the unattended message showed a disruption in their shadowing of the attended message. In other words, if they processed information in the unattended message, did this processing have a cost to their performance on the main task? The answer was a clear yes. Wood and Cowan counted the percentage of errors made in shadowing and noted that the percentage rose to a peak during the 30 seconds of the backward-speech presentation. The effect was especially dramatic for those people who reported noticing the backward speech. Control participants, who were never presented with backward speech, showed no rise in their shadowing errors, nor did most of the participants who did not report noticing the backward speech.

What caused the shift in attention to the backward speech? Did the participants (or even some of them) switch their attention back and forth between the two messages periodically? Or did the backward speech cause the attentional filter to be reset automatically (that is, without awareness, intention, or effort)? To address these questions, Wood and Cowan (1995) analyzed shadowing errors by 5-second intervals for the 30 seconds preceding, during, and following the backward-speech segment (for the groups who were presented with back-

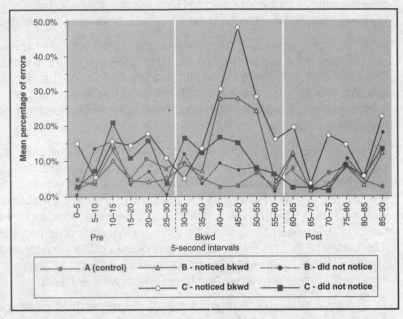

ward speech). These findings, presented in Figure 4.2, show that control participants and participants who did not notice the backward speech made no more errors over the time studied. However, participants who did report hearing backward speech made noticeably more errors, which peaked 10 to 20 seconds after the backward speech began.

■ Figure 4.2: Mean percentage of errors in shadowing for each 5-second interval within the 30-second periods immediately before, during, and after backward speech, shown separately for participants who did and did not notice the backward speech. A = control condition; B = backward speech during the first half of the 6th minute; C = same as B but ending after 6 minutes rather than 8.5 minutes. Bkwd = backward.

Wood and Cowan (1995) conclude that the attentional shift to the unattended message was unintentional and completed without awareness. They based this conclusion on the facts that detection of the backward speech interrupted and interfered with shadowing and that error rates peaked at a uniform time for all participants who noticed the backward speech. Put another way, Wood and Cowan believe that the participants who noticed the backward speech had their attention "captured" by the backward speech, which led to poorer performance on the main shadowing task.

Indeed, A. R. A. Conway, Cowan, and Bunting (2001) show that research participants who detect their name in the unattended message are those who have a lower working-memory span. (We'll talk about working memory in the next chapter. For now, you can think of it as the memory "space" or capacity a person has for keeping things in immediate mind.) In fact, 20% of participants with high working-memory spans detected their names in the unattended channel, compared with 65% of participants with low working-memory spans. The authors interpret this finding as follows: A lower working-memory capacity means less ability to actively block the unattended message. In other words, people with low working-memory spans are less able to focus.

Given her research findings, psychologist Anne Treisman (1960) proposed a modified filter theory, one she called **attenuation theory**. Instead of considering unattended messages as being completely blocked before they can be processed for meaning (as in filter theory), Treisman argued that their "volume" is "turned down." In other words, some meaningful information in unattended messages might still be available, even if hard to recover. She explained this idea as follows.

Incoming messages are subjected to three kinds of analysis. In the first, the message's physical properties, such as pitch or loudness, are analyzed. The second analysis is linguistic, a process of parsing the message into syllables and words. The third kind of analysis is semantic, processing the meaning of the message.

Some meaningful units (such as words or phrases) tend to be processed easily. Words that have subjective importance (such as your name) or that signal danger ("Fire!" "Watch out!") have permanently lowered thresholds; that is, they are recognizable even at low volumes. You might have noticed yourself that it is hard to hear something whispered behind you, although you might recognize your name in whatever is being whispered. Words or phrases with permanently lowered thresholds require little mental effort by the hearer to be recognized. Thus, according to Treisman's theory, the participants in Moray's experiments heard their names because recognizing their names required little mental effort.

Only a few words have permanently lowered thresholds. However, the context of a word in a message can temporarily lower its threshold. If a person hears "The dog chased the . . . ," the word *cat* is **primed**—that is, especially ready to be recognized. Even if the word *cat* were to occur in the unattended channel, little effort would be needed to hear and process it. This explains why people in Treisman's (1960) experiment "switched ears": Hearing the previous words in a sentence primed the participants to detect and recognize the words that followed, even when those words occurred in the unattended message.

According to Treisman (1964), people process only as much as is necessary to separate the attended from the unattended message. If the two messages differ in physical characteristics, then we process both messages only to this level and easily reject the unattended message. If the two messages differ only semantically, we process both through the level of meaning and select which message to attend to based on this analysis. Processing for meaning takes more effort, however, so we do this kind of analysis only when necessary. Messages not attended to are not completely blocked but rather weakened in much the way that turning down the volume weakens an audio signal from a stereo. Parts of the message with permanently lowered thresholds ("significant" stimuli) can still be recovered, even from an unattended message.

Note the contrasts here between attenuation theory and filter theory: Attenuation theory allows for many different kinds of analysis of all messages, whereas filter theory allows for only one kind of analysis. Filter theory holds that unattended messages, once processed for physical characteristics, are discarded and fully blocked; attenuation theory holds that unattended messages are weakened but the information they contain is still available.

Broadbent (1958) originally described attention as a bottleneck that squeezed some information out of the processing area. To understand the analogy, think about the shape of a bottle. The smaller diameter of the bottle's neck relative to the diameter of the bottle's bottom reduces the spillage rate. The wider the neck, the faster the contents can spill. We can applying this analogy to cognitive processes: The wider the bottleneck, the more information can "spill through" to be processed further at any point in time.

SPOTLIGHT APPROACHES

Modern cognitive psychologists often use different metaphors when talking about attention. For example, some compare attention to a spotlight that highlights whatever information the system is currently focused on (W. A. Johnson & Dark, 1986). Accordingly, psychologists are now concerned less with determining what information *can't* be processed (as the bottleneck metaphor highlighted) than with studying what kinds of information people choose to *focus* on (as the spotlight metaphor directs).

To see this, let's consider the spotlight metaphor in a bit more detail. Just as a spotlight's focal point can be moved from one area of a stage to another, so can attention be directed and redirected to various kinds of incoming information. Just as a spotlight illuminates best what is at its center, so too is cognitive processing usually enhanced when attention is directed toward a task.

Attention, like a spotlight, has fuzzy boundaries. Spotlights can highlight more than one object at a time, depending on the size of the objects. Attention, too, can be directed at more than one task at a time, depending on the capacity demands of each task. Of course, the spotlight metaphor is not a perfect one, and some researchers think it has many shortcomings (Cave & Bichot, 1999). For example, the spotlight metaphor assumes that attention is always directed at a specific location, which may not be the case.

Daniel Kahneman (1973) presented a slightly different model of what attention is. He viewed attention as a set of cognitive processes for categorizing and recognizing stimuli. The more complex the stimulus, the harder the processing, and therefore the more resources are engaged. However, people have some control over where they direct their mental resources: They can often choose what to focus on and devote their mental effort to.

An analogy could be made to an investor depositing money in one or more of several bank accounts—in Kahneman's model, the individual "deposits" mental capacity to one or more of several different tasks. Many factors influence this allocation of capacity, which itself depends on the extent and type of mental resources available. The availability of mental resources, in turn, is affected by the overall level of *arousal,* or state of alertness.

Kahneman (1973) argued that one effect of being aroused is that more cognitive resources are available to devote to various tasks. Paradoxically, however, the level of arousal also depends on a task's difficulty. This means we are less aroused while performing easy tasks, such as adding 2 and 2, than we are when performing more difficult tasks, such as multiplying a Social Security number by pi. We therefore bring fewer cognitive resources to easy tasks, which, fortunately, require fewer resources to complete.

Arousal thus affects our capacity (the sum total of our mental resources) for tasks. But the model still needs to specify how we allocate our resources to all the cognitive tasks that confront us. Kahneman (1973) posited that individuals have different "allocation policies," which are affected in turn by enduring dispositions (for example, your preference for certain kinds of tasks over others), momentary intentions (your vow to find your meal card right now, before doing anything else!), and evaluation of the demands on one's capacity (the knowledge that a task you need to do right now will require a certain amount of your attention).

Essentially, this model predicts that we pay more attention to things we are interested in, are in the mood for, or have judged important. For example, opera lovers listen carefully during an operatic performance, concentrating on nuances of the performance. People less interested in opera may sometimes have a hard time even staying awake. In Kahneman's (1973) view, attention is part of what the layperson would call "mental effort." The more effort expended, the more attention we are using.

Kahneman's view raises the question of what factors limit our ability to do several things at once. We've already discussed arousal. A related consideration is alertness as a function of time of day, hours of sleep obtained the night before, and so forth. Sometimes we can attend to more tasks with greater concentration. At other times, such as when we are tired and drowsy, focusing is hard.

Effort is only one factor that influences performance on a task. Greater effort or concentration results in better performance of some tasks, those that require resource-limited processing, performance of which is constrained by the mental resources or capacity allocated to them (Norman & Bobrow, 1975). Taking a midterm is one such task. On some other tasks, one cannot do better no matter how hard one tries. An example is trying to detect a dim light in a bright room or a soft sound in a noisy room. Even if you concentrate as hard as you can on such a task, your vigilance may not help you detect the stimulus. Performance on this task is said to be *data limited,* meaning that it depends entirely on the quality of the incoming data, not on mental effort or concentration. Norman and Bobrow pointed out that both kinds of limitations affect our ability to perform any cognitive task.

SCHEMA THEORY

Ulric Neisser (1976) offered a completely different conceptualization of attention, called **schema theory**. He argued that we don't filter, attenuate, or forget unwanted material. Instead, we never acquire it in the first place. Neisser compared attention to apple picking. The material we attend to is like apples we pick off a tree—we grasp it. Unattended material is analogous to the apples we don't pick. To assume the unpicked apples are "filtered out" of our grasp would be ridiculous; a better description is that they simply get left on the tree. Likewise, Neisser believed, with unattended information: It is simply left out of our cognitive processing.

Neisser and Becklen (1975) performed a relevant study of visual attention. They created a "selective looking" task by having participants watch one of two visually superimposed films. Figure 4.3 shows an example of what participants in this study saw. One film showed a "hand game," two pairs of hands playing a familiar hand-slapping game many of us played as children. The second film showed three

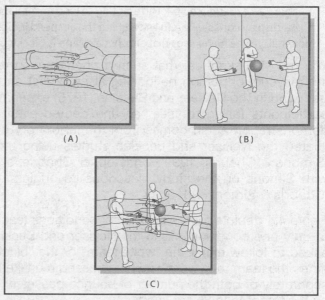

(A)   (B)

(C)

■ Figure 4.3: Outline tracings of typical video images used in the Neisser and Becklen (1975) study. (A) shows the hand game alone; (B) the ballgame alone; (C) the hand game and ballgame superimposed.

people passing or bouncing a basketball, or both. Participants in the study were asked to "shadow" (attend to) one of the films and to press a key whenever a target event (such as a hand slap in the first film or a pass in the second film) occurred.

Neisser and Becklen (1975) found, first, that participants could follow the correct film rather easily, even when the target event occurred at a rate of 40 per minute in the attended film. Participants ignored occurrences of the target event in the unattended film.

Participants also failed to notice unexpected events in the unattended film. For example, participants monitoring the ballgame failed to notice that in the hand game film, one of the players stopped hand slapping and began to throw a ball to the other player. Neisser (1976) believed that skilled perceiving rather than filtered attention explains this pattern of performance. Neisser and Becklen (1975) argued that

> once picked up, the continuous and coherent motions of the ballgame (or of the hand game) guide further pickup; what is seen guides further seeing. It is implausible to suppose that special "filters" or "gates," designed on the spot for this novel situation, block the irrelevant material from penetrating deeply into the "processing system." The ordinary perceptual skills of following visually given events "are simply applied to the attended episode and not to the other." (pp. 491–492)

INATTENTIONAL BLINDNESS

A recent area of research in attention concerns a phenomenon known as **inattentional blindness** (Bressan & Pizzighello, 2008; Rensink, 2002; Simons & Ambinder, 2005; Simons, Nevarez, & Boot, 2005). This is phenomenon of not perceiving a stimulus or a change in a stimulus that might be literally right in front of you, unless you are paying attention to it.

Mack (2003) gives the following everyday example of inattentional blindness:

> Imagine an experienced pilot attempting to land an airplane on a busy runway. He pays close attention to his display console, carefully watching the airspeed indicator on his windshield to make sure he does not stall, yet he never sees that another airplane is blocking his runway! (p. 180)

You may be skeptical that such a phenomenon really happens. After all, how can a (nonpsychotic) person be looking at an object and not really see it? One answer can be found in the Neisser and Becklen (1975) experiment described previously—research participants failing to "see" an unexpected event. A more dramatic (and humorous) demonstration again comes from the laboratory of Daniel Simons, who partially replicated the Neisser and Becklen studies using more sophisticated video technology (Simons & Chabris, 1999). Christopher Chabris, a graduate student who collaborated with Simons on the study, describes its origins in a recent book for a lay audience (Chabris & Simons, 2010).

Figure 4.4 depicts four experimental conditions (each research participant was assigned to only one condition). As in the Neisser and Becklen (1975) studies, participants were asked to follow either the "white team" or the "black team" and to count the number of times the team they were watching passed a basketball (Easy condition) or to keep track separately of both the number of bounce passes and the number of aerial passes made by the target team (Hard condition).

At a little under a minute into the presentation, an unexpected event occurred:

After 44–48 s of this action, either of two unexpected events occurred: in the Umbrella-Woman condition, a tall woman holding an open umbrella walked from off camera on one side of the action to the other, left to right. The actions of the players, and this unexpected event, were designed to mimic the stimuli used by Neisser and colleagues. In the Gorilla condition, a shorter woman wearing a gorilla costume that fully covered her body walked through the action in the same way. In either case, the unexpected event lasted 5 s, and the players continued their actions during and after the event. (Simons & Chabris, 1999, p. 1066)

■ Figure 4.4: Single frames from each of the display tapes used. The transparent conditions (top row) were created by superimposing three separately filmed events by means of digital video editing. The opaque conditions (bottom row) were filmed as a single action sequence with all seven actors. This figure shows the display for each condition halfway through the unexpected event, which lasted for 5 s of the 75-s-long video.

After viewing the entire videotape, students first wrote down their counts and then were asked to describe anything unusual they had seen on the video. Questions became increasingly specific, beginning with "While you were doing the counting, did you notice anything unusual on the video?" and ending with "Did you see a gorilla (or a woman carrying an umbrella) walk across the screen?"

Overall, 46% of participants failed to notice either the umbrella woman or the gorilla. Only 44% of participants ever reported seeing a gorilla, although this number was much greater for the subjects watching the black team, who presumably shared more visual features with the gorilla (dark color) than did the white team (see Table 4.1 for a full presentation of results). Simons and Chabris (1999) conclude that unexpected events can be overlooked. Presumably, we only perceive those events to which we attend, especially if the unexpected event is dissimilar to the focus of our attention and especially if our attention is tightly focused somewhere else.

■ Table 4.1: Percentage of subjects noticing the unexpected event in each condition. Each row corresponds to one of the four video display types. Columns are grouped by monitoring task and attended team (White or Black). In the Easy task, subjects counted the total number of passes made by the attended team. In the Hard task, subjects maintained separate simultaneous counts of the aerial and bounce passes made by the attended team.

	Easy task		Hard task	
	White team	Black team	White team	Black team
Transparent				
Umbrella Woman	58	92	33	42
Gorilla	8	67	8	25
Opaque				
Umbrella Woman	100	58	83	58
Gorilla	42	83	50	58

The original phenomenon has been widely replicated with a variety of stimuli (e.g., Bressan & Pizzighello, 2008; Chabris & Simons, 2010; Chabris, Weinberger, Fontaine, & Simons, 2011; Graham & Burke, 2011; Hyman, Boss, Wise, McKenzie, & Caggiano, 2010; Simons, 2010; Simons & Jensen, 2009). You might wonder if this phenomenon occurs only when watching movies or videos. Another study—this one by Simons and Levin (1998)—suggests that at least sometimes, it happens to real people in real interactions (see Chabris et al. for a second example). Simons and Levin describe a scenario they studied as follows (see a depiction of the study in Figure 4.5):

> Imagine that a person approaches you and asks for directions. Kindly, you oblige and begin describing the route. While you are talking, two people interrupt you rudely by carrying a door right between you and the person you were talking to. Surely you would notice if the person you were talking to was then replaced by a completely different person. (Simons and Levin, 1997, p. 266)

But in fact, only about 50% of their "participants" *did* notice that the person they had been talking to was replaced by a second person. (The replacement was achieved by having the second "interviewer" carry the back half of the door up to the first interviewer and the participant; the first "interviewer" then changed places with him, in a scene reminiscent of a *Candid Camera* segment.) The change in person went undetected even though the two interviewers were of different heights and builds, had noticeably different voices, had different haircuts, and wore different clothing, as you can see in the last photograph!

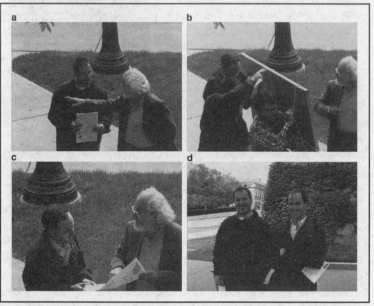

■ Figure 4.5: Frames from a video of participants in the Simons and Levin (1998) study.

Source: Simons, D. J., & Levin, D. T. (1998). Failure to detect changes to people during a real-world interaction. *Psychonomic Bulletin and Review*, 5, Fig. 1, p. 646. Copyright ©1998, Psychonomic Society, Inc. Reprinted with permission.

Interestingly, student participants were more likely to notice the change than were older participants (the study was conducted on the Cornell University campus). But when the two interviewers donned construction-worker clothing, fewer than half the *students* noticed the change. Simons and Levin (1997) speculate that participants encoded the status (including age or profession) of the interviewer only for gist, in other words, once the students decided a person was a worker, they ignored details of what the person looked like. Conversely, students would pay more attention to the interviewers when they looked like other students.

Investigators have also looked to see whether they can predict who will and who won't be affected by inattentional blindness, with mixed results. Chabris and Simons (2010) argue that there is almost no evidence that individual differences in attention or other abilities affect inattentional blindness. Simons and Jensen (2009) offer evidence in support of this conclusion in an experimental task. Interestingly, however, Graham and Burke (2011) report that older adults seem to be more subject to the phenomenon. Hannon and Richards (2010) report that lower working-memory capacity predicts susceptibility to inattentional blindness, a finding reminiscent of the Wood and Cowan (1995) study we reviewed earlier in the chapter. Seegmiller, Watson, and Strayer (2011) published similar findings and speculate that what helps individuals notice the "gorilla in our midst" is attentional control, a part of working memory we will discuss in Chapter 5.

NEURAL UNDERPINNINGS OF ATTENTION

Cognitive neuroscientists are interested in examining which areas of the human brain are active when a person is attending to a stimulus or event. Researchers have long suspected the parietal lobe of the brain (review Figure 2.3 to see where this lobe is situated) is one such location.

Clinical neurologists have documented the phenomenon of sensory neglect (sometimes called hemineglect) in patients who have parietal lobe damage. (You may recall some discussion of hemineglect in Chapter 3.) These patients often ignore or neglect sensory information located in the visual field opposite to the damaged hemisphere. Thus, if an area of the right parietal lobe is the damage site (as it often is in cases of hemineglect), the patient overlooks information in the left visual field. The patient may, for example, neglect to wash one side of the face or body, neglect to brush the teeth on one side of the mouth, or eat from only one side of the plate.

In clinical studies, patients showing hemineglect have been studied in more detail. Typically, they are presented with stimuli and asked to copy them. Figure 4.6 shows examples of stimuli presented to a patient with right parietal lobe damage and the patient's drawings. Note that in both cases, the left part of the drawing is missing, something the patient did not appear to notice.

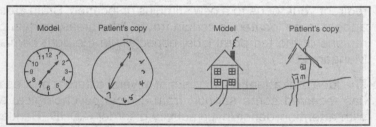

■ Figure 4.6: When a patient with a lesion of the right parietal lobe is asked to copy simple line drawings, such as a clock or a house, he omits details on the left.

Clinical work has established that hemineglect is attentional, rather than sensory (Banich, 1997). Were it simply a sensory deficit, we would expect patients to turn their gaze to the part of the visual field they were missing—in other words, to be aware that their visual information is incomplete. Indeed, some patients have just this type of deficit, and they do compensate by just such strategies. In contrast, patients with hemineglect seem unaware of one side of their body and disinclined to try to attend to information from that side. In extreme cases, patients with hemineglect even deny that some of their own limbs belong to them. In one case study, a patient thought hospital staff had cruelly placed a severed leg in his bed; he tried to throw it to the floor, but the rest of his body followed the (still attached) leg.

Although the parietal lobe is one brain region known to be associated with attention, it is not the only one. Areas of the frontal lobe (again, review Figure 2.3) also play a role in people's ability to select motor responses and develop plans (Milham et al., 2001). But how do the various brain regions communicate with each other to produce attentional performance? This question is clearly significant, and I will provide only a short, focused answer by looking specifically at one kind of attention.

NETWORKS OF VISUAL ATTENTION

Much work on brain processes of attention has centered on visual attention. Researchers have identified more than 32 areas of the brain that become active during visual processing of an attended stimulus (LaBerge, 1995). We obviously don't have the time or room to perform a detailed review of each. Instead, we will focus on some "networks" or systems of visual attention, initially proposed by Posner and Raichle (1994).

One such network is the operational, or enhancing-of-processing network (Kastner, McMains, & Beck, 2009). Luck and Mangun (2009) call this "implementation of attention" and argue it is used when a person has already decided where and on what to focus attention. This network serves to ensure that the to-be-focused-upon stimulus actually receives the cognitive processing and resources it requires. Kastner et al. (2009) believe that this attentional network is distributed across areas of both the frontal and parietal areas. These areas generate top-down instructions to the visual system to guide its focus on relevant stimuli.

A separate network, also located in the frontal, parietal, and subcortical lobes (that is, beneath the cerebral cortex), is used to control attention. When you decide or are instructed to, for example, look at the board in the front of the classroom, you recruit this attentional system to disengage from whatever you were previously attending to and redirect your focus to a new stimulus or location. Brain areas involved in this network also appear to be located in certain frontal lobe areas, certain parietal lobe areas, and certain regions of the temporal lobe, especially in the right hemisphere (Karnath, 2009; Luck & Mangan, 2009).

The idea that attention consists of several different processes that operate independently has received some support from clinical psychological studies of children and adults with attention-deficit/hyperactivity disorder (ADHD; Barkley, 1998; Rubia & Smith, 2001; Woods & Ploof, 1997). An estimated 3% to 5% of the general school-age population has some form of ADHD (Casat, Pearson, & Casat, 2001), with the disorder approximately 3 times more common in boys than girls. Barkley's classic work suggests that ADHD clients suffer not so much from an inability to be alert or to devote mental resources to a task as from an inability to sustain vigilance on dull, boring, repetitive tasks, such as "independent schoolwork, homework, or chore performance" (Barkley, p. 57). Logan, Schachar, and Tannock (2000) suggest that in fact the major deficit in ADHD children is an inability to inhibit an ongoing response (for example, talking or playing a game when asked to do homework).

EVENT-RELATED POTENTIALS AND SELECTIVE ATTENTION

Cognitive neuropsychologists have reported some fairly dramatic findings suggesting that information is processed very differently in attended versus unattended channels. Some of this work relies on measures such as a series of electrical potential recordings (electroencephalogram, or EEG) taken from the scalp of a participant. For technical reasons, researchers often average EEG records over many trials to reduce noise, ending up with the average electrical potential recorded 1 millisecond after presentation of a stimulus, 2 milliseconds after a stimulus, and so forth. This procedure results in a measure, already introduced briefly in Chapter 2, called an **event-related potential (ERP)**.

Banich (1997) has described the methodology of a typical study. Participants are asked to listen to one channel and to count long-duration tones. Short-duration tones and long-duration tones are both presented in each channel, attended and unattended. Researchers keep track of the ERPs to each stimulus. Results from many studies show that ERPs differ as a function of whether a stimulus is attended to (Pashler, 1998). Figure 4.7 presents an example of some typical results. Notice that the amplitude of the waveforms (that is, how much the waveform deviates from the horizontal) is usually much larger for the attended than for the unattended stimulus. This difference usually begins 80 milliseconds after presentation of the stimulus, which is enough time for information to travel from the sensory receptors in the ears to the cerebral hemispheres, suggesting that the effect occurs in the brain, not in the ears (Banich).

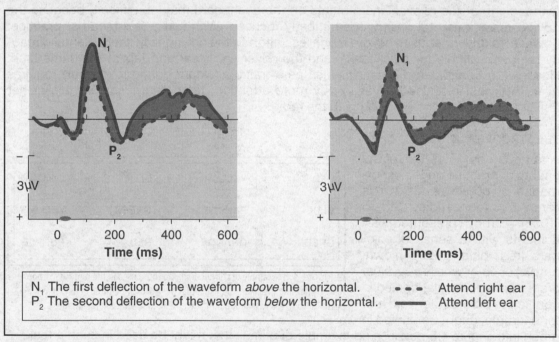

N₁ The first deflection of the waveform *above* the horizontal. ● ● ● Attend right ear
P₂ The second deflection of the waveform *below* the horizontal. ▬▬ Attend left ear

■ Figure 4.7: Modulation of early event-related potential (ERP) components by attention. The response to the stimulus is enhanced when it is presented in the attended location as compared with when it is not. (Left) For example, the amplitude of the N1 is greater to a left-ear tone when the individual is attending to the left ear (solid line) than when the same tone is heard but the individual is attending to the right ear (dotted line). (Right) Likewise, the response to a right-ear tone is greater when the right ear is attended (dotted line) than when the left is (solid line). The difference between these two waveforms (shaded area) is the Nd component. This effect begins relatively soon after stimulus presentation, within the first 100 milliseconds.

Source: Banich, M. T. (1997). *Neuropsychology: The neural bases of mental function* (1st ed.), p. 239. Copyright ©1997 Wadsworth, a part of Cengage Learning, Inc. Reproduced by permission. http://www.cengage.com/permissions/.

AUTOMATICITY AND THE EFFECTS OF PRACTICE

As we become well practiced doing something, that act takes less of our attention to perform. Typing is a good example. If you are skilled at typing, you can probably type fairly quickly and accurately and can do so while you carry on a conversation or even look out the window. If you aren't very skilled, then you type more slowly, make more errors, and are less able to process other incoming information. More formally said, an important variable that governs the number of things we can do simultaneously is the capacity a given task consumes. Adding 2 and 3 consumes little of my capacity, leaving some for other tasks (such as planning dinner tonight and wondering if I have all the ingredients at home).

What affects the capacity any given task requires? One factor is obviously the difficulty of the task. Another is the individual's familiarity with the task. Although easy for me, adding 2 and 3 still challenges a 5-year-old. The difference between us on this task is practice— I've added 2 and 3 far more often than any 5-year-old has. Practice is thought to decrease the amount of mental effort a task requires.

Recall the earlier example of a novice automobile driver. The unpracticed task of controlling a car in motion requires so much mental effort that little capacity is available for other tasks, such as tuning a radio or responding to a conversation. Even coordinating driving with looking at the relevant instruments on the dashboard may be difficult, because the novice driver's mental energy is so intently focused. With just a few months' practice, however, a driver needs to devote much less effort to the driving task itself. Mental capacity is now available for other tasks, and the driver can steer and talk at the same time. However, a complicated situation (such as a traffic accident during rush hour) requires even the most practiced driver to pay more attention, temporarily reducing his or her ability to converse or sing along with the radio.

THE STROOP TASK

A famous demonstration of the effects of practice on the performance of cognitive tasks was given by John Ridley Stroop (1935). Stroop presented participants with a series of color bars (red, blue, green, brown, purple) or color words (*red, blue, green, brown, purple*) printed in conflicting colors (the word *red*, for example, might be printed in green ink). Figure 4.8 provides an example of stimuli that might be used in such a task.

RED	YELLOW	BLUE	ORANGE
BLUE	PURPLE	GREEN	YELLOW
GREEN	ORANGE	RED	PURPLE

■ Figure 4.8: Example of stimuli similar to those used in the famous "Stroop" task. Try naming the colors of the ink that the words are printed in as fast as possible. Go to www.sagepub.in/galotti_CP5e to see the colored image

Participants were asked to name, as quickly as possible, the ink color of each item in the series. When shown bars, they did so quickly, with few errors and apparently little effort. Things changed dramatically, however, when the items consisted of words that named colors other than that of the ink in which the item was printed. Participants stumbled through these lists, finding it difficult not to read the word formed by the letters.

According to Stroop (1935), the difficulty stems from the following: Adult, literate participants have had so much practice reading that the task requires little attention and is performed rapidly. In fact, according to Stroop, literate adults read so quickly and effortlessly that *not* reading words is hard. Thus when confronted with items consisting of words, participants couldn't help reading them. We describe this kind of response—one that takes little attention and effort and is hard to inhibit—as *automatic.*

The actual task given to participants, to name colors, was one they had practiced much less. Participants in one of Stroop's (1935) subsequent experiments, given eight days of practice at the naming task, in fact showed less interference in performing the so-called **Stroop task** and became faster at naming colors with all stimuli. Moreover, a summary of the literature suggests that Stroop interference begins when children learn to read, peaking at around second or third grade (when reading skills develop) and then declining over the adult years until about age 60 (MacLeod, 1991). Virtually everyone who can read fluently shows a robust Stroop effect from an early age.

AUTOMATIC VERSUS ATTENTIONAL (CONTROLLED) PROCESSING

What exactly does it mean to perform a task "automatically"? We often talk about being "on autopilot" when we do something without being aware of it—but what is actually going on cognitively? Posner and Snyder (1975) offered three criteria for cognitive processing to be called **automatic processing**: (1) It must occur without intention; (2) it must occur without involving conscious awareness; and (3) it must not interfere with other mental activity.

Let's consider our driving example once again. A practiced driver driving a familiar route under normal, nonstressful conditions may well be operating the car automatically. Driving home, for example, I've often found myself in the middle of making a turn without actually intending to: My hand seems to hit the turn signal and my arms to turn the steering wheel without my consciously deciding to do so. Indeed, sometimes I follow my usual route home even when I intended to go a different way. For example, I may intend to go to the dry cleaners but start thinking of something else and then, to my surprise and embarrassment, find myself in my own driveway, simply because I forgot to change my automatic routine!

Schneider and Shiffrin (1977) examined automatic processing of information under well-controlled laboratory conditions. They used a version of something cognitive psychologists call a *visual search task,* in which participants see different arrays of letters or numbers and are asked to search for one or more targets. Figure 4.9 presents some examples of general visual search stimuli. You can see that the task can vary by whether the participant is asked to search for one or multiple targets, by

Target 3	Target B
R T E U	S D C X
I O P M	M R E A
Q 3 V Z	Z F G L
E N C A	N Q W O
(a) Single target-present	(b) Single target-absent

Target B	Target 3 or 9 or 1
2 5 4 9	T R P Q
0 3 4 B	G 9 H J
7 1 5 8	X M C E
4 2 7 0	W V L N
(c) Single target-present	(d) Multiple targets-present

■ Figure 4.9: Examples of visual search stimuli.

whether a target is present or not, and by whether the target and the other stimuli are from the same category or type (e.g., letters) or not.

Previous work had suggested that when people search for targets of one type (such as numbers) in an array of a different type (such as letters), the task is easy. For example, the search required in Figure 4.9 (a), (c), or (d) ought to be easier than the search required in 4.9 (b). Numbers against a background of letters (or letters against a background of numbers) seem to "pop out" automatically. In fact, the number of nontarget characters in an array, called distractors, makes little difference *if* the distractors are of a different type from the targets. So finding a *J* among the stimuli *1 6 3 J 2* should be about as easy as finding a *J* among the stimuli *1 J 3.* Finding a specific letter against a background of other letters seems much harder. So searching for *J* among the stimuli *R J T* is easier than searching for the *J* among the stimuli *G K J L T.* In other words, when the target and the distractors are of the same type, the number of distractors does make a difference.

Schneider and Shiffrin (1977) had two conditions in their experiment. In the *varied-mapping condition,* the set of target letters or numbers, called the *memory set,* consisted of one or more letters or numbers, and the stimuli in each frame were also letters or numbers. Targets in one trial could become distractors in subsequent trials. So a participant might search for a *J* on one trial, then search for an *M* on the second trial with a *J* distractor included. In this condition, the task was expected to be hard and to require concentration and effort.

In the *consistent-mapping condition,* the target memory set consisted of numbers, and the frame consisted of letters, or vice versa. Stimuli that were targets in one trial were never distractors in other trials. The task in this condition was expected to require less capacity. Figure 4.10 provides examples of some of the stimuli Schneider and Shiffrin (1977) might have used.

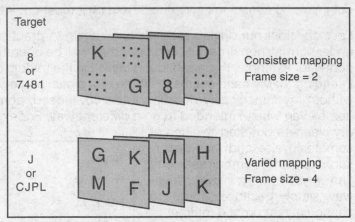

■ Figure 4.10: Depiction of stimuli presented to research participants in the Schneider and Shiffrin (1977) study.

In addition, Schneider and Shiffrin (1977) varied three other factors to manipulate the attentional demands of the task. The first was *frame size*—that is, the number of letters and numbers presented in each display. This number was always between 1 and 4. Slots not occupied by a letter or number contained a random dot pattern. Second was the *frame time*—that is, the length of time each array was displayed. This varied from approximately 20 milliseconds to 800 milliseconds. The last variable manipulated was the *memory set*—that is, the number of targets the participant was asked to look for in each trial (for example, find a *J* versus find a *J, M, T,* or *R*).

Figure 4.11 presents the results of the Schneider and Shiffrin (1977) study. The graphs are a little hard to follow, but try to do so in conjunction with what you read in the next few paragraphs. In the consistent-mapping condition, thought to require only automatic processing (because the targets and distractors were not the same type of stimuli), participants' performance varied only with the frame time, not with the number of targets searched for (memory set) or the number of distractors present (frame size). This means participants were just as accurate in searching for one as for four targets and in searching among one, two, or four items in a frame. Accuracy depended *only* on the length of time the frames were displayed.

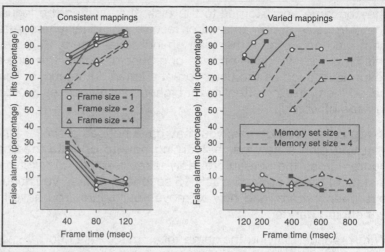

■ Figure 4.11: Results of Schneider and Shiffrin's (1977) experiments. Notice that for subjects in the consistent-mapping condition, only the variable of frame time affects reaction time. Subjects in the varied-mapping condition are also affected by frame size and memory set size.

In the varied-mapping condition, thought to require more than automatic processing (because the targets and distractors could both be letters or both numbers, and because targets on one trial could become distractors on another), participants' performance in detecting the target depended on all three variables: memory set size (number of targets searched for), frame size (number of distractors present), and frame time. You can see this in the second panel of Figure 4.11, where all the lines are separated, indicating that participants responded differently on trials with different memory set sizes and/or different frame sizes.

Schneider and Shiffrin (1977) explained these results by distinguishing between two kinds of processing. *Automatic processing,* they asserted, is used for easy tasks and with familiar items. It operates in parallel (meaning it can operate simultaneously with other processes) and does not strain capacity limitations. This kind of processing is done in the consistent-mapping condition: Because the targets "popped out" from the background, little effort or concentration was required. That searching for four targets was as easy as searching for one illustrates the parallel nature of this kind of processing: Several searches can be conducted simultaneously.

Schneider and Shiffrin (1977) dubbed the second kind **controlled processing**. Controlled processing is used for difficult tasks and ones that involve unfamiliar processes. It usually operates serially (with one set of information processed at a time), requires attention, is capacity limited, and is under conscious control. Controlled processing occurred in the varied-mapping condition (where targets and distractors could alternate across different trials). More generally, controlled processing is what we use with nonroutine or unfamiliar tasks.

Can we learn to use automatic processing in place of controlled processing for a task? Much work suggests we can, if we practice a task extensively. Bryan and Harter (1899) first made this point in an early study of the development of the ability to receive and send telegraph messages. They found, first, that with practice, people got better at both sending and receiving telegraph messages. Second, their participants reported that as they became accustomed to the task, they shifted the focus of their attention. At first, they struggled simply to send or receive individual letters. After a few months, they concentrated on words rather than on individual letters. Still later, their focus shifted again, this time from words to phrases or groups of words. Practice apparently made individual responses (such as the detection of a letter) automatic, or "habits," as Bryan and Harter called them, freeing attention for higher-level responses (words instead of letters, phrases instead of words).

If you play video games, you may have noticed a similar kind of learning effect. When you first play a new game, learning how to operate the controls to move your video figure across the screen probably takes a while. (My first game of Mario Brothers, for instance, lasted approximately 15 seconds.) At first, you need full concentration to figure out when, where, and how to move your figure. You have little capacity left to notice impending danger.

With practice, playing the game takes much less effort. I know "expert" Mario Brothers players (sadly for my ego, they are a fraction of my age and have a fraction of my educational level) who can play 30-minute games and still have enough cognitive resources left to carry on an extended discussion with me! My information processing in playing Mario Brothers is still of the controlled sort. My young friends, because of their extensive practice, now process much of the information automatically.

FEATURE INTEGRATION THEORY

By now you may have noticed lots of similarities among the investigations of perception and attention. In fact, these two areas of cognitive psychology are heavily intertwined, and researchers studying one of these topics typically have to be very well informed about research into the other. You may also be wondering about the role attention and automaticity play in perception, and vice versa, because many experiments we've talked about in this chapter certainly involve the perception and recognition of familiar stimuli. Anne Treisman, inspired by the work of Schneider and Shiffrin, investigated this question, developing what has come to be called **feature integration theory**. Her general idea is that we perceive objects in two distinct stages. In the first stage, which is preattentive, or automatic, we register features of objects, such as their color or shape. In the second stage, attention allows us to "glue" the features together into a unified object (Tsal, 1989a).

Treisman reported several experimental results that support feature integration theory. In one experiment (Treisman & Gelade, 1980), researchers presented participants with a series of simple objects (such as letters) that differed in several features (such as color or shape). Participants were asked to search for a particular object—for example, a pink letter or the letter *T*. If the item being searched for differed from the background items in the critical feature (such as a pink item among green and brown items, or a *T* among *O*s), the target item seemed to pop out of the display, and the number of background items did not affect participants' reaction times. Treisman and Gelade interpreted this pattern of results as evidence that the detection of individual features is automatic—that is, requiring little attention or concentration and occurring in parallel. As a result, detecting a circle or the color blue or any other single feature is relatively easy. You can check out this phenomenon for yourself with the stimuli shown in Figure 4.12.

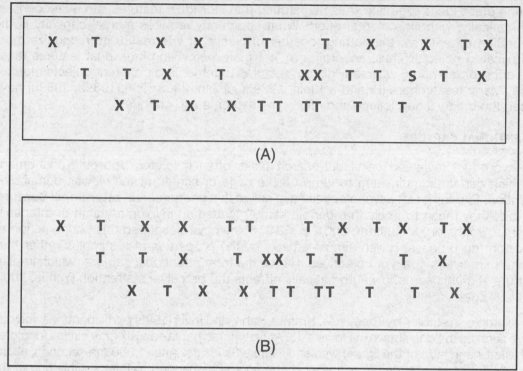

■ Figure 4.12: Example of stimuli from a feature integration study. Notice how easy it is to spot the blue S in (A) relative to finding the green X in (B).

In another condition, participants were asked to search for an object with a combination of features—such as a pink *T*—against a background of objects that had one or the other feature (in this example, both pink items that were not *T*s, and *T*s that were not pink). In this condition, participants' reaction times varied with the number of background items. Treisman and Gelade (1980) argued that searching for a conjunction, or combination, of features requires controlled, nonautomatic processing.

Interestingly, in a later study, Treisman and Schmidt (1982) showed that when attention is diverted or "overloaded," participants make integration errors, resulting in what Treisman called *illusory conjunctions.* Consider the example of glancing quickly and without much attention out the window at a red Honda Civic and a blue Cadillac. Later, when asked to report what you saw, you might say, "A blue Honda Civic." Such combining of two stimuli is erroneous; the conjunction reported is illusory.

In the experimental demonstration of this phenomenon (Treisman & Schmidt, 1982), participants saw two black digits displayed on either side of a row of three larger, colored letters, presented briefly (for 200 milliseconds). They were asked to pay attention to and recite the black digits, with the experimenter emphasizing the importance of accuracy. Participants were also asked, *after* they had reported the digits, to report the positions (left, right, or middle), colors, and names of any letters they had seen. They were asked to report only information about which they were highly confident. Participants were able to provide correct information on letters 52% of the time, but in 39% of the trials, they reported illusory conjunctions (such as a red *X* instead of either a blue *X* or a red *T*). In other words, when mentally taxed, people mistakenly combined features in illusory conjunctions.

Putting these ideas together, Treisman argued that individual features can be recognized automatically, with little mental effort. What apparently requires mental capacity is the integration of features, the putting together of pieces of information to recognize more complicated objects. Thus, according to Treisman, perceiving individual features takes little effort or attention, whereas "gluing" features together into coherent objects requires more. Many researchers (Briand & Klein, 1989; Quinlan, 2003; Tsal, 1989a, 1989b) have tested the theory's predictions and offered refinements and critiques.

ATTENTIONAL CAPTURE

The work just reviewed on visual search tasks often involves "pop-out" phenomena in which certain stimuli seem to jump off the page or screen at the viewer, demanding attention. Experimental psychologists have called this phenomenon **attentional capture**. By this, they mean to imply that certain stimuli "cause an involuntary shift of attention" (Pashler, Johnston, & Ruthruff, 2001, p. 634). Many have described this phenomenon as a bottom-up process, driven almost entirely by the properties of a stimulus rather than by the perceiver's goals or objectives. Hence the term *attentional capture,* which implies that the stimulus somehow automatically attracts the perceiver's attention (Yantis, 2000; Yantis & Egeth, 1999).

For example, in studies by Theeuwes, Kramer, Hahn, and Irwin (1998) participants viewed displays such as the one shown in Figure 4.13. At first, participants saw six gray circles (depicted in the left-hand side of the figure) with small figure 8s inside. After 1,000 milliseconds, all but one of the circles changed to red, and all the figure 8s changed to letters. Only one of the circles remained gray. Participants were instructed to move their eyes to the only gray circle and to decide as quickly as possible if the letter it contained was a *C* or a reverse *C.*

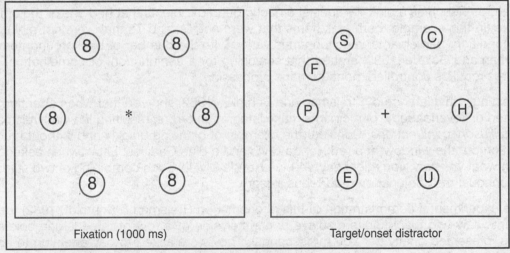

■ Figure 4.13: Stimuli from the Theeuwes et al. (1998) study of attentional capture.

On half the trials, when the gray circles changed to red, another (seventh) red circle suddenly appeared, without forewarning, somewhere on the screen. Even though this new object was irrelevant to the task, it tended to draw the participants' eyes toward it, extending their reaction time to make a decision. However, when participants in a follow-up study (Theeuwes, Atchley, & Kramer, 2000) were first warned to attend to a specific location (where the single remaining gray circle would be), they did not have their attention "captured" by the appearance of a new, irrelevant stimulus. This suggests that, with enough time, top-down processes intentionally controlled by a participant can override passive and reflexive attentional capture (see also studies by Eimer & Kiss, 2010; Liao & Yeh, 2011).

Fukuda and Vogel (2011) examined the role of working-memory capacity in attentional capture. They recruited students who had either a high or low working-memory capacity and found that both groups were equally susceptible to the phenomenon of attentional capture. What distinguished the two groups was that high-capacity students recovered more quickly from the initial attentional capture than did low-capacity students. This, in turn, suggested to the authors that a lower working-memory capacity has to do with attentional control and, in particular, with one's ability to disengage attention from a distractor. We'll return to this point in Chapter 5, where we discuss the central executive component of working memory.

DIVIDED ATTENTION

If attention is a flexible system for allocating resources, and if tasks differ in the amount of attention they require, then people should be able to learn to perform two tasks at once. Parents of teenagers, for example, often marvel over how their children seem able to listen to music, talk on the phone to their friends, and study all at the same time. How difficult is doing two or more tasks at once, and on what factors does this ability depend?

DUAL-TASK PERFORMANCE

Spelke, Hirst, and Neisser (1976) examined this question in a clever and demanding laboratory study. Two Cornell University students were recruited as participants. Five days a week, for 17 weeks, working in 1-hour sessions, these students learned to write words dictated while they read short stories. Their reading comprehension was periodically tested. After 6 weeks of practice, their reading rates (shown in Figure 4.14) approached their normal speeds. Also by the end of 6 weeks, their scores on the reading comprehension tests were comparable whether they were only reading stories (and thus presumably giving the reading task their full attention) or reading stories while writing down dictated words. Further investigation revealed that participants could also categorize the dictated words by meaning and could discover relations among the words without sacrificing reading speed or comprehension.

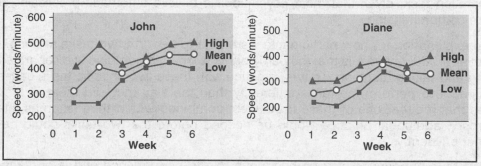

■ Figure 4.14: Reading speeds during practice phase of learning to do two things at once. Weekly means and interquartile ranges of reading speeds are plotted for each week of practice for two subjects, John and Diane.

Many psychologists were surprised that the participants in this study could process information about meaning without conscious attention, and some offered alternative explanations for the findings. One hypothesis is that participants alternated their attention between the two tasks, attending first to the story, then to the dictation, then to the story again, and so on. Although this possibility was not directly tested, the authors argued the fact that the participants' reading speeds were comparable whether or not they were taking dictation suggests that if they were alternating their attention, they were doing so without any measurable lag (Spelke et al., 1976).

Hirst, Spelke, Reaves, Caharack, and Neisser (1980) found evidence against this alternation hypothesis. Their participants were given training similar to that given to the participants in Spelke et al.'s (1976) experiment. All participants copied dictated words while reading. Some participants read short stories, presumably containing some redundant material and therefore requiring relatively little attention. Other participants read encyclopedia articles, thought to contain less redundant material and thus to require more concentration. After they reached normal reading speeds and reading comprehension during dictation, the participants' tasks were switched: Those who had been reading short stories were now given encyclopedia articles, and those trained using encyclopedia articles now read short stories. Six of the seven participants performed comparably with the new reading material, indicating that the participants were probably not alternating their attention between the two tasks. If they were, then learning to take dictation while reading short stories should not transfer well to doing so while reading encyclopedia articles.

A second possible explanation for participants' ability to learn to do two tasks at once is that one of the two tasks (for example, the dictation task) is being performed automatically. According to one of Posner and Snyder's (1975) criteria for automaticity—that processing not interfere with other mental activity—taking dictation in this study might be considered automatic. However, participants were clearly aware that words were being dictated, and they typically recognized about 80% of the dictated words on tests immediately following trials. Moreover, participants clearly intended to copy the dictated words. Therefore, taking dictation does not meet Posner and Snyder's last two criteria: lack of intention and lack of conscious awareness.

Hirst et al. (1980) also offered evidence against the possibility that one task becomes automatized. Participants trained to copy complete sentences while reading were able to comprehend and recall those sentences, suggesting that the participants had processed the dictation task for meaning. This in turn suggests they paid at least some attention to the dictation task, given that most psychologists believe automatic processing occurs without comprehension.

A third explanation for how participants were able to perform two tasks at once, which Hirst et al. (1980) favored, is that the participants learned to combine two separate tasks: reading and taking dictation. That is, practice with these two specific tasks caused the participants to perform the tasks differently than the way they did them at first. This implies that if either one of these tasks were combined with a third (such as shadowing prose), additional practice would be needed before the two tasks could be done together efficiently.

Practice thus appears to play an enormous role in performance and is one important determinant of how much attention any task requires. Studies such as those by Hirst et al.

(1980) are not without critics (see Shiffrin, 1988). However, this work and related studies are beginning to change our understanding of the role that practice plays in cognitive tasks (see Pashler et al., 2001, for a more detailed discussion).

THE ATTENTION HYPOTHESIS OF AUTOMATIZATION

Work by Gordon Logan and Joseph Etherton (Logan & Etherton, 1994; Logan, Taylor, & Etherton, 1996) has sought to tie together many concepts we have talked about in this chapter. These researchers propose what they call the **attention hypothesis of automatization**, which states that attention is needed during the practice phase of a task and determines what gets learned during practice. Attention also determines what will be remembered from the practice. Logan et al. (1996) puts it this way: "Learning is a side effect of attending: People will learn about the things they attend to and they will not learn much about the things they do not attend to" (p. 620). Specifically, Logan et al. argue that attention affects what information gets encoded into a memory and what information is later retrieved (topics we will take up in detail in Chapters 5 and 6).

In a series of experiments, Logan and Etherton (1994) presented college student participants with a series of two-word displays and asked them to detect particular target words (for example, words that named metals) as fast as possible. For some participants, the word pairs remained constant over trials; for example, if the words *steel* and *Canada* were paired on one trial, then neither word ever appeared with any other word on subsequent trials. Other participants saw word pairs that varied from trial to trial, such as *steel* with *Canada* on one trial and *steel* with *broccoli* on another. The question was, Would participants in the first condition gain an advantage in performance because the words were consistently paired?

The answer was yes, but only when the specifics of the target-detection task forced the participants to pay attention to both words in the display. If, for example, the experimenters colored one of the two words green and asked participants only to decide whether the green word in a stimulus display was a target word on each trial, then participants did not gain an advantage from consistent pairings of words and, indeed, later recalled fewer of the distractor words. Apparently the color cue made it easy for participants to ignore the meaning of the second word in the display. To ignore something means not to pay attention to it, and thus apparently little gets learned about it. Even with extensive practice (five sessions), participants in the consistent pairing condition were unlikely to learn which words had been paired if they had no reason to pay attention to the distractor word.

DIVIDED ATTENTION OUTSIDE THE LABORATORY: CELL PHONE USAGE WHILE DRIVING

Let's see if we can apply some of the theoretical concepts just reviewed to an actual instance of **dual-task performance** in the real world. Recently, many states have enacted or have considered enacting legislation to prohibit drivers from talking on cell phones while behind the wheel. Using a cell phone while driving is becoming more commonplace and is also believed to be a major cause of a four- to sixfold increase in accident risk (Maciej, Nitsch, & Vollrath, 2011). The argument against driving while using a cell phone is that talking on a cell phone distracts the driver's attention from what should be the primary task, navigating the vehicle on the road.

In a clever simulation, Strayer and Johnston (2001) investigated this interference. In their first experiment, they had research participants perform a pursuit tracking task: The participants used a joystick to move a cursor on a computer; their goal was to keep it positioned over a moving target. (Ethical considerations no doubt precluded doing the study with actual drivers on actual highways!) At various intervals, the target flashed either red or green, a signal to the "driver" to push a "brake" button on the joystick (red) or ignore the flash (green). Participants first performed the tracking ("driving") task by itself, then performed the dual-task portion of the study: either listening to a radio broadcast or talking on a cell phone with a confederate of the experimenters. The confederate, who was in a different location, talked with the participants, either about the then-current Clinton presidential impeachment or about the Salt Lake City Olympic Committee bribery scandal, and tried to ensure that the participant talked and listened approximately equally. Listening to the radio broadcast did not cause people to miss red lights or to react to them more slowly than they had when they performed the pursuit task by itself (the single-task condition). However, talking on the cell phone did cause both problems, as shown in Figure 4.15.

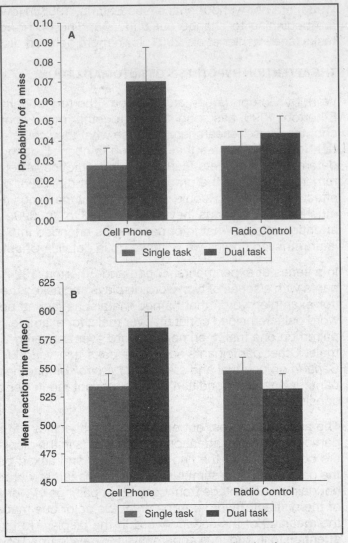

Figure 4.15: Results from the Strayer and Johnston (2001) study.

In a second experiment, the authors had participants talk on a cell phone, either "shadowing" lists of words the confederate read to them or else performing a word-generation task. In the latter task, the participant listened to the word the confederate read (let's say the word was *cream*) and then had to generate a new word that began with the last letter of the word read (in our example, participants had to say a word beginning with the letter *m*). For some participants, the pursuit task was easy, with few unpredictable changes, whereas for others it was more difficult, with many such changes. Shadowing words did not lead to reliable decrements in performance. However, generating words did, and the decrement was especially pronounced when the task was difficult.

You might wonder why, if talking on a cell phone is so dangerous, talking to a passenger in the car isn't. Indeed, having a passenger in the car results in less accident risk relative to driving alone. Maciej et al. (2011) explain the apparent paradox by arguing that passengers who are able to see what the driver sees *modulate,* or adjust, their style of conversation to match the attentional demands on the driver. When the driver faces a challenging situation, such as traffic, an accident, or bad weather, passengers change the way they talk—speaking in less complex ways, for example. As the driver adjusts to road conditions—speaking less, speaking in shorter utterances, pausing more—passengers also made adjustments. So, in fact, did cell phone partners who had visual information about what the driver was facing (this study was again done in a simulator).

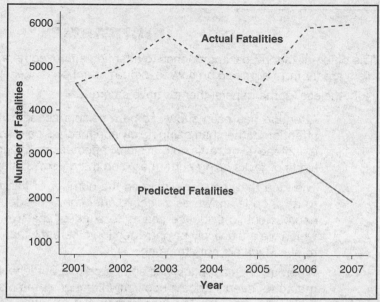

■ Figure 4.16: Estimated and actual traffic fatalities.

What about texting and driving? F. A. Wilson and Stimpson (2010) report on data that should give everyone who drives or rides in cars pause: In 2008, approximately 1 in 6 fatal vehicle collisions involved "distracted" driving (which included cell phone usage and texting). These authors, using statistical techniques including regression analyses, estimated the number of traffic fatalities there would have been in the period 2001–2007 if text messaging were not to have occurred and compared them with actual fatalities. The results are shown in Figure 4.16.

Despite the dangers of texting while driving, the practice is a common one, especially among relatively young and inexperienced drivers. Harrison (2011) reports in a recent survey that 91% of her college student participants reported having used text messaging while driving, even when passengers were in the car (including children), despite the fact that they agreed that texting is dangerous and should be illegal. Atchley, Atwood, and Boulton (2011) found that 70% of their undergraduates reported sending texts while driving, 81% reported replying to texts, and 92% reported reading texts. Additional respondents reporting texting while at stop lights or signs only, leaving only 2% of their sample who reported never texting in any form while driving.

In summary, research on divided attention suggests that there are serious limits on the number of things we can successfully do at once. It may seem that we can do things simultaneously, but in many cases we do both tasks by rapidly switching our attention back and forth between the two. Of course, when those individual tasks become more demanding, it becomes harder and harder to do them simultaneously.

Summary

The different theoretical approaches to attention surveyed here suggest that psychologists are far from agreeing on how to explain attentional phenomena.

Nonetheless, some general themes have emerged.

1. Attention has been shown to be a flexible aspect of cognition. We see that attention, rather than being rigidly and mechanically limited, as first described, is instead a more flexible system, affected by things such as practice, the kinds of tasks being performed, and the person's intention.

2. The idea that there are limits on the number of things we can pay attention to at once is known as *selective attention*. Anecdotal, laboratory, and even neuroscientific evidence seems to suggest that we process information to which we are actively paying attention differently than we process information to which we are not attending.

3. Whereas once attention was compared to a bottleneck, today the appropriate metaphor seems to be a spotlight (although some disagree over how far that metaphor extends). The idea here is that attention can vary in effectiveness, just as a spotlight, aimed at one spot, more or less lights surrounding areas, depending on its size and intensity.

4. Cognitive neuropsychologists have identified different neural (brain) networks of attention, which they have localized in specific regions of the brain. They have also demonstrated a different pattern of event-related potentials for attended and unattended information.

5. Practice with a physical or cognitive task seems to change the amount of attention we need to perform that task. Tasks that require little mental capacity to perform are said to be *automatic*.

6. Some criteria proposed to call a task or process "automatic" include the following: (a) It occurs without intention; (b) it occurs without conscious awareness; and (c) it does not interfere with other mental activity. Recently, however, these criteria have been the subject of criticism.

7. A real-world example of the relevance of laboratory research on attention comes from work on conversing via cell phone or text messaging while driving a car.

Review Questions

1. Cognitive psychologists have offered several definitions of the term *attention*. Which one seems the most useful? Describe and defend your criteria.

2. Describe the dichotic listening task and explain why cognitive psychologists find it a useful way to study attention.

3. Describe the differences and similarities among filter theory, attenuation theory, and schema theory.

4. Describe and evaluate Kahneman's capacity model of attention. What, if any, real-world phenomena does it predict or explain?

5. What questions are answered by the work on the neurological underpinnings of attention? What questions are raised?

6. Evaluate Posner and Snyder's criteria for what makes a cognitive process automatic. Which criterion is the strongest, and why?

7. Consider the studies on divided attention. Can these findings be used in training workers who need to process a great deal of information from different sources simultaneously? Why or why not?

Key Terms

attention hypothesis of automatization

attentional capture

attenuation theory

automatic processing

controlled processing

dichotic listening task

divided attention

dual-task performance

event-related potential (ERP)

feature integration theory

filter theory

inattentional blindness

priming

schema theory

selective attention

Stroop task

CHAPTER 5

WORKING MEMORY
Forming and Using New Memory Traces

CHAPTER OUTLINE

Traditional Approaches to the Study of Memory

Sensory Memory

Iconic Memory

Echoic Memory

Short-Term Memory

Capacity and Coding

Retention Duration and Forgetting

Retrieval of Information

Working Memory

Executive Functioning

Neurological Studies of Memory Processes

Many cognitive psychologists regard memory as one of the most basic cognitive processes. We rely on memory whenever we think back to a personal event—when we remember, for example, our first day of school, our 10th birthday, or a trip to Disneyland. Memory is also obviously involved when we remember information about historical events, such as the 9/11 attacks or the sudden death of Osama bin Laden. All these cases illustrate **retrieval**, the calling to mind of previously stored information. The processes by which we do so are the focus of this chapter and the next two chapters.

In one way or another, memory enters into almost every cognitive activity. Clearly, activities such as taking an exam or remembering the name of your third-grade teacher require memory. But other activities, such as balancing a checkbook or comprehending a sentence, also involve some aspect of memory. While doing the calculations necessary to balance a checkbook, we have to keep some numbers in mind, at least for a moment. Similarly, when we hear or read a sentence, we have to keep the beginning of the sentence in mind while we process its middle and end. We use memory so frequently that, as with other cognitive processes, we tend to take it for granted.

Try, for example, to recall your first day at college. What do you remember about that day? Now ask yourself how you are able to recall any of these memories (if in fact you can). If you drew a total blank, why? What exactly goes on when you try to recall? What makes some information memorable and other information hard to recall? (For example, can you describe what your cognitive psychology professor wore two lectures ago?)

Sometimes we fail to notice how extraordinary a particular ability is until we encounter someone who lacks it. Baddeley (1990) has documented the tragic case of Clive Wearing, a musician and broadcaster who, because of brain damage caused by encephalitis, has been left with severe amnesia. Although many people suffer from amnesia, Wearing's case is one of the most devastating on record. As Baddeley describes it,

> his amnesia was so dense that he could remember nothing from more than a few minutes before, a state that he attributed to having just recovered consciousness. Left to his own devices, he would often be found writing down a time, for example, 3:10, and the note, "I have just recovered consciousness," only to cross out the 3:10 and add 3:15, followed by 3:20, etc. If his wife left the room for a few minutes, when she returned he would greet her with great joy, declaring that he had not seen her for months and asking how long he had been unconscious. Experienced once, such an event could be intriguing and touching, but when it happens repeatedly, day in, day out, it rapidly loses its charm. (pp. 4–5)

Interestingly, a few of Wearing's memory abilities seem to have been spared. He has apparently conducted a choir through a complex piece of music and can still play the harpsichord and piano. These abilities are the exception rather than the rule, however. Wearing cannot go out alone because he would quickly become lost and unable to find his way back. He cannot recognize much in photographs of familiar places, and his memories of his own life are quite sketchy.

In this chapter and the next, I will try to explain these phenomena. To do so, we will look in detail at the processes people use to form, store, and retrieve information. We will examine theoretical approaches to the study of memory, considering memory that lasts only briefly as well as memory that endures for hours, weeks, and even years. Much of the research described in Chapters 5 and 6 comes from the laboratory, where experiment participants, often college student volunteers, are presented with lists or series of words, syllables, or pictures under highly controlled conditions. In some parts of Chapter 6, we will consider how well laboratory-based models apply to memory phenomena outside the laboratory, most often to memories of episodes from people's own life stories.

In this chapter, we will take up topics that have several deep connections to topics we have been talking about in the last two chapters (perception and attention). We've already seen some previews, for example, that working memory capacity seems to be related to degree of attentional focus and control. Here, we'll be exploring what this term *working memory* refers to. The important point for now is that some of the topics in the last chapter could quite easily have been put here, and, conversely, some of the topics in this chapter would have fit comfortably in Chapters 3 or 4. I hope, though, that when you are done reading both chapters carefully, all of the interconnections will be clear.

A brief review of terminology is in order before we begin. We say that **encoding** occurs when information is first translated into a form that other cognitive processes can use. We call this the formation of a **memory trace**. This trace held in **storage** in one form or another for later retrieval. We say that **forgetting** occurs when we cannot retrieve information.

TRADITIONAL APPROACHES TO THE STUDY OF MEMORY _____

Fascination with what memory is and how it works has a long tradition in philosophy, predating any psychological investigations. Neath and Surprenant (2003) note that the Greek philosopher Plato wrote about memory, comparing it both to an aviary and to a wax tablet on which impressions are made. Throughout the Middle Ages and Renaissance, other analogies were made between memory and a cave, an empty cabinet, and a body in need of exercise.

In the 1950s, memory was compared to a telephone system, and later it was compared to a computer. One theoretical approach to studying memory, which dominated cognitive psychology throughout the 1960s and 1970s, distinguished among kinds of memory according to the length of time information is stored.

This **modal model of memory** assumes that information is received, processed, and stored differently for each kind of memory (Atkinson & Shiffrin, 1968; Waugh & Norman, 1965). Unattended information presented very quickly is stored only briefly in **sensory memory**.

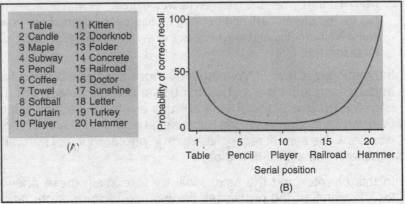

■ Figure 5.1: Word list for a serial position curve experiment (A); typical results (B).

Attended information is held in **short-term memory (STM)** for periods of up to 20 or 30 seconds. (Synonyms for STM include *primary memory* and *short-term storage,* or *STS.*) Information needed for longer periods of time—the correct spelling of the words on tomorrow's test, for example, or the name of your fourth-grade teacher—is transferred to **long-term memory (LTM)**, sometimes called *secondary memory* or *long-term storage* (*LTS*). We'll begin our look at psychological investigations of memory using this metaphor, largely because of its enormous influence on the field of cognitive psychology and its ability to make sense of a wide range of memory findings.

Many empirical findings seem to support the idea of different memory systems. One well-known finding comes from free-recall experiments, in which people are given a list of words to remember, such as that shown in Figure 5.1(A), and are asked to recall the words in any order. Next, the experimenter, using data from all the participants, computes the probability of recall of each word as a function of the word's serial position in the original list. In our example, *table* is in serial position 1 because it is the first word on the list, *candle* is in serial position 2, and so forth. Figure 5.1(B) shows an idealized version of typical results (Murdock, 1962).

Notice that the two ends of the curve are higher than the middle, indicating that people recall more words at either the beginning or the end of the list than they do words in the middle. This is known as the **serial position effect**. The improved recall of words at the beginning of the list is called the **primacy effect**; that at the end of the list, the **recency effect**.

What accounts for these two effects? Participants typically report subvocalizing to themselves as follows when they start the experiment:

Experimenter
(reading list at a fixed rate) :   Table.

Participant *(to self)* :   Table-table-table-table.

Experimenter: Candle.

Participant *(a little faster)* :   Table-candle-table-candle.

Experimenter: Maple.

Participant *(very rapidly)* :   Table-candle-maple-table-candle.

Experimenter: Subway.

Participant
(giving up on rehearsing earlier words) :   Subway.

We'll see later that the participant's repetition of items, or **rehearsal**, is thought to help the items enter long-term storage. In fact, if the experimenter reads the list rapidly enough to prevent the participant from having enough time to rehearse, the primacy effect disappears, although the recency effect stays intact (Murdock, 1962).

The recency effect is thought to result from participants' using either sensory memory or short-term memory. Participants often report that they can still "sort of" hear the last few words, and they often report these first and quickly. If the experimenter prevents the participant from reporting words right away, by having her first perform an unrelated counting task, the recency effect (but not the primacy effect) disappears (Postman & Phillips, 1965).

That the primacy and recency effects can be independently affected suggests they reflect two kinds of memory. In addition, some psychologists argue for a third kind of memory, sensory memory, which is thought to work differently from both the other systems. Those who endorse the idea of sensory memory believe that incoming information first passes through this rapidly decaying storage system. If attended to, the information next moves to STM. To be held for longer than a minute or two, the information must be transferred again, this time to LTM.

We will take up the first two hypothesized kinds of memory in this chapter, examining first sensory memory and then STM. After a look at the modal model and its predictions and explanations, we will focus on a newer proposal from psychologist Alan Baddeley called *working memory.* Next we'll turn our attention to recent proposals for the existence and importance of executive processes that govern and direct the operation of other cognitive processes, picking up on a discussion begun in Chapter 4. This chapter will conclude by looking at neuropsychological evidence of memory for material actively being processed. We'll defer until Chapter 6 discussion of memories stored over longer periods.

SENSORY MEMORY

Sensory "memory" is closely connected to what we call "perception." This kind of memory has been described as a record of our percepts (Baddeley, 1990), because it refers to the initial brief storage of sensory information—what you might retain, for example, if you glanced up at a billboard and quickly looked away. In fact, there have been debates within cognitive psychology as to whether the findings from a typical sensory memory study are perceptual or memorial (relating to memory) in nature (Neath & Surprenant, 2003). The more common view today is that the phenomena are in fact more like other memories than they are like perceptions.

Many cognitive psychologists hypothesize that separate sensory memories exist for each sensory modality. In other words, they believe there is a visual sensory memory, an auditory sensory memory, an olfactory (pertaining to smell) sensory memory, a gustatory (pertaining to taste) sensory memory, and a tactile (pertaining to touch) sensory memory. The overwhelming bulk of the research on sensory memories to date has focused on the first two types of sensory memory, called iconic and echoic memory, respectively.

Iconic Memory

Let's first talk about iconic memory. Imagine sitting in a classroom equipped with an overhead projector. The lecturer enters and puts her first transparency on the projector. To check that it is working, she quickly clicks it on and off (she doesn't want to give anyone too much of a sneak preview). If you were looking at the projection screen when the lecturer clicked the projector on and off, you might experience a rapidly fading visual event, and you might have thought it was due to a physical extinguishing of a stimulus—perhaps the bulb in the projector slowly fading. But controlled studies have demonstrated that the effect is a mental experience (Massaro & Loftus, 1996), as we shall see.

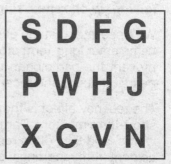

■ Figure 5.2: Example of the kind of stimulus display used by Sperling (1960).

Sperling (1960) conducted an elegant experiment, now considered classic, to investigate the properties of visual sensory memory. He presented participants with displays containing letters, such as shown in Figure 5.2, and asked them to recall the letters they saw. The displays were presented for only 50 milliseconds. Sperling found that, on average, people could report only 4 or 5 of the 12 letters presented. Extending the display time, even to 500 milliseconds, did not improve performance. The problem wasn't perceptual; 500 milliseconds, or half a second, is plenty of time to perceive something about all the letters (Klatzky, 1980).

Sperling (1960) did find a way to improve participants' performance, however, inventing what has become known as the *partial-report technique.* After seeing the display, participants were presented with a low-, medium-, or high-pitched tone. A low pitch indicated they were to report only the letters in the bottom row of the display; a high pitch, those in the top row; and a medium pitch, those in the middle row. Regardless of which tone sounded, participants' reports were almost always completely accurate. This finding suggests participants must have stored the whole display, because they did not know ahead of time which tone would sound. If their accuracy on a randomly chosen row was, say, 90%, we can infer their accuracy for any row would have been 90%. In fact, Sperling found that with the partial-report technique, participants accurately recalled an average of about three out of four letters in any given row, suggesting an average total recall of about 75% or more.

What caused the better performance? Sperling (1960) believed that in the original condition (called the *whole-report condition* because participants had to report the whole display), participants lost the information in their memory during the time they took to report the first few letters. Put another way, even as participants were recalling the display, the information was fading from wherever it was being stored. This implies that information lasts only briefly in this memory system. In fact, Sperling found that if the tone was delayed 1 second, participants giving partial reports did no better than participants giving whole reports.

Neisser (1967) called this brief visual memory the **icon.** The icon is a sensory memory storage system for visual material, holding information for up to about 1 second. The information it holds is in a relatively unprocessed form, as another of Sperling's (1960) experiments showed: If the displays contained both consonants and vowels, and if two different tones cued the participants to report either all the vowels or all the consonants, participants' performance roughly matched their performance when giving whole reports. That indicated that people are not as good at reporting by category (vowel or consonant) as they are at reporting by physical location (e.g., top row, bottom row). Therefore, Sperling inferred, the icon holds information that has not yet been categorized.

Averbach and Coriell (1961) showed that the icon can be "erased" by other stimuli presented immediately after the icon, a phenomenon known as *masking.* For instance, if the display with letters was followed by a display with circles, and if the participant was told to report which letters had been in the locations of the circles, the circles appeared to "erase" the memory trace of the letters originally shown.

Other work investigated how many ways participants could be cued to give partial reports (see Coltheart, 1980, for a review). Different investigators showed that such things as the color or brightness of the letters could be used to cue partial reports. Interestingly, cueing partial reports by category or phonological sound (for instance, "Report all the letters that rhyme with *B*") is all but impossible. This suggests the information available in the icon is only visual—not auditory or related to type of stimulus.

More recent work has complicated the picture of the icon described so far. Neath and Surprenant (2003) review studies that found evidence research participants could be successfully cued to report by category. They also describe other studies showing that, although information for the particular location in the matrix fades over time, information about *which* letters were presented does not seem to. As a result, some cognitive psychologists are now coming to view the icon as a mental representation lasting only about 150 to 200 milliseconds, followed by a recoding of the stimulus into another, more meaningful code.

Echoic Memory

There is also a sensory memory for auditory material, which Neisser (1967) called the **echo.** Moray, Bates, and Barnett (1965) offered a clever demonstration of the echo. Participants were given a "four-eared" listening task, similar to a dichotic listening task (see Chapter 4 to review this). They heard, simultaneously over headphones, four channels of incoming information, each apparently coming from a different location. Each channel consisted of a string of random letters. (The four channels were created by stereophonic mixing.)

In one condititon, similar to Sperling's (1960) whole-report condition, participants were asked to report all the letters they had heard. In another condition, each participant held a board with four lights on it, each light corresponding to one of the channels, cueing the participant to report only the letters from a particular channel. As did Sperling, Moray et al. (1965) found that participants giving partial reports could report proportionately more letters. This suggests that the echo, like the icon, stores information only briefly.

Darwin, Turvey, and Crowder (1972) later replicated Moray et al.'s (1965) result, using better experimental controls, although they found a much smaller partial-report advantage. Darwin et al. also found that recall could be cued by category, at least to some degree, suggesting that the echo works somewhat differently than the icon. Crowder (1976), reviewing the literature on echoic memory, proposed that echoic memory has a larger capacity than iconic memory. Other investigations (Watkins & Watkins, 1980) provided evidence that echoes can last longer than icons, perhaps even as long as 20 seconds, although other researchers disagree with these conclusions (Massaro & Loftus, 1996).

A demonstration called the "suffix effect" also reveals something about the nature of echoic memory. Imagine you are a research participant in a memory experiment and a list of random digits, letters, or the like is being presented to you. If the list is presented to you auditorily (as opposed to visually) and if there is an auditory recall cue such as a spoken word or specific item, recall of the last few items on the list is seriously hindered (Crowder, 1972).

Researchers think the recall cue, called the *suffix,* functions as an auditory "mask" of sorts, because when the suffix is simply a beep or tone or a visual stimulus, there is usually not much effect. Nor is there any effect if the items on the list are presented visually—say, on a computer screen. Finally, the more auditory similarity there is between the suffix and the items on the list, the greater the suffix effect.

Although research continues to refine our understanding of both the icon and the echo, sensory memory can currently best be described by a number of properties. First, sensory memories are *modality specific:* the visual sensory memory contains visual information; the auditory sensory memory, auditory information; and so forth. Second, sensory memory capacities appear relatively large, but the length of time information can be stored is quite short, much less than a second. Third, the information that can be stored appears to be relatively unprocessed, meaning that most of it has to do with physical aspects of the stimuli rather than with meaningful ones.

Some proposals (Haber, 1983; Neisser, 1983) have disputed the idea that the icon and the echo play a necessary role in perception or memory. Although no one disputes the findings reported by Sperling (1960) and others, some argue that problems arise with the interpretations of the findings. In particular, some researchers assert that the very brief (typically less than a second) presentation of stimuli created an artificial task for participants, unlike anything people would need or want to do outside the laboratory. In contrast, Neath and Surprenant (2003) argue that sensory memory research could have a very practical use outside the laboratory: Having directory assistance operators say, "Have a nice day," after giving a phone number should (and apparently does) disrupt recall for the phone number because their pleasant sign-off acts as a suffix!

Another counterargument to the idea that sensory memory is only a laboratory phenomenon is that sensory memory guarantees a minimum of time during which information presented to us (that we pay attention to) is available for processing (Baddeley, 1990). In other words, by this argument, sensory memory *does* play an important role in the everyday workings of normal memory: It ensures that we will be able to "reinspect" incoming data, if not with our actual eyes and ears, then with the mind's eye and the mind's ear. As you can see, then, the role that sensory memory plays in later processing of information is very much debated.

SHORT-TERM MEMORY

Most of the time, when people think about memory, they think about holding on to information for longer than a second or two. In the rest of this chapter and the next, we'll talk about kinds of memory more familiar to nonpsychologists.

We'll first look at STM. You use this kind of memory system when you look up a phone number, walk across a room to a telephone, and dial the number. Suppose I asked you to call one of my colleagues, whose phone number is 555-4362. Suppose further that you couldn't take this book with you but had to remember the number until you could dial it on a nearby phone. How would you accomplish this task? Chances are you'd begin by rehearsing the number aloud several times as you walked across the room. You'd dial the number, but as soon as the conversation started, you'd likely have forgotten the number you just dialed. This example illustrates one aspect of STM: It lasts only a short while. (Cognitive psychologists typically regard STM as lasting for a minute or two, if rehearsal is not prevented; however, neuropsychologists sometimes consider information in STM as lasting for up to a day, which can lead to some confusion. When I talk about STM, I'll be talking about material stored for up to about a minute.)

Does any other distinguishing characteristic, besides length of time information is stored, separate STM from LTM? Psychologists who make the distinction believe there are a number of such characteristics, including how much information can be stored (capacity), the form in which the information is stored (coding), the ways in which information is retained or forgotten, and the ways in which information is retrieved.

How psychologists working within the information-processing paradigm conceptualize STM has changed a great deal over the past two decades. We'll begin with a look at the traditional description of STM and then consider a newer proposal of what has been renamed *working memory* to avoid confusion.

Capacity and Coding

If you are going to store information for only a short period of time (as in the phone number example), how much room do you have in which to do so? In other words, how much information can you remember for only a brief period of time? A classic paper by George Miller (1956) begins with the following rather unusual confession:

> My problem is that I have been persecuted by an integer. For seven years this number has followed me around, has intruded in my most private data, and has assaulted me from the pages of our most public journals. This number assumes a variety of disguises, being sometimes a little larger and sometimes a little smaller than usual, but never changing so much as to be unrecognizable.
>
> The persistence with which this number plagues me is far more than a random accident. There is, to quote a famous senator, a design behind it, some pattern governing its appearances. Either there really is something unusual about the number or else I am suffering from delusions of persecution. (p. 81)

The integer plaguing Miller was 7 (plus or minus 2). Among other things, 7 (plus or minus 2, depending on the individual, the material, and other situational factors) seems to be the maximum number of independent units we can hold in STM. We call this the **capacity** of STM.

G. Miller (1956) reviewed evidence demonstrating that if you are presented with a string of random digits, you'll be able to recall them only if the string contains about seven or fewer digits. The same is true if you are presented with random strings of any kinds of units: letters, words, abbreviations, and so on. The only way to overcome this limitation is by somehow **chunking** the individual units into larger units. For instance, consider the following string of letters: *N F L C B S F B I M T V.* This 12-letter string would normally exceed almost everyone's short-term memory capacity. But if you look closely at the letters, you'll see they really form four sets of abbreviations for well-known entities: *NFL* (the National Football League), *CBS* (one of the major television networks currently operating in the United States), *FBI* (the Federal Bureau of Investigation), and *MTV* (the rock video cable television station). If you notice that the 12 letters are really four organized sets, you'll be more likely to recall the entire string. In recognizing that the three sets of letters really "go together" and in forming them into a single unit, you are said to be chunking them.

Chunking depends on knowledge. Someone not familiar with our culture might regard *MTV* as merely three randomly presented letters. G. Miller (1956) regarded the process of forming chunks (he called it "recoding") as a fundamental process of memory—a very powerful means of increasing the amount of information we can process at any given time that we use constantly in our daily lives. The process of chunking can be seen as an important strategy in overcoming the severe limitation of having only seven or so slots in which to temporarily store information.

The term **coding** refers to the way in which information is mentally represented—that is, the form in which the information is held. When you try to remember a phone number, as in the preceding example, how do you represent it? A study by R. Conrad (1964) addressed this question. He presented participants with lists of consonants for later recall. Although the letters were presented visually, participants were likely to make errors that were similar in *sound* to the original stimuli. So, if a *P* had been presented and participants later misrecalled this stimulus, they were much more likely to report a letter that *sounded* like *P* (for example, *G* or *C*) than to report a letter that *looked* like *P* (such as *F*). Remember, the original presentation was visual, but participants apparently were confused by the sound. Participants were apparently forming a mental representation of the stimuli that involved acoustic rather than visual properties.

Later work by Baddeley (1966a, 1966b) confirmed this effect even when the stimuli were words rather than letters: Similar-sounding words make for poor immediate recall, although similar-meaning words don't, and the reverse is true for delayed recall. Although an acoustic code is not the only one used in STM, researchers have regarded it as the dominant code used, at least by hearing adults and older children (Neath & Surprenant, 2003).

Retention Duration and Forgetting

We regard STM as the storage of information for short periods of time. But how short is short? John Brown (1958) and Peterson and Peterson (1959), working independently, came to the same conclusion: If not rehearsed, information is lost from STM in as little as 20 seconds. That length of time is called the **retention duration** of the memory.

The Brown–Peterson task works as follows. Participants are presented with a three-consonant trigram, such as *BKG*. They are also given a number, such as 347, and asked to count backward out loud by 3s, at the rate of two counts per second, in time to a metronome. The purpose of the counting task is to prevent the participant from rehearsing the trigram. The length of time a participant must count varies. If asked to count backward for only 3 seconds, roughly 80% of participants can recall the trigram. If asked to count for 18 seconds, this drops to about 7%. Both Brown and the Petersons interpreted this finding as meaning that the memory trace—the encoded mental representation of the to-be-remembered information that is not rehearsed—**decays**, or breaks apart, within about 20 seconds. Putting this interpretation into our phone number example gives us the following: If I tell you my phone number and you fail to do something to remember it (say, by rehearsing it or writing it down), you'll be able to remember it only for a maximum of about 30 seconds. After that time, the memory trace will simply decay, and the information will be lost.

However, other cognitive psychologists soon began to challenge this decay explanation of forgetting. They proposed a different mechanism, called **interference**, that works as follows: Some information can "displace" other information, making the former hard to retrieve. You can think of the interference explanation as being akin to finding a piece of paper on my desk. At the start of each academic term, my desk is (relatively) free of clutter. Any piece of paper placed on the desktop is trivially easy to find. However, as the term goes on and my time grows short, I tend to allow all kinds of memos, papers, journals, and the like to accumulate, as shown from a late-in-term photograph of my desk (Photo 5.1). Papers placed on my desk at the beginning of the term become buried; they're there, all right, but can be very difficult to find at any given moment. The late-arriving papers have "displaced" the early papers.

■ Photo 5.1: A photo of my desk, providing a metaphor for memorial interference.

Can we explain the Brown–Peterson task results in terms of interference? Think once again about the counting task. Notice that it supposedly has very little purpose other than to distract the participant from rehearsing the trigram. Yet maybe the counting task does more than prevent participants from rehearsing; it may actually interfere with their short-term storage of the trigram. As participants count aloud, they compute and announce the values. As they compute and announce the values, they put them into STM. Thus, the counted values may be displacing the original information.

A study by Waugh and Norman (1965) demonstrated the role of interference in STM. They invented the *probe digit task,* which works as follows. Participants are given a 16-digit number, such as 1596234789024815. The last digit in the number is a cue for the participant to report the digit that first came after the first occurrence of the cue in the number. (It's a little complicated to follow that instruction, but it can be done; stop reading for a moment and actually try it.) In our example, the cue is 5 (it's the last digit of the number), and the first occurrence of 5 in the number is followed by a 9, so the response should be 9.

Waugh and Norman (1965) presented the numbers either quickly, at the rate of four digits per second, or slowly, at the rate of one digit per second. Their reasoning was that if decay caused forgetting in STM, then participants receiving a slow rate of presentation should be not as good at recalling digits from early in the number. This is because more time would have elapsed on trials with the slow presentation, causing more decay from the beginning of the number. Figure 5.3 (which plots the rate of recall as a function of the number of interfering items) shows, however, that this is not what happened. Participants showed equivalent performance on recalling digits throughout the number regardless of rate of presentation. On all trials, participants were not as good at recalling digits from early in the number as from later in the number, implicating interference rather than decay in forgetting information in STM.

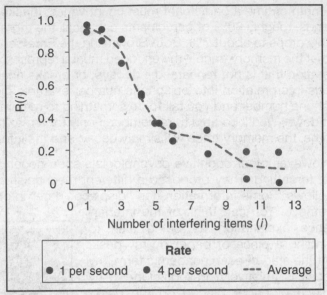

■ Figure 5.3: Results from Waugh and Norman's (1965) probe digit task study.

All this evidence might lead you to think all cognitive psychologists agree that only inter-ference causes forgetting in STM. The picture, however, is not that neat. Reitman (1971, 1974) initially offered evidence supporting an interference explanation of forgetting in STM. Her participants performed a Brown–Peterson task while simultaneously working on what was supposed to be a noninterfering task: detecting a syllable such as "doh" in a spoken stream of repetitions of a similar syllable ("toh"). The auditory detection task was supposed to prevent participants from rehearsing the trigram but not to interfere with material stored in STM. An interference account of forgetting in STM would predict no loss of the trigrams over the retention periods, and this is indeed what Reitman (1971) found. However, in an important follow-up, Reitman (1974) found that some of her participants confessed to "cheating" a bit: surreptitiously rehearsing the letters while they performed the detection task. When Reitman looked only at the performance of the participants who hadn't been rehearsing, she found clear effects of decay: Only 65% of the trigrams were retained after a 15-second interval. From this, Reitman concluded that information really could decay if not rehearsed in STM.

Reitman's research leaves us with an unresolved issue: What causes forgetting in STM, trace decay or interference? We cannot rule out either one, at least for now. One problem is that it is hard to think of a task in which no interference can occur. Thus, designing a definitive experiment (or series of definitive experiments) is beyond our current capabilities.

Also, maybe the question "Is it decay, or is it interference?" is badly posed, because it rules out the possibility that both may be involved. That is, maybe STM loses information by more than one mechanism. Baddeley (1990) argues that some (although very little) trace decay does occur in STM along with interference. E. M. Altmann and Gray (2002) propose that decay does occur and in fact is essential to avoid catastrophic types of interference. These authors believe that when information must be updated frequently in memory (e.g., you are driving and have to remember the speed limit on each new road you take), its current value (e.g., you're on an interstate, going 70 mph) decays to prevent interference with later values (e.g., you get off the highway, and the speed limit is now 55 mph).

Retrieval of Information

We've talked about the ways in which people hold on to information for brief periods of time: how they encode it, how much they can encode, and how long they can retain it. That brings us to the question "How do we retrieve this information from STM when we need it again?" Saul Sternberg (1966, 1969), in a series of experiments, found some surprising things about how we retrieve information from short-term memory. Before turning to his experiments, let's consider various possibilities of how information might be retrieved from STM.

S. Sternberg's first question was whether we search for information held in STM in a *parallel* or a *serial* manner. Imagine, for example, that STM is full of some (small) number of movie titles. Let's say STM holds a list of my all-time favorite movies, which I have just orally given you. Let's call the number of movie titles the *memory set size.* Now suppose that someone asks you if *Toy Story 3* is on that list and that to answer the question, you mentally search the list.

If you compare *Toy Story 3* simultaneously to all the titles on your list, you are performing a **parallel search**. Essentially, no matter what the number of titles is, you examine them at the same time, and it takes you no more time to compare *Toy Story 3* to 1 title than to 10 titles. Figure 5.4(A) depicts how the data would look if you used parallel search, plotting time to search against memory set size.

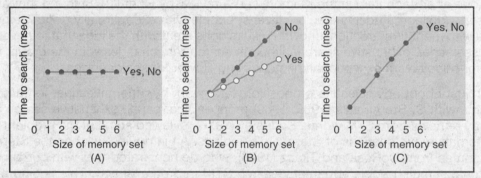

■ Figure 5.4: Theoretically predicted results from the Sternberg (1966) short-term memory-scanning experiment. "Yes" and "No" refer to whether the subject will report finding the probe letter in the memory set. (A) depicts a parallel search; (B), a serial, self-terminating search; and (C) a serial, exhaustive search. The data that Sternberg reported looked most like those in (C).

Suppose, instead, that you use a **serial search**. In our movie titles example, this would mean comparing *Toy Story 3* to the first movie title on the list, then to the second title on the list, and so on, until you come to the last title. The comparisons are done one at a time. In this model, the longer the list is, the longer it should take to decide if *Toy Story 3* matches a title on that list. Successful searches are indicated by the "yes" line; unsuccessful searches (where a target is not found) by the "no" line.

We can also ask whether the search is self-terminating or exhaustive. **A self-terminating search** stops when a match is found. Suppose the list of movie titles is *Citizen Kane, Titanic, Toy Story 3,* and *The Big Chill.* If you do a self-terminating search, you will stop after the third comparison because you've found a match. On average, then, successful searches take less time (because you don't continue searching after you've found the match) than unsuccessful searches (where you have to search through everything). Figure 5.4(B) depicts the results we should see if retrieval from memory uses serial, self-terminating search.

Another kind of serial search is an **exhaustive search**, meaning that even if a match is found, you continue looking through every other item in the set. In our example, this would mean that even after you find *Toy Story 3,* you check the remaining titles on the list. With this kind of search, it takes just as long for successful as for unsuccessful searches. Figure 5.4(C) shows this possibility.

S. Sternberg's (1966) experimental task was the following. First, participants were presented with a set of seven or fewer letters. These were to be encoded and held in short-term memory and hence could be called the "memory set." After the participant had the set in memory, he indicated readiness for an upcoming trial. A single letter, called a probe, was presented, and the participant's task was to decide, as quickly as possible, whether the probe was in the memory set. For example, the memory set might be *B K F Q,* and probes might be *K* (yes, in the memory set) and *D* (no, not in the memory set).

As counterintuitive as it sounds, S. Sternberg's (1966) results argue for serial, exhaustive search as the way we retrieve information from STM. Sternberg's explanation is that the search process itself may be so rapid and have such momentum it is hard to stop once it starts. From a processing point of view, it may be more efficient just to let the search process finish and then make one decision at the end, instead of making several decisions, one after each item in the memory set. A review by Hunt (1978) found that people of all sorts (college students, senior citizens, people with exceptionally good memories, people with mental retardation) showed results consistent with the idea that retrieval from STM uses serial, exhaustive search, although search rate changes with the group, being faster for people with exceptional memories and slower for senior citizens.

As with just about any scientific proposition, later work by other investigators turned up problems with S. Sternberg's (1966, 1969) proposal that serial, exhaustive search is the only way retrieval from STM works. Baddeley (1976) reviewed some of the problems with and alternative explanations of Sternberg's findings. An intriguing twist on the Sternberg study comes from DeRosa and Tkacz (1976), who demonstrated that with certain kinds of pictorial stimuli, people apparently search STM in a parallel way. This finding makes an important point: Memory processes apparently work differently as a function of the material (stimuli) to be remembered. Therefore, we cannot automatically generalize results from the laboratory to everyday life. Instead, to know which laboratory models bear on which kinds of phenomena, we need to consider what kinds of information are processed in what ways.

Let's summarize our review of the STM system so far. The general picture that emerged in the 1960s and 1970s was that STM is a short-term, limited-capacity storehouse where information is coded acoustically and maintained through rehearsal. Information can be retrieved from this storage using high-speed, serial, exhaustive search. The nature of the information in STM, however, can affect the capacity and processing of stored information.

WORKING MEMORY

The idea that memory consists of a number of information-processing stores was most completely described by Atkinson and Shiffrin (1968). These authors distinguished between the information being stored, calling this "memory" (for example, STM, LTM), and the structure that did the storing, which they termed a "store" (for example, STS, LTS). Their conception of STS was that it does more than merely hold on to seven or fewer pieces of information for a few seconds. In addition, they thought that information in STS somehow activates relevant information from LTS, the long-term store, and gathers some of that information into STS. They equated STS with consciousness and saw it as the location of various *control processes* that govern the flow of information, such as rehearsal, coding, integration, and decision making. STS is involved in transferring information to LTS, in integrating various pieces of information, and in keeping certain information available.

Baddeley and Hitch (1974) performed a series of experiments to test this model. The general design was to have participants temporarily store a number of digits (thus absorbing some of the STS storage capacity) while simultaneously performing another task, such as reasoning or language comprehension. These tasks were also thought to require resources from STS—specifically, the control processes mentioned earlier. The hypothesis was that if the STS capacity is taken up by stored digits, fewer resources are available for other tasks and performance on other tasks suffers.

Let's look at one of Baddeley and Hitch's (1974) studies in detail. Participants saw a sentence describing the order of appearance of two letters—for example, "*A is preceded by B*"—together with two letters in a particular order—for example, "*B A.*" The task was to decide, as quickly as possible, if the sentence correctly described the two letters. Participants were given from one to six digits to hold in memory while they verified the sentences. The results showed that participants were able to verify the sentences while holding one or two digits in memory about as well as they could without holding any digits in memory. However, a six-digit memory load did hurt performance: The sentence took longer to verify. The effect was especially pronounced if the sentence was negative and passive (for example, "*B is not preceded by A*"), both of which properties are known to be harder to process. Although performance was hurt by storing six digits, the effects were not catastrophic (Baddeley, 1990). That is, it took people much longer to reason while rehearsing six digits, but they still could perform the task. According to the predictions from Atkinson and Shiffrin's (1968) model, they should not have been able to do so. Related experiments described in the 1974 article showed that storing digits in memory also interfered with reading comprehension and the recall of recently learned material.

Baddeley and Hitch (1974) and Baddeley (1981) interpret the findings from the various studies as follows. First, a common system does seem to contribute to cognitive processes such as temporarily storing information, reasoning, and comprehending language. Filling up STM with six digits does hurt performance on a variety of cognitive tasks, suggesting that this system is used in these tasks. However, the memory loads used, thought to be near the limit of STM capacity, do not totally disrupt performance. Because researchers think STM has a capacity of about seven items, plus or minus two, the six-digit memory load should have essentially stopped any other cognitive activity. Baddeley and Hitch therefore argue for the existence of what they called **working memory (WM)**. Baddeley (2007) defines working memory as a "limited capacity temporary storage system that underpins complex human thought" (pp. 6–7).

Baddeley (1981, 1986, 1990, 2000, 2007) conceives of WM as consisting of multiple components, as depicted in Figure 5.5. The first is the **central executive**. This component directs the flow of information, choosing which information will be operated on when and how. Researchers assume it has a limited amount of resources and capacity to carry out its tasks. Some of this capacity can be used to store information. The central executive is thought to function more as an attentional system than a memory store (Baddeley, 1990), meaning that rather than dealing with the storage and retrieval of information, the central executive deals with the way resources are allocated to cognitive tasks. So the central executive would be the system that controls many of the phenomena reviewed in Chapter 4. The central executive is also thought to coordinate information coming from the current environment with the retrieval of information about the past, enabling people to use this information to select options or form strategies. Baddeley (1993a) equates this coordination with conscious awareness.

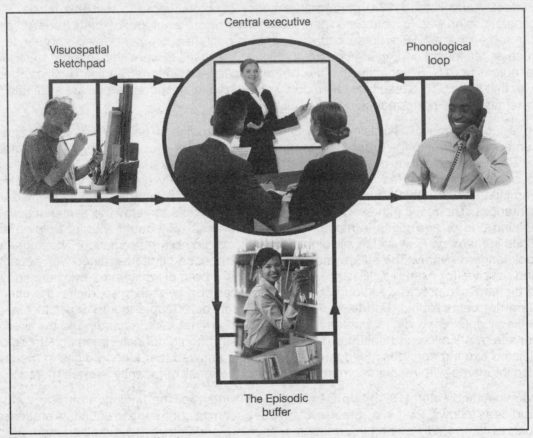

■ Figure 5.5: Baddeley's model of working memory.

Other components of Baddeley's model are concerned with the storage and temporary maintenance of information: the **phonological loop**, used to carry out subvocal rehearsal to maintain verbal material, and the **visuospatial sketch pad**, used to maintain visual material through visualization. Researchers think the phonological loop plays an important role in such tasks as learning to read, comprehending language, and acquiring vocabulary. The visuospatial sketch pad involves the creation and use of mental images. Finally, the **episodic buffer** is thought to be a temporary system that is capable of integrating information from different sources (Baddeley, 2000).

Notice that postulating the existence of a separate phonological loop explains why having a person remember digits (which presumably loads the phonological loop) does not totally devastate performance on other tasks requiring WM. Researchers think that the tasks spared are drawing on another part of working memory.

Investigators believe that the phonological loop consists of two structures: a short-term phonological buffer (which holds onto verbal information for short periods of time, such as a few minutes, assuming rehearsal is not prevented), and a subvocal rehearsal loop used to compensate for the rapid decay of information in the phonological buffer (Demetriou, Christou, Spanoudis, & Platsidou, 2002). The idea here is that when the person initially encounters information, particularly verbal information, she translates it into some sort of auditory code and processes it through the phonological loop. Because the information from the phonological buffer decays rapidly, the person must subvocally rehearse the information, and the faster the rehearsal process, the more information can be maintained. If the phonological buffer is "filled up"—say, by having a person repeat a syllable or count aloud—then less capacity from this system is available to devote to other tasks.

Researchers have devised various working-memory-span tasks involving the phonological loop. A very well-known one, created by Daneman and Carpenter (1980), works like this: A person is given a set of sentences to read (usually aloud) but at the same time is asked to remember the last word in each sentence for later recall. For example, the participant might be presented with the following three sentences:

The leaves on the trees turn various hues in autumn.
A group of students congregated outside the front entrance of the delicatessen.
Although lying and fabrication are generally not acceptable, they are sometimes necessary.

After reading them aloud, the participant is cued to recall the last word in each sentence. In this example, the correct answers are *autumn, delicatessen,* and *necessary.* The number of sentences a participant can process and reliably recall words from is said to be a measure of his span. This measure has been shown to correlate significantly with other cognitive measures, such as reading comprehension and other complex cognitive tasks (Miyake, 2001).

The visuospatial sketch pad is to visual material as the phonological loop is to auditory and/or verbal material: Researchers think it maintains and is involved in the manipulation of visual information and imagery (Baddeley & Andrade, 2000). We will be taking up the topic of visual imagery in Chapter 8 and so will defer a detailed discussion until then.

In 2000, Baddeley revised his original model of working memory to include the fourth component: the episodic buffer. This is thought to be another temporary storage system, but one that interacts with both the phonological loop and the visuospatial sketch pad, as well as with LTM. It, too, is controlled by the central executive, and it is used to integrate information across different modalities and to facilitate the transfer of information into and from LTM.

Teasdale et al. (1995) report an interesting application of Baddeley's conception of working memory. They focus on stimulus-independent thoughts (SITs), which they define as "a flow of thought or images, the contents of which are quite unrelated to immediate sensory input" (p. 551). SITs include things such as daydreams or even intrusive thoughts such as when we worry or ruminate over a problem or concern.

Teasdale et al. (1995) wondered whether the production of SITs could be disrupted by having research participants perform another task. Some of the tasks they had their participants perform were verbal and were thought to involve the phonological loop of working memory. An example is the "silly sentences" task, in which people view a sentence (such as "Bishops can be bought in shops") and judge as quickly as possible whether it is true or false. Other tasks were more visual or spatial. For example, people viewed complex drawings and were asked to find "hidden" geometric figures or to tap different keys on a keyboard in a particular manner.

During the experimental sessions, participants were stopped at different points and asked to tell the experimenter "exactly what was passing through [their] mind when [they] heard the experimenter say 'stop.'" Experimenters transcribed and later categorized these thoughts as to whether they pertained to the task at hand or were unrelated to it (that is, were SITs). Teasdale et al. (1995) found that both the auditory and the visuospatial tasks significantly disrupted SIT production. Thus neither the phonological loop nor the visuospatial sketch pad is solely responsible for SIT production.

In subsequent experiments, Teasdale et al. (1995) determined that producing these intrusive thoughts involves the central executive. They had research participants practice either a spatial task (keeping a light beam in a pencil-like instrument focused on a revolving circle; this is called a *pursuit rotor task*) or a memory task (keeping a specific digit in mind when the specific digit changed every 4 seconds). Next all participants performed both tasks and were again interrupted at various points and asked to report their thoughts. The researchers found that whichever task had been practiced produced far less interference with SITs than did the unpracticed task. In other words, when you or I perform a novel and challenging task, we are far less likely to experience intrusive, unrelated thoughts (for example, about the fight we just had with our partner or about a dream vacation we hope to take someday) than if we are working at a task at which we are well practiced.

Note the fit of this explanation with the topics we discussed in Chapter 4. Presumably, tasks that have been practiced require less attention or, in Baddeley's terminology, require fewer resources from the central executive of working memory. That capacity is thus available for the mind to do other things—for instance, to think about unrelated things. Unpracticed, demanding tasks, in contrast, "soak up" more central executive resources, leaving them unavailable to produce unrelated intrusive thoughts.

Teasdale et al. (1995) point out a practical implication of their research. Suppose you want to stop worrying about an issue. Tasks in which you simply repeat memorized phrases or chant the same word or phrase over and over again are not likely to be very effective, because they don't require enough of your central executive resources to block out the worrisome thoughts. Instead, Teasdale et al. propose that you engage in a task in which you need to "make continuous demands on the control and coordinating resources of the central executive" (p. 558). One suggestion is to try to generate a word or phrase at random intervals, thus requiring you to continuously monitor your performance and coordinate your current response with your past responses.

Baddeley (1992) regards his proposal about working memory as an evolution of the STM idea, rather than a competing proposal. Moving away from a view of STM as a passive, temporary, limited-capacity storehouse, Baddeley and others are now investigating the active role played by the processing system that is operating on current information and are separating this function from the temporary storage of information. Working memory is thought to be involved in translating visual information into an acoustic code, forming chunks, rehearsing to keep attention focused on material to remember (as in the phone number example, earlier), and sometimes elaborating on incoming information by calling up relevant knowledge from LTM. Thus, the term *working memory* conveys more than a temporary storehouse; rather, it connotes a place where the person exerts active mental effort to attend to, and often to transform, the material.

EXECUTIVE FUNCTIONING

Recall from Chapter 4 the finding that in a dichotic listening task, people with higher working-memory (WM) capacity are *less* likely to detect their names in the unshadowed message (A. R. A. Conway et al., 2001) and are less susceptible to inattentional blindness (Hannon & Richards, 2010). A variety of other studies, reviewed by Baddeley (2007) and by Engle and colleagues (Barrett, Tugade, & Engle, 2004; Engle, 2002; Unsworth & Engle, 2005), show other individual differences as a function of WM capacity on very different tasks. The general picture emerging seems to be that higher WM capacity means an individual is better able to control her cognitive focus.

One task studied by Kane, Bleckley, Conway, and Engle (2001) is called an "antisaccade" task. Research participants sit before a visual display and are asked to fixate their eyes in the middle of the screen. Then a stimulus (a letter to identify) is presented briefly on one side or the other of the screen, forcing the participant to attend to that stimulus in order to make the proper response as quickly as possible. Now, just before that stimulus is presented, the experimenters flash a cue of some sort. Sometimes this cue is presented on the same side of the screen the stimulus will appear on. The authors call this the "prosaccade" task, because the cue presumably causes the participant to automatically look at (by moving his eyes sideways with a saccade) the correct side of the visual display. In this condition, no differences appeared in reaction time to identify the target letter between participants with very high WM capacity and those with very low WM capacity.

However, large differences arose in performance between persons with high WM and low WM capacity in the antisaccade task, in which a cue appeared on the opposite side of the screen from where the target would appear. To perform optimally at this task, the research participant had to resist the temptation to have her attention drawn to the misleading cue. Now, this is a tough temptation, and everyone shows a slower reaction time in this condition relative to the prosaccade condition. However, the performance of low WM-capacity participants was hurt more than that of high WM-capacity participants.

Other researchers have also found correlations between WM capacity and the ability to reason from premises or to make consistent decisions, both topics we will consider in Chapter 12 (Del Missier, Mäntylä, & Bruine de Bruin, 2010; Markovits, Doyon, & Simoneau, 2002); the ability to overcome the effects of postevent misleading information in an eyewitness memory task, a topic discussed in Chapter 6 (Jaschinski & Wentura, 2002); and the role of executive functioning in different kinds of problem solving, covered in Chapter 11 (Gilhooly & Floratou, 2009). Indeed, some authors link WM capacity to general fluid intelligence, a topic we'll explore in more depth in Chapter 13 (Baddeley, 2007; Suess, Oberauer, Wittmann, Wilhelm, & Schulze, 2002).

We have seen a lot of growth and evolution of the concept of STM into WM. It makes sense to pause here and consider the key differences between the two concepts. Cowan (1995), Engle (2002), and Kail and Hall (2001), among others, have presented strong empirical evidence and theoretical arguments to suggest that STM and WM are distinct. STM can be thought of as information that is actively being processed, perhaps even information from long-term memory that is currently activated. WM includes these active memory traces *as well as* the attentional processes used to maintain that activation and to keep the person focused on the primary cognitive task at hand.

In terms of the diagram in Figure 5.5, we can describe the development of the WM concept as the articulation of different STM components. Instead of regarding STM as a single entity, we are conceptualizing it in a new way and giving it a new name to indicate that it includes several components and is involved in a variety of forms of cognitive processing.

NEUROLOGICAL STUDIES OF MEMORY PROCESSES

Memory processes ultimately are instantiated in the brain, of course, and we will pause now to consider some relevant background and findings from the study of neuropsychology. Previous discussion of "stores" or "components" of memory can make it seem as if memory were located in one place in the brain—a sort of neural "filing cabinet" that holds on to memory traces of information being stored.

Actually, however, the picture emerging from neuropsychological studies is quite different and much more complicated. Memories don't all seem to be "stored" in one place. Desimone (1992) notes that in humans and animals, lesions of the cerebellum, a motor control structure, impair the acquisition of classically conditioned motor responses; lesions or disease of portions of the striatum, which normally functions in sensorimotor integration, impair stimulus–response learning of habits; lesions of the inferior temporal cortex, an area important for visual discrimination, impair visual recognition and associative memory; and lesions of the superior temporal cortex, an area important for auditory discrimination, impair auditory recognition memory.

Much of the interest in "localizing" memory in the brain dates back to a famous case study. In 1953, William Beecher Stover, a neurosurgeon, performed surgery on H.M., a 27-year-old epileptic patient. Before the operation, H.M. was of normal intelligence. Stover removed many structures on the inner sector of the temporal lobes of both sides of H.M.'s brain, including most of the hippocampus, the amygdala, and some adjacent areas (look back to Figure 2.2 to see where these are located). This noticeably reduced H.M.'s seizures, and H.M.'s postoperative IQ actually rose about 10 points (Schacter, 1996).

Unfortunately, however, H.M. suffered another decrement: He lost his ability to transfer new episodic memories into long-term memory and thus became one of the most famous neuropsychological case studies in the literature. H.M. could remember semantic information (see Chapters 6 and 7 for a fuller discussion) and events that he had experienced several years before the operation. However, H.M. could no longer form new memories of new events. He could remember a series of seven or so digits, as long as he was not distracted, but if he turned his attention to a new task, he could not seem to store that (or much other) information. In addition to this anterograde amnesia (amnesia for new events), H.M. had retrograde amnesia (amnesia for old events) for the period of several years just before his operation.

H.M.'s case, widely publicized by psychologist Brenda Milner in the hope of preventing similar surgeries this extensive, suggests strongly that the structures removed from his brain, especially the rhinal cortex and underlying structures, played a major role in forming new memories. Other researchers have reported other case studies and animal studies that seem to provide corroborating evidence.

H.M.'s case was also taken as evidence to support the distinction between long-term (perhaps very long-term) memories, which seemed accessible, at least for events several years before the operation, and short-term memories, which seemed unstorable. As we will see in Chapters 6 and 7, this statement seems to work only for certain kinds of memories, so the picture is a bit more complicated.

Findings from other brain-damaged people have implicated areas in the frontal lobe as having much to do with WM, perhaps because frontal-lobe damage is often reported to disrupt attention, planning, and problem solving (that is, the central executive in Baddeley's model; see Gathercole, 1994). Shimamura (1995) suggests that these problems may arise not because attention and planning are located in the frontal lobe but rather because areas of the frontal lobe inhibit activity in the posterior part of the brain. People with frontal-lobe damage seem more distractible and less able to ignore irrelevant stimuli.

PET scan studies also give us more information about the neural underpinnings of memory. Recall from Chapter 2 that for PET studies, patients are injected with a radioactive compound, then asked to lie still with their head in a doughnut-shaped scanner (Posner & Raichle, 1994). This scanner measures blood flow in different brain regions. The idea is that when a particular area of the brain is being used in a cognitive activity, more blood flows to that area. E. E. Smith and Jonides (1997) report that PET study results confirm many aspects of Baddeley's model of working memory—in particular, different patterns of activation for verbal WM (localized primarily in the left frontal and left parietal lobes; see Figure 2.3 to review these) versus spatial WM (localized primarily in the right parietal, temporal, and frontal lobes). Nyberg and Cabeza (2000) review brain-imaging studies of memory conducted in many different laboratories and report similar findings. Baddeley (2007) also reviews much of this work.

How does the activity of different brain regions change as memories are formed? We are far from reaching a complete answer to this question. However, some preliminary answers are emerging. Neil Carlson (2013) describes some basic physiological mechanisms for learning new information. One basic mechanism is the *Hebb rule*, named after the man who posited it, Canadian psychologist Donald Hebb. The Hebb rule states that if a synapse between two neurons is repeatedly activated *at about the same time* the postsynaptic neuron fires, the structure or chemistry of the synapse changes. A more general, and more complex, mechanism is called **long-term potentiation**. In this process, neural circuits in the hippocampus that are subjected to repeated and intense electrical stimulation develop hippocampal cells that become more sensitive to stimuli. This effect of enhanced response can last for weeks or even longer, suggesting to many that this could be a mechanism for long-term learning and retention (Baddeley, 1993b). As you might suspect, disrupting the process of long-term potentiation (say, through different drugs) also disrupts learning and remembering.

Despite the intriguing results from neuropsychological studies, we are far from having a complete picture of how the brain instantiates all, or even many, memory phenomena. It is not clear which aspects of memory are localized in one place in the brain and which are distributed across different cortical regions. It is not clear what kinds of basic neural processes are involved in any one particular complex cognitive activity. Tulving (1995) makes the point quite explicitly:

> Memory is a biological abstraction. There is no place in the brain that one could point at and say, Here is memory. There is no single activity, or class of activities, of the organism that could be identified with

the concept that the term denotes. There is no known molecular change that corresponds to memory, no behavioral response of a living organism that is memory. Yet the term *memory* encompasses all these changes and activities. (p. 751)

Tulving notes further that neuroscientists today reject the idea of studying memory as though it were a single process. Instead, they are likely to look for neurological underpinnings at a more precise level—at such processes as encoding or retrieval.

Summary

1. Memory is a very basic cognitive process used in almost every cognitive activity. It involves encoding information, storing it, and later retrieving it from that storage. Cognitive psychologists consider memory an active, constructive process. This means the information does not "sit still" in a storehouse, waiting to be retrieved, but instead is elaborated and sometimes distorted or constructed.

2. One approach to the study of memory, called the *modal approach,* divides memory into different types: *sensory memory,* which holds information in specific modalities for fractions of a second up to several seconds (depending on the modality); *STM,* which holds a limited amount of information for brief periods of seconds or minutes; and *LTM,* which holds onto memories for longer periods of time.

3. The number of unrelated pieces of information that can be held in the short term (without rehearsal or recoding) seems to be seven, plus or minus two. This limit can be overcome through techniques such as *chunking,* which requires some knowledge about the pieces of information and how they relate.

4. There is controversy in the explanations proposed for why we forget information. The question is whether information in a memory store ever decays or "disintegrates" or whether all supposedly "forgotten" information is actually buried information displaced by interference from other information. Although these two possibilities are quite distinct, as a practical matter, it is very difficult to design critical experiments that would rule out one of them. Perhaps both kinds of processes play some role in forgetting.

5. Saul Sternberg's work suggests that retrieval from STM is serial and exhaustive. Later work suggests that the nature of STM may depend on the nature of the stimuli presented.

6. A newer conception of STM, proposed by Alan Baddeley, is called *working memory (WM)*. Working memory is thought to consist of a *central executive,* concerned with coordinating and controlling incoming information; a *phonological loop,* acting as an inner "ear"; and a *visuospatial sketch pad,* used as an inner "eye"; as well as an episodic buffer, a temporary storage place used to transfer information between working memory and long-term memory.

7. Recent work suggests that WM capacity is a powerful variable relating to the ability to resist distraction and distortion, to reason with abstract or concrete premises, and to maintain control of attention more generally.

8.   Neuropsychological studies of memory provide a glimpse at some very exciting cutting-edge research. Investigators are examining the role of particular brain structures, such as the hippocampus and medial temporal cortex, in memory formation, as well as attempting to localize the brain regions involved in encoding and retrieval.

Review Questions

1.   Review the evidence that has led some psychologists to posit the existence of different memory stores (such as sensory memory, short-term memory, and long-term memory).

2.   Discuss the importance of research on icons and echoes for understanding how people process incoming information. Consider issues of both experimental control and ecological validity.

3.   Psychologists have posited two distinct mechanisms for forgetting: decay and interference. Describe each, briefly review the experimental evidence supporting each, and state the problem in distinguishing between them.

4.   Describe the methods used in S. Sternberg's memory-scanning experiment. What do the results tell us about retrieval of information from STM?

5.   How does Baddeley's conception of working memory differ from traditional descriptions of STM?

6.   Explain why WM capacity, but not STM capacity, would relate to performance on so many other cognitive tasks (such as dichotic listening, inattentional blindness, problem solving, and reasoning).

7.   Describe two ways in which our knowledge of findings from research on working memory can help us design effective real-world strategies for coping with everyday tasks and problems.

8.   Summarize the findings of neuropsychological research on localizing memory in the brain.

Key Terms

capacity

central executive (of WM)

chunking

coding

decay

echo

encoding

episodic buffer (of WM)

exhaustive search

forgetting

icon

interference

long-term memory (LTM)

long-term potentiation

memory trace

modal model of memory

parallel search

phonological loop (of WM)

primacy effect

recency effect

rehearsal

retention duration

retrieval

self-terminating search

sensory memory

serial position effect

serial search

short-term memory (STM)

storage

visuospatial sketch pad (of WM)

working memory (WM)

6

RETRIEVING MEMORIES FROM LONG-TERM STORAGE

CHAPTER OUTLINE

Aspects of Long-Term Memory
  Capacity
  Coding
  Retention Duration and Forgetting
  Retrieval of Information
    The Use of Mnemonics
    Other Retrieval Principles
    The Testing Effect

Subdivisions of Long-Term Memory
  Semantic Versus Episodic Memory
  Implicit Versus Explicit Memory
  Declarative Versus Procedural Memory

The Levels-of-Processing View

The Reconstructive Nature of Memory
  Autobiographical Memory
  Flashbulb Memories
  Eyewitness Memory
  The Recovered/False Memory Debate

Amnesia
  Anterograde Amnesia
  Retrograde Amnesia

In the last chapter, we focused on the formation of new memories and on memories held for brief periods of time—fractions of a second, a few seconds, or a minute. In this chapter, we will focus on memories held for longer periods—several minutes, hours, weeks, years, and even decades. The kind of memory we'll be talking about corresponds better than STM does to the layperson's definition of a memory: information retrieved after some long period of storage.

We will begin by looking at the traditional view of long-term memory, the modal model of memory. Recall that this model of memory emphasizes the different memory stores: sensory, short-term, and long-term. We will then examine different proposals for subdividing LTM into different systems. Next we'll turn our attention to other models of memory that focus less on the type of memory store and more on the way information is processed, both at the time of encoding and at the time of retrieval. We'll look at how various cues become associated, either intentionally or unintentionally, with the information to be remembered and then at how these cues can be used to maximize the chances of retrieving information.

Our fourth major topic will be a look at the malleability of memory. In this section, we'll review research on memory for events and how those memories can be distorted without a person's awareness. Finally, we will look in greater detail at the topic of amnesia, reviewing the different types of amnesia. We'll examine what the clinical data so far tell us about the laboratory-based theories of memory organization.

ASPECTS OF LONG-TERM MEMORY

In the modal model, long-term memory (LTM) is thought to differ from short-term memory (STM) in many ways. LTM is described as a place for storing large amounts of information for indefinite periods of time. Note the contrast here with the modal description of STM as holding a very limited amount of information (seven, plus or minus two, pieces of unrelated information) for a very short period of time (seconds or at most a few minutes). In other words, LTM is commonly thought to be a sort of mental "treasure chest" or "scrapbook": The material you have cognitively collected in your lifetime is stored there in some form. In this section, we will examine the capacity, coding, storage, and retrieval of information from long-term storage, as well as review evidence bearing on forgotten material.

CAPACITY

What is the capacity of LTM? The question cannot be answered with a single number. Think about information you have stored in your LTM. It would have to include your memory of all the word meanings you know (probably between 50,000 and 100,000); all the arithmetic facts; and all the historical, geographic, political, and other kinds of information you've learned. You also probably stored in LTM at one time or another the names and faces of all sorts of people: family members, significant teachers, neighbors, friends, enemies, and others. You also surely have stored various pieces of other information about each of them: physical attributes, birthdays, favorite color or musical group, and so on. All your information about various ways of doing familiar things—getting a transcript from the registrar's office; checking out a book from the library; asking for, accepting, or turning down a date; finding a phone number; addressing a letter—must also be in LTM. Indeed, a complete list of all information you have at one time or another put into long-term storage would be very long. This fact has led psychologists to estimate that the capacity of LTM is virtually unlimited.

Thomas Landauer (1986) has tried to provide a more quantitative estimate of LTM capacity. He begins with two previous estimates. The first is that the size of human memory is equal to the number of synapses in the cerebral cortex of the brain. As you may remember from your introductory psychology course, a synapse is the gap between two neurons, or nerve cells, across which neurotransmitters pass chemical messages. The cerebral cortex has 1013 synapses, so some believe that human memory can hold 1013 distinct bits of information.

Another estimate is 10^{20} bits of information, the estimated number of neural impulses, or electrical messages, transmitted within the brain during a person's lifetime. Landauer argued that both these estimates are probably too high: Not every neural impulse or synaptic connection results in a memory. Through various different analyses, in which he tried to estimate the rate at which new information is learned and the rate at which information is forgotten or lost, he came to an estimate of about 1 billion bits of information for an adult at midlife (say, about age 35).

Whatever the actual number of bits of information stored in LTM, not all that information is retrievable at any given moment. Indeed, there are many everyday examples of failures to retrieve information. You meet someone you know you know but can't place, or you think of a word but can't name it. The information probably is in your long-term storage somewhere, but you can't access it. We'll return to the issues of retrieval and forgetting later.

CODING

Many studies of recall from LTM report a common finding: Errors made while recalling information from LTM are likely to be semantic confusions. That is, words or phrases that mean things similar to the words or phrases actually presented are likely to be "recalled" in error, if errors are made. Baddeley (1966a) demonstrated this phenomenon experimentally. He presented participants with lists of words that sounded similar (such as *mad, map, man*) or that were matched in word length to the first list but did not sound alike (such as *pen, day, rig*). Others also saw a list of words with similar meanings (such as *huge, big, great;* such words are called "semantically similar") and another list of control words that were matched to the third list but did not share meaning (such as *foul, old, deep*). Recall was tested after a 20-minute interval, during which participants worked on another task to prevent rehearsal and to ensure the material would be drawn from long-term rather than short-term storage. The results showed that acoustic similarity produced little effect on performance but that the list of semantically similar words was harder to learn. Baddeley (1976), reviewing this and other work, concluded that the following generalization, although not absolute, is roughly true: Acoustic similarity affects STM; semantic similarity affects LTM.

RETENTION DURATION AND FORGETTING

How long can information be stored in LTM? Although most laboratory experiments test recall after several hours or days, evidence is abundant that at least some information can last for decades or even a lifetime. Harry Bahrick (1983, 1984) has studied people's memory for material learned to varying degrees at varying times, including memory for the faces of college classmates 20 or 30 or even 50 years after graduation.

In one study, Bahrick (1984) tested 733 adults who had taken or were taking a high school or college course in Spanish. The participants who were not currently enrolled in a Spanish course had not studied Spanish for periods ranging from 1 to 50 years. They also varied in their original degree of learning of Spanish. Bahrick plotted "forgetting curves" for different aspects of knowledge of Spanish—for example, grammar recall and idiom recognition. Although forgetting differed slightly as a function of the measure, the pattern of results was remarkably consistent. For the first 3 to 6 years after completing Spanish study, participants' recall declined. But for the next three decades or so, the forgetting curve was flat, suggesting no further loss of information. Retention showed a final decline after about 30 to 35 years.

Bahrick (1984) interpreted the findings as follows:

> Large portions of the originally acquired information remain accessible for over 50 years in spite of the fact the information is not used or rehearsed. This portion of the information in a "permastore state" is a function of the level of original training, the grades received in Spanish courses, and the method of testing (recall vs. recognition), but it appears to be unaffected by ordinary conditions of interference. (p. 1)

So you thought that after the final exam you'd forget everything about cognitive psychology? If your professor contacts you in 20 years or so, you might surprise both of you: You'll probably remember at least some of the course material!

Another study of Bahrick's (1983) examined people's recall of the spatial layout of a city over a period of time ranging from 1 to 50 years. Bahrick's research participants were 851 current students and alumni of Ohio Wesleyan University, where he was on the faculty. Bahrick asked his participants to describe the campus and the surrounding city of Delaware, Ohio. Among other things, he asked participants to list all the street names in Delaware that they could recall and to categorize each as running north–south or east–west; to recall names of buildings and landmarks in the city and on the campus, and to mark provided maps with names of streets, buildings, and landmarks.

Bahrick (1983) also asked participants how long they had lived in Delaware (excluding alumni who had lived in the town for more than 2 years before or after their undergraduate years), the frequency of their visits back to Delaware (for the alumni), and the frequency with which they had driven a car around Delaware and/or used maps. Bahrick used these data to adjust for the fact that some participants had more and/or different kinds of experience with the city than others.

Using the data from the current students, Bahrick (1983) plotted information acquisition as a function of time spent in Delaware. His results show learning of street names occurred at a steady rate over 36 months of residence. In contrast, the learning of building and landmark names showed a steeper curve, with most learning occurring during the 1st year. Bahrick speculated that the difference in learning rates stems from the facts that campus locations are much more important to learn for students than are the names of streets and that students spend much more time walking around a small area of the city and campus than they spend driving around the city streets.

Bahrick (1983) assessed retention of information by surveying alumni who had graduated from 1 to 46 years previously. These findings were in some ways the inverse of the learning data. Street names (which had been learned slowly and steadily) were forgotten quickly: Most information about street names was lost after 10 years. Names of landmarks and buildings faded more slowly; 46 years after graduation, alumni retained about 40% of the information that current graduating seniors had (the test included only landmarks and buildings that had existed for 50 years).

If information can last indefinitely in LTM, why does so much of it seem unavailable, even a week later? There are several familiar examples: "knowing" you know the answer to an exam question but being unable to quite remember it; meeting someone on the street who is extremely familiar but you don't know from where. What has happened to your memory in these instances? Has it been erased somehow?

Forgetting or even "misremembering" is a topic that dates back to the early days of experimental psychology. Hermann Ebbinghaus, a Prussian psychologist, pioneered the empirical study of memory under controlled conditions (Hoffman, Bamberg, Bringmann, & Klein, 1987). His master work (Ebbinghaus, 1885/1913) reported on 19 of his studies using himself as a subject.

Ebbinghaus created stimuli he thought were carefully controlled and free from any contamination from prior learning; he called them *nonsense syllables* (such as *rur, hal,* and *beis*). He carefully and precisely presented, at a controlled rate, hundreds of lists of these syllables to a single and dedicated subject: himself. Day after day, Ebbinghaus memorized, tested himself, recorded the results, and prepared new stimuli. Altogether, he spent about 830 hours memorizing 85,000 syllables in 6,600 lists (Hoffman et al., 1987). The primary questions he asked had to do with the number of repetitions needed for perfect recall, the nature of forgetting, the effects of fatigue on learning, and the effects of widely spaced versus closely spaced practice.

One of Ebbinghaus's many findings is presented in Figure 6.1. Depicting a "forgetting curve," the graph plots the amount of time it took him to relearn a list of nonsense syllables after initial learning followed by a retention interval of varying amounts of time (the retention interval is plotted on the *x*-axis). Ebbinghaus assumed that the more forgetting, the more effort it would take to relearn a list; conversely, the less forgetting, the less effort to relearn. The curve suggests that forgetting is not a simple linear

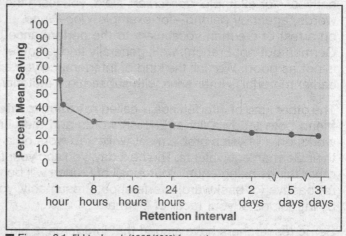

■ Figure 6.1: Ebbinghaus's (1885/1913) forgetting curve.

function of time. Instead, forgetting is rapid at first and then levels off. Notice how well this laboratory finding anticipates the real-world memory studies of Bahrick, reported earlier.

As with STM, many psychologists believe that interference, not decay, accounts for "forgetting" from LTM (McGeoch, 1932). They believe material that can't be retrieved successfully from LTM is there but "buried" or in some other way unavailable. (You may want to review Chapter 5 for a discussion of decay versus interference accounts of forgetting.)

Much of the literature on interference has used a task called **paired associates learning**. Participants hear lists of pairs of words such as *flag–spoon* and *drawer–switch*. After one or more presentations of a list, the experimenter then presents participants with the first word in each pair—for example, *flag*—and the participant is asked to recall the word originally paired with it, such as *spoon*.

Researchers have used this task to study interference in two ways (see Table 6.1). The first is through *proactive interference (PI)*. The term *PI* refers to the fact that previous learning can make retention of subsequent learning more difficult. Thus if a group of participants learns a list of paired associates ("List A–B" in the table) and then learns a second list with the same set of first terms but new second ones ("List A–C" in the table), recalling information from the second list is harder.

■ Table 6.1: Experimental Paradigms for Assessing Proactive and Retroactive Interference

Phase	Experimental Group	Control Group
Proactive Interference		
I	Learn List A–B	(Unrelated activity)
II	Learn List A–C	Learn List A–C
Test	List A–C	List A–C
Retroactive Interference		
I	Learn List A–B	Learn List A–B
II	Learn List A–C	(Unrelated activity)
Test	List A–B	List A–B

A more familiar example of proactive interference might come from foreign language vocabulary learning. Imagine you are taking beginning courses in French and in German at the same time and for some perverse reason you decide to study their vocabularies sequentially. You first learn a list of French words by pairing them with their English alternatives—for example, *dog–chien.* Next, you learn the German equivalents for the English words, again by pairing—for example, *dog–Hund.* If we compare how well you perform on a test of German vocabulary to the performance of your roommate (who is studying German but not French), we'll generally find, all other things being equal, that your recall is not as good. We call the kind of interference you experience *proactive* to indicate that earlier material is interfering with subsequent material.

The other kind of interference is called **retroactive interference**. Imagine you and another friend both study a list of English words and their French equivalents. Your friend now works on a physics problem set while you work on a list of the same English words with their German equivalents. The next day, you and your friend take a quiz in French class. All other things being equal, your recall of French will be worse than your friend's because of retroactive (or backward) interference. Presumably, your recall of French is contaminated by intrusions of your recall of German.

Some researchers have argued that interference plays a role in most, if not all, forgetting of material from the long-term storage system (Barnes & Underwood, 1959; Briggs, 1954; Postman & Stark, 1969). Of course, it is impossible to rule out the idea that decay occurs, because it is impossible to design a task in which interference cannot occur.

How exactly does interference work? M. C. Anderson and Neely (1996) present several possibilities. They start with the assumption that a **retrieval cue** points to, and leads to the recovery of, a target memory. However, when that retrieval cue becomes associated with other targets, during retrieval the second target "competes" with the first. Anderson and Neely offer the following example:

> Consider, for example, the deceptively simple task of recalling where you parked your car at a local shopping center. If you have never before been to that shopping center, recalling your car's location may be fairly easy. If you park there frequently, however, you may find yourself reunited with the spot where you parked yesterday or, if you are like the present authors, standing befuddled at the lot's edge. Further, if asked where you parked on previous visits, you would almost certainly fail to recall the locations, as though your intervening parking experiences had overwritten those aspects of your past. (p. 237)

Their point is that the more times you park in a particular parking lot, the more "targets" (actual parking spots) get associated with a retrieval cue (such as the question you ask yourself as you leave the store, "Now where did I park?"). The more possible targets associated with the cue, the less the chances of finding any particular one of them. Complicating matters even further, a given retrieval cue can become associated with different targets (or other cues), leading to even more complexity and making it that much harder to traverse a path from the cue to the correct target.

To account for some of these results, psychologist John Anderson (1974; Anderson & Reder, 1999) describes a phenomenon known as the **fan effect**. Anderson's idea is that as research participants study more facts about a particular concept, the time they need to retrieve a particular fact about that concept increases. So, for example, if you study lots of facts about forgetting, your ability to recall any individual fact about it (for example, that many psychologists think it is caused by interference) is slowed.

M. C. Anderson and Neely (1996) speculate that forgetting may not be so much a short-coming of memory as a side effect of our ability to direct memory. In particular, they wonder whether sometimes it is beneficial to be able to forget voluntarily. Example: You are working for the summer break as a short-order cook. Servers spend their time shouting orders at you: "Egg salad on wheat, lettuce, no mayo!" It behooves you both to maintain this information in immediate memory as you construct the sandwich *and* to clear this information when you are done so it does not interfere with newer incoming orders. Laboratory work that Anderson and Neely review suggests that when people lose information through "directed" (voluntary or intentional) forgetting, they experience much less proactive interference. Forgetting, then, can be a useful thing to do!

In this section, we've explored mechanisms for forgetting or at least being unable to retrieve previously stored information. It makes sense now to ask, What happens to information that is retained instead of forgotten? Let's look at how information from LTM is retrieved successfully.

RETRIEVAL OF INFORMATION

Suppose you want to improve your chances of recalling information at a later date (for example, to study for an upcoming midterm in cognitive psychology). What do we know from cognitive psychology that can help? We might use some specific techniques to aid memory known collectively as **mnemonics**.

The Use of Mnemonics

Around 500 BCE, the Greek poet Simonides was called out from entertaining diners at a banquet. While he was out of the hall, the roof caved in, crushing the guests so badly that they could not be identified by members of their families. Simonides, by recalling where each guest sat, was able to help relatives find the remains of their family members (Paivio, 1971). Thus was invented one of the first mnemonic techniques, often called the **method of loci**.

The method of loci, as the name might suggest, requires the learner to imagine a series of places (locations) that have some sort of order to them. For example, I might use a series of landmarks I pass on my way from my office to the campus snack bar. I would then mentally picture different pieces of the material I wanted to remember at the different landmarks.

Suppose that I needed to remember to bring certain things to a meeting—for example, a tablet, a pen, certain computer printouts, a book, and a calculator. I could use the method of loci to remember these materials in the following way. First, I would imagine myself walking through my office doorway (first locus) and propping the first object (the tablet) against the door as a doorstop. Next I would see myself walking by my administrative assistant's desk and leaving my pen on the desk atop a letter or note. Then I would see myself walking into the hall and down the nearby stairwell, draping the printouts over the railing at the top of the stairs. I would mentally exit the building, pass a big oak tree to my left, and place the book on one of its branches. Finally, as I entered the student union, I would picture the calculator hung from the front door. When I needed to remember these five items, all I would need to do would be to mentally "take a walk" over the same route, noticing the objects I passed. Essentially, I would take the same path again, this time looking around in my image as I did so.

Another technique for improving memory could be called the technique of *interacting images.* A study reported in 1894 anticipated the usefulness of this technique. The results indicated that recall of concrete nouns on a list improved when participants were told to form images of the words, in comparison to when they were not given such instructions (Kirkpatrick, 1894). Bower (1970) found similar results in experiments of paired associates learning. In other words, if participants were given pairs of words such as *goat–pipe,* participants who formed images of, say, a goat smoking a pipe recalled almost twice as many paired associates as control participants who were not instructed to use imagery. These figures may underestimate the effect, because some control participants may have spontaneously used imagery.

Bower's (1970) research showed in particular that for images to be maximally effective in paired associates, participants should try to form images that interact—for example, a goat *smoking* a pipe rather than simply a picture of a goat next to a picture of a pipe with the two pictures separated in space. The principle of interactive imagery applies equally to the method-of-loci technique: The images should depict the to-be-remembered items interacting in some way with items at the various loci.

A third mnemonic technique, one that also involves imagery, is called the *pegword method.* Like the method of loci, it involves picturing the items with another set of ordered "cues"—pegging them to the cue. In this case, the cues are not locations but rather nouns that come from a memorized rhyming list: "One is a bun, two is a shoe, three is a tree, four is a door, five is a hive, six is sticks, seven is heaven, eight is a gate, nine is wine, and ten is a hen." The method calls for the participant to picture the first item interacting with a bun, the second with a shoe, the third with a tree, and so forth (notice that the method works only for lists of 10 items or fewer). Bugelski, Kidd, and Segmen (1968) showed that the method also improves recall in paired associates tasks as long as participants are given 4 seconds or more per item to form the images.

Not all mnemonic techniques have to do with imagery. One set of techniques that does not involve visual imagery per se involves *recoding* the material to be recalled, adding extra words or sentences to *mediate,* or go between, your memory and the material. One example, familiar to most schoolchildren, involves taking the first letter of each word you want to remember and forming a word or sentence from these letters. This technique can be used to recall the names of the Great Lakes (*HOMES:* Huron, Ontario, Michigan, Erie, Superior) or to recall the names of the notes on the lines of a musical staff ("Every good boy deserves fudge"). Research investigating the usefulness of this technique reports mixed results, although the technique is popular (L. Carlson, Zimmer, & Glover, 1981). Notice, by the way, that the words and sentences serve functions similar to those of the images in the techniques described previously. All are *mediators:* internal codes that connect the items to be remembered and your (later) overt responses (Klatzky, 1980).

Other Retrieval Principles

Let's consider a few principles of retrieval that can be used to aid recall.

The first is the principle of categorization. This states that material organized into categories or other units is more easily recalled than information with no apparent organization. This effect happens even when organized material is initially presented in a random order.

Bousfield (1953) presented participants with a list of 60 words. The words came from four categories—animals, names, professions, and vegetables—but were presented in scrambled order. Nevertheless, participants tended to recall the words in clusters—for example, a number of animals together, then a group of vegetables, and so on. It turns out that even if the material doesn't have apparent organization, asking people to organize it into their own subjective categories improves recall (G. Mandler, 1967).

How can we apply the principle of categorization to your studying for a midterm? Simply put, the best advice is to categorize and organize your information! Make a list of theories of forgetting, for example, and organize your notes about memory phenomena around this list. That way, if you are asked to write an essay about theories of forgetting, you will likely recall more of the relevant information.

A second principle of retrieval, discovered by Thomson and Tulving (1970), is called **encoding specificity**. The idea is that when material is first put into LTM, encoding depends on the context in which the material is learned. The manner in which information is encoded is specific to that context. At the time of recall, it is a great advantage to have the same context information available. Aspects of the context function as cues to the retrieval.

Roediger and Guynn (1996) summarize the encoding specificity hypothesis slightly differently:

> A retrieval cue will be effective if and only if it reinstates the original encoding of the to-be-remembered event. When a word like *black* is presented without context, it is presumably encoded with regard to its dominant meaning (as associated with *white*). Therefore, *white* serves as an effective retrieval cue, and a weak associate like *train* does not. However, when *black* is encoded in the context of a weak associate like *train,* subjects are likely to engage in a more idiosyncratic encoding of the target word (e.g., they might imagine a black train). In this case, the weak associate could serve as an excellent retrieval cue, but now the strong associate is completely ineffective. (p. 208)

Apparently, even information unrelated to the material, such as the environmental stimuli present at the time of encoding, can become a retrieval cue. One of my favorite studies is that by Godden and Baddeley (1975), who presented lists of 40 unrelated words to 16 scuba divers, all wearing scuba gear. Divers learned some of the lists on the shore and the others 20 feet under water. They were later asked to recall the words either in the same environment where they were learned or in the other environment. Results showed that recall was best when the environment was the same as the learning environment. Lists learned underwater were best recalled underwater, and lists learned on the shore were recalled best on the shore. This finding, that recall is best when performed in the original environment, is called a context effect.

Interestingly, researchers later found that recognition memory does not show the same context effect (Godden & Baddeley, 1980), suggesting that recognition and recall work differently. In particular, this finding suggests that physical context affects recall but not recognition (Roediger & Guynn, 1996). Presumably, in the former task the participant must do more work to generate his or her own retrieval cues, which may include certain features of the learning environment, whereas in the latter task, the test itself supplies some retrieval cues (in the form of the question and the possible answers).

Other studies have demonstrated similar effects (called **state-dependent learning**) with pharmacological states: Material learned while someone is chemically intoxicated (for example, by alcohol or marijuana) is usually recalled better when the person re-creates that state (J. E. Eich, 1980). By the way, to ensure that you don't use this scientific finding as an excuse to party, I must note that overall performance was best for those participants who learned and recalled material while sober! However, the finding of interest was that participants who learned material while in a chemically altered state showed significantly better recall if they were again chemically intoxicated at the time of recall. Later studies suggest that this **state-dependent memory** effect, like context effect, is found only with recall and not with recognition tasks (Roediger & Guynn, 1996).

Bower (1981) even claimed that a person would recall more information if he or she were in the same mood at recall time as at encoding time. That is, Bower claimed that if you learned information while happy, you would recall that information better if you were in a happy mood again. Over the years, however, this **mood-dependent memory effect** has proven more complicated than this, although recent work suggests the phenomenon does occur under certain conditions (E. Eich, 1995).

Further support for the encoding specificity hypothesis comes from a phenomenon known as the **spacing effect** (B. H. Ross & Landauer, 1978). You may already be familiar with this effect because it restates advice that teachers often give. Simply, if you repeatedly study the same material, you are much better off doing so in a number of short study sessions spaced some time apart than you are studying for one long session. (In other words, don't cram!) Ross and Landauer noted, "In most cases, two immediately successive presentations [of a piece of information] are hardly more effective than a single presentation, while two well-spaced presentations are about twice as effective as one" (p. 669).

A variety of theories seek to explain the spacing effect (Glenberg, 1977; B. H. Ross & Landauer, 1978). One of the most common is called **encoding variability**. Spacing allows the context of encoding to change so that a wider variety of cues can be attached to the material. The greater the number of cues, the greater the chances that one or more of them will be activated at the time of retrieval. Thus, the spacing effect is explained primarily in terms of the encoding specificity principle.

Another concept relevant to retrieval from long-term memory is **cue overload** (Roediger & Guynn, 1996). The basic principle here is that a retrieval cue is most effective when it is highly distinctive and not related to any other target memories. For example, we all remember dramatic, unusual events better than we do routine, more mundane events.

The Testing Effect

Psychologist Henry Roediger and colleagues have recently reported a series of studies exploring the **testing effect**—a finding that taking tests on material actually improves the learning of it, even when compared with simply repeatedly studying that material (Butler & Roediger, 2008; Roediger, Agarwal, McDaniel, & McDermott, 2011; Roediger & Butler, 2010).

Roediger et al. (2011) demonstrated the testing effect in a series of studies carried out with sixth graders in their social studies class. The researchers compared students' performance on material they had studied, but not previously been quizzed on, to the same students' performance on material they had previously been quizzed on. Whether the test came 2 days after the quiz or almost 2 weeks later, and whether the format of the test was multiple-choice (same as the quizzes) or free recall (e.g., "Recall all the facts you learned about ancient China"), students performed better on the previously quizzed material. In a later experiment in which performance on previously quizzed material was compared with performance on material that had been re-read, the testing effect still emerged.

Other studies using other populations (adults, college students) learning other kinds of material also show the testing effect. Roediger et al. (2011) believe that one of two things (or both) may account for the testing effect. First, taking a quiz requires more effort than simply reading or re-reading material. This effort might involve elaboration of the material, or the creation of retrieval strategies that will prove useful on a subsequent test. A second idea is that quizzing combats a certain "overconfidence" that can develop when students re-read (or highlight or underline) text, thinking they have mastered it. Whatever the mechanism, the take-home message is clear for students studying material for an upcoming test (presumably, you): Throw out your colored markers and quiz yourself instead to prepare most effectively!

SUBDIVISIONS OF LONG-TERM MEMORY_____

We saw in Chapter 5 a proposal by Alan Baddeley to postulate the existence of different components, or parts, of working memory. In a similar vein, other cognitive psychologists have offered proposals for "subdividing" LTM into different systems. In this case, the argument is that the systems function independently and/or according to different rules or processes. In this section, we'll take a look at three such proposals.

SEMANTIC VERSUS EPISODIC MEMORY

Endel Tulving (1972, 1983, 1989) drew a distinction between memories for events and memories for general knowledge. He argued that long-term memory consists of two separate and distinct yet interacting systems. One system, **episodic memory**, holds memories of specific events in which you yourself somehow participated. The other system, **semantic memory**, holds information that has entered your general knowledge base: You can recall parts of that base, but the information recalled is generic—it doesn't have much to do with your personal experience. For example, your memory that Sigmund Freud was a founding practitioner of psychoanalysis is presumably in your general knowledge base but divorced from your personal memories of what happened to you at a certain time. It's probable, actually, that you can't even remember when the fact about Freud entered your memory.

Contrast this situation with when information about your first date or the 9/11 attacks on the World Trade Center and Pentagon entered your memory. For those instances, you may recall not only the information itself but also the circumstances surrounding your acquisition of the information (where, when, why, how, and from whom you heard, saw, or otherwise acquired it), as we will see in just a bit when we review flashbulb memories.

Any of your memories that you can trace to a single time are considered to be in episodic memory. If you recall your high school graduation, your first meeting with your freshman roommate, or the time you first learned of an important event, you are recalling episodic memories. Even if you don't recall the exact date or even the year, you know the information was first presented at a particular time and place, and you have a memory of that presentation.

Semantic memory, in contrast, is thought to store general information about language and world knowledge. When you recall arithmetic facts (for example, $2 + 2 = 4$), historical dates ("In fourteen hundred and ninety-two/Columbus sailed the ocean blue"), or the past tense forms of various verbs (*run, ran; walk, walked; am, was*), you are calling on semantic memory.

Notice in these examples that in recalling $2 + 2 = 4$, you aren't tracing back to a particular moment when you learned the fact, as you might do with the 9/11 attacks. Instead of "remembering" that $2 + 2 = 4$, most people speak of "knowing" that $2 + 2 = 4$. This distinction between memories of specific moments and recall from general knowledge marks the major difference between semantic and episodic memory. Why make such a distinction? Doing so captures our intuition that the recall of some things differs from the recall of others. Recalling your graduation simply has a different "feel" than recalling the sum of 2 and 2.

Tulving (1972, 1983, 1989) described episodic and semantic memory as **memory systems** that operate on different principles and hold on to different kinds of information. Tulving (1983) pointed to a number of differences in the ways episodic and semantic memory seem to work, and I'll describe a few of the major differences here.

Organization of episodic memory is temporal; that is, one event will be recorded as having occurred before, after, or at the same time as another. Organization of semantic memory is arranged more on the basis of meanings and meaning relationships among different pieces of information.

Schacter (1996) offers a number of case studies of people suffering from different kinds of amnesia that support the episodic/semantic distinction. Gene, for example, survived a motorcycle accident in 1981 (when he was 30 years old) that seriously damaged his frontal and temporal lobes, including the left hippocampus. Gene shows anterograde amnesia and retrograde amnesia. In particular, Gene cannot recall *any* specific past events, even with extensive, detailed cues. That is, Gene cannot recall any birthday parties, school days, or conversations. Schacter notes further that

> even when detailed descriptions of dramatic events in his life are given to him—the tragic drowning of his brother, the derailment near his house of a train carrying lethal chemicals that required 240,000 people to evacuate their homes for a week—Gene does not generate any episodic memories. (p. 149)

In contrast, Gene recalls many facts (as opposed to episodes) about his past life. He knows where he went to school; he knows where he worked. He can name former coworkers; he can define technical terms he used at the manufacturing plant where he worked before the accident. Gene's memories, Schacter argues, are akin to the knowledge we have of other people's lives. You may know, for example, about incidents in your mother's or father's lives that occurred before your birth: where they met, perhaps, or some memorable childhood incidents. You know *about* these events, although you do not have specific *recall* of them. Similarly, according to Schacter, Gene has *knowledge* of some aspects of his past (semantic memory) but no evidence of any *recall* of specific happenings (episodic memory).

Schacter (1996) also describes neuropsychological case studies of people with deficits that are "mirror images" of Gene's. A case was reported, for instance, of a woman who, after a bout of encephalitis and resultant damage to the front temporal lobe, no longer knew the meanings of common words and forgot a great many historical facts and names of famous people.

These two cases and others like them (some described by Schacter, 1996; see also Riby, Perfect, & Stollery, 2004) provide some clinical neuropsychological evidence supporting the idea that episodic memory and semantic memory operate independently. That is, the existence of people in whom one type of memory seems seriously impaired while the other appears intact gives concrete evidence for the existence of two separate systems of memory.

Tulving (1989) also reported some cases in which the cerebral blood flow patterns were different when volunteer participants were asked to lie quietly and retrieve either an episodic or a semantic memory. Episodic retrieval tended to be associated with more frontal lobe activity than did semantic memory. Unfortunately, not all participants showed these effects; some showed no discernible differences, making any straightforward interpretation of these results impossible as of yet. Other work has suggested that different neural areas are activated during episodic versus semantic memory retrieval, although the patterns of neural activity underlying different kinds of memory retrieval share similarities and are not completely distinct (Menon, Boyett-Anderson, Schatzberg, & Reiss, 2002; Nyberg, Forkstam, Petersson, Cabeza, & Ingvar, 2002).

Tulving's (1972, 1983, 1989) proposals have provoked strong controversy within the field of cognitive psychology. McKoon, Ratcliff, and Dell (1986) presented a series of arguments centering on the usefulness of considering episodic and semantic memories to be two separate memory systems and on the kind of evidence needed to support the distinction. Many psychologists find it hard to draw sharp lines between knowledge that includes information about the time it was first learned and knowledge that is more "generic" in character (Baddeley, 1984). However, almost everyone agrees that at the very least there seem to be two kinds of memories—semantic and episodic—even if they are stored within a single system.

IMPLICIT VERSUS EXPLICIT MEMORY

Other cognitive psychologists have proposed another distinction between kinds of memory: implicit and explicit (Roediger, 1990; Schacter, 1987). **Explicit memories** are things that are consciously recollected. For example, in recalling your last vacation, you explicitly refer to a specific time (say, last summer) and a specific event or series of events. Your recall is something you are aware of and may even be deliberate. **Implicit memory**, by contrast, is memory that is not deliberate or conscious but shows evidence of prior learning and storage. Schacter (1996) poetically describes implicit memory as "a subterranean world of nonconscious memory and perception, normally concealed from the conscious mind" (pp. 164–165).

Laboratory work on implicit memory has been mainly concerned with a phenomenon known as *repetition priming.* **Repetition priming** is facilitation of the cognitive processing of information after a recent exposure to that same information (Schacter, 1987). For example, participants might be given a very brief exposure (of 30 milliseconds or less) to a word (such as *button*) and soon afterward be given a new word completion task (for example, "Fill in the blanks to create the English word that comes to mind: _U _T O_"). This task is called a *word stem completion* task. The repetition priming effect is demonstrated by an increased probability of responding "button" to the stimulus given in the word completion task, relative to the performance of participants not shown the word *button.* (Note that there are other possible ways to complete the word, such as *mutton* or *suitor.*)

Do laboratory demonstrations of implicit memory have any real-world relevance? Investigators who study implicit memory believe so. One real-world example of implicit memory was reported by Sergei Korsakoff, who in 1889 described patients with amnesic symptoms that have come to be known as *Korsakoff's syndrome.* One patient to whom he had administered an electric shock professed not to remember the shock but, on seeing the case containing the shock generator, told Korsakoff that he feared the scientist had probably come to electrocute him (Schacter, 1987).

Other work with amnesic patients demonstrated findings to support the idea that a dissociation exists between implicit and explicit memory. For example, Warrington and Weiskrantz (1970) conducted a more controlled investigation: They presented a variety of memory tasks to four amnesic patients, as well as to eight patients without brain damage who served as a control group. In one experiment (Experiment 2), participants received two "explicit memory" tasks (the quotation marks indicate the authors did not use this term to describe the tasks), a free-recall task and a recognition task.

Participants also worked on two "implicit memory" tasks. One was a word completion task, similar to the one just described. The other presented participants with words in which the letters were visually degraded; participants were asked to guess the word being displayed. All four tasks involved a prior presentation of various words. In the two "explicit" tasks, participants were asked to recall consciously or recognize the words previously presented. In the two "implicit" tasks, participants were *not* reminded of the prior presentation of words but merely asked to guess the word being presented (that is, in degraded letters or partial word stem).

Figure 6.2 presents the results. It shows quite clearly that amnesic participants performed more poorly than nonamnesic participants on the explicit memory tasks but quite comparably to nonamnesic participants on the implicit memory tasks. In other words, their amnesia seemed to selectively hurt performance on explicit memory tasks. These results have been replicated several times and on a variety of tasks (Shimamura, 1986).

Phenomena such as the one depicted in Figure 6.2 are sometimes called "dissociative," because performance on one task appears independent of (or dissociated from) performance on another. Dissociative phenomena do not by any means occur only with amnesic participants. Many studies (reviewed by Roediger, 1990) have demonstrated striking differences in performance on implicit and explicit memory tasks with normal participants. Schacter (1996) reports that repetition priming effects could persist as long as a week,

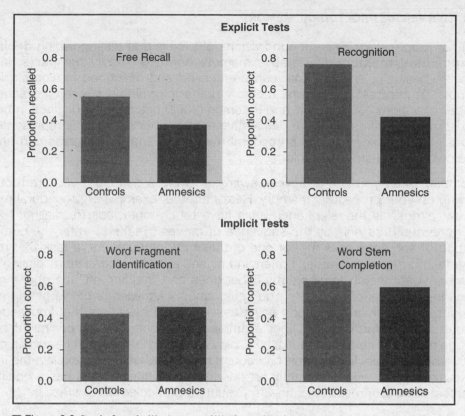

■ Figure 6.2: Results from the Warrington and Weiskrantz (1970) study.

SOURCE: Figure created by Roediger (1990). In Warrington, E. K., & Weiskrantz, L. (1970). Amnesic syndrome: Consolidation or retrieval? *Nature, 228*, p. 630. Copyright © 1970, Nature Publishing Group. Reprinted with permission.

even when his experimental participants denied that they had previously seen the primed words in the laboratory!

How are such dissociation phenomena best explained? Roediger (1990) presents two distinct possibilities. One is to postulate two memory systems. Schacter (1996) even speculates that different brain structures are associated with the two memory systems. The dissociation in performance on the two tasks would then be assumed to reflect two memory systems operating in different ways.

The second possibility is that the two kinds of memory tasks require different cognitive procedures, although they both tap into a common memory system (Roediger, 1990). One idea consistent with this proposal is that most implicit memory tasks require *perceptual* processing (that is, interpreting sensory information in a meaningful way) and that explicit memory tasks require *conceptual* processing (in other words, drawing on information in memory and the knowledge base). In this view, the type of processing required in the two types of tasks explains dissociation phenomena. Much debate focuses on the question of whether the two approaches can be reconciled (Schacter, 1989; Whittlesea & Price, 2001). Essentially, this debate hinges on whether there are multiple and distinct systems of memory, each operating on different principles, or a single memory system that supports different kinds of processing.

DECLARATIVE VERSUS PROCEDURAL MEMORY

Yet another proposal for different subdivisions of LTM is that distinguishing **declarative** from **procedural memory**. Declarative memory contains knowledge, facts, information, ideas—basically, anything that can be recalled and described in words, pictures, or symbols. In contrast, procedural memory holds information concerning action and sequences of actions. Sun, Merrill, and Peterson (2001) describe the distinction between the two somewhat differently, with declarative memory being explicitly represented and consciously accessible, whereas procedural memory is implicitly represented and thus perhaps not consciously accessible.

For example, when you ride a bicycle, swim, or swing a golf club, you are thought to be drawing on your procedural memory. Here's another example of procedural memory. Right now, almost all the telephones I use have touch-tone pads for dialing. I "know" many phone numbers only by the sequence of moves I make to enter the number on the keypad. If someone asks me for one of these phone numbers (a task that requires me to state information in words), I often find myself at a loss; then I start "dialing" on an imaginary keypad, watching where my finger goes and "reading off" the phone number based on the motions of my finger. You could say my knowledge of the phone number is procedural, not declarative. Upon being asked, I can't easily put that knowledge into words but can only perform it. Other examples of procedural memory might be your knowledge of how to tie a shoe, ride a bike, play a guitar chord, or shift gears in a car. The distinction between declarative and procedural memory should help explain the intuition that your memory of who is currently president of the United States has a qualitatively different feel than your memory of how to execute a particular dance step.

THE LEVELS-OF-PROCESSING VIEW

The modal approach to memory makes a distinction among different kinds of memory—for example, sensory memory, STM, and LTM stores. Many cognitive psychologists think these components process information differently, store information differently, and retain information for different lengths of time. The component used at any given time depends primarily on how long information is stored.

The modal approach is not universally endorsed, however. Some psychologists argue that there is only one kind of memory storage (Melton, 1963) but that different kinds of information processing take place within that store. Others take issue with the way the modal approach describes certain kinds of memory stores, such as STM.

Crowder (1993), for example, points out many experimental findings that he says are inconsistent with the modal model of STM. To cite just one: If you ask undergraduates to list the names of all the US presidents they can recall, you are likely to obtain a curve such as that shown in Figure 6.3. Note that its overall shape looks quite similar to a typical serial position curve; it shows both a primacy and a recency effect. But it is completely implausible to suggest that the existence of the recency effect indicates the undergraduates were drawing on STM to recall the most recent presidents. Although you might want to argue that the size of the recency effect is larger than is typically found (Healy & McNamara, 1996) or that the classic conception of STM can be extended and elaborated to account for such findings (Shiffrin, 1993), the fact remains that the modal model is no longer the only viable explanation of how memory works.

One alternative to the modal view of memory is the **levels-of-processing theory of memory**. In this model, memory is thought to depend not on how long material is stored or on the kind of storage in which the material is held but on the initial encoding of the information to be remembered (Craik & Lockhart, 1972). That is, the levels-of-processing approach does not posit different memory stores (such as STM and LTM) but rather posits different kinds of cognitive processing that people perform when they encode information.

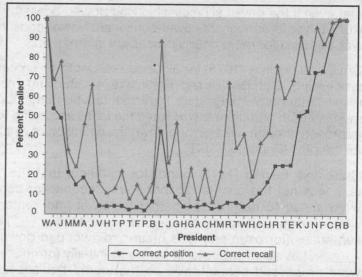

■ Figure 6.3: Recall of the names of US presidents as a function of their ordinal position.

SOURCE: Crowder, R. G. (1993). Short-term memory: Where do we stand? *Memory and Cognition, 21,* p. 143. Copyright © 1993, Psychonomic Society Inc. Reprinted with permission.

The fundamental assumption is that retention and coding of information depend on the kind of perceptual analysis done on the material at encoding. Some kinds of processing, done at a superficial or "shallow" level, do not lead to very good retention. Other kinds of "deeper" (more meaningful or semantic) processing improve retention. According to the levels-of-processing view, improvement in memory comes not from rehearsal and repetition but from greater depth of analysis of the material.

Craik and Tulving (1975) performed a typical levels-of-processing investigation. Participants were presented with a series of questions about particular words. Each word was preceded by a question, and participants were asked to respond to the questions as quickly as possible; no mention was made of memory or learning. Any learning that is not in accord with the participant's purpose is called **incidental learning**.

In one experiment, three kinds of questions were used. One kind asked the participant whether the word was printed in capital letters. Another asked if the target word rhymed with another word. The third kind asked if the word fit into a particular sentence (for example, "The girl placed the _____ on the table"). The three kinds of questions were meant to induce different kinds of processing. To answer the first kind of question, you need look only at the typeface (physical processing). To answer the second, you need to read the word and think about what it sounds like (acoustic processing). To answer the third, you need to retrieve and evaluate the word's meaning (semantic processing). Presumably, the "depth" of the processing needed is greatest for the third kind of question and least for the first kind of question.

As predicted, Craik and Tulving (1975) found that on a surprise memory test later, words processed semantically were remembered best, followed by words processed acoustically. However, the experiment gave rise to an alternative explanation: Participants spent more time answering questions about sentences than they did questions about capital letters. To respond to this explanation, in subsequent experiments the authors showed that even if the physical processing was slowed down (by asking participants, "Does this word follow a consonant-vowel-consonant-vowel-consonant-vowel pattern?"), memory was still best for more deeply processed information.

Craik and Tulving (1975) initially equated depth of processing with degree of semantic processing. But Bower and Karlin (1974), studying memory for faces, found similar results with nonverbal stimuli: Participants who rated faces for "honesty" showed better memory than participants who rated the faces according to gender. One problem with this approach, though, was pinning down the definition of what defined a level and what made for "depth" (Baddeley, 1978).

Craik and Tulving (1975) found, for instance, that the "meaningfulness" of the initial task was not the only factor that could account for better retention. Participants who were asked to determine whether words fit into sentences showed poorer recall for simple sentences (for example, "She cooked the _____") than they did for more complex sentences (for example, "The great bird swooped down and carried off the struggling _____"). Levels-of-processing theory as initially formulated would argue that both words were processed semantically, so that could not account for the difference in recall. Craik and Tulving therefore extended the levels-of-processing idea, arguing that the elaboration of material could also aid recall. Presumably, the second, more complicated sentence calls to mind a richer idea: The sentence itself has more underlying propositions (there was a bird, the bird was very large, the bird swooped down, the bird carried something off) than the first sentence (there is a female, she is baking something). Sentences that specified more precisely the relation of the target word to the context were found especially likely to increase the probability of recalling the target word (Stein & Bransford, 1979).

Craik and Lockhart (1972) viewed memory as a continuum of processes, from the "transient products of sensory analyses to the highly durable products of semantic . . . operations" (p. 676). This view ties memory in with other cognitive systems quite neatly. For example, recall the work on dichotic listening tasks, reviewed in Chapter 4. Recall that material from the unattended channel is typically not remembered after the task is completed. The levels-of-processing approach can account for this finding, holding that material not analyzed for meaning receives only "shallow" processing, which results in poor retention.

Baddeley (1978) presented a thorough critique of the levels-of-processing approach. First, he argued that without a more precise and independent definition of *depth of processing,* the usefulness of the theory is very limited. Second, he reviewed studies that showed, under certain conditions, greater recall of information processed acoustically than semantically. Finally, he described ways in which the modal view of memory could explain the typical levels-of-processing findings.

Nonetheless, the levels-of-processing approach did help to reorient the thinking of memory researchers, drawing their attention to the importance of the *way* material is encoded. The approach has helped cognitive psychologists think about the ways in which people approach learning tasks. It has reinforced the idea that the more "connections" an item has to other pieces of information (such as retrieval cues), the easier it will be to remember, a point that fits nicely with the idea of encoding specificity discussed earlier.

And, the framework continues to inspire research today (e.g., Rose, Myerson, Roediger, & Hale, 2010).

Other memory research has also encouraged psychologists to pay attention to how encoding changes with the type of material presented. Some aspects of information, for instance, seem to be encoded without much effort or even intention. Frequency of occurrence is one such aspect (Hasher & Zacks, 1984). For example, if you are a movie fan, you see lots of movies, and you may even see some more than once. Although you probably have no reason to keep track of how many times you saw a particular movie, you may have a clear sense you've seen one a few more times than you've seen another. Chances are quite good that your sense is correct. If so, Hasher and Zacks would explain your impression as an instance of *automatic encoding:* Certain aspects of experience, such as frequency of occurrence, have a special representation and are kept track of in memory without effort or even intention.

Other work in various laboratories is aimed at explicating other so-called unitary models of memory, which do not assume different processes for short- and long-term memory. Like Craik and Tulving, psychologist James Nairne (2002) argues against positing distinct short- and long-term memory stores. What differs for memories recalled after a few seconds versus after several years, Nairne believes, are the retrieval cues that are in effect. Thus, unlike Craik and Tulving, who emphasized encoding processes, Nairne focuses on retrieval.

THE RECONSTRUCTIVE NATURE OF MEMORY

Thus far, we have concentrated on laboratory studies of memory. This tradition dates back at least to Ebbinghaus. One can't help admiring Ebbinghaus's dedication and feeling gratitude for his many insights about memory. However, a similarly common reaction is to find his efforts somewhat amusing. After all, what relevance do his heroic studies have to memory in "real life"? Does the study of memory for nonsense syllables really tell us very much about how to study for an upcoming midterm, how to remember where we left our house key, or how we recall our first day of kindergarten (if in fact we remember anything about it)?

Another pioneer in the study of memory, Frederick Bartlett, rejected the emphasis on laboratory studies of memory. Bartlett (1932) believed that in the real world (as opposed to the laboratory) memory largely uses world knowledge and **schemata**—frameworks for organizing information. According to Bartlett, at retrieval time, this knowledge and organizational information are used to reconstruct the material. Bartlett tested both friends and students, first presenting them with stories such as the one in Box 6.1.

Bartlett used the method of serial reproduction, meaning participants were asked to recall the stories on more than one occasion. Participants were asked to recall the tales at varying intervals, some as long as years. Bartlett was interested in what information was remembered and what information was "misremembered"—distorted or reordered in the participants' recollections. Box 6.2 provides examples of repeated recollections of the "War of the Ghosts" story as retold by one participant. This retelling shows concretely that over time, the same person's recall becomes more distorted.

Box 6.1

"The War of the Ghosts": A Story Used by
Bartlett (1932) to Investigate Long-Term Memory

One night two young men from Egulac went down to the river to hunt seals, and while they were there it became foggy and calm. Then they heard war-cries, and they thought: "Maybe this is a war-party." They escaped to the shore, and hid behind a log.

Now canoes came up, and they heard the noise of paddles, and saw one canoe coming up to them. There were five men in the canoe, and they said: "What do you think? We wish to take you along. We are going up the river to make war on the people." One of the young men said: "I have no arrows." "Arrows are in the canoe," they said.

"I will not go along. I might be killed. My relatives do not know where I have gone. But you," he said, turning to the other, "may go with them." So one of the young men went, but the other returned home.

And the warriors went on up the river to a town on the other side of Kalama. The people came down to the water, and they began to fight, and many were killed. But presently the young man heard one of the warriors say: "Quick, let us go home: that Indian has been hit." Now he thought: "Oh, they are ghosts." He did not feel sick, but they said he had been shot.

So the canoes went back to Egulac, and the young man went ashore to his house, and made a fire. And he told everybody and said: "Behold I accompanied the ghosts, and we went to fight. Many of our fellows were killed, and many of those who attacked us were killed. They said I was hit, and I did not feel sick." He told it all, and then he became quiet. When the sun rose he fell down. Something black came out of his mouth. His face became contorted. The people jumped up and cried.

He was dead.

Box 6.2

One Participant's Recall of "The War of the Ghosts"

Recalled 15 minutes after hearing story:
The Ghosts

There were two men on the banks of the river near Egulac. They heard the sound of paddles, and a canoe with five men in it appeared, who called to them, saying: "We are going to fight the people. Will you come with us?" One of the two men answered, saying: "Our relations do not know where we are, and we have not got any arrows." They answered: "There are arrows in the canoe." So the man went, and they fought the people, and then he heard them saying: "An Indian is killed, let us return." So he returned to Egulac, and told them he knew they were ghosts.

He spoke to the people of Egulac, and told them that he had fought with the Ghosts, and many men were killed on both sides, and that he was wounded, but felt nothing. He lay down and became calmer, and in the night he was convulsed, and something black came out of his mouth.

The people said: "He is dead."

Recalled 2 weeks later:

The Ghosts

There were two men on the banks of a river near the village of Etishu (?). They heard the sound of paddles coming from the up-stream, and shortly a canoe appeared. The men in the canoe spoke, saying: "We are going to fight the people: will you come with us?"

One of the young men answered, saying: "Our relations do not know where we are; but my companion may go with you. Besides, we have no arrows."

So the young man went with them, and they fought the people, and many were killed on both sides. And then he heard shouting: "The Indian is wounded; let us return." And he heard the people say: "They are the Ghosts." He did not know he was wounded, and returned to Etishu (?). The people collected round him and bathed his wounds, and he said he had fought with the Ghosts. Then he became quiet. But in the night he was convulsed, and something black came out of his mouth.

And the people cried: "He is dead."

Bartlett used this evidence to argue for a constructive view of long-term memory (LTM). He believed that participants unintentionally introduced the distortions to make the material more rational and more coherent from their own point of view. Interestingly, the original story, a Native American folktale, was often "misrecalled" in ways more consistent with people's cultural conventions for stories. Thus, the "foggy and calm" weather might be changed to a "dark and stormy night"—something more in keeping with a Western assumption of how weather portends bad events. Bartlett thus rejected the idea of LTM as a warehouse where material is stored unchanged until retrieval. Rather, he saw memory as an active and often inaccurate process that encodes and retrieves information so as to "make sense."

Psychologist Ulric Neisser, a major figure in the study of memory, offered related arguments regarding studying memory in natural settings (1982a). Neisser was skeptical of the assumption that laboratory studies of memory are necessarily relevant to memory in natural settings; rather, he believed that laboratory studies are of limited value in understanding the use of memory in everyday life. Neisser called for the study of how people construct and use memories of their own past experiences, how they remember events of historical significance, how they use memory to plan and carry out everyday errands, and so on. In this section, we will take up some of these questions.

AUTOBIOGRAPHICAL MEMORY

Marigold Linton (1982) conducted a study that nicely demonstrates this principle. Like Hermann Ebbinghaus, she studied her own memory. Like those of Ebbinghaus, her methods of data collection have a heroic quality: Every day for six years (!), she wrote brief descriptions of two (or more) events that had happened that day. Each month, she conducted tests of her memory.

> Memory tests proceeded as follows: Once a month items were drawn semi-randomly from the accumulated event pool. After reading a pair of randomly paired event descriptions, I estimated their chronological order and attempted to reconstruct each item's date. Next, I briefly classified my memory search (for example, I might "count backwards" through a series of similar events, as school quarters, Psychonomic Society meetings, and the like) and reevaluated each item's salience. After six years the experiment had reached imposing dimensions. I had written more than 5,500 items (a minimum of two times each day) and tested (or retested) 11,000 items (about 150 items each month). Item generation required only a few minutes each day but the monthly test was extremely laborious, lasting 6–12 hours. (pp. 78–79)

Linton (1982) found that some items were easily retrievable: Any description such as "I did X for the first time" (for example, went to New York, met a famous psychologist) was very memorable. Other items became harder and harder to recall, especially when the written description did not pertain to a single, distinctive event.

This is a good example of a classic study of **autobiographical memory**—that is, memory for events that the rememberer has been part of. During the first 20 months of the study, Linton recorded 2,003 events and tested 3,006 (1,468 of these were retests of previously tested items). She had expected, before running the study, that she would quickly forget many of the items, but in fact that did not happen, perhaps because she needed only to recognize the events (not recall them) and to date them, not answer detailed questions about them. In fact, Linton's results suggest that real-world memories are much more durable than those of most laboratory experiments.

Linton also recorded protocols of herself thinking aloud (a technique discussed in Chapter 10) as she tried to date items. She found that she often used problem-solving strategies to arrive at a date, even when she had no explicit recall of the event. You might be able to re-create this phenomenon by trying to answer the following question: Where were you on June 28, 2012, at 9:20 am? Your first reaction may be to laugh and to claim you can't possibly answer the question. But think about it. No doubt you can find some "markers" that point you toward some sort of answer. For instance, you might note that June is during the summer. You might be able to figure out June 28 must have been a Thursday, because (say) your mother's birthday is June 25, and you remember that being on a Monday. You might remember you held a summer job at a local department store and conclude that at 9:20 on June 28, you must have been working, probably stocking shelves. Notice that what you've done is to zero in on the date and time by finding and using different markers. You haven't necessarily remembered what you were doing; instead, you've reconstructed it.

Linton (1982) also reported on "unrecalled" items and found them to be of (at least) two types. Some were simply not recalled; that is, the description she originally reported did not serve to bring to mind any recollection of the event when it was tested. However, at least as many "forgotten" items were ones Linton found herself unable to distinguish from other, similar memories.

Robinson and Swanson (1990) offer an explanation of Linton's findings on "unrecalled" items. They suggest that as similar events are repeated, the similar aspects start to form an event schema. That is, as Linton repeatedly experienced an event, such as sending what she believed to be a "final" draft of her book to her publisher, which in fact she would subsequently need to rewrite and submit, memory traces of the specific instances of the different events fused together and became indistinguishable. Linton herself (1982) talked about a transformation from episodic to semantic memory.

Barsalou (1988) reported findings consistent with Robinson and Swanson's (1990) proposal. He and his collaborators stopped people on the campus of Emory University during the fall semester and asked whoever agreed to participate to describe events they were involved with during the preceding summer. Although people were asked to report and describe specific events, only 21% of the recollections collected could be categorized as specific recollections. Instead, people were more likely to give "summarized events," statements that referred to two or more events of a certain kind, such as "I went to the beach every day for a week." These summarized events made up almost a third of the recollections collected. People also reported what Barsalou called an "extended event," a single event lasting longer than a day, such as "I worked at a camp for disadvantaged children." Even when Barsalou and his associates pointedly tried to elicit only specific event recollections, their participants still tended to report extended or summarized events.

Brewer (1988) took a different methodological approach to studying recall for ordinary events. He found eight very cooperative undergraduates to serve in a demanding multiweek experiment. During the data acquisition phase, participants were asked to wear beepers programmed to go off on a random schedule about once every 2 hours. When the beeper sounded, participants were asked to fill out a card with information about the event that was occurring when the beeper went off. Specifically, participants were asked to report the time and their location, actions, and thoughts and then to complete a number of rating scales (rating such things as how often this kind of event occurred, how pleasant the event was, and how trivial or significant it was). Fortunately, participants were given the option of recording the word "private" on a card instead of giving a detailed account, if the activity they were engaged in was one they preferred for any reason not to report. Brewer noted that most participants exercised this option at least occasionally, which no doubt led to some systematic undersampling of certain kinds of events, such as dating or parties.

This methodology, Brewer (1988) argued, had certain advantages over the one Linton used. Obviously, it involves separating the experimenter from the participant, which methodologically has many advantages. More important, however, Brewer argued that Linton wrote down the most "memorable" events of each day, which would tend to skew the set of items to be remembered. Brewer compares Linton's technique to one in which a laboratory participant in an experiment is given lists of hundreds of words each day and is asked at the end of each day to select one word to use in later testing. To compare these techniques, Brewer also asked his participants to list the most memorable event of each day.

Brewer (1988) later tested his participants' recall of the events they had recorded on cards. Each participant was tested three times: once at the conclusion of the data acquisition period, once about 21.2 months later, and once about 41.2 months after the end of the acquisition period. Items tested were randomly selected from all items the participants had initially described. Brewer (1988) reported very good overall retention from his participants, who recognized more than 60% of the events. Memory was better for actions than for thoughts and better for "memorable" events than for events randomly prompted by beepers. Consistent with some of the results Linton reported (1975, 1982), Brewer found that events that occurred in a unique or infrequent location were better remembered than occurrences in frequented locations. Similarly, rare actions were more likely to be recalled than frequent actions. Interestingly, the time period of study encompassed the Thanksgiving break for Brewer's participants. Memories from that mini vacation were recalled especially well. The reason for this, Brewer argued, was that these trips were taken during the participants' first trip home from college (all the participants were first-year students). Those trips, he believed, were likely to be quite distinctive, especially in comparison with the routine events of going to class and studying that preceded and followed the vacation. Brewer concluded that the more distinct the mental representation of an event, the more likely it is to be recalled, a conclusion similar to the one Linton reached.

In summary, Brewer (1988) concluded that autobiographical memories, while showing many of the phenomena demonstrated in laboratory studies, also showed important differences. Few overt recall errors were found, suggesting to Brewer that "personal memories are reasonably accurate copies of the individual's original phenomenal experiences" (p. 87).

FLASHBULB MEMORIES

Where were you when you learned of the terrorist attack on the World Trade Center on September 11, 2001? Many of us recall information not only about the tragic disaster itself but also about where we were, whom we were with, and what we were doing when we first heard about it. For example, I was standing in line at Goodbye, Blue Monday, my town's local coffee store. I'd just had my hair done and was thinking about all the things I had to do that day when a woman in a pink dress behind me tapped me on the arm and asked if I'd heard the news. When I got to my car, I turned on the radio, and I hurried to school to use my computer to surf the Web. For most of the day I listened to the radio, surfed the Web, and talked in horrified tones to coworkers. That evening, I took my 8-year-old son to an on-campus service of remembrance. The day seems etched permanently in my memory.

R. Brown and Kulick (1977) coined the term **flashbulb memory** to describe this phenomenon. Other examples might be found in your parents' or other relatives' recollections of where they were when they heard about the assassinations of John F. Kennedy or Martin Luther King Jr. A recent study reports on flashbulb memories among Danish World War II veterans of the invasion and liberation of Denmark (Berntsen & Thomsen, 2005). Given the historical importance and surprising nature of these events, it may be small wonder that most of us old enough to have experienced them remember them. Why, though, do we remember details about our own circumstances when we first heard the news? Some have argued that part of the explanation involves our physiological response when we hear such news: Parts of the brain that are involved in emotional responses activate, and the cognitive effects of this activation result in the storage of a great deal of information only indirectly related to the main information (R. Brown & Kulik, 1977). Pillemer (1984) found, for example, that his participants who reported a stronger emotional reaction to the news of the assassination attempt on President Reagan had stronger and more detailed flashbulb memories of that event.

Neisser (1982b) offered a different explanation for the origin of flashbulb memories: People are finding a way to link themselves to history. Flashbulb memories come about because the strong emotions produced by the event prompt people to retell their own stories of where they were when they heard the news. Flashbulb memories, then, result from the retellings of stories. Over time, the memories can become distorted, in much the same way that participants in Bartlett's (1932) study distorted their retellings of the "War of the Ghosts" story: People elaborate and fill in gaps in their stories, making them approximate a standard story format.

Stephen Schmidt (2004) offers results of a study on people's flashbulb memories for 9/11. Undergraduates at his university (Middle Tennessee State) filled out survey instruments asking for their recall of the events of 9/11 beginning the very next day (September 12, 2011). Students were also resurveyed 2 months later. In this way, Schmidt was able to compare recollections across a 2-month time span. Almost all of his participants were able to report basic "flashbulb" information: who told them about 9/11, where they were when they first heard the news, what activity they were engaged in when they first heard the news, what they were wearing, what the weather was like. Students showed greater consistency in answering what Schmidt calls "central" questions, such as the first three in the list above, and less for "peripheral" questions, such as what they were wearing. However, contrary to prediction, Schmidt found that those participants who initially reported the strongest emotional reaction to the events of 9/11 showed the most impairment in their memory. Interestingly, Daniel Greenberg (2004) has analyzed news reports to show that George W. Bush has demonstrated substantial inaccuracies in his own flashbulb memories of the events of that day. Arguably, as the sitting president during the events of 9/11, his reaction was powerfully emotional.

The question of whether flashbulb memories differ in kind from other types of memories has been actively debated (see, for example, N. J. Cohen, McCloskey, & Wible, 1990; McCloskey, Wible, & Cohen, 1988; Pillemer, 1990). McCloskey et al., for example, found evidence that some flashbulb memories are quite inaccurate and that the kinds of forgetting and distortion evident in flashbulb memories can be predicted on the basis of traditional studies of ordinary memory.

Weaver (1993) reports on a relevant and well-timed study of flashbulb memories. In January 1991, Weaver asked students enrolled in an upper-division psychology class to try to remember, in detail, their very next meeting with their roommate (or friend, if they were living alone). Specifically, students were urged to do their best to remember "all the circumstances surrounding" that meeting (without being told specifically what kinds of things to try to remember). Weaver's intention was to see whether the memories formed of these routine meetings would function in ways similar to flashbulb memories, and he distributed a sealed questionnaire for students to fill out as soon as feasible after the meeting.

As it happened, that very evening the first President Bush announced the initial attacks on Iraq in the Persian Gulf War. Although expected and thus not terribly surprising, it was an event of great consequentiality, especially to people with friends or relatives involved. Thus, this event seemed likely to be one for which flashbulb memories would be formed. Weaver, reacting quickly, created another questionnaire asking about their memories of hearing about Bush's announcement. Students filled out this second questionnaire 2 days later. Weaver (1993) gave similar questionnaires about both memories (bombing of Iraq and meeting with roommate/friend), which students completed in April 1991 (3 months after the original events) and January 1992 (1 year after the original events).

Weaver (1993) found very few differences in accuracy for the two memories (as measured by the degree of correspondence between the January 1991 descriptions and the two subsequent ones). Weaver reports that accuracy for both fell off in an Ebbinghaus-like pattern: less accuracy after 3 months but relatively little change from 3 months to 12 months. What did differ, however, was students' confidence in their memories. Students were much more confident in their memories of the Persian Gulf bombing than in their memory of meeting their friend or roommate. However, the increased confidence did not lead to increased accuracy.

Weaver (1993) concludes that no "flash" is necessary to form a flashbulb memory: Having an intention to remember a particular meeting or event seems enough to ensure forming some memory of it. The "flash," he believes, affects only our confidence in our memory. What makes flashbulb memories special, he argued, is in part the "undue confidence placed in the accuracy of those memories" (p. 45). Although this last assertion is sure to be controversial, probably no cognitive psychologist would disagree with another of Weaver's conclusions: "Flashbulb memories for exceptional events will continue to be studied, for obvious and interesting reasons. They are rare, unique, and universal" (p. 45). However, Weaver and others reject the idea that flashbulb memories rely on special memory mechanisms.

EYEWITNESS MEMORY

Imagine yourself a juror assigned to a robbery/murder case. The defendant, a young man, is alleged to have robbed and killed a convenience store clerk at gunpoint at around 11 pm. No physical evidence (such as fingerprints or fiber samples) links the defendant to the crime. Instead, the case hinges on the sworn testimony of a convenience store patron who insists that the defendant is the man she saw on the night in question. In cross-examination, the defense attorney gets the witness to agree that the lighting was poor, the robber was wearing a stocking cap over his face, she was nervous and paying more attention to the gun than to the face of the robber, and so on. Nevertheless, the witness remains convinced that the defendant is the man she saw that night rob and murder the store clerk.

How much would the eyewitness testimony convince you of the defendant's guilt? Elizabeth Loftus, a cognitive psychologist specializing in the study of **eyewitness memory**, would argue that the testimony would have a disproportionate effect on your behavior. She stated that "eyewitness testimony is likely to be believed by jurors, especially when it is offered with a high level of confidence," even when the confident witness is inaccurate. Indeed, she believed that "all the evidence points rather strikingly to the conclusion that there is almost nothing more convincing than a live human being who takes the stand, points a finger at the defendant, and says 'That's the one!'" (1979, p. 19). Several studies Loftus reviewed, however, suggest that confidence in eyewitness testimony may be far too strong.

In one study, for example, participants viewed a series of slides depicting a (simulated) automobile accident. The automobile, a red Datsun, came to either a stop sign (for half the participants) or a yield sign (for the other half) before becoming involved in an accident with a pedestrian. The experimental manipulation came in the questioning that followed the slide show. About half the participants (half of whom had seen a stop sign; the other half, a yield sign) were asked, "Did another car pass the red Datsun while it was stopped at the stop sign?" The other half of the participants were asked, "Did another car pass the red Datsun while it was stopped at the yield sign?" After answering these and other apparently routine questions, participants worked on an unrelated activity for 20 minutes. Then they were given a recognition test of several slides. Included in the test was a critical test pair depicting a red Datsun stopped either at a stop sign or at a yield sign. Participants were to decide which of the two slides they had originally seen. Those who received a question consistent with the slide originally seen (for example, a question about the stop sign when the slide they had previously seen contained a stop sign, not a yield sign) correctly recognized the slide 75% of the time. Participants who received an inconsistent question, however, had an overall accuracy rate of 41%, a dramatic decrease given that guessing alone would have produced an overall accuracy rate of 50%.

Other studies by Loftus (1975) have demonstrated that people's memories can apparently be altered by presenting misleading questions. For example, some participants viewed a film and were then asked, "How fast was the white sports car going when it passed the barn while traveling along the country road?" Other participants were merely asked, "How fast was the white sports car going while traveling along the country road?" Actually, no barn was presented in the film. One week later, all participants were asked whether they had seen a barn. Fewer than 3% of the participants in the second condition reported having seen a barn, whereas 17% of the participants who had been asked the misleading question reported having seen a barn. Lane, Mather, Villa, and Morita (2001) found that experimental "witnesses" who were asked to focus on specific details of a videotaped crime were more likely to confuse what they'd witnessed with the information given them in postevent questions than were "witnesses" asked only to summarize the major aspects of the crime.

"Memory malleability" fits well with some laboratory studies of sentence recall; both support Bartlett's conception of memory as a constructive process. A classic study by Bransford, Barclay, and Franks (1971) illustrates this idea. They gave participants a list of sentences, all derived from four basic sentences, such as "The ants were in the kitchen," "The jelly was on the table," "The jelly was sweet," and "The ants ate the jelly." The sentences the participants saw included two of the preceding sentences, combinations of two of the simple sentences (for example, "The sweet jelly was on the table"), and combinations of three of the simple sentences (example, "The ants ate the sweet jelly on the table"). On a later recognition test, the participants were asked to decide, for each sentence presented, if they had seen that exact sentence before and to rate their confidence in their judgment. They were most confident in "recognizing" the sentence that combined all four of the simple sentences, "The ants in the kitchen ate the sweet jelly that was on the table," even though it had never been presented.

Bransford et al. (1971) explained that the participants had not stored a copy of the actually presented sentences in memory. Instead, they had abstracted and reorganized the information in the sentences, integrating the ideas and storing the integration. The participants later could not distinguish between the presented sentences and their own integration. One might argue this is just what Loftus's participants were doing: integrating the original memories with later questions. If the later questions were misleading, that incorrect information became integrated with the original memory to produce a distorted memory.

Recent work in cognitive psychology laboratories has focused on how to improve the chances of accuracy in eyewitness identification. Wells (1993) reviews some of the findings and makes specific suggestions on how police might set up lineups and photo lineups so as to reduce the chances of eyewitness error. For example, he suggests having "mock" witnesses, people who were not present during the crime but who have been given limited information about the crime. The logic here is that the mock witnesses should be equally likely to choose any of the people in a lineup. If, however, the mock witnesses all "identify" the actual suspect, that is evidence that the lineup has been put together in a biased way. Other investigators have offered other suggestions for how to decrease eyewitness suggestibility (K. L. Chambers & Zaragoza, 2001), such as warning people against being misled by tricky questions.

However, there remains active and often very sharp debate over how well the findings of laboratory studies can be extrapolated to real-world settings. Typically, research participants view staged events or even movies or slides of incidents. This experience may not be very similar to that of a bystander who observes an actual robbery, assault, murder, terrorist attack, or other kind of crime. Moreover, it seems quite possible that victims or possible victims of crime may attend to different aspects of the situation than bystanders. Yuille (1993) argues that we need more justification to assume that research participants are subject to the same influences as witnesses (or victims) of real crimes.

THE RECOVERED/FALSE MEMORY DEBATE

One of the biggest debates to erupt in cognitive psychology in recent years concerns issues of forgetting, retrieving, and creating autobiographical memories. The debate has far-reaching implications well beyond the boundaries of an experimental laboratory. At stake are issues that touch, and indeed tear apart, the lives of real people. The issues concern whether victims of abuse can and/or do repress memories of incidents of abuse, retrieving these so-called **recovered memories** later in therapy, or whether instead some therapists (in fact, a small minority), misinformed about the workings of memory, inadvertently prompt their clients to create **false memories** of things that never really happened.

Note that the topics of eyewitness testimony and false versus recovered memory share many similarities: Both essentially involve the alleged witnessing of an event, sometimes traumatic, often followed later by newer, distorting information. But differences between the topics should also be kept in mind. In the case of eyewitness testimony, the issue is typically focused on recall for information acquired within the past few days, weeks, or months. In the case of false or recovered memories, the issue is whether one can recall information from several years to several decades earlier.

Elizabeth Loftus is again an active participant in the debate over whether such "recalls" represent recovered or false memories. She begins a review article (Loftus, 1993) on the phenomenon with an anecdote:

> In 1990, a landmark case went to trial in Redwood City, California. The defendant, George Franklin, Sr., 51 years old, stood trial for a murder that had occurred more than 20 years earlier. The victim, 8-year-old Susan Kay Nason, was murdered on September 22, 1969. Franklin's daughter, Eileen, only 8 years old herself at the time of the murder, provided the major evidence against her father. What was unusual about the case is that Eileen's memory of witnessing the murder had been repressed for more than 20 years.
>
> Eileen's memory did not come back all at once. She claimed that her first flashback came one afternoon in January 1989 when she was playing with her 2-year-old son, Aaron, and her 5-year-old daughter, Jessica. At one moment, Jessica looked up and asked her mother a question like, "Isn't that right, Mommy?" A memory of Susan Nason suddenly just came back. Eileen recalled the look of betrayal in Susie's eyes just before the murder. Later, more fragments would return, until Eileen had a rich and detailed memory. She remembered her father sexually assaulting Susie in the back of a van. She remembered that Susie was struggling as she said, "No, don't" and "Stop." She remembered her father saying "Now Susie," and she even mimicked his precise intonation. Next, her memory took the three of them outside the van, where she saw her father with his hands raised above his head with a rock in them. She remembered screaming. She remembered walking back to where Susie lay, covered with blood, the silver ring on her finger smashed.
>
> Eileen's memory report was believed by her therapist, by several members of her family, and by the San Mateo district attorney's office, which chose to prosecute her father. It was also believed by the jury, who convicted George Franklin, Sr., of the murder. The jury began its deliberations on November 29,

1990, and returned its verdict the next day. Impressed by Eileen's detailed and confident memory, they found her father guilty of murder in the first degree. (p. 518)

Loftus goes on in her article to examine various questions—among them, how authentic recovered memories are. The idea that memories of traumatic events can be repressed—buried in the unconscious mind for long periods of time, even forever—is a tenet of psychoanalytic forms of therapy dating back to Freud. But from a cognitive psychology perspective, the question is whether such **repressed memories** can be carefully described, documented, and explained.

Loftus (1993) and Lindsay and Read (1994) point to advice given in different self-help books, one of the best known being *The Courage to Heal* (Bass & Davis, 1988). That book encourages readers who are wondering whether they have ever been victims of childhood sexual abuse to look for the presence of various symptoms, such as having low self-esteem, depression, self-destructive or suicidal thoughts, or sexual dysfunction. The problem, Lindsay and Read note, is that these symptoms can also occur for people who have *not* been victims of abuse; the symptoms are just not specific enough to be diagnostic. In *The Courage to Heal,* Bass and Davis make a further, very strong claim: "If you are unable to remember any specific instances [of abuse] like the ones mentioned above but still have a feeling that something abusive happened to you, it probably did" (p. 21) and "If you think you were abused and your life shows the symptoms, then you were" (p. 22). The book goes on to recommend that readers who are wondering about their past spend time exploring the possibility that they were abused. It offers techniques for recalling specific memories, such as using old family photographs and giving the imagination free rein, or using a recalled childhood event as a beginning point and then deliberately trying to remember abuse connected with that event.

We have seen earlier that there is plenty of room to doubt the absolute accuracy of people's autobiographical memories, even when people seem very sure of them. Research on eyewitness memory has shown how receptive people can be to postevent suggestions. But is it possible for false "memories" of events that never happened to be somehow implanted? Loftus and Pickrell (1995; see also Loftus, 2000; Loftus & Ketcham, 1994) report on a study that suggests just such a possibility.

Twenty-four people served as the target research participants. Experimenters first interviewed relatives of the participants (who, to be included in the study, had to be familiar with the participant's early childhood) and from the interviews generated three true events that had happened to the research participant when the latter was age 4 to 6. Relatives were instructed that these events were not to be "family folklore" or to be so traumatic that they would be effortlessly recalled. Relatives also provided details about shopping malls and favorite treats of the research participant when he or she was a 5-year-old.

From the interviews with relatives, experimenters then created false accounts of an event that had never actually happened, in which the target participant had allegedly become lost in a shopping mall at age 5. Included in the accounts were details about the name of the mall that had been the closest one to the participant then, as well as names of family members who plausibly might have accompanied the target participant on the alleged trip. Here is an example of a "false memory" created for a 20-year-old Vietnamese American woman:

You, your mom, Tien, and Tuan all went to the Bremerton K-Mart. You must have been 5 years old at the time. Your mom gave each of you some money to get a blueberry Icee. You ran ahead to get into the line first, and somehow lost your way in the store. Tien found you crying to an elderly Chinese woman. You three then went together to get an Icee. (Loftus & Pickrell, 1995, p. 721)

Participants were given booklets containing instructions and four stories. Three of the stories recounted actual events, and the fourth story recounted the false event. Each event was described in about a paragraph, with room left for the participant to describe his or her own recall of the event. One to 2 weeks later, the participants were individually interviewed about their recollections (again being asked to recall as much as they could about the four "events"); the participants were reinterviewed about 2 weeks after that.

As a group, research participants recalled 68% of the true events. However, when completing the booklets, 29% of the participants (7 out of the 24) "recalled" the false event of being lost in a shopping mall. One of the seven later said she did not recall the false memory at the first interview, but the rest (6, or 25%) maintained at least partial recall of the false event through both interviews. Participants' length of recall (measured in number of words they used to describe events) was higher for the true than for the false memories, and they rated the clarity of their memories as lower for the false than for the true memories.

Loftus and Pickrell (1995) make no explicit claims about how easy it is to induce false memories or about how prevalent such memories are. They take the results as proof that false memories *can* be formed through suggestive questioning, and they offer a speculative account of the mechanism(s) responsible.

> The development of the false memory of being lost may evolve first as the mere suggestion of being lost leaves a memory trace in the brain. Even if the information is originally tagged as a suggestion rather than a historic fact, that suggestion can become linked to other knowledge about being lost (stories of others), as time passes and the tag that indicates that being lost in the mall was merely a suggestion slowly deteriorates. The memory of a real event, visiting a mall, becomes confounded with the suggestion that you were once lost in a mall. Finally, when asked whether you were ever lost in a mall, your brain activates images of malls and those of being lost. The resulting memory can even be embellished with snippets from actual events, such as people once seen in a mall. Now you "remember" being lost in a mall as a child. By this mechanism, the memory errors occur because grains of experienced events or imagined events are integrated with inferences and other elaborations that go beyond direct experience. (p. 724)

Other researchers have also been able to induce "recollections" of events that never happened. Hyman, Husband, and Billings (1995), for instance, were able to induce about 25% of their undergraduate participants to falsely "recall" different childhood events: being hospitalized for an ear infection; having a fifth birthday party with pizza and a clown; spilling punch at a wedding reception; being in the grocery store when sprinklers went off; and being left in a parked car, releasing the parking brake, and having the car roll into something. Garry and Wade (2005) induced false memories with both narratives and (doctored) photographs, finding that the narratives were more effective in inducing false memories.

Clancy, Schacter, McNally, and Pitman (2000) report a study in which a laboratory-based model of a false memory was induced. They made use of what is called the Deese/Roediger–McDermott paradigm, in which a participant is presented with a number of related words—for example, *nap, bed, quiet, dark, snore, dream, pillow, night.* Later, the person is given a recognition test consisting of both these "old" words and some "new" ones that weren't on the list. Results show that semantically related words, such as *sleep,* are likely to be falsely recognized by up to about 80% of college student participants (Roediger & McDermott, 1995).

Clancy et al. (2000) recruited four groups: a control group of women who had never experienced childhood sexual abuse (CSA), a group of women who had experienced CSA and who had a continuous memory of it, a group of women who believed they had experienced CSA but had no specific memory of it (the "repressed memory" group), and a group of women who claimed to have repressed and then recovered memories of experienced CSA (the "recovered memory" group). The recovered-memory group showed much higher false recognition of the semantically related words than did all other groups. The authors concluded that, although great caution must be taken in interpreting the results, they are at least consistent with the hypothesis that women who report recovered memories are more likely to experience false recognition of words than women who do not to have certain kinds of false memories.

Not all cognitive psychologists have received the research just described on false memories with complete enthusiasm, however. Pezdek (1994), for example, has argued that just because an explanation exists for how false memories *could* be formed does not mean that false memories, especially for ones as traumatic as childhood abuse, actually *are* formed in this way. By analogy, Pezdek notes that an aeronautical engineering explanation exists for why it is impossible for bumblebees to fly (even though they obviously do). Pezdek cautions against assuming that "memory recovery therapy" is very widespread and argues that existing evidence for therapist-implanted memories is quite weak.

Obviously, much more work needs to be done on the issue of whether, how, and when false information can be made a part of one's memory. Loftus and Pickrell's (1995) and Hyman et al.'s (1995) work is suggestive and provocative, but the question of to what degree it can be generalized remains open. An fMRI study (Cabeza, Rao, Wagner, Mayer, & Schacter, 2001) shows that different areas of the brain become activated in a word recognition task, with "false" words (ones that were not presented but are semantically related to the "true" words that were actually presented) activating different regions of the brain. Nonetheless, the extension of findings from word recognition tasks to real-world narrative memory recalls may not be straightforward.

It is becoming clearer to cognitive psychologists that autobiographical memories do not function the way video cameras do, faithfully recording details and preserving them for long-term storage and later review. Instead, human memories are malleable and open to "shaping" by later questioning or information. Just how often such shaping occurs, and by what mechanisms, remain open and exciting questions with important real-world implications and consequences.

AMNESIA

In the preceding sections, we discussed material forgotten from LTM. Here, we pause to take a more detailed look at cases in which people suffer profound impairments in their LTM—people suffering from memory disorders collectively known as **amnesia**. One of the most studied clinical cases was that of H.M., a patient who underwent surgery in 1953 that removed many brain structures in the medial temporal lobe region of the brain bilaterally (on both sides), including most of the hippocampus, the amygdala, and some adjacent areas. As a result, H.M. has suffered since that date from profound amnesia, both for any events after the surgery (anterograde amnesia) and for events that happened within a span of several years before the surgery (Schacter, 1996).

H.M. is not the only person to suffer from amnesia, of course, and over the years neurologists and psychologists have amassed a great number of clinical cases from which to draw generalizations and principles. Amnesia can result from damage either to the hippocampal system (which includes the hippocampus and amygdala; see Figure 2.2 to review the location of these brain structures) or to the closely related midline diencephalic region. This damage can arise from oxygen deprivation, blockage of certain arteries through a stroke, the herpes simplex encephalitis virus, a closed head injury such as those typically suffered in automobile accidents, Alzheimer's disease, Korsakoff's syndrome (a disease of chronic alcoholism), certain tumors, or, in the short term, bilateral electroconvulsive shock treatments (ECT; Cohen, 1997).

The severity of the amnesia varies from case to case, with H.M. exhibiting some of the most severe memory impairments. Some patients recover some memories over time; for example, those undergoing bilateral ECT (a treatment used today for severe forms of depression) recover completely within a few months, and people who suffer a closed head injury likewise often recover some or all of their memories. Some amnesias, such as those brought on by accidents or strokes, have very sudden onsets; others, typically those originating through brain tumors or disease, appear more gradually (Cohen, 1997). Many neuropsychologists make a distinction between anterograde and retrograde amnesia in terms of the way each functions, and we will therefore review each of these in turn.

ANTEROGRADE AMNESIA

N. J. Cohen (1997) notes that the **anterograde** form of amnesia, a memory deficit extending forward in time from the initial point of memory loss, has five principal features. The first is that anterograde amnesia affects LTM but not working memory. Cohen relates an illustrative anecdote about a conversation he had with H.M.

> One day during a lengthy car drive to MIT's Clinical Research Center to be tested, H.M. proceeded to tell me about some guns that were in his house (actually, he had them only in his youth). He told me that he had two rifles, one with a scope and certain characteristics, and the other with just an open sight.
>
> He said that he had magazines from the National Rifle Association (actually, just a memory of his earlier family life), all about rifles. But, he went on, not only did he have rifles, he also had some handguns. He had a .22, a .32, and a .44. He occasionally took them out to clean them, he said, and had taken them with him on occasion to a shooting range. But, he went on, not only did he have some handguns, he also had rifles. He had two rifles, one with a scope and the other with an open sight. He had magazines from the National Rifle Association, all about rifles, he said. But, not only did he have rifles, he also had handguns. . . . On and on this went, cycling back and forth between a description of the rifles and a description of the handguns, until finally I derailed the conversation by diverting his attention. (p. 323)

N. J. Cohen argues that H.M.'s memory of his handguns and of his rifles were both intact because they derived from his very remote past, several years before his surgery. They were related in his LTM—not surprising, given what researchers know about memory for general knowledge (a topic we will take up in Chapter 7 in greater detail). Thus, his discussion of one piece of knowledge called to mind the other. Each piece, however, filled up the working-memory capacity, so that when H.M. finished talking about one, he forgot he had just told about the other.

The second feature is that anterograde amnesia affects memory regardless of the modality—that is, regardless of whether the information is visual, auditory, kinesthetic, olfactory, gustatory, or tactile. N. J. Cohen (1997) notes that global anterograde amnesia results from bilateral damage to the medial temporal lobe or midline diencephalic structures; unilateral (one-sided) damage to these areas typically impairs only one kind of memory—for example, either verbal or spatial. Moreover, whether the mode of testing memory is free recall, cued recall, or recognition, the memory of someone with anterograde amnesia is similarly hampered.

Third, according to N. J. Cohen (1997) and as illustrated in the story about H.M. and the guns, anterograde amnesia spares memory for general knowledge (acquired well before the onset of amnesia) but grossly impairs recall for new facts and events. Thus H.M. could not report any personal event that had occurred after his surgery, and he performed very poorly on tasks in which he was asked to recall lists of words for any length of time beyond a few minutes. H.M. also had difficulty retaining newly learned pairings of information, such as learning new vocabulary (*jacuzzi, granola,* and other words that had come into usage after 1953, the year of his surgery).

A fourth principal feature of anterograde amnesia is that it spares skilled performance. Recall the story of the musician Clive Wearing, described in Chapter 5, who cannot remember much of his own life or remember his wife's frequent visits but can still play the harpsichord and piano and conduct a choir through a complex piece of music. Other studies have shown that amnesic patients can be taught to perform a skill, such as mirror tracing (tracing the outline of a geometric figure that is only visible in a mirror) or a rotary pursuit task (tracking a target that is moving circularly and erratically). H.M. learned the first task and showed a normal learning curve for it, although at each session he denied any previous experience with the task. N. J. Cohen and Squire (1980) have shown similar results in teaching amnesic patients and nonamnesic control participants to perform a mirror-image reading task. The performance of the amnesic patients was in many instances virtually identical to that of the control participants.

The fifth principal feature of anterograde amnesia is that even when amnesic patients do learn a skill, they show *hyperspecific* memory: They can express this learning only in a context extremely similar to the conditions of encoding. In a sense, this seems to be a version of the encoding specificity principle carried to the extreme.

RETROGRADE AMNESIA

Loss of memory for information acquired and stored before the onset of amnesia is known as **retrograde amnesia**. Although such loss has some similarities with anterograde amnesia, important differences appear as well. Interestingly, all amnesic patients seem to show at least some retrograde amnesia; they may or may not exhibit anterograde amnesia. N. J. Cohen (1997) describes four basic features of retrograde amnesia.

The first is that the temporal extent—the time span for which memory is lost—can vary enormously in retrograde amnesia. Patients suffering from Korsakoff's, Alzheimer's, Parkinson's, or Huntington's disease are likely to exhibit temporally extensive amnesia, with loss of memory acquired and stored over several decades. Other patients, such as those who have undergone bilateral ECT or suffered a closed head injury, show temporally limited retrograde amnesia, losing information from a span of only months or perhaps weeks. In many cases, over time the patient either fully (in the case of ECT) or partially recovers the lost memories. Damage to the hippocampal region can also cause retrograde amnesia. H.M.'s retrograde amnesia was found to cover a span of 11 years, less than for some other cases reported in the literature.

A second feature of retrograde amnesia is observable when scientists examine which particular memories are lost. Patients undergoing ECT treatments were asked to recall information about television shows that had aired for a single season only (that way, the experimenters knew precisely when the memories were formed; this study was conducted well before the proliferation of cable channels!). As shown in Figure 6.4, before the ECT treatments, the patients were best at recalling facts from very recently aired shows, as you would be. After the ECT treatments, however, these same patients' data showed a temporal gradient, with the most recent memories being the most likely to be lost (N. J. Cohen, 1997).

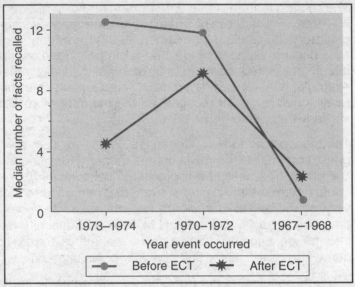

■ Figure 6.4: Evidence of temporally limited retrograde amnesia in patients who have undergone electroconvulsive therapy (ECT). Before and after a series of ECT treatments, 20 individuals were asked to recall information about former television programs that aired for just one season. Shown here is a graph of the median number of facts recalled. Before ECT, patients showed a normal forgetting curve; their best recall was for shows from the most recent time period, and their poorest recall was for shows from the most remote time period. After ECT, a selective impairment occurred in the recall of shows from the most recent time period.

SOURCE: Banich, M. T. *Neuropsychology: The neural bases of mental function* (1st ed.), p. 337. Copyright © 1997 Wadsworth, a part of Cengage Learning, Inc. Reproduced by permission. http://www.cengage.com/permissions/.

In the case of ECT patients, we would expect full recovery, in time, of the lost memories. With patients suffering from a closed head injury, the story is a little different. There, the temporal extent of the retrograde amnesia often shrinks slowly over time, with the most remote memories being the most likely to return. For example, initially the retrograde amnesia might span several years before the head trauma occurred; after a year in recovery, the total span of retrograde amnesia might be the two weeks immediately preceding the trauma.

N. J. Cohen (1997) describes a third feature of retrograde amnesia: It typically spares information that was "overlearned" before the onset. Finally, as with anterograde amnesia, retrograde amnesia seems not to affect skill learning, such as mirror tracing. Even when patients cannot remember ever having practiced the skill, their performance still seems to show normal rates of improvement.

Many neuropsychologists believe the study of amnesia supports some specific ideas about the organization of memory in general. That amnesia can disrupt long-term memory without any impairment in working memory provides some support for considering these as two distinct types of memory. That retrograde amnesia covers a defined time span and shows a temporal gradient implies that even after being formed, new memories continue to undergo neurological change for some period of time, perhaps years. That some kinds of information (personal memories, memories for events or random tidbits of information) are lost in amnesia and others are not (such as overlearned and well-practiced information and skills) has suggested the existence of many different kinds of memory systems to some (though not all) psychologists. Finally, there is a strong suggestion that the structure in the brain known as the hippocampus plays a very important role in the retrieval of memories for information, although clearly not all long-term memories require involvement of the hippocampus (otherwise, amnesic patients would never recall any previously learned information).

McGaugh (2000) notes that studies of amnesic patients also tell us something about **memory consolidation**, a process originally proposed a century ago. The idea is that new information "initially persist[s] in a fragile state and consolidate[s] over time" (p. 248). Blows to the head disrupt this process, causing newly learned information to be lost. Some of McGaugh's work suggests an important role for the amygdala, a structure we discussed earlier, in the memory consolidation process.

Throughout this chapter, we've been focusing on memory for specific events (such as hearing a particular word list or witnessing a crime). Often, however, our memories of a particular event call on our memories of general knowledge. For example, if I were to recall the last lecture I gave, I might use my general knowledge about lectures (where students sit or the kinds of equipment, such as whiteboard markers or overhead projectors, that I typically use) to reconstruct my memory of that particular class. In the next chapter, we will examine more closely the ways in which this general knowledge is stored and organized.

As stated before, memory touches just about every cognitive activity we can think of. Thus it should come as no surprise that memory appears in many other chapters in this book. In particular, in Chapter 7 we will take up the question of how memory for general knowledge is organized and stored and how we form new concepts. In Chapter 8 we will discuss visual imagery and will come back to issues of how information is encoded and mentally represented. We will see in other chapters that memory plays a significant role in almost every instance of cognitive processing. Thus, as new research on the topic of memory changes our conceptions of how it works, we can expect new developments in almost every other area of cognition.

Summary

1.   We've seen in this chapter, as well as in Chapter 5, that cognitive psychologists approach the study of memory in a variety of ways and that this diversity dates back at least to "founding" cognitive psychologists such as Ebbinghaus and Bartlett. Some of the diversity arises in theoretical orientations: Some psychologists seek evidence for the proposition that there are different memory stores (for example, sensory memory, STM, LTM), whereas others focus on the kind of processing done with to-be-remembered information.

2.   Within the modal model of memory, LTM is described as the storage of vast amounts of information, usually coded by meaning, for durations ranging up to several decades if not indefinitely.

3.   Theories of forgetting from LTM emphasize interference as a very important mechanism. An elaboration of this idea is that when retrieval cues become linked to multiple targets, they become less reliable aids to enable the person to pick out a given target.

4.   Techniques known as mnemonics are often used to help people retrieve information from long-term memory. Commonly used mnemonics include the method of loci, the pegword method, the method of interacting images, and recoding.

5.   Retrieval of information is made easier when the information to be retrieved is categorized, when the retrieval cues match the cues that were available at the time of encoding (the encoding specificity principle), and when the retrieval cues are very distinctive.

6.   Consistent with the encoding specificity principle, investigators have found that recall (but not recognition) is made easier when the recall context is the same as the learning context (the context effect), when the pharmacological state of the person at recall matches his or her pharmacological state during encoding (the state-dependent learning effect), and, under some conditions, when the person's mood at the time of recall matches his or her mood at the time of learning (the mood-dependent memory effect). Recall is also enhanced when material is learned in several temporally spaced sessions as opposed to one long learning session (the spacing effect).

7.   Practice at retrieval, for example through repeated testing, has also been shown to enhance recall or recognition memory, a phenomenon known as the testing effect.

8.   A number of different theoretical proposals posit distinct systems within long-term memory. These include the episodic versus semantic memory proposal, the implicit versus explicit memory proposal, and the declarative versus procedural proposal.

9.   Work on the levels-of-processing theory has demonstrated that the more active and meaningful the original processing of information, the more memorable the information will be. This idea has obvious and practical relevance for students: If you want to improve your recall of material for later testing (in midterms and finals), organize it and think about its meaning (deep processing) rather than merely reading, underlining, or highlighting the words (shallow processing).

10. The work reported here on people's recall of their own life events dovetails in several ways with the laboratory-based investigations of memory described in this chapter and the last. Some of the findings that have emerged—for example, the constructive nature of recall—fit well with laboratory findings. However, different results are found in laboratory- and everyday-based studies. Autobiographical recall seems to be better than recall of laboratory stimuli, but whether different cognitive mechanisms are at work remains an open question.

11. Work on flashbulb and eyewitness memories suggests that people's recollections of moments of their past can be wrong, even when those people seem absolutely convinced of the accuracy of the memory. This suggests that our own confidence in our memories may sometimes be too high; at the very least, there are probably occasions when we are both very sure of our memories and also very wrong. Work on eyewitness testimony suggests that memory traces of a witnessed event are highly malleable and subject to disruption by postevent leading questions.

12. Debates over whether memory traces can be repressed for long periods of time, then recalled, have erupted in recent years. Some studies purport to show that under repeated urgings, people can be induced to "recall" emotional events that never happened. One study suggests there may well be limits to the types of "false" memories that can be so implanted, but as yet we do not have a firm understanding of what these limits are.

13. Neuropsychologists who study memory deficits recognize two kinds of amnesia. Both seem to involve damage to either the hippocampal system or the midline diencephalic region. This damage can arise in several ways: through closed head injury, a stroke, oxygen deprivation to the brain, bilateral electroconvulsive shock treatments, a virus such as encephalitis, or other diseases such as Alzheimer's or Korsakoff's.

14. Anterograde amnesia, which extends forward in time from the onset of amnesia, selectively affects long-term (but not working) memory, regardless of modality or type of memory test, and it spares memory for general knowledge and skilled performance (although the learning of the latter will not be explicitly remembered). However, anterograde amnesia can result in memories for skills that are hyperspecific to the original learning context and cannot be transferred to other, similar contexts.

15. Retrograde amnesia, the loss of memory acquired and stored before the point of onset, is almost always a component of amnesia. The temporal extent of the amnesia varies in different patients; it is worst for memories of information acquired closest to the point of onset. Some recovery of some of the lost retrograde memories is often possible. Retrograde amnesia also spares material that has been "overlearned" before the onset, including such things as language, general knowledge, and perceptual and social skills. As with anterograde amnesia, retrograde amnesia seems to spare skill learning.

Review Questions

1. In what ways do the underlying assumptions of the levels-of-processing theory differ from the underlying assumptions of the modal model?

2. Describe the different kinds of interference and how they are theorized to operate.

3. Describe and evaluate encoding specificity as a principle of retrieval of information. How does it relate to such phenomena as the spacing effect, state-dependent learning, and context effects on retrieval?

4. Explore the interrelationships among the context effect, the state-dependent learning effect, the mood-dependent memory effect, and the spacing effect.

5. Apply the cognitive research on memory to the practical problem of giving a college student advice about how to study for an upcoming midterm. What advice would you give, and which principles would this advice draw on?

6. Describe two mnemonics and contrast the underlying mechanisms thought to account for their effectiveness.

7. Describe the semantic/episodic memory distinction and discuss the reasons why some psychologists make the distinction and others don't.

8. Describe the distinction between declarative and procedural memory and that between implicit and explicit memory. Do these two distinctions fit together well? Explain why you think so.

9. What do the findings of Linton and Brewer suggest about the workings of autobiographic memory for ordinary events?

10. How do findings from the eyewitness testimony and the flashbulb memory literature fit with laboratory-based findings reported earlier? What are the differences, if any?

11. Is there a need to posit special mechanisms for flashbulb memories? Defend your view.

12. Describe the debate over "recovered" versus "false" memories of traumatic events. What are the most important issues for cognitive psychologists to address, and what issues (pragmatic, ethical, theoretical) are they likely to face in doing so?

13. Review the similarities and differences between anterograde and retrograde amnesia.

14. What exactly do findings from memory studies with amnesic patients tell us about the way memory operates in nonamnesic people? (Note: This question is a controversial one within the field—can you see why?)

Key Terms

amnesia

anterograde amnesia

autobiographical memory

cue overload

declarative memory

encoding specificity

encoding variability

episodic memory

explicit memory

eyewitness memory

false memory

fan effect

flashbulb memory

implicit memory

incidental learning

levels-of-processing theory of memory

memory consolidation

memory system

method of loci

mnemonics

mood-dependent memory effect

paired associates learning

procedural memory

recovered memory

repetition priming

repressed memory

retrieval cue

retroactive interference

retrograde amnesia

schemata

semantic memory

spacing effect

state-dependent learning

state-dependent memory

testing effect

CHAPTER 7

KNOWLEDGE REPRESENTATION
Storing and Organizing Information in Long-Term Memory

CHAPTER OUTLINE

Organizing Knowledge

Network Models

ACT Models

Connectionist Models

Forming Concepts and Categorizing New Instances

The Classical View of Concepts and Categorization

The Prototype View of Concepts and Categorization

The Exemplar View of Concepts and Categorization

The Schemata/Scripts View of Concepts
and Categorization

The Knowledge-Based View of Concepts
and Categorization

As a psychologist, teacher, and amateur dog trainer, I have a great deal of mentally stored knowledge about different topics. I often surprise my students (and sometimes myself) by remembering the approximate title, author, journal, and year of an article that would complement their independent study projects. Less often, when I teach dog obedience classes and am stumped by a dog who just can't seem to learn a simple task, I can call up from memory an idea I heard about years ago at a dog-training seminar. Obviously, when I remember or recall these pieces of information, I am using my memory.

How do I hold on to information in such a way that I can access it, sometimes years after I've stored it? Consider the vast range of information everyone must have stored in permanent memory. In addition to information regarding events in your life (your sixth birthday party, the time you broke your arm, going to the circus, your first day of junior high), you have also stored a great deal of knowledge: definitions of the words you know; arithmetic facts and procedures; historical, scientific, and geographic knowledge; and (I hope) even some knowledge of principles of cognitive psychology. In this chapter, we will take a more detailed look at this kind of permanent memory—memory for knowledge and information.

The first question that will concern us is how stored knowledge is organized. There are several distinct ways of arranging and storing information, and each has different implications for ease of access and retrieval. An analogy to your bookshelves may help. Think about your books and how they are arranged. You may have a section for textbooks, a section for nonfiction, a section for mysteries, and a section for trashy romances. Or you may have all the books arranged alphabetically by author. Or you may have tall books on one shelf, paperbacks on another. Each possibility represents a different way of organizing, and each possibility has different implications for how you look for a particular book and how easy it is to find it. Suppose you want to find *Gone With the Wind*, but you've forgotten the author's name. If you've arranged your books alphabetically by author, you'll have a much more difficult time than if you've arranged them by title or by category.

A variety of models have been proposed for how our knowledge is mentally represented and organized. Each model makes different predictions about how we search for particular pieces of information. Specifically, we'll look at a number of proposals for how our knowledge base or bases are organized and the implications that organization has for the ways we access information. We'll be taking a detailed look here at semantic (as opposed to episodic) memory, a topic that was introduced in Chapter 6.

Next, we'll turn our attention to concepts and categorization. We will discover that mental representations categories are called concepts and the process used to assign individual examples to concepts is called categorization. Medin (1989) argued that "concepts and categories serve as building blocks for human thought and behavior" (p. 1469). Lamberts and Shanks (1997) have argued that how things such as concepts are mentally represented is a central concern of cognitive psychology.

To illustrate, consider this real-life example of medical diagnosis. Suppose you wake up one day feeling achy, lethargic, congested, and feverish. Your symptoms could indicate nothing more serious than flu. Or your symptoms could be the harbinger of a much more serious illness. It is your doctor's job to make the diagnosis, which essentially means assigning your pattern of symptoms to a category corresponding to known diseases or medical problems. The categorization allows the physician to determine appropriate treatment and predict the course of recovery. To make the diagnosis, your physician must have an idea of the various categories (possible medical problems) to be considered and, presumably, calls upon stored mental representations of these categories (concepts). By the way, physicians are not the only ones who categorize illnesses, as shown by a recent study of laypeople's categorization of forms of mental illness (Kim & Ahn, 2002).

ORGANIZING KNOWLEDGE

Many of the semantic memory models developed because psychologists and computer scientists interested in the field of artificial intelligence wanted to build a system having what most people refer to as "commonsense knowledge." The premise was that associated with your knowledge of an explicit fact is a great deal of *implicit* knowledge, information you know but take for granted.

Here's an example of implicit knowledge in our understanding of everyday routines. Consider the typical directions on a shampoo bottle: "Wet hair. Apply shampoo. Lather.

Rinse. Repeat." If you slavishly followed these directions, you would emerge from the shower only when the bottle was empty or the water ran out! However, most of us do manage to wash our hair, even before our first cup of coffee. What we rely on is not just the directions but our world knowledge or common sense that one or two repetitions of the lather–rinse cycle are sufficient (Galotti & Ganong, 1985).

Our vast knowledge of language and concepts also appears to have associated with it a great deal of implicit knowledge. For instance, if I asked you, "Does a Bernese mountain dog have a liver?" you would very likely answer yes (correctly). Your answer comes (I assume) not from your extensive study of Bernese mountain dogs but from your knowledge that Bernese mountain dogs are dogs, dogs are mammals, and mammals have livers. In this section, we will consider models of how knowledge is represented in semantic memory such that we can make these inferences and demonstrate our common sense.

To build such models, we need to make a number of inferences about our mental representations of information from our performance on specific tasks. For example, if we can retrieve some information very quickly (say, think of words beginning with the letter *L*) relative to other information (say, think of words with *L* as the fourth letter), that suggests something about the organization of knowledge. In this example, for instance, we can infer that our **lexicons**, or mental dictionaries, are organized by the first letter, not the fourth, in a word. In the specific models presented next, you'll see that the tasks invented were meant to answer very specific questions about the nature of the mental organization of information.

NETWORK MODELS

Because our world and language knowledge is so great, the storage space requirements to represent it are large. Computer scientists trying to create databases of knowledge decades ago were constrained by the very limited memory available to computers of that day, so the models of semantic memory may well have been shaped by this constraint. One way to conserve memory space would be to try to avoid storing redundant information wherever possible. Therefore, rather than storing the information "has live young" with the mental representation for Bernese mountain dog and again with the mental representations for human, lion, tiger, and bear, it makes more sense to store it once, at the higher-level representation for mammal. This illustrates the principle of **cognitive economy**: Properties and facts are stored at the highest level possible. To recover information, you use inference, much as you did to answer the earlier question about Bernese mountain dogs' having livers.

A landmark study on semantic memory was performed by Collins and Quillian (1969). They tested the idea that semantic memory is analogous to a network of connected ideas. As in later connectionist networks, this one consists of nodes, which in this case correspond roughly to words or concepts. Each node is connected to related nodes by means of *pointers,* or links that go from one node to another. Thus, the node that corresponds to a given word or concept, together with the pointers to other nodes to which the first node is connected, constitutes the semantic memory for that word or concept. The collection of nodes associated with all the words and concepts one knows about is called a **semantic network**. Figure 7.1 depicts a portion of such a network for a person (such as me) who knows a good deal about Bernese mountain dogs. Readers familiar with computer science may be reminded of linked lists and pointers, a metaphor that Collins and Quillian intended.

Collins and Quillian (1969) also tested the principle of cognitive economy. They reasoned that if semantic memory is analogous to a network of nodes and pointers and if semantic memory honors the cognitive economy principle, then the closer a fact or property is stored to a particular node, the less time it should take to verify the fact and property. Collins and Quillian's

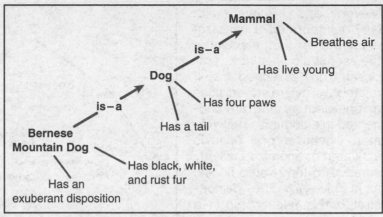

■ Figure 7.1: Partial semantic network representation for Bernese mountain dog.

reasoning led to the following prediction: If a person's knowledge of Bernese mountain dogs is organized along the lines of Figure 7.1, he or she should be able to verify the sentence "A Bernese mountain dog has an exuberant disposition," more quickly than the sentence "A Bernese mountain dog has live young." Note that the property "has an exuberant disposition" is stored right with the node for Bernese mountain dog, indicating that this property is specific to this kind of animal. The property "has live young" is not specific to Bernese mountain dogs, so it is stored a number of levels higher in the hierarchy.

In their study (see Figure 7.2), Collins and Quillian (1969) presented people with a number of similar sentences, finding, as predicted, that it took people less time to respond to sentences whose representations should span two levels (for example, "A canary is a bird") than they did to sentences whose representations should span three (for example, "A canary is an animal").

This model was called a **hierarchical semantic network model of semantic memory**, because researchers thought the nodes were organized in hierarchies. Most nodes in the network have superordinate and subordinate nodes. A superordinate node corresponds to the name of the category of which the thing corresponding to the subordinate node is a member. So, for example, a node for "cat" would have the superordinate node of "animal" and perhaps several subordinate nodes, such as "Persian," "tabby," and "calico."

■ Photo 7.1: Two actual Bernese Mountain dogs.

Meyer and Schvaneveldt (1971) performed a series of experiments that elaborated the semantic network proposal. They reasoned that if related words are stored close to one another and are connected in a semantic network, then whenever one node is activated or energized, energy spreads to the related nodes, as in Figure 7.3. They demonstrated this relationship in a series of experiments based on **lexical decision tasks**. In this kind of experiment, participants see a series of letter strings and are asked to decide, as quickly as possible, if the letter strings form real words. Thus they respond yes to strings such as *bread* and no to strings such as *rencle*.

Meyer and Schvaneveldt (1971) discovered an interesting phenomenon. In their study, participants saw two words at a time, one above the other, and had to decide if both strings were words or not. If one of the strings was a real word (such as *bread*), participants were faster to respond if the other string was a semantically associated word (such as *butter*) than if it was an unrelated word (such as *chair*) or a nonword (such as *rencle*). One interpretation of this finding invokes the concept of **spreading activation**, the idea that excitation spreads along the connections of nodes in a semantic network. Presumably, when the person read the word *bread,* he activated the corresponding node in semantic

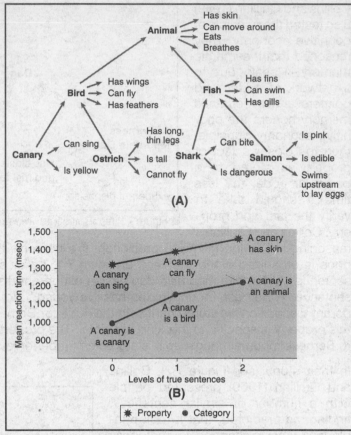

(A)

(B)

■ Figure 7.2: Illustration of the Collins and Quillian (1969) experiment. Panel A shows the hypothesized underlying semantic network, and Panel B shows reaction times to verify sentences about information in the semantic network.

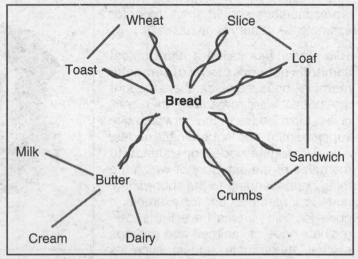

■ Figure 7.3: Depiction of spreading activation. Once the node for "bread" is excited, the activation travels to related nodes.

memory. This activity primed, or changed the activation level of, the nodes corresponding to words related to *bread.* Thus, when processing of the word *butter* began, the node corresponding to it was already excited, and processing was consequently faster. This priming effect, originally discovered by Meyer and Schvaneveldt, has been widely replicated in the years since (see Neely, 1990) and is a very important idea in understanding connectionist networks, to be described later.

You may note here a connection to the research on the word superiority effect described in Chapter 3. Recall that people are generally faster to recognize a particular letter (such as *D* or *K*) in the context of a word (such as *WOR_*) than they are to recognize it with no context or in the context of a nonword (such as *OWR_*). The explanations offered went roughly along the following lines: The word context helps letter recognition because a node corresponding to a word is activated in the former case. This automatic activation facilitates recognition of all parts of the word, thus facilitating letter recognition. The Meyer and Schvaneveldt (1971) results extend this idea a little more: Individual nodes can be activated not just directly, from external stimuli, but indirectly, through spreading activation from related nodes.

Soon after Collins and Quillian (1969) presented their model, others found evidence that contradicted the model's predictions. One line of evidence was related to the prediction of cognitive economy, the principle that properties and facts are stored with the highest and most general node possible. Carol Conrad (1972) found evidence to contradict this assumption. Participants in her sentence verification experiments were no slower to respond to sentences such as "A shark can move," than to "A fish can move," or "An animal can move." However, the principle of cognitive economy would predict that the property "can move" would be stored closest to the node for "animal" and thus that the three sentences would require decreasing amounts of time to verify. Conrad argued that the property "can move" is one frequently associated with "animal," "shark," and "fish" and that frequency of association rather than cognitive economy predicts reaction time.

A second prediction of Collins and Quillian's (1969) model had to do with hierarchical structure. Presumably, if the network represents such words (which in turn represent concepts) as *animals, mammals,* and *pigs,* then it should do so by storing the node for "mammal" under the node for "animal" and the node for "pig" under the node for "mammal." However, Rips, Shoben, and Smith (1973) showed that participants were faster to verify "A pig is an animal," than to verify "A pig is a mammal," thus demonstrating a violation of the predicted hierarchical structure.

A third problem for the hierarchical network model was that it failed to explain other consistent findings. One such finding is the **typicality effect**. Rips et al. (1973) found that responses to sentences such as "A robin is a bird," were faster than responses to "A turkey is a bird," even though these sentences should have taken an equivalent amount of time to verify. In general, typical instances of a concept are responded to more quickly than atypical instances; in most people's lives, robins are typical birds, while turkeys are not. The hierarchical network model did not predict typicality effects; instead, it predicted that all instances of a concept should be processed similarly.

Collins and Loftus (1975) presented an elaboration of the Collins and Quillian (1969) hierarchical network model that they called *spreading activation theory.* In general, these authors sought both to clarify and to extend the assumptions made about the manner in which people process semantic information. They also conceived of semantic memory as a network, with nodes in the network corresponding to concepts. They also saw related concepts as connected by paths in the network. They further asserted that when one node is activated, the excitation of that node spreads down the paths or links to related nodes. They believed that as activation spreads outward, it decreases in strength, activating very related concepts a great deal but activating distantly related nodes only a little bit.

Figure 7.4 shows a representation of part of a semantic network, as Collins and Loftus (1975) conceived it. Notice that in this model, very similar concepts—such as "car" and "truck"—have many connecting links and are placed close to each other. Less similar concepts, such as "house" and "sunset" (both may, or may not, be red), have no direct connections and are therefore spaced far apart. Each link or connection between two concepts is thought to have a certain weight or set of weights associated with it. The weights indicate how important one concept is to the meaning of a concept to which it is connected. Weights may vary for different directions along these connections. Thus, it may be very important to the meaning of *truck* that it is a type of vehicle but not very important to the meaning of *vehicle* that *truck* is an example.

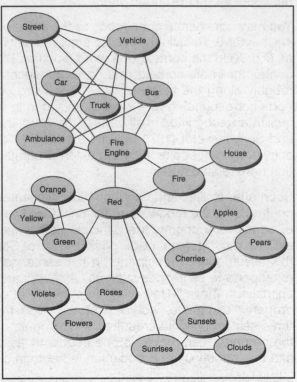

■ Figure 7.4: Partial network representation of related concepts. Length of time segments indicates the degree of relatedness or connection between two concepts.

Collins and Loftus (1975) described a number of other assumptions this model makes to explain how the model accounts for data from many other experiments. They dispensed with the assumptions of cognitive economy and hierarchical organization, helping their model avoid the problems of the Collins and Quillian (1969) model. However, many psychologists find the breadth of this model, which is its major strength, to be its major shortcoming as well, because it is difficult to make clear and strong predictions from the model regarding empirical findings. Thus, although the model is consistent with a number of findings, such as the typicality effect and the category size effect, it is hard to think of data that would falsify the model. The proposal is therefore regarded more as a descriptive framework than as a specific model.

ACT MODELS

Another network theory of memory has been developed and refined over several years by John Anderson (1976, 1983, 1993, 2005; Anderson, Budiu, & Reder, 2001). Called the **adaptive control of thought (ACT) model of memory**, it has evolved over the almost 40 years of its existence, and various versions (ACT-*, ACT-R) exist. Based on analogies to computers, ACT has given rise to several computer simulations of cognitive processing of different tasks. ACT models do not make the semantic/episodic distinction described in Chapter 6, but they distinguish among three kinds of memory systems: working memory, declarative memory, and procedural memory.

J. R. Anderson (1983) believed that declarative memory stores information in networks that contain nodes. There are different types of nodes, including those corresponding to spatial images or to abstract propositions. As with other network models, ACT models allow both for activation of any node and for spreading activation to connected nodes. Anderson also posited the existence of a procedural memory. This memory store represents information in **production rules**. Production rules specify a *goal* to achieve, one or more *conditions* that must be true for the rule to apply, and one or more *actions* that result from applying the rule.

For example, a typical college student could use this production rule: *"If* the goal is to study actively and attentively (goal) *and* the noise level in the dormitory is high (condition) *and* the campus library is open (condition), *then* gather your study materials (action) *and* take them to the library (action) *and* work there (action)." Okay, that example was a bit contrived. But psychologists, computer scientists, and others have used production rules to build computer programs that simulate human problem solving. Box 7.1, from J. R. Anderson (1995), presents some examples of production rules for multicolumn subtraction.

Box 7.1

Production Rules for Multicolumn Subtraction

If the goal is to solve a subtraction problem,
Then make the subgoal a process to the rightmost column.

If there is an answer in the current column
    and there is a column to the left,
Then make the subgoal to process the column to the left.

If the goal is to process a column
    and there is no bottom digit,
Then write the top digit as the answer.

If the goal is to process a column
    and the top digit is not smaller that the bottom digit,
Then write the difference between the digits as the answer.

If the goal is to process a column
    and the top digit is smaller than the bottom digit,
Then add 10 to the top digit
    and set as a subgoal to borrow from the column to the left.

If the goal is to borrow from a column
    and the top digit in that column is not zero,
Then decrement the digit by 1.

If the goal is to borrow from a column
    and the top digit in that column is zero,
Then replace the zero by 9
    and set as a subgoal to borrow from the column to the left.

J. R. Anderson's (1983) proposal was not meant merely to address the question of knowledge representation. Instead, his aim was to create a theory of *cognitive architecture,* a theory of how human cognition actually operates in practice. He proposed a system that includes both memory storage and particular processing structures. Interestingly, this broad goal led him to develop proposals about knowledge representation that fit well with those of researchers whose aims were more focused.

In the ACT models, working memory is actually that part of declarative memory that is very highly activated at any particular moment. The production rules also become activated when the nodes in the declarative memory that correspond to the conditions of the relevant production rules are activated. When production rules are executed, they can create new nodes within declarative memory. Thus, ACT models have been described as very "activation-based" models of human cognition (Luger, 1994).

CONNECTIONIST MODELS

Earlier in the chapter I referred to the library metaphor, which represents each piece of information stored in long-term memory as a particular item stored in a particular location, much like a book in a library. This metaphor is a useful one within the information-processing framework, which assumes the existence of one or more distinct "stores" of memory.

Connectionist models make very different assumptions and thus do not incorporate the library metaphor as easily. Let's take a brief look at connectionist models of memory to try to understand why. James McClelland, a pioneer of connectionist models of cognition, argues that connections models of memory

> [let] go of the idea that items are stored in memory as such. Instead the fundamental idea is that what is stored in memory is a set of changes in the instructions neurons send to each other, affecting what pattern of activity can be constructed from given inputs. When an event is experienced, on this view, it creates a pattern of activity over a set of processing units. This pattern of activity is considered to be the representation of the event. The formation of this pattern of activity provides the trigger for the creation of the instructions. The set of instructions is then stored in the connections among the units, where it is available for use in the construction of subsequent patterns of activity. Under some circumstances—for example, when the constructive process takes place in response to a recall cue—the cue may result in the construction of a pattern of activation that can be viewed as an attempted reconstruction of the pattern that represented the previously experienced event. Such a reconstructed representation corresponds to a recollection. The patterns themselves are not stored, and hence are not really "retrieved"; recall amounts not to retrieval but to reconstruction. (2000, p. 583)

Let's look at a concrete example to compare network and connectionist models of semantic memory. Figure 7.5(A) presents a semantic network model of various concepts and should look familiar. Figure 7.5(B) presents a connectionist model of these same concepts. The concept "robin," depicted in Figure 7.5(A) as a particular node with several related links to other nodes, is depicted in Figure 7.5(B) as a specific set of units being activated. A unit might correspond to an ability possessed by certain living creatures (e.g., flying) or to certain aspects such as color. Darkened units are activated units, and a connectionist network learns, over trials, that when the unit for "robin" becomes active, then other units should become active as well (for example, "can" and "grow," "move" and "fly," but not "swim").

How does this learning occur? Essentially, a connectionist network must be taught to develop patterns of activation through many trials with training examples. The procedure used, called "back propagation," is quite complicated, but I will offer a very simplified version here.

Initially, the connections between units (depicted in Figure 7.5(B) as the lines between the units) have weights that are all set at random and neutral values (such as 0.5, if the minimum and maximum values are 0 and 1). Activation weights result in the units they connect becoming active (or not). Training occurs by presenting a specific example (input pattern) to the network, which then generates a particular output. So, for example, at the beginning of training, the example "robin" might be activated, and the units for "can" and "pretty" and "fly" and "branches" might then become activated. This output is compared to target (correct) output, such as "can," "grow," "move," and "fly" all being activated, and no others. The network connections

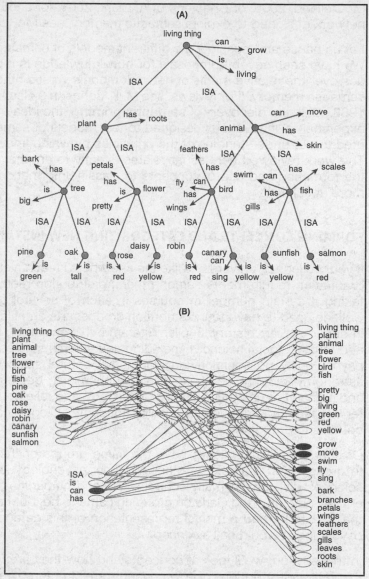

are then adjusted in this direction (they take on values closer to 1), all other connections are incrementally decreased (they take on values closer to 0), and the training process repeats, with new examples.

■ Figure 7.5: (A) A network description of "robin." (B) A connectionist network showing an alternative depiction of the same information as in (A).

Typically, training takes place in a series of what connectionist researchers call "epochs," similar to trials of learning. Each epoch follows the procedure just described: An input pattern is presented, and an output pattern of activation is generated, then compared with a correct, target pattern of activation. Connection weights between units are adjusted accordingly, and another input pattern presented to start the next epoch. (For a more detailed and technical discussion of how this training procedure works, consult

McClelland, 2000, or Chapter 4 of A. Clark, 2001; for another example of a connectionist network designed to explore semantic memory, see McRae, 2004.)

Let us pause and consider the different models of semantic memory we've just covered. We have seen several proposals for how knowledge is represented. The debate continues over the relative merits of network models versus other kinds of models to describe semantic memory. (For reviews, see M. K. Johnson & Hasher, 1987; Rumelhart & Norman, 1988.) Still, the discovery of **semantic priming**, the idea of spreading activation, and the experimental innovations designed to test models of semantic memory have all contributed to our understanding of the principles by which knowledge is stored and retrieved. The work reviewed here so far relates directly to another topic in cognitive psychology, the formation and use of concepts to classify information. We will examine this area in more detail next.

FORMING CONCEPTS AND CATEGORIZING NEW INSTANCES

If your college or university is like the one where I teach, you probably have to fulfill certain graduation requirements—among them, distribution requirements, which mandate your taking a certain number of courses in each of several groups. For example, Carleton College used to have four distribution groups: arts and literature (including most courses in studio art, art history, English, literature in translation, literature in foreign languages, and music), social sciences (including educational studies, economics, political science, psychology, and sociology/anthropology), natural science and mathematics (including astronomy, biology, computer science, chemistry, geology, mathematics, and physics), and humanities (including history, philosophy, and religion). The groupings of subject matter into larger distribution groups illustrates my college's categorization, or assignment of courses to groupings.

Of course, not all colleges have the same groups or the same assignment of courses to groups. For example, at other colleges, psychology is often assigned to the natural sciences division. At many schools, arts and humanities are grouped together. I'm not entirely sure how the Carleton grouping came to be, but I am sure the dean or committee that created it had a mental representation of this category, something that a cognitive psychologist would call a *concept*.

In this section, we'll look at concepts and how they are formed. We'll examine different theoretical descriptions of how concepts are structured and their implications for how we assume our mental representations work. We'll then focus on how concepts are accessed and used in categorizing new objects, patterns, or events. Many ideas discussed in the early part of the chapter will extend and elaborate on proposals presented in Chapter 3, "Perception: Recognizing Patterns and Objects" (pattern recognition and classification have many similarities, as we shall see), and in the last section on semantic memory. Similarly, our examination of categorization will anticipate some later discussions about language, thinking, reasoning, and decision making (Chapters 9–11).

What are concepts and categories, and how do they differ? The distinction, though a little blurry, can be made. Medin (1989) defined a concept as "an idea that includes all that is characteristically associated with it" (p. 1469). In other words, a **concept** is a mental representation of some object, event, or pattern that has stored in it much of the knowledge typically thought relevant to that object, event, or pattern. Most people's concept of "dog," for example, includes information to the effect that a dog is an animal, has four legs and a tail, has a reputation as "man's best friend," is a common pet, and so on.

A **category** can be defined as a class of similar things (objects or entities) that share one of two things: either an essential core (example: why all science courses are considered "science") or some similarity in perceptual, biological, or functional properties (Lin & Murphy, 2001). When a psychologist thinks about categories, she usually thinks about several into which various things get sorted. In the game twenty questions, a common opener is, "Is it an animal, vegetable, or mineral?" This question seeks to categorize, or sort, the to-be-guessed item into one of three things. Sometimes categories are described as existing objectively in the world, and concepts are described as mental representations of categories (Medin, 1989).

Concepts help us establish order in our knowledge base (Medin & Smith, 1984). Concepts also allow us to categorize, giving us mental "buckets" in which to sort the things we encounter, letting us treat new, never-before-encountered things in the same way we treat familiar things that we perceive to be in the same set (Neisser, 1987). Categorization also allows us to make predictions and act accordingly. If I see a four-legged creature with a tail coming toward me, my classification of it as either a dog or a wolf has implications for whether I'll want to call to it, run away, pet it, or call for help.

Throughout this section, we'll be focusing on concepts of objects and nouns, because they are the most commonly studied at present in cognitive psychology. We will see, however, that the kind of concept studied may affect the theories that are subsequently created. So it will be useful to keep in mind that psychologists have yet to explore fully the entire range of people's concepts.

Models of semantic memory, reviewed earlier, describe the ways in which representations of different concepts are interrelated. Here we will concentrate on the representation and organization of individual concepts. We will explore five distinct proposals about how concepts are represented and structured. Each provides a different answer to the question "What information do we have when we have a particular concept?" Each proposal will therefore have different implications for the question of how concepts are formed, acquired, or learned.

THE CLASSICAL VIEW OF CONCEPTS AND CATEGORIZATION

The classical view of concepts, which dates back to Aristotle, was the dominant view in psychology up until the 1970s (Smith & Medin, 1981). This proposal is organized around the belief that all examples or instances of a concept share fundamental characteristics, or features (Medin, 1989). In particular, the **classical view of concepts** holds that the features represented are individually necessary and collectively sufficient (Medin). To say a feature is individually necessary is to say that each example must have the feature if it is to be regarded as a member of the concept. For example, "has three sides" is a necessary feature of the concept *triangle;* things that do not have three sides are automatically disqualified from being triangles. To say that a set of features is collectively sufficient is to say that anything with each feature in the set is automatically an instance of the concept. For example, the set of features "has three sides" and "closed, geometric figure" is sufficient to specify a triangle; anything that has both is a triangle. Table 7.1 presents some other examples of sets of features or of concepts that are individually necessary and collectively sufficient.

The classical view of concepts has several implications. First, it assumes that concepts mentally represent lists of features. That is, concepts are not representations of specific examples but rather abstractions containing information about properties and characteristics that all examples must have. Second, it assumes that membership in a category is clear-cut: Either something has all the necessary and sufficient features (in which case it is a member of the category), or it lacks one or more of the features (in which case it is not a member). Third, it implies that all members within a category are created equal; that is, there is no such thing as a "better" or "worse" triangle.

■ Table 7.1: Examples of Concepts and Their Features

Concept	Feature(s)
Bachelor	Male
	Adult
	Unmarried
	Human
Even number	Integer
	Divisible by 2
Triangle	Planar figure
	Closed geometric figure
	Three sided

Work by Eleanor Rosch and colleagues (Rosch, 1973; Rosch & Mervis, 1975) confronted and severely weakened the attraction of the classical view. Rosch found that people judged different members of a category as varying in "goodness." For instance, most people in North America consider a robin or a sparrow a very good example of a bird but find other examples, such as chickens, penguins, and ostriches, not as good. Notice the problem this result presents for the classical view of concepts. The classical view holds that membership in a category is all or none: Either an instance (such as robin or ostrich) belongs to a category, or it doesn't. This view has no way to explain people's intuitions that some birds are "birdier" than others.

People's judgments of typicality, the "goodness" of the instance in the category, were later shown to predict several aspects of their performance on different tasks. We saw earlier in the chapter that participants in a sentence verification task were faster to respond (true or false) to a sentence such as "A robin is a bird," than to a sentence such as "A chicken is a bird" (McCloskey & Glucksberg, 1978; Rosch, 1973; E. E. Smith, Shoben, & Rips, 1974). Asked to list instances of a concept, people were more likely to list typical than atypical instances (Mervis, Catlin, & Rosch, 1976). In semantic priming studies, highly typical instances often led to better priming (Rosch & Mervis, 1975; Rosch, Simpson, & Miller, 1976).

These results are not easily explained within a classical framework. In addition, other studies cast doubt on the idea that people typically store and refer to a list of necessary features when judging category membership. McCloskey and Glucksberg (1978) gave participants a list of items and asked them to judge whether the items belonged to certain categories (for example, "Does 'chair' belong to the category 'furniture'?"). The classical view would predict very strong agreement across people, but McCloskey and Glucksberg's participants in fact disagreed considerably on atypical instances (for example, "Do 'bookends' belong to the category 'furniture'?"). In fact, participants were often inconsistent in their own responses in different sessions. This result argued especially strongly against the classical assumption that categories have clearly defined boundaries. Finally, even when given specific instructions to do so, most people cannot generate lists of features that are individually necessary and collectively sufficient to specify membership in a category (Ashcraft, 1978; Rosch & Mervis, 1975).

THE PROTOTYPE VIEW OF CONCEPTS AND CATEGORIZATION

A second theoretical view of the nature of concepts, known as the *prototype view,* was proposed in the 1970s. The **prototype view of concepts** denies the existence of necessary-and-sufficient feature lists (except for a limited number of concepts such as mathematical ones), instead regarding concepts as a different sort of abstraction (Medin & Smith, 1984). Like perceptual researchers (see Chapter 3), conceptual researchers believe in the existence of mental prototypes, idealized representations of some class of objects or events. Specifically, researchers studying the prototype view of concepts hold that prototypes of concepts include features or aspects that are *characteristic*—that is, typical—of members of the category rather than necessary and sufficient. No individual feature or aspect (except very trivial ones, such as "is an object") need be present in the instance for it to count as a member of the category, but the more characteristic features or aspects an instance has, the more likely it is to be regarded as a member of the category.

The prototype view of concepts and categories often refers to the **family resemblance structure of concepts** (Wittgenstein, 1953), a structure in which each member has a number of features, sharing different features with different members. Few, if any, features are shared by every single member of the category; however, the more features a member possesses, the more typical it is. Figure 7.6 provides an example of family resemblance. Note that the Smith brothers (modeled after the men on Smith Bros. Cough Drop boxes) have several shared features: light hair, bushy mustaches, large ears, and eyeglasses. Not every Smith brother has every feature, but the brother in the middle, having them all, would likely be judged

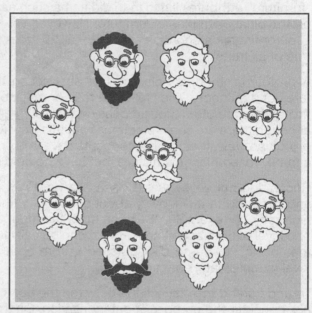

■ Figure 7.6: An example of family resemblance.

by Smith friends to be the most typical Smith of the bunch. Note that he shares big ears, eyeglasses, and light hair with the brother in the "ten o'clock" position and a mustache and big ears with the "seven o'clock" brother. Indeed, different pairs of brothers share different features.

The prototype view of concepts explains typicality effects by reference to family resemblance. The idea is that the more characteristic features an instance of a concept has, the stronger the family resemblance between that instance and other instances, and therefore the more typical an instance it is. Presumably, then, a robin is thought of as being a more typical bird than a penguin because the robin possesses more characteristic bird features, such as "is small," "flies," "eats worms," and "lives in a tree." Even with well-defined concepts such as "bachelor," some examples seem more bachelor-like than others. For example, is a 13-year-old boy a good example of a bachelor? He is male and unmarried. And he's probably a better example of a bachelor today than he was 10 years ago. What about the pope? The point here is that both people may meet the technical definition of a bachelor (there's some disagreement over whether the definition includes "adult"), but neither is as good an example as might be the current male teenage heartthrob.

In one set of studies, Rosch and Mervis (1975) presented their undergraduate participants with terms (such as *chair, car, orange, shirt, gun, peas*) from six different superordinate categories (such as "furniture," "vehicle," "fruit," "clothing," "weapon," "vegetable") and asked them to list attributes "common to and characteristic of" those objects. So, for example, for the word *chair* a participant might list "has four legs; used to sit in; sometimes has arms; used in homes and offices." Then Rosch and Mervis tallied a list of all the attributes any participant listed for all basic-level terms belonging to a superordinate category (for example, all the attributes listed for *chair, sofa, table, dresser, desk, bed, clock, closet, vase, telephone*). Next, they computed, for each item, the number of attributes commonly listed for it. They found that items such as chair and sofa—ones that seem more prototypical of the superordinate category "furniture"—had many more of the "furniture" attributes listed than did items such as clock or telephone, which are not at all prototypical examples of furniture. However, very few (0 or 1) attributes in any of the six superordinate categories were true of all 20 items for the category (for example, attributes true of all fruits).

A prototype, then, is some sort of abstraction that includes all the characteristic features of a category. The prototype may or may not be an actual instance of the category. Prototypes are often thought of as mental "summaries" or "averages" of all the instances, although there are some problems with this view (Barsalou, 1985). The general idea of the prototype view, then, is that concepts have one or more "core" representations, based on a family resemblance structure, but have no rigid boundaries.

Rosch and her colleagues (Rosch, Mervis, Gray, Johnson, & Boyes-Braem, 1976) made another important discovery about concepts. Although concepts exist at many levels of a hierarchy (for example, "Bernese mountain dog," "dog," "canine," "mammal," "animal"), one level of abstraction appears psychologically fundamental. The researchers called this the "basic" level and distinguished it from both higher-level (superordinate) and lower-level (subordinate) concepts.

To understand the distinctions between the **basic level of categorization** and other levels, consider the purpose of categorization. On the one hand, we want to group together similar objects, events, people, ideas, and so on. On the other hand, we want our categorization to distinguish among objects, events, people, and ideas that differ in important ways. There must be some compromise between these two goals. Rosch and colleagues consider the basic level to be the best compromise.

"Piano" and "guitar" are examples of two basic-level categories. Such categories include members that are maximally similar to one another. **Superordinate levels of categories** (such as "musical instruments"), on the other hand, contain members (such as pianos and guitars) that are dissimilar in several respects. At the same time, basic-level categories are most differentiated from one another, especially relative to subordinate categories. "Grand piano" and "upright piano," two categories at the **subordinate level of categories**, are less distinct than are two basic-level categories, such as "piano" and "guitar." The list in Table 7.2 presents examples of basic-level categories along with related superordinate and subordinate categories.

■ Table 7.2: Basic-Level Categories With Related Superordinate and Subordinate Categories

Superordinate Categories	Basic-Level Categories	Subordinate Categories
Musical Instrument	Guitar	Classical guitar Folk guitar
	Piano	Grand piano Upright piano
	Drum	Bass drum Kettle drum
Fruit	Apple	Delicious apple McIntosh apple
	Peach	Cling peach Freestone peach
	Grapes	Concord grapes Green seedless grapes
Tool	Hammer	Claw hammer Ball-peen hammer
	Handsaw	Hack handsaw Cross-cutting handsaw
	Screwdriver	Phillips screwdriver Regular screwdriver
Clothing	Pants	Levi's Double-knit pants
	Socks	Knee socks Ankle socks
	Shirt	Dress shirt Knit shirt
Furniture	Table	Kitchen table Dining room table
	Lamp	Floor lamp Desk lamp
	Chairs	Kitchen chair Living room chair
Vehicle	Car	Sports car Four-door sedan
	Bus	City bus Cross-country bus
	Truck	Pickup truck Tractor-trailer truck

The prototype view does a very good job at explaining why certain members of a category are seen as more typical than others. It also explains why people have a hard time providing strict definitions of their concepts: Strict definitions do not exist. Finally, the prototype view can explain why some classifications are especially easy to make and others are unclear. Take tomatoes, which some people classify as a vegetable and others classify as a fruit. Tomatoes are often eaten with other vegetables instead of with other fruits, and they share some similarities with other vegetables. However, to a biologist, tomatoes are a fruit because they develop from the flower of the plant (technically, the pistil). Vegetables, in contrast, are any nonreproductive parts of a plant, such as the stem or root. The prototype view explains the ambiguity of tomatoes: They share features with both vegetables (leading to classification as a vegetable) and fruits (leading to classification as a fruit).

The prototype view is not wholly free of problems. For one thing, it fails to capture people's knowledge about the limits of conceptual boundaries. To illustrate, even though a Chihuahua seems in many ways more similar to a cat than to a Great Dane, the Chihuahua and Great Dane are classified together as dogs. The prototype view has a hard time telling us why. Unlike the classical view, which sets constraints or boundaries around which things can and can't belong to a category, the prototype view does not specify clear constraints.

Rosch and colleagues (Rosch, 1973; Rosch & Mervis, 1975; Rosch, Mervis, et al., 1976) have argued that some constraints around different categories come from the environment itself.

■ Photo 7.2: Although very different in appearance, this harlequin Great Dane and Chihuahua are both classified as dogs.

Having wings and being able to fly, for example, tend to co-occur, often in those things we call *birds* (but also in airplanes, butterflies, and insects). Boundaries between categories, then, come not just from us as cognitive processors of information but from our knowledge of the way the world works: Certain patterns of attributes or features occur in the world, and others don't (Komatsu, 1992; Neisser, 1987). People's main job in categorizing, then, is to pick up information about the world's regularities, not to impose arbitrary groupings, as the classical view might imply. (The idea of "picking up information" about the world might remind the alert student of Gibsonian theories of perception, discussed in Chapter 3.)

A second problem for the prototype view has to do with typicality ratings. Barsalou (1985, 1987) and Roth and Shoben (1983) showed that the typicality of an instance depends to some extent on context. So although a robin may be seen as a typical bird in the context of birds you see in the neighborhood, it is atypical of birds you see in a barnyard. These findings contrast with the idea that a member of a category has a certain level of typicality. Instead, typicality apparently varies with the context in which the concept is being considered.

Studies by Armstrong, Gleitman, and Gleitman (1983) demonstrated additional problems with typicality ratings. In these studies, the investigators asked participants to rate the typicality of instances of both natural concepts (such as "vehicle" or "fruit"), previously studied by Rosch and her colleagues, and of well-defined concepts (such as "even number," "female," "geometric figure"). Armstrong et al. found that participants happily rated the typicality of members of well-defined categories, generally agreeing that 3 is a more typical odd number than 57, for example. The same participants also agreed, however, that the category "odd number" is well defined and that it makes little sense to talk about degree of membership in the category: Numbers either are or are not odd. The investigators concluded that the typicality ratings task is flawed, at least for discovering the underlying representation of concepts.

THE EXEMPLAR VIEW OF CONCEPTS AND CATEGORIZATION

The previous two views of concepts both hold that concepts are some sort of mental abstraction or summary. In other words, individual instances are not specifically stored or mentally represented but instead are averaged into some sort of composite representation. The **exemplar view of concepts** makes just the opposite assumption: It asserts that concepts include representations of at least some actual individual instances. The exemplar approach assumes that people categorize new instances by comparing them to representations of previously stored instances, called *exemplars*. That is, people store representations of actual instances (Fido, the golden retriever with the long ears; Rover, the black and white sheltie who's missing a tail due to an unfortunate encounter with a raccoon; Precious, the Yorkshire terrier who always has painted toenails and a bow in his hair).

Like the prototype view, the exemplar view explains people's inability to state necessary and defining features: There are none to be stated. It also explains why people may have difficulty categorizing unclear, atypical instances, since such instances are similar to exemplars from different categories (for example, a tomato is similar both to fruit exemplars, such as oranges or apples, and to vegetable exemplars, such as beets or squash) or are not similar enough to any known exemplars (Medin & Smith, 1984). Typical instances are thought more likely to be stored than less typical ones (Mervis, 1980) or to be more similar to stored exemplars, or both. This explains why people are faster to process information about typical instances: In trying to retrieve information about a typical instance, finding very similar stored exemplars is relatively fast. Atypical instances, in contrast, being dissimilar from stored exemplars, take longer to process.

The biggest problem with the exemplar view is that, like the prototype view, it is too unconstrained. It fails to specify, for example, which instances will eventually be stored as exemplars and which will not. It also does not explain how different exemplars are "called to mind" at the time of categorization. However, many psychologists believe people often store information about some specific category members in their conceptual representations.

Arthur Reber (1967, 1976) conducted a series of studies bearing on this

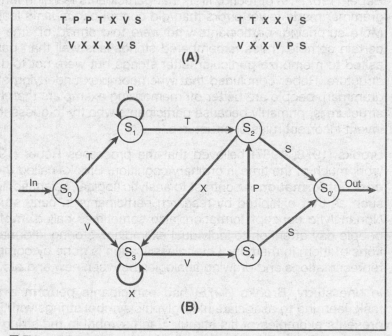

■ Figure 7.7: Possible stimuli (A) and their underlying "grammar" (B) used by Reber (1967).

issue. In his experiments, participants were given strings of letters to learn, such as the ones shown in Figure 7.7(A). Unknown to people in some of the experimental groups, the letters were not randomly arranged but were generated by a structure sharing similarities with certain language grammars.

Figure 7.7(B) depicts one such grammar. To generate a "legal" letter string—that is, in accordance with the grammar—imagine yourself starting at the path marked "In" and moving to the path marked "Out," following the directional arrows as you go. As you take each path, you add the letter of that path to your string. So the first letter of a "legal" string is always either a *T* or a *V*. Notice two loops in the grammar, one labeled *P* and one *X*. These loops can be followed any number of times (each time adding either a *P* or an *X* to the letter string), allowing letter strings that are infinitely long.

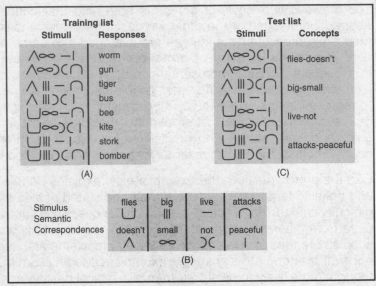

■ Figure 7.8: Stimuli from Brooks's (1978) experiments.

Reber (1967, 1976) found, first, that participants learning letter strings that followed the grammar made fewer errors than did control participants learning random letter strings. More surprising, participants who were told ahead of time that letter strings followed certain complex rules remembered strings *less* well than participants who were simply asked to memorize particular letter strings but were not told that the strings followed a structure. Reber concluded that when complex underlying structures exist (such as his grammar), people are better off memorizing exemplars than trying to figure out what the structure is, primarily because participants who try to guess the structure often induce or invent incorrect rules or structures.

Brooks (1978, 1987) believed that the processes Reber (1967) had discovered are at work much of the time in ordinary cognition. Brooks called these processes **nonanalytic concept formation** in contrast to analytic (logical, scientific, focused) concept formation, such as that exhibited by research participants in early studies of concept formation. Nonanalytic concept formation, also sometimes called **implicit learning**, requires that people pay attention to individual exemplars, storing information about and representations of them in memory. Later classification is done by comparing new instances to the representations and drawing analogies between new and old.

In one study, Brooks (1978) had participants perform a paired-associates learning task, learning to associate hieroglyphic symbol strings with English words. Figure 7.8(A) presents examples of his stimuli. Each symbol in the string had a certain meaning, as shown in Figure 7.8(B), but participants were not alerted to this fact. Later they were unexpectedly given new strings, such as those in Figure 7.8(C), and were asked four questions: Does it fly? Is it big? Is it alive? Does it attack? Most of the participants reported they answered the questions by thinking of a previous example that looked similar. However, they generally couldn't point to any particular symbol in the string as a basis for their response.

Brooks's results pose a puzzle for cognitive psychologists. Apparently, participants sometimes explicitly test specific hypotheses when forming concepts. Sometimes they form prototypes (as in the Posner & Keele, 1968, experiments, described in Chapter 3), and sometimes they memorize exemplars (as in the Reber, 1967, 1976, and Brooks, 1978, experiments). The question is, When and why do people adopt such different approaches?

Brooks (1978) believed the answer had to do with the concept formation task itself. Some simple laboratory tasks seem to lead participants to adopt an analytical, hypothesis-testing framework. Other, more complex stimuli lead people to abandon this approach for another. Brooks went on to describe five factors that encourage people to store information about individual exemplars.

The first factor involves task requirements to learn information that distinguishes among individual instances. Brooks (1978) reminded us that in natural situations, different items in the same category must sometimes be treated differently. It is all very well to recognize that Rover, the lovable family mutt, and Killer, the attack dog of the pawn shop down the street, are both dogs, but the child or adult who treats them as interchangeable could be in for a painful surprise.

A second factor involves the original learning situation. In many real-life situations, instances are not presented one at a time in rapid succession (as in many laboratory experiments). Instead, the same instance (Rover, the family mutt) may appear repeatedly (especially at mealtimes!), affording the person a chance to get to know certain instances very well.

Third, some stimuli lend themselves to hypothesis testing better than others do. In simple laboratory experiments, stimuli may only differ in a small number of very obvious ways. In real life, things vary in many complicated ways. Often, the relevant dimensions of variation are not apparent to the novice, an idea we discussed in the section of Chapter 3 on perceptual learning. A fourth factor is that in real-life concept learning, instances may belong to a number of categories all at the same time. Rover might belong to any of the following categories: "dog," "family pet," "partner to take to obedience classes," "source of mud on rainy days," or even "incurrer of large food bills." Finally, Brooks pointed out that in natural settings, we learn about instances without knowing how we will be called on to use the information later.

THE SCHEMATA/SCRIPTS VIEW OF CONCEPTS AND CATEGORIZATION

Another proposal for the way people represent knowledge and concepts invokes the notion of a schema. This approach dates back to Sir Frederick Bartlett (1932), as we saw in Chapter 6. The term *schema* usually refers to something larger than an individual concept. Schemata (the plural of *schema*) incorporate both general knowledge about the world and information about particular events. Bartlett defined a schema as an "active organization of past reactions, or of past experiences, which must always be supposed to be operating in any well-adapted organic response" (p. 201). The key term here is *organization*. A **schema** is thought to be a large unit of organized information used for representing concepts, situations, events, and actions in memory (Rumelhart & Norman, 1988).

Rumelhart and Ortony (1977) viewed schemata as the fundamental building blocks of cognition, units of organized knowledge analogous to theories. Generally, they saw schemata as "packets of information" that contain both variables and a fixed part. Consider a schema for the concept "dog." The fixed part would include the information that a dog is a mammal, has (typically) four legs, and is domesticated; the variables would be things like breed (poodle, cocker spaniel, Bernese mountain dog), size (toy, medium, extra large), color (white, brown, black, tricolored), temperament (friendly, aloof, vicious), and name (Spot, Rover, Tandy). Just and Carpenter (1987) compared a schema to a questionnaire with blanks that a person is supposed to fill in. Labels next to the blanks indicate what sort of information to fill in—for example, name, address, and date of birth.

Schemata can also indicate the relationships among the various pieces of information. For example, to end up with a dog, the "parts" of the dog (tail, legs, tongue, teeth) must be put together in a certain way. A creature with the four legs coming out of its head, its tail sticking out of its nose, and its tongue on the underside of its belly would not count as an instance of a dog, even if all the required dog parts were present.

Moreover, schemata can be connected to other schemata in a variety of ways. The schema for my dog, Tandy, for instance, is a part of a larger schema for dogs I have owned (Tandy, Bussey, Eskie, Flit, Tackle, Lizzy), which in turn is part of a larger schema of Bernese mountain dogs, which is part of a still larger schema of all dogs, and so on. The schema for Bernese mountain dogs can also be connected with similar, related schemata, such as the one for Saint Bernard dogs (both breeds come from the canton of Bern, Switzerland) or the one for Rottweiler dogs (both classified as "working" breeds by the American Kennel Club and other registries).

Schemata are assumed to exist at all levels of abstraction; thus, schemata can exist for small parts of knowledge (what letter does a particular configuration of ink form?) and for very large parts (what is the theory of relativity?). They are thought of as active processes rather than as passive units of knowledge. That is, they are not simply called up from memory and passively processed; instead, people are thought to be constantly assessing and evaluating the fit between their current situation and a number of relevant schemata and subschemata.

Some researchers think schemata are used in just about every aspect of cognition. Schemata are deemed to play an important role in perception and pattern matching as we try to identify the objects we see before us. They are considered important in memory functioning as we call to mind relevant information to help us interpret what is happening around us and make decisions about what to do next. We will see in Chapter 9 as well that schemata are thought to explain some aspects of text and discourse comprehension as we try to follow the meaning of a conversation, story, or textbook.

One kind of schema, a schema for routine events, has been called a **script** (Schank & Abelson, 1977). Consider the best-known example of a script: going to a restaurant. Think for a moment (and even better, before reading further, make a few notes) about what happens when you go to a restaurant. Now do the same thing for these other events: attending a lecture, getting up in the morning, grocery shopping, and visiting a doctor. Schank and Abelson noticed that people's knowledge of what is involved in going to a restaurant was widely shared and was structured in very similar ways. They explained this similarity by saying that people share scripts.

Scripts are thought to be used in a variety of situations. For instance, if you go to a new restaurant in a city you've never visited before, you can call on a script to tell you what to expect. In general, you should expect on entry to be greeted by a host, shown to a table when one is available, given menus, and so on. This knowledge cues you for how to behave appropriately. So if you enter a restaurant but don't see a host, it is normally a good idea to wait (at least a little while) before sitting down; your script tells you this.

Scripts also let us make a number of inferences (Rumelhart & Norman, 1988). Consider this story: "Tim really wanted a chicken-fried steak. So he went to a restaurant and ordered it. Finally, he asked for the check, paid it, and left." Other, apparently omitted information can be inferred by use of the script. For instance, we can infer that Tim entered the restaurant and was seated, that someone took and delivered his order, that someone cooked his steak, that he had money or a credit card before entering the restaurant, and so on. The story didn't need to say all this, because it gave enough information for us to call up the appropriate script ("going to a restaurant") and that script filled in the rest.

Bower, Black, and Turner (1979) investigated how much people typically use scripts. They first asked participants to write their scripts for a number of specific events: going to a restaurant, attending a lecture, getting up in the morning, grocery shopping, visiting a doctor. They compared the notes generated by all the participants and found a high degree of overlap in what people mentioned. The participants generally agreed about which characters to describe, which props and actions to mention, and the order in which different actions would occur.

The investigators also found a high degree of agreement in description level. Thus, most people would mention "eating the food" instead of "picking up a spoon, dipping it into soup, raising the spoon to lips, and sipping." In another study, Bower et al. (1979) showed that if information from a story was presented in scrambled order, people tended to recall it in the scripted order. In a further experiment, the investigators presented stories that mentioned only some of the events in a typical script. They found that in a later recall task, people often "recalled" information that wasn't in the story but was in the relevant script. Rizzella and O'Brien (2002) found that when people were given a narrative text to read and remember, central concepts relevant to the script (being served a meal in a restaurant script, for instance) were typically better remembered than concepts of less importance to the script (such as giving one's name to a host).

The preceding finding was replicated in a study by Owens, Bower, and Black (1979). They presented participants with stories about a character's doing such routine things as making coffee, visiting a doctor, and going to a lecture. Participants in the experimental condition read a three-line description of a problem, such as "Nancy woke up feeling sick again, and she wondered if she really was pregnant. How would she tell the professor she had been seeing? And the money was another problem." Participants were later asked to recall the stories as close to verbatim as possible. Participants who read the problem description recalled more of the story episodes than control participants but also "recalled" more than was in the stories. These intrusions appeared to come from the underlying scripts (e.g., of a young, pregnant woman) and became more frequent with longer retention intervals.

The authors suggested that although scripts play an important role in helping us organize recall, they force us to pay a price: Other, script-related information intrudes into our memory. Thus, part of the reason Bartlett's (1932) participants produced such distorted recalls of "The War of the Ghosts" (discussed in Chapter 6) is that they used their schemata and scripts for stories and "regularized" the original folktale, making it conform more to their own cultural expectations of how a story should proceed.

Some (Komatsu, 1992) have seen the **schemata/scripts view of concepts** as sharing features with both the prototype view (in that both schemata and prototypes store information that is abstracted across instances) and the exemplar view (in that both schemata and exemplars store information about actual instances). The schemata view shares some of the problems facing the prototype and exemplar views. It does not specify clear enough boundaries among individual schemata. Moreover, some psychologists argue that, in its current state, the schema framework is not sufficiently delineated to be empirically testable (Horton & Mills, 1984). Answers to the following questions are still needed: What kinds of experiences lead to the formation of new schemata? How are schemata modified with experience? How do people know which schemata to call up in different situations—that is, what sorts of environmental cues are used?

THE KNOWLEDGE-BASED VIEW OF CONCEPTS AND CATEGORIZATION

A number of cognitive psychologists (Barsalou, 2008; Keil, 1989; Lin & Murphy, 2001; Murphy & Medin, 1985) have argued that concepts have much more to do with people's knowledge and worldviews than previously recognized. Murphy and Medin suggested that the relationship between a concept and examples of the concept is analogous to the relationship between a theory and data supporting that theory. The idea of the **knowledge-based view of concepts** is that a person classifying objects and events doesn't just compare features or physical aspects of the objects and events to features or aspects of stored representations. Instead, the person uses his or her knowledge of how the concept is organized to justify the classification and to explain why certain instances happen to go together in the same category. The knowledge-based view helps explain how an apparently disparate collection of objects can form a coherent category in particular circumstances.

To take an example from Barsalou (1983), consider the category comprising children, pets, photo albums, family heirlooms, and cash. On the face of it, these things don't seem to go together very well, but in the context of a scenario in which a fire is about to engulf a house, these things fall neatly into the category "things to save." We know that each object mentioned is precious to its owner or parents and is irreplaceable. Notice, however, that the category becomes coherent only when we know its purpose. A similar context effect arises when concepts are combined. Here's an example: If I ask you to think of "pets," you are likely to think of dogs and cats. If I ask you to think of "fish," you might think of trout or salmon. But, if I ask you to think of "pet fish," a goldfish is the best exemplar and most prototypical. Notice, though, that a goldfish isn't a particularly prototypic pet or fish (Hampton, 2007; Wu & Barsalou, 2009).

Recall that the prototype, exemplar, and schemata/scripts approaches to concepts and categories fail to offer much of an answer to the question of how things in the same category go together. The knowledge-based view proposes that people's theories or mental explanations about the world are intertwined with their concepts and provide the basis for categorization (Heit, 1997). This view lets people explain to themselves and to others the instances that go together and why, the features or aspects of instances that are important and why, and the features or aspects that are irrelevant and why.

A proposal by Medin (1989), drawing on work by the philosopher Hilary Putnam (1975), has examined people's reliance on underlying nature as a basis for many concepts. Medin proposed a framework he called **psychological essentialism** and described several assumptions. The first is that people generally act as if objects, people, or events have certain essences or underlying natures that make them what they are. Presumably, for instance, a human being is a human being by virtue of having a certain molecular structure.

That essence constrains or limits the kinds of variation that different instances of a category can show. So, for instance, people can vary in height, weight, hair color, eye color, bone structure, and the like, but they must have certain other properties in common by virtue of the underlying essence they share. People's theories about the essences of various categories help them connect deeper properties (such as the structure of DNA) to more superficial properties (such as eye color or hair color). For example, Medin (1989) pointed out that although most of us believe that the categories "male" and "female" are genetically determined, most of us look at characteristics such as hair length, facial hair, and so on rather than conducting genetic tests when classifying a new person as a woman or a man. We may sometimes make errors in using superficial characteristics, but we will be correct most of the time.

People's knowledge of the essence of a category varies by level of expertise. Biologists, in general, know a lot more about the genetic structure of a human being than do laypeople. For this reason, experts can generally be expected to make different and more accurate classifications, especially if the criteria for the classifications are subtle. Medin's (1989) idea is that classifying on the basis of perceptual or other superficial similarity may be a pretty effective strategy much of the time. Still, when the situation calls for it and if the expertise is possessed, people classify on the basis of deeper principles. This suggestion implies, then, that people's classification of instances will change as they become more experienced and knowledgeable—an idea that fits well with our discussion of perceptual learning, as well as with the currently available data.

The way people acquire and mentally represent concepts may also vary as a function of what the concepts are (Murphy, 2005). Some psychologists have adopted the perspective of philosophers in distinguishing among kinds of concepts. **Nominal-kind concepts** include concepts that have clear definitions. **Natural-kind concepts**, such as "gold" or "tiger," are of things naturally occurring in some environment (Putnam, 1975). A third kind of concept is **artifact concepts**, things constructed to serve some function or accomplish some task (see Keil, 1989; S. P. Schwartz, 1978, 1979, 1980). Different information may be represented in different kinds of concepts.

For instance, nominal-kind concepts (such as bachelor or odd number) may include information about necessary and sufficient features, because these things exist as part of the concept definition. Natural-kind concepts may include more information about definitional or essential features, especially about molecular or chromosomal structure. Natural-kind concepts may also be more likely to have a family resemblance structure but can be equally well explained within a knowledge-based approach.

Artifact concepts, in contrast, may highlight information about the object's purpose or function and may be adequately described only within the knowledge-based approach. In one study, Barton and Komatsu (1989) presented participants with five natural-kind concepts (such as *goat, water, gold*) and five artifacts (such as *TV, pencil, mirror*). With each concept, they asked the participants to imagine different transformations. Some transformations were phrased in terms of function or purpose (for example, a female goat that did not give milk or a TV with no visible picture); others were in terms of physical features (for example, gold that was red in color or a pencil that was not cylindrical). A third type of change was molecular (for example, water that did not consist of the formula

H2O or a mirror not made out of glass). The investigators found that with natural-kind terms, participants were most sensitive to molecular transformations, whereas with artifact terms, they were most sensitive to functional changes. Apparently, then, all concepts are not treated equally, and, under at least some conditions, people use their knowledge about why instances of a category should be grouped in their representation of the related concept (Medin, Lynch, & Solomon, 2000).

The five approaches to conceptual structure just reviewed have been themselves categorized into two major types: similarity-based and explanation-based (Komatsu, 1992). The similarity-based category consists of the classical, prototype, and exemplar views (and some parts of the schemata/scripts view). It includes approaches in which categorization is assumed to be based on the similarity of an instance to some abstract specification of the category (such as a definition or a prototype) or to one or more stored exemplars.

However, to say that objects are categorized on the basis of similarity raises some problems, some of which Goodman (1972) pointed out. Consider two objects, a fork and a spoon. We say they are similar, probably because they share many properties: Both are made of metal, both are less than a foot long, and both are used as eating utensils. Now consider two other objects, a plum and a lawnmower. Are these similar? Well, they share several properties: Both weigh less than 100 kilos (and in fact, both weigh less than 101 kilos, 102 kilos, and so forth). In fact, these two apparently dissimilar items share an infinite number of properties (Hahn & Chater, 1997). But the property of weighing less than 100 kilos seems somehow beside the point when you are evaluating the similarity between a plum and a lawnmower. The key point is that similarity is meaningful only in certain respects. Goodman concluded that the term *similarity* is pretty empty without some specification of what the relevant respects are.

Komatsu (1992) defines a different type of approach to concepts, which he calls the *explanation-based category,* comprising some of the schemata/scripts view and some of the knowledge-based view. In this approach to the study of concepts, people are seen as basing classifications on meaningful relationships among instances and categories. The contrast between the similarity-based and the explanation-based approaches has to do with the degree to which people focus on superficial, perceptual information about a particular object versus the degree to which they focus on deeper, knowledge-derived information about an object's function or role.

The five approaches to concepts differ on several dimensions. The first dimension is the cognitive economy of the mental representation. Recall our earlier discussion of cognitive economy. The idea is to save on mental resources (such as storage space, processing time) by limiting the amount of information we must store. If we treated every single object or event as unique, thereby forming a unique mental representation for each, we would not be using our cognitive resources very economically. In contrast, if we categorized all objects into one category (called "things"), the category wouldn't be very informative. So any theory of concepts and categorization must strike a balance between cognitive economy and informativeness (Komatsu, 1992). At the same time, any theory of concepts must explain a concept or category's coherence—what holds the class of things together into a natural grouping. Some approaches, such as the classical approach, do this very directly; others have fuzzier boundaries around and between concepts.

We can expect much research in this area of knowledge and conceptual representation in the coming years. Questions such as "What is the nature of the mental representation?"

"Which inferences are easy to make using general knowledge, and which inferences are harder?" and "How does knowledge representation change as a function of practice and expertise?" must all be answered. Knowledge representation and organization are critically important to cognitive psychologists. For one thing, the issue of how knowledge is mentally represented underlies the important question "What is common sense?" Workers in artificial intelligence are discovering over and over again that a truly intelligent program or system must have a wide and deep knowledge base and must be able not only to store but also retrieve a great deal of information about the world. Thus, the knowledge base must be organized efficiently. So far, the only creatures who have demonstrated efficient organization of such vast knowledge bases are human beings. The challenge now is to find out just how we accomplish this marvelous feat.

Summary

1. There are a number of different theoretical frameworks and empirical tests of the ways in which information in permanent memory is stored and organized.

2. Network models of semantic memory posit that different concepts or ideas are mentally represented as nodes, with connections among related ideas along which mental activation can spread.

3. ACT models also posit the existence of nodes; they further postulate the existence of production (if-then) rules used to represent information in procedural memory.

4. Connectionist models represent concepts or ideas by a pattern of activation across different units.

5. Categories are classes of similar objects, events, or patterns. Concepts are mental representations of those categories. Concepts are thought to help us order our knowledge and to relate new objects or patterns to previously encountered ones.

6. There are five distinct approaches to the study of concepts. These have been themselves categorized into two major types: similarity-based and explanation-based.

7. The similarity-based category, comprising the classical, prototype, and exemplar views (and some parts of the schemata view), includes the approaches in which categorization is assumed to be based on the similarity of an instance to some abstract specification of the category (for example, a definition or a prototype) or to one or more stored exemplars.

8. The explanation-based category, comprising aspects of the schemata/scripts view and aspects of the knowledge-based view, instead sees people as classifying instances based on meaningful relationships among instances and categories.

9. The classical approach to concepts posits that each concept is defined by a set of necessary and sufficient features.

10. The prototype approach to concepts holds that we categorize objects by comparing them to mental abstractions, called prototypes, which are idealized representations of some class of objects or events.

11. The exemplar approach to concepts assumes we store specific individual instances and use these stored representations to categorize.

12. The schemata/scripts view regards concepts as schemata, packets of information with specific parts, that fill in default values for aspects of the situation.

13. Proponents of the knowledge-based view of concepts hold that people use their own theories to guide their classification of objects. Experts have more elaborated theories and therefore different mental representations than do novices.

Review Questions

1. Explain the concept of spreading activation and review the evidence that leads some psychologists to maintain that it is a property of semantic memory.

2. The research on knowledge representation typically involves laboratory research with participants working on somewhat artificial tasks (for example, lexical decision, sentence verification). Does such research have much bearing on cognition in real life? Defend your answer and use specific examples to illustrate your points.

3. Describe the distinction many cognitive psychologists make between concepts and categories. What are the cognitive benefits of having concepts? Explain.

4. Contrast the classical, prototype, and exemplar proposals for how concepts are mentally represented. What kinds of arguments and/or empirical findings support each? What kinds of arguments and/or empirical data are troublesome for each?

5. Describe what a family resemblance structure is and how it relates to the prototype approach to concepts.

6. Compare and contrast the schemata view and the knowledge-based view of concepts. Are the two compatible? Why or why not?

7. Briefly review Reber's work on implicit learning and its implications for concept formation.

8. Give some new examples of scripts and justify your examples.

9. Discuss this statement: "Any approach to concepts must strike some balance between cognitive economy and informativeness."

Key Terms

adaptive control of thought (ACT) model of memory

artifact concept

basic level of categorization

category

classical view of concepts

cognitive economy

concept

exemplar view of concepts

family resemblance structure of concepts

hierarchical semantic network model of semantic memory

implicit learning

knowledge-based view of concepts

lexical decision task

lexicon

natural-kind concept

nominal-kind concept

nonanalytic concept formation

production rules

prototype view of concepts

psychological essentialism

schema

schemata/scripts view of concepts

script

semantic network

semantic priming

spreading activation

subordinate level of categories

superordinate level of categories

typicality effect

CHAPTER 8

VISUAL IMAGERY AND SPATIAL COGNITION

CHAPTER OUTLINE

Codes in Long-Term Memory
> The Dual-Coding Hypothesis
> The Relational-Organizational Hypothesis

Empirical Investigations of Imagery
> Mental Rotation of Images
> Scanning Images

The Nature of Mental Imagery
> Principles of Visual Imagery
>> Implicit Encoding
>> Perceptual Equivalence
>> Spatial Equivalence
>> Transformational Equivalence
>> Structural Equivalence
> Critiques of Mental Imagery Research and Theory
>> Tacit Knowledge and Demand Characteristics
>> The Picture Metaphor
>> Propositional Theory

Neuropsychological Findings

Spatial Cognition

Think of the house or apartment you consider your permanent residence. In particular, think about its kitchen. How many cabinet doors does it have? Obviously, this question draws on your memory. Most people can answer it after some mental work. What sort of work is required? In the process I used, I first recognized that I didn't have the information needed already stored; that is, I didn't know the answer "off the top of my head." So I had to determine the answer in another way. I mentally pictured my kitchen by drawing on memory. Then, starting at one end of the room, I scanned my mental picture, counting cabinet doors. My procedure is neither difficult nor original (Shepard, 1966) but seems to be the one commonly used.

The nature of these "mental pictures," or **visual images**, is one focus of this chapter. We will look at the role of images in memory. We will also consider experiments investigating the ways in which people construct and use visual images and what these findings suggest about cognition. Finally, we will turn to the nature of visual images, considering the kinds of mental representations used to create and store them.

Throughout the chapter, we will confine ourselves to a discussion of visual images. Recognize, however, that other kinds of mental images exist. Examples include auditory images (such as the imagined sound of your dog barking), olfactory images (such as the imagined smell of fresh-baked bread), and cutaneous images (such as the imagined feeling of your toe being stubbed into the wall). Visual images, like visual perception, have received the most attention within cognitive psychology. Thus, just as when we examined perception (Chapter 3) we focused on visual perception, in this chapter we will focus on visual imagery.

The study of visual imagery has had a controversial history within psychology (Paivio, 1971). Although occasional references to imagery were made at the turn of the 20th century, the rise of behaviorism essentially dictated that even the concept of an image be rejected. Visual images are problematic as objects of scientific inquiry. After all, the experience of a visual image is just about as private an experience as one can have. If I assert that I am forming a visual image of my kitchen, no one but me can tell if I really have the image or am just pretending. Visual images, unlike behaviors, cannot be seen, counted, or controlled by other people. Because visual images can be reported only by the person who asserts she is experiencing them, that person can distort or bias them, either consciously or inadvertently. Behaviorists argued that imagery is not the sort of topic that can be investigated with sufficient scientific rigor or control.

Nonetheless, interest in visual imagery never completely vanished (Paivio, 1971) and in fact became stronger after the popularity of behaviorism waned in the 1960s. It is difficult to explain how people perform certain cognitive tasks, such as the one described earlier, without talking about visual images. Moreover, research on memory suggests that people who report using imagery are better able to recall information than people who do not.

Sports psychologists, too, have a strong interest in the use of visual imagery. An athlete who before competing spends time mentally imagining a smoothly executed, well-timed, elegant performance has been shown to perform better a bit later when engaging in the sport (Martin, Moritz, & Hall, 1999). Some research suggests further that imagery can be used to help people cope with negative emotional events, such as remembering a real incident of being rejected, abandoned, or excluded. Research participants asked to visualize so-called cool aspects of the experience—for example, where they were standing or sitting in relation to other people during the incident—were better able to reduce their hostile feelings than were participants asked to form images of their visceral reactions during the incident or participants not asked to form any images (Ayduk, Mischel, & Downey, 2002).

Psychologists now recognize that to eliminate imagery as a subject of discussion and investigation is to overlook a potentially fundamental aspect of cognition. Hence, visual imagery has regained credibility as a worthwhile topic among most cognitive psychologists.

CODES IN LONG-TERM MEMORY

If you recall our discussion of different mnemonic techniques from Chapter 6, you remember that mnemonics are techniques used to help people remember certain information. For our current purposes, I hope you remember that several (though not all) mnemonic techniques involve visual imagery: method of loci, interacting images, and the pegword method. You might have wondered why so many mnemonic techniques use visual imagery or how imagery-based mnemonics function differently from non-imagery-based mnemonics. We will consider two opposing views on this matter now.

THE DUAL-CODING HYPOTHESIS

Allan Paivio (1969, 1971, 1983) originated the **dual-coding hypothesis** of memory to explain the workings of various mnemonics. According to Paivio, long-term memory contains two distinct coding systems (or codes) for representing information to be stored. One is verbal, containing information about an item's abstract, linguistic meaning. The other involves imagery: mental pictures of some sort that represent what the item looks like. Items to remember can be coded by either verbal labels or visual images and, in some cases, both. Paivio's idea is that pictures and concrete words give rise to both verbal labels and visual images; that is, they have two possible internal codes or mental representations. Abstract words, in contrast, typically have only one kind of code or representation: a verbal label.

One study by Paivio (1965) provided evidence to support this hypothesis. Participants were asked to learn one of four lists of noun pairs. The first list (CC) included pairs in which both nouns referred to concrete objects (for example, *book–table*). The second list (CA) included pairs in which the first noun was concrete and the second abstract (such as *chair–justice*). The third list (AC) was the converse of the second (such as *freedom–dress*). The fourth (AA) contained pairs of abstract nouns (for example, *beauty–truth*). Of a possible 16 correct responses, participants averaged 11.41, 10.01, 7.36, and 6.05 correct responses for the CC, CA, AC, and AA lists, respectively.

Paivio (1965) explained the results as follows. Whenever possible, participants spontaneously formed visual images of the noun pairs. The formation was easiest with concrete nouns. Paivio (1969) assumed that visual imagery, unlike verbal labeling, increases as a function of concreteness: the more concrete the noun, the richer the image and the more elaborated the internal code. This helps explain why pictures (very concrete) are often remembered better than words (see, for example, Kirkpatrick, 1894; Shepard, 1967). When items are coded by both images and verbal labels (as concrete nouns can be), the chances of the learner's retrieving them are obviously better. If the learner forgets the verbal label, he or she might still access the visual image, or vice versa. Items coded only by verbal labels are disadvantaged; if the verbal label is forgotten or "misplaced," the learner has less to go on.

Further, Paivio (1969) believed that the first noun in a pair (called the "stimulus" noun) serves as a *conceptual peg* on which the second ("response") noun is hooked. In this sense, the stimulus noun serves as a "mental anchor," a place to which the representation of the response noun can be attached. Thus the imaginability of the first noun is particularly important in improving memorability, explaining why recall in the CA condition was significantly higher than in the AC condition.

THE RELATIONAL-ORGANIZATIONAL HYPOTHESIS

Bower (1970) proposed an alternative to the dual-coding hypothesis, which he called the **relational-organizational hypothesis**. He believed that imagery improved memory not because images are necessarily richer than verbal labels but because imagery produces more associations between the items to be recalled. Forming an image (say, between two words in a pair or between a word and a location, as in the method of loci) typically requires the person to create a number of links or hooks between the information to be remembered and other information. Recall from Chapter 6 that the more retrieval cues a piece of information in memory has, the greater are the chances of recalling it. Bower's argument, then, is that imagery works by facilitating the creation of a greater number of hooks that link the two to-be-remembered pieces of information.

Bower (1970) performed an experiment to distinguish between the dual-coding and the relational-organizational hypotheses. Participants were divided into three groups, each given different instructions for a paired-associates learning task. One group was told to use "overt rote repetition" (that is, to rehearse aloud); the second, to construct two images that did not interact and were "separated in imaginal space"; the third, to construct an interactive scene of the two words in a pair (p. 530). Results showed that all participants recognized about 85% of the previously seen words. However, recall of those words differed greatly. Those who used rote memorization recalled about 30% of the paired associates; those who used noninteractive imagery, 27%; and those who formed interacting images, about 53%.

If imagery simply led to more elaborated coding of the paired associates, as the dual-coding hypothesis predicts, then participants in the two conditions that involved instructions to form two images ought to have performed similarly. In fact, only those who formed interacting images showed an improvement over the rote memorizers. Apparently, it is not imagery per se that helps memory but rather the way in which imagery is used. Interacting images presumably create or suggest more links between the target information and other information, making the target information easier to retrieve.

Although the dual-coding hypothesis continues to attract proponents (see Yuille, 1983), still unresolved are how well it explains the workings of imagery mnemonics and what kind of explanations it provides for nonimagery mnemonics. However imagery mnemonics work, there is at least little doubt that many do aid memory. To understand how these mnemonics work, it will be necessary to explore further what imagery is and how it works, topics we turn to next.

EMPIRICAL INVESTIGATIONS OF IMAGERY

A series of studies by Lee Brooks (1968) is widely regarded as yielding some of the best evidence that images are distinct from verbal materials or at least invoke different processes from those invoked by verbal materials. Figure 8.1 depicts different conditions of Brooks's primary experiment. In one condition, participants were asked to imagine a letter, such as the outlined capital *F* in Figure 8.1(A), and then to move clockwise mentally from a particular corner (marked in Figure 8.1 with an asterisk) and to indicate, for each corner, whether it was at the extreme top or extreme bottom of the letter. In this example, the correct responses are "yes, yes, yes, no, no, no, no, no, no, yes."

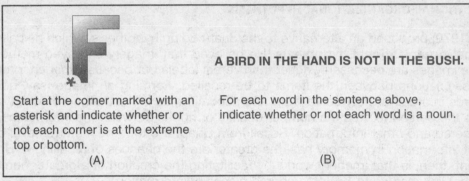

Start at the corner marked with an asterisk and indicate whether or not each corner is at the extreme top or bottom.

(A)

A BIRD IN THE HAND IS NOT IN THE BUSH.

For each word in the sentence above, indicate whether or not each word is a noun.

(B)

■ Figure 8.1: Stimuli from Brooks's 1968 study.

Participants indicated their responses in different ways. One mode of response was verbal: Participants said "yes" or "no," as noted. Another response mode was spatial. Participants were given a response sheet on which the letters *Y* and *N* were printed in an irregular pattern and were told to point to either a *Y* or an *N* in each row to indicate their responses. Brooks (1968) found that participants took almost 2.5 times longer when they responded by pointing than they did when responding verbally.

On a second task, Figure 8.1(B), participants were asked to remember a sentence, such as "A bird in the hand is not in the bush," and, for each word, to indicate whether it was a concrete noun. In this example, the correct responses are "no, yes, no, no, yes, no, no, no, no, yes." As with the previous task, sometimes participants responded verbally, and other times they pointed to *Y* or *N* on a response sheet. With this task, however, people were faster to respond by pointing than they were to respond verbally (although the difference in response times was not as great).

One explanation for these results is as follows. The first task requires the formation of a visual image of an *F*. The visual image probably has at least some picturelike qualities (spatial or visual), so a spatial or visually guided response (pointing) would be interfered with to a greater extent than would a verbal response. In other words, the visual image is more disruptive of, and disrupted by, another spatial or visual type of task (pointing) than by a verbal kind of task (talking). The converse is also true: Holding a sentence in memory (a verbal task) is easier to do with a concurrent visual/spatial task (such as pointing) than with another verbal task. Notice that pointing or talking do not differ in difficulty overall but vary in difficulty as a function of the task with which they are being performed. Brooks's (1968) work supports the idea that images and words use different kinds of internal codes (as the dual-coding hypothesis suggests).

Brooks's (1968) task is not the only one that apparently requires people to form visual images. Here is another. Answer the following question: Which is larger, a pineapple or a coconut (Finke, 1989)? To answer the question, you most likely constructed a visual image of a coconut next to a pineapple and "read" the answer from your image.

Moyer (1973) asked similar questions and found that people were faster to respond when the two objects (in his study, animals) differed greatly. This effect, called the *symbolic-distance effect,* works as follows. Other things being equal, you'd be faster to answer the question "Which is bigger, a whale or a cockroach?" than the question "Which is bigger, a hog or a cat?" Interestingly, the same pattern of response times is also obtained when people look at actual objects (Paivio, 1975). In other words, you'd be faster to answer the first question even if, instead of consulting mental images, you looked at the actual animals or at photographs of the animals. This result suggests that images seem to function, at least in some ways, like pictures. If people merely retrieved verbal information (for example, from a semantic network such as those networks described in Chapter 7), it would be difficult to explain this pattern of results.

MENTAL ROTATION OF IMAGES

The preceding studies suggest that people create and use visual images to answer certain questions and perform certain tasks. They also suggest that the images created are in some ways picturelike (although this conclusion has been energetically debated, as we'll see). At the same time that these findings were reported, other studies showed that people could do more than simply create images; they could also, apparently, mentally transform them.

One of the most famous studies of this type was performed by Shepard and Metzler (1971). They showed participants perspective line drawings of three-dimensional objects (Figure 8.2 presents examples). On each trial, participants would see two drawings. In some cases, the two drawings depicted

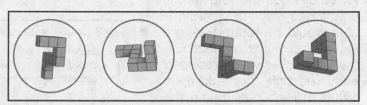

■ Figure 8.2: Stimuli from the Shepard and Metzler (1971) study.

SOURCE: Shepard, R. N., & Metzler, J. (1971). Mental rotation of three-dimensional objects. *Science, 171*, p. 701. Copyright © 1971, American Association for the Advancement of Science. Reprinted with permission.

the same object but with one rotated by some degree. In the other cases, the drawings depicted mirror-image reversals; in other words, the objects were similar but not identical. The mirror images were also sometimes rotated. The kinds of rotations used were either in the picture plane (that is, as if the drawing were rotated on the page) or in depth (that is, as if the object were going toward or away from the viewer). Shepard and Metzler found that the amount of time it took participants to decide if the two drawings depicted the same object or a mirror-image reversal was directly proportional to the angle of rotation between the drawings.

Figure 8.3 shows their results. This close correspondence between the angle of rotation of the two drawings and the participants' reaction times strongly suggests that they performed the task by **mental rotation** of one drawing. Moreover, the time it took participants to come to a decision was the same for rotations in the picture plane and in depth. This suggests they were mentally

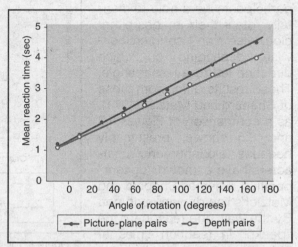

■ Figure 8.3: Results from the Shepard and Metzler (1971) study.

SOURCE: Shepard, R. N., & Metzler, J. (1971). Mental rotation of three-dimensional objects. *Science, 171*, p. 701. Copyright © 1971, American Association for the Advancement of Science. Reprinted with permission.

rotating three-dimensional images, not just the two-dimensional drawings. Had participants been rotating only the latter, their performance would have differed as a function of whether the rotation was in the picture plane or in depth.

Later studies by Cooper and Shepard (1973, 1975) showed that participants also mentally rotated more recognizable stimuli, such as alphabet letters or drawings of hands. In one study (Cooper & Shepard, 1973), participants were sometimes given a drawing of the letter to be used on a trial, followed by a cue showing the orientation to which the test stimulus would be rotated, before the test stimulus appeared. If these two cues were presented early enough (for example, 1,000 milliseconds before the test stimulus appeared), then the participants' performances were the same for all angles of rotation. Figure 8.4 depicts the experimental conditions, and Figure 8.5 shows the results.

Note the shape of the curves in Figure 8.5, which suggests that participants were able to mentally rotate their images either clockwise or counterclockwise, depending on which direction led to a lesser angle. These results differ from those of Shepard and Metzler (1971), as a comparison of Figures 8.3 and 8.5 shows, presumably because alphanumeric characters have a known "upright" position, whereas Shepard and Metzler's line drawings do not. By the way, one reason for the "peaks" in reaction times at 180 degrees might be that participants were uncertain about which direction to rotate the figure and thus hesitated.

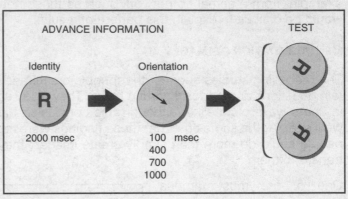

■ Figure 8.4: Cooper and Shepard's 1973 experimental design.

SOURCE: Cooper, L. A., & Shepard, R. N. (1973). The time required to prepare for a rotated stimulus. *Memory and Cognition, 1*, p. 247. Copyright © 1973, Psychonomic Society, Inc. Reprinted with permission.

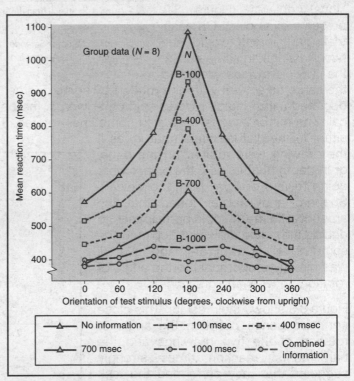

■ Figure 8.5: Results from Cooper and Shepard's 1973 study.

SOURCE: Cooper, L. A., & Shepard, R. N. (1973). The time required to prepare for a rotated stimulus. *Memory and Cognition, 1*, p. 248. Copyright © 1973, Psychonomic Society, Inc. Reprinted with permission.

Are participants in these experiments mentally rotating the whole stimulus, or are they looking only at certain parts? To answer this question, Lynn Cooper (1975) performed studies that presented participants with irregular polygons, such as those shown in Figure 8.6. The polygons were formed by connecting a randomly scattered number of points, with more complex polygons resulting from a greater number of points. Participants were first trained to discriminate between original and mirror-image reflections of the polygons. Next, they were shown either the original polygons or the reflections at different angles of rotation and were asked to determine whether the object depicted was the original or a reflection of the original.

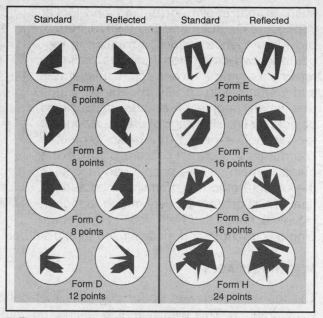

■ Figure 8.6: Stimuli from Cooper's 1975 study.

Cooper (1975) found that the reaction times once again increased linearly with the angle of rotation and that the rate of rotation was the same for all the polygons, regardless of their complexity. If participants were attending only to parts of the polygons, then performance ought to have differed as a function of the polygon complexity. Instead, it appears that participants mentally rotated entire polygons, treating the very simple polygons in exactly the same manner as they did the very complex ones.

In another study, Cooper (1976) showed that mental rotations, like physical rotations, are continuous in nature. Her demonstration worked as follows. She determined, for each person, his or her rate of mental rotation. To do this, she showed participants a polygon at a particular orientation. The polygon was removed, and participants were asked to start mentally rotating it in a clockwise direction. As they were doing this, a test shape (the polygon or its mirror image reflection) was presented in some orientation. If the test shape was presented at the orientation corresponding to the orientation at which the participants' visual images would be expected to be, their reaction times were always fast. As the disparity between the actual orientation of the test shape and the expected orientation of the visual image grew, the reaction times to respond grew longer.

These results in particular suggest that mental rotation works like physical rotation. If you draw a shape on a piece of paper and slowly rotate the paper 180 degrees, the drawing will pass through intermediate orientations: 10 degrees, 20 degrees, and so on. Similarly, it appears from Cooper's (1976) work that rotating images pass through intermediate angles of orientation.

Since Cooper's landmark studies, other cognitive psychologists have studied whether and how people use mental rotation in recognizing objects presented at unusual angles. Consider, for example, the object(s) depicted in Figure 8.7 (A) and (B). How do you recognize (A) as depicting the same object as (B)? One possibility is that you mentally rotate an image of (A) until it reaches some canonical, or standard, orientation of depiction, such as that shown in (B). Tarr and Pinker (1989) and Gauthier and Tarr (1997a, 1997b) provide evidence of mental rotation in recognizing two-dimensional shapes drawn to resemble asymmetric characters. Biederman and Gerhardstein (1993), in contrast, argue that when people view three-dimensional objects (or line drawings of them), as long as the distinctive geons (the basic geometric components shown in Figure 3.10) of the object remain visible, people can recognize the object without performing mental rotation. This debate is very much ongoing. However, notice that both sides of the debate

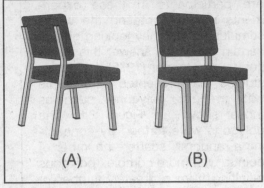

■ Figure 8.7: Two views of a chair.

employ concepts and models used to explain perceptual phenomena.

SCANNING IMAGES

The research reviewed so far suggests that people can construct and transform their visual images. This evidence also seems to suggest that images are in many ways like pictures: They contain visual information, and the kinds of transformations performed on them seem to correspond to similar transformations on pictures. Another series of studies, carried out by Stephen Kosslyn, investigated the spatial properties of images. The series typically required participants first to form a visual image and then to scan it, moving from one location to another in their image, a process known as **imaginal scanning**. The idea is that the time people take to scan reveals something about the ways images represent spatial properties such as location and distance (Finke, 1989).

In one study, Kosslyn (1973) had participants study drawings of objects such as those shown in Figure 8.8. Notice that these drawings are elongated either vertically or horizontally and that each has three easily describable parts: two ends and the middle. After the initial learning phase, participants were told to form an image of one of the drawings and then to "look for" a particular part (for example, the petals of the flower). Some participants were told to focus first on one part of the image (for

■ Figure 8.8: Stimuli from Kosslyn's 1973 study.

example, the top or the left) and then to scan, looking for the designated part. Kosslyn's results showed that the longer the distance from the designated end to the location of the part, the longer it took people to say whether the part they were looking for was in the drawing. So, for example, participants told to form an image of the flower and to start scanning at the bottom took longer to "find" the petals (at the top of the drawing) than they did to "find" the leaves (in the middle of the drawing). Presumably, this is because the visual image formed preserves many of the spatial characteristics of the drawings such that parts of the drawings that are separated in space are also separated in the image.

The results of the study were not entirely clear, however. Lea (1975), for instance, argued that perhaps the reaction times increased, not because of increased distance in the image, but because of the number of items in the image that had to be scanned. Notice in the flower example that, if one started from the bottom, one would scan over the roots and the leaves on the way to the petals but only over the roots to get to the leaves. Lea reported results supporting this interpretation.

In reply, Kosslyn, Ball, and Reiser (1978) performed another series of studies of image scanning. In one, they first created a map of a fictional island and had participants memorize the locations of seven objects shown on the map, depicted in Figure 8.9. Notice that the seven objects allow for the construction of 21 distinct paths—for example, from the tree to the lake and from the tree to the hut. The paths vary in length, from 2 cm to 19 cm.

Participants were instructed to focus mentally on one object. A few seconds later, the experimenter named another object on the island, and participants were then asked to imagine scanning to this second object by imagining a small black speck moving across the map in a straight line. They were instructed to push a button when they "arrived" at the second object, and their reaction times were recorded. The reaction times to scan between objects were correlated with the distance between objects (Kosslyn et al., 1978); that is, participants took more time to scan between two distant objects than they did to scan between two nearby ones. This reinforced the idea that images preserve spatial rela-

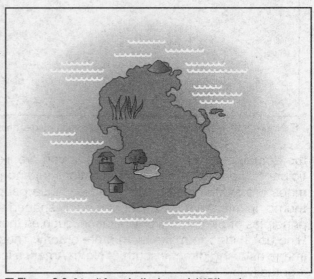

■ Figure 8.9: Stimuli from the Kosslyn et al. (1978) study.

tions. Related studies by Pinker (1980) showed similar results when the stimulus was a three-dimensional array of objects (toys suspended inside an open box).

Kosslyn's work suggests that people's scanning of their visual images is in some ways similar to their scanning of actual pictures: The greater the distance between two parts, the longer it takes to scan between them. Images apparently depict at least some spatial information, and people can retrieve this information from their images. These conclusions have strengthened the metaphor of images as kinds of "mental pictures" (Kosslyn, 1980).

Adding some interesting wrinkles to Kosslyn's conclusions, however, is work by Barbara Tversky (1981) on people's systematic errors in memory for maps. Before reading further, close this book, draw a map of the United States, and put in it the following cities: Seattle; Portland, Oregon; Reno; Los Angeles; San Diego; Chicago; Boston; Portland, Maine; Philadelphia; New York; and Washington, D.C. Presumably, to carry out this task you are drawing on a previously stored mental image of a map of the United States, formed perhaps in your fourth-grade geography class or maybe even from staring at a vinyl place mat showing the 50 states.

Now, referring to your image, answer the following questions: (a) Which city is farther north, Boston or Seattle? (b) Which city is farther west, New York City or Philadelphia? (c) Which city is farther east, Reno or San Diego? Now look at Figure 8.10, which shows

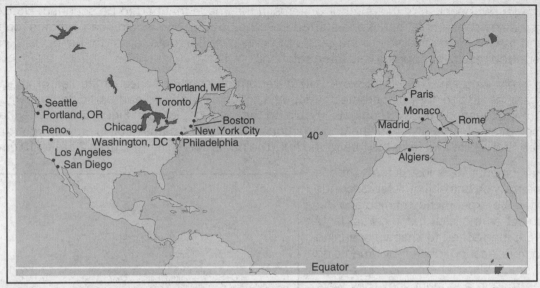

■ Figure 8.10: Map of Europe and the United States with selected cities (cylindrical projection).

the actual locations of these cities. If you are like B. Tversky's Stanford University participants, you made errors on questions (a) and (c). Tversky (1981) argued that people's maps are systematically distorted because people use different **heuristics**, or rules of thumb, in orienting and anchoring oddly shaped units such as continents or states. Using principles of perceptual organization, such as those discussed in Chapter 3, people try to "line up" things to make them more orderly. Thus, South America is "remembered" in an image as being directly south of North America instead of southeast of North America, as it actually is.

A similar principle applies to your siting of the various cities on your map. You probably know that the state of California is west of the state of Nevada, a fact largely true. However, *parts* of Nevada are west of *parts* of California. In fact, San Diego is *east* of Reno, not west. And Seattle is significantly *north* of Boston. But your knowledge of the states' relative locations, combined with your propensity to make your mental image of the map more aligned, contributes to systematic distortions. These distortions are one way in which mental images are *not* like mental pictures.

Another way is found in the work of Chambers and Reisberg (1992). They first asked their research participants to form an image of the creature shown in Figure 8.11(A). You might recognize the creature as the ambiguous "duck/rabbit" shown in many introductory psychology textbooks. Sometimes experimenters told participants that the creature was a duck; other times, they

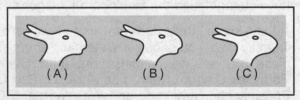

■ Figure 8.11: Test stimuli for Chambers and Reisberg's experiments: (A) unmodified figure, (B) modification on the duck's bill, (C) modification on the rabbit's nose.

said it was a rabbit. They presented the actual drawing for only about 5 seconds (enough time to form an image of the figure but not enough time to "reverse" the figure).

Once participants had formed an image, they were presented with a pair of duck/rabbits, either (A) and (B) or (A) and (C), and were asked to choose which had actually been presented. You'll notice that the distinctions between any pair are subtle and hard to detect. Chambers and Reisberg (1992) found that when participants thought they were imaging a *duck,* they were well above chance at detecting the difference between (A) and (B) [the alteration in (B) is to the duck's bill] but could not clearly distinguish between (A) and (C) [the alteration in (C) is to the rabbit's nose]. Exactly the opposite pattern emerged for those who had formed an initial image of a rabbit. Chambers and Reisberg believe the reason for this effect is that people paid more attention to the region they took to be the creature's "face" and less to the back of the creature's head. In any case, the result shows that people who form images of the same physical stimulus, but who give different construals or meanings to the stimulus, actually form different images. In fact, Chambers and Reisberg report from their previous work that even with hints and prompts, few participants spontaneously reversed their image of the duck/rabbit, although almost everyone looking at the picture of the duck/rabbit did.

This review sounds so far as if it were always beneficial to be able to construct and use mental images. But a recent study by Knauff and Johnson-Laird (2002) provides a counterexample. They studied people reasoning with what are called *three-term series problems*, such as the following:

Tandy is furrier than Bussey.
Bussey is less furry than Eskie.
Which dog is furriest?

The authors varied the kinds of terms used in the problems. Some were easy to envisage both visually and spatially, such as *above–below* or *front–back.* In other words, it's easy to mentally image one person being in front of or behind another, *and* it is easy to mentally depict the three terms. Let's say, for example, that the premises state:

Tandy is in back of Bussey.
Bussey is in back of Eskie.

Then it is easy to spatially depict the relative positions of the three dogs without forming a visual image of them, as in this "map":

(front) Eskie Bussey Tandy *(back)*

Notice that this representation doesn't show visual details of any of the dogs. Knauff and Johnson-Laird (2002) created other problems with different content, which were easy to form mental images of but not quite as easy to form spatial representations of (e.g., *cleaner–dirtier, fatter–thinner*). If you form a representation of "Tandy is dirtier than Bussey," for instance, you probably do it by constructing a visual image of one dog more covered in mud than another one. There were also control problems, which were not easy to form any kind of image or spatial representation of (e.g., *better–worse, smarter–dumber*).

Results showed that visual relations (for example, cleaner–dirtier) slowed down performance relative to either control problems (for example, better–worse) or visuospatial problems (in back of–in front of). Plausibly, the mental effort devoted to constructing the visual images used up mental capacity that could have been focused solely on drawing a logical conclusion. Thus, imagery is not always a boon to cognitive performance—a lot depends on the nature of the task at hand.

THE NATURE OF MENTAL IMAGERY

All the results reviewed so far suggest that images share some properties with pictures. People typically report their experience of images as looking at mental pictures, and the kinds of mental transformations done on images seem very similar to transformations done on pictures. This leads directly to the questions: Just what are images? What kinds of properties do images have, and how are these like and unlike the properties that real pictures have?

Presumably, answers to such questions have implications for the way information is stored, retrieved, and used. Research on visual imagery, then, can potentially tell us a great deal about how information is mentally represented and organized. Our coverage of knowledge representation and concepts (Chapter 7) focused primarily on verbal information. Research on visual imagery suggests there may be another kind of information that is stored and used.

Debate over the nature of visual images has been intense in cognitive psychology. We will review highlights of the debate here, taking a close look at the image-as-mental-picture metaphor. To organize this discussion, we will first review Ronald Finke's (1989) principles of visual imagery. Then we will examine critiques of this research and of the image–mental picture metaphor.

PRINCIPLES OF VISUAL IMAGERY

Finke's (1989) principles of visual imagery, taken together, are meant to describe the fundamental nature and properties of visual images. There are five principles, and each covers a different aspect or characteristic of imagery.

Implicit Encoding

Finke's first principle of visual imagery states that "mental imagery is instrumental in retrieving information about the physical properties of objects, or about physical relationships among objects, that was not explicitly encoded at any previous time" (1989, p. 7). This principle implies that images are places from which some information can be obtained, even if that information was never intentionally stored. Imagery can thus be used to answer questions for which you probably don't have a directly stored answer. The task at the beginning of this chapter—you were asked about the number of cabinet doors in the kitchen of your permanent residence—is a case in point. My guess is that if you are like most people, you've never had much reason to count kitchen cabinet doors. So this information was probably not represented directly in long-term memory. However, the information was **implicitly encoded**, meaning it was stored unintentionally along with other information that allows you to construct a visual image of your kitchen. To answer the question, then, all you need to do is form the visual image, scan it, and count cabinets.

Brooks's (1968) task, in which people had to answer questions about an outlined capital *F*, provides another illustration. Most people have never bothered to check whether each corner of an outlined capital *F* is at the top or bottom of the letter. Yet people are able to perform this task, presumably because the required information has been implicitly encoded together with the information that allows them to form a visual image of an *F*.

Perceptual Equivalence

Finke's second principle of visual imagery has to do with the similarities between the construction of visual images and the perception of real objects and events. It states that "imagery is functionally equivalent to perception to the extent that similar mechanisms in the visual system are activated when objects or events are imagined as when the same objects or events are actually perceived" (1989, p. 41). In other words, many of the same kinds of internal processes used in mental visualization are used in visual perception as well.

An early study by Perky (1910) bears on this principle. Perky had participants imagine that they were looking at an object (such as a tomato, a banana, an orange, a leaf) while staring at a blank screen. After they reported having formed the image, they were briefly distracted by one experimenter while another two experimenters operated an apparatus that projected faint pictures of the objects the participants were imagining. Perky found that many of the participants were unable to distinguish between their own images and the faint pictures. Presumably, this is because images share many similarities with faint pictures.

A related group of studies, including many more experimental controls, was reported by Martha Farah (1985). Participants were asked to form an image of a certain letter—for example, an *H* or a *T*. Very soon after, they were sometimes presented with one of these letters but at a low level of contrast, making the letters very difficult to see. Those who imagined a letter first were more accurate at detecting the actual presented letter than they were at detecting another letter. These results suggest that imagery can "prime" the visual pathway used in detecting an actual stimulus (Finke, 1989). Some authors even regard visual imagery as perceptual "anticipation": the visual system "getting ready" to actually see something (Neisser, 1976).

Spatial Equivalence

Finke's third principle of visual imagery has to do with the way that spatial information, such as location, distance, and size, is represented in visual imagery. The principle states that "the spatial arrangement of the elements of a mental image corresponds to the way objects or their parts are arranged on actual physical surfaces or in an actual physical space" (1989, p. 61).

Much of the evidence for this principle comes from the scanning studies by Kosslyn and associates, reviewed above. The general finding is that the amount of time it takes people to scan from one element of a visual image to another corresponds to the distance between the elements in a physical representation. Thus, the spatial relationships among elements of a drawing or object (for example, relative locations, distances, sizes) all seem to be preserved in the visual image of the drawing or object.

Separating the visual characteristics from the spatial characteristics of an image (or object or drawing) is quite difficult. But an ingenious series of studies by Nancy Kerr (1983) has apparently succeeded at this task. Hers was a map-scanning study, very similar to that of Kosslyn et al. (1978) described earlier. However, in this case some of the participants were congenitally blind and learned the "map" by feeling objects (each of which had a distinct shape) placed on a flat surface. Once participants had learned the locations, they heard the experimenter name a pair of objects and were asked to focus mentally on one and to imagine moving a raised dot from that object to the second. Kerr found that the greater the distance between objects, the longer it took both blind and sighted participants to scan.

Results of this study echoed those of Kosslyn et al. (1978), suggesting that visual imagery has spatial properties. The spatial properties are similar to visual representations but need not be visual, because congenitally blind people—without vision—apparently are able to make use of spatial images.

Transformational Equivalence

Finke's fourth principle of visual imagery has to do with the way that images are mentally transformed. It states that "imagined transformations and physical transformations exhibit corresponding dynamic characteristics and are governed by the same laws of motion" (1989, p. 93).

The best evidence for this principle comes from the studies of mental rotation. Recall that the findings from those studies suggest that mental rotation apparently works in the same way physical rotation does: It is continuous, with rotating objects moving through intermediate orientations on their way to their final orientation. The time it takes to perform mental rotation depends on how much rotation is to be done, as with physical rotation. And, as with physical rotation of an object, the whole object, and not just parts of it, is rotated. The principle of transformation equivalence extends beyond mental rotation, however, in asserting that other kinds of transformations will work with images in much the same way they work with real objects.

Structural Equivalence

Finke's fifth principle of visual imagery has to do with the ways that images are organized and assembled. It states that "the structure of mental images corresponds to that of actual perceived objects, in the sense that the structure is coherent, well organized, and can be reorganized and reinterpreted" (1989, p. 120).

Imagine that you need to draw a picture of an object or (if your artistic skills and inclinations are as poor as mine) that you need to look carefully at an object. How would you do this, and what properties of the object would influence the difficulty of your task? Generally speaking, the larger the object, the more time it would take to look over or to draw. Also, the more complicated the object—that is, the more different parts the object had—the harder it would be (and the longer it would take) to look at carefully or to draw. Apparently, the construction of visual images works the same way. Visual images are formed, not all at once, but in pieces that are assembled into a final rendition (Finke, 1989).

■ Figure 8.12: Stimuli from the Kosslyn et al. (1983) study.

Kosslyn, Reiser, Farah, and Fliegel (1983) studied image generation as it relates to the complexity of the object to be imagined. Participants were asked to form images of pictures that differed in amount of detail, such as those in Figure 8.12(A). It took participants about 1.3 times as long to form an image of the detailed pictures as it did other participants to form images of outline drawings. In a related study, the authors used geometric forms such as those shown in Figure 8.12(B) as stimuli, all of which allowed for different descriptions. For instance, Figure 8.12(B) could be described either as "five squares in the shape of a cross" or as "two overlapping rectangles." Participants first read a description, then saw the corresponding figure, then covered it up and formed a visual image of the figure. Kosslyn et al. found that people given the first description took longer to form the image than did people given the second description, even though the physical stimulus was the same. Notice, by the way, that it would probably be faster to draw or look over Figure 8.12(B) if you conceived of it as two rectangles than as five squares. With images, apparently, the greater the complexity of the *conceived* structure of the object, the longer it takes to assemble an image of it.

CRITIQUES OF MENTAL IMAGERY RESEARCH AND THEORY

In the introduction to this chapter, I noted that the study of imagery has been controversial in psychology, and it is time now to examine the controversy. Although almost every imagery study has been subject to some debate (Finke, 1989, provides several examples), we will focus on three general and interrelated themes. The first concerns criticism of imagery research. In particular, the criticism is that the experiments themselves give enough "hints," either explicitly or implicitly, for people to perform by relying on their beliefs and knowledge rather than relying strictly on visual Imagery. A second critique questions the metaphor of images as pictures. A third kind of criticism is more theoretical, questioning the need to talk about imagery as a distinct kind of internal code. We will consider each critique in turn.

Tacit Knowledge and Demand Characteristics

Pylyshyn (1981) argued that the results from many imagery studies reflect participants' underlying and implicit **tacit knowledge** and beliefs about the task rather than their construction and manipulation of visual images. He paid special attention to image-scanning experiments. Participants' scanning time is proportional to distance scanned, Pylyshyn asserted, because they know that the amount of time it takes to physically scan between two points in a visual display depends on distance *and* because they expect the experiment to demand this kind of performance.

Finke (1989) explained how this knowledge and expectation could distort results. Imagine you want to move an object (say, your coffee cup) from one location (the right side of your desk) to another (the left side of your desk). You could (à la movie scenes in western bars) try to slide the cup across the desk, but it would probably be safer to pick up your cup and place it in the new location. Imagine, for the sake of argument, that you could move the cup instantaneously, regardless of the distance (maybe "teleporting" it from one set of coordinates to the other, à la *Star Trek*). Suppose, however, you believed or expected that the amount of time it will take to move the coffee cup to the new location should depend on the total distance from the old to the new location. You could adjust your time by pausing and holding the cup over the new location for some amount of time before you placed it down on the desk. Then your reaction time in moving the cup would be proportional to the distance the cup moved, although the time would depend arbitrarily on the time you chose to pause.

Pylyshyn's (1981) argument was that people may be "mentally pausing" in image-scanning experiments because of their beliefs and expectations about what the experimenters want them to do. Tasks that are affected by people's beliefs and expectations are termed by Pylyshyn to be *cognitively penetrable*. Some tasks make it obvious to participants how the tasks ought to be performed. The instructions, the tasks themselves, or something else about the situation cues the person how to behave. Such a task is said to have **demand characteristics** (Orne, 1962). In other words, the task "demands" somehow that the person behave in a certain way. Typically, participants in psychology experiments try to please and may behave artificially just to perform in ways they believe will satisfy the experimenter.

Moreover, sometimes experimenters unconsciously give subtle cues to participants. Intons-Peterson (1983) has argued that these **experimenter expectancy effects** have influenced at least some of the imagery investigations. She had undergraduate experimenters conduct a number of imagery studies. Some of the experimenters were led to believe that the results would turn out one way; the other experimenters were led to believe the opposite. In all the studies, participants performed as the experimenters expected them to.

In one study, Intons-Peterson (1983) used four undergraduate experimenters, all known "for their intelligence, dependability, good judgment, and maturity" (p. 396). None was familiar with the imagery literature. Each experimenter was assigned to supervise a total of 18 participants in three different conditions in a mental rotation study. Some participants were "primed" by either seeing or imagining a stimulus before each trial; participants in a control condition received no primes. Two of the four experimenters were told to expect that imaginal primes (primes that participants were asked to imagine) would be more effective than perceptual primes (primes actually presented to participants). The other two experimenters were told the opposite: Perceptual primes would be more effective than imaginal primes. Although all stimuli were presented by microcomputer, and although experimenters were not in the same room with the participants, except initially when they read instructions, the results mirrored the experimenters' beliefs. Participants supervised by experimenters who believed imaginal primes would be more effective than perceptual primes produced data to support that belief; participants supervised by the other experimenters produced data that resulted in the opposite findings.

Intons-Peterson (1983) found similar results in imaginal scanning experiments. She concluded that participants in imagery experiments were sensitive to subtle, unintentional cues given by experimenters, including slight differences in intonation or pauses when reading instructions. Intons-Peterson further argued that imagery research, by virtue of the subjective nature of the phenomenon under study, may be especially vulnerable to demand characteristics and experimenter expectations. Although she did *not* assert that results from all visual imagery experiments are the result of experimenter effects and demand characteristics, she did warn that visual imagery researchers must take special care to minimize these effects.

The Picture Metaphor

Much of the discussion so far has suggested an analogy between pictures and images. Some psychologists speak casually of visual images as "mental pictures." The question is, How far does the analogy go? As Pylyshyn (1973) pointed out, pictures and images differ in several ways. Perhaps the most important difference is that you can physically look at a picture without first knowing what it's a picture of (say, if someone wordlessly hands you a photograph and you ask, "What's this?"), but you cannot "look" at an image unless you first know what it is. After all, images are internal constructions formed with some intention in mind. You don't just spontaneously create random images; rather, you form images of particular things.

Second, pictures and images are disrupted, and disruptable, in different ways. You can cut a photograph in half, with the result that arbitrary parts of the objects depicted disappear. Images are organized more meaningfully, and when they fade, only the meaningful parts disappear (Finke, 1989).

Last, images seem to be more easily distorted by the viewer's interpretations than are pictures or photographs. Remember Bartlett's (1932) work on story recall? (See Chapter 6 if you need to review.) We saw that people's memory for stories changes over time and often depends on their initial or subsequent interpretations. So also with images. Carmichael, Hogan, and Walter (1932) presented participants with patterns such as those in Figure 8.13 with one of two labels (different participants were given different labels). Participants' later reproductions of the patterns (presumably based on imagery) were distorted in accordance with the label initially provided, as shown in the figure.

Similarly, Nickerson and Adams (1979) have shown that people make many errors when trying to reproduce their images of familiar objects. Try drawing a picture of a US penny without looking at one and then compare it to a real penny. Is Lincoln facing the right way? Is the right motto in the right place? How about the date? Notice in this case that your image probably has far less information in it than would a photograph of a penny, as you can see in Photo 8.1. Even when given a multiple-choice recognition test, with several drawings of pennies, Nickerson and Adams's participants were not very good at selecting the correct representation.

A student in my recent Cognitive Processes class, Rebecca Plotnick (2012), performed a very creative study based on the Nickerson and Adams (1979) study but using familiar corporate logos as stimuli. She asked undergraduates to choose the real logo from a set of foils, either in context (e.g., on a coffee cup or computer screen, as they would normally be encountered, as in the examples shown in Figure 8.14 (A) and (B)) or presented in isolation (see Figure 8.14 (C) or (D)). Overall, the participants were slightly better at identifying the correct choice when the logos were presented in context (58% correct) than when the logos were presented in isolation (48% correct).

■ Photo 8.1: Compare this photograph of a penny with the sketch you just made.

What's the significance of finding differences between images and pictures? Visual images are thought to be one means of internal coding and representation of information. Although many cognitive psychologists believe that visual imagery exists as a distinct mental code, and although they believe the code has many visual and/or spatial qualities, the evidence to date suggests that the visual image-as-picture analogy works only roughly.

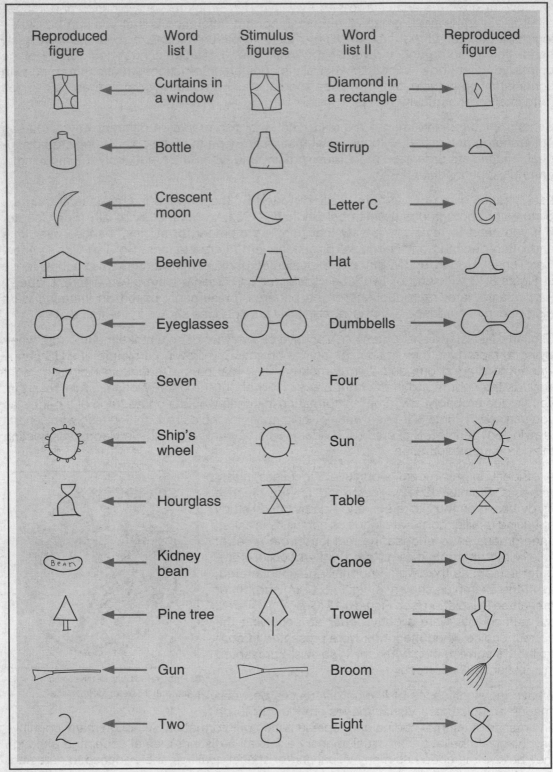

Reproduced figure	Word list I	Stimulus figures	Word list II	Reproduced figure
	← Curtains in a window		Diamond in a rectangle →	
	← Bottle		Stirrup →	
	← Crescent moon		Letter C →	
	← Beehive		Hat →	
	← Eyeglasses		Dumbbells →	
	← Seven		Four →	
	← Ship's wheel		Sun →	
	← Hourglass		Table →	
	← Kidney bean		Canoe →	
	← Pine tree		Trowel →	
	← Gun		Broom →	
	← Two		Eight →	

■ Figure 8.13: Materials from the Carmichael et al. (1932) study.

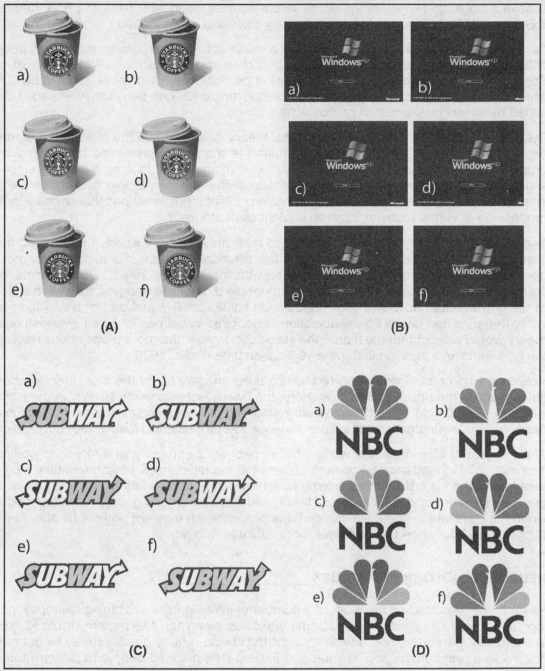

■ Figure 8.14: Corporate logos from Plotnick (2012) study. Go to www.sagepub.in/galotti_CP5e for colored image.

Propositional Theory

A broader criticism of work on imagery is theoretical and is aimed at the very premise behind the field. Proponents of *propositional theory* reject the idea that images serve as a distinct mental code for representing information. Instead, propositional theorists believe a single code, neither visual nor verbal but propositional in nature (J. R. Anderson & Bower, 1973), is used to store and mentally represent all information.

As we saw in Chapter 7, propositions are a means of specifying relationships between different concepts. For example, the idea that New York is a city located to the west of Boston might be represented by the following propositions: CITY (New York); WESTOF (New York, Boston). Propositions can be linked in networks, with two closely related ideas joined by sharing a number of propositions.

Pylyshyn (1973) asserted that propositional theory could explain the results of imagery experiments. His idea was that all information is mentally represented and stored by propositions. Participants in visual imagery experiments might *look* as if they were consulting or manipulating internal visual representations, but they would actually be using internal propositional representations, the same kind of representations that underlie their processing of verbal material, such as sentences or stories.

Two studies by Kosslyn (1976) attempted to test this assertion. Kosslyn first tested the *association strength* between animals and their physical attributes. For instance, for most people "claws" are more strongly associated with "cat" than is "head," although cats, of course, have both. Kosslyn found that when people did *not* use imagery, they were faster to verify that cats had claws (high association value, small visual part of a cat) than to verify that cats had heads (low association value, large visual part of a cat). Propositional theory would predict that the higher the association value, the more propositions relating the two items and thus the faster the verification time (Finke, 1989).

However, when participants reported having used imagery to do the task, their reaction times went in the opposite direction. Here, they were faster to verify visually larger parts with low association values than visually smaller parts with higher association values. Apparently, using imagery results in performance that propositional theory does not predict.

What does it matter in the real world whether people use imagery as a means of coding information? Understanding how and under what circumstances people mentally represent information is crucial to explaining how they carry out a variety of cognitive tasks. If they use different codes for different tasks, and if we can make good predictions about when they use which code, we can perhaps predict when they are likely to be able to do things easily and when they will have more difficulty with a task.

NEUROPSYCHOLOGICAL FINDINGS

Farah (1988) reported on the work of a number of investigators examining neuropsychological aspects of visual imagery. Some work has examined the pattern of blood flow in the brain. Cerebral blood flow is thought to provide a fairly precise measure of brain activity in a particular region. Roland and Friberg (1985) asked people to perform three cognitive tasks while their cerebral blood flows were being monitored. The tasks were mental arithmetic, memory scanning of an auditory stimulus, and visual imagery (visualizing a walk through a familiar neighborhood). The experimenters made sure the tasks were approximately equal in difficulty. They found that each person tested showed massive activation in the parts of the brain important for visual processing of information (mostly in the occipital lobe and other posterior regions) during the imagery task. During the other two tasks, however, there were no such increases in cerebral blood flow to those parts. Farah and her colleagues have replicated these results using other neuropsychological measures, such as event-related potentials (ERPs) measuring electrical activity in the brain (Farah, Péronnet, Gonon, & Giard, 1988).

Other investigators report a wealth of studies showing that the creation of visual images activates those areas of the brain involved in visual processing (Kosslyn & Ochsner, 1994; Miyashita, 1995). These regions are often located in the occipital lobe, that region of the cerebral cortex devoted to visual processing. In one study, for example, Kosslyn, Thompson, Kim, and Alpert (1995) tested 12 volunteers asked to form images of previously memorized line drawings of common objects. They were also asked (in different parts of the testing session) to form their images at different sizes. During the tasks, the cerebral blood flow of the volunteers was monitored using PET scans. Results indicated that all the imagery tasks produced activation in the visual cortex, replicating many previous findings, such as those just described. Of greater interest was the fact that the specific area of the occipital lobe showing maximal activation differed depending on whether the image created was small, medium, or large.

Zatorre, Halpern, Perry, Meyer, and Evans (1996) conducted a study similar in spirit, during which the cerebral blood flow of 12 participants was measured while the participants either (a) saw two words and judged which was longer, (b) saw two words from a song while hearing the song and judged whether a pitch change occurred in the song between the two words, or (c) again saw the two words from the song *without* hearing the song but were still asked to judge whether a pitch change occurred in the song. Tasks (b) and (c) led to similar patterns of cerebral blood flow changes with respect to the control condition, (a). During both Task (b) and Task (c), there was noticeable activity in both hemispheres in the secondary auditory cortex, which is in the temporal lobes. Imagining the songs led to somewhat weaker activation than did actually hearing the songs.

O'Craven and Kanwisher (2000) showed additionally in an fMRI study that when people form a mental image of faces, a different area of the brain becomes activated than when they imagine a place. When participants formed images of faces, the *fusiform face area* of the brain was activated—the same area that becomes activated when subjects view photographs of faces. (The fusiform face area is located in the occipital-temporal areas.) Conversely, when participants formed a mental image of a place, the *parohippocampal place area* of the brain (located in the ventromedial area) was active—just as it is when people view photographs of complex scenes.

How can neuropsychological findings bear on the controversies in the literature on visual imagery? Neuropsychological work by Farah (1985) is particularly effective in addressing the issues of demand characteristics. Farah argued that the data from her laboratory, showing that visual imagery involves activation of the same parts of the brain used in vision, are not susceptible to a demand characteristics explanation unless certain questionable assumptions are made:

> A tacit knowledge account of the electrophysiological and blood flow data, implicating the use of cortical visual areas during visual imagery activity, would need to include the following two assumptions: (a) that subjects know what parts of their brains are normally active during vision and (b) that subjects can voluntarily alter their brain electrical activity, or modulate or increase regional blood flow to specific areas of their brains. (1988, p. 314)

Kosslyn et al. (1995) argue that their data are also evidence against the propositional account of visual images. The fact that visual processing areas become active when visual images are formed makes a strong case for the proposal that images are processed visually and/or spatially and that the findings from purely cognitive tasks are not simply produced by people's tacit theories of how imaginal processing ought to function.

SPATIAL COGNITION

The study of visual imagery can be construed as part of a broader picture: **spatial cognition** or how people represent and navigate in and through space (Montello, 2005). That is, how do we acquire, store, and use mental representations of spatial entities, and use them to get from point A to point B? One example of a spatial entity might be a "cognitive map"—a mental depiction of some part of our environment, presumably showing major landmarks and spatial relationships among them.

For example, right where you are sitting (or standing, or lying down), point in the direction of the building in which your cognitive psychology class is held. To do this, presumably you call upon some stored knowledge of the relationship between your current location and the specified location. Opinions vary as to how maplike a cognitive map really is. (You might note a similarity here to the debate over how picturelike a visual image is.) In any case, most agree that cognitive maps are mental constructs people use to navigate spatially through an environment, especially one that is too large to be immediately perceived (Kitchin, 1994).

Barbara Tversky (2005) notes that in the realm of spatial cognition, there are really a number of different kinds of spaces to be distinguished. The way people think about space depends on which kind of space is under consideration. Each kind of space seems to have different attributes and organization.

The first kind of space is the **space of the body**. This space includes knowing where the different parts of one's body are located at any given moment (such as knowing that my right foot currently rests flat against the floor but my left foot is wrapped around the bottom of my desk chair); knowing what other objects different body parts are interacting with (my fingers with the keyboard; my derriere with the seat of the chair); as well as feeling internal sensations (my stuffy sinuses, the slight chill from my underheated office). I use my knowledge of the space of the body to direct different parts of my body spatially—as I reach for something, duck to avoid something, or walk or run toward something.

The second kind of space is the **space around the body**. This space refers to the area immediately around you: the room you are in, say, or the region in which you can easily perceive and act on objects. Tversky's work suggests that people localize objects in this space along three axes that are extensions of the body. One axis is the front–back axis, another is the up–down axis, and the third is the left–right axis. Studies by Tversky and colleagues had people imagine being in a particular space and then locating an imaginary object in that space. People heard narratives describing them standing, say, in a hotel lobby or a museum, with objects on all six sides of their body (front, back, at the head, at the feet, to the right, to the left). Next they were asked to imagine themselves facing a different direction and then to locate objects while facing this new direction. Times to "retrieve" objects at the head and feet were consistently fastest, and times to retrieve objects along the left–right axis were consistently slowest (Tversky, 2005).

The **space of navigation** refers to larger spaces—ones we walk through, explore, and travel to and through. In Tversky's (2005) words:

> Constituents of the space of navigation include places, which may be buildings or parks or piazzas or rivers or mountains, as well as countries or planets or stars, on yet larger scales. Places are interrelated in terms of paths or directions in a reference frame. The space of navigation is too large to perceive from one place so it must be integrated from different pieces of information that are not immediately comparable. Like the space around the body, it can be acquired from descriptions and from diagrams, notably maps, as well as from direct experience. One remarkable feature of the human mind is the ability to conceive of spaces that are too large to be perceived from one place as integral wholes. In order to conceive of spaces of navigation as wholes, we need to paste, link, join, superimpose, or otherwise integrate separate pieces of information. (p. 9)

When we give directions to someone, we are dealing with the space of navigation. Whether we adopt a "route" perspective and give those directions in terms of landmarks ("go straight two blocks till you come to the gas station, then take a right and go until you see the red barn, then turn left") or a "survey" perspective and give directions in terms of a bird's-eye view ("Watson dorm is two blocks east of the chapel and one block southeast of Goodsell Observatory"), we communicate some spatial information. However, the representations we form within the space of navigation aren't always accurate or complete. Thus, Tversky (2005) prefers the term *cognitive collage* to the term *cognitive map.* Cognitive collages are subject to systematic errors and distortions, as we saw earlier with people's inaccurate beliefs about whether Seattle or Boston is farther north.

These ideas were instantiated in a senior honors thesis conducted by one of my students, Drew Dara-Abrams (2005). Drew created a task in which participants (students at Carleton College) were shown cutout versions of different campus buildings and asked to place each on a map as accurately as possible. Figure 8.15 shows an actual map of the campus with the cutouts correctly placed; Figure 8.16 shows the cutout task as it was presented to research participants.

Results showed that participants were likely to make "neater" maps in the cutout task (Dara-Abrams, 2005). That is, they systematically arranged the cutouts along orthogonal lines, making buildings line up more neatly on lines running north–south and east–west than the buildings are actually arranged. They were also likely to rotate buildings so that they all lined up along vertical or horizontal orientations—that is, to avoid placing the buildings diagonally, even though several of our campus buildings do have a "diagonal" orientation. Such work replicated earlier findings by A. Tversky (1992) on people's memory for maps. For example, people frequently think of South America as directly south of North America, even though it is really more southeast. The twist in Dara-Abrams's thesis is that the space of navigation used by his participants was learned through their actual navigation on the campus, not from a map-learning session.

Some recent work in spatial cognition concerns **spatial updating** (Sargent, Dopkins, Philbeck, & Chichka, 2010; Wang et al., 2006). The idea is that as organisms move through space, they must continually revise their mental representation of where things in the environment are with respect to their current location. Zhang, Mou, and McNamara (2011) give the following illustration:

> For example, suppose you are entering your department's main office and see a colleague who is to your left. You stop and turn left to have a chat. After turning, you need to know that the main office is to the right of you. (p. 419)

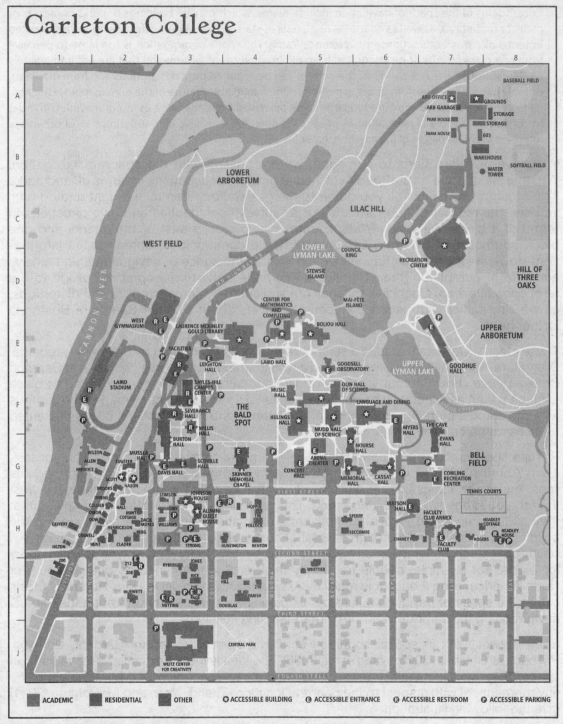

Figure 8.15: Actual map of the Carleton College campus.

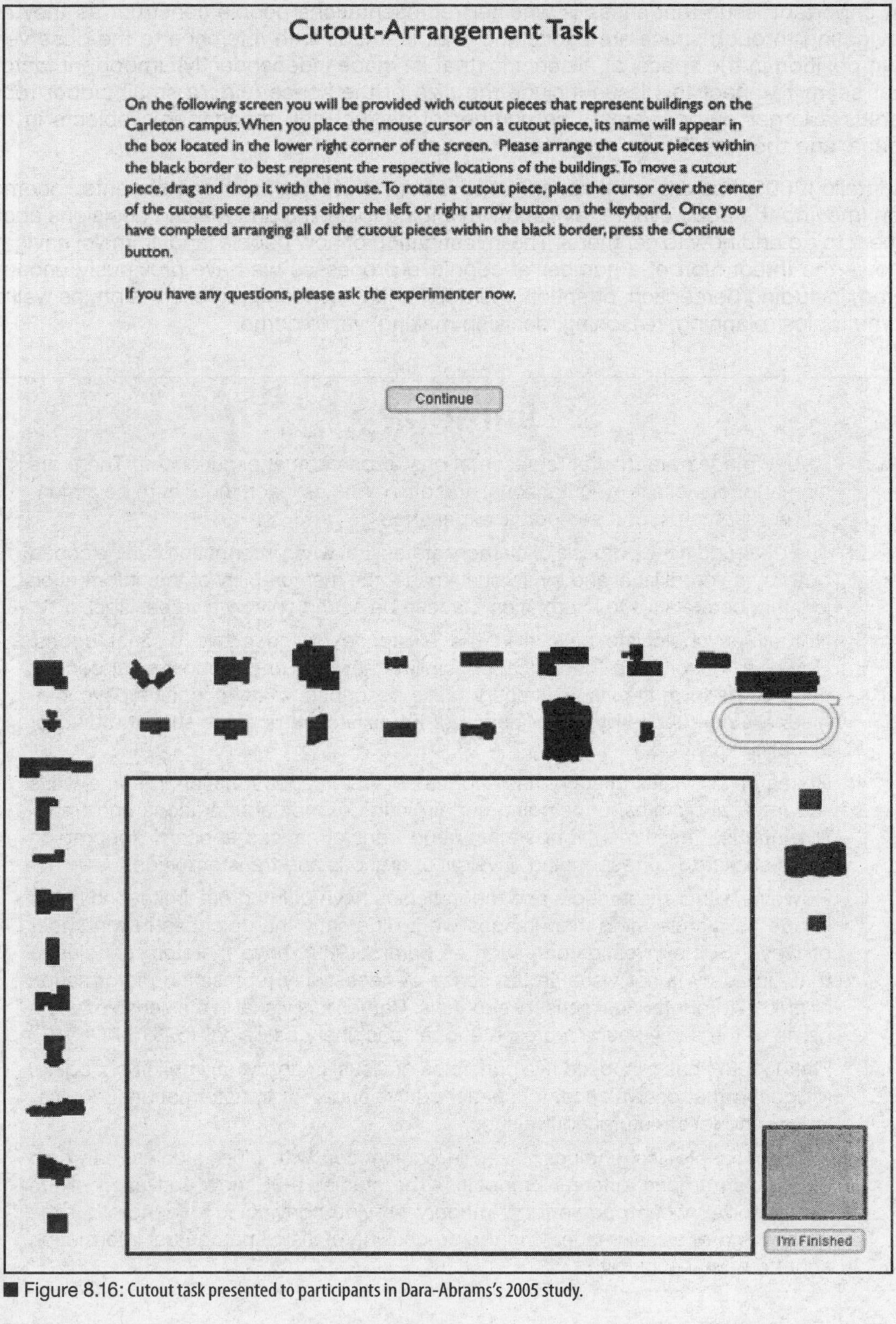

Cutout-Arrangement Task

On the following screen you will be provided with cutout pieces that represent buildings on the Carleton campus. When you place the mouse cursor on a cutout piece, its name will appear in the box located in the lower right corner of the screen. Please arrange the cutout pieces within the black border to best represent the respective locations of the buildings. To move a cutout piece, drag and drop it with the mouse. To rotate a cutout piece, place the cursor over the center of the cutout piece and press either the left or right arrow button on the keyboard. Once you have completed arranging all of the cutout pieces within the black border, press the Continue button.

If you have any questions, please ask the experimenter now.

Continue

I'm Finished

■ Figure 8.16: Cutout task presented to participants in Dara-Abrams's 2005 study.

An important issue that arises is whether representations people construct as they are navigating through space are egocentric (that is, made with reference to the observer's own position in the space) or allocentric (that is, made independently). Important factors that seem to affect this issue include the size of the space (e.g., a small indoor room versus a larger outdoor area), the number of distinct and recognizable objects in the space, and the specific updating task.

Montello (2005) has argued that navigation consists of two major components: locomotion (moving the body over terrain) and wayfinding (planning and making decisions about where to go and how to get there). The investigation of how people (and animals) navigate shows the integration of a number of cognitive processes we have previously encountered, including perception, attention, memory, and knowledge representation, as well as some topics (planning, reasoning, decision making) yet to come.

Summary

1. Visual images are mental representations of perceptual experiences. There are also auditory, olfactory, cutaneous, and other images, each thought to be a mental representation of a perceptual experience.

2. The dual-coding hypothesis of memory states that when information can be coded both by a verbal label and by a visual image, the memorability of that information is enhanced relative to information that can be coded only by a verbal label.

3. Not all psychologists believe in the existence of these two distinct codes. However, despite the theoretical possibility that only one propositional code is used to perform the visual imagery tasks described, many cognitive psychologists are persuaded by the evidence of the existence of some sort of a distinct visual-spatial code.

4. Research on visual imagery has suggested that images function in some ways like internal pictures, undergoing certain kinds of mental operations and transformations. These mental operations and transformations appear to operate in ways similar to corresponding physical operations and transformations.

5. However, other researchers and theoreticians have pointed out limitations in the image-as-picture metaphor. Images work differently than pictures in a number of ways. Some investigators, such as Farah (1988), have therefore concluded that "imagery is not visual in the sense of necessarily representing information acquired through visual sensory channels. Rather, it is visual in the sense of using some of the same neural representational machinery as vision" (p. 315).

6. Finke (1989) has proposed five principles of visual imagery: (a) implicit encoding, (b) perceptual equivalence, (c) spatial equivalence, (d) transformational equivalence, and (e) structural equivalence.

7. Neuropsychological findings, taken in conjunction with older studies, can help distinguish among different proposals. The studies that show activation of the visual cortex when people form imagery provide convincing evidence that the processing of visual images and the processing of visual perceptual information share a neural substrate.

8. Images are necessarily a private mental experience. It is all the more exciting, then, when results from cognitive psychology and neuropsychology converge. Many consider the empirical investigations of imagery a major victory in the larger task of understanding how cognition, a collection of private mental experiences, functions.

9. Visual imagery can be seen as part of a broader topic of spatial cognition. Spatial cognition encompasses the ways in which people acquire, store, and use information about spatial properties to navigate.

Review Questions

1. Describe and contrast the dual-coding hypothesis and the relational-organizational hypothesis and describe experimental means of distinguishing between them.

2. What interpretations have cognitive psychologists performing mental rotation studies (for example, Shepard, Metzler, and Cooper) drawn from their findings? In what ways are such interpretations consistent with those drawn by Kosslyn from his image-scanning experiments?

3. Describe and discuss Finke's five principles of imagery.

4. Pylyshyn asserted that many of the results from visual imagery experiments are attributable to tacit knowledge and demand characteristics. Describe and critique his arguments.

5. What objections did Intons-Peterson raise to some of the findings from visual imagery experiments? In your view, how strong are such objections? Defend your view.

6. In what ways are visual images like pictures? In what ways are they different?

7. Some researchers have used neuropsychological findings to try to resolve some of the controversies in the imagery field. How decisive are such findings? Explain.

8. Describe Tversky's proposal for different "spaces" of which people have knowledge. Why is it important to distinguish among them?

Key Terms

demand characteristic

dual-coding hypothesis

experimenter expectancy effect

heuristic

imaginal scanning

implicit encoding

mental rotation

relational-organizational hypothesis

space around the body

space of navigation

space of the body

spatial cognition

spatial updating

tacit knowledge

visual image

CHAPTER 9

LANGUAGE

CHAPTER OUTLINE

The Structure of Language
Phonology
Syntax
Semantics
Pragmatics
Language Comprehension and Production
Speech Perception
Speech Errors in Production
Sentence Comprehension
Comprehending Text Passages
Story Grammars
Gricean Maxims of Conversation
Language and Cognition
The Modularity Hypothesis
The Whorfian Hypothesis
Neuropsychological Views and Evidence

Right now, as you read this sentence, you are engaged in the process of language comprehension. As I write this sentence, I am engaged in language production. Probably neither of us finds our behavior remarkable. We comprehend and produce language all day long—when we read or speak, when we listen to dialogue or conversations, when we struggle to write a term paper (or a textbook chapter), or even when we compose the most mundane pieces of prose ("Gone to the library—meet me at 5 at the car"). In short, we take our language abilities for granted.

Evidence is abundant, however, that language use and abilities are not so straightforward. Researchers studying artificial intelligence have found it extremely difficult to build computer systems that can understand language (spoken or written) as easily as a 4-year-old child can. Parents of toddlers can attest that although language acquisition is rapid, a person takes several years to become proficient. Many high school and college students come to appreciate fully the complexities of language only when they try to master a second one.

Language use is intimately connected to cognition. Much of the information we receive comes from spoken or written (or signed) language; we use language to ask questions, explain conclusions, clarify problems, and so on (Damian, 2011; Fox, 2007; Sandler & Lillo-Martin, 2006). Like perception or memory, then, language seems to be a crucial cognitive ability so easily used that we typically overlook its complexity.

In this chapter, we will first look at the structural elements of a language: the pieces or aspects that go into the elaborated, rule-governed, and creative communication systems we recognize as different human languages. We will then examine models of language comprehension and production: how we understand and create spoken discourse and written material. Finally, we will consider the relationship between language and other cognitive processes.

Continuing themes from earlier chapters, we will see that some language processes are bottom-up, or driven by incoming data, whereas others are top-down, or driven by the listener's or speaker's expectations. Some language processing appears automatic, carried out without awareness or intention. Other language processing, of course, is performed intentionally and with effort. Thus, processing language is very clearly constrained by other cognitive processes we have studied—perception, attention, and memory, in particular. At the same time, language is used in cognitive processes described in later chapters—thinking, planning, reasoning, and making decisions.

It is important to define language precisely and, in particular, to distinguish between *language* and *communication*. Although language is often used as a communication system, there are other communication systems that do not form true languages. Many bees, for example, use elaborate dances to tell other bees about a newfound source of food. Although this dance communicates where the food is, it can only communicate that kind of message—the dance can't inform the bees about an interesting sight to see along the way to the food source. Birds have songs and calls to broadcast territorial boundaries and to attract mates (Demers, 1988). But again, these communication systems can send only very specific messages. How do these systems of communication differ from language? To decide, we must first define a language.

A natural language has two necessary characteristics: It is *regular* (governed by a system of rules, called a **grammar**), and it is *productive,* meaning that infinite combinations of things can be expressed in it. Other characteristics of human languages include *arbitrariness* (the lack of a necessary resemblance between a word or sentence and what it refers to) and *discreteness* (the system can be subdivided into recognizable parts—for example, sentences into words, words into sounds; see Demers, 1988, or Hockett, 1960).

Using these criteria, we can conclude that bees do not have a language, because the physical motions in the dance carry information about the nectar source (lack of arbitrariness). For instance, the direction of the food source is indicated quite literally by the direction of the bee's dance, and the distance is indicated in the dance by the rate at which the bee wiggles (Harley, 1995). Further, the dances are restricted to communicating about food sources, thus failing on the grounds of productivity. Bird songs and calls also cannot be classified as languages, primarily on the grounds of productivity, because the songs and calls communicate only about certain topics (mostly mates, predators, and territories;

see Demers, 1988). These illustrations help clarify the relationship between language and communication systems: All human languages are communication systems, but not all communication systems have the prerequisites to be classified as natural languages.

Investigators have studied animal communication during various endeavors, such as play or tool use (Bekoff & Allen, 2002; Hauser, 2000), and many others have attempted specifically to teach various language and communication systems to chimpanzees (B. T. Gardner & Gardner, 1971; Premack, 1976; Savage-Rumbaugh, McDonald, Sevcik, Hopkins, & Rubert, 1986; Terrace, 1979). Some investigators have taught their participants to use sign language; others have relied on systems of plastic tokens or geometric symbols. Most agree that chimpanzees can be taught to use symbols or signs to make requests or label objects (for example, "Kanzi chase Sue," "Me more eat," or "Orange juice"). A study by Sue Savage-Rumbaugh et al. suggests that pygmy chimpanzees can even learn to spontaneously use symbols to communicate, learn to use symbols simply by watching others (people or chimpanzees) use them, and learn to understand spoken English words.

Despite these impressive findings, most researchers would agree that substantial differences exist between the language that even the brightest and most linguistically sophisticated chimpanzees have acquired to date and the language of most 3-year-old children. Most would agree, too, that although chimpanzees can acquire many vocabulary items and some rudimentary language structure, their communication system still falls far short of any known human language. To understand why, we need to review the structure of human language in detail.

THE STRUCTURE OF LANGUAGE

As with any complex ability, language comprises a number of systems working together. I will illustrate some of the ways in which the systems work together through the example of conversation. I use a conversation as an example because it is considered a basic setting for language and one that is common to all people, even the estimated one sixth of the world's population who lack the literacy necessary for reading and writing (H. H. Clark & Van Der Wege, 2002).

When you have a conversation, you first have to listen to and perceive the sounds the speaker directs at you. Different languages have different sounds (called **phonemes**). The study of the ways in which phonemes can be combined in any given language constitutes the study of *phonology*. Next you have to put the sounds together in some coherent way, identifying the meaningful units of language, an aspect known as *morphology*. Word endings, prefixes, tense markers, and the like are critical parts of each sentence. Some of the **morphemes** (smallest meaningful units of language) are words, and you also need to identify these and to determine the role each word plays in a sentence. To do so, you need to determine the **syntax**, or structure, of each sentence. Figure 9.1 illustrates the different "levels" of language a simple sentence can be broken into. We will come back to the topic of sentence structure very shortly.

A syntactically correct sentence does not by itself make for a good conversation. The sentence must also mean something to the listener. **Semantics** is the branch of linguistics and psycholinguistics devoted to the study of meaning. Finally, for the conversation to work, there must be some flow or give-and-take. Listeners must pay attention and make

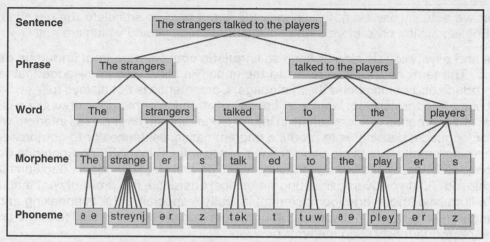

Figure 9.1: An analysis of a simple English sentence. As this example shows, verbal language has a hierarchical structure. At the base of the hierarchy are the phonemes, which are units of vocal sound that do not, in themselves, have meaning. The smallest units of meaning in a language are morphemes, which include not only root words but also such meaning-carrying units as the past-tense suffix -*ed* and the plural -*s*. Complex rules of syntax govern how the words constructed from morphemes may be combined into phrases and phrases into meaningful statements, or sentences.

certain assumptions, and speakers must craft their contributions in ways that will make the listener's job feasible. This aspect of language, **pragmatics**, will conclude our discussion of the structure of language. Keep in mind throughout that although the various aspects of language will be discussed separately, in actual conversation they must work together.

We will repeatedly encounter the idea of different linguistic rules (such as phonological rules or syntactic rules) in this section. These rules make up the grammar of the language and, taken together, define the way a language works. It is important to note that linguists and psychologists use the term *grammar* in a very restricted sense, meaning "the set of rules for a language." In particular, *grammatical* in this context has nothing to do with the "rules" of "good English" such as "Don't use *ain't*" or "Use end punctuation at the end of a complete statement." To a linguist or a psycholinguist, the sentence "I ain't going to happily do it" is perfectly meaningful and "legal"—that is, it follows the "rules" of English that native speakers observe—and is therefore grammatical. (You understand it perfectly well, right?) Here *grammar* refers not to polite ways of speaking but to ways of speaking that form intelligible phrases or utterances recognizable as examples of language that a native speaker of the language might produce.

Linguists and psychologists distinguish between people's explicit and implicit knowledge of linguistic rules. It is doubtful, for instance, that most of us could state with precision or accuracy just what the rules for English syntax are. (If it were easy, many linguists would be out of a job!) Still, most of us can easily and almost immediately detect violations of the rules—for example, syntactically ill-formed sentences such as "Ran the dog street down cat after yellow the very the." Moreover, not only would we recognize the example as ungrammatical, but we would never produce such gross violations (although we frequently produce sentences with minor grammatical violations). Our knowledge of the rules is therefore not explicit (we cannot articulate what all the rules are, nor are we consciously aware of all of them) but implicit (whatever the rules are, we somehow follow them). We can often articulate the so-called *prescriptive* rules (such as "Don't say *ain't*"), which tell us how we *should* talk or write, even though we may violate them (for instance, whenever we actually say *ain't*). In contrast, we find it hard to articulate the *descriptive* rules of English, which characterize which sentences are legal and which are not.

Linguists and psychologists also distinguish **linguistic competence** from **linguistic performance**. The term *competence* refers to the underlying linguistic knowledge that lets people produce and comprehend their language. Competence is not always fully evident in actual use or performance of language. Lapses of attention or memory, nervousness or tiredness, environmental changes, shifts in interest, and random error can all interfere with our use of language, causing us to produce ungrammatical sentences or to comprehend a sentence incorrectly. Linguistic performance would reflect linguistic competence only under completely ideal conditions (Chomsky, 1965). In real life, such ideal conditions are never achieved. So if you overhear an ungrammatical utterance, it is probably not that the speaker's linguistic knowledge (competence) is faulty (especially if he is speaking in his native language) but rather that various other factors and pressures in his life at the time he spoke (performance) caused the error or errors.

PHONOLOGY

To me, French sounds musical and German sounds harsh. No doubt, you too would describe various languages with various adjectives. Part of what distinguishes languages is their idiosyncratic sounds. Here we will consider the sounds of language (in our case, English) and how they are combined. We will draw on findings from two disciplines: **phonetics**, the study of speech sounds and how they are produced, and **phonology**, the study of the systematic ways in which speech sounds are combined and altered in language.

The English language has about 40 phonetic segments (sometimes called *phones*). Although a language may have a large number of phones, only certain ones are "meaningful" to it. Linguists use the term *phoneme* to refer to the smallest unit of sound that makes a meaningful difference in a given language. So if one phoneme in a word is exchanged for another, the word itself is changed. Thus, if the phoneme \d\ is replaced with the phoneme \t\, the word *duck* becomes *tuck*.

In English, we distinguish between the \l\ and the \r\ sound; other languages, such as the Cantonese dialect of Chinese, do not. Some of the dialect jokes about a Chinese speaker's saying "flied lice" instead of "fried rice" are based on the fact that a native speaker of Cantonese dialect simply wouldn't hear the difference (Fromkin & Rodman, 1974). Of course, other languages make sound distinctions that English doesn't, and native English speakers learning those languages can make errors that are just as ridiculed by the native speakers. Table 9.1 presents a list of English phonemes.

Linguists and phoneticians distinguish between consonants and vowels. Vowels work without obstructing the airflow, simply depending on the shape and position of the tongue and lips (Halle,

■ Table 9.1: Examples of Some English-Language Phonemes

Symbol	Examples
p	pat, apple
b	bat, amble
d	dip, loved
g	guard, ogre
f	fat, philosophy
s	sap, pass, peace
z	zip, pads, xylophone
y	you, bay, feud
w	witch, queen
l	leaf, palace
ē	beet, beat, believe
e	ate, bait, eight
i	bit, injury
u	boot, two, through
U	put, foot, could
oy	boy, doily
ay	bite, sight, island
š	shoe, mush, deduction

SOURCE: Adapted from Moates and Schumacher (1980).

1990). Try articulating vowel sounds and observe how your mouth changes configurations as you do.

Consonants are more complicated. In general, they are phonemes made by closing, or at least almost closing, part of the mouth. They differ first in what linguists call "place of articulation," meaning where the obstruction of the airflow occurs. For example, the \b\ and \p\ sounds are made by closing the lips, and the \s\ and \z\ sounds are made by placing the tongue against the hard palate of the roof of the mouth, just behind the ridge of gums. Consonants differ also in "manner of articulation," the mechanics of how the airflow is obstructed. The \m\ sound, for example, is made by closing the mouth while opening the nasal cavity; the \f\ sound is made through an obstruction of the airflow that produces a hissing sound. A third distinction between groups of consonants is known as *voicing.* Compare the \s\ in the syllable "sa" with the \z\ in "za." The \s\ does not require the vocal cords to be vibrated as the \z\ does; therefore, the \z\ is said to be voiced and the \s\ unvoiced.

Features of phonemes, such as those just reviewed, are involved in certain *phonological rules* that govern the ways in which phonemes can be combined. For example, if two "true" consonants (that is, all the consonants except \h\, \w\, \y\, \r\, or \l\ plus certain other sounds, such as the \th\ in *thy,* the \th\ in *thigh,* and the \ch\ in *chip*) are at the beginning of an English word, then the first must be an \s\ (H. H. Clark & Clark, 1977). This rule prevents word strings such as *dtop* or *mpeech* from being "legal" words in our language (although they may be so in other languages), whereas *stop* and *speech* are. These phonological rules also explain how to pronounce new words and how to pronounce prefixes and suffixes to words, such as plural or past-tense endings. To illustrate, the way to form a plural for an English word depends on the phoneme with which the singular form of the word ends. From work in phonetics, we can state the following rule (after Halle, 1990):

If the word ends with . . .	The plural ending of the word is . . .	Examples
\s z c j\	\z\	places, porches, cabbages
\p t k f\	\s\	lips, lists, telegraphs
Anything else	\z\	clubs, herds, phonemes

Different languages have different phonological rules; hence, there are two answers to the question, Why do different languages sound different? One answer is that they contain different sounds (phonemes). A second answer is that they have different rules for combining those sounds (phonology).

SYNTAX

The term *syntax* refers to the arrangement of words within sentences or, more broadly, to the *structure* of sentences—their parts and the way the parts are put together. Syntactic rules, similar to phonological rules, govern the ways in which different words or larger phrases can be combined to form "legal" sentences in the language. Thus, sentences such as "The book fell off the table" are clearly acceptable to English speakers, and word strings such as "Chair the on sits man" are not. Syntactic rules should meet two requirements: They should be able to describe every "legal" sentence, and they should never be able to describe an "illegal" sentence (Chomsky, 1957).

What does it mean to say that sentences have structure? Consider the following sentence:

(1) The student will carry the shiny laptop.

If you were to try to divide the words of this sentence into groups (linguists call these *constituents*), you might proceed as follows. Certainly the word *student* goes with the word *the.* Similarly, *shiny* appears to modify *laptop,* and *the* forms another constituent with *shiny laptop. Carry* could also form a constituent with *the shiny laptop,* and *will* seems to modify this larger grouping. Notice that there are various levels of groupings or constituents, as depicted in Figure 9.2(A). This kind of diagram is called a *tree diagram,* and the small gray circles, called *nodes,* depict the various constituents of the

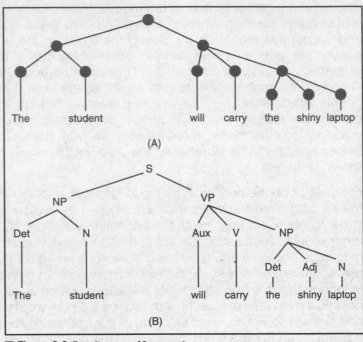

■ Figure 9.2: Tree diagrams of Sentence 1.

sentence. Notice also that each word is a constituent by itself but that there are higher-level constituents as well, made out of different word groupings. So the word *laptop* is a member of four constituents: [laptop], [the shiny laptop], [carry the shiny laptop], and [The student will carry the shiny laptop].

Figure 9.2(B) shows a similar diagram of the sentence, but here labels that tell the type, or category, of each constituent have replaced the gray dots. At the very bottom level in the tree, you see labels for familiar terms: V for verb, N for noun, Adj for adjective, and so forth. The labels give us some idea of the role that each word plays in the sentence and allow us to see that, generally speaking, if we replace a noun with another noun, we will still have a syntactically grammatical sentence. So, substituting *shoe* for *laptop* gives us "The student will carry the shiny shoe." Higher up in the tree, other labels categorize the larger constituents. Thus, the constituents "the student" and "the shiny laptop" are both noun phrases (NP). The labeling is meant to capture our intuition that these constituents are similar to other constituents, such as "the angry firefighter," "her grandfather's birthday," or "my first tooth." Figure 9.2(B) is called a *labeled tree diagram,* and it depicts what is called the *categorical constituent structure* of the sentence.

Notice that one NP can be substituted for another in a sentence, yielding a sentence that is semantically anomalous (its meaning, if any, is hard to determine) but syntactically grammatical. So we could substitute the NP "my first tooth" for "the student" in Sentence 1 and get "My first tooth will carry the shiny laptop," an odd but certainly "legal" sentence.

What's the point of such diagrams? For one thing, they help explain why certain kinds of changes can be made in a sentence and others can't. One illustration comes from a change called *preposing*—taking a certain part of a sentence and moving it to the front, usually for emphasis (Radford, 1988). In the following examples, the italicized material has been preposed:

(2) *My naughty dog,* I'm mad at.

(3) *That inflated price,* I will not pay.

(4) *Up the mountain,* the hikers climbed furiously.

Preposing works (results in a grammatical or legal sentence) only when certain kinds of whole phrases or constituents are moved to the front. Thus, it isn't legal to say, "Naughty dog, I'm mad at my," "Price, I will not pay that inflated," or "Mountain, the hikers climbed furiously up the." Tree diagrams such as the ones in Figure 9.2 provide answers to which parts of the sentence form constituents and are therefore candidates for preposing.

It is interesting that this kind of analysis of sentences explains an apparent paradox. The following four sentences are all "legal":

(5) Kimmie rang up Emily.

(6) Timothy stood up his job interviewer.

(7) Carol looked up the definition.

(8) Isaac ran up the street.

Preposing the phrase "up the street" in Sentence 8 results in a legal sentence:

(8a) Up the street, Isaac ran.

But none of the other sentences can undergo preposing in this way, as the following illegal sentences (marked with asterisks) show:

(5a) *Up Emily, Kimmie rang.

(6a) *Up his job interviewer, Timothy stood.

(7a) *Up the definition, Carol looked.

Figure 9.3 provides tree diagrams of Sentences 5 through 8 and shows that in Sentences 5 through 7, the word *up* is part of the constituent involving the verb and hence must stay with the verb in the sentence. However, in Sentence 8, the word *up* is a part of the constituent "up the mountain," so it is perfectly acceptable to prepose it as long as the entire constituent gets moved.

How can we concisely summarize this discussion of what can and can't be legally preposed? Linguists do so by formulating constraints on syntactic rules like this: Only constituents labeled as being whole phrases—for example, nodes marked as NP or VP (verb phrase)—can undergo movement from one position in a sentence to another. Such rules describe the ways in which parts of sentences are formed and work together.

Various linguists have proposed a variety of syntactic rules, as well as a variety of *kinds* of syntactic rules. For example, Chomsky (1965) proposed one set of rules, called *phrase structure rules,* that function to generate the structures depicted in tree diagrams such as Figures 9.2 and 9.3. These rules, sometimes called *rewrite rules,* describe the ways in which certain symbols can be rewritten as other symbols. The rule S → NP VP says that a symbol S (which stands for "sentence") consists of different constituents and can be rewritten as the symbol NP (the symbol for the constituent "noun phrase") followed by the symbol VP (the symbol for the constituent "verb phrase"). The point is that phrase structure rules allow certain symbols to be rewritten as other symbols. To replace a symbol with an actual word in the English language (for example, N → poodle) requires a different type of syntactic rule, a *lexical-insertion rule,* which allows the insertion of words (linguists call these *lexical items*) into the structures generated by the phrase structure rules.

Another type of syntactic rule is a *transformational rule.* Transformational rules turn structures such as those depicted in tree diagrams into other structures. Preposing phrasal constituents, for example, might be allowed through a transformational rule. Even a brief explanation of these or other syntactic rules, or other proposals for what the rules could be, would take us far afield (interested readers are referred to an introductory

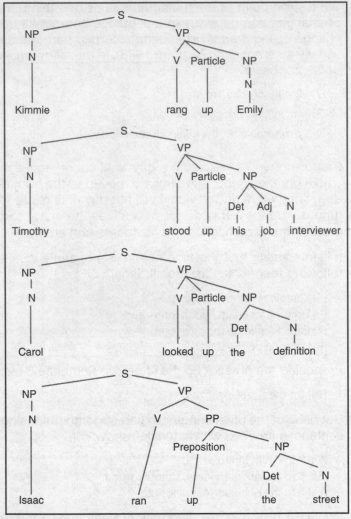

■ Figure 9.3: Tree diagram of Sentences 5 through 8.

linguistics course or to Cowper, 1992). The point here is to show that just as the sounds of a language are organized and rule governed in the way they are combined, so too are phrases and sentences.

Again, rules of syntax, like rules of phonology, are probably not rules you are consciously aware of. However, the evidence accumulated by linguists and psycholinguists strongly suggests that you have some access to these rules, because your language behavior indicates a great deal of compliance with them and your judgments of grammaticality (under reasonable conditions) are remarkably consistent.

SEMANTICS

Semantics, the study of meaning, also plays an important role in our language use. After all, the sounds we produce are meant to communicate ideas, and for communication to take place, the listener (or audience) must somehow receive the speaker's (or sender's) meaning. The task of creating a complete theory of meaning is daunting and currently unfinished. Many of these topics relate to ones we covered in Chapter 7, so what we will cover here will be theories of meaning narrowly defined.

Theories of meaning have to explain several things, at a minimum (Bierwisch, 1970):

- *Anomaly* (Why can't one really say things like "Coffee ice cream can take dictation"?)
- *Self-contradiction* (Why is it contradictory to say, "My dog is not an animal"?)
- *Ambiguity* (Why isn't it clear where I intend to go in "I need to go to the bank"—to a financial institution or to the side of a river?)
- *Synonymy* (Why does "The rabbit is not old enough" mean the same thing as "The rabbit is too young"?)
- *Entailment* (Why does "Pat is my uncle" mean that Pat is male?)

Such theories should also explain how we use word meanings to process whole sentences and discourses. Much of cognitive psychologists' interest in semantics has to do with how knowledge is organized and stored and theories of how people form concepts and categorize things accordingly, topics we discussed in Chapter 7.

Let's examine how semantics enters into our understanding of a sentence. Consider the sentence "Sara exchanged a dress for a suit." Generally, we interpret this to mean that Sara took her dress somewhere (most likely, to the store where she had bought it) and gave it to someone (probably a salesperson), and in return that person gave Sara a suit. Exchanging thus seems to have something to do with two people, each giving something to the other, although *mutual giving* and *exchanging* are not defined as precisely the same thing (G. A. Miller & Johnson-Laird, 1976). What exactly does *exchanging* mean? Miller and Johnson-Laird (p. 577) offered the following definition: Someone, X, "exchanges" something, w, for something, z, with someone, Y, if two conditions are met: (1) X gives w to Y and (2) this obligates Y to give z to X. Notice that this analysis explains why exchanging and mutual giving are similar but not identical: Exchanging creates an *obligation* for Y to give something back to X, but Y might renege on the deal; in mutual giving, X and Y must give something to each other.

For listeners to figure out the meaning of a sentence, they need to pay attention to more than just the meanings of individual words. Syntax also gives clues as to what a sentence means. Were this not the case, the following two sentences, because they make use of the same words, would mean exactly the same thing:

(9)   The professor failed the student.
(10) The student failed the professor.

Clearly, the meaning of *failed* in the two sentences is not identical. Something in the way words are arranged, then, must cue the listener or reader about who the actor of the sentence is, what the action is, and to whom or what the action is done.

The study of semantics also involves the study of *truth conditions* of sentences and of the relationships between sentences. As the term itself suggests, truth conditions are simply the circumstances that make something true. Refer to our earlier example sentence, "Sara exchanged a dress for a suit." Under what circumstances would this sentence be true? First of all, Sara has to be the person either actually carrying out the exchange or causing the exchange to happen (perhaps she sends Jane, her personal assistant, to the store). Second, Sara must, at the beginning of the transaction, have a dress to give and must give it to someone who gives her back a suit. If Sara gets back a hat instead of a suit or gives a skirt rather than a dress, then the sentence is false. The point here is that our understanding of the meaning of this sentence requires (a) an understanding of the meaning of each word in the sentence, (b) an understanding of the syntax of the sentence, and (c) an understanding of the truth conditions of the sentence.

PRAGMATICS

To communicate verbally with another speaker of the English language, you must produce utterances that follow rules of phonology, syntax, and semantics. In addition, a fourth set of rules must be honored if you want to communicate successfully. Known as *pragmatics*, these rules are the social rules of language; they include certain etiquette conventions, such as not interrupting another speaker and beginning conversations with certain conventional greetings (such as "Hi. How are you?").

Searle (1979) pointed out that in listening to another person, we must understand not only the sounds, words, and structure of the utterances but also the kinds of utterances. Different kinds of utterances demand different responses from us. For instance, in *assertives* the speaker asserts a belief in some proposition—for example, "It's hot in here," or "I'm a Libra." These require little overt response from the listener, who is assumed to add the information asserted by the speaker into her or his own model of the world. *Directives*, another kind of speech act, are instructions from the speaker to the listener—for example, "Close the door," or "Don't believe everything you hear." *Commissives* are utterances that commit the speaker to some later action—for example, "I promise to clean my room," or "I guarantee this will work." *Expressives* describe psychological states of the speaker—for example, "I apologize for eating the last piece of pie," or "I thank you for the favor you did for me." Finally, *declarations* are speech acts in which the utterance is itself the action. Examples include "I now pronounce you husband and wife," or "You're fired." According to Searle's *speech act theory*, part of our job as listeners is to figure out which of the five types a particular utterance is and to respond appropriately.

Moreover, there are usually a number of distinct ways of stating or asking something. Imagine, for instance, that you are sitting in a room and a cold breeze is blowing through an open window. You want the window closed, but for one reason or another you do not wish to close it yourself. What could you say to someone else to get him or her to close the window? Here are a few possibilities (all of which would be classified as directives in Searle's 1979 classification): (a) "Close the window," (b) "Could you close the window, please?" (c) "Hey, would you mind if we closed the window?" (d) "I'm getting cold," or (e) "Gee, there's quite a breeze today, isn't there?" How are you to choose among these (or other) options?

Note that in this example, how you choose to make your request will no doubt depend on whom you are talking to and where the conversation takes place (say, to your child in your house versus to your host in his house). Option (e), for instance, might be too subtle to communicate your intention if you were speaking to a preschooler (who might take it as a general and rather uninteresting comment on the weather). However, (a) might communicate clearly but mark you as an overbearing and rude guest if you were to say this to your host while dining at his house.

Gibbs (1986) studied the ways in which adults choose to frame requests. His data suggest that speakers anticipate the potential obstacles their listeners face in fulfilling a request and formulate it accordingly. For instance, imagine you are working in the library when your pen runs out of ink. You don't have a backup, so you look around for someone from whom to borrow a pen. You don't know the student at the next table, and she is engrossed, but she is the only person in sight and has two extra pens next to her books and papers. Would you say (a) "I need a pen," (b) "Please give me a pen," (c) "Excuse me, would you mind lending me a pen?" or (d) "Do you have an extra pen?" Gibbs's participants, given similar scenarios, chose (c), responding to the biggest perceived obstacle of imposing on a stranger. A not-so-good choice if you could see the extra pens would be (d), but it might be appropriate if you didn't know whether the student had extra pens with her.

Pragmatic understanding is something often exploited by advertising as well. Consider a television commercial for a new product, Eradicold pills. The video shows athletic, healthy-looking people vigorously skiing, sledding, skating, and generally wending their way through a snow-covered winter wonderland. The voice-over says, "Aren't you tired of sniffles and runny noses all winter? Tired of always feeling less than your best? Get through a whole winter without colds. Take Eradicold pills as directed." Odds are, you would draw the inference that taking Eradicold as directed would cause you to evade colds all winter. But the ad doesn't directly say that. Advertisers rely on the fact that the way they word ads implies causal relationships that may or may not be true. Harris (1977), who studied comprehension of such ads, showed that people are not very good at distinguishing between what an ad directly states and what it only implies.

So far, we've seen that our language is structured and rule governed at several different but interacting levels. Although much more can be said about each of these levels (each of which gives rise to several linguistics courses), we need to turn our attention to how the structure of language directs and is influenced by other kinds of cognitive processing. We'll look first at how speakers of a language process incoming utterances or written sentences to comprehend their meaning.

LANGUAGE COMPREHENSION AND PRODUCTION

Like other information, language must be transformed from raw input into meaningful representations. One of the first stages of this transformation is perceptual. In this section, we'll examine the perception of speech, noticing the special ways in which speech input is initially processed. We will then turn to further stages of processing—in particular, comprehension and the processing of discourse, such as conversations. Finally, we will examine the processing of written language through reading.

SPEECH PERCEPTION

One way we encounter and use language is in the form of speech. Understanding the speech of someone talking to you is usually easy, unless the speech is in a foreign language or the speaker has a very marked speech impediment. We can almost always understand the speech of children, adults, fluent speakers, and those with strong foreign or regional accents. As we will see, this ability is pretty remarkable.

It might seem reasonable to suppose we perceive speech in the way (we think) we perceive written text: one sound at a time, using the pauses between sounds (like the white space between letters) to identify letters and the pauses between words to identify when one word ends and another begins. Unfortunately, this tidy explanation doesn't work. (Actually, evidence suggests we really don't process written text letter by letter, either.)

Joanne Miller (1990) described two fundamental problems in speech perception. First, speech is continuous. Rarely are there pauses around each sound; different sounds from the same word blend into each other. This is shown most clearly in Figure 9.4, which displays a spectrogram of a spoken sentence. A spectrogram is a graphic representation of speech, showing the frequencies of sound, in hertz (cycles per second), along the y-axis, plotted against time on the x-axis. Darker regions in the figure indicate the intensity of each sound at each frequency. Note that the boundaries (white spaces) do not correspond to word or syllable boundaries.

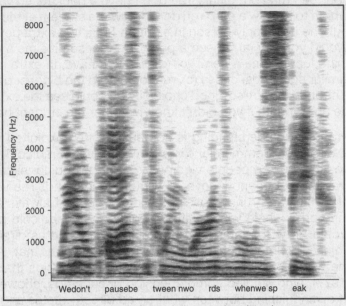

■ Figure 9.4: Spectogram of a person pronouncing the indicated sentence.

Indeed, nothing in the physical stimulus itself indicates where these boundaries are. In other words, when you listen to someone talk, it sounds as if there were pauses between syllables and words, but many of those pauses are illusory!

A second problem in speech perception is that a single phoneme sounds different, depending on context. Although it casually appears as if *dog*, *dig*, *dug*, *deep*, and *do* all began with the same identical sound, this is not the case. Figure 9.5 presents a spectrogram of my pronouncing these five words, and examination of the spectrogram reveals few if any properties present for all five words. Moreover, men and women generally speak with different pitches (women's voices generally have higher pitch, or frequencies); different

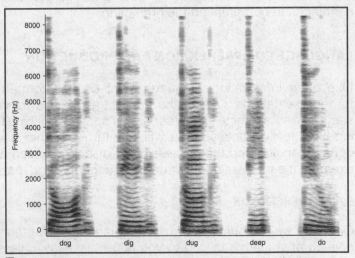

■ Figure 9.5: Spectogram of person proununcing the words *dog, dig, dug, deep, do.*

people have different accents; and speakers talk differently when shouting, coaxing, whispering, or lecturing. Thus, you can realize just how complicated it is to ascertain which phoneme is being produced simply from the physical properties of the acoustic stimulus.

Although we clearly pay careful attention to critical sound distinctions in our language, it isn't just sounds that influence us. A clever study by Massaro and Cohen (1983) demonstrated that we also make use of visual information in the perception of speech. These investigators examined the categorical perception of the stop consonants \b\ and \d\, two sounds that differ only in the place of articulation. Participants heard nine computer-synthesized syllables that ranged in their acoustic properties from a clear "ba" sound to a clear "da" sound. In the "neutral" condition, participants heard the syllables with no visual information. In two other conditions, participants heard the syllables while watching a silent but synchronized videotape of a speaker who was pronouncing either "ba" or "da." One question was whether participants would notice a discrepancy when the auditory information presented was "ba" but the videotaped speaker was saying "da." The participants did not. It is interesting, however, that what the speaker appeared to be saying influenced what was heard: Syllables in the middle of the "ba"–"da" continuum were perceived slightly differently as a function of what the speaker appeared to be saying relative to the perception reported in the neutral condition.

Apparently, then, visual cues affect how sounds are perceived. One might describe this as a kind of *context effect,* first described in Chapter 3. A number of other studies have demonstrated that speech perception is subject to a number of other context effects. Studies by Warren and his colleagues (Warren, 1970; Warren & Obusek, 1971) have demonstrated that in some cases people "hear" phonemes that are not there! In the 1970 study, Warren presented participants with a recording of the sentence "The state governors met with their respective legi*latures convening in the capital city," in which a 120-millisecond portion had been replaced with a coughing sound (indicated by the asterisk). Only 1 of 20 listeners reported detecting a missing sound covered by a cough, and the one who did misreported its location. The other 19 demonstrated *phoneme restoration effect,* so called because listeners apparently "restore" the missing phonemes predicted by other linguistic information during the course of perception.

People are capable of using a great deal of information to "predict" what the correct sound of a missing segment should be. Warren and Warren (1970) demonstrated this by presenting people with one of four sentences. Each was the same recording, with the exception of the final word, which had been spliced on, and each contained a missing segment, as indicated by an asterisk:

(11) It was found that the *eel was on the *axle.*
(12) It was found that the *eel was on the *shoe.*
(13) It was found that the *eel was on the *orange.*
(14) It was found that the *eel was on the *table.*

Depending on the sentence (which provided a context for the missing sound), participants reported hearing *wheel, heel, peel,* or *meal.* Here again, we see that the context directs the listener's perception of a sound—typically without the listener's even being aware of this influence.

Other studies also suggest that people use context to help them perceive speech. One study, by Marslen-Wilson and Welsh (1978), required participants to "shadow" speech— that is, to repeat it aloud. (We encountered shadowing tasks in Chapter 4, as you may recall.) The investigators introduced some distortions into the speech presented to participants (for example, the pseudoword *cigaresh*). They found participants were often likely to restore the distortion to the proper pronunciation *(cigarette)*, especially if the word was highly predictable from the preceding context (for example, "Still, he wanted to smoke a _____"). This result suggests that readers and listeners typically use the context of the previous words in a sentence to predict the next word and can even "mishear" or "misread" that word if it is presented in a distorted fashion. You might note here a parallel to context effects in visual perception, a topic reviewed in Chapter 3.

In the last decade, a couple of companies I use (mostly airline and credit card) have installed voice recognition systems. So, for example, I can call a toll-free number and check my credit card balance, or receive flight departure and arrival information, simply by speaking the numbers of the card or flight clearly into the phone. If speech recognition is so complicated, you might wonder, how come a computer can do it?

The answer parallels that for handwriting recognition systems, as we discussed in Chapter 3. Simply put, the incoming stimuli are limited to a number of discrete categories. The voice recognition systems really only recognize names of different digits. They don't have to figure out which language I'm speaking in (they only work in one or two languages, and I specify that at the beginning of the call), and they expect only certain responses, such as "one" or "two" or "three" but not "zebra" or "melting pot" or "hurricane."

SPEECH ERRORS IN PRODUCTION

So far, we have examined the ways in which we perceive language, specifically spoken sounds, but this is only part of the story regarding the ways in which we process speech. As native speakers of a language, we do more than comprehend and process it—we also produce speech for others to comprehend and process. One kind of study of speech production focuses on *speech errors,* defined as instances in which what the speaker intended to say is quite clear but the speaker makes some substitution or reorders the elements. Some examples of speech errors are the following (adapted from M. F. Garrett, 1990):

(15) Sue keeps food in her *v*esk. (Substitution of "v" for "d")
(16) Keep your cotton-pickin' hands off my weet *s*peas. (Shift of "s")
(17) . . . got a lot of po*ns* and pa*ts* to wash. (Exchange of sounds)
(18) We'll sit around the *song* and sing *fires.* (Exchange of words and morphemes)

Much of the data from speech error studies is observational rather than experimental for the simple reason that it seems to be difficult to control experimentally the ways in which people produce speech. Because of the observational nature of the studies, assertions about causation are problematic. However, one can look at the relative frequency of occurrence of different kinds of errors and make inferences regarding the underlying mechanisms. M. F. Garrett (1990) advocated this approach.

In studying one kind of speech error, word substitution, M. F. Garrett (1988) found two broad classes: errors that showed meaning relations (for example, using *finger* in place of *toe,* or *walk* instead of *run*) and errors that showed form relations (for example, *guest* instead of *goat, mushroom* for *mustache*). Garrett argued that the two kinds of errors were very distinct: Those that showed similarities of meaning rarely involved similarities of form, and vice versa. Although errors in both meaning and form relations are possible (such as *head* for *hair, lobster* for *oyster*), they seldom occur.

According to M. F. Garrett (1990), the relative infrequency of word substitution errors showing *both* meaning and form similarities indicates the language production system processes information about meaning and information about form at different points in sentence construction. His reasoning: If meaning and form processes operate simultaneously, then sentences in which both kinds of similarity are present ought to produce the most errors because there is greater opportunity for error to come about. This doesn't happen, suggesting that the two kinds of processing are separate and operate at different points.

SENTENCE COMPREHENSION

How do people understand or recover the meaning from sentences? This is a complicated task and, as we have seen, requires us to retrieve not only the meaning of individual words but also syntactic structure. Much evidence suggests people pay attention to syntactic constituents, such as those described earlier.

In a series of studies, Jarvella (1971) had people listen to long passages of speech. Interruptions during the passages were cues to the participants to recall, as precisely as possible, whatever they could from the sentence just heard. Jarvella created passages that contained identical phrases, except that the phrases "belonged" to different clausal constituents. Consider Passages 19 and 20 and notice that the middle clauses in each are the same, although they belong to different sentences:

(19) With this possibility, Taylor left the capital. After he had returned to Manhattan, he explained the offer to his wife.

(20) Taylor did not reach a decision until after he had returned to Manhattan. He explained the offer to his wife.

Participants' recall for the initial clauses (the ones that differ in the two passages) was similar and averaged around 16% verbatim recall. Recall for the third clause ("he explained the offer to his wife") was similar for both groups of participants, averaging 85%, presumably because participants were still actively processing this part of the sentence and were therefore still holding it in working memory. A more interesting result concerned the middle clause ("after he had returned to Manhattan"). It contained the same words and sounds but was part of the first sentence in Passage 20 and of the second sentence in Passage 19. Those listening to passages such as Passage 19 showed overall accuracy of about 54%, but those listening to Passage 20 only 20%, for the clause at issue. Jarvella (1971) argued that in Passage 19, the second clause is still being processed because the sentence is not yet finished; therefore, the clause is still in working memory. However, in Passage 20, the second clause belongs to a sentence for which processing is finished. (Work by Just and Carpenter, 1987, described in the next section, suggests that we don't always process sentences clause by clause.)

Ordinarily, it seems, when we finish processing a sentence, we "discard" the exact wording and store only a representation of its gist (Sachs, 1967). Apparently, then, some of the syntactic rules described earlier in this chapter are similar to those people ordinarily rely on as they interpret speech. Although people might never consciously think about the function of a word or phrase in a sentence, the evidence overwhelmingly suggests they are sensitive to it and use information about syntax as they understand.

Comprehending a sentence often involves resolving its possible ambiguities. Box 9.1 offers examples of phonetic, lexical (that is, word-level), and syntactic ambiguities present in different sentences. The interesting thing about the sentences is that we would ordinarily not notice the ambiguities; our processing would result in one unambiguous representation.

Box 9.1 [o]

Examples of Ambiguous Sentences

Phonetic ambiguity
Remember, a spoken sentence often contains many words not intended to be heard.
Ream ember us poke can cent tense off in contains men knee words knot in ten did tube bee herd.

Lexical ambiguity
I've got to go to the bank this morning.
I've got to go to First National this morning.

or

I've got to go to the river's edge this morning.

Syntactic ambiguity
Have the missionaries eaten.
(Spoken by the bishop as a question or spoken by a cannibal chief as an order)

Source: Garrett, M. F. (1990). Sentence processing. In D. N. Osherson & H. Lasnik (Eds.), An invitation to cognitive science: Vol. 1. Language. Cambridge, MA: MIT Press, pp. 133–175.

Only rarely, and with certain kinds of sentences, do we even notice ambiguities. Consider the following sentences (M. F. Garrett, 1990, p. 137):

(21) Fatty weighed 350 pounds of grapes.
(22) The cotton shirts are made from comes from Arizona.
(23) The horse raced past the barn fell.

These sentences are sometimes called *garden path sentences* because they lead the listener or reader down one path, to one interpretation, until somewhere in the middle or the end of processing, he or she realizes the interpretation is incorrect and the sentence must be reprocessed. Normal sentence processing somehow goes astray with these examples.

The three preceding sentences have initial fragments (such as "The cotton shirts are made from") that are *syntactically ambiguous:* They are consistent with at least two different parses. In this sentence, the word *cotton* could be treated as an adjective, modifying *shirts* (as in "The cotton shirts are made from dyed fibers"), or as a noun (as in "The cotton shirts are made from comes from Arizona"). Some have argued that we have a preference for parsing the fragment in certain ways. According to this line of thinking, we come to the second interpretation only when forced to because the first parse does not work. We notice that the first parse does not work only when we get to the fragment "comes from Arizona" and don't know what to do with it (G. Altmann, 1987).

A sentence processor encounters other ambiguities as well. One type is called **lexical ambiguity**. It occurs with words that have two meanings, such as *bank,* which can refer to either a financial institution or the edge of a river. How are lexical ambiguities normally resolved?

A study by Swinney (1979) offers some insights. Swinney presented people with spoken passages. Some of these contained ambiguous words; other, similar passages (heard by different experimental participants) did not. In each case, the unambiguous version included a word synonymous with one of the meanings of the ambiguous word. Here is an example of such a passage (with the ambiguous/unambiguous words italicized):

(24) Rumor had it that, for years, the government building had been plagued with problems. The man was not surprised when he found several roaches, spiders, and other *(bugs/insects)* ‡ in the corner of his room. (Swinney, p. 650)

Simultaneously, people participated in a visual lexical decision task (we discussed such tasks in Chapter 7) in which they were presented with a string of letters and asked to decide, as quickly as possible, whether the string formed an English word. The letter strings were presented at the point marked with a double dagger ‡ in the preceding example. Previous work by Swinney and others had demonstrated the existence of priming across the modalities (that is, a spoken word can prime a visually presented word). Swinney's question here was, Would all the meanings (such as "insect," "recording device") of an ambiguous word (such as *bug*) be subject to priming, or would priming occur only for the meaning activated by the context?

Swinney's (1979) results suggested that even in highly biased contexts such as the preceding one, both meanings of an ambiguous word (in this case, *bug*) were able to prime performance in the lexical decision task if the visual presentation happened immediately after the auditory presentation of the ambiguous word. So, for example, Passage 24 primed both *spy* and *ant,* which are semantically related to different meanings of the word *bug,* when they were presented immediately after the participants heard *bug.* If the visual presentation of letter strings was delayed for even as few as four syllables after the auditory presentation of the ambiguous word, however, priming occurred only for the contextually appropriate meaning of the ambiguous word. So, with a delayed presentation of words visually, the spoken word *bug* would prime *ant* but not *spy* in the context of Passage 24. Subsequent research by Gernsbacher (1993) supports Swinney's findings. Gernsbacher and her colleagues have shown that good readers suppress the inappropriate meaning of a word (in this case, "spy" for *bug*) and use the appropriate meaning ("ant") more efficiently and readily than do poor readers.

These results have several implications. First, when we process ambiguous sentences, all the meanings of an ambiguous word are temporarily available through what looks to be an automatic, bottom-up process or set of processes. So however context effects operate, they do not immediately restrict the listener or reader to the most appropriate "reading" of the words. Instead, for a period of time all meanings are accessible; however, the period is very short.

Three syllables after presentation of the ambiguous word (for most people, about 750 to 1,000 milliseconds), only one meaning remains active, suggesting that people resolve sentence ambiguity fairly quickly. Garrett (1990), reviewing these and other results, concluded that sentence comprehension normally occurs with left-to-right processing (each word in the sentence is processed sequentially), with each word usually processed once and one interpretation usually assigned. Processing results in each sentence's being assigned a "logical structure" so that the reader knows the role of each word in the sentence and how the sentence fits with preceding sentences. Garden path sentences, however, demonstrate that normal processing can sometimes fail. Still, the rarity of garden path sentences suggests that most of the time, we process sentences very rapidly and efficiently.

COMPREHENDING TEXT PASSAGES

We've just examined some evidence of how we process individual sentences. One question we can now ask is, How does processing of individual sentences work when they are bundled into connected passages, such as paragraphs or stories? Much of the time, when we encounter text passages, they are in written form. Thus, to examine text processing, we will first need to review briefly some findings on how people read.

Just and Carpenter (1987) have conducted a number of studies on how people read. They often use computer-driven instruments to measure and record eye *fixations* on parts of the written text. Fixations are brief pauses that everyone makes as their eyes scan text. Reading consists of a series of fixations and jumps between fixations. The average fixation lasts about 250 milliseconds (about a quarter of a second); the average jump lasts 10 to 20 milliseconds.

Just and Carpenter's model of reading assumes that as soon as readers encounter a new word, they try to interpret it and assign it a role. The authors called this the *immediacy assumption.* In addition, Just and Carpenter (1987) proposed what they called the *eye–mind hypothesis,* which holds that the interpretation of each word occurs during the time it is fixated. Therefore, the time spent on each fixation provides information about ease of interpretation. (Rayner and Sereno, 1994, gave reasons against both these assumptions or hypotheses, although these probably do not undermine the results reported next. Tanenhaus, Magnuson, Dahan, and Chambers, 2000, present a similar model of eye movements that they believe indicate access of stored words from memory during spoken language comprehension.) Just and Carpenter argued that among the factors that increase fixation duration, and thus ease of interpretation, are longer words, infrequently encountered words, and syntactically or semantically anomalous words.

Box 9.2

Gaze Durations of a Typical Reader

Eye fixations of a college student reading a scientific passage. Gazes within each sentence are sequentially numbered above the fixated words with the durations (in msec) indicated below the sequence number.

1	2	3	4	5	6	7	8	9		1
1566	267	400	83	267	617	767	450	450		400
Flywheels	are	one	of the	oldest	mechanical	devices	known	to man.		Every

2	3	5	4	6	.7	8		9		10
616	517	684	250	317	617	1116		367		467
internal	combustion	engine		contains	a small	flywheel	that	converts	the	Jerky

11	12	13	14	15	16	17		18	19	20	21
483	450	383	284	383	317	283		533	50	366	566
motion	of the pistons	into	the	smooth	flow	of	energy	that	powers the	drive	shaft.

The researchers (Carpenter & Just, 1983; Just & Carpenter, 1980) presented college students with passages from magazines such as *Newsweek* and *Time* describing scientific inventions, technical innovations, or biological mechanisms. Box 9.2 shows sample results for one student. Numbers above each word indicate the fixation time (measured in milliseconds) for that word. Note that content words, such as *flywheels, devices,* or *engine,* almost always receive longer fixations than function words, such as *the, on,* or *a,* which often are not fixated at all. These results suggest that more time is spent on the meaningful or semantically rich parts of the text, as would be expected, given the reader's goal of understanding meaning.

Other research on reading also suggests that semantic factors influence the reading task. Kintsch and Keenan (1973) showed that two sentences of equal length might be differentially difficult to process. The source of the difficulty, they suggested, lies in the **propositional complexity** of the sentences, the number of basic ideas conveyed. The two sentences in Figure 9.6 are approximately equal in length, but they differ greatly in the number of underlying propositions, or basic ideas. This model predicts that the second sentence,

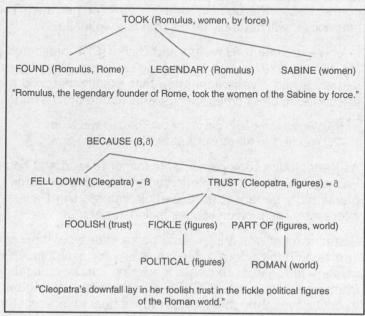

■ Figure 9.6: Propositional structure of two sentences.

having the same number of words but more propositions than the first, will be more difficult to process, and, indeed, this is what Kintsch and Keenan found.

Participants were asked to press a button after reading a sentence (or passage) silently and then to immediately recall as much of the sentence as they could. The more propositions a sentence contained, the longer it took for the participants to read and comprehend it. Further, they were much more likely to recall the more "central" propositions, those critical to the meaning of the sentence, than the more peripheral ones that merely elaborated on the central ideas. This result suggests that propositions are mentally represented in some sort of hierarchy, with more central propositions at the top of the hierarchy, as shown in Figure 9.6. The peripheral, lower-level propositions apparently serve the function of elaborating the more central propositions and so are less important to remember.

Another factor influencing the processing of text has to do with the relationships among sentences. How do people integrate related ideas that may come from different sentences? Haviland and Clark (1974) described what they called the *given–new* strategy, a pragmatic approach to processing sentences whereby listeners and readers divide sentences into two parts: the given and the new. The given part of a sentence contains information that is (or should be) familiar from the context, the preceding information (including other sentences just presented), or background knowledge. The new part, as the term implies, contains unfamiliar information. Listeners first search memory for information corresponding to the given information and then update memory by incorporating the new information, often as an elaboration of the given.

The given–new strategy can work only if the information in the given part of the sentence corresponds to some information in the listener's memory, called the *antecedent*. One way to help the listener make this connection is to use the same description in the given part of the sentence as in memory. However, as a practical matter, it is often easier to use slightly different ways of referring to things and to expect the listener to make some connections—the obvious ones—on his or her own. The connections, called *bridging inferences*, will naturally take some time to make.

In one experiment, Haviland and Clark (1974) presented people with passages consisting of context followed by target sentences. Sometimes (as in Passage 25) the target sentence had given information that exactly matched the antecedent information (from the context); other times, participants had to draw a bridging inference (as in Passage 26).

> (25) We got some beer out of the car. The beer was warm.
> (26) We checked the picnic supplies. The beer was warm.

As predicted, it took participants longer to read and comprehend the target sentence in Passage 26 than it did participants who read the same target sentence in Passage 25, presumably because those participants reading Passage 26 had to draw the bridging inference "The picnic supplies included beer."

Readers must sometimes also make inferences between sentences that are far apart in a text. Think about a mystery story, for example. To understand how the clues of a mystery fit together to create a solution, readers must infer how the central propositions from each clue connect to the essential ideas of another clue. These connections need to occur even though the clues may appear at different times in the story. Readers vary in the number of such inferences they can create at any one time, and the inferences themselves vary in how strongly they connect one piece of information to another. Researchers have consistently shown that the number of inferences readers make and the strength of those inferences affect how well readers remember and understand what they read (Goldman & Varnhagen, 1986; Graesser & Clark, 1985; Trabasso, Secco, & van den Broek, 1984; Trabasso & van den Broek, 1985). In short, inferences of all types, including bridging inferences between sentences or inferences that tie more distant parts of a text together, are crucial to how well you and I understand what we read.

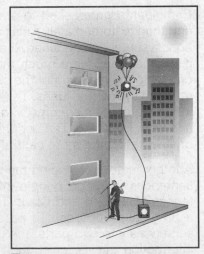

The role of context in processing language has been extensively documented by John Bransford and Marcia Johnson. Read the passage in Box 9.3; then cover it and try to recall as much as you can. If you are like Bransford and Johnson's (1972) participants, you may find the task very difficult, and your recall may include only a few of the ideas. However, if you were first provided with a context for the passage, such as the one depicted in Figure 9.7, your recall would be much more complete.

■ Figure 9.7: Context for story in Box 9.3.

Bransford and Johnson showed that with the context provided before the passage, participants recalled an average of 8.0 out of 14.0 distinct ideas. Without any context, or even with the context provided after the passage, participants only recalled about 3.6 ideas.

Box 9.3

An Ambiguous Story

If the balloons popped, the sound wouldn't be able to carry since everything would be too far away from the correct floor. A closed window would also prevent the sound from carrying, since most buildings tend to be well insulated. Since the whole operation depends on a steady flow of electricity, a break in the middle of the wire would also cause problems. Of course, the fellow could shout, but the human voice is not loud enough to carry that far. An additional problem is that the string could break on the instrument. Then there could be no accompaniment to the message. It is clear that the best situation would involve less distance. Then there would be fewer potential problems. With face-to-face contact, the least number of things could go wrong.

SOURCE: Bransford and Johnson (1972, p. 718).

Van den Broek and Gustafson (1999) offer three conclusions from research on reading texts. The first is that "the mental representation is a construction by the reader that differs from, and goes beyond, the information in the text itself" (p. 17), meaning that people recruit their own background knowledge to draw inferences to comprehend text. Second, "a good representation is coherent" (p. 18), implying that structures such as schemata or story grammars (see later) are used to make the information in a text fit together. A third principle, which we have seen evidence for in earlier chapters, is that a reader's attentional resources are limited. Therefore, to cut down on their workload, readers do not draw every logically possible inference they could from a text (the number of inferences drawn would be overwhelming). Instead, van den Broek and Gustafson posit, inferences are created only when they are needed to create coherence.

STORY GRAMMARS

In Chapter 7, we encountered the idea of scripts, defined as schemata for routine events. Earlier in this chapter, we discussed the idea of grammars—systems of rules that result in legal entities, such as sentences. Some cognitive psychologists have put these two ideas together, forming the concept of a **story grammar** to describe the way people comprehend large, integrated pieces of text.

Story grammars are similar to scripts in that both have variables or slots that are filled in differently for different stories. For example, different stories have different protagonists, settings, plots, conflicts, and resolutions. Story grammars are also similar to syntactic grammars in that they help identify the units (constituents) and the role each unit plays in the story (Just & Carpenter, 1987). Like syntactic grammars, story grammars attempt to describe the hierarchical structure of the story, specifying how each part of the story relates to the other parts. Story grammars produce a division of (or parse) the story into parts or constituents. Text passages that cannot be parsed by a grammar are then seen as "illegal" or "ungrammatical" stories, just as strings of words that cannot be parsed by a syntactic grammar are identified as "ungrammatical" sentences.

Like other schemata, story grammars provide listeners or readers with a framework within which to expect certain elements and sequences, enabling them to fill in with "default values" things that are not explicitly stated. For example, young children expect stories to begin with some sort of setting, such as "Once upon a time" or "A long time ago." One example of a story grammar is shown in Table 9.2 (Thorndyke, 1977). It divides a story into several constituents: setting, theme, plot, resolution, and so forth. Each of these parts may also have subparts; for example, settings may have location, characters, and time. Some parts may also have a number of different instances of certain subparts; for example,

■ Table 9.2: Example of a Story Grammar

Rule Number	Rule
(1)	STORY → SETTING + THEME + PLOT + RESOLUTION
(2)	SETTING → CHARACTERS + LOCATION + TIME
(3)	THEME → (EVENT)* + GOAL
(4)	PLOT → EPISODE*
(5)	EPISODE → SUBGOAL + ATTEMPT* + OUTCOME
(6)	ATTEMPT → { EVENT* / EPISODE
(7)	OUTCOME → { EVENT* / STATE
(8)	RESOLUTION → { EVENT / STATE
(9)	SUBGOAL } / GOAL } → DESIRED STATE
(10)	CHARACTERS / LOCATION TIME } → STATE

SOURCE: Thorndyke (1977, p. 79).

the plot may have several episodes. The asterisks in the table indicate that certain subparts (such as "episode" in Rule 4) can be repeated an indefinite number of times. Parentheses around a subpart indicate that the subpart is optional.

J. M. Mandler and Johnson (1977) found that stories conforming to the structure of a story grammar were better recalled than were stories that conformed less well. In fact, people were more likely to "misremember" details such that they fit better with the story grammar. Interestingly, when these authors analyzed Bartlett's (1932) "War of the Ghosts" story (see Chapter 6), they found that it contained several violations of their story grammar. Some of the recall attempts Bartlett reported showed errors of recall at precisely these points. We can analyze the problem in a story grammar framework as follows: At least part of the reason why Bartlett's participants had so much trouble remembering the story was that it did not fit the structure they were expecting. They tried to make the story fit the expected structure a little more and, in the process, inadvertently distorted their representation of the story.

Thorndyke (1977) has argued that people use story grammars to guide their reading and their interpretation. One way he tested this idea was to ask people to read and recall various stories he had previously analyzed according to a story grammar. Box 9.4 depicts an example of one of his stories. Thorndyke predicted that the higher up in the levels of the story hierarchy (i.e., the higher the level depicted in Box 9.4) a part of the story occurred, the better it would be recalled, and results confirmed this prediction. Notice that this result is similar to those reported in studies by Kintsch and Keenan (1973), discussed earlier, on which parts of sentences people typically remember.

Box 9.4

Example Story and Its Structure

(1) Circle Island is located in the middle of the Atlantic Ocean, (2) north of Ronald Island. (3) The main occupations on the island are farming and ranching. (4) Circle Island has good soil, (5) but few rivers and (6) hence a shortage of water. (7) The island is run democratically. (8) All issues are decided by a majority vote of the islanders. (9) The governing body is a senate, (10) whose job is to carry out the will of the majority. (11) Recently, an island scientist discovered a cheap method (12) of converting salt water into fresh water. (13) As a result, the island farmers wanted (14) to build a canal across the island, (15) so that they could use water from the canal (16) to cultivate the island's central region. (17) Therefore, the farmers formed a procanal association (18) and persuaded a few senators (19) to join. (20) The procanal association brought the construction idea to a vote. (21) All the islanders voted. (22) The majority voted in favor of construction. (23) The senate, however, decided that (24) the farmers' proposed canal was ecologically unsound. (25) The senators agreed (26) to build a smaller canal (27) that was 2 feet wide and 1 foot deep. (28) After starting construction on the smaller canal, (29) the islanders discovered that (30) no water would flow into it. (31) Thus the project was abandoned. (32) The farmers were angry (33) because of the failure of the canal project. (34) Civil war appeared inevitable.

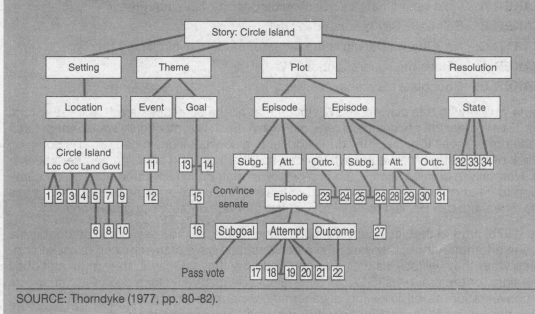

SOURCE: Thorndyke (1977, pp. 80–82).

GRICEAN MAXIMS OF CONVERSATION

Not all the connected text people must process occurs in written form. We can think of ordinary conversations as examples of spoken connected text. Conversations are interesting to study because they occur so frequently and because (unlike written texts) they normally involve the production of a great deal of language with little time for planning and revision. Indeed, H. H. Clark and Van Der Wege (2002) argue, the essence of language use is found in face-to-face talk. It is here that speaking and listening arise in their natural, universal states. It is here that researchers can study why speakers say the things they say and how listeners interpret these things—ultimately, as a way of coordinating joint activities. . . .

The problem is that too little is known about spontaneous language and how it differs from reciting, reading aloud, listening to idealized speech, and other such forms. Understanding language in its natural habitat is a major challenge for the second century of psycholinguistics. (p. 250)

We've already seen a number of examples of linguistic rules that people follow in producing or comprehending language. Some of these have to do with ways of combining sounds to produce words, combining words to produce sentences, or even combining ideas to produce meanings. Many researchers believe, however, that yet another set of rules is necessary for people to use language appropriately or effectively, especially in conversations: pragmatic rules.

Here we will examine some pragmatic rules specific to conversations called the **Gricean maxims of cooperative conversation** (Grice, 1975). Grice believed that for people to converse, they must do more than produce utterances that are phonologically, syntactically, and semantically appropriate. Consider the following "conversation."

SPEAKER A: I just heard that Joe got promoted today. Isn't that great?

SPEAKER B: Salt Lake City is located in Utah.

SPEAKER C: No, Charles Darwin is the father of modern evolutionary theory.

SPEAKER A: What's the square root of 34?

SPEAKER B: Chocolate ice cream is sweet.

What is wrong with this conversation? Notice that all the sentences are "legal" at several levels. Each obeys the phonological rules of English. Each is syntactically well formed. Each is meaningful. Yet all together, they don't add up to a conversation. In part, what is going on is a lack of connection between anything one speaker says and anything another speaker says. Normally in conversation, each of a person's contributions or utterances bears some relation to what others have already said or to what the speaker plans to say later. In this sense, speakers can be said to provide a context for one another's contributions.

Grice (1975) argued that for a conversation to take place, all the speakers must cooperate with one another. Although speakers in a conversation have many choices to make concerning what they will say, as well as when and how they will say it, they must still obey constraints, or general rules (G. A. Miller & Glucksberg, 1988). Grice described speakers in a conversation as all following a general "cooperative principle." Speakers do this, Grice believed, by following four specific conversational *maxims* or rules:

1.   *Maxims of quantity.* Make your contribution as informative as required. Do not make your contribution more informative than is required.

2.   *Maxims of quality.* Try to make your contribution one that is true. Do not say what you believe to be false. Do not say that for which you have no evidence.

3.   *Maxim of relation.* Be relevant.

4.   *Maxims of manner.* Be clear. Avoid obscurity of expression. Avoid ambiguity. Be brief. Be orderly.

Violations of the maxims produce conversations that are noticeably odd. For instance, if someone asks, "Do you have a watch?" and you respond, "Yes, I do," you are violating the first maxim of quantity: You are being less informative than is required. Your conversation partner is not, in all likelihood, taking a census for Timex or Rolex; he or she probably wants to know the time. As a member of the language community that you live in, you are expected to know that the question asked is really a request for the time and to respond appropriately.

It is also possible to violate the first maxim by being *too* informative. For example, some of my students occasionally invite me to eat with them in the campus dining halls. When we arrange a luncheon date, they often ask something like "Where should we meet?" My response ought to be something on the order of "How about if you come to my office?" rather than something much more detailed like "Please come to my office door, and I will be standing 27 centimeters inside of it." The latter would be bizarre, presumably because it's too specific.

The second maxim has to do with truthfulness. Generally, conversation partners assume that the other is telling the truth, or at least what the speaker believes to be the truth. On some occasions, it is permissible to violate this maxim—for example, to be ironic. Imagine that a friend who's missed a lecture in a class in which you are both enrolled asks, "How was class today?" You can respond, "Utterly fascinating!" even if it really was dry as toast, *if* you somehow signal your answer isn't to be taken literally. Rolled eyes, exaggerated intonation, winks, and the like help to communicate that your violation of the maxim of quality is itself meant to communicate something—in this case, ironic humor. However, if you simply utter an untruthful response without letting your listener know you aren't being candid, then your conversation will not be successful, and your conversation partner could legitimately complain about your conversation skills.

Someone who consistently violates the maxims of quantity or quality may well be perceived as uncooperative or obnoxious and, after a while, may find it difficult to attract conversation partners. Someone who consistently violates the third maxim of relation by responding with irrelevant utterances will have a bigger problem: He or she will simply be regarded as, at best, very bizarre. To illustrate, imagine a conversation between Tom and Joe, two college roommates.

TOM *(looking around):*   Hey, Joe, have you seen my sweater?

JOE *(looking at Tom, and smiling):*   Lo, a flaming squirrel!

If Joe persists in violating the maxim of relation, he will likely find himself at a complete loss for conversation partners, if not roommates and friends.

The fourth maxim, the maxim of manner, generally governs the way you choose to construct your conversation contributions. The general idea is that you should speak as clearly as possible, using language appropriate to your listener and the context. Among other things, this maxim forbids you to answer your professors in pig Latin or your younger siblings in "academese." It also prevents you from holding a filibuster (unless you are a member of Congress) and requires that you at least *attempt* to organize what you say before you begin speaking.

Gricean maxims are not always obeyed, but the assumption is that people try to obey them most of the time. When the maxims are violated, the speaker apparently wishes to end the conversation, wishes to avoid the conversation, or expects the listener to understand that the violation is occurring and why (Levinson, 2000; G. A. Miller & Glucksberg, 1988). Again, though, it is doubtful that the average person is consciously aware of the rules. As with most linguistic rules, maxims are implicitly understood even if they can't be precisely stated.

LANGUAGE AND COGNITION

Language is used in ways other than social conversation. Lecturers use language to get ideas across to students, authors to readers, newscasters to audiences, and so on. It should be evident by now that language is used in a number of cognitive processes. When we perceive a familiar object and name it (either aloud or to ourselves), we use language; when we follow one conversation rather than another, we are processing language; when we repeat information aloud or take notes to organize it, we are using language. Similarly, when we reason, make plans, or brainstorm new ideas, we rely heavily on language, as we will see in the next several chapters.

Our use of language in a wide variety of cognitive tasks raises the following important question: What influences does language have over other cognitive processes? Two extreme positions exist: (a) Language and other cognitive processes operate completely independently, and (b) language and other cognitive processes are completely related, with one determining the other. Between the extremes is a broad middle ground, where language and other cognitive processes are seen as related in some ways but independent in others.

The relationship between language and thought has been heavily debated. In the early days of American psychology, John B. Watson (1930) asserted that thought was language and nothing more. In particular, he rejected the idea that thought (internal mental representation or other cognitive activity) could occur without some sort of conditioned language responses occurring. Watson believed that all apparent instances of thinking (such as mentally computing sums, daydreaming about a vacation, weighing the pros and cons of a plan) were really the results of subvocal speech. Thinking was equated with talking to yourself, even if so quietly and covertly that no one (including you) knew you were using language.

S. M. Smith, Brown, Toman, and Goodman (1947) conducted a heroic experiment to test Watson's theory. Smith served as the subject and allowed himself to be injected with a curare derivative, which paralyzed all his muscles, necessitating the use of an artificial respirator for the duration of the experiment. Because he could not move any muscles, he could not engage in subvocal speech. The question was, Would this also prevent him from other kinds of cognitive activity? The answer was a decisive *no*. Smith reported remembering and thinking about events that took place while paralyzed. Apparently, then, subvocal speech and thought are not equivalent.

THE MODULARITY HYPOTHESIS

A proposal from the philosopher Jerry Fodor (1983, 1985) made a quite different argument about the relationship of language to other aspects of cognition. Fodor argued that some cognitive processes—in particular, perception and language—are *modular*. What does it mean for a process to be a module? First, it means the process is *domain-specific:* It operates specifically with certain kinds of input and not others. With regard to language, for example, Fodor argued that sentence parsing involves processes that are specific to the division of phrases and words into constituents. Such processes are meant only for parsing and are of little use in other cognitive tasks.

Modularity of a process also implies that it is an **informationally encapsulated process**: It operates independently of the beliefs and the other information available to the processor. Another way of explaining this is to say that an informationally encapsulated process operates relatively independently of other processes. Fodor (1983) compared informationally encapsulated processes to reflexes:

> Suppose that you and I have known each other for many a long year . . . and you have come fully to appreciate the excellence of my character. In particular, you have come to know perfectly well that under no conceivable circumstances would I stick my finger in your eye. Suppose that this belief of yours is both explicit and deeply felt. You would, in fact, go to the wall for it. Still, if I jab my finger near enough to your eyes, and fast enough, you'll blink. . . .
>
> [The blink reflex] has no access to what you know about my character or, for that matter, to any other of your beliefs, utilities, and expectations. For this reason the blink reflex is often produced when sober reflection would show it to be uncalled for. (p. 71)

The **modularity hypothesis**, then, argues that certain perceptual and language processes are modules. (In the case of language, one such process is that which parses input utterances.) These processes are thought to be set apart from other cognitive processes, such as memory, attention, thinking, and problem solving, that are thought to be nonmodular. Modular processes operate automatically and independently (at least at the first stages of processing) of other cognitive processes, such as thought. Modular processes are domain-specific, which means that they are specialized to work with only certain kinds of input. The syntactic parsing aspects of language are not used in other kinds of cognitive processing. In this sense, then, language really is a special and very independent cognitive process.

Is there evidence for the modularity hypothesis? The experiment by Swinney (1979) on lexical ambiguity resolution offers findings that support the modularity hypothesis. Recall that Swinney found that when people are presented with an ambiguous word (even in a context that should disambiguate the meaning of the word), all possible meanings are triggered for a fraction of a second. This triggering appears to be automatic and reflexive and completely independent of whatever other cognitive processes might be operating at the time. That all the meanings are activated, independent of the context, demonstrates some informational encapsulation.

THE WHORFIAN HYPOTHESIS

The modularity hypothesis can be taken as a proposal for treating language (or at least certain aspects of language) as quite independent of any other cognitive process. Other investigators have argued for a different proposal: Strong relations exist between language and other cognitive processes. One hypothesis, called the **Whorfian hypothesis of linguistic relativity**, was originated by Benjamin Whorf, a chemical engineer whose hobby was studying Native American languages of North America. The Whorfian hypothesis is that language both directs and constrains thought and perception. Whorf (1956) stated the hypothesis as follows:

> We dissect nature along lines laid down by our native languages. The categories and types that we isolate from the world of phenomena we do not find there because they stare every observer in the face;

on the contrary, the world is presented in a kaleidoscopic flux of impressions which has to be organized by our minds—and this means largely by the linguistic systems in our minds. We cut nature up, organize it into concepts, and ascribe significance as we do, largely because we are parties to an agreement to organize it in this way—an agreement that holds through our speech community and is codified in the patterns of our language. The agreement is, of course, an unstated one, but its terms are absolutely obligatory. (pp. 213–214)

Whorf believed that the language or languages one grows up learning and speaking thus determine the way one perceives the world, organizes information about the world, and thinks. Whorf (1956) based his hypothesis on the observation that each language differs in how it emphasizes various aspects of the world. For example, he observed that the Eskimo language has several words for snow, whereas English has one. (In a very amusing essay, Pullum, 1991, offers evidence and arguments to refute this belief about Eskimos and snow.) English has a number of words to describe basic colors, but the language of the Dani, an Indonesian agricultural group, has only two: *mili* for dark or black and *mola* for white or light (Heider, 1972). Whorf's hypothesis predicts that these language differences could limit the information available to speakers of different languages: As English speakers, we might fail to make distinctions between kinds of snow that Eskimos are thought to make routinely. Similarly, the Dani might process information about colors in very different ways than we do because of differences in color terms in our respective languages.

Eleanor Rosch (formerly Heider) conducted a series of studies that directly tested the Whorfian hypothesis. If Whorf is correct, then the Dani should have great difficulty perceiving or remembering colors not named in their language (such as green versus yellow) relative to speakers of English, whose language names each color. Dani-speaking and English-speaking participants were shown various color chips. Some depicted basic or *focal* colors—chips considered to be the best examples of basic color terms (say, a very green green, as opposed to a blue green). Others depicted nonfocal colors, those that English speakers would describe as a combination of focal colors or as a shade of a focal color (such as light pink, scarlet, olive green, aquamarine).

Heider (1972) presented participants with a chip of either a focal or a nonfocal color, typically for 5 seconds. Thirty seconds later, participants were shown 160 color chips and asked to point to the one that matched the chip they had just seen. Like English speakers, and contrary to Whorf's hypothesis, Dani speakers performed much better if the initial chip showed a focal rather than a nonfocal color. In another experiment, Rosch (1973) asked participants to learn new, arbitrary names for colors. Once again, Rosch found that Dani speakers, like English speakers, performed better when the colors shown were focal rather than nonfocal.

Apparently, contrary to Whorf's hypothesis, even if a language does not mark particular differences, it does not always prevent its speakers from either perceiving those differences or learning them. Indeed, work by anthropologists Berlin and Kay (1969) suggests that all languages observe certain rules about the way colors are named. Berlin and Kay found that in every language, no more than 11 basic color terms (that is, terms not derived from other color terms) are recognized.

Moreover, the way colors are recognized is hierarchical. The hierarchy is depicted in Table 9.3. It shows that if a language has only two color terms, they are always something corresponding to "black" (or "dark") and "white" (or "light"). If a language has three color terms, then a term meaning "red" is added to this list. Languages with four color terms also have either a term for "green" or one for "yellow," but not both, and so on. English, which recognizes all 11 terms as names for focal colors, includes words for all the colors in the hierarchy. No other language recognizes more colors as basic. The implication is that color terms and concepts are in an important way universal. However, some have argued that because Rosch's task depended so heavily on color perception (which may

■ Table 9.3: Hierarchy of Color Terms in Different Languages

Number of Color Terms	Names of Color Terms
2	white, black
3	white, black, red
4	white, black, red, and either yellow or green
5	white, black, red, yellow, green
6	white, black, red, yellow, green, blue
7	white, black, red, yellow, green, blue, brown
8 through 11	white, black, red, yellow, green, blue, brown plus some combination of one or more of the following: pink, purple, orange, gray

SOURCE: After Berlin and Kay (1969).

have physiological determinants), it is not as crucial a test of Whorf's hypothesis as it was claimed to be (Hunt & Agnoli, 1991).

A more recent controversy regarding linguistic relativity comes from Alfred Bloom (1981), who proposed to study a weaker form of the Whorfian hypothesis: The presence of certain linguistic markers makes some kinds of comprehension and thinking easier or more natural. Specifically, Bloom noticed that the various dialects of Chinese language lack a structure equivalent to those in Indo-European languages that mark a *counterfactual inference,* such as "If your grandmother had been elected president, there would be no taxation." Counterfactuals require inferences to be drawn on the basis of a premise known to be false. By using the past tense of the verb, or by using the phrase "were to" in the first clause, English marks the fact that the premise is false. In contrast, Chinese has no direct marker of a counterfactual, although there are various indirect ways of getting the idea across.

On the basis of anecdotal evidence from Chinese-speaking associates, Bloom (1981) hypothesized that Chinese speakers would have a more difficult time drawing counterfactual inferences than would speakers of English, especially when text passages containing counterfactual inferences were difficult. In a series of studies, Bloom gave both Chinese-speaking and English-speaking participants different stories to read in their native languages. He reported that only 7% of the Chinese-speaking participants offered counterfactual interpretations of the story, whereas 98% of the English-speaking participants did so. At first blush, these findings offered nearly perfect confirmation of Bloom's predictions (which, recall, were predictions derived from the Whorf hypothesis).

Later investigations by native Chinese speakers, however, disputed Bloom's findings. They maintained that various *artifacts,* or unrelated aspects of the way he had conducted the studies, accounted for his results. Au (1983, 1984), for instance, argued that Bloom's Chinese versions of his story were unidiomatic—that is, awkwardly phrased. When she provided new and more idiomatic stories to her Chinese-speaking participants, they showed very little difficulty responding correctly. Liu (1985) replicated Au's findings on counterfactual interpretations with Chinese-speaking participants who had minimal or no exposure to the English language. Recently, a spirited debate has emerged between Li and Gleitman (2002) and Levinson, Kita, Haun, and Rasch (2002) over whether speakers of different languages encode spatial directions differently, constructing fundamentally different structures of space.

Apparently, then, little evidence suggests that language constrains either perception (as demonstrated in the color-naming studies) or higher-level forms of thinking (as demonstrated in the counterfactual-reasoning studies). This is not to say that language has no effects on people's thinking, only that empirical evidence causes us to reject the original, strong form of Whorf's hypothesis (Bates, Devescovi, & Wulfeck, 2001).

Nonetheless, it is true that language at least reflects thought in many instances. For example, although most of us have only a single word for snow, those interested in the white stuff (such as skiers) have developed a more extensive vocabulary, presumably to communicate better about conditions on the slope. In general, experts or connoisseurs in given areas tend to develop specialized vocabularies that reflect distinctions and differences that novices might have difficulty (at first) seeing or labeling. Presumably, this is because the experts need to communicate about the subtle differences and so develop the enabling vocabulary. Novices, who have little need to discuss the differences, don't develop the vocabulary (nor, by the way, do they develop the perceptual differentiation skills, as we saw in Chapter 3).

NEUROPSYCHOLOGICAL VIEWS AND EVIDENCE

That we process complex language information with amazing speed is an understatement. Caplan (1994) reports, for example, that people typically recognize spoken words after about 125 milliseconds (about one eighth of a second!)—that is, while the word is still being spoken. Normal word production, estimated over a number of studies, requires us to search through a mental "dictionary" of about 20,000 items, and we do so at the rate of three words per second.

Obviously, the brain architecture to support this rapid and complex cognitive processing must be sophisticated indeed. Neuropsychologists have been trying to understand what the underlying brain structures involved with language are, where they are located, and how they operate. In this section, we will take a brief look at some of the major findings.

Interest in *localizing* language function in the brain dates back at least to the 1800s, when a French physician with interests in anthropology and ethnography, Pierre Paul Broca, read a paper in 1861 at the meeting of the Société d'Anthropologie in Paris. The paper reported on a patient nicknamed "Tan" because he had lost the ability to speak any words save for *tan.* Shortly after the patient died, his brain was examined and found to have a lesion in the left frontal lobe. The very next day, Broca reported this exciting (for science, not for the patient or his family, probably) finding (Posner & Raichle, 1994). The area of the brain, henceforth known as *Broca's area,* is shown in Figure 2.3 (see page 27). Subsequently, several other patients were reported who had similar difficulties in speaking and who were found to have lesions in the same brain region.

About 13 years later, German neurologist Carl Wernicke identified another brain area that, if damaged by a small lesion (often the result of a stroke), left patients with extreme difficulty *comprehending* (but not producing) spoken language (Posner & Raichle, 1994). (Not surprisingly, this area has come to be called *Wernicke's area,* and it too is shown in Figure 2.3.)

Both these language disorders were termed **aphasia**, although the first was called **expressive aphasia** (or **Broca's aphasia**) and the second **receptive aphasia** (or **Wernicke's aphasia**). Broca's aphasia appeared to leave language reception and processing undisturbed; Wernicke's, to spare fluent production of words and sentences (although the language was often gibberish). More recent evidence provides qualifications to these statements, suggesting, for example, that patients with Broca's aphasia do have some difficulties in understanding spoken language. Thus, our understanding of different kinds of aphasia is becoming more elaborated. Other kinds of aphasia have also been reported and correlated with brain damage in specific brain regions, often ones adjacent to Broca's or Wernicke's areas (Banich, 1997).

Researchers studying aphasia also noticed an interesting generalization about aphasic patients: Usually the area of damage to the brain was in the left and not the right hemisphere. This led to the idea that the two cerebral hemispheres of the brain play different roles and have different functions. The term for this specialization of function between the two hemispheres is *lateralization.*

Briefly, it appears that in most people, the left cerebral hemisphere is associated with the ability to produce and comprehend language and the right hemisphere with the ability to process complex spatial relationships (Springer & Deutsch, 1998). Evidence for this lateralization began with the clinical observation (beginning with Broca) of aphasic patients. Other evidence comes from a test used with people about to undergo brain surgery for epilepsy, called the *Wada test.* This involves injecting a barbiturate drug, sodium amobarbital, into one of two carotid arteries: either the one going to the left hemisphere or the one going to the right hemisphere. The injection anesthetizes one of the hemispheres. The patient is kept conscious during this procedure and, just before the injection, is asked to hold up his or her two arms and to start counting. When the drug reaches the intended hemisphere, the patient drops the arm that is on the opposite side of the body from the side anesthetized. The human brain, like those of other animals, is organized in such a way that the right hemisphere controls the left side of the body and vice versa, so the dropping of the arm signals the physician that the drug has arrived at the brain. If the anesthetized hemisphere is the one controlling language abilities, the patient will, soon after his or her arm drops, experience a 2- to 5-minute period during which he or she is unable to speak (Springer & Deutsch).

Not all people have language in the left hemisphere. About 96% of right-handers do, with the other 4% showing a mirror-image pattern: language in the right hemisphere. Left-handers show a different pattern, with 70% still showing language in the left hemisphere, 15% showing language in the right hemisphere, and the remaining 15% showing language in both hemispheres (Banich, 1997).

Technologies such as CAT and PET scans have also been used to study language functioning in both aphasic and nonaphasic people. Kempler et al. (1990) studied three patients with an aphasia known as *slowly progressive aphasia,* noting either normal or mild atrophy of the left language regions (shown by CAT scans) and hypometabolism (that is, less use of glucose) by the left hemispheres of the three patients.

A now classic study conducted by Petersen, Fox, Posner, Mintun, and Raichle (1988) examined the processing of single words using PET scans. Participants were presented with single words, either in writing or auditorily, and were asked to make no response, to read written stimuli, or to generate a word related to the presented word. Results showed that different areas of the brain were activated for different tasks. Simply viewing visually presented words led to activation of the inner left hemisphere in the occipital lobes (the part of the brain known to be specialized for visual information). When the task was only to listen to words, participants showed elevated cortical activity in the temporal lobes (known to be the area of the brain having to do with auditory processing, which includes Wernicke's area) of both hemispheres.

One important finding from the study is that the areas activated do *not* overlap. In other words, the area of the brain activated in written-word recognition is separate from that area activated when words are heard. When presented with a visual word and asked to pronounce it, participants showed activation in both hemispheres but this time in the motor cortex, the part of the brain that directs motor behaviors. Interestingly, the PET scans did not show elevated levels of activity in either Wernicke's or Broca's areas (Posner & Raichle, 1994). However, when participants were asked to generate another word in response to the one presented, many areas of the brain previously quiet became active, including Broca's area. Many of the findings reported by Petersen et al. (1988) have been replicated using functional magnetic resonance imaging (fMRI), a newer noninvasive technique (Cuenod et al., 1995).

Other research, however, has clouded this neat picture. Not all patients with lesions in Broca's area, for example, develop Broca's aphasia, and not all patients with Broca's aphasia have damage in Broca's area. Moreover, not all Broca's aphasia patients show the same degree of impairment; many of them show an inability to process subtle nuances of language. The story is similarly complicated with Wernicke's aphasia.

Caplan (1994) concludes that the localization of specific language processing in particular brain regions is not straightforward. One possible idea entertained by Caplan is that language processes do not necessarily have a specific location in the brain. Instead, they may be distributed across a region of the brain in a neural network configuration similar to the connectionist models presented in Chapters 1 and 7 (see Christiansen and Chater, 2001, for a description of some such models). The exact location differs from individual to individual, but it probably lies somewhere on a pathway connecting the frontal, parietal, and temporal lobes (Catani, Jones, & Ffytche, 2005). Small lesions in any one area are unlikely to "knock out" an entire language process, but larger lesions might.

Obviously, much work is needed with the newer neuroimaging techniques to test many of these intriguing ideas (Gernsbacher & Kaschak, 2003). It looks as if Fodor's modularity idea is gaining some support from the neurolinguistic and neuropsychological data reported to date. How well this proposal will withstand further tests is an open question.

Summary

1. To be a language, a system must exhibit regularity (that is, be governed by a system of rules, called a *grammar*) and productivity (be able to express an infinite number of ideas).

2. When researchers say that people "follow" the rules of a language, they distinguish between conscious awareness of a rule (which neither psychologists nor linguists believe is the way people apply most linguistic rules) and implicit access to a rule (such that a person follows a rule, though perhaps being unaware of its existence and unable to articulate just what the rule is).

3. Language is structured on several levels: the phonological (sound), syntactic (ordering and structuring of words and phrases in sentences), semantic

(meaning), and pragmatic (the ways in which language is actually used), to name a few. Each of these levels has a different set of rules associated with it.

4. People use different linguistic rules both when they produce and when they comprehend language. The ways in which a number of our perceptual systems are set up help people master the very complicated task of processing language relatively easily. Despite ambiguity in many of the utterances we encounter, we can use the context of the utterance as well as other strategies to settle on the most likely intended meaning.

5. Perceptual context effects exist at many levels. Context can affect even the perception of individual sounds. The phoneme restoration effect demonstrates that people effortlessly "fill in" experimentally created gaps in a stream of speech. Context affects the ways in which individual words are interpreted, although Swinney's (1979) study suggests that context effects operate not instantaneously but after a brief period (a fraction of a second).

6. People seem to parse sentences into syntactic constituents as they construct the sentence's meaning. They appear to discard the exact wording of a sentence and to retain only its gist when they finish the processing. Many sentences involve some sort of ambiguity, which people seem to resolve very quickly.

7. In processing text passages, listeners and readers seem to be affected by the difficulty of the individual words and the syntactic complexity, as well as by the propositional complexity, the relationships among sentences, and the context in which the passage is presented. Some cognitive psychologists believe that people use story grammars to comprehend large, integrated pieces of text.

8. Conversations, spoken versions of texts, also seem governed by a system of implicit rules known as the *Gricean maxims of cooperative conversation*. Speakers who consistently violate the maxims are doing so for humorous or ironic effect, trying to end or avoid a conversation, being inattentive or inappropriate, or showing a gross disregard for the expectations of their conversation partners.

9. Two distinct proposals regarding the relation of language to other cognitive processes are the modularity hypothesis and the Whorfian hypothesis of linguistic relativity. The modularity hypothesis proposes that some aspects of language, especially syntactic processes, function autonomously, independently of any other cognitive process. This proposal, being relatively recent, awaits rigorous empirical testing, although some evidence is consistent with it. The strong version of the Whorfian hypothesis of linguistic relativity, despite its intriguing nature, has so far failed to receive strong or lasting empirical support.

10. The development of various neuroimaging techniques has allowed researchers to construct detailed "brain maps" that localize different functions. There is some ongoing disagreement over just how localized any one language process is.

Review Questions

1. Describe and evaluate the criteria that linguists and psychologists use to distinguish between (human) languages and communication systems.

2. What does the term *grammar* mean to linguists and psychologists? How does their understanding of the term differ from that of a layperson?

3. Explain the competence/performance distinction and the arguments linguists and psychologists give for making it.

4. What does it mean to say that our knowledge of linguistic rules is implicit rather than explicit? Discuss the implications of this statement.

5. Contrast the Gricean maxims of conversation with syntactic and phonological rules.

6. Describe the modularity hypothesis and its implications for the study of language as part of cognitive psychology.

7. What is the Whorfian hypothesis of linguistic relativity? Evaluate the empirical evidence bearing on it.

8. In what ways do (and don't) neuropsychological findings support Fodor's modularity hypothesis?

Key Terms

aphasia

Broca's aphasia

expressive aphasia

grammar

Gricean maxims of cooperative conversation

informationally encapsulated
process

lexical ambiguity

linguistic competence

linguistic performance

modularity hypothesis

morpheme

phoneme

phonetics

phonology

pragmatics

propositional complexity

receptive aphasia

semantics

story grammar

syntax

Wernicke's aphasia

Whorfian hypothesis of
linguistic relativity

CHAPTER 10

THINKING AND PROBLEM SOLVING

CHAPTER OUTLINE

Classic Problems and General Methods of Solution

Generate-and-Test Technique

Means–Ends Analysis

Working Backward

Backtracking

Reasoning by Analogy

Blocks to Problem Solving

Mental Set

Using Incomplete or Incorrect Representations

Lack of Problem-Specific Knowledge or Expertise

The Problem Space Hypothesis

Expert Systems

Finding Creative Solutions

Unconscious Processing and Incubation

Everyday Mechanisms

Critical Thinking

This chapter is about different kinds of thinking and **problem solving**, the kind of mental work you do in each of the following tasks:

1. Think of your favorite restaurant. What is its name? Where is it? What are its best dishes? What makes it your favorite?

2. Solve this problem: If 10 apples cost $2, how much do 3 apples cost?

3. Create unusual but appropriate titles for the drawings shown in Figure 10.1; for example, "Giant robot head" for Figure 10.1(A).

4.   Consider whether a change in one of your school's policies (for example, dropping all distribution requirements) would have overall beneficial or harmful effects.

In this chapter, we will examine descriptions and explanations for the mental work you have just done. How did you accomplish the tasks? What processes did you use? We will look at a number of different thinking tasks and discuss what makes thinking either easy or hard.

Thinking is a broad term. Psychologists who study thinking often study what look like very different tasks. Defining *thinking* turns out to be a tough job and one that itself requires thought. **Thinking** has been defined as "going beyond the information given" (Bruner, 1957), as "a complex and high-level skill" that "fill[s] up gaps in the evidence" (Bartlett, 1958, p. 20), as a process of searching through a problem space (Newell & Simon, 1972), and as

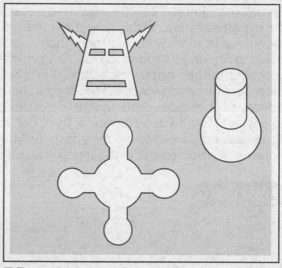

■ Figure 10.1: Ambiguous drawings.

what we do "when we are in doubt about how to act, what to believe, or what to desire" (Baron, 2000, p. 6).

Clearly, the term *thinking* is used to refer to more than one specific activity. This suggests there may be different types of thinking. One distinction that may prove useful is between *focused* and *unfocused* thinking. Focused thinking begins with a clear starting point and has a specific goal. (We will see examples of focused thinking in this chapter, as well as in much of the material in Chapter 11.) Unfocused thinking has the character of daydreaming or unintentionally calling to mind a number of different and loosely related ideas. We will primarily explore focused thinking, especially in the first sections of the chapter that deal with problem solving. We will then turn to creative thinking, which some have described as including aspects of unfocused thinking. Finally, we will examine how people evaluate the products of their thinking. In particular, we will look at the ways in which people assess their ideas, reflect on the implications of their conclusions, and guard against bias or impulsivity.

You may wonder why psychologists study thinking through the use of problems and puzzles that appear *not* to mirror the kind of thinking that occurs in everyday life (such as when you think about what shirt to wear, what to order in a restaurant, or what route to take to get to work). One reason stems from the intuition that everyday thinking often occurs so rapidly and automatically that it would be hard to study. Moreover, people likely bring much of their background knowledge to bear in their everyday thinking. You presumably choose what to wear for the day on the basis of what you expect to be doing and perhaps on external standards or expectations regarding dress. Because people have varying background knowledge and goals, then, it would be nearly impossible to devise a problem that is equal in difficulty for different individuals. By presenting standardized sets of problems, investigators have more control over the information participants have available and how it is given to them. Various problems are presented throughout the chapter as opportunities to work with the phenomena of thinking. I suggest that to maximize the value of these undertakings, you rely on a time-honored method of observation in experimental psychology: introspection. As discussed in Chapter 1, introspection is the detailed, concurrent, and nonjudgmental observation of the contents of your consciousness as you work a problem. Although introspection has problems and critics (see Ericsson & Simon, 1984, for a detailed summary), it can at the very least provide the basis for hypotheses and tests using more objective measures. The key to proper use of this technique is to avoid doing more than is asked for: Don't explain or justify what you're thinking about; just report it. Box 10.1 provides instructions on how to introspect. Before you read further, obtain paper and a pen or pencil for note taking or, preferably, a tape recorder into which you can record your thoughts as you work the problems. Work in the privacy of your room or some other quiet place. You won't be showing your notes or tapes to anyone else, so don't censor or try to control your thoughts—just be a careful observer. To assess how well the theories describe your performance, you can then compare your notes with descriptions of the theories presented.

Box 10.1

Instructions for Introspecting

1. Say whatever's on your mind. Don't hold back hunches, guesses, wild ideas, images, intentions.

2. Speak as continuously as possible. Say something at least once every 5 seconds, even if only, "I'm drawing a blank."

3. Speak audibly. Watch out for your voice dropping as you become involved.

4. Speak as telegraphically as you please. Don't worry about complete sentences and eloquence.

5. Don't overexplain or justify. Analyze no more than you would normally.

6. Don't elaborate past events. Get into the pattern of saying what you're thinking now, not of thinking for a while and then describing your thoughts.

SOURCE: Perkins (1981, p. 33).

The problems presented are similar in at least one respect: They fall into the class of problems called *well defined*. **Well-defined problems** have a clear goal (you know immediately if you've reached the solution), present a small set of information to start from, and often (but not always) present a set of rules or guidelines to abide by while you are working toward a solution. In contrast, **ill-defined problems** don't have their goals, starting information, or steps clearly spelled out.

The difference between well- and ill-defined problems can be illustrated as follows. Consider the problem of calculating the sales tax on a purchase, given that you know the price of the item you are buying, whether it is taxable, the rate of taxation, and basic rules of multiplication. If you are armed with this background information, it should be relatively easy for you, a college student, to arrive at the tax. Contrast this with another problem often encountered: composing a letter that articulately and sensitively conveys a difficult message (for example, a "Dear John" or "Dear Jane" letter to someone you're still fond of or a letter to your boss asking for a promotion). It's not clear in any of these cases of ill-defined problems what information you should start from (how much of your education and how many of your qualifications and past year's accomplishments do you tell your boss about?). It's also not clear when you've reached the goal (is the current draft good enough, or can it be made better?) or what rules (if any) apply.

Psychologists have focused on well-defined problems for several reasons: They are easy to present, they don't take weeks or months to solve, they are easy to score, and they are easy to change. It is assumed that problem solving for ill-defined problems works in similar ways to problem solving for well-defined problems, although this assumption has not been extensively tested (Galotti, 1989). In one study, Schraw, Dunkle, and Bendixen (1995) demonstrated that performance on well-defined problems was not correlated with performance on an ill-defined one.

CLASSIC PROBLEMS AND GENERAL METHODS OF SOLUTION_____

The way to solve a problem depends, to a great extent, on the problem. For instance, if your problem is to fly to Los Angeles, you might call various airlines or travel agents or even surf the web pages of relevant airlines or general travel websites such as Orbitz or Travelocity. In contrast, if your problem is to balance your checkbook, you normally would not ask for assistance from a travel agent, but you might from a banker. These are *domain-specific* problem-solving approaches—they only work for a limited class of problems. Here, I will only be reviewing a certain class of general, domain-independent techniques. These methods are stated at a general enough level that, in principle, they can be used with a wide variety of problems, not just with problems of a certain type or domain.

GENERATE-AND-TEST TECHNIQUE

Here is the first problem for you to try. Think of 10 words beginning with the letter c that are things to eat or drink. Write down all the things that occur to you, even if they end up not meeting the criteria. How are you solving this problem?

I faced a real-life problem somewhat like this several years ago. I was in Minnesota and had to get 100 Swiss francs to a hotel in Bern, Switzerland, within a week to hold a room reservation. I went to the post office to get an international money order but discovered it would take about a month for the order to make its way to the hotel. I deliberated over how to solve the problem, talked to lots of friends who've traveled more extensively than I have, and came up with a number of ideas. I could call people at American Express and see if they could help. I could see if by chance any of my friends would be traveling to Bern in the next week. I could call Western Union and wire the money. I could get a cashier's check from a bank. I could go to my automobile club, purchase a traveler's check in Swiss francs, and mail it. The first four options, as it turned out, wouldn't work or were much too expensive. The fifth one met my criteria of being possible, working within a week's time, and being (relatively) affordable, so that was the one I chose.

The process that I used in solving this problem is a good example of the **generate-and-test technique**. As the name suggests, it consists of generating possible solutions (for example, "Let's call people at American Express and see if they can help") and then testing them (for example, "Hello, American Express? Can you help me with the following problem . . . ?"). The tests didn't work for the first four possibilities but did for the fifth (it would work, the cost was reasonable, and the money would get there in time).

You may have used generate-and-test to solve the problem of listing 10 words that begin with *c* and that name things to eat or drink. When I worked on this problem, some names came to mind that sound as if they start with *c* but don't (for example, *ketchup* [unless you spell it *catsup*] and *sarsaparilla*), and some words came to mind that start with *c* but aren't edible or drinkable (*cable, canoe*). Again, the process used was thinking of possible solutions (generating) and then seeing if those possibilities met all the criteria (testing).

■ Photo 10.1: Here are some examples of foods that begin with the letter *c*.

Generate-and-test is a technique that loses its effectiveness very rapidly when there are many possibilities and when there is no particular guidance for the generation process. If you forget the combination to your locker, for instance, the technique will eventually work, but your frustration level by that time might exceed your willingness to persevere with the task. Moreover, if you don't have a way to keep track of the possibilities you have tried, along with the ones you have yet to try, you might be in real trouble. There's a joke in the movie *UHF* in which a blind man working on a Rubik's cube puzzle sits next to a sighted man. The blind man twists the Rubik's cube into a particular pattern, thrusts it in front of the sighted man, and asks, "Is this it [the correct pattern]?" "No," says the latter. The interchange is repeated, rapidly, several times. The joke is that this method of problem solving is all but doomed to failure, given the large number of possible configurations and the lack of any systematic way of trying them.

Generate-and-test can be useful, however, when there aren't a lot of possibilities to keep track of. If you've lost your keys somewhere between the cafeteria and your room and you made intermediate stops in a classroom, the snack bar, and the bookstore, you can use this technique to help you search.

MEANS–ENDS ANALYSIS

Suppose you want to visit a friend who lives in Summit, New Jersey, and you are currently residing in Pomona, California. There are several possible means of transportation: walking, bicycling, taking a taxi, taking a bus, taking a train, driving a car, or taking a plane or helicopter. The most practical means might be to fly on a commercial airline; it's the fastest and fits your budget. However, to board your flight, you have to get to the nearest airport, which is 5 miles east of your residence. Again, you could walk, bicycle, take a taxi, and so on. The most efficient and cost-effective means to get to the airport is to drive your car. However, the car is parked in the garage, not where you are sitting when you are ready to depart, so you have to get to the car. You would probably choose to walk there (as opposed to, say, calling a cab).

The technique of problem solving described here is called **means–ends analysis**. It involves comparing the goal (Summit, New Jersey) with the starting point (Pomona, California), thinking of possible ways of overcoming the distance (walking, bicycling, taking a taxi, and so on), and choosing the best one. The selected option (taking a plane) may have certain prerequisite conditions (for example, being at the airport, with a ticket). If the preconditions aren't met, then a *subgoal* is created (for example, "How can you get to the airport?"). Through the creation of subgoals, the task is broken down into manageable steps that allow a full solution to be constructed.

Newell and Simon (1972) and their associates studied means–ends analysis while solving certain arithmetic problems, such as the following:

$$
\begin{array}{r}
\text{DONALD} \\
+ \text{GERALD} \\
\hline
\text{ROBERT}
\end{array}
$$

Given that $D = 5$, determine the values for the other letters. (Problems in which letters stand for digits are known as *cryptarithmetic* problems.)

The researchers created a computer program, called **GPS**, or **General Problem Solver**, that solves problems in cryptarithmetic and in logic using means–ends analysis. GPS uses the following basic strategy. First, it looks at the object it is given (such as the preceding cryptarithmetic problem) and compares it with the desired object (an arithmetic problem with numbers in place of all letters in which the solution is actually the addition of the two numbers above the line). By doing so, GPS detects any differences between the actual and the desired object.

Next, GPS considers the operations available to change objects. Here, the available operations include those that replace certain letters with certain digits, for example, $D = 5$. The operations used are chosen with the aim of reducing differences between actual and desired objects. In cases where none of the available operations applies to the actual object, GPS tries to modify the actual object so that operations can apply. GPS also tries to keep track of various kinds of differences between desired and actual objects and to work on the most difficult differences first. Thus, if several possible operations are found, all of which could apply to an actual object, GPS has some means of ranking the different operations such that certain ones are used first.

Newell and Simon (1972) gave several problems in logic and in cryptarithmetic to both human participants and GPS and compared the "thinking" of both. Human participants generated verbal protocols, much like the ones you have been asked to generate as you read this chapter; GPS produced a printout of its goals, its subgoals, and the operations it applied as it worked.

Comparing the protocols generated, Newell and Simon (1972) concluded that there were many similarities between the performance of GPS and the performance of the Yale students who served as participants. Notice that means–ends analysis, the general heuristic (shortcut strategy) used by GPS, is a more focused method of solution than generate-and-test: It gives the problem solver more guidance in choosing what step to take next.

Means–ends analysis also forces the problem solver to analyze aspects of the problem before starting to work on it and to generate a plan to solve it. Often this requires establishing subgoals. Notice here that the problem solver is acting less "blindly" and only after some thought.

Means–ends analysis is not always the optimal way to reach a solution, however, because sometimes the optimal way involves taking a temporary step backward or further from the goal. For example, imagine you live in an eastern suburb of Los Angeles but want to take a flight from Los Angeles to Denver. To do so, you have to go first to the airport, and that means moving, temporarily, a greater distance (further west) from your goal than your current distance. Means–ends analysis can make it difficult to see that the most efficient path toward a goal isn't always the most direct one.

WORKING BACKWARD

Another general problem-solving technique is called **working backward**. Its user analyzes the goal to determine the last step needed to achieve it, then the next-to-last step, and so on. In the problem of getting to my high school friend's house, for instance, the very last step is to walk from outside her front door into the house. The problem in getting to her front door from the Manchester, New Hampshire, airport can be solved by taking a cab to her house. I can get a cab at the airport, and so on. Working backward often involves establishing subgoals, so it functions similarly to means–ends analysis.

Working backward is a very important technique for solving many problems, including the famous Towers of Hanoi problem, depicted in Figure 10.2. A successful episode of problem solving might be something like the following: "First I have to get

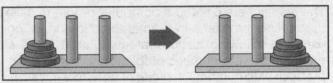

■ Figure 10.2: The Towers of Hanoi problem. Determine a sequence of moves to transfer the three disks from the first to the third peg, moving only one disk at a time and never placing a bigger disk on top of a smaller one.

the bottom disk moved over. But to do that, I have to move the top two disks. I can do that if I move the second disk to the spare peg, but to do that, I have to move the top disk out of the way. I could do that by temporarily moving it to the goal peg, then moving the second disk to the spare peg, then moving the top disk back to the spare peg, then moving the bottom disk over." Notice that the solution process usually does not start with the problem solver making a move and seeing what happens. Instead, after only a little practice, the usual pattern is to plan moves in advance, setting up many intermediate goals along the way (Egan & Greeno, 1974). Of course, it takes a few trials before the problem solver adopts the correct solution; if the puzzle consists of more than three disks, the participants are unlikely to solve it with the minimum number of moves on the first few trials (Xu & Corkin, 2001).

Working backward is most effective when the backward path is unique, which makes the process more efficient than working forward. And, as you may have noticed, working backward shares with means–ends analysis the technique of reducing differences between the current state and the goal state.

BACKTRACKING

Try this next problem. Imagine there are five women: Cathy, Debbie, Judy, Linda, and Sonya. Each of the five women owns a different breed of dog (a Bernese mountain dog, a golden retriever, a Labrador retriever, an Irish setter, or a Shetland sheepdog). And each has a different occupation (clerk, executive, lawyer, surgeon, or teacher). Also, each has a different number of children (zero, one, two, three, or four). Given the information in Box 10.2, figure out how many children the person who owns the Shetland sheepdog has.

In solving a problem, you often need to make certain provisional assumptions. Sometimes they turn out to be wrong and need to be "unmade." In those instances, it is useful to have some way to keep track of when and which assumptions were made so you can back up to certain points of choice and start over, a process known as **backtracking**. The women, dogs, children, and jobs problem in Box 10.2 is a case in point. Many people solve such problems by setting up a chart like the one shown in Figure 10.3. The chart is incomplete, corresponding to the chart of someone who has read only the first 12 lines of Box 10.2. At this point, a problem solver can determine that the golden retriever's owner, who is an executive with four children, is either Debbie or Linda. The problem solver might temporarily assume that it's Debbie, only to find out when he reads the 13th line in Box 10.2 that Debbie owns the Bernese mountain dog. He would enter that information into his chart. But if the problem solver backed up to the point at which he made the incorrect assumption (that is, knew that either Debbie or Linda was the golden retriever–owning, mother-of-four executive), he would now know it is Linda, and this information would be necessary to solve the rest of the problem. The key to backtracking, then, is for the problem solver to keep close track of choice points—places where she made a provisional assumption—so that, if subsequent work leads to a dead end, she can "back up" to that choice point and make a different assumption.

Box 10.2

The Women, Dogs, Children, and Jobs Problem

From the following information, determine how many children the owner of the Shetland sheepdog has.

> There are five women: Cathy, Debbie, Judy, Linda, and Sonya.
> There are five occupations: clerk, executive, lawyer, teacher, and surgeon.
> Everyone has a different number of children: 0, 1, 2, 3, or 4.
> Cathy owns the Irish setter.
> The teacher has no children.
> The owner of the Labrador retriever is a surgeon.
> Linda does not own the Shetland sheepdog.
> Sonya is a lawyer.
> The owner of the Shetland sheepdog does not have three children.
> The owner of the golden retriever has four children.
> Judy has one child.
> The executive owns a golden retriever.
> Debbie owns the Bernese mountain dog.
> Cathy is a clerk.

Woman	Cathy	Debbie	Judy	Linda	Sonya
Dog	Irish setter				
Number of Children			1		
Occupation					Lawyer

Golden retriever	Labrador retriever	Shetland sheepdog	
4		≠3	0
Executive	Surgeon		Teacher

■ Figure 10.3: Partial solution to the women, dogs, children, and jobs problem.

REASONING BY ANALOGY

The next problem, known as "the tumor problem," is famous in the literature:

> Given a human being with an inoperable stomach tumor and rays that destroy organic tissue at suf-ficient intensity, by what procedure can one free him of the tumor by these rays and at the same time avoid destroying the healthy tissue that surrounds it?

Originally posed to participants by Duncker (1945, p. 1), the problem is often a dif-ficult challenge. Duncker argued from studying the performance of several participants Box 10.3 presents an example protocol) that problem solving is not a matter of blind trial and error; rather, it involves a deep understanding of the elements of the problem and their relationships. To find a solution, the solver must grasp the "functional value of the solution" (p. 4) first and then arrange the specific details. The solution to the tumor problem is to send weak rays of radiation (weak enough so that no individual ray will inflict damage) from several angles, such that all rays converge at the site of the tumor. Although the radiation from any one ray will not be strong enough to destroy the tumor (or the healthy tissue in its path), the convergence of rays will be strong enough.

Gick and Holyoak (1980) presented participants with Duncker's tumor problem after each person had read a story such as the one in Box 10.4. Although the story appeared very dissimilar to the tumor problem, the underlying method of solution was the same. Gick and Holyoak found that participants who had read the story of the general *and* were told that it contained a relevant hint were more likely to solve the tumor problem than were participants who simply read the story but did not have the analogy between the problems explicitly pointed out. The former group of participants are said to be using the problem-solving technique of **reasoning by analogy**.

Box 10.3

Protocol From One of Duncker's (1945) Subjects

1. Send rays through the esophagus.

2. Desensitize the healthy tissues by means of a chemical injection.

3. Expose the tumor by operating.

4. One ought to decrease the intensity of the rays on their way; for example—would this work?—turn the rays on at full strength only after the tumor has been reached. (Experimenter: False analogy; no injection is in question.)

5. One should swallow something inorganic (which would not allow passage of the rays) to protect the healthy stomach-walls. (E: It is not merely the stomach walls which are to be protected.)

6. Either the rays must enter the body or the tumor must come out. Perhaps one could alter the location of the tumor—but how? Through pressure? No.

7. Introduce a cannula.—(E: What, in general, does one do when, with any agent, one wishes to produce in a specific place an effect which he wishes to avoid on the way to that place?)

8. (Reply:) One neutralizes the effect on the way. But that is what I have been attempting all the time.

9. Move the tumor around to the exterior. (Compare 6.) {The E repeats the problem and emphasizes " . . . which destroy at *sufficient intensity*.")

10. The intensity ought to be variable. (Compare 4.)

11. Adaptation of the healthy tissues by previous weak application of the rays. (E: How can it be brought about that the rays destroy only the region of the tumor?)

12. (Reply:) I see no more than two possibilities: either to protect the body or to make the rays harmless. (E: How could one decrease the intensity of the rays en route? [Compare 4.])

13. (Reply:) Somehow divert . . . diffuse rays . . . disperse . . . stop! Send a broad and weak bundle of rays through a lens in such a way that the tumor lies at the focal point and thus receives intensive radiation. (Total duration about half an hour.)

SOURCE: Duncker (1945, pp. 2–3).

The tumor problem and the problem of the general differ in their surface features but share an underlying structure. The components of one correspond at least roughly with the components of the other: The army is analogous to the rays, the capturing of enemy forces to the destruction of the tumor, and the convergence of soldiers at the fortress to the convergence of rays at the site of the tumor. To use the analogy, participants must engage in the "principle-finding" analysis described by Duncker, moving beyond the details and focusing on the relevant structures of the problem. Gick and Holyoak (1980) referred to this process as the induction of an abstract *schema* (using the term in the ways defined in Chapters 6 and 7). They presented evidence that participants who construct such a representation are more likely to benefit from work on analogous problems.

Box 10.4

The Story of the General

A small country was ruled from a strong fortress by a dictator. The fortress was situated in the middle of the country, surrounded by farms and villages. Many roads led to the fortress through the countryside. A rebel general vowed to capture the fortress. The general knew that an attack by his entire army would capture the fortress. He gathered his army at the head of one of the roads, ready to launch a full-scale direct attack.

However, the general then learned that the dictator had planted mines on each of the roads. The mines were set so that small bodies of men could pass over them safely, since the dictator needed to move his troops and workers to and from the fortress. However, any large force would detonate the mines. Not only would this blow up the road, but it would also destroy many neighboring villages. It therefore seemed impossible to capture the fortress.

However, the general devised a simple plan. He divided his army into small groups and dispatched each group to the head of a different road. When all was ready he gave the signal and each group marched down a different road. Each group continued down its road to the fortress so that the entire army arrived together at the fortress at the same time. In this way, the general captured the fortress and overthrew the dictator.

SOURCE: Gick and Holyoak (1980, pp. 351–353).

It is interesting that participants often had to be explicitly told to use the story of the general to solve the tumor problem. Only 30% of participants spontaneously noticed the analogy, although 75% solved the problem if told that the story of the general would be useful in constructing the solution (for comparison, only about 10% solved the problem without the story). This is similar to a finding reported by Reed, Ernst, and Banerji (1974): Participants' performance was facilitated by their previous work on an analogous problem, but only if the analogy was pointed out to them.

In later work, Gick and Holyoak (1983) found that they could do away with explicit hints if they gave two analogous stories rather than one. Participants read the story of the general and a story about a fire chief's putting out a fire by having a circle of firefighters surround it and all throw buckets of water at once. Participants were told the experiment was about story comprehension and were asked to write summaries of each story and a comparison of the two before being given the tumor problem to solve. The authors proposed that providing multiple examples helps participants to form an abstract schema (in this case, what the authors called a "convergence" schema), which they later apply to new, analogous problems. Catrambone and Holyoak (1989) further suggested that unless participants were explicitly asked to compare stories, they did not form the necessary schema with which to solve the problem.

BLOCKS TO PROBLEM SOLVING

A problem, by definition, is something that can't be solved in a single, obvious step. For instance, we don't count combing our hair as an instance of problem solving because the step of using a comb does not require much thought and no particular obstacles need to be overcome.

Problem solving, in contrast, carries the meaning of a goal with some barriers or constraints. Sometimes the barriers and constraints are so strong that they prevent, or at least seriously interfere with, successful solution. In this section, we will review some factors that apparently hinder solving a variety of problems.

MENTAL SET

Figure 10.4 presents a number of problems on the same theme: obtaining an exact amount of water, given three different-size measuring jugs. Before reading on, work on each problem in the order given and write down the time it takes you to complete each one. Also, record any thoughts about the relative difficulty of the problems.

If you actually worked the problems, you probably found the following: The first one took a relatively

Problem	Capacity of jar A	Capacity of jar B	Capacity of jar C	Desired amount
1	21	127	3	100
2	14	163	25	99
3	18	43	10	5
4	9	42	6	21
5	20	59	4	31
6	23	49	3	20
7	18	48	4	22
8	14	36	8	6

■ Figure 10.4: The water jar problem.

long time, but you were faster and faster at solving the subsequent problems; your problem-solving speed corresponded to the number of problems that you had previously worked. You also probably noticed a common pattern to the problems: All could be solved by the formula $B - A - 2C$. Did you use this formula to solve the second-to-last problem? If you did, that is interesting because an apparently more direct solution would be $A + C$. The very last problem is also interesting in that it does not fit the first formula at all but is quickly solved with a very easy formula, $A - C$. Did it take you some time to realize this? If so, your performance might be characterized as being constrained by *mental set*.

Mental set is the tendency to adopt a certain framework, strategy, or procedure or, more generally, to see things in a certain way instead of in other, equally plausible ways. Mental set is analogous to **perceptual set**, the tendency to perceive an object or pattern in a certain way on the basis of your immediate perceptual experience. Like perceptual set, mental set seems to be induced by even short amounts of practice. Working on several water jug problems in a row that follow a common pattern makes it easy to apply the formula but harder to see new relationships among the three terms.

Luchins (1942) reported on experiments in which problems such as those in Figure 10.4 were given to university students. After solving the first four problems using the formula $B - A - 2C$, all the students solved the fifth problem using this method instead of the more direct $A + C$ method. Even more striking, when the $B - A - 2C$ solution wouldn't work, students suffering from mental set were unable even to see the more obvious $A + C$ solution, which would have worked!

Mental set often causes people to make certain unwarranted assumptions without being aware of making them. Figure 10.5 gives a famous example. Most people, when asked to solve the nine-dot problem, make the assumption that the four lines must stay within the "borders" of the dots. This constraint makes it impossible to come up with the solution, shown in Figure 10.6.

Another problem relevant to mental set is borrowed from Perkins (1981). I will describe a situation, and you determine what the situation is:

> There is a man at home.
> That man is wearing a mask.
> There is a man coming home.
> What is happening?

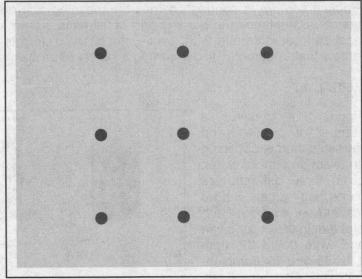

■ Figure 10.5: The nine-dot problem.

Because I can't interact with you, I'll report on the questions (constrained to be of the yes/no type) that my students ask when I present this. Is the man at home at his own home? *(Yes.)* Does the man at home know the other man? *(Yes.)* Does the man at home expect the other man? *(Yes.)* Is the mask a disguise? *(No.)* Is the man at home in a living room? *(No.)* Is the man at home in the kitchen? *(No.)*

Part of where my students start to go wrong is in making assumptions about the home in the situation. Many equate *home* with *house*, although the answer to the problem is a baseball game. Perkins (1981) would argue

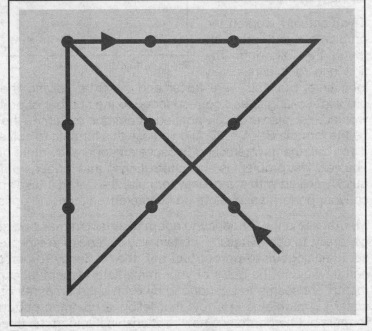

■ Figure 10.6: Solution to the nine-dot problem.

that the assumptions people make in interpreting the problem are a kind of mental set and that this mental set hinders problem solving.

Another example of mental set is illustrated in another famous problem in the literature known as the two-string problem (Maier, 1930, 1931). You are shown to a room that has two strings attached to the ceiling. The strings are spaced so far apart that you cannot hold on to both at the same time. Your task is to tie these strings together somehow. All you have in the room with you are a table, a book of matches, a screwdriver, and a few pieces of cotton. What can you do?

The solution, which many people have difficulty discovering, is to use the screwdriver as a weight to make one of the strings into a pendulum. Swing this string, walk to the other string and grab it, wait for the pendulum to swing toward you, grab it, and tie the two strings together. Fewer than 40% of the participants in Maier's experiment solved this without a hint. One source of difficulty seemed to be their unwillingness to think of other functions for a screwdriver; they failed to notice that the screwdriver could be used as a weight as well as for its intended function. This phenomenon is called **functional fixedness**. It appears to be an instance of mental set, in that a person subject to functional fixedness has apparently adopted a rigid mental set toward an object.

USING INCOMPLETE OR INCORRECT REPRESENTATIONS

A related difficulty in problem solving has to do with the initial interpretation of the problem. If the problem is misunderstood or if the wrong information is focused on, the solver is at a disadvantage. The checkerboard problem illustrates this block to problem solving.

The problem is depicted in Figure 10.7, which shows a standard checkerboard with two diagonally opposite corner squares cut off. Next to the checkerboard are a number of dominoes of such dimensions that each takes up exactly two checkerboard squares. Intact checkerboards, you'll recall, have 64 squares. This one has 62. Is there a way to arrange 31 dominoes such that every checkerboard square is covered by a domino?

The key to the solution is to realize that whatever the arrangement, each domino will cover exactly one black square and one red square, given the way checkerboards are arranged. But now notice that the two excised squares are the same color. Because a domino must cover two differently colored squares, there is no way to arrange 31 dominoes to cover the mutilated checkerboard.

■ Figure 10.7: The mutilated checkerboard problem. Can 31 dominoes be arranged to cover the remaining checkerboard squares? Each domino covers exactly two squares.

The difficulty most people have with this problem is that they fail to include these two pieces of crucial information in their initial representation of the problem. Thus the representation is incomplete. Similarly, in the baseball game (man at home) problem given earlier, representing the problem in terms of a person sitting in a house would lead you down the wrong path. It would be a case of using an incorrect representation—one that included information not presented in the problem *and* not correct.

The choice of representation can often make a great difference. S. H. Schwartz (1971), studying problems such as the women-dogs-children-jobs problem of Box 10.2, found that people who constructed charts like the one in Figure 10.3 were much more successful in solving the problems than people who merely wrote down names, dogs, jobs, and so forth with arrows or lines connecting them (for example, Cathy—Irish setter; golden retriever—four children).

Here's another well-known example of a case in which the form of the representation can make a problem either very easy or very hard. It's called the "numbers game," and the objective of each player is to choose three digits from a set of digits such that the digits chosen total exactly 15. Two players are given a sheet of numbers, 1 2 3 4 5 6 7 8 9. They take turns crossing one of the digits off the list and adding it to their own list. The first player to have three digits totaling 15 (for example, 4, 5, 6 or 1, 6, 8) wins.

If you were to play this game, what would your strategy be? If you played first, which digit would you choose? What if you played second and your opponent had first chosen a 5? The first time or two you play this game, you might find it surprisingly challenging. Now look at Figure

■ Figure 10.8: A tic-tac-toe board representation of the numbers game.

10.8, which presents an alternative way of representing this game. Notice that, depicted this way, the difficult "numbers game" is actually the game of tic-tac-toe in disguise. Rendered as in Figure 10.8, the game is easy, but without this representation, the problem is much harder to solve.

LACK OF PROBLEM-SPECIFIC KNOWLEDGE OR EXPERTISE

Until now, we have been discussing general problem-solving abilities in terms of problems that have a puzzlelike character. The assumption is that most of these problems are about equally unfamiliar to everyone and that people go about solving them in basically the same way. Other kinds of problems—for example, those in chess or other skilled games; textbook problems in physics, geometry, or electronics; computer programming; and problems in diagnosis—seem to be different in kind from the puzzles we have been talking about. In particular, experts and novices approach most such problems differently (Chi, Glaser, & Farr, 1988).

We saw in Chapter 3 that experts and novices differ in their perceptual abilities, with experts able to "pick up on" more perceptual information than a novice would. Effects of expertise are not limited to perceptual abilities, however. Familiarity with a domain of knowledge seems to change the way one solves problems within that frame of reference. A good example is to compare the ability of undergraduate psychology majors and their professors to design experiments. Typically, professors are much better at solving the problems connected to the task. Their experience in designing experiments lets them sort out the relevant from the irrelevant information and call to mind various situations that need to be noticed. Experience also provides a number of shortcut rules to use in estimating the number of participants to be used, the kinds of statistical analyses that can be performed, the duration of the experiment, and so on. Problem solvers who come to a problem with a limited knowledge base are clearly at a disadvantage.

A classic study of expert–novice differences was carried out by de Groot (1965). He examined the thinking processes of both chess masters and weaker players, finding that the master players considered about the same number of possibilities but somehow chose the best move more easily. Chase and Simon (1973), in a replication study, found that the more expertise a chess player had, the more information he extracted from even brief exposures to chessboards set up to reflect an ongoing chess game. That is, when a chess master and chess beginner are both shown a chessboard for 5 seconds, the chess master will remember more about where the pieces are placed—but only if the pieces are configured to depict a possible chess game.

Gobet and Simon (1996) examined the sophistication of play of Gary Kasparov, a Professional Chess Association world champion, as he played simultaneous games against four to eight opponents who were all chess masters. His opponents were each allowed 3 minutes per move (on average), while Kasparov was allowed one fourth to one eighth that amount of time for each move (because he was playing multiple games simultaneously). Despite the tremendous time constraints, Kasparov played almost as well as he did under tournament conditions, where he would face only one opponent and have 4 to 8 times as much time to think through and plan his moves. Gobet and Simon concluded that Kasparov's superiority came from his ability to recognize patterns more than from his ability to plan future moves. They based this conclusion on the fact that the time pressure of simultaneous games would severely hamper Kasparov's ability to think ahead, yet the overall quality of his play did not suffer.

Lesgold et al. (1988) compared the performance of five expert radiologists with that of first-, second-, third-, and fourth-year medical residents as they diagnosed X-ray pictures. They found the experts noted more specific properties of the X-ray films, hypothesized more causes and more effects, and clustered more symptoms together than did any of the nonexpert groups of medical residents.

Glaser and Chi (1988), reviewing this and other studies of expert–novice differences, described several qualitative distinctions between the two groups. First, experts excel in their own domains; that is, their knowledge is domain specific. A grand master chess player, for example, would not be expected to solve chemistry problems as well as a chemist would. We have already noted in Chapter 3 that experts perceive larger meaningful patterns in their domain of expertise than novices do. Experts are faster than novices at performing skills in their domain of expertise, and they show greater memorial abilities for information within that domain.

In problem solving, experts see and represent a problem in their domain at a deeper and more principled level than do novices, who tend to represent information superficially (Chi, Feltovich, & Glaser, 1981). For example, when solving physics problems, experts tend to organize the problems in terms of physics principles, such as Newton's first law of motion; novices instead tend to focus on the objects mentioned in the problem, such as an inclined plane or a frictionless surface. Experts also spend proportionately more time qualitatively analyzing a problem, trying to grasp or understand it, relative to novices, who are more likely to plunge in and start looking for solutions. Finally, throughout the process of problem solving, experts are more likely to check for errors in their thinking.

Expertise by itself is not always enough for problem solving, as shown dramatically in a case study of an experienced architect with a lesion to the right prefrontal cortex (Goel & Grafman, 2000). Patient P.F. was a 57-year-old architect who suffered a grand mal seizure and was treated for a stroke. Subsequent MRI scans showed a predominantly right-hemisphere lesion to the prefrontal cortex, a part of the brain previously implicated in deficits in the ability to plan and solve problems. Goel and Grafman asked P.F. (and a control architect, matched for age and education) to come to the lab to develop a new design for their lab space. Both P.F. and the control participant regarded this task as relatively easy.

P.F. was observed to have "his sophisticated architectural knowledge base . . . intact, and he used it quite skillfully during the problem structuring phase" (Goel & Grafman, 2000, p. 415). However, P.F. was unable to move from this phase to the problem-solving phase, was unable to generate a preliminary design until two thirds of the way through the two-hour session, and created an erratic and minimal preliminary design that was never developed or detailed. These authors concluded that the preliminary designs represented ill-structured problem solving (of the type described at the beginning of the chapter) and that P.F.'s lesion "has resulted in a selective impairment of the neural system that supports ill-structured representations and computations" (p. 433).

THE PROBLEM SPACE HYPOTHESIS

Researchers studying problem solving often think about the processes in terms of mentally searching a problem space (Baron, 2008; Lesgold, 1988; Newell, 1980; Newell & Simon, 1972). The main idea behind this **problem space hypothesis** is that every possible state of affairs within a problem corresponds to a node in a mental graph. The entire set of nodes occupies some mental area, and this area, together with the graph, is the problem space.

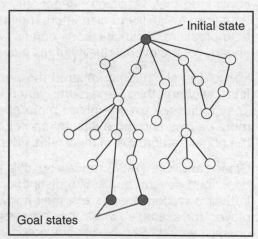

■ Figure 10.9: A generic problem space.

Figure 10.9 presents a schematic diagram of a generic problem space. Each circle, or node, corresponds to a certain state of affairs at some point during the problem-solving process. If the problem is to win a chess game, for example, each node corresponds to a possible chess-board configuration at each point in the game. The node labeled "initial state" corresponds to the conditions at the beginning of a problem—for example, a chessboard before the first move. The goal states correspond to conditions when the problem is solved—for example, configurations in which a game is won. Intermediate states (unlabeled in this diagram) are depicted by the other nodes.

If it is possible to move from one state to another by means of some operation, that move can be depicted in any paper-and-pencil representation of the problem space by a line connecting the two nodes. Any sequence of "mental moves" is shown as a sequence of moves from one node to another. Any sequence of moves beginning at the initial state and ending at the final goal state constitutes a path through the problem space. Figure 10.10 depicts a generic solution path; Figure 10.11 depicts a part of the problem space for the Towers of Hanoi problem.

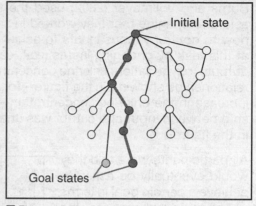

■ Figure 10.10: A solution path through the problem space.

Good problem solving is thought to be the creation of efficient paths: ones that are as short as possible and take as few detours as possible between the initial state and the goal state. It is assumed the best paths are found through searching, with thorough searches being more likely to turn up solutions.

Researchers in the field of artificial intelligence have created different search algorithms to search through problem spaces (Nilsson, 1998; Winston, 1992). One is depth-first search, which goes as far down a graph as it can to search for a goal state before backing up to examine alternatives. Another is breadth-first search, which examines all nodes at a given level to search for a goal state before delving deeper into the graph. Different algorithms have different probabilities of success depending on the nature of the graph, of course.

A study by Burns and Vollmeyer (2002) yielded some nonintuitive findings relevant to the idea of searching through problem spaces to generate solutions.

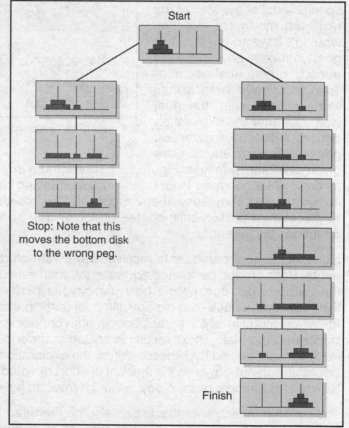

■ Figure 10.11: A part of the problem space for the Towers of Hanoi problem, showing the solution.

These authors believed that exploration of a problem space would yield better performance. Moreover, they believed, exploration was more likely when the process was not curtailed by a person's eagerness to achieve a specific goal.

Burns and Vollmeyer (2002) used the task depicted in Figure 10.12. Participants were asked to imagine that they worked in a laboratory and that they were trying to figure out how to control various inputs to achieve a certain water-quality effect. They could work at this task by changing inputs (salt, carbon, lime) and observing what happened to the outputs (oxygenation, chlorine concentration, temperature). In reality, the inputs had linear relationships showing in the figure—for example, a change in the salt input produced an increase in the chlorine concentration—but participants were not told what the relationship between input and output was (that is, they weren't shown the values on the arrows in the figure).

All participants were told they would eventually be asked to achieve a certain goal in terms of specific values for the outputs. Some of the participants (called "specific goal" participants) were given the specific goal at the start of the task, but they were told they wouldn't have to achieve this goal until after an exploration period; others (called "nonspecific goal" participants) weren't told what the goal was until after the exploration period. After the exploration phase, all participants were

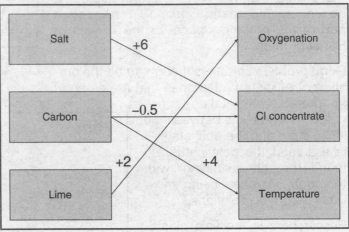

■ Figure 10.12: The water-tank system (note that Cl concentrate is the chlorine concentrate output).

given a diagram similar to Figure 10.12 but without any of the links shown and were asked to draw links between inputs and outputs, placing directions and weights on the links if they thought they knew them. From this, the researchers derived a "structure score" to calculate a participant's degree of knowledge about the correct values of the links' directions and weights.

Nonspecific goal participants received higher structure scores than specific goal participants. Both groups performed equivalently when asked to achieve specific goal values for the outputs, but nonspecific goal participants performed better on a transfer problem with new goal values than did specific goal participants. Burns and Vollmeyer (2002) did a follow-up study in which participants in both conditions were asked to think aloud as they performed the task. These results indicated that nonspecific goal participants were more likely to test specific hypotheses during the exploration phase. Presumably, having a specific goal can cut down on the amount of effort devoted to searching the problem space, in Newell and Simon's terminology, although this can have its costs, depending on the task.

The problem space hypothesis can also be recruited to help us understand how blocks to problem solving work. Searches that fail to explore parts of the space (because of mental set, for example) can block problem solving when the solution lies in a part of the space that isn't searched. Incomplete or incorrect representations are likely to result in the construction of an incomplete or incorrect problem space, which in turn also harms problem solving.

The acquisition of expertise is another way to explore problem spaces. Expertise presumably allows people to develop better hunches about which areas of the problem space will be most useful to explore and in what order exploration is most likely to yield results.

EXPERT SYSTEMS

The problem space hypothesis has been used to create **expert systems**, computer programs designed to model the judgments of one or more human experts in a particular field. Expert systems contain a knowledge base, which stores facts relevant within that field. They typically also contain a set of **inference rules** (of the form "If X is true, then Y is true"), a search engine that the program uses to search the knowledge base using the inference rules, and some interface, or means of interacting with a human user who has a question or problem for which he or she is consulting the expert system (Benfer, Brent, & Furbee, 1991).

One example of an expert system is MUckraker, an expert system designed to give advice to investigative reporters regarding the best way to approach people for interviews, to prepare for interviews, and to examine public documents while investigating an issue (Benfer et al., 1991). Table 10.1 presents some (simplified) rules MUckraker uses to give advice on how to approach a person for an interview.

The format of the rules used includes several antecedents, or conditions. Rule 2, for example, has three antecedents: (a) The probable source will not talk by telephone with the reporter; (b) the interview is crucial; and (c) there are more than 6 days in which to get the interview. Each of these antecedents specifies a condition that must be met for the rule to be activated.

Rules also have a consequent part, indicated by the word THEN. These consequents are actions to be taken if the rule is applied. For example, the action of Rule 2 is to set a variable (send_by_mail2) to a certain value (namely, 80). Some rules also include an explanation or justification, preceded by the word BECAUSE. Notice the references to "send_by_mail1," "send_by_mail2," and so forth. These are names of variables used by the program. Rules 1 through 4 assign values to send_by_mail1 through send_by_mail4, respectively. Rule 5 checks to see whether any of these four variables have been assigned a value greater than 79. If so, Rule 5 directs the reporter to send the potential interviewee a request by mail.

Creating expert systems is a complex undertaking. Typically, one or more human experts in the domain are interviewed, often repeatedly. They are often asked to generate a verbal online protocol, thinking aloud as they classify instances or solve problems (Stefik, 1995). Part of the difficulty comes from the fact that it is difficult for any expert to state all of his or her knowledge.

For example, you are probably "expert" at studying for academic exams, right? Suppose I simply asked you to state all your knowledge that pertains to the activity of studying for an exam. Hard to do, isn't it? Expert system developers therefore often find themselves adopting techniques from anthropologists. They follow experts around as they "do their thing," often asking them to elaborate on their thinking as it happens (Benfer et al., 1991). Through repeated interviews, the developers are able to formulate rules such as those shown in Table 10.1.

■ Table 10.1 Simplified Examples of Rules From MUckraker

Rule 1: Prefer_mail
IF <u>unknown</u> whether source will talk
    with reporter on telephone
AND the interview is critical
AND there are ≥ 6 days to get the
interview

THEN (send_by_mail)$_1$ request = 60
ELSE telephone request = 40
BECAUSE may get the interview with
    a formal, written request.

Rule 2: Definitely_prefer_mail
IF <u>probable</u> source <u>will not</u> talk with
    reporter on telephone
AND the interview is critical
AND there are ≥ 6 days to get the
    interview

THEN (send_by_mail)$_2$ request = 80
BECAUSE see Rule 1.

Rule 3: Telephone_anyway
IF probable source will not talk with
reporter on telephone
    AND if the interview is <u>not-critical</u>
OR there are ≤ 6 days to get the
    interview

THEN (send_by_mail)$_3$ request = 10
BECAUSE there isn't time for mail
AND telephoning worth a try.

Rule 4: Older_sources
IF the age of the source is $>$ <u>49 years</u>
AND the interview is critical
AND there are ≥ 6 days to get the
    interview

THEN (send–by–mail)$_4$ request = 90
BECAUSE older individuals respond
    more positively to written requests.

Rule 5: Combine_Send-by_mail
IF maximum of (send_by_mail)i > 79

THEN send written request and ASK:
    Do you want to see a sample letter?
ELSE telephoning worth a try
BECAUSE most sources will talk to a
    reporter on the telephone.

SOURCE: Benfer et al. (1991, p. 6).

Why would anyone *want* to develop computerized expert systems and use them in place of human experts? One reason may be that the supply of highly trained human experts is limited in many domains. Not every city, for example, has an expert in every domain, and if the knowledge possessed by experts can be distributed through software, the wealth is spread.

A second argument will be further elaborated in Chapter 11. There we will see that human decision making is often, if not always, tainted by biases, some quite insidious. Especially when a problem is complex, with many factors, the cognitive load placed on the person facing the problem can quickly become overwhelming. Having an expert system means gaining a handle on the complexity and preventing it from crushing the process of finding the best solution.

FINDING CREATIVE SOLUTIONS

Many of the problems psychologists ask people to solve require *insight,* a change in frame of reference or in the way elements of the problem are interpreted and organized.

The process by which insight occurs is not well understood. Whatever it is, it appears to play a vital role in what is commonly called **creativity**. Although the term is difficult to define precisely, many psychologists agree that creativity has to do with appropriate novelty—that is, originality that suits some purpose (Hennessey & Amabile, 1988; Nielsen, Pickett, & Simonton, 2008; Runco, 2004; Simonton, 2011). Appropriate ideas that lack novelty are mundane; conversely, original ideas that do not address some problem in a useful way are bizarre. Other cognitive scientists talk of creativity as consisting of a combination, or recombination, of knowledge, information, or mental representations— things the creator "already has," knows of, or has depicted (Dartnall, 2002).

Great artistic, musical, scientific, or other discoveries often seem to share a critical moment, a mental "Eureka!" experience when the proverbial "lightbulb" goes on. Many biographies of composers, artists, scientists, and other eminent experts begin with "Eureka!" stories (Perkins, 1981, presented a review of some of these). Such stories lead to the notion that creative people have something that less creative people don't have or that their cognitive processes work in very different ways (at least while they are being creative) than those of less creative people.

In this section, we will focus on two types of explanations for creative insight: one that describes creativity as special cognitive processing and one that describes it as the result of normal, everyday cognition.

UNCONSCIOUS PROCESSING AND INCUBATION

As a college junior, I took courses in calculus, which, although extremely useful, were often extremely frustrating to me. I would work on a homework assignment only to find one of the problems absolutely unworkable. The problem would nag at me, and I'd try every technique I could think of. In frustration, I would put the problem aside and go on to other things. Late that night, sometimes waking from sleep, I would see the problem in a whole new light. Often I had discovered the correct solution. (On occasions when I'd hit on another incorrect solution, my feelings of frustration were renewed. On those occasions, I was known to grab the textbook and fling it against the nearest wall. The book did not survive the semester.)

The experience I am describing is a "textbook case" of **unconscious processing**, or **incubation**. The idea is that while my mind was actively running other cognitive processes, some other sort of processing was happening in the background. (Those of you who like computer metaphors might describe this as "batch processing" as opposed to "interactive processing.") The unconscious processing churned away, even as I slept, until the answer was found; then the answer announced itself all at once, even if it had to wake me up. Those who believe in incubation typically believe in the existence of an unconscious layer of the mind that can process information without giving rise to conscious awareness.

S. M. Smith and Blakenship (1989) offered one empirical demonstration of incubation effects by means of picture-word puzzles called *rebuses*. After the participants had solved 15 rebuses, they were presented with a 16th, which had a misleading cue that induced fixation on an incorrect interpretation. They were later given this critical rebus a second time, without the cue, and were again asked to solve the puzzle and also to recall the cue. Control participants saw the second presentation of the rebus immediately, but experimental participants received either a 5- or 15-minute "break" from the puzzle, when they either did nothing or were asked to complete a demanding music perception task (to prevent them from continuing to work on the rebus surreptitiously). Smith and Blakenship predicted that those who were given longer "filled" intervals (during which the music task was presented) would be more likely to forget the misleading cue and thus to solve the rebus. In fact, this pattern of results is exactly the one they reported.

Most empirical studies, however, fail to find positive effects of incubation. Participants who take physical and mental breaks during problem solving, and who therefore have more opportunity for incubation, rarely show increased ability to solve problems more thoroughly or more quickly than participants who work steadily at the problem (Olton, 1979). Moreover, participants in another study on incubation effects reported that during the "break" periods, they surreptitiously thought aloud about the problem. In fact, participants in another experimental condition who during the break were prevented from engaging in covert thinking about the problem (by having to memorize a text passage) showed very few effects of incubation (Browne & Cruse, 1988).

Designing critical tests of the incubation hypothesis is very difficult: Experimenters must make sure participants really do cease consciously thinking about the problem during the incubation interval, a challenging task for experimenters who cannot read minds!

EVERYDAY MECHANISMS

Does creative insight depend on special cognitive processes, such as incubation? An alternative view asserts that it results from ordinary cognitive processes that virtually every person uses in the normal course of life (Perkins, 1981). Perkins's ideas provide a coherent overview of this approach to the study of creativity and will be reviewed in detail here. Other authors offer slightly different proposals but share Perkins's idea that the processes leading to creativity are not extraordinary (Langley & Jones, 1988; Sternberg, 1988; Ward, Smith, & Finke, 1999; Weisberg, 1988).

Perkins (1981) described examples of cognitive processes that underlie normal everyday functioning as well as creative invention. One such process is *directed remembering.* This is the ability to channel your memory in order to make conscious some past experience or knowledge that meets various constraints. The first task in this chapter, asking you to think of foods and drinks whose names begin with *c,* is a directed-remembering task. Perkins argued that the same process goes on in creative invention. Darwin's construction of evolution theory, for instance, had to provide an explanation consistent with existing scientific knowledge. That knowledge constrained the types of explanations he could develop.

A second relevant cognitive process is *noticing.* An important part of creation, artists and scientists assert, is revising drafts. In revising, one needs to notice where the problems are. Noticing also plays a role in many "Eureka!" or "Aha!" experiences, according to Perkins, in which creators notice a similarity between one problem and another.

Contrary recognition, or the ability to recognize objects not for what they are but as something else, is another important creative process. Seeing a cloud as a castle is a familiar example. This ability obviously relates to analog thinking in that it requires the creator to move beyond the bounds of reality, of what is, and to imagine reality in other ways.

This approach to creativity, then, assumes that creative individuals use the same cognitive processes that so-called noncreative people use. Its proponents argue that "flashes of insight" actually occur in a progressive, step-by-step fashion. Incubation, following this line of argument, has to do with making a fresh start on the solution process, forgetting old approaches that did not work. Note that this description is quite similar to descriptions of what it means to break a mental set.

Indeed, the relationship between problem solving and the contrary recognition approach to creativity is strong. Both include the idea of a mental search for possibilities that are novel and that meet various requirements or constraints. A person's creativity has to do with a willingness to search harder and longer for solutions that meet multiple constraints. What constitutes creativity, then, are a creator's own values for original, useful results; an ability to withstand potentially long periods without success; and plans and abilities.

Many proposed accounts of creativity remain, for the most part, untested empirically. Thus, the question of whether acts of creativity use special-purpose or regular cognitive processes remains open, as researchers struggle to develop appropriate empirical methods to investigate creativity (Runco & Sakamoto, 1999). The proposals just described, then, should be seen as ideas that can guide future investigations rather than as well-developed theories that have survived rigorous testing.

CRITICAL THINKING

Much creativity hinges on the ability to generate a number of ideas that might at first seem "off the wall" or "out of touch." Once a novel idea is generated, however, it must be evaluated and assessed in terms of its appropriateness. Does the proposed solution really meet all the objectives and constraints? Are there hidden or subtle flaws in the idea? What are the proposal's implications?

A person asking these kinds of questions can be described as doing what psychologists, philosophers, and educators call **critical thinking**. Many definitions of critical thinking exist. Dewey (1933), who called it "reflective thinking," defined it as "active, persistent, and careful consideration of any belief or supposed form of knowledge in the light of the grounds that support it and the further conclusions to which it tends" (p. 9). Dewey distinguished between reflective thought and other kinds: random ideas, rote recall, or beliefs for which a person has no evidence.

Wertheimer (1945), a Gestalt psychologist, presented several examples that illustrate critical thinking quite well. One concerns learning how to find the area of a parallelogram. One way to teach someone how to do this is by teaching a formula, such as the familiar one from high school geometry: Area = Base × Altitude. Figure 10.13(A) presents an example of a parallelogram with the base and altitude labeled.

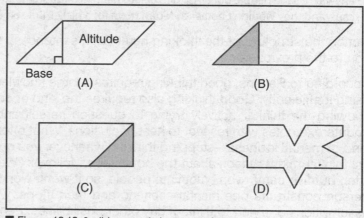

■ Figure 10.13: Parallelograms and other geometric figures.

If the student memorizes this formula carefully, he will have a "rote" means, or what Wertheimer (1945) called a "mechanically repetitive" means, of solving the problem. One problem with rote solutions, however, is that if a student forgets the formula, he may be at a complete loss. A better approach, Wertheimer argued, is to teach the student to grasp the "essential structure" of the problem—to identify and understand the fundamental issues.

Consider the parallelogram in Figure 10.13(B), noting the shaded area. Suppose this area is cut off the parallelogram and added to the other side, as shown in Figure 10.13(C). The transformation of the object creates a familiar and simple geometric object, a rectangle. The formula for finding the area of a rectangle is well known (Base × Altitude). Note that the transformation has added exactly the same area to the right side of the figure as was subtracted from the left. As a result, the total area has not been changed. Instead, a more "regular" geometric figure, with exactly the same area, has been created.

What is the advantage of teaching this method of solution? For one thing, it is more generalizable. The method applies not just to parallelograms but to many geometrically irregular figures, such as the one depicted in Figure 10.13(D). For another, the solution shows a deeper understanding of *why* the formula works. In this instance, the formula is not simply blindly applied to the problem but rather grows out of the student's understanding of the nature of a parallelogram as a geometric object.

In a more recent study of critical thinking, David Perkins and his colleagues (Perkins, Allen, & Hafner, 1983) presented students and adults of various levels of educational background with various controversial issues. Participants were asked to reason aloud about each issue. One example was "Would a law requiring a five-cent deposit on bottles and cans reduce litter?" (Perkins et al., p. 178). The authors measured critical thinking by looking at the number of times a participant raised objections or challenges to his own thinking. An example of what the researchers would consider good critical thinking is the following:

> The law wants people to return the bottles for the five cents, instead of littering them. But I don't think five cents is enough nowadays to get people to bother. But wait, it isn't just five cents at a blow, because people can accumulate cases of bottles or bags of cans in their basements and take them back all at once, so probably they would do that. Still, those probably aren't the bottles and cans that get littered anyway; it's the people out on picnics or kids hanging around the street and parks that litter bottles and cans, and they wouldn't bother to return them for a nickel. But someone else might. (p. 178)

Notice the structure of the thinking here: Each sentence in some way presents an objection to the previous one.

According to Perkins, good thinking requires a large knowledge base and some means of using it efficiently. Good thinking also requires the kind of objection raising just illustrated, showing the thinker actively trying to question herself and to construct examples and counterexamples with respect to her conclusions. What often hampers critical thinking is a kind of mental laziness—stopping thinking whenever you get any answer at all. An uncritical thinker might reason about the bottle bill as follows: "Well, it'd be nice to try to reduce litter, but five cents won't motivate people, so it won't work." Notice that in this case, the person constructs one mental scenario and then stops, without questioning any of the assumptions or trying to think of any other possibilities. Perkins et al. (1983) urged people to overcome this tendency to think about an issue only until things make superficial sense and, instead, to search harder and look longer for other possibilities and interpretations.

Summary

1. Thinking, the manipulation of information, occurs for a wide range of what appear to be very different tasks. Psychologists draw distinctions among types of problems (for example, between well-defined and ill-defined ones) and among types of thinking (for example, focused versus unfocused). It is not yet clear, however, whether the cognitive processes used for different tasks are themselves really different in kind. An alternative possibility is that what look like different kinds of thinking really stem from different combinations of the same cognitive processes.

2. Some psychologists studying problem solving have discovered general strategies (for example, generate-and-test, means–ends analysis, reasoning by analogy) that they believe people use in a wide variety of situations. Psychologists have also explored different blocks to problem solving (mental set, functional fixedness, incorrect or incomplete problem representations).

3. Other psychologists argue for the importance of domain-specific knowledge and strategies as a better predictor of whether a given person will have success solving a given problem. These investigators point out that problem-solving strategies often vary with the expertise, or background knowledge, of the problem solver.

4. Similarities among kinds of thinking can also be identified. Some psychologists argue that the similarities can be explained by a common framework: the idea that all sorts of instances of thinking (including episodes of problem solving, inventing, and even reasoning and decision making, covered in Chapter 12) are all a kind of mental search (Baron, 2008). This proposal accepts the problem space hypothesis, or something close to it, as a good account of how people mentally manipulate information. The problem space hypothesis views thinking as finding a path through a "mental graph" of possibilities (the mental graph being the problem space). Sometimes the search for a path is very focused and constrained; at other times (for example, during episodes of daydreaming), it meanders without a definite goal.

5. Expert systems, computer programs designed to mimic a human expert in a specific field, are one kind of instantiation of a problem space. Expert systems contain a knowledge base, inference rules, some means of searching through the knowledge base, and a user interface so that the human user can ask questions and be queried to provide the program with more information.

6. Psychologists studying creativity differ over whether there is one general creativity, independent of domain, or whether creativity, like expertise, is specific to a domain. Some argue for special-purpose creative cognitive processes, such as incubation and unconscious processing; others believe that creativity makes use of everyday, ordinary cognitive processes such as directed remembering and contrary recognition.

7. Some psychologists have argued that the factors that seem to promote good performance on one type of thinking task also seem to help on others. Among these factors are remaining open-minded, exploring unusual possibilities, questioning the first conclusion you come to, trying to avoid bias, and trying to find new and fresh approaches.

8. Although no one would argue that thinking skills can substitute for a broad and deep knowledge base, what is suggested is that good thinking skills help you get the most out of the knowledge you have. This suggestion, based largely on anecdotal proposals from educators, philosophers, and psychologists, awaits future research on the processes used in all kinds of thinking.

Review Questions

1. Do well-defined and ill-defined processes make use of the same cognitive processes? How might psychologists go about trying to answer this question?

2. Compare and contrast the generate-and-test, the means–ends analysis, and the reasoning-by-analogy approaches to problem solving.

3. What might the Gick and Holyoak results on reasoning by analogy suggest about people applying theoretical principles in real-world situations? Explain.

4. In what ways is mental set similar to perceptual set (described in Chapter 3)? In what ways are the two phenomena dissimilar?

5. Describe some of the expert–novice differences in problem solving.

6. Discuss the problem space hypothesis. How might it account for and explain the various blocks to problem solving?

7. Explore the connections and differences between various possible problem solving strategies reviewed in the chapter.

8. What kinds of cognitive processes have been proposed to account for creativity? How can an experimental psychologist test the role of any one of these processes?

Key Terms

backtracking	ill-defined problem	problem space hypothesis
creativity	incubation	reasoning by analogy
critical thinking	inference rule	thinking
expert system	means–ends analysis	unconscious processing
functional fixedness	mental set	well-defined problem
generate-and-test technique	perceptual set	working backward
GPS (General Problem Solver)	problem solving	

CHAPTER 11

REASONING AND DECISION MAKING

CHAPTER OUTLINE

Reasoning

Types of Reasoning

Deductive Reasoning

    Propositional Reasoning

    Syllogistic Reasoning

Inductive Reasoning

    Analogical Reasoning

    Hypothesis Testing

Everyday Reasoning

Decision Making

Setting Goals

Gathering Information

Structuring the Decision

Making a Final Choice

Evaluating

Cognitive Illusions in Decision Making

Availability

Representativeness

Framing Effects

Anchoring

Sunk Cost Effects

Illusory Correlation

Hindsight Bias

Confirmation Bias

Overconfidence

Utility Models of Decision Making
   Expected Utility Theory
   Multiattribute Utility Theory
Descriptive Models of Decision Making
   Image Theory
   Recognition-Primed Decision Making
Neuropsychological Evidence on Reasoning and Decision Making

I t is six o'clock, and you've been waiting for more than an hour for your friend to arrive for dinner. She's almost always on time, and she's the kind of person who would call if she knew she'd be late. You remember her telling you she would be driving her car to get to your place. Putting all this information together, you conclude that, more than likely, she's caught in traffic. Psychologists use the term *reasoning* to describe these and other cognitive processes "that [transform] given information (called the set of **premises**) in order to reach conclusions" (Galotti, 1989, p. 333). You make a decision to sit tight and wait another half hour before doing anything else.

The terms *reasoning* and *decision making* are often used interchangeably with the term *thinking,* and you may therefore notice a great deal of overlap between the topics covered in this chapter and those covered in Chapter 10, "Thinking and Problem Solving." The psychologists who do make distinctions among these terms see the first two as special cases of the third. Specifically, when cognitive psychologists speak of *reasoning,* they mean a specific kind of thinking: the kind done to solve certain kinds of puzzles or mysteries. Reasoning often involves the use of certain principles of logic. At other times, the term *reasoning* is used more broadly, to cover instances of thinking in which people take certain information as input and, by making various inferences, either create new information or make implicit information explicit. Cognitive psychologists use the term *decision making* to refer to the mental activities that take place when one chooses among alternatives. We'll look at each of these cognitive processes in turn.

REASONING

When reasoning, we have one or more particular goals in mind—our thinking is focused. Reasoning involves drawing inferences or conclusions from other information. Some of the conclusions we draw involve new information; however, many are so mundane that we may not even notice we have done any mental work to draw them. For instance, a friend says to you, "Last night at softball, I managed to catch a pop fly." From this, you almost automatically infer that your friend in fact tried to catch that ball. Her word *managed* presupposes effort on her part, and this presupposition cues your inference. All this happens so quickly and automatically that you would probably not even notice you had drawn an inference. In fact, you took your friend's statement (the premise) and drew the conclusion you did on the basis of your understanding of the words in the premise and their presuppositions.

Psychologists studying reasoning often give people logical puzzles to solve. One of my favorite examples (based on Lewis Carroll's *Alice in Wonderland*) is shown in Box 11.1. Try to solve it on your own before comparing your thinking with the solution, which is laid out at the end of the chapter in Box 11.2. In these kinds of tasks, the inferences people draw often follow principles of formal logic. This tendency has led some cognitive psychologists to develop a "psychologic," or set of logical principles that they believe people rely on to draw inferences. We will consider examples of such systems later.

Box 11.1

A Logic Puzzle

"How about making us some nice tarts?" the King of Hearts asked the Queen of Hearts one cool summer day.

"What's the sense of making tarts without jam?" said the Queen furiously. "The jam is the best part!"

"Then use jam," said the King.

"I can't!" shouted the Queen. "My jam has been stolen!"

"Really!" said the King. "This is quite serious! Who stole it?"

"How do you expect me to know who stole it? If I knew, I would have had it back long ago and the miscreant's head in the bargain!"

Well, the King had his soldiers scout around for the missing jam, and it was found in the house of the March Hare, the Mad Hatter, and the Dormouse. All three were promptly arrested and tried.

"Now, now!" exclaimed the King at the trial. "I want to get to the bottom of this! I don't like people coming into my kitchen and stealing my jam!" . . .

"Did you by any chance steal the jam?" the King asked the March Hare.

"I never stole the jam!" pleaded the March Hare. . . .

"What about you?" the King roared to the Hatter, who was trembling like a leaf. "Are you by any chance the culprit?"

The Hatter was unable to utter a word; he just stood there gasping and sipping his tea.

"If he has nothing to say, that only proves his guilt," said the Queen, "so off with his head immediately!"

"No, no!" pleaded the Hatter. "One of us stole it, but it wasn't me!"

"And what about you?" continued the King to the Dormouse. "What do you have to say about all of this? Did the March Hare and the Hatter both tell the truth?"

"At least one of them did," replied the Dormouse, who then fell asleep for the rest of the trial.

As subsequent investigation revealed, the March Hare and the Dormouse were not both speaking the truth.

Who stole the jam?

(The solution is on page 317.)

Other psychologists have noted, however, that some situations that require inferences do not have logical principles that apply. For example, consider the following **analogical reasoning** task: Washington is to 1 as Jefferson is to what? It seems unlikely that any general rule will apply to this problem; rather, drawing the correct inference will depend on your knowledge of US presidents and either their serial order of office (Washington was the first president, Jefferson the third) or their appearance on US paper currency (Washington on the $1 bill, Jefferson on the $2 bill).

We will examine a variety of reasoning tasks in the upcoming sections. To describe people's performance, you will first need to understand something about logical principles and arguments and kinds of reasoning tasks. These will be reviewed in the next section. We will then examine three general frameworks that attempt to explain the mental processes we use when we draw inferences and conclusions.

TYPES OF REASONING

Cognitive psychologists, along with philosophers, draw many distinctions between kinds of reasoning. One common distinction divides reasoning into two types: deductive and inductive. There are several ways to explain the difference between the two. One way is to say that **deductive reasoning** goes from the general to the specific or particular (for example, "All college students like pizza; Tim is a college student; therefore, Tim likes pizza"). **Inductive reasoning** goes from the specific to the general (for example, "Gage is a college student; Gage lives in a dormitory; therefore, all college students live in dormitories").

Another way to describe the difference between the two types of reasoning is to say that in deductive reasoning, no new information is added; any conclusion drawn represents information that was already implicit in the premises. Inductive reasoning, in contrast, can result in conclusions that contain new information.

A third, related way of talking about the differences between deductive and inductive reasoning has to do with the claims that can be made for the kinds of conclusions drawn. Deductive reasoning, if performed correctly, results in conclusions that are said to have **deductive validity** (Skyrms, 1975). An argument is deductively valid if and only if it is impossible for the premises to be true and the conclusion (or conclusions) to be false. Deductive validity thus provides the reasoner with a nice guarantee: Start with true premises and reason according to logical principles, and the conclusion you come to cannot be false. The argument about Tim and the pizza is a deductive argument: If it is true that all college students like pizza and that Tim is a college student, then we know, with absolute certainty, that Tim likes pizza.

It would be very nice, in many ways, if all kinds of reasoning resulted in guaranteed conclusions. However, deductive validity is a property that holds only for deductive reasoning. Many kinds of reasoning are inductive rather than deductive, and in these cases we cannot be certain of our conclusions; we can have only stronger or weaker confidence in them. Take the argument about Gage's living in a dormitory. Even if Gage *is* a college student and *does live* in a dormitory, that does not in any way guarantee the conclusion that all college students live in dormitories.

In general, inductive reasoning deals with probable, not guaranteed, truth. Assuming that inductive reasoning has begun with true premises and followed acceptable principles, it has the property of **inductive strength**. An argument has inductive strength if it is improbable (but not impossible) for the premises to be true and the conclusion false (Skyrms, 1975). In the next two sections, we will review examples of specific deductive and inductive reasoning tasks. These examples should clarify the distinction between the two types of reasoning, which many argue call upon different modes of evaluation (Rips, 2001).

DEDUCTIVE REASONING

Deductive reasoning has been of interest to psychologists, philosophers, and logicians since at least Aristotle (Adams, 1984). Various systems of logic were devised to set a standard to evaluate human reasoning. Of the several kinds of deductive reasoning, we will discuss two: propositional and syllogistic reasoning. Before examining people's performance on these reasoning tasks, first we need to understand the tasks themselves. To do so, let's briefly review some logical terms.

Propositional Reasoning

Propositional reasoning involves drawing conclusions from premises that are in the form of propositions. A *proposition* can be thought of as an assertion—for example, "John likes chocolate cake," "The population of Northfield, Minnesota, is around 19,000," or "Today is Friday." Propositions are either true or false. For the sake of convenience, they may be abbreviated to single letters—for example, letting p stand for the proposition "Mary is a philosophy major."

Simple propositions, such as the ones just given, can be hooked together into more complicated (compound) propositions by using certain **logical connectives**. These connectives include **&** (ampersand), which functions somewhat as the English word *and* does (for example, "John likes chocolate cake, and Mary likes root beer"); **V**, which functions somewhat as the English word *or* does, only less so (for example, "George lives in Omaha, or my skirt is made of cotton"); ¬, the negation operator, akin to *not* (for example, "It is not true that the moon is made of green cheese"); and →, called the material implication connective, which works roughly like the English construction "If . . . , then . . ." (for example, "If it is after five o'clock, then I should go home").

In these definitions, I said that each logical symbol functions *somewhat* as an English word does. What do I mean by this? Unlike English words, logical connectives are defined *truth-functionally:* The truth or falsity of a compound proposition such as p & q depends only on the truth or falsity of p and the truth or falsity of q (Suppes, 1957). Notice that truth-functionality works differently than the way English is typically interpreted to work. Consider two sentences: "John got dressed, and John left the house," and "John left the house, and John got dressed." We tend to interpret these two sentences differently, seeing the first as a typical day in the life of John and the second as a possibly bizarre episode. However, if we let p equal "John got dressed," and q equal "John left the house," then "p & q" has exactly the same interpretation in logic as "q & p." We call these two compound propositions *logically equivalent.* The expression "p & q" is given the truth value "true" if and only if p is true and q is true.

The connective V matches up even less well with the English word *or.* The English term is typically used in the exclusive sense, as in "You can have a cookie or a candy bar," implying that you can't have both. In contrast, V is used in the inclusive sense. Thus, a person who heard the previous statement and interpreted it in a strictly logical fashion could get more to eat than a person who interpreted the sentence in the typical way. The expression p V q is true if and only if p is true, q is true, or both are true. Said another way, "p V q" is false if and only if p is false and q is false.

Next, let's consider the connective →. In logical terms, "p → q" is equivalent (carries the same truth value) to "¬p V q (read: "not-p or q"). The equivalence is not at all intuitive but results from the way that V is defined. We call p in the expression "$p \rightarrow q$" the antecedent and q the consequent, and we say that "$p \rightarrow q$" is true whenever the antecedent is false or the consequent is true. Alternatively, we could say that "$p \rightarrow q$" is false only when p is true and q is false. Thus, the sentence "If my maternal grandmother lived to be 569 years old, then my car is a Mercedes-Benz," is automatically true (even though my only car is a Toyota Sienna), because the antecedent ("My maternal grandmother lived to be 569 years old") is false. Notice that in logic, no cause-and-effect relationship must be present or is even implied. This contrasts with English, because we normally expect the antecedent (what precedes) to be related to the cause of the consequent (what follows) when we use the expression "If . . . , then. . . ." Also, when using the English expression, we consider "If p, then q," to be false if p is false and q true (unlike in logic, where it would be considered true).

Here's an example: I say, "If you don't stop practicing your tuba playing, I'll scream." In response, you cease your irritating playing. I scream anyway. I have behaved perfectly reasonably according to logic, even though I've violated your expectations. To see why, remember that the logical interpretation of "If p, then q," is equivalent to the logical interpretation of "not-p or q." Substituting for p and q with our example, then "If you don't stop practicing your tuba playing, (then) I'll scream," is the same thing (in logic) as "You [will] stop practicing your tuba playing [or] I'll scream [or both]." Compound propositions can be formed out of simple propositions joined by connectives. Evaluating the truth status of such compound propositions can be difficult. The final truth values of any compound expression depend only on the truth values of the individual propositions. Logicians have often used truth tables as a systematic way to consider all possible combinations of truth values of individual propositions. In a **truth table**, every possible combination of truth values of individual propositions is listed, and the definitions of the connectives are used to fill in the overall truth value of the final expression. This method of solution is algorithmic, in the sense that it's guaranteed to reveal whether a compound proposition is always true (in which case it's called a **tautology**), sometimes true, or always false (in which case it's called a **contradiction**).

One big problem with truth tables, however, is that they grow at a very fast rate as the number of individual propositions increases. If there are n simple propositions in an expression, the truth table for that expression will be 2^n lines long. Various "shortcut" methods have therefore been developed, many of them in the form of rules of inference. Two well-known rules are *modus ponens* and *modus tollens.* Box 11.3 presents examples of valid rules of inference. To say that a rule is valid is to say that if the premises are true and the rules are followed, the conclusion will also be true.

Box 11.3

Examples of Inferences Rules and Fallacies

Symbols above the lines are premises; symbols below the lines are conclusions.

Modus Ponens (valid)	Modus Tollens (valid)	Denying the Antecedent (fallacy)	Affirming the (valid) Consequent (fallacy)
$p \rightarrow q$	$p \rightarrow q$	$p \rightarrow q$	$p \rightarrow q$
p	$\neg q$	$\neg p$	q
q	$\neg p$	$\neg q$	p

Also shown in Box 11.3 are two other "rules" that turn out not to be valid; that is, they can produce conclusions that are false even if the premises are true. "Rules" of this sort are called **fallacies**. Let's work through examples of why these rules are fallacies. Consider *affirming the consequent* as it applies to the following example: "If a man wears a tie, then he's a Republican. Mitt is a Republican. Therefore, he wears a tie." Notice that the first premise ("If a man wears a tie, then he's a Republican") is *not* equivalent to the converse ("If a man is a Republican, then he wears a tie"). In fact, the first premise allows for the possibility of T-shirt-clad Republicans, which contradicts the conclusion.

The second fallacy, *denying the antecedent,* is exemplified in the argument "$p \rightarrow q; \neg p,$ therefore $\neg q$." Using the example, these propositions would be instantiated as "If a man wears a tie, then he's a Republican. Newt does not wear a tie. Therefore, he is not a Republican." For the reason just given (namely, the possible existence of T-shirt-wearing Republicans), this argument is also false.

Now that we have discussed the nature of propositional reasoning, it is time to examine psychological investigations of how people actually perform on such tasks. Wason (1968, 1969, 1983; Wason & Johnson-Laird, 1970) studied people's propositional reasoning in a task he invented called the selection task, or the

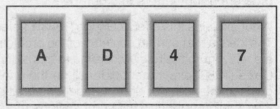

■ Figure 11.1: Depiction of the Wason (1968) selection task.

four-card task. Figure 11.1 presents an example. Participants see four cards, two with a letter and two with a digit. They are told that all four cards have a letter on one side and a digit on the other. They are given a rule such as "If a card has a vowel on one side, then it has an even number on the other side." We can restate this rule in propositional terms by letting p equal "A card has a vowel on one side," and q equal "A card has an even number on the other side." Then the rule can be written as "$p \rightarrow q$." The four cards presented to participants might be something like "A" (exemplifying p), "D" (exemplifying $\neg p$), "4" (exemplifying q), and "7" (exemplifying $\neg q$). The person is asked to turn over all the cards, and only those cards, that would allow her to see if the rule is true. Before reading on, write down the one or more cards you would turn over. Also write down the reasons for your selections.

This is a task on which people make many errors. The correct answer is to select "A" and "7." To see why, refer to Box 11.3. Card "A" is relevant because, together with the rule ("If a card has a vowel on one side, then it has an even number on the other side"), it forms an instance of *modus ponens:* "$p \rightarrow q$, and p." Card "7" is similarly relevant because, together with the rule, it forms an instance of *modus tollens*. The "D" card is irrelevant because it exemplifies $\neg p$ and thus is an instance of denying the antecedent. And choosing the "4" card is equivalent to committing the fallacy of affirming the consequent. Generally, most people know to select "A" but neglect to select "7" or mistakenly select "4." We will discuss some general explanations for this pattern of performance later.

The puzzle given in Box 11.1 is also an instance of propositional reasoning. This puzzle is an example of a class of puzzles, often called "truar/liar" or "knight/knave" puzzles, in which the task is to determine which speakers are telling the truth and which are lying, assuming that every speaker is either a "truar" (knight) or a liar (knave) and that truars always tell the truth and liars always lie (Rips, 1989). Once again, we can translate the "stolen jam" story into propositions, letting p stand for "The March Hare is telling the truth," q stand for "The

Mad Hatter is telling the truth," and *r* stand for "The Dormouse is telling the truth." (Notice then that ¬*p* would be "The March Hare is *not* telling the truth," and so on.)

Propositional reasoning is frequently subject to a phenomenon known as a **content effect**. Recall the Wason four-card task, in which four cards labeled "A," "D," "4," and "7" are laid in front of you. Your task is to turn over all and only the cards that could test the rule "If a card has a vowel on one side, it has an even number on the other side." It turns out that performance improves dramatically if the four cards contain different information: on one side, a person's age; on the other, what the person is drinking. Then the four cards shown say "drinking a beer," "drinking a Coke," "16 years of age," and "22 years of age." The rule to be investigated is "If a person is drinking a beer, then the person must be over 21 years of age." This experiment was conducted by Griggs and Cox (1982, Experiment 3), who found that about three quarters of their college student participants solved the problem correctly when it was about drinking age but that none could solve the equivalent problem about letters and numbers.

What explains this effect? Griggs (1983) offered what he calls a "memory cueing" explanation. The idea is that certain contents of the problem cue, or call to mind, personal experiences that are relevant to the rule. According to this argument, college student participants in Griggs and Cox's (1982) experiment did well on the drinking-age version of the problem because their own experience with drinking-age laws (and perhaps with violations of those laws) facilitated their thinking about what combinations of ages and beverages would violate the rule. The same participants had no comparable relevant experience to draw on when they reasoned about vowels and numbers in the other version of the task.

Interestingly, work by Blanchette and Richards (2004) shows that simply changing the words in a conditional reasoning task from neutral words to emotional words (e.g., "If one is in a library, then one sees books," versus "If a person is being punished, then she will feel hurt") causes a decrease in reasoning performance. Given emotional content, people are likely to draw more invalid inferences than they are with neutral words.

Leda Cosmides and her colleagues (Cosmides, 1989; Cosmides & Tooby, 2002; Fiddick, Cosmides, & Tooby, 2000) offer an evolutionary account of reasoning rules. Her argument is based on the idea that people (as well as all other organisms) have been shaped by evolutionary forces.

> Even if they have not paid much attention to the fact, cognitive psychologists have always known that the human mind is not merely a computational system with the design features of a modern computer, but a biological system "designed" by the organizing forces of evolution. This means that the innate information-processing mechanisms that comprise the human mind were not designed to solve arbitrary tasks, but are, instead, adaptations: mechanisms designed to solve the specific biological problems posed by the physical, ecological, and social environments encountered by our ancestors during the course of human evolution. However, most cognitive psychologists are not fully aware of just how useful these simple facts can be in the experimental investigation of human information-processing mechanisms. (Cosmides, 1989, p. 188)

Cosmides goes on to argue that much of cognition is not supported by domain-general or independent mechanisms, rules, or algorithms but instead by many, very specific mechanisms, adapted evolutionarily to solve very specific problems. For example, she believes that evolution has pressured humans to become very adept at reasoning about social contracts and social exchange.

Social exchange—cooperation between two or more individuals for mutual benefit—is biologically rare: few of the many species on earth have evolved the specialized capacities necessary to engage in it. . . . Humans, however, are one of these species, and social exchange is a pervasive aspect of all human cultures.

The ecological and life-historical conditions necessary for the evolution of social exchange were manifest during hominid evolution. Pleistocene small-group living and the advantages of cooperation in hunting and gathering afforded many opportunities for individuals to increase their fitness through the exchange of goods, services, and privileges over the course of a lifetime. (Cosmides, 1989, pp. 195–196)

Cosmides (1989) asserted that any evolutionarily adaptive mechanism for reasoning about social exchange must fulfill two criteria: (a) It must concern itself with the costs and benefits of social exchanges, and (b) it must be able to detect cheating in social exchanges. A person who was not able to think in terms of costs and benefits would not be able to reason successfully about the worthiness of a proposed social exchange, and a person unable to detect cheating would presumably be at a big disadvantage in any society.

Cosmides (1989) predicted that people would be especially adept at the Wason selection task when the content of the task could be construed in terms of social costs and benefits. So, she reasoned, people do well on the underage-drinking version of the task because this version causes people to invoke their special-purpose reasoning mechanism about social exchange. The drinking-problem version of the Wason selection task asks reasoners to look for violations of a social contract (cheating) that stipulates only those who have attained legal majority (thus paying a kind of "cost") are authorized to partake of a "benefit" (consuming alcoholic beverages). Reviewing the literature on content effects in reasoning, Cosmides concluded that unless the content had an implicit or explicit cost-benefit structure, people's reasoning was not enhanced.

Syllogistic Reasoning

Another type of puzzle or problem commonly used to study reasoning is called a *syllogism.* The reasoning done with this kind of problem is called **syllogistic reasoning**. This type of problem presents two or more premises and asks the reasoner either to draw a conclusion or to evaluate a conclusion that the problem supplies to see if the conclusion must be true whenever the premises are true. Although logicians recognize different types of syllogisms, we'll deal only with what are called *categorical syllogisms.* Box 11.4 presents some examples. As you look at these, try to solve them, making notes on which ones are hard, which ones are easy, and why.

Categorical syllogisms present premises that deal with classes of entities. As a result, the premises have words called *quantifiers* in them. Quantifiers provide information about how many members of a class are under consideration: all, none, or some. All the following are examples of quantified premises: "All Gordon setters are dogs," "No polar bears are inanimate objects," "Some flowers are blue," and "Some ballerinas are not tall." As you might expect by now, the words *all* and *some* are being used in ways that differ slightly from normal English usage. Here, *all* means "every single"; *some* means "at least one, and perhaps all." (It is important to note that, logically speaking, the proposition "Some X are Y," does not mean that "Some X are not Y," even though this inference might seem natural.)

Box 11.4

Examples of Categorical Syllogisms

Premises are above the lines; valid conclusions, if they exist, are below the lines.

All red books are astronomy books. All astronomy books are large.	Some documents are not paper. Some documents are not legal.
All red books are large.	Nothing follows.
Some pilots are magicians. All magicians are Pisces.	All psychology majors are curious. No tennis players are curious.
Some pilots are Pisces.	No tennis players are psychology majors.
No liberals are Republicans. Some wealthy people are not Republicans.	No union members are fearful. No children are fearful.
Nothing follows.	Nothing follows.

Certain rules can be used to draw valid conclusions from categorical syllogisms (Damer, 1980). For example, a categorical syllogism with two negative premises (such as "No X are Y," or "Some X are not Y") has no conclusion that necessarily follows. Similarly, a categorical syllogism in which both premises are quantified by "some" has no valid conclusion. In fact, the majority of categorical syllogisms do not have valid (always true in every case) conclusions.

Performance on many categorical syllogisms is error-prone (Ceraso & Provitera, 1971; Woodworth & Sells, 1935). In general, people tend to be slower and make more errors when one or more premises are quantified by *some* or when one or more premises are negative. So, for example, when presented with syllogisms such as "Some businesspeople are Republicans. Some Republicans are conservative," most people erroneously conclude it must be true that "Some businesspeople are conservative." (To see why this is not the case, notice that the first premise allows for the possibility that some Republicans may exist who are not businesspeople. Maybe they are all lawyers. Perhaps only these Republican lawyers are conservative.)

Syllogistic reasoning is prone to at least four types of errors. First, there are content effects (similar to the one that occurs for propositional reasoning). Second, there are so-called **believability effects**. People are likely to judge as valid any conclusion that reinforces their initial assumptions, regardless of whether the conclusion follows from the premises (Evans, Barston, & Pollard, 1983). Consider this syllogism: "Some college professors are intellectuals. Some intellectuals are liberals." The correct response to this syllogism (as you now know) is that no particular conclusion follows from it. Generally, though, most people (who haven't just read a chapter on reasoning) tend to conclude that these premises lead inevitably to the conclusion "Some college professors are liberals." This conclusion agrees with their previous beliefs and stereotypes about college professors: Professors are absentminded and theoretical; they are intelligent but sometimes impractical; they are unconcerned about money but are concerned about social justice.

Notice that a change in this syllogism's content makes it much clearer why this conclusion isn't always true: "Some men are teachers. Some teachers are women." This syllogism calls to mind a different mental picture. Our world knowledge lets us filter out the suggested conclusion, "Some men are women," because we know this to be false in the world. You might also notice that this error could be described in terms of a limited search within the problem space hypothesis, discussed in Chapter 10.

A third variable that affects syllogistic reasoning performance has to do with premise phrasing. Premises that have negatives (the word *no* or *not* in them) are generally more difficult to work with, result in more errors, and take people longer to comprehend than premises that don't have negatives in them (Evans, 1972). Similarly, quantifiers such as *all* or *none* are easier for most people to deal with than quantifiers such as *some* (Neimark & Chapman, 1975).

More generally, it appears that the way information is stated can make a reasoning task easy or hard. Presumably, part of the explanation is that syntactically complex statements require more processing resources for the reasoner to comprehend, encode, represent, and store in working memory. As a result, fewer mental resources are available to tackle the other reasoning processes necessary to draw conclusions or to check for validity.

Lastly, syllogistic reasoning gives rise to a number of errors in understanding what the premises mean. That is, people often make assumptions or alter the meanings of certain terms such that their interpretations of what the premises mean do not correspond very well with what the problem actually states. For example, when told "All daxes are wugs,"

Dax = Creature with a pointed head
Wug = Creature with sneakerlike feet

All daxes are wugs.
(And all wugs are daxes.)

All daxes are wugs.
(And there are other wugs that are not daxes.)

Figure 11.2: Illustration of possible meanings of "All daxes are wugs."

whatever daxes and wugs are, people often automatically assume that daxes and wugs are the same thing and/or that all wugs are daxes. In fact, the exact statement given allows two possibilities: Every dax is a wug, and every wug is a dax (the common interpretation); or every dax is a wug, and there are other wugs that are not daxes. See Figure 11.2 for an illustration.

The quantifier *some* in a premise compounds the difficulties. To say "Some bers are sabs," is to say only the following: "At least one ber is a sab, but there may or may not be other bers that aren't sabs, and there may or may not be other sabs that aren't bers." Generally, people wrongly interpret the statement as if it means only that some bers are sabs and that some bers aren't sabs. People make a similar mistake with if–then statements. The statement "If A, then B," does not mean the same thing as "If B, then A," but confusing the two constructions is common. As in the case with *some,* people overlook possible interpretations of the premise, depicted in Figure 11.3.

It has been argued that many errors in drawing deductively valid conclusions can be traced to misinterpretations of premises (Revlis, 1975). Moreover, the problem persists when people are given detailed definitions and even a fair amount of practice in applying these definitions (Galotti, Baron, & Sabini, 1986). Maybe the usual everyday understand-

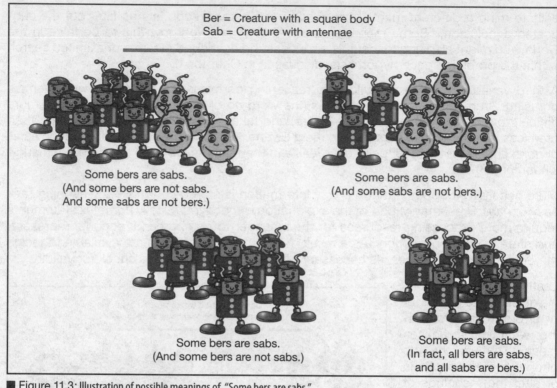

Ber = Creature with a square body
Sab = Creature with antennae

Some bers are sabs.
(And some bers are not sabs.
And some sabs are not bers.)

Some bers are sabs.
(And some sabs are not bers.)

Some bers are sabs.
(And some bers are not sabs.)

Some bers are sabs.
(In fact, all bers are sabs,
and all sabs are bers.)

■ Figure 11.3: Illustration of possible meanings of "Some bers are sabs."

ings of words such as *all, some,* and *if–then* are so powerful that people have difficulty ignoring the terms' slightly different definitions vis-à-vis reasoning tasks.

INDUCTIVE REASONING

Inductive reasoning, or reasoning about conclusions that are likely (but not guaranteed) to be true, probably occurs in everyone's thinking several times in the course of an ordinary day. Although inductive conclusions aren't guaranteed to be true, they may be more useful than deductive conclusions because they add new information to our thinking. In general, it is easier to think of real-life examples of inductive reasoning than to think of real-life examples of deductive reasoning. Holyoak and Nisbett (1988) provided several examples of ordinary induction:

> A child who has never heard verbs rendered incorrectly into the past tense exclaims, "I goed to bed." A stock analyst, observing that for several years market prices for petroleum stocks have risen steadily in the final two months of the year and then dropped in January, urges her clients to buy petroleum stocks this year at the end of October and sell in late December. A physicist, observing the patterns formed by light as it undergoes refraction and diffraction, hypothesizes that light is propagated as waves. (p. 50)

Holyoak and Nisbett (1988) defined *induction* as "inferential processes that expand knowledge in the face of uncertainty" (p. 50). They noted that induction often involves categorization and the formation of rules or hypotheses. Thus, you'll probably observe a great deal of overlap among induction, categorization (Chapter 7), and thinking (Chapter 10). There are a number of different inductive reasoning tasks, but I'll focus here on two: analogical reasoning and hypothesis testing.

Analogical Reasoning

Figure 11.4 presents examples of both verbal and pictorial analogies. You may be familiar with this type of problem from standardized tests. The format of such a problem is "A is to B as C is to ____." The general idea is that the first two terms (A and B) suggest some relationship, and the third term (C) provides a partial description of another relationship. The job of the reasoner is to figure out what the fourth term (the one that goes in the blank) should be such that its relationship to the third term is the same (or nearly so) as the relationship of the second to the first term.

Analogies can also be extended into what are called *series completion* and *matrix completion* problems. Figure 11.5 gives an example. Although these problems include more terms, the same general mental processes used in analogies are probably used to solve them (Sternberg & Gardner, 1983).

The ease of reasoning about an analogy depends on the complexity of the problem. Complexity, in turn, depends on a number of factors, among them the following: How complicated to comprehend are the individual terms? How knowledgeable is the reasoner about the terms? How easy is it to find a relationship between the first two terms? How many possibilities are there for the blank term, and how easy are they to call to mind? (Pellegrino & Glaser, 1980; Sternberg, 1977a).

You have probably noted here a specific link to a topic we covered in Chapter 10—namely, reasoning by analogy as a problem-solving technique. Analogical reasoning is so common in our experience that we may use it in all sorts of tasks.

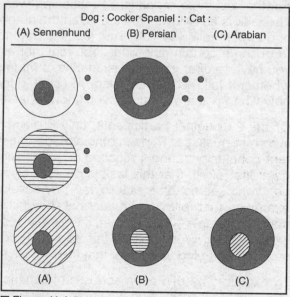

■ Figure 11.4: Examples of verbal and pictorial analogies.

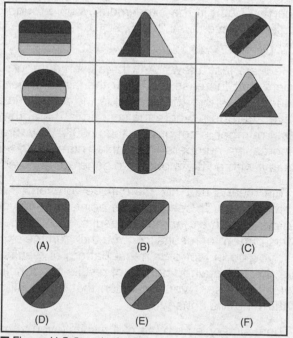

■ Figure 11.5: Example of a matrix completion problem.

Just as we try to find relationships between terms in an analogy problem, so we try to find relationships between apparently dissimilar problems (for example, between the tumor problem and the problem of the general in the last chapter). In both cases, we try to apply the relationship found to determine the solution.

Hypothesis Testing

Another example of inductive reasoning was developed by Peter Wason (1960, 1977). The task is as follows: You are given the numbers 2, 4, and 6 and are told that this triplet of numbers follows a rule. Your job is to determine what the rule is, but to do so you need to observe certain guidelines. You may not ask direct questions about the rule. Instead, you have to offer your own examples of triplets, and for each one you give, you'll be told whether it follows the rule. Also, you should try not to guess; you should announce a rule only when you are confident you know what it is.

Of the 29 original participants, only 6 discovered the correct rule without first making incorrect guesses. Thirteen others made one wrong guess, 9 reached two or more incorrect conclusions, and 1 reached no conclusion at all (Wason, 1960). These results suggest, first of all, that this task is deceptively difficult. The manner in which most people go wrong seems to be as follows: They develop a general idea of the rule, then construct examples that follow the rule. What they fail to do is to *test* their rule by constructing a counterexample—a triplet that, if their rule is correct, *won't* receive a yes answer from the experimenter. Wason called this approach **confirmation bias**, because the participants seem to be trying to confirm that their rule is true, rather than trying to test their rule.

To explain why this approach is problematic, Wason pointed out a feature of the task that mirrors the situation facing any researcher testing scientific hypotheses: An infinite number of hypotheses can be constructed consistent with any set of data (in this case, the triplets judged by the experimenter to follow the rule). For instance, suppose at a certain point in the experiment, you've found out that all the following triplets follow the rule (whatever it is): 2, 4, 6; 8, 10, 12; 20, 22, 24; 100, 102, 104. What rules are consistent with this set?

Here are just a few: "Any three even numbers that increase by 2"; "Any three even numbers that increase by 2, but the last number is not greater than 500"; "Any three even numbers where the second is the arithmetic average of the first and third"; "Any three even numbers where the second is the arithmetic average of the first and third, but the last number is not greater than 500"; "Any three even numbers that increase"; "Any three increasing numbers"; "Any three numbers"; "Any three things." This list suggests it's very easy, with a little thought, to generate hundreds of rules for any given set of numbers.

This means that no rule can be "proven" true, just as no scientific hypothesis can be proven true. To see this latter point, pretend you are a scientist with a hypothesis that predicts certain experimental results. You think, "If my hypothesis is true [*p*], then I'll obtain this pattern of results [*q*]." You then run the experiment, and, as luck or nature would have it, you do in fact obtain that pattern of results. Can you, on the basis of your rule (*p* à *q*) and your obtained pattern of results (*q*), conclude that your hypothesis is proven true (*p*)? No, because if you did reach that conclusion, you would be committing the fallacy of affirming the consequent.

There simply is no pattern of results (even from hundreds of experiments) that can *prove* a theory *true,* just as no rule about three numbers can be proven true, even by a large number of examples that apparently follow it. Instead, the best one can do is to try to disprove as many incorrect rules (or, if you are a scientist, as many alternative hypotheses) as possible. So if you think the correct rule is "any three increasing even numbers," you are better off testing the rule with a triplet that is a *counter*example to the rule (for example, 3, 5, 7). Why?

If this triplet *follows* the rule, then you know immediately that your hypothesis is wrong. Suppose you instead generate another example of the rule (such as 14, 16, 18). If you're told it does follow the rule, you won't be able to use it to prove your hypothesis true (because no hypothesis can ever be proven true), and you haven't managed to rule anything out.

EVERYDAY REASONING

All the reasoning tasks presented so far are typical of tasks that psychologists use in experiments or that teachers might use in classes. These kinds of tasks have been grouped together under the label **formal reasoning** (Galotti, 1989). Philosophers, psychologists, and educators assume that these kinds of tasks are at the heart of all kinds of reasoning, even the kind of reasoning we do in everyday life. Consider the following example of **everyday reasoning**: You're preparing dinner, and the recipe you are following calls for mozzarella cheese. You search your refrigerator but can't find any. You conclude that you don't have any mozzarella cheese and that you need to go to the grocery store.

We can analyze the inferences you drew as follows. The inference that you had no mozzarella cheese can be seen as an instance of deductive reasoning, more specifically as an instance of *modus tollens* (for example, "If I had mozzarella cheese, it would be in the refrigerator. There is no mozzarella cheese in the refrigerator. Therefore, I have no mozzarella cheese"). Your inference that you need to go to the grocery store can be seen as an inductive inference (for example, "The grocery store usually stocks mozzarella cheese. Therefore, it will have mozzarella cheese in stock today"). These analyses assume that the mental processes you use in making inferences about mozzarella cheese are the same ones you would use in laboratory investigations of reasoning, such as knight/knave, categorical syllogism, or pictorial analogies tasks. The mozzarella cheese example is a more familiar variant of some of these tasks.

There is some reason to question, however, how similar the reasoning we use in everyday life is to the reasoning we use in laboratory tasks (Galotti & Komatsu, 1993). Collins and Michalski (1989) have identified certain kinds of inferences that people draw in everyday reasoning that do not seem to occur on formal reasoning tasks. For example, two people (identified as Q, the questioner, and R, the respondent) are having the following dialogue about geography (Collins & Michalski, p. 4):

Q: Is Uruguay in the Andes Mountains?

R: I get mixed up on a lot of South American countries (pause). I'm not even sure. I forget where Uruguay is in South America. It's a good guess to say that it's in the Andes Mountains because a lot of the countries are.

In this example, the respondent first expresses doubt, then draws an (incorrect, as it turns out) inference: Because many South American countries include a part of the Andes range within their territories, and because Uruguay is a typical South American country, the respondent concludes that it, too, includes some of the Andes Mountains. Collins and Michalski (1989) labeled this a kind of "plausible deduction" (in our terminology, we might better call it a plausible induction, because the conclusion is not guaranteed to be true).

A number of distinctions between everyday reasoning tasks and formal reasoning tasks have been suggested (see Table 11.1). The differences may require cognitive psychologists who study reasoning to reevaluate the usefulness of laboratory reasoning tasks as a model of real-life reasoning performance. Research on people's everyday reasoning is beginning, but we will need to await more findings before assessing the fit between everyday and formal reasoning.

■ Table 11.1: Formal and Everyday Reasoning Tasks Compared

Formal	Everyday
All premises are supplied.	Some premises are implicit, and some are not supplied at all.
Problems are self-contained.	Problems are not self-contained.
Typically there is one correct answer.	Typically there are several possible answers, which vary in quality.
Established methods of inference that apply to the problem often exist.	Established procedures for solving the problem rarely exist.
It is typically unambiguous when the problem is solved.	It is often unclear whether the current "best" solution is good enough.
The content of the problem is often of limited, academic interest.	The content of the problem typically has potential personal relevance.
Problems are solved for their own sake.	Problems are often solved as a means of achieving other goals.

Everyday reasoning has been shown to be subject to a variety of biases. A **bias** in thinking is defined as a tendency to perform in a certain way regardless of the information presented. You might think of it as an error that frequently distorts thinking in a particular way. For example, a person might be biased toward coming to the most general conclusions possible and might then erroneously decide that broad generalizations necessarily follow from any set of premises.

Investigators have identified some biases relevant to reasoning. One, mentioned earlier with regard to the Wason 2-4-6 task, is confirmation bias—the tendency to look only for information that supports existing beliefs. So, for example, if you believe that all college professors are liberal, you may try to "test" your conclusion but fail to do so adequately because you seek out only college professors who are liberal, somehow overlooking or forgetting about conservative college professors. In general, people have been shown to be much less likely to think of counterexamples to their own tentative conclusions (Baron, 1985, 2008). Thus, when assessing their own reasoning or other performance, people typically find it much easier to think of or gather information consistent with their predictions than to think of or gather information that goes against their predictions.

There are many other examples of biases in thinking, several of which are more relevant to decision making. We will therefore defer an extended discussion of biases to that section. The important point for our present purposes is to note that people often appear to exhibit thinking that is distorted in the direction of making it seem that their thinking or reasoning has been more careful or thorough than it actually has been.

DECISION MAKING

You've arrived at your sophomore year of college and realize you must soon declare a major—and perhaps a minor. What cognitive processes do you use to consider the options, evaluate your priorities, and make a choice? Cognitive psychologists use the term **decision making** to refer to the mental activities that take place in choosing among alternatives. In the instance just given, the decision about an undergraduate major often is part of a larger set of decisions about a career and future life. Typically, decisions are made in the face of some amount of *uncertainty.* It is not 100% certain, say, how well you will do in the courses required for various majors, or how well you will like them, or how much various majors will help you obtain a good job after graduation. You will not know for sure if you will enjoy the faculty who teach the courses you have not yet taken, or if the topics will be interesting or useful, or if they will be relevant to your long-term goals and aspirations.

Nonetheless, at some point you have to decide. At the college where I teach, students who seek my advice about choosing a major often appear in my office showing unmistakable signs of agitation, nervousness, and confusion. They know they need to decide but don't know how. They wish the uncertainty over, but they don't want to close off options prematurely. They are aware that a lot of information relevant to the decision exists but don't know quite how to collect, organize, and use it all in the time allotted. They know there are no guarantees but don't want to make an unfortunate choice.

The dilemma is familiar to anyone who has had to make a significant and difficult life choice. The degree of uncertainty is vexing. So, too, is the number of conflicting goals and objectives. The sophomore student typically wants not only a major that is interesting but also one in which she shows some aptitude, enjoys the faculty and other students who are majoring in the same field, and sees some relevance to a future job and some flexibility for future career paths.

The number of options available also comes into play. Many schools have more than 25 majors available (some have many more). There are also options to double-major, declare minors, participate in off-campus study programs, and so on, adding to the complexity of the decision. The amount of information that is potentially relevant can quickly grow to be staggering, in which case the decision maker needs some help in organizing it all.

Because decisions are often made under conditions of uncertainty, some don't yield the hoped-for results, even if made carefully and after thorough, unbiased consideration of the evidence. Psychologists generally argue that "goodness" of decision making cannot be measured by the success of individual decisions—luck, for instance, often plays too big a role. Instead, the yardstick of success is often taken to be the **rationality** of the decision. Various people define this term differently, but a typical definition comes from von Winterfeldt and Edwards (1986a): Rational decision making "has to do with selecting ways of thinking and acting to serve your ends or goals or moral imperatives, whatever they may be, as well as the environment permits" (p. 2). In other words, to be rational means to consider all your relevant goals and principles, not just the first ones that come to mind. If you buy a new computer and choose one that looks sleek on your desk but neglect other goals—speed, reliability, and availability of software, for example—you are undercutting your own decision making. Rational decision making also involves gathering information as painstakingly and fairly as possible under the circumstances. It requires you to examine not only evidence that supports your initial inclinations but also evidence that does not.

We will look at descriptions of how people gather and use information in making decisions. Many of these descriptions will show how decision making falls short of optimality. Psychologists have argued that the lack of optimality stems, in large part, from **cognitive overload**—when the information available overwhelms the cognitive processing available.

Strategies for coping with information overload, though often useful, can lead to error and irrationality. Next, we will examine what people do after they have gathered the evidence—how all the pieces are put together. Finally, we will look briefly at ways of improving decision making.

We can divide decision making tasks into five categories (Galotti, 2002). Figure 11.6 provides a schematic view. These tasks often occur in a particular order, but there may be "cycles" within the order, in which certain tasks are revisited and redone, as depicted by the arrows in the figure. I use the term *phases* of decision making to convey the ideas that there may or may not be a set order to the tasks, that the performance of one task can overlap with the performance of another, that some tasks can be skipped, and that tasks can be done in different orders.

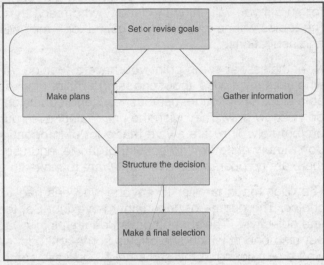

■ Figure 11.6: Phases of decision making.

SETTING GOALS

When we try to understand why a person makes one decision rather than another, it often turns out that the reasons have to do with the decision maker's *goals* for the decision (Bandura, 2001; Galotti, 2005). Many students I talk with say they plan to declare a biology major because their goal is to go to medical school. Others tell me they are thinking about economics because they want to get into a competitive corporate training program. (As it turns out, such majors aren't required, or even necessarily prized, by the organizations in question, many of which value a variety of majors, but we'll leave that issue aside for now.)

The idea in setting goals is that the decision maker takes stock of his or her plans for the future, his or her principles and values, and his or her priorities. That is, the decision maker needs to develop answers to the question "What am I trying to accomplish?" Those answers are the decision maker's goals, and they influence decision making in various ways.

GATHERING INFORMATION

Before making a decision, the decision maker needs information. Specifically, she or he needs to know what the various options are. For example, what are the likely consequences of each option, both short- and long-term? Who is affected in each option, and how? Do the effects change over time? Will taking or not taking a particular course of action obligate the decision maker to other decisions or plans? In other words, does each option open or close off other options?

Some decisions are highly complex. For example, consider the decision of which computer to buy. In any given year, many models are available. If you consider all the different ways a given computer can be customized, the options multiply rapidly. Somehow, the decision maker needs to gather some information about at least some of the options.

In addition to information about options, decision makers may need or want to gather information about possible criteria to use in making their choice. If you've never bought a computer before, you might talk with computer-savvy friends or people in your company's IT department to get information about what features they consider important. Or you might try to develop your own "wish list" of features that an ideal computer would have, based on your goals.

STRUCTURING THE DECISION

For complex decisions, decision makers need a way to organize all their information. This is especially true when they face a great number of options and considerations. Reflect again on the example of choosing a college major. In one of my studies, I surveyed first-year college students over a period of 1 year as they thought about this decision (Galotti, 1999). Many of the students I surveyed listed a wide variety of criteria they considered in making this decision. Among these criteria were considerations such as "Do I enjoy the material?" "Will it lead to a career I am interested in?" "Does it have a lot of requirements?" and "Do I like the faculty who teach the classes?" In the study, students listed about seven different criteria and about four different options, or possible majors. To comprehensively consider all these criteria and options, a typical decision maker needs to think about 28 pieces of information (for example, "Is biology a subject I enjoy?" "Is chemistry a subject I enjoy?" "Is psychology a subject I enjoy?").

Twenty-eight different things to think about is quite a lot. Somehow the decision maker needs to determine or invent a way of managing this information. The way she or he does this is called **decision structuring**.

MAKING A FINAL CHOICE

After gathering all the information he or she is going to gather, the decision maker needs to select from among the final set of options. This may involve a procedure as simple as flipping a coin or throwing a dart at a wall, or it may be considerably more complex. This process may involve other decisions—such as deciding when to cease the information-gathering phase of the process or deciding which information is most relevant or reliable.

EVALUATING

A helpful (and often omitted) last phase of decision making is an evaluation of the entire process. What went well? What didn't go so well? The aim here is to reflect on the process and identify those aspects that could be improved, as well as those that ought to be used again for similar decisions in the future.

With this overview, let's take a more detailed look at some of the processes involved in decision making. I'm going to concentrate on the middle three—gathering information, structuring the decision, and making a final choice—largely because cognitive psychologists have so far studied these processes the most.

COGNITIVE ILLUSIONS IN DECISION MAKING _____

How do people gather the information they will use to make a decision? Often the information comes from their own memories. Students choosing a major, for instance, may think about their experiences in different courses or things they have heard older students say about their experiences in different majors. Once information is gathered, the decision maker must decide on the importance and/or relevance of each piece of information. If you don't care about becoming a biologist, for instance, the information on the biology department's course offerings may not seem very important to you. The way people gather and assess the relevance of different pieces of information is the topic of this section.

Research on people's decision-making skills and styles has consistently demonstrated the existence of certain systematic and common **heuristics** (shortcuts) or biases, ways of thinking that lead to systematic errors (D. G. Goldstein & Gigerenzer, 2011; Kruglanski & Gigerenzer, 2011). The heuristics and biases are typically understandable and often justifiable ways of thinking under most conditions, but they can lead to error when misapplied. These systematic biases have been labeled **cognitive illusions** (von Winterfeldt & Edwards, 1986b). The term itself is meant to invoke an analogy to perceptual illusions: errors of cognition that come about for understandable reasons and that provide information relevant to understanding normal functioning. We can and do consider these illusions "errors," in the sense that one's percept does not correspond with what's really there. However, these illusions are not used as evidence that the whole perceptual system is faulty and unreliable. Rather, illusions (perceptions under certain specific conditions) tell us something about the way the perceptual system works generally—what cues are attended to, how they are interpreted, and so forth.

In a similar way, errors in decision making tell us something about the ways people gather, sort, and integrate the information they use for making a choice. The cognitive illusions described next also give us information on when unaided human decision making is likely to be optimal and when it is not. Finally, these descriptions can help us design and implement educational programs or interventions to improve the quality of decisions and plans people make.

Just what is a cognitive illusion? Von Winterfeldt and Edwards (1986b) specified that something counts as a cognitive illusion only if there is a "correct" way of answering a question or making a decision, there is also an intuitive estimate or decision, and there is a discrepancy between the two that always goes in the same direction. Answers that randomly fluctuate around the correct value, then, do not count as illusions.

AVAILABILITY

Consider the problems in Box 11.5 and give your first intuitive response to each before reading further. Tversky and Kahneman (1973) presented problems such as these to undergraduate students. The general findings were that people's intuitions were systematically wrong. In Problem 1, for instance, the letter *L* occurs more frequently in the third position than in the initial position. In Problems 2 and 3, the A and B options have the same number (of committees in the former case, of paths in the latter).

What accounts for the errors? Tversky and Kahneman (1973) argued that when faced with the task of estimating probability, frequency, or numerosity, people rely on shortcuts or rules of thumb—heuristics—to make these judgments easier. One such heuristic is known as the **availability heuristic**—"assessing the ease with which the relevant mental operation of retrieval, construction, or association can be carried out" (Tversky & Kahneman, p. 208). In other words, instances (for example, particular words, particular committees, or particular paths) that are more easily thought of, remembered, or computed stand out

Box 11.5

Problems Demonstrating Availability

1. Consider the letter *L*. In the English language, is this letter more likely to appear in the first position of a word or the third position of a word? Give your intuition or "gut reaction."
2. Ten students from a nearby college have indicated a willingness to serve on a curriculum committee. Their names are Ann, Bob, Dan, Elizabeth, Gary, Heidi, Jennifer, Laura, Terri, and Valerie.
a. The dean wants to form a two-person committee. What is your estimate of the number of distinct committees that could be formed? (Don't use formulas; just respond intuitively.)
b. The dean wants to form an eight-person committee. What is your estimate of the number of distinct committees that could be formed? (Don't use formulas; just respond intuitively.)
3. Consider the two structures shown below:

```
A                          B
x x                        x x x x x x x x
x x                        x x x x x x x x
x x                        x x x x x x x x
x x
x x
x x
x x
x x
x x
```

A *path* in a structure is a line that connects one "x" from each row, starting with the top row and finishing at the bottom row. How many paths do you think each structure has? (Again, give an intuitive estimate.)

more in one's mind. Those instances are particularly salient and hence are deemed to be more frequent or probable.

In Problem 1, it turns out to be easier to think of words that begin with *l* (such as *lawn*, *leftover*, and *licorice*) than to think of words that have *l* as the third letter (*bell*, *wall*, *ill*). The reason for this may stem from the way our lexicons, or "mental dictionaries," are organized or with how we learn or practice words—alphabetically by the first letter. As with paper or electronic dictionaries, it's easier to search for words by initial letter than by interior letters.

In Problem 2, the appropriate formula for determining the number of distinct committees that can be formed is

$$\frac{10!}{(x!)(10-x)!}$$

where *x* is the size of the committee. Notice that for $x = 2$, $10 - x = 8$, and that for $x = 8$, $(10 - x) = 2$, implying there should be an equal number of two-person committees and eight-person committees (namely, 45). Tversky and Kahneman (1973) argued that two-person committees are more distinct. There are 5 two-person committees with no overlap in membership, but any 2 eight-person committees will have at least some overlap. Distinctiveness makes different committees easier to think of. Therefore, two-person committees are more available (because they are more distinctive) and hence deemed more numerous. You can easily see, however, that two-person and eight-person committees must be equally numerous. Consider that every two-person committee defines an eight-person noncommittee, and vice versa.

The same kind of analysis applies to Problem 3. The number of paths in either structure is given by the formula x^y, where x is the number of x's in a row and y is the number of rows. The number of paths in structure A, then, is $8^3 = 512$. The number of paths in structure B is 2^9, also equal to 512. Again, though, it is easier to see more nonoverlapping paths in A than in B; different paths in A are less confusable than different paths in B. Paths in A are shorter and therefore easier to visualize than those in B. The ease of visualization makes paths more available and hence deemed more numerous in A than in B.

Everyday analogs that involve the use of the availability heuristic have also been reported. Ross and Sicoly (1979), for instance, surveyed 37 married couples (husbands and wives separately and independently) about the estimated extent of their responsibility for various household activities, such as making breakfast, shopping for groceries, and caring for children. Husbands and wives both were more likely to say they had greater responsibility than did their spouse for 16 of the 20 activities. Moreover, when asked to give examples of their own and their spouse's contributions to each activity, each participant listed more of her or his own activities than activities of the spouse.

Ross and Sicoly (1979) explained these findings in terms of the availability heuristic. Our own efforts and behaviors are more apparent and available to us than are the efforts and behaviors of others. After all, we are certain to be present when we perform an action, but we may or may not be present when a friend or spouse does. Our own thoughts and plans are important to us, and we may be formulating them just as other people do or say something, thus distracting us from their contributions. In general, what we do, think, say, or intend is more accessible to us than to anyone else and also more accessible than anyone else's deeds, thoughts, words, or intentions. Small wonder, then, that in joint ventures each partner often feels she or he shoulders a greater share of the burden.

Availability can be both an efficient and effective heuristic. If we can be sure that ease of constructing or calling instances to mind is unbiased, then it may be the best, or even only, tool to use when judging frequency or probability. If you are trying to decide which course you typically do more papers for, psychology or philosophy, it probably is fair to judge the frequency of papers by trying to recall specific paper assignments for each course. In this case, there is probably no reason to believe psychology papers are more memorable than philosophy papers. If there is (for example, you took philosophy 3 years ago but psychology this semester), then the comparison is probably not fair.

However, if you are trying to decide which occurs more often, hours you spend working on a group project or hours someone else spends working on the same project, using availability to judge may be unfair. You have been there whenever you have worked, but you may not have been there all the times when other group members have worked. And even if you had been there, you probably would have been paying more attention to your own work and planning than to your partners' work and planning. Thus, examples of your own work are likely to be more memorable and more available to you than examples of anyone else's work.

The point of demonstrating the availability heuristic, then, is not to warn you away from its use. Instead, as with all other heuristics, the idea is to suggest you think carefully first about whether the range of examples you are drawing from are equally accessible.

REPRESENTATIVENESS

Two students, Linda and Joe, are having a boring Saturday afternoon in the student union. For lack of something better to do, they each begin flipping a quarter, keeping track of the way it lands over time. Then they compare results. Linda reports that her sequence of coin flips was heads, heads, heads, tails, tails, tails. Joe gets the following results: tails, tails, heads, tails, heads, heads. Which student has obtained a more statistically probable series of results?

Most people who respond to this question intuitively believe Joe did. After all, his sequence of responses is less patterned and more "random looking." In fact, however, both outcomes are equally likely. The problem is that people generally expect that a random *process,* such as a coin flip, will always produce results that are random looking. That is, they expect the results to be representative of the process that generated them. People who make judgments this way are said to be using the **representativeness heuristic**.

Kahneman and Tversky (1973) demonstrated people's use of the representativeness heuristic in a series of studies. In one study, undergraduate participants were assigned to three conditions. Those in the *base rate* condition were told, "Consider all first-year graduate students in the United States today. Please write down your best guesses about the percentage now enrolled in each of the following nine fields of specialization." The nine fields are shown in Box 11.6. Those in the *similarity* condition were presented with the personality sketch shown in Box 11.6(A) and were asked to rank the nine fields in terms of "how similar Tom W. is to the typical graduate student in each of the following nine fields of graduate specialization." Participants in the *prediction* condition were also given the personality sketch but were told it was written several years ago, during Tom W.'s senior year of high school, based on his response to projective tests (such as the Rorschach test). They were then asked to predict the likelihood that Tom W. was currently a graduate student in each field.

Box 11.6(B) shows that the mean similarity rankings are very similar to the mean likelihood rankings and are independent of the mean judged base rate, again suggesting use of the representativeness heuristic. Participants who were asked to estimate the likelihood that Tom W.was a graduate student in field *X* do so, apparently, by comparing his personality description to their beliefs about what typical graduate students in field *X* are like, ignoring base rates. Base rates are important information, however. The failure to include base rate information in your estimates of probability can lead to answers that are in error, often by an order of magnitude or more.

A related error in judgment is called the **gambler's fallacy**. Imagine yourself standing beside a roulette wheel in Atlantic City. You watch the wheel come up red on eight successive trials. Assuming you are still willing to believe the wheel is equally likely to come up black or red, where would you place a bet for the next spin? Many people would bet on black, reasoning that if black and red are equally likely, then the previous outcomes have skewed the process a bit and it is now "black's turn." However, on the next trial, the chances of black are exactly the same as the chances of red. The wheel is not "keeping track" in any way of past results, so it is not going to "correct" or "make up for" past

Box 11.6

Data From a Prediction Study

(A) Personality sketch of Tom W.

Tom W. is of high intelligence, although lacking in true creativity. He has a need for order and clarity, and for neat and tidy systems in which every detail finds its appropriate place. His writing is rather dull and mechanical, occasionally enlivened by somewhat corny puns and by flashes of imagination of the sci-fi type. He has a strong drive for competence. He seems to have little feel and little sympathy for other people and does not enjoy interacting with others. Self-centered, he nonetheless has a deep moral sense.

(B) Estimated base rates of nine areas of graduate specialization, and summary of similarity and prediction data for Tom W.

Graduate Specialization Area	Mean Judged Base Rate (in %)	Mean Similarity Rank	Mean Likelihood Rank
Business administration	15	3.9	4.3
Computer science	7	2.1	2.5
Engineering	9	2.9	2.6
Humanities and education	20	7.2	7.6
Law	9	5.9	5.2
Library science	3	4.2	4.7
Medicine	8	5.9	5.8
Physical and life sciences	12	4.5	4.3
Social science and social work	17	8.2	8.0

results. Although *in the long run* the number of times black comes up should equal the number of times red comes up, this does not mean that *in the short run* the proportions will be even. This explanation applies also to the coin-flipping example given earlier. A random process (such as a coin flip or a roulette wheel spin) will not always produce results that look random, especially in the short run.

Tversky and Kahneman (1971) described people's (mistaken) belief in the *law of small numbers.* The idea is that people expect small samples (of people, of coin flips, of trials in an experiment) to resemble in every respect the populations from which they are drawn. In actuality, small samples are much more likely to deviate from the population and are therefore a less reliable basis on which to build a conclusion than are larger samples. The gambler's fallacy problem can be thought of as an instance of belief in the law of small numbers. People expect that a small sample of roulette wheel spins (such as 8) will show the same proportion of reds as will a very large sample (such as 100,000). However, the chances of finding large deviations from the expected proportion are much greater with a small *N* sample. Said another way, only very large samples can be expected to be representative of the population from which they come. Sedlmeier and Gigerenzer (2000) explored the issue of people's intuitions about sample size in greater depth, arguing that people sometimes do have correct intuitions about sample size, but often don't.

FRAMING EFFECTS

Driving down the road, you notice your car is running low on gasoline, and you see two service stations, both advertising gasoline. Station A's price is $4.00 per gallon; station B's, $3.95. Station A's sign also announces, "5 cents/gallon discount for cash!" Station B's sign announces, "5 cents/gallon surcharge for credit cards." All other factors being equal (for example, cleanliness of the stations, whether you like the brand of gasoline carried, number of cars waiting at each), to which station would you choose to go? Many people report a preference for Station A, the one that offers a cash discount (Thaler, 1980).

It is interesting that people have this preference, because both stations are actually offering the same deal: a price of $3.95 per gallon if you use cash and $4.00 per gallon if you use a credit card. Tversky and Kahneman (1981) explained this phenomenon in terms of **framing effects**: People evaluate outcomes as changes from a reference point, their current state (Keren, 2011; McCloy, Beaman, Frosch, & Goddard, 2010). Depending on how their current state is described, they perceive certain outcomes as gains or losses. The description is therefore said to "frame" the decision, or to provide a certain context for it. We have already seen with previous cognitive topics (such as perception, thinking, and reasoning) that context effects can play a large role in affecting cognitive performance. Framing effects, in essence, can be thought of as context effects in decision making.

Here's what appears to be going on in the gas station example. Described as a "cash discount," the price seems a bargain—you assume you are starting from a reference point of $4.00 a gallon and then saving or gaining a nickel. In the case of station B, however, you describe the situation to yourself as follows: "Okay, so they're charging three bucks and ninety-five cents. Sounds good. But hey, wait a minute. If I want to use my card, they'll jack up the price to four dollars. I'd lose a nickel a gallon that way. What rip-off artists! Forget them—I'll just go to station A." Kahneman and Tversky (1979) argued that we treat losses more seriously than we treat gains of an equivalent amount (whether of money or of some other measure of satisfaction). That is, we care more about losing a dollar than we do about gaining a dollar, more about losing a nickel than gaining a nickel.

The problem is that simply changing the *description* of a situation can lead us to adopt different reference points and therefore to see the same outcome as a gain in one situation and a loss in the other. That in turn may lead us to alter our decision, not because any facts of the problem have changed but simply because the way we describe the situation to ourselves has changed.

ANCHORING

Suppose I ask you to answer a numerical question with an estimate (assuming you don't know the exactly correct value): As of April 2000, what was the population of Philadelphia? (I'll give you the correct answer later.) Imagine I give two people, call them Tim and Kim, this question, but I give each one a "starting value," obtained by spinning a roulette wheel. Now, Kim and Tim watch me spin the wheel, and they know that it operates (and stops) purely by chance and that the "starting value" is arbitrary. Kim's starting value is 1 million and Tim's, 2 million. If they are like most research participants in Tversky and Kahneman's (1973) study, Kim will arrive at an estimate of 1.25 million; Tim, 1.75 million. In other words, their initial starting point will have a huge effect on their final estimates, showing evidence of the phenomenon known as **anchoring**. (The correct value is 1,517,550, according to the April 1, 2000, US Census.)

Likewise, consider two groups of high school students, each given 5 seconds to estimate a complex expression. Group 1 estimates $8 \times 7 \times 6 \times 5 \times 4 \times 3 \times 2 \times 1$ and reports a mean estimate of 2,250; Group 2 estimates $1 \times 2 \times 3 \times 4 \times 5 \times 6 \times 7 \times 8$ and reports the answer to be (on average) 512. As you can tell, the two problems are identical. You probably can't tell quickly, both estimates are too small: The correct value is 40,320.

Tversky and Kahneman (2000) explain these results this way: People tend to perform the first few steps of multiplication, then extrapolate. The extrapolation tends to be too little rather than too much. Thus, both groups of participants underestimated the answer. In addition, those who started with $1 \times 2 \times 3$ began with a smaller value than did those who began with $8 \times 7 \times 6$, so the first group more severely underestimated the actual result.

SUNK COST EFFECTS

A major educational initiative is begun in your hometown; $3 million is invested in a 4-year program to help students avoid using cigarettes, liquor, and other drugs. In year 3, evidence begins to accumulate that the program is not working. A local legislator proposes ending funding to the program before the scheduled date. Howls of protest go up from some individuals, who claim that to stop a program after a large expenditure of funds would be a waste. These individuals are falling prey to what Arkes and Blumer (1985) have dubbed the **sunk cost effect**: "[the] greater tendency to continue an endeavor once an investment in money, effort, or time has been made" (p. 124).

Why is this an error? The explanation goes something like this: Money spent is already gone. Whether or not a great deal of money (or time, or energy, or emotion) has been spent does not affect the likelihood of future success. Those resources have been used, regardless of which option is chosen. All that should affect a decision, therefore, are the expected future benefits and costs of each option (Arkes & Hutzel, 2000).

ILLUSORY CORRELATION

You and a friend, both students of (if not majors in) psychology, observe fellow students around campus and discover a behavioral pattern you call "hair twisting": The person pinches a strand of hair between thumb and forefinger and proceeds to twist it around the forefinger. You believe this behavior is especially likely in people undergoing a great deal of stress. Needing a research paper for your psychology class, you undertake a study with your friend. You observe a random sample of 150 students for a day, categorizing them as hair twisters or not hair twisters. (Assume that you and your friend make your observations independently and that your interrater reliability, the agreement of categorization between you two, is high.) Later, each participant is given a battery of psychological tests to decide whether he or she is under significant amounts of stress.

The results are shown in Box 11.7. Given these data, what is your intuitive estimate of the relationship between stress and hair twisting? If you have had a course in statistics, you can try estimating the correlation coefficient or chi square test of contingency statistic; if not, try to put into words your belief about how strong the relationship is.

I posed this question to 30 students taking a cognitive psychology course. Most believed there was at least a weak relationship between the two variables. In fact, there is absolutely no relationship. Notice that the proportion of hair twisters is .25 (20/80 and 10/40) for both the participants under stress and the participants not under stress. Nevertheless,

Box 11.7		
Example of Illusory Correlation		
	Under Stress	**Not Under Stress**
Hair twister	20	10
Not a hair twister	80	40

Given the data above, give your intuitive estimate of the correlation between the two variables (from 0 to 1).

my students' intuitions are typical: People report seeing data associations that seem plausible even when associations are not present. In this example, hair twisting and stress are plausibly related because hair twisting sounds like a nervous behavior and because nervous behaviors are likely to be produced under conditions of anxiety.

The phenomenon of seeing nonexistent relationships is called **illusory correlation**. Notice that in the example given, it occurs even under ideal conditions (all the data are summarized and presented in a table, so you do not need to recall the relevant cases from memory). There is no ambiguity over where individual cases fall (everyone is classified as a hair twister or not and as being under stress or not), and there is no reason to expect personal biases on your part to interfere with your estimate. The data are dichotomous (that is, yes or no) for both variables and therefore easy to work with.

Chapman and Chapman (1967a, 1967b, 1969) presented an even more compelling demonstration of the phenomenon of illusory correlation. The authors were puzzled by a controversy within the field of clinical psychology over the use of the Draw-a-Person Test. In this a psychodiagnostic test, the client is asked to "draw a person," and the drawings are scored according to a number of dimensions (for example, whether the figure drawn is muscular, has atypical eyes, is childlike, is fat). Clinicians had reported strong correlations between some features of drawings and particular symptoms and behavioral characteristics of clients (for example, atypical eyes being drawn by suspicious clients; big heads being drawn by intelligent clients). However, these reports were never confirmed by researchers studying the test itself.

In one study, Chapman and Chapman (1967a) gave undergraduates who were unfamiliar with the Draw-a-Person Test a series of 45 drawings that they randomly paired with symptoms allegedly displayed by the people who drew them. These undergraduates "discovered" the same correlations that clinicians had been reporting. Because the drawings and symptoms were randomly paired, it appeared the undergraduates shared with the clinicians a preexisting bias as to what relationships would be found in the data. That is, they "discovered" relationships they expected to find, even when no such relationships existed.

Variables that tend to be falsely associated typically seem to have some prior association in people's minds (Chapman & Chapman, 1967b). On the surface, it seems to make sense that suspicious clients might draw wide-eyed figures: The wide eyes might be an artistic or symbolic representation of their suspiciousness. The point here is that the associations we bring to a situation often color our judgment to such as extent that we see them even if they are not there.

HINDSIGHT BIAS

Consider the following decision: You need to choose between declaring a major in psychology or a major in economics. You consult your own performance, goals, likes, and dislikes and have long discussions with faculty in both departments, majors in both departments, teachers from both areas who have instructed you, friends, parents, and relevant others. You finally decide to become an economics major, primarily because of your interest in the topics in your classes but also because you like the economics faculty so much.

A few months later, you start to discover you like your economics classes less and less, and you find your psychology courses more interesting than you previously had. You reopen the decision about your major, spend another couple of weeks rethinking your goals and interests, and decide to switch to psychology. When you announce this decision to your best friend, she says, "Well, I knew this was going to happen. It was pretty much inevitable. You don't seem the type to fit in with the other majors in that department, and also, given the stuff you said about last term's assignments, I knew you wouldn't like it for long." Other friends of yours also express little surprise at your latest decision, confiding that they "knew all along" that you would change your major.

How is it that you yourself didn't foresee this inevitable change in majors? How did your friends see into your future while you could not? In fact, one likely answer is that your friends are in error, suffering from something called **hindsight bias**. Fischhoff (1982b) described this bias as a tendency to "consistently exaggerate what could have been anticipated in foresight" when looking back (in hindsight) on an event (p. 341). The idea is that once you know how a decision has turned out, you look back on the events leading up to the outcome as being more inevitable than they really were.

How does hindsight bias apply to your friends in the hypothetical situation just described? Recall that they told you they "knew all along" that your decision to major in economics would not turn out well. It is likely, however, that your friends are looking at your decision in hindsight, knowing how your original decision turned out, and are therefore more able to think of reasons that it turned out this way. Their ability to predict, in foresight, how your decision would turn out is probably far weaker. In short, to quote an old maxim, "Hindsight is always 20/20." Recent investigations, by the way, have demonstrated the occurrence of hindsight bias in real-life contexts, with participants' (mis)recollections of such events as the economic effects of the introduction of the euro (Hoelzl, Kirchler, & Rodler, 2002), the impeachment verdict regarding President Clinton (Bryant & Guilbault, 2002), and the outcome of the O. J. Simpson trial (Demakis, 2002).

CONFIRMATION BIAS

In my hometown, parents can place their public school children in one of about a half dozen options for first grade. Parents of kindergartners, therefore, spend a lot of time and energy trying to find the "best" option for their child. Some parents do this by talking to other parents. For example, parents interested in the Spanish-immersion option may seek out other parents who have children enrolled in the immersion program and ask if they like it. After a prospective parent has talked to, say, five happy Spanish-immersion parents, his or her own sense grows that the immersion program is right for his or her child.

What's wrong with that, you may ask? Who better to tell a parent what the experience is like than another parent? Well, the name for the way in which the prospective parent is gathering information is called *confirmation bias,* as we discussed earlier when we looked at the Wason four-card task. This is the tendency to search only for information that will confirm one's initial hunch or hypothesis and to overlook or ignore other information.

Parents go wrong if they *only* seek information that would potentially confirm their hunch that a particular option is the best. If they only talk to parents of children in the program, they talk to parents most likely to be happy customers of the program. (If they weren't happy with the program, then presumably those parents would have placed their children in other programs.) The most rational decision, then, would be made by talking to a randomly selected set of parents or to parents who have transferred out of a particular option as well as to parents with children still in that option.

OVERCONFIDENCE

Consider the questions in Box 11.8, and choose from the two possible answers. After answering, rate your confidence. If you have absolutely no idea what the answer is, choose the value .5, to indicate that you think the odds you are right are 50–50. (Any number lower than .5 would indicate you think you are more likely to be wrong than right, so you should have chosen the other answer.) A rating of 1.00 means you are 100% certain your answer is correct. Values between .5 and 1.00 indicate intermediate levels of confidence, with higher numbers reflecting higher confidence.

For the purposes of this discussion, it matters very little how accurate your answers are. (If you simply *must* have the correct answers, see the note at the bottom of this page.*) What matters here is the relationship between your accuracy and your confidence rating. In several studies (reviewed by Lichtenstein, Fischhoff, & Phillips, 1982), participants were given a long list of questions similar to those in Box 11.8. After they answered all the questions and gave confidence ratings, their accuracy was plotted as a function of their confidence ratings.

Box 11.8

Some Trivia Questions

Choose one answer for each question, and rate your confidence in your answer on a scale from .5 (just guessing) to 1.0 (completely certain).

Which magazine had the largest circulation in 1978?
   a. Time   b. Reader's Digest

Which city had the larger population in 1953?
   a. St. Paul, MN   b. New Orleans, LA

Who was the 21st president of the United States?
   a. Arthur   b. Cleveland

Which Union ironclad ship fought the Confederate ironclad ship Merrimack?
   a. Monitor   b. Andover

Who began the profession of nursing?
   a. Nightingale   b. Barton

For example, the experimenters looked at all the questions for which a participant rated his confidence as .6 and calculated the proportion of those questions he answered correctly.

Typical findings are shown in Figure 11.7. This kind of curve—plotting confidence against accuracy—is called a **calibration curve**. The closer the curve is to the 45-degree line, the better the calibration, or "fit," between confidence and accuracy. Results on the 45-degree line would indicate that confidence and accuracy were perfectly synchronized; for example, questions for which a participant had a confidence rating of .6 would be answered accurately 60% of the time. This result is rarely, if ever, found.

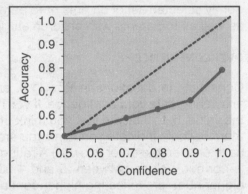

Instead, typical curves are "bowed" out from the 45-degree line, as shown in Figure 11.7. Deviations from the curve below this line are said to indicate **overconfidence**, because confidence ratings are higher than actual accuracy. Deviations above the line would indicate *underconfidence,* a phenomenon that rarely occurs. The general idea is this: For all the questions to which participants give a .8 confidence rating (meaning they estimate the probability of their answering correctly as 80%), they are correct only about 60% of the time. Further, when participants say they are 100% certain of the answer, they are correct only about 75% to 80% of the time.

■ Figure 11.7: Example of a calibration curve.

Said another way, people's impressions of their own accuracy are inflated. Overconfidence is a real impediment to good decision making. If your confidence in your judgment is inappropriately high, you probably will spurn any offers of help in making decisions because you will fail to see the need for it. Even when good decision aids are available to help you overcome other biases and errors of judgment, overconfidence will make you weight your own intuitions more heavily than any objective information that might be available. Overconfidence, then, can be thought of as arrogance in decision making.

So far, we have reviewed a (very incomplete) list of heuristics and biases in decision making and planning. Again, the point here is not that these ways of gathering and assessing information are always wrong or bad. Instead, the examples point out situations in which decision making may not produce as optimal results as it could. The existence of these biases also tells us something about how human beings "naturally" cope with information, particularly when information is abundant. Documenting such errors can be the first step to setting up effective remedial programs.

UTILITY MODELS OF DECISION MAKING

The previous section described errors and patterns of thinking that people use when gathering information. Another issue, though, is how people sift through all the gathered information to reach a decision. In this section, we will review two models that describe, or purport to describe, exactly what people are doing when they structure a decision and choose from alternatives.

It will be useful first to describe in a more general way the kinds of models of decision making (and thinking) that exist. **Normative models** define ideal performance under ideal circumstances. **Prescriptive models** tell us how we "ought" to make decisions. They take into account the fact that circumstances in which decisions are made are rarely ideal, and they provide guidance about how to do the best we can. Teachers try to get students to follow prescriptive models. **Descriptive models**, in contrast, simply detail what people actually do when they make decisions. These are not necessarily endorsements of good ways of thinking; rather, they describe actual performance. The distinctions among normative, prescriptive, and descriptive models are important as we consider specific theories.

EXPECTED UTILITY THEORY

Making a decision such as choosing a major can be compared to a gamble. In most gambles, you win (or lose) particular amounts of money depending on certain outcomes. Probability theory tells us (assuming fair coins, decks of cards, and the like) the odds of any outcome. The dollar amount won or lost tells us the monetary worth of each outcome.

It would be nice if we could somehow combine information about probabilities and amounts that can be won or lost. In fact, we can. One way is to calculate the *expected value* of each outcome. By multiplying the probability of each outcome by the amount of money won or lost for that outcome and summing these values over all possible outcomes, we can determine the expected value of the gamble. Presumably, then, if we were offered a choice between two gambles, we could choose the better one by calculating the expected value of each and choosing the gamble with the higher value.

This idea of expected value can be expressed in the form of an equation,

$$(1)\ EV = \Sigma\ (pi \times vi),$$

where EV is the expected value of the gamble, p_i is the probability of the ith outcome, and v_i is the monetary value of that outcome. For example, imagine a lottery with 10 tickets numbered 1 through 10. If the ticket drawn is numbered 1, you win $10. If the ticket drawn is numbered 2, 3, or 4, you win $5. Any other numbers drawn are worth nothing. The EV of this lottery, then, is

$$(.1 \times \$10) + (.3 \times \$5) + (.6 \times \$0) = \$1.60$$

What good does it do to calculate the expected value? For one thing, it provides you with a guide to how much money (if any) you should be willing to spend to buy a lottery ticket. If you are making rational decisions, you should not spend more for the ticket than the expected value of the lottery. (In some lotteries for charity, of course, you may want to donate more money simply to support the cause. In that case, you would need to add the expected value of the lottery and the amount of money you are willing to donate to arrive at the maximum price you should pay for a ticket.)

Not every decision involves monetary outcomes. We often care about other aspects of possible outcomes: our chances for happiness, success, or fulfillment of goals. Psychologists, economists, and others use the term **utility** to capture ideas of happiness, pleasure, and the satisfaction that comes from achieving one or more personal goals. A choice that fulfills one goal has less utility than a choice that fulfills that same goal plus another. For these decisions, we can use the kind of equation just given, using utility instead of monetary value. Equation 1 now becomes

$$(2)\ EU = \Sigma\ (pi \times ui),$$

where *EU* is the expected utility of a decision and u_i is the utility of the *i*th outcome. The summation is again over all the possible outcomes.

Let's translate our original example of choosing a major into the expected utility (EU) model. Imagine that you have listed all possible majors, estimated the probability of success in each, and determined your overall utility for success or failure. Table 11.2 provides an example. You estimate you have a good chance of success in some majors (such as classics). You do not think you have much chance of success in others (perhaps biology). At the same time, you place different values on success in various majors. In this example, you value cognitive science the most, followed by sociology and economics.

Your utility for failure also differs among the possible majors. For some, such as biology and mathematics, your overall utility even for failure is positive. For others, such as psychology and sociology, your overall utility for failure is strongly negative. The last column gives the overall expected utility for each major. It suggests that the best decision, given the estimates of probability and utility, is to be a chemistry major, with psychology and biology as second and third choices, respectively.

■ Table 11.2: An Example of Expected Utility Calculations for the Decision to Major in Selected Subjects

Major	Probability of Success	Utility		Expected Utility
		For Success	For Failure	
Art	.75	10	0	7.50
Asian studies	.50	0	−5	−2.50
Biology	.30	25	5	11.00
Chemistry	.45	30	4	15.70
Economics	.15	5	−10	−7.75
English	.25	5	0	1.25
French	.60	0	−5	−2.00
German	.50	0	−5	−2.50
History	.25	8	0	2.00
Mathematics	.05	10	5	5.25
Philosophy	.10	0	−5	−4.50
Physics	.01	0	0	0.00
Psychology	.60	35	−20	13.00
Religion	.50	5	−5	0.00
Sociology	.80	5	−25	1.00

NOTE: The probability of each outcome (success and failure) is multiplied by the utility for each outcome, and summed across both, giving the overall expected utility of choosing that major. Probabilities and utilites come from the individual making the decision and are subjective estimates.

You may be wondering how utility is measured in this example. The measurement of utilities turns out to be fairly straightforward. If you select one outcome and assign it the value of zero, then you can assign other values using this as the reference point. It does not matter which outcome is chosen as the zero point, because the final decision depends on differences in *EU*, not on the absolute value of the utilities (see Baron, 2008, for more on this process).

Many see **expected utility theory** as a normative model of decision making. It can be shown (see Baron, 2008) that if you always choose so as to maximize expected utility, then over a sufficiently large number of decisions, your own satisfaction will be highest. In other words, there is no better way of choosing among options that in the long run will increase overall satisfaction than using EU.

MULTIATTRIBUTE UTILITY THEORY

Like many others, you may be feeling that using EU theory to choose a major oversimplifies the decision. Specifically, you may find it hard to quantify your utility for success or for failure in any specific major. You may care about several goals and find it hard to figure out how they all fit together.

In three studies (Galotti, 1999; Galotti et al., 2006; Galotti & Kozberg, 1987), undergraduates were asked to list the factors they had thought about (or, in the case of freshmen and sophomores, that they were thinking about) when they chose a major. Respondents listed a number of factors. One principal source of difficulty in making this decision appeared to involve how the various factors and goals were integrated. Calculating *EU,* using Equation 2, may be difficult because information about several aspects of the decision must be integrated. Fortunately, there is a model that provides a means of integrating different dimensions and goals of a complex decision. It is called **multiattribute utility theory (MAUT).**

MAUT involves six steps: (1) breaking a decision into independent dimensions (such as those just listed for choosing a major), (2) determining the relative weights of each dimension, (3) listing all the alternatives (such as possible majors), (4) ranking the alternatives along the five dimensions, (5) multiplying the ranking by the weighting of each alternative to determine its final value, and (6) choosing the alternative with the highest value.

Table 11.3 provides an example of MAUT applied to the decision of choosing a major. It's fictional, but looks a lot like ones we've seen in our research program.

In the first column of the worksheet, the fictional decision maker has listed her four criteria, or factors for making the decision. The second column shows an importance weight, on a scale from 1 to 10 (the higher the number, the more important the factor). Notice that she places the most importance on her interest in the topic. The next most important criterion, for this student, is the job prospects for graduates with this major. The criterion "faculty in department" has been given only moderate weight. Of significance here is that these weights are subjective and would be different for different students. Your own weightings might be very dissimilar to the ones given in this example.

Across the next five columns are the student's perceptions of various options or alternative majors, rated with respect to each of the four criteria.

The fifth step in the MAUT process is to calculate an assessment of each alternatives with consideration for all the dimensions and the their respective weights. There are different ways to do this, three of which are illustrated in the bottom three rows of Table 11.3. The top criterion model focuses on the most important criterion (in this case, "interest in topic") and uses only those ratings, ignoring all others. In this case, psychology comes out slightly ahead of biology as the "best" alternative for this student.

■ Table 11.3: Example of a Multiattribute Utility Analysis for the Decision of Choosing a Major

| Criterion | Importance Weight | Options | | | | |
		Major: Psychology	Major: Biology	Major: Mathematics	Major: Classics	Major: Sociology
Interest in topic	9	9	8	7	4	6
Job prospects	8	7	9	8	1	3
Faculty in department	5	3	4	3	9	5
Requirements	7	5	4	3	7	8
Model	Summary Scores					
Full Multiattribute Utility Theory		187	192	163	138	159
Equally Weighted Criteria		24	25	21	21	22
Top Criterion		9	8	7	4	6

A second model uses more of the student's perceptions. In the equally weighted criteria model, the sum of the ratings across all criteria is computed. In this model, biology comes out slightly ahead of psychology.

Finally, the most complicated model, the full multiattribute utility model, combines all the information from the table above by multiplying each rating by the associated importance weighting and then summing. According to this model, biology is best, followed by psychology, and both of these are far ahead of the other options.

To use MAUT in decision making, it is critical that the dimensions listed be independent of one another. For instance, the possible dimensions "difficulty of courses" and "past grades in course" are presumably related. Thus, the decision maker must choose each dimension carefully. The decision maker then must be willing to make tradeoffs among the various dimensions. Although the decision maker in our example may care most about her interest in the major, MAUT assumes the person would be willing to choose an alternative that was not highest on this dimension *if* its relative position on other dimensions was enough to compensate.

I asserted earlier that many psychologists see MAUT as a normative model of decision making (although there are other views, discussed later). That is, if people follow MAUT, they will maximize their own utility to as to optimally achieve all their goals. Unfortunately, little is known about whether people ever use MAUT spontaneously when making important decisions, especially if the information they must consider is extensive.

A study by Payne (1976) suggests people do not always spontaneously use MAUT. Payne examined how people chose apartments when given different amounts of information about different numbers of alternatives. Participants were presented with an "information board" displaying a number of cards, as depicted in Photo 11.1. Each card represented information about a different one-bedroom, furnished apartment and carried the name of a factor, such as "noise level," "rent," or "closet space." The back of the card gave the value of that dimension for that apartment; possible values for the rent factor, for example, might be (in today's dollars) $500, $650, or $980.

Participants could examine one piece of information at a time (for example, the rent for apartment 1) and could examine as many or as few pieces of information as they needed to make a

■ Photo 11.1 : John Payne pioneered the use of a "decision board" as a technique to study decision making.

decision. The experimenter kept track of which pieces of information were examined. Two factors were varied in the experiment: the number of alternatives (that is, apartments) presented—2, 6, or 12—and the number of factors of information available per alternative—4, 8, or 12.

When choosing between only two apartments, participants examined the same number of factors for each. That is, if they asked about rent, closet space, parking, and laundry facilities for one, they asked about rent, closet space, parking, and laundry facilities for the other. They were willing to make tradeoffs in this decision, letting a desirable value of one factor (such as low rent) offset a less desirable value of another (such as less closet space).

When participants had to decide among 6 or 12 apartments, however, they used another strategy. In these cases, they eliminated some alternatives on the basis of only one or a few dimensions. For instance, they looked first at rent and immediately eliminated all apartments with high rents, without considering tradeoffs with other factors. This strategy has been called **elimination by aspects** (Tversky, 1972). It works as follows: First a factor is selected, say, rent. All the alternatives that exceed a threshold value for this factor (for example, more than $500) are eliminated. Next another factor is selected—say, noise level—and any alternatives found to exceed a threshold value on that dimension (for example, very noisy) are eliminated. This process continues until only one alternative is left. Payne (1976) believed that when decision makers have too much information to deal with, they reduce "cognitive strain" by resorting to such nonoptimal heuristics as elimination by aspects.

MAUT is a normative model; elimination by aspects is a descriptive model. It provides a picture of what people actually do. Whether elimination by aspects is the best one can do, with limited time or memory, to make a decision is an open question. In some cases, it may be entirely rational. If an apartment seeker simply cannot afford a rent above a certain amount, then it makes no sense to expend energy considering apartments that cost more, regardless of how well they rate on other dimensions. In other cases, it may be important for decision makers to take the time and trouble to engage in a MAUT analysis of a decision. Various kinds of decision aids (including computer-assisted ones) exist and may prove useful.

DESCRIPTIVE MODELS OF DECISION MAKING

As I implied earlier, not all investigators regard EU theory as normative. Frisch and Clemen (1994) offer several shortcomings of EU theory. The first is that EU theory provides an account only of making the final selection from a set of alternatives, not of making decisions in which one chooses between maintaining the status quo and making a change. Moreover, EU theory does not describe the process(es) by which people *structure* a decision—that is, gather information and lay out the possibilities and parameters.

IMAGE THEORY

A more recently proposed descriptive model of decision making, quite different from EU models, is that of **image theory** (Beach, 1993; Beach & Mitchell, 1987; Mitchell & Beach, 1990). The fundamental assumption of this theory is that in making real-life decisions, people rarely go through a formal structuring process in which they lay out all their options and criteria and then weigh and integrate various pieces of information, as MAUT and other EU models predict. Instead, most of the decision-making work is done during a phase known as the "prechoice screening of options." In this phase, decision makers typically winnow the number of options under active consideration to a small number, sometimes one or two. They do this by asking themselves whether a new goal, plan, or alternative is compatible with three images: the *value image* (containing the decision maker's values, morals, and principles), the *trajectory image* (containing the decision maker's goals and aspirations for the future), and the *strategic image* (the way in which the decision maker plans to attain his or her goals).

To return to our example of choosing a major, image theory might describe the college student as "trying on for size" various majors. That student might quickly reject certain majors because they aren't perceived as fitting well with the student's values or principles (for example, "I can't major in economics because all econ majors care about is money"). Alternatively, options might be dropped from further exploration if they don't fit well with the student's view of his or her own future (for example, "Art history? No way. I don't want to end up driving a taxi for life") or the path a student plans to take to achieve his or her future vision (for example, "If I want to go to med school, an English lit major isn't going to help me much"). (By the way, I use these quotes as examples of what students say, but I don't endorse the ideas they express: I know philanthropists who were econ majors, art history majors who went on to lead financially successful lives, and English lit majors who became physicians!)

According to image theory, options judged incompatible with one or more of these three images (value, trajectory, strategic) are dropped from further consideration. This prechoice screening process is noncompensatory: Violations of any image are enough to rule out that option, and no tradeoffs are made. Screening may result in a single option remaining active; in this case the decision maker's final choice is simply whether to accept the option. If there is more than one survivor of the prechoice screening phase, then the decision maker may go on to use a compensatory (i.e., making tradeoffs) or other decision strategy to make the final choice. If there are no survivors, decision makers presumably attempt to discover new options.

Image theory offers some intriguing ideas to researchers studying real-life decision making. Some preliminary work supports this model, but more studies are needed to fully assess how well it captures the early processes of decision making.

RECOGNITION-PRIMED DECISION MAKING

Researcher Gary Klein (1998, 2009) studied experts making time-pressured, high-stakes (often life-or-death) decisions: firefighters, intensive care pediatric nurses, and military officers. What he found was that few of their decision processes were captured by utility-like models, with the listing and evaluating of several options simultaneously. Instead, he argues, experts are most likely to rely on intuition, mental simulation, making metaphors or analogies, and recalling or creating stories. Klein and his associates expanded these studies into a series of investigations they dub "naturalistic decision making" (Lipshitz, Klein, Orasanu, & Salas, 2001), and the model they created is called **recognition-primed decision making**.

Much of the work in expert decision making is done, Klein argues, as the experts "size up" a situation. As they take stock of a new situation, they compare it to other situations they've previously encountered, calling to mind narrative stories about what happened in those situations and why. Typically, Klein found, experts consider one option at a time, mentally simulating the likely effect of a particular decision. If that simulation fits the scenario, the decision maker implements it; if not, she tries to find either another option or another metaphor for the situation. Box 11.9 provides an example in which a firefighter describes a sort of "sixth sense" he used to arrive at a decision. We'll talk more about expert/novice differences in cognition in Chapter 13.

Box 11.9

Example of Real-Life Expert Decision Making

It is a simple house fire in a one-story house in a residential neighborhood. The fire is in the back, in the kitchen area. The lieutenant leads his hose crew into the building, to the back, to spray water on the fire, but the fire just roars back at them.

"Odd," he thinks. The water should have more of an impact. They try dousing it again, and get the same results. They retreat a few steps to regroup.

Then the lieutenant starts to feel as if something is not right. He doesn't have any clues; he just doesn't feel right about being in that house, so he orders his men out of the building—a perfectly standard building with nothing out of the ordinary.

As soon as his men leave the building, the floor where they had been standing collapses. Had they still been inside, they would have plunged into the fire below.

NEUROPSYCHOLOGICAL EVIDENCE ON REASONING AND DECISION MAKING

Trying to localize the brain region(s) corresponding to higher-order cognitive processes, such as reasoning and decision making, is a difficult task. The processes themselves call upon other cognitive processes—memory, knowledge representation, language, and perception come immediately to mind—making it likely that no one place in the brain is associated with all and only instances of reasoning or decision making. However, neuropsychologists increasingly look to areas of the prefrontal cortex (see Figure 2.3 for a picture of where this region is located) as playing a major role in these and other higher-order cognitive functions.

Waltz and colleagues (1999) found that patients with prefrontal cortex damage were catastrophically hampered in their ability to reason with problems requiring the integration of multiple propositions (e.g., Beth is taller than Tina, Amy is taller than Beth) when the premises were not in a direct order permitting easy integration (Amy is taller than Beth, Beth is taller than Tina). Interestingly, patients with prefrontal cortex damage did not show deficits in their IQs or in their semantic memories. The deficit persisted on inductive reasoning tasks that required integration of different relations as well. The authors believe that the prefrontal cortex, shown to be important in many complex cognitive tasks, might be specialized for the integration of relations—that is, putting together different pieces of information into a unified mental representation.

Neuroscientst Antonio Damasio (1994) argues as well for the importance of prefrontal cortext functioning. Among other examples, he cites the famous case of Phineas Gage, a construction worker who, in 1848, suffered a bizarre and tragic accident while working on a railroad expansion in Vermont. In the accident, a long iron bar hurtled through the air after an unplanned explosion, entered Gage's left cheek, pierced his prefrontal cortex, and left a hole at its exit from the top of the skull. Miraculously, Gage did not die (or even lose conciousness), even though his brains and blood were splattered on the rod. He was able to talk shortly after the accident and able to sit up and to walk. He survived the ensuing infection (thanks to the care taken by Gage's doctor to clean the wound regularly).

However, after the accident, as Damasio (1994) puts it, "Gage was no longer Gage" (p. 7). He became fitful and irreverent, took to using profanity regularly, and was obstinate and unwilling to take advice when it went against his immediate inclinations. Though he proposed many plans, he abandoned most right away. He lost his job, lost other jobs, travelled for a while in a circus, and died in 1861. According to Damasio,

> it was selective damage in the prefrontal cortices of Phineas Gage's brain that compromised his ability to plan for the future, to conduct himself according to the social rules he previously had learned, and to decide on the course of action that ultimately would be most advantageous to his survival. (p. 33)

Much more remains to be discovered about the role of different neural centers in reasoning and decision making. But these investigations combined with hundreds more reviewed by Damasio give a strong hint that the prefrontal cortex plays a significant role.

Summary

1. Reasoning involves goal-directed thinking and drawing conclusions from various information. The inferences made may be automatic or intentional.

2. There are a variety of types of reasoning. Deductive reasoning involves conclusions that are logically necessary, or valid; examples include propositional or syllogistic reasoning. Inductive reasoning can lead only to conclusions that possess some degree of inductive strength; examples include analogies and hypothesis testing.

3. Formal reasoning includes tasks in which all the premises are supplied and the problems are self-contained; they usually have one correct, unambiguous answer and often contain content of limited interest. Everyday reasoning tasks often involve implicit premises, are typically not self-contained, and are often of personal relevance.

4. Psychologists seek general principles of human reasoning, not limited to only one reasoning task. Some findings from the reasoning literature seem to hold true for a variety of reasoning tasks. For example, the way premises are phrased can greatly influence performance: People often misinterpret what

premises mean or overlook possible interpretations of the premises' meanings. Reasoning is also subject to content and believability effects: People may perform very differently given different versions of the same problem, depending on the problem's content.

5. Decision making requires setting goals; gathering information; organizing, combining, and evaluating information; and making a final selection.

6 Because the process can be so complex, it is perhaps not surprising that decision making can go wrong or be suboptimal in a number of ways. People's intuitions about uncertainty and probability, their means of acquiring and/or remembering relevant information, and the processes they use to integrate different pieces of information can easily be shown to be error-prone. You can think of at least some biases and errors in decision making as cognitive illusions: They arise for understandable reasons and may be quite useful in some circumstances. For example, using availability to estimate the relative frequency of something may work perfectly well as long as you can be sure that examples have been collected in an unbiased fashion.

7. The existence of framing effects suggests that the way people evaluate options often is inappropriately colored by the way they describe (or "frame") those options. If the description frames the status quo in a positive light, then people see changes as more risky and shy away from those options; the converse is true if the status quo is defined in more negative terms.

8. One of the most general biases that people typically exhibit is overconfidence in their own judgment. Several demonstrations make the point that people often feel much more sure of their thinking and their predictions for the future than is justified (on the basis of their track records, for instance). Overconfidence can also play a role in more specific biases, such as hindsight bias and illusory correlation. In general, overconfidence can prevent people from critically examining their own thinking or from admitting of possibilities other than their favored one.

9. Some normative models of decision making purport to show how people should make decisions under ideal circumstances. One example is multiattribute utility theory (MAUT), which describes how information about the probability and the utility of various possible outcomes can be combined and compared.

10. Other, descriptive models describe how people actually make decisions. One such model, elimination by aspects, assumes that the amount of information people seek depends on the number of alternative possibilities under consideration. Another descriptive model of decision making, image theory, places more emphasis on the initial phases of decision making, the screening of options, than on the later stages of decision making, in which one option is selected. Recognition-primed decision making, a model developed from studies of experts, suggests that much of the work of decision making is done when an expert "sizes up" a situation.

11. The prefrontal cortex is believed to play a very important role in a person's ability to integrate relations—that is, to build a mental representation that incorporates multiple propositions or relationships—and to use that representation to draw conclusions or make important decisions.

Review Questions

1. Describe the similarities and differences between inductive and deductive reasoning.

2. Describe and contrast two methods by which people can derive conclusions in propositional reasoning tasks.

3. Distinguish between formal and everyday reasoning. How might the former be relevant to the latter?

4. (*Challenging*) Consider factors that hinder people's reasoning. In what ways are these factors present for other kinds of thinking and problem-solving tasks? (*Hint:* Review Chapter 10.) What does your answer imply about the relationship between thinking and reasoning?

5. Describe and give a new example of confirmation bias.

6. In what ways are inference rules (for example, *modus ponens*) similar to, and different from, the syntactic rules discussed in Chapter 9?

7. What are the major phases of decision making?

8. Why do some psychologists regard heuristics and biases in decision making as "cognitive illusions"?

9. Give two examples of the use of the availability heuristic in everyday life—one example where it would be appropriate and another example where it might not be. Explain why your examples are illustrative of availability.

10. Discuss the relationship between hindsight bias and overconfidence.

11. Explain the distinctions among normative models, prescriptive models, and descriptive models of thinking.

12. Describe image theory and contrast it with expected utility theory.

13. What are the major similarities and differences between image theory and the recognition-primed model of decision making?

Box 11.2

Solution to the logic puzzle in Box 11.1.

The Hatter said, in effect, that either the March Hare or the Dormouse stole it. If the Hatter lied, then neither the March Hare nor the Dormouse stole it, which means that the March Hare didn't steal it, hence was speaking the truth. Therefore, if the Hatter lied, then the March Hare didn't lie, so it is impossible that the Hatter and the March Hare both lied. Therefore the Dormouse spoke the truth when he said that the Hatter and March Hare didn't both lie. So we know that the Dormouse spoke the truth. But we are given that the Dormouse and the March Hare didn't both speak the truth. Then, since the Dormouse did, the March Hare didn't. This means that the March Hare lied, so his statement was false, which means that the March Hare stole the jam.

Key Terms

analogical reasoning

anchoring

availability heuristic

believability effect

bias

calibration curve

categorical syllogism

cognitive illusion

cognitive overload

confirmation bias

content effect

contradiction

decision structuring

deductive reasoning

deductive validity

descriptive model of decision making

elimination by aspects

everyday reasoning

expected utility theory

fallacy

formal reasoning

framing effect

gambler's fallacy

heuristic

hindsight bias

illusory correlation

image theory

inductive reasoning

inductive strength

logical connectives (&, V, ¬, →)

multiattribute utility theory (MAUT)

normative model of decision

making

overconfidence

premise

prescriptive model of decision making

propositional reasoning

rationality

recognition-primed decision making

representativeness heuristic

sunk cost effect

syllogistic reasoning

tautology

truth table

utility

CHAPTER 12

COGNITIVE DEVELOPMENT THROUGH ADOLESCENCE

CHAPTER OUTLINE

Piagetian Theory

General Principles

Stages of Development

The Sensorimotor Stage

The Preoperational Stage

The Concrete Operations Stage

The Formal Operations Stage

Reactions to Piaget's Theory

Non-Piagetian Approaches to Cognitive Development

Perceptual Development in Infancy

Toddlers' Acquisition of Syntax

Preschoolers' Use of Memorial Strategies

The Development of Reasoning Abilities in Middle and Late Childhood

Some Post-Piagetian Answers to the Question "What Develops?"

Neurological Maturation

Working-Memory Capacity and Processing Speed

Attention and Perceptual Encoding

The Knowledge Base and Knowledge Structures

Strategies

Metacognition

A little more than 19 years ago, an infant son came into my life. Despite my delight in this arrival, I have to admit that his limited behavioral and communicative repertoire made the very early months sometimes frustrating and stressful. His frequent crying often gave no clue as to the source of his problem, and it was hard to know if he was happy, sad, mad, or glad (to paraphrase Dr. Seuss) to be in the world.

Sixty-odd months later, I was parenting a son who could print his name, tell unsuspecting strangers long tales of his life (real and pretend), invent pretend schools (at which his imaginary teacher was Cinderella and his imaginary coach scheduled six basketball games a day), argue with great sophistication over bedtime and mealtime rules, and remember details of trips and conversations that had occurred months earlier.

As I write this edition, I travel this journey with my now 19-year-old son and my almost 11-year-old daughter. It's amazing to watch them use their abilities and confront challenges. These personal experiences, combined with my professional interest in cognitive abilities, have led me to wonder about the origins of those abilities. So far in this book, the capacities, skills, and strategies used in cognitive tasks have all been described in terms of a person who has presumably mastered or acquired most, or even all, of the skills considered necessary for a fully functioning cognitive being. It can be argued, however, that our understanding of adult cognition is fundamentally incomplete unless we understand its development. The reasons that adults use their memory, reach one conclusion rather than another, or perceive something in a certain way may have a great deal to do with their previous experience with cognitive tasks as well as with their current ability to understand the demands of the task in front of them.

In this chapter, we will pause to consider how cognitive capacities, skills, and strategies come to be—when and how they are acquired or mastered and what sorts of influences affect their growth. We will examine how infants and children at different points in their development cope with different cognitive tasks.

Our review of cognitive development will necessarily be quite selective. There simply isn't room in one chapter to consider the development of performance on all the cognitive tasks that we have previously discussed. Whole books have been written on the subject (including one by me—Galotti, 2011)! Instead, we will first look at broad theoretical approaches to cognitive development, considering the general question "How do cognitive abilities change and grow as an infant matures through adolescence?" To do this, we will focus on two major kinds of theoretical approaches: stage theories, such as that developed by Piaget, and nonstage theories, such as information-processing models.

Stage theories of cognitive development are so named because they describe development as consisting of a series of qualitatively different periods, called **stages**. Each stage consists of a different way of making sense of the world. Stage theories view children as fundamentally and qualitatively different from adults in one or more respects by virtue of their being in different developmental stages. Stage theories assume that children go through stages in a fixed or stable order, never skipping stages or going backward. Presumably, the cognitive abilities and capacities gained in one stage prepare the child to acquire the abilities and capacities of the next stage. In this sense, stages build on one another. Most stage theorists also claim *universality* for their stages, seeing them as applicable to children from a wide variety of cultures and environments.

Nonstage theories of cognitive development do not see qualitative changes at different developmental periods. Instead, these theories view development as the gradual acquisition of one or more things—for example, mental associations, memory capacity, perceptual discrimination, attentional focus, knowledge, or strategies. Generally speaking, nonstage theories view children as quantitatively but not qualitatively different from adults.

After reviewing these two theoretical approaches in greater detail, we will examine cognitive development on selective specific cognitive tasks. In doing so, we will review several proposals for what children acquire and master in the course of their development. We will see that there currently are a number of distinct, although not mutually exclusive, answers to the question "What is it that develops?" (Siegler, 1978).

Like other theories, developmental theories are organized ways of explaining phenomena. They include assumptions and predictions that can be translated into testable hypotheses. In particular, developmental theories try to explain how and why certain changes occur in children's behavior and performance at different periods. Further, developmental theories focus mainly on long-lasting changes, not momentary oscillations of behavior (P. H. Miller, 2011).

There are hundreds of developmental theories in psychology. Most have a narrow focus, describing only one aspect of development (such as memory or perception), and many focus on only one developmental period (such as infancy or adolescence). Here, we will first consider one very broad developmental approach that set out to describe and explain many aspects of cognitive development over a broad time span. This approach, Piagetian theory, is arguably the single most important theory in the field of cognitive development. Next we will consider alternatives to Piagetian theory, not one opposing theory but rather a collection of proposals from different researchers. Each of these usually focuses on a more limited aspect of cognitive development.

PIAGETIAN THEORY

Jean Piaget (1896–1980), pictured in Photo 12.1, was fascinated by the question of how intelligence and cognitive functions come to be. He quickly rejected the idea that intelligence consists of the passive acquisition, storage, and organization of knowledge from the environment. Nor did he accept the view that intelligence arises solely as a function of physical maturation. Instead, he saw intelligence as something that adapts to its environment over time, through the active participation of both the child and his or her environment (Piaget,

■ Photo 12.1: Jean Piaget is shown here interacting with a group of children in a classroom.

1970/1988a). We will review a few general principles of Piagetian theory before describing specific cognitive stages of development.

GENERAL PRINCIPLES

Piaget's long-standing interest in the development of children's thinking actually began, in a way, in his own childhood, as he studied and wrote about birds, fossils, and mollusks.

In adolescence, he added the study of philosophy to his ever-widening circle of interests. His knowledge of natural history and science led him to think about psychological concepts, such as thinking and intelligence, in very ethological terms. Specifically, Piaget saw the problem of how any organism adapts to its environment as sharing many similarities to the problem of how human children's intelligence develops. Both processes involve a sort of adaptation. Intelligence, Piaget believed, represented an adaptation of mental structures to the physical, social, and intellectual environments (Ginsburg & Opper, 1988).

Piaget saw children as active participants in their own development. He rejected the idea that cognitive structures somehow slowly emerge or unfold or that they are thrust on an unsuspecting and passive child by a parent, teacher, or other aspect of the environment. Instead, Piaget believed that children construct their own *mental structures,* the building blocks of cognition and intelligence, through a constant and active series of interactions with their environment.

Construction of mental structures begins shortly after birth. The infant comes into the world with very little cognitive "equipment." Indeed, about all the neonate has is a set of reflexes, such as sucking and grasping. These reflexes (the precursors to mental structures) encounter the environment, and the interaction of the two results in the gradual growth and change of the original reflexes. Throughout the process, the infant (and later the child, and still later the adolescent) actively participates through practice, experimentation, and accidental discovery.

Piaget saw the major mechanism of development as the *adaptation* of mental structures. The analogy here is to evolutionary adaptation—how animals, over several generations, evolve new structures or behaviors that better fit their current environment. Adaptation in the Piagetian sense consists of two distinct but interrelated processes: assimilation and accommodation. Piaget (1970/1988b) defined *assimilation* as the "integration of external elements into evolving or completed structures" (p. 7). The idea here is that mental structures are applied to new objects in the world.

An infant who has a structure (Piaget called it a *scheme*) for sucking may at first suckle only at the mother's breast. However, when new objects are placed within easy reach of his mouth, the infant may apply that structure to the new object, say, a bent finger. We say the finger has been *assimilated* into the sucking scheme.

Accommodation, by contrast, involves changing the structures to fit new objects. A finger has a different shape and texture than does a breast and must be sucked in a slightly different way. Each time the infant sucks on a new object, she changes, even if ever so slightly, the sucking scheme. That internal change in the structure is known as *accommodation.* Assimilation and accommodation are always present, at least to some degree, in every act of adaptation, because it is impossible for one to exist in the absence of the other. Optimally, the two are balanced, or in equilibrium.

Piaget assumed that all cognitive functioning is organized in a particular manner at every level of development. By "organized," Piaget meant to suggest that the various mental structures have some relationships to one another. With development, these relationships become more complex, more numerous, and more systematic. Although some organization among mental structures always exists, the specific interrelationships of mental structures change in different developmental stages. As a result, the ways in which the child understands the world also change with development. According to Piaget, this is because knowledge is always acquired and interpreted through whatever mental structures currently exist.

STAGES OF DEVELOPMENT

Piaget described four major periods (we will refer to them here as *stages*) of development. Some of these stages can be divided into a series of substages. For our purposes, we will concentrate on the four main stages, but interested students can learn more about the substages by consulting other sources (such as Ginsburg & Opper, 1988; P. H. Miller, 2011).

The Sensorimotor Stage

The first stage is the **sensorimotor stage**, beginning at birth and lasting roughly 18 months. The stage is so named because Piaget believed that an infant in this phase of development experiences the world almost entirely through sensory and motor experiences. According to Piaget, knowledge gained during this stage is acquired through, and is often equivalent to, sensation or action. The infant is described as lacking the capacity for mental representation. Thus, all experience must happen in the here and now and must be centered on things that are present.

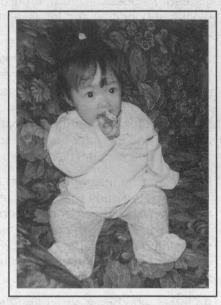

The implications of this description are profound. They suggest that infants experience the world in ways completely different from those of older children or adults. Older children can have thoughts, conscious recollections of past experiences, and ideas about the past and future. All these abilities, however, require the capacity for mental representation. The infant, lacking the capacity for mental representation, cannot have any of these things. For the infant, thought *is* action or sensation, because there is no means of representing thought except through action or sensation.

■ Photo 12.2: According to Piaget, the sucking scheme demonstrated by this infant will undergo assimilation and accommodation.

Piaget saw all cognitive development as beginning with the infant's biological heritage: a simple set of reflexes such as sucking and rooting (moving the head in the direction of a touch on the cheek). This primitive "mental equipment" slowly changes and evolves as the infant matures and acquires many experiences in the world. Sucking, for instance, is applied to many different objects—fingers, toys, keys, strands of hair—demonstrating assimilation of new objects to the sucking scheme. Each of these objects has a different shape, size, and texture, so the way the infant sucks on each one is slightly different, forcing accommodation of the sucking scheme.

Gradually, over a period of 18 months, the schemes grow more complex, are executed more smoothly and more efficiently, and become integrated with other developing schemes. At first, for example, infants may suck only on objects placed near their mouth. Later in infancy, they learn how to grasp objects in front of them. As these two schemes—sucking and grasping—develop, they can also be coordinated so that older infants can reach out for an interesting novel object, pull it toward them, and place it in their mouth as a new thing to suck on.

One of the important developments in the sensorimotor stage is the acquisition of the concept of *object permanence,* shown in Photos 12.3 (A) and (B). An adult holds a novel and interesting toy in front of a seated infant, attracting his attention. As the infant reaches for the toy, however, the adult frustrates his attempts to grab it by first moving it out of reach, then blocking the infant's view by placing a screen between the infant and the toy. The reaction of the 4-month-old infant is quite surprising: A few seconds after the toy disappears from sight, the infant looks away and shows no inclination to search for it. Piaget interpreted this reaction as follows: Having no capacity for mental representation, the infant experiences objects only when they are present in the here and now. Quite literally, objects out of sight are also objects out of mind.

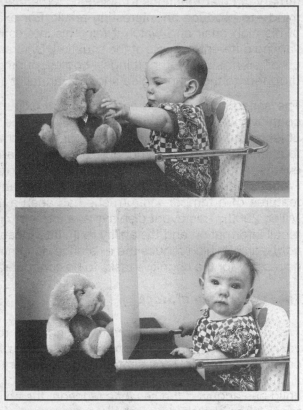

■ Photo 12.3: According to Piaget, until object permanence develops, babies fail to understand that objects still exist when they're no longer in view.

An older infant (say, around 8 months) demonstrates more, if not complete, understanding of the idea that objects continue to exist even when they are not immediately in view. An infant at roughly this age continues to search for objects that are partly hidden. A slightly older infant (10–12 months) even searches for completely hidden objects. This is also about the time that infants start to show *stranger anxiety*—looking fearfully around for a parent who has left the room and showing wariness of the person left with them (often a hapless babysitter). The infant seems to treat the missing parent as yet another object that has disappeared—except in this case, the emotional consequences of the disappearance are much greater than they are for a ball or other toy.

Another important developmental achievement in the sensorimotor period is the increasing intentionality and understanding of causality. Piaget's description of this aspect of development (as well as other aspects) involves the concept of *circular reactions*—behaviors that are repeated over and over. At first, young infants (1–4 months) display *primary circular reactions*—behaviors that are set off by chance, are centered on the infant's own body, lead to an interesting (from the infant's point of view) result, and are then continued. Thumb sucking is an example. Young infants' thumbs find their way into their mouths almost at random. Once a thumb is properly situated, however, most infants keep it there and continue to suck on it.

Secondary circular reactions emerge at roughly 4 to 8 months. These are oriented to objects outside the infant's body and may include such things as shaking a rattle to produce a noise or banging the side of a crib to make a mobile attached to the crib move. At around 18 months, *tertiary circular reactions* appear. Piaget compared the infant's tertiary circular reactions to scientific experiments. Here the infant begins with a goal in mind—to produce an interesting result. For example, he may drop a toy over the side of his high chair and watch it fall. This interesting result leads the infant to experiment, varying different aspects of the situation. Different toys are dropped, from varying heights, on different sides. Other things—bottles, cups of juice, and bowls of food—can also be dropped, to the infant's glee and the caretaker's frustration.

The sensorimotor period ends after approximately 18 to 24 months. Having begun her cognitive life with little more than reflexes, the infant now has a new understanding of objects and their existence independent of her actions; a better sense of her own ability to affect things in the world; and, most important, the mental ability to represent objects, events, and people. Older infants show some recall of past events. For example, one of Piaget's daughters, Jacqueline, was able at about 14 months to re-create many of the features of a temper tantrum she had seen a little boy produce 12 hours before (P. H. Miller, 2002). This event displays a number of cognitive abilities—the ability to store and recall information and the ability to imitate these behaviors at a later time *(deferred imitation)*—all of which require the existence of mental representation. These achievements are necessary for the cognitive tasks to be confronted in the next period of development.

The Preoperational Stage

The next stage of development, lasting from roughly age 18 months to roughly age 7 years, is known as the **preoperational stage** of cognitive development. Armed with the capacity for mental representation, the preoperational child understands the world in new and more complex ways than did the infant or toddler. In particular, the preoperational child has acquired the *semiotic function,* the ability to use one thing to represent or stand for another. The child now shows a great deal of symbolic functioning: pretending to drink from an empty cup, cradling a doll or stuffed toy as if it were a baby, "riding" on a "pretend horse" made of a stick.

A second, and related, ability is the use of language. Children at this age are rapidly acquiring a vocabulary of words that "stand for" real objects or events in the world. In this sense, language requires symbolic thought capacities. Piaget saw children's language development as a reflection, rather than a cause, of their intellectual structures. The child's capacity for representational thought now allows a greater variety of cognitive activities and thus a greater range of exploration. Children can now play in more complex ways than before, including elements of fantasy and reenactment. They can talk with others about their experiences, those in the present and those that have previously happened. They can also talk about and begin to plan for future events, such as a trip to the store after nap time, and use language to guide themselves through challenging tasks.

At the same time, as the name of the stage suggests, there are important gaps in children's thinking. In fact, the name *preoperational* suggests a contrast with the later period of concrete operations. Preoperational children are typically described as lacking mental operations that older children have (to be described later; Gelman, 1979) and, consequently, as having significant limits on their thinking. Of course, adults have been shown throughout the book to have limits on their thinking, too. Apparently, though, the greater limitations to which children seem subject change their cognitive performance in very noticeable ways.

Piaget described the preoperational child as *egocentric* in his thinking. Children of this age apparently have a difficult time taking into account any viewpoint other than their own. For example, a 4-year-old coming home from nursery school might tell his mother, "Ted did it," not explaining who Ted is or what he did. According to Piaget, this egocentric language results from his inability to take his mother's perspective, to understand that his mother might not know who Ted is. The 4-year-old assumes that everyone knows what he knows, sees things as he does, and remembers what he remembers.

An experimental demonstration of egocentrism came from the work of Piaget and Inhelder (1948/1967). They presented children with a three-dimensional model of three mountains. Arranged around the mountains were different objects, such as a small house and a cross, that were visible from some angles but not others. Preschool children were asked to describe whether an observer (a small wooden doll) on the other side of the table could see particular objects (see Figure 12.1). Children typically responded that the observer could see everything the child could see, failing to take into account the observer's different vantage point.

■ Figure 12.1: Example of the stimulus apparatus for the three-mountain task.

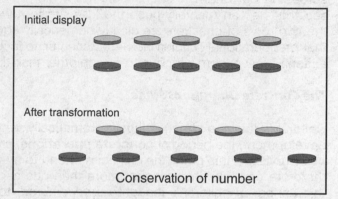

■ Figure 12.2: Depiction of conservation of number task.

Preoperational children's thinking has also been described as *centered* on their perceptions of the world. That is, the children attend to, or focus on, only a limited amount of the information available at any given point (Ginsburg & Opper, 1988). Moreover, the thought of preoperational children is said to be *static,* focusing on states rather than transformations or changes. Finally, preoperational children are described as lacking *reversibility,* the ability to "mentally reverse" an action.

One well-known illustration of these aspects of preoperational thinking comes from Piagetian number *conservation* tasks, depicted in Photo 12.4 and Figure 12.2. They work as follows: The experimenter sets two rows of checkers in front of the child, one set black and one red, each containing five checkers. Initially, the checkers in each row are set out in one-to-one correspondence (each black checker is lined up with a red checker), and the child judges both rows of checkers to be equal in number. Next the experimenter spreads out one of the rows of checkers (see Figure 12.2) and asks the child which row has more or if the two rows still have the same number of checkers. The typical 4-year-old responds that the longer row has more checkers than the shorter row. He does not appreciate that operations such as moving checkers around the table are number irrelevant; that is, they do not affect the numerosity of the rows.

One explanation for this puzzling response is that the child is overwhelmed by what the two rows of checkers look like. One row does indeed look "bigger" (longer) and perhaps therefore more numerous. The child has centered on the length of the rows and ignored the density (the space between checkers) or the numerosity. The child has paid attention to what the rows of checkers now look like (the static stimulus display) and has ignored the fact that the transformation involved did not add or subtract any checkers and thus could not have affected the number of checkers in either row. Finally, the child has not mentally reversed the action of spreading out one row of checkers—to

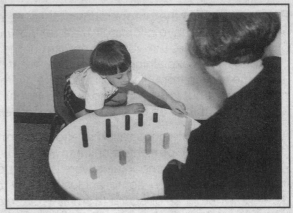

■ Photo 12.4: To a preoperational child, it might seem as though the row of pegs closer to him, in which the pegs are closer together, contains fewer than the row farther away.

see that he can mentally push the less dense row into its original formation, in which the two rows of checkers are clearly numerically equal. According to Piaget, the abilities that preoperational children lack—to decenter, to focus on transformations, and to reverse actions—leave them with little to rely on other than their perceptual experience.

The Concrete Operations Stage

Children's thinking changes, again dramatically, when they move into the next stage of development, the period of **concrete operations**, around the age of 7 until about the age of 11 or 12. At this point, the child can attend to much more information than before and therefore can take into account more than one aspect of a situation. Piaget described this aspect of children's thought as *decentered,* to draw a contrast with the centered nature of preoperational thought. Concrete-operational children also can pay attention to transformations and not just to initial and final states.

The conservation task provides a familiar example. The child who conserves number moves beyond her perception, recognizing that certain changes (for example, in number or in amount of liquid) result only from certain transformations, such as adding or taking away, and not from others, such as spreading out or changing shape. Piaget says that this child's thought shows *reversibility.* A concrete-operational child can construct (as the preoperational child cannot) a mental representation of the transformation and of the "reverse" of the transformation (moving checkers to their original position, pouring a liquid back into its original container) and can use this knowledge to judge correctly the relative numbers or amounts.

Another ability that matures during the stage of concrete operations is *classification.* The younger, preoperational child has a great deal of trouble consistently sorting a group of objects into categories (for example, all the round things, all the square things; or all the blue things, all the red things). This child has difficulty maintaining a consistent basis of classification. He may start out sorting wooden blocks on the basis of shape but, midway through the task, start sorting on the basis of color. The groups he ends up with will include blocks that vary in both shape and color. The older, concrete operational child is much more consistent and hence better able to keep track of the task.

The typical concrete-operational child seems like a very mature thinker when compared with a younger child; however, there are still areas of limitation in this period of development. In particular, the child has difficulty thinking in abstract terms. Her thinking is limited to actual or imagined concrete things. And, when compared with that of an older adolescent, her thinking is less systematic.

The Formal Operations Stage

The final stage of cognitive development, which begins around puberty, is that of **formal operations**. Adolescents show much more systematic thinking. For instance, when given a number of beakers containing different liquids and asked to determine how they can be mixed together to produce a liquid of a certain color, adolescents do a number of things that younger children do not. First, they can generate all the possible combinations of liquids and often do so in a systematic way. They can test one combination at a time and keep track of the results of each one. They are better able to isolate and hold constant all factors except one and to report on their results accurately. This may be why middle school and high school students seem so much better than younger students at designing and carrying out experiments in science classes.

The formal-operational thinker is also able to think more abstractly than the concrete-operational thinker. Adolescents now see reality as one of several possibilities and can imagine other kinds of realities. This new liberation of thought has been described as one of the sources of adolescent idealism and political awakening. Adolescents' awareness of different possibilities opens up for them many different possible paths to the future because they can "think beyond old limits" (Moshman, 2005).

Typically, adolescents are also more adept at logical thinking than are younger children. In part, this has to do with their ability to think abstractly and to reason from arbitrary propositions such as "If all the Xs are Ys, and none of the Ys are Zs, then at least some of the Xs are not Zs." Adolescents, unlike younger children, are able to understand the idea of *logical necessity* in reasoning. This is the notion that for some arguments, if the premises are true, then the conclusion is guaranteed to be true as well (Moshman, 2005).

Logical thinking also derives from a newly emerging ability Piaget called *reflective abstraction* (Piaget, 1964/1968). Adolescents can, for the first time, acquire new knowledge and understanding simply from thinking about their own thoughts and abstracting from these reflections. By doing so, they may begin to notice inconsistencies in their beliefs. Reflective abstraction is also useful in other realms of thinking, notably those of social and moral thinking. The adolescent is now quite capable of taking the points of view of others and trying to think about issues as others would.

There is much debate over whether all adolescents reach the period of formal operations, although Piaget (1972) maintained that they do. However, Piaget did not mean to suggest that even those who do will always display their highest competence. Instead, his idea was that adolescents who acquire formal operations have the ability to think abstractly, systematically, and logically, even if they do not always do so.

Piaget's theory of cognitive development thus describes how thought evolves from simple reflexes into an organized, flexible, logical system of internal mental structures that allow thinking about a wide variety of objects, events, and abstractions. A child at each stage of development has a remarkable set of abilities but often (especially in stages before formal operations) faces several limitations in thinking. The mental structures that allow and organize thought develop slowly through the child's active exploration of the world.

REACTIONS TO PIAGET'S THEORY

Piaget's major writings date from the 1920s, although his fame in the United States was not really established until the early 1960s. Halford (1989) described the 1960s as a period of intense optimism about Piagetian theory in this country, as many psychologists and educators sought ways of using it to design appropriate educational curricula for children and adolescents of varying ages. However, beginning around the 1970s, enthusiasm for Piaget's ideas began to fade as a number of studies appeared to disconfirm some of the theory's predictions (see Gelman & Baillargeon, 1983, and Halford, 1989, for reviews; see Newcombe, 2002, and D. Roth, Slone, & Dar, 2000, for other perspectives on Piagetian theory).

Many researchers were concerned about methodological problems in Piaget's studies. His reports of sensorimotor cognitive development, for example, were based on the observation of only three infants, all Piaget's own children (P. H. Miller, 2011). Accordingly, it is hard to know how free from bias or overinterpretation Piaget's observations were, although later research has replicated nearly all the phenomena he reported (Ginsburg & Opper, 1988).

In work with older children and adults, Piaget again employed the *clinical method,* often modifying the tasks or questions for each child in response to his or her performance or explanation. Although this approach allows a great deal of flexibility, it also opens the door to various threats to validity, especially the possibility that the experimenter will unconsciously and subtly provide the child with cues or leading questions.

Siegel and Hodkin (1982) pointed out other methodological problems in the tasks Piaget developed. Many seem to require much more than simply the understanding of the concept under investigation. Children in a conservation task, for instance, not only must observe the materials undergoing different transformations and make the correct judgments but also must explain their answers carefully and, in some cases, resist countersuggestions from the experimenter. Siegel and Hodkin argued that when a child is asked the same question several times, to assess the particular cognitive ability with different stimuli, the child may change the answer because he or she believes the adult is asking the question again because the first answer was wrong. Usually, as most children are aware, adults do not repeat a question when the answer is correct but only when it is wrong.

Other investigators and theorists have raised problems with parts of Piaget's theory. Many have agreed that evidence for distinct stages of cognitive development is not strong (Brainerd, 1978; P. H. Miller, 2011). A strict interpretation of stage theory would require, for example, that all stage-related abilities appear together, a prediction not well borne out. There is also an arguable lack of evidence for the specific cognitive structures that Piaget described as underlying the different stages (Halford, 1989). Further, a variety of empirical studies have demonstrated a great deal of competence and knowledge among young children for which Piaget's theory has difficulty accounting.

Nonetheless, even his sharpest critics acknowledge a tremendous debt to Piaget. Most investigators admire the wide-ranging scope of the theory and the cleverness Piaget showed in devising tasks to reveal important aspects of children's thinking at different periods in development.

NON-PIAGETIAN APPROACHES TO COGNITIVE DEVELOPMENT _____

Many psychologists who study cognitive development appreciate the keen observations that Piaget reported but do not accept his interpretation of their underlying causes. In particular, many believe neither that cognitive development proceeds through a series of qualitatively different stages or periods nor that qualitatively different intellectual structures underlie cognition at different periods. Instead, these investigators assert that cognitive skills and abilities emerge or are acquired gradually.

Many of these psychologists use adult models of cognitive processes as a framework within which to understand how children process information. Many take information-processing models, such as those described in earlier chapters, as the starting point for a model of cognitive development. The basic strategy is to discover how information-processing models of adult cognition must be modified to describe and explain the performance of children of different ages and abilities.

As with models of adult cognition, information-processing models of children's cognition use the digital computer as a metaphor for the child's mind. Information presented to the child (either explicitly or implicitly) can be regarded as input. Just as computers have various storage devices (buffers, disks), so too children are assumed to have one or more distinct memory stores. Just as computers retrieve information from their stores, so too children are assumed to be able to access (at least some of) their information and to use it in a number of cognitive tasks, including calculation, classification, identification, and integration. Finally, just as computers write information on disks or on printers or terminal screens, so too do children often produce output of one sort or another: a verbal response, a drawing, a gesture, or some other behavior.

Other psychologists focus on physiological (particularly neurological) and other innate factors that contribute to cognitive development. These psychologists begin with the premise that young infants do not have "blank slates" for minds but instead bring to their cognitive life certain mental structures that are present from birth. Not surprisingly, these psychologists investigate the cognitive competencies of young infants and toddlers, who presumably have had relatively little opportunity to learn cognitive skills.

Still other developmental psychologists are rediscovering another "great theorist" of cognitive development, the Russian psychologist Lev Vygotsky (1896–1934). Vygotsky's theory differs from Piaget's mainly in that he sees as inseparable the child and the context in which that child functions. Thus, a child's ability to understand the concept of the permanent object, or to conserve number, or to reason systematically cannot be evaluated by focusing on the child alone. Instead, Vygosky held, the environment, both physical and social, within which an activity is carried out must be taken into account.

Vygotsky introduced the concept of the "zone of proximal development" to account for the fact that children can often perform in more advanced ways with guidance or collaboration from an adult (P. H. Miller, 2011). When a more competent individual collaborates with a younger, less cognitively mature child, that child's performance is typically enhanced, even if the interaction is informal (Rogoff, 1990). Developmental psychologists in the Vygotskian tradition, therefore, are more apt to investigate children working with adults on everyday tasks. Thus, their work falls within the ecological paradigm discussed in Chapter 1.

In this section, we will review a few examples of work that departs from the Piagetian tradition. The examples span a range of types of cognitive tasks, as well as different periods of development. Although they represent only a minute proportion of the possible examples of important research on cognitive development, they provide a sense of the kinds of questions cognitive developmental psychologists ask and how they seek answers.

PERCEPTUAL DEVELOPMENT IN INFANCY

We saw in Chapter 3 that our perceptual activities are crucial to our acquiring information from and about the world around us. It behooves a cognitive psychologist interested in perception, then, to understand how perceptual abilities, skills, and capacities develop. Work with infants conducted by Renee Baillargeon traces the development of perceptual understanding of objects and events across age groups (Baillargeon & Wang, 2002). Consider the ability of infants to understand the concept of physical support; for example, one object can physically support another if (typically) the supporting object is underneath the supported object and if enough of the supported object's surface makes contact with the supporting object.

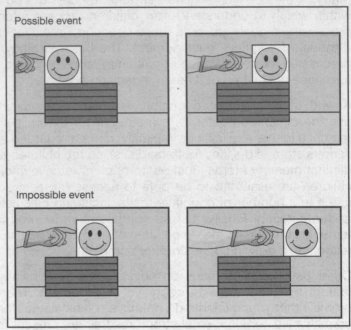

■ Figure 12.3: Paradigm for studying infants' understanding of support phenomena. In both events, a gloved hand pushes a box from left to right along the top of a platform. In the possible event (top), the box is pushed until its leading edge reaches the end of the platform. In the impossible event (bottom), the box is pushed until only the left 15% of its bottom surface rests on the platform.

To make this more concrete, consider Figure 12.3. Imagine showing a research participant one of two events. In the top row, depicting a possible event, a gloved hand pushes one box (with a smiley face) across the top of another one. This is called a *possible* event because in real life it could easily happen. The bottom row depicts an *impossible* event, one that under normal circumstance could not occur (the experimenters used sleight of hand to make it occur): A box is pushed across the top of a supporting box until only 15% of its bottom surface rests on the supporting box.

What do infants do when they witness these two events? Piagetian theory would predict that young infants (below 10 months, say) would see both events as equally possible. But they don't. Their facial expressions register surprise (as rated by research assistants who can't see what the infants are looking at). In fact, the results show a developmental pattern quite at odds with Piagetian theory:

> Our results indicate that by 3 months of age, if not before, infants expect the box to fall if it loses all contact with the platform and to remain stable otherwise. At this stage, any contact between the box

and the platform is deemed sufficient to ensure the box's stability. At least two developments take place between 3 and 6.5 months of age. First, infants become aware that the locus of contact between the box and the platform must be taken into account when judging the box's stability. Infants initially assume that the box will remain stable if placed either on the top or against the side of the platform. By 4.5 to 5.5 months of age, however, infants come to distinguish between the two types of contact and recognize that only the former ensures support. The second development is that infants begin to appreciate that the amount of contact between the box and the platform affects the box's stability. Initially, infants believe that the box will be stable even if only a small portion (for example, the left 15%) of its bottom surface rests on the platform [see Figure 12.3]. By 6.5 months of age, however, infants expect the box to fall unless a significant portion of its bottom surface lies on the platform. (Baillargeon, 1994, pp. 133–134)

Similarly, Quinn et al. (2002; see also Bhatt & Quinn 2011) report that infants aged 3 months do not show evidence of using Gestalt principles of similarity, whereas infants aged 6–7 months do. These authors and others (Yoshida et al., 2010) suggest that different Gestalt principles become functional at different times in an infant's development.

TODDLERS' ACQUISITION OF SYNTAX

In Chapter 9, we discussed several aspects of language abilities and usage. Each of these aspects shows interesting developmental changes. Most psychologists and linguists who study language development agree on a proposition that at first might seem startling: Children do not *learn* syntax (Chomsky, 1959). That is, the way in which syntax develops from infancy through adolescence is difficult to account for in terms of simple learning mechanisms. One reason is that syntactic development typically occurs in a very short time frame—in only a few years. Further, children undergoing language development hear many different utterances of a language—from parents, siblings, teachers, and others. However, what children appear to acquire are not specific sentences or utterances but rather the underlying rules that govern a particular language. As I hope Chapter 9 convinced you, the rules that govern a language are complex and very difficult to articulate. Thus, it is quite unlikely that parents and other adults are teaching these syntactic rules.

Moreover, studies of parents interacting with their children demonstrate that parents rarely correct syntactic errors of children's speech (such as "Yesterday I goed to the playground"), responding instead to the content of what is said (such as "No, honey, yesterday we went to the *zoo*"; Ingram, 1989). These and other arguments cause developmental psychologists to speak of *language acquisition* rather than *language learning*.

Many developmental psychologists studying language acquisition agree with Chomsky's (1957, 1959) assertions that people are born with *language universals;* that is, they are biologically prepared to acquire a human language (as opposed to a computer language or other kind of artificial language). The actual language a child acquires almost certainly is subject to environmental influences: Children born to English speakers invariably acquire English, and those born to parents who speak Hungarian unfailingly acquire that language. Chomsky believes people have a *language acquisition device* (LAD), an inborn set of mechanisms and knowledge that requires only an environmental trigger to be set in motion. The environment controls *which* language(s) is (are) acquired, but the *capacity* to acquire a human language is regarded as innate.

Although children typically begin to use recognizable words at around 1 year of age, usually not until their 2nd year do they begin producing utterances of more than one word. It is not possible to speak of *syntax* in a toddler's language until he produces multiword utterances, simply because it is not possible to structure a one-word utterance in different ways.

If children's two-word utterances had absolutely no structure, then what we should observe are random pairings of words in a child's vocabulary. In fact, what we observe is quite the opposite: Children's two-word utterances display a considerable amount of regularity. Consider Box 12.1, which presents a number of two- and three-word utterances spoken by my niece, Brandi Lee, when she was about 18 months old. You'll notice that certain words or phrases, such as *rockabye* or *oh deah,* always occur initially in the utterance; that other words or phrases, such as *down* or *didit,* always occur at the end of the utterance; and that certain other words, such as *Dassie, Mummy,* and *Santa,* occur either initially or at the end of the utterance.

Box 12.1

Sample Two-Word Utterances

Dassie (her word for "Kathie") down. (meaning "Kathie, sit on the floor.")

Mummy down. (meaning "Mommie, sit on the floor.")

Rockabye baby.

Rockabye turkey.

Rockabye Santa.

Oh deah ("dear") Santa.

Oh deah Dassie.

Oh deah Mummy.

Oh deah turtle.

Mummy didit. ("didit" meaning, roughly, to have performed an action)

Dassie didit.

Brannie (her word for "Brandi") didit.

Braine (1963) hypothesized a *pivot grammar* to account for these regularities. Braine argued that children begin to form two-word utterances by first somehow selecting a small set of frequently occurring words in the language they hear. These words are called "pivots." Children's knowledge about pivots includes not only the pronunciation and something about the word's meaning but where in an utterance the pivot should appear. Other words the child uses are called "open" words. Braine argued from data much like that in Box 12.1 that toddlers form "syntactic" rules of the following sort: "Pivot1 + Open" or "Open + Pivot2," where Pivot1 includes all sentence-initial pivots (such as *oh deah* and *rockabye*) and Pivot2 includes all sentence-final pivots (such as *didit* and *down*).

Braine's (1963) pivot grammar accounts for some of the regularities apparent in the speech of some children. However, work by other investigators (Bowerman, 1973; R. Brown, 1973) soon showed that it fails to account for the utterances of all children. Although current consensus is that the grammar is at best incomplete and in many cases incorrect, some investigators have argued that it may provide some useful ideas about how children begin to construct a grammar from the language they hear around them (Ingram, 1989).

Roger Brown (1973) took a different tack in accounting for regularities in children's two-word utterances. Brown asserted that children at the two-word stage are constructing their utterances *not* by following rules of syntax but by using a small set of semantic relations. Table 12.1 presents the semantic relations he proposed. Brown argued that this particular set of relations is an outgrowth of the knowledge toddlers of this age should have about the world. He believed that children at this point in development focus on actions, agents, and objects and are concerned with issues such as where objects are located and when and how they can disappear and reappear. As such, Brown's proposals fit nicely with the Piagetian view of sensorimotor development (Ingram, 1989).

■ Table 12.1: Proposed Semantic Relations for Early Grammars

Relation	Definition and Examples
1. Nomination	The naming of a referent, without pointing, usually in response to the question "What's that?" Often indicated with words such as "this," "that," "here," "there." (Also see (11) Demonstrative and Entity below.)
2. Recurrence	The reappearance of a referent already seen, a new instance of a referent class already seen, or an additional quantity of some mass already seen (e.g., "more" or "another" X).
3. Nonexistence	The disappearance of something that was in the visual field (e.g., "no hat," "allgone egg").
Semantic Functions	
4. Agent + Action	The agent is "someone or something, usually but not necessarily animate, which is perceived to have its own motivating force and to cause an action of process" (p. 193; e.g., "Adam go," "car go," "Susan off").
5. Action + Object	The object is "someone or something (usually something, or inanimate) either suffering a change of state or simply receiving the force of an action" (p. 193).
6. Agent + Object	A relation that uses the two definitions above. It can be considered a direction relation without an intervening action.
7. Action + Location	"The place or locus of an action" (p. 194), as in "Tom sat in the chair." Often marked by forms like "here" and "there."
8. Entity + Locative	The specification of the location of an entity (i.e., any being or thing with a separate existence). These take a copula in adult English (e.g., "lady home," meaning "The lady is home.").
9. Possessor + Possession	The specification of objects belonging to one person or another (e.g., "mommy chair").
10. Entity + Attribute	The specification of "some attribute of an entity that could not be known from the class characteristics of the entity alone" (p. 197; e.g., "yellow block," "little dog").
11. Demonstrative and Entity	This is the same as (1) Nomination, except that the child points and uses a demonstrative.

One problem with Brown's approach is that it requires an adult to interpret what the child intended to communicate at the time of the utterance; it makes adults interpret children's language in terms of adult assumptions and beliefs, and it assumes that adults and children use language to refer to events and objects in the world in similar ways. Ingram (1989) pointed out that this assumption can be erroneous.

Much work since the 1970s has attempted to avoid problems in both syntactic and semantic approaches (see, for example, Camaioni, 2001; E. V. Clark, 1993; Tomasello, 2006). The complexity and specificity of many of the existing models preclude their being discussed here. However, there is agreement that even from the early days of language use, children's utterances show many regularities. Because many of the regularities observed occur across children of very different cultures and language communities, it is further hypothesized that children's language acquisition cannot be merely the result of learning.

PRESCHOOLERS' USE OF MEMORIAL STRATEGIES

Many researchers who study the development of memory in children have been struck by the different approaches to memory tasks adopted by younger and older children (see, for example, Biazak, Marley, & Levin, 2010). A particularly striking difference concerns the use of memorial *strategies,* defined as "deliberate plans and routines called into service for remembering" (A. L. Brown, Bransford, Ferrara, & Campione, 1983, p. 85). One important remembering strategy is rehearsal of the to-be-remembered material. Rehearsal can involve silent or out-loud repetition and is thought to maintain information in working memory, making it more likely to be stored for longer periods of time (Ornstein & Naus, 1978).

A number of studies (reviewed by Ornstein & Naus, 1978) have repeatedly demonstrated two things. First, younger children (preschoolers and younger elementary school–age children) are less likely to rehearse material than are older children (older elementary school–age children and middle school–age children). Second, when children who do not spontaneously rehearse can be induced to do so, their memory performance often rises to the level of similar-age children who do rehearse spontaneously.

A classic study by Flavell, Beach, and Chinsky (1966) demonstrated the first of these points. The authors worked with children in kindergarten, second grade, and fifth grade. Each child was shown two sets of seven pictures and was asked to point to the pictures in the same order that the experimenter did. In one condition, the wait was 15 seconds between the time the experimenter finished pointing and the time the child was asked to re-create the order. During the waiting interval, the children donned special "space helmets" that prevented them from looking at the pictures or seeing the experimenter but allowed the experimenter to observe whether they were verbalizing the items they had to remember (one of the experimenters, trained in lip reading, spent each session watching and listening for such verbalizations). Results were dramatic: Very few of the kindergarten participants showed evidence of rehearsal; a little more than half of the second graders and almost all the fifth graders did show such evidence.

A later study (Keeney, Cannizzo, & Flavell, 1967), using a similar procedure, illustrates the second point. These researchers found that 6- and 7-year-old "rehearsers" performed significantly better in recalling information than same-aged "nonrehearsers." When the nonrehearsers were later trained to rehearse, their performance became indistinguishable from that of the initial "rehearsers." However, when left to their own devices, the initial "nonrehearsers" abandoned the rehearsal strategy. A. L. Brown et al. (1983) believed that the use of rehearsal during early childhood is fragile, disappears easily, and occurs under only very limited circumstances (see p. 94).

Other research on memory development has shown that children's performance on a memory task is often a function of their preexisting knowledge of, and expertise with, the materials of the task. Michelene Chi (1978) demonstrated this in a study with children (in

Grades 3 through 8) with chess tournament experience and adults with casual experience with chess. When given standard digit-span tasks, the adults tended to outperform the children. However, when the memory task involved recalling positions of chess pieces on boards, the children outperformed the adults. One possible explanation could be that their knowledge allowed the chess-experienced children to notice more relationships between chess pieces (such as "the king's rook is attacking the queen"), facilitating more retrieval cues than were available to the less experienced adults.

THE DEVELOPMENT OF REASONING ABILITIES IN MIDDLE AND LATE CHILDHOOD

The final set of examples illustrating information-processing models of cognitive development describes the development of reasoning abilities. In a classic study by Osherson and Markman (1975), first, second, and third graders had apparent difficulty distinguishing between statements that were empirically true or false (that is, true in fact) and those that were logically true or false (that is, true by necessity or definition). The experimenter showed children, adolescents, and adults small plastic poker chips in assorted solid colors. Children were told that the experimenter would be saying some things about the chips and that the children should indicate after each statement if it was true or false or if they "couldn't tell." Some of the statements were made about chips held visibly in the experimenter's open hand. Other, similar statements were made about chips hidden in the experimenter's closed hand. Among the statements used were logical *tautologies* (statements true by definition)—for example, "Either the chip in my hand is yellow, or it is not yellow"; logical *contradictions* (statements false by definition)—for example, "The chip in my hand is white, and it is not white"; and statements that were neither true nor false by definition but depended on the color of the chip.

First, second, third, and even sixth graders did not respond correctly to tautologies and contradictions, especially in the hidden condition. They tended to believe, for example, that a statement such as "Either the chip in my hand is blue, or it is not blue" cannot be assessed unless the chip is visible. Tenth graders and adults, in contrast, were much more likely to respond that even when the chip couldn't be seen, if the statement was a tautology or contradiction, the statement could be evaluated on the basis of form. These results were consistent with Piaget's assertion that logical reasoning, particularly abstract, hypothetical reasoning, awaits the attainment of formal operations in adolescence.

A later study by Hawkins, Pea, Glick, and Scribner (1984) painted a different picture. These authors gave 4- and 5-year-olds a number of verbal syllogisms, such as "Pogs wear blue boots. Tom is a pog. Does Tom wear blue boots?" The syllogisms required logical reasoning. Contrary to expectation, the preschoolers could correctly answer many of the syllogisms and provide appropriate justifications for their answers, especially if the problems were about make-believe animals, as in the example above. The authors believed these syllogisms in particular prevented the children from using their preexisting knowledge of animals (they had probably not had previous knowledge of, or experience with, a pog).

With other syllogisms that were about real animals or objects, the children performed noticeably worse, especially when the premises in the problem were incongruent with the children's preexisting world knowledge (for example, "Glasses bounce when they fall. Everything that bounces is made of rubber. Are glasses made of rubber?"). This result implies that although some ability to reason logically might begin in early childhood, much is undeveloped or unreliable, at least until early adolescence and maybe all through adulthood (see the discussion of adults' reasoning abilities in Chapter 11).

Another study, by Moshman and Franks (1986), supports this view. They gave children (fourth and seventh graders) a more stringent test of logical reasoning competence. The children were presented with sets of three cards. On each card was typed an argument that was either (a) empirically true or false or (b) logically *valid* (the conclusion followed necessarily from the premises; see Chapter 11) or invalid. Participants were asked to sort the cards in as many ways as they could. In some of the studies, they were given definitions of the concepts of validity and were prompted to sort on this basis. However, even when specifically asked to do so, fourth graders had difficulty sorting on the basis of validity (as opposed to, say, truth of the conclusion or format of the argument). Moshman and Franks interpreted these results as indicating that even when children can draw logically valid conclusions, they don't fully appreciate the idea of validity before age 12 or so. (Incidentally, recent work by Barrouillet [2011] and Gauffroy and Barrouillet [2011] supports this view.)

My collaborators and I (Galotti, Komatsu, & Voelz, 1997) followed up on this line of work, looking to see when children recognized the difference between a deductive and an inductive inference. The following two versions illustrate these two types of inference: (1) "All wortoids have three thumbs. Hewzie is a wortoid. Does Hewzie have three thumbs?" versus (2) "Hewzie is a wortoid. Hewzie has three thumbs. Do all wortoids have three thumbs?" Most adolescents and adults see a distinction between the first problem (which calls for a deductive inference) and the second (which calls for an inductive inference). The former can be made with much greater confidence (in fact, with certainty); the latter, with only some (however strong) degree of probability. Our studies showed that until fourth grade, children did not consistently and clearly articulate the inductive/deductive distinction; however, by about second grade, they showed an implicit understanding of the distinction, answering more quickly and more confidently when asked to draw deductive inferences.

This examination of recent work in the non-Piagetian traditions of cognitive development has yielded narrower and more specific descriptions of what actually develops. Typically, instead of focusing on general and widespread cognitive achievements, researchers in these traditions offer accounts that are more specific to the particular tasks being used. Thus, an account of how reasoning ability develops may show little resemblance to an account of how children acquire and organize new information into concepts. Researchers such as those whose work has been described, however, see this narrowness of scope as positive. By attending to specific tasks and domains, they believe a clearer and more accurate picture will emerge of what children know and can do.

Some developmentalists see a large hole left by the demise of grand theories such as Piaget's (Bjorklund, 1997). They call for us to examine children's performance on various cognitive tasks in the context of their everyday experiences and to look at the evolutionary "advantages" of what may appear to adults to be "failures." For example, Bjorklund and Green (1992) argue that preschoolers' unrealistic optimism about their own abilities, frequently taken as an indication of their lack of realistic self-judgment, has some beneficial side effects. Children who think their abilities in some domain are terrific will work longer and harder at practicing their skills in that domain. My son Timmy gave many daily examples when he was a 5-year-old. Convinced his basketball skills were "awesome," he regularly spent many tireless sessions shooting "hoops," despite a low success rate. As an adult, my own skills at estimating my basketball skill are much better. (Perhaps as a result, I spend as little time as possible practicing my free throws.)

SOME POST-PIAGETIAN ANSWERS TO THE QUESTION "WHAT DEVELOPS?" _____

Recall from our discussion earlier that Piagetian theory describes cognitive development as the acquisition of progressively more sophisticated mental structures. Researchers in other traditions do not necessarily believe that children at different ages possess qualitatively different mental structures. These researchers instead provide a variety of answers to the question "How do children develop cognitively?" Here we will review some of the most common answers.

NEUROLOGICAL MATURATION

One factor to which cognitive and cognitive developmental psychologists are paying increasing attention is that of neurological, or brain, development. Although many neurons or nerve cells in the brain emerge during gestation, the brain continues to grow and develop after birth, especially in the first 4 years (Nowakowski, 1987). Early exposure to stimuli helps to develop a normal level of interconnections among neurons, such that a more complex network of nerve cells is formed. The network allows for the efficient transmission of a great deal of information.

Do neurological developments bear directly on cognitive developments? Goldman-Rakic (1987) described research with monkeys suggesting that the age at which infant monkeys can perform certain cognitive tasks (such as a Piagetian object permanence task) coincides with the peak of the development of neuronal connections in an area of the brain known as the *prefrontal cortex.*

Adele Diamond (1991) has extended this line of work, using a classic object permanence task in which an infant, having previously seen an object hidden in location A, watches it hidden in location B, but continues to look for the hidden object in location A instead of B. Diamond compared older (7–12 months) infants' ability on the "A, not B" object permanence task to the development of the frontal cortex. This area of the brain has been shown to undergo tremendous growth, both in density of synapses and in myelination of axons. Diamond's work has shown that improved performance on the "A, not B" task correlates with age (and therefore with frontal-lobe development) in infancy. In her work with monkeys with frontal-lobe lesions, she has produced monkeys with specific neurological deficits who show the same pattern of behavior on the "A, not B" task as do infants of different ages.

Diamond (1991) believes that the frontal cortex underlies cognitive performance both in the ability to integrate information over time and space *and* in the ability to inhibit strong response tendencies. The infant searching for an object in location A (where it has been previously hidden) instead of in B (where it was just hidden) must keep track of the information that the hiding place has changed and also stop himself from making the same behavioral response (reaching toward A) that was previously successful.

More recent work involving brain-imaging techniques paints the following picture: With development, the brain becomes more fine-tuned and organized (Farber & Beteleva, 2011). Brain regions associated with so-called basic functions, such as sensation and motor behavior, develop first, in line with Piagetian tenets. Association areas—brain regions that facilitate integration of information—develop a little more slowly. Areas involved in top-down control of behavior, such as the frontal and prefrontal cortex, are the last to develop (Casey, Tottenham, Listen, & Durston, 2005). Moreover, as the individual develops and has certain experiences, certain synaptic connections between neurons in the brain are strengthened, while other, unused ones are pruned. This pruning results in more efficient neural circuits, but ones that become increasingly specialized and unique to the individual. Kuhn (2006) speculates that this brain reorganization might account for why, during adolescence, individual differences in performance become more and more common. Although it's possible to talk about the cognitive abilities of a typical 6-month-old, by the time children reach adolescence, there are much wider variations in performance—some adolescents can perform like adults on some tasks, while others cannot. One important factor in this variation, Kuhn believes, stems from the experiences the adolescents engage in, which in turn direct the maintenance or pruning of different neural circuits.

The issue of neurological underpinnings of cognitive performance is at the cutting edge of research at the moment. Whether certain cognitive tasks require a certain level of neurological development and the role of environmental experience in neurological functioning and development are matters that will surely be addressed in the coming decade.

WORKING-MEMORY CAPACITY AND PROCESSING SPEED

Our review of memory in Chapters 5 and 6 suggested that working memory is an essential ingredient of many cognitive tasks. Recall that working memory is the system in which currently active information is stored and manipulated. It stands to reason, then, that the larger the working-memory capacity, the more complex are the cognitive tasks of which a person is capable. Researchers such as Pascual-Leone (1970), Gathercole and her colleagues (Gathercole & Pickering, 2000; Gathercole, Pickering, Knight, & Setgmann, 2004), and Simmering (2012) have tried to measure the amount of "mental space" children seem to have available to perform cognitive tasks. These authors report increases in this capacity with age.

Some of the research has involved estimation of *memory span,* done by giving children lists of items, such as numbers, letters, or words, and asking the children to repeat them. The memory span is thus the number of items that a child of a particular age can reliably reproduce. Figure 12.4 displays data from several studies suggesting that memory span increases with age.

Some proposals assert that working-memory span is constrained by how quickly information deteriorates from the mental workspace (Hitch, Towse, & Hutton, 2001). Still other researchers have argued that what develops is not working-memory capacity per se but the speed and/or efficiency with which information is processed (Case, 1978; Dempster, 1981). For example, children at different ages have been shown to differ widely in the speed with which they can name items presented to them, rotate mental images, or search through a visual display (Kail, 1986, 1988). Adults and older children typically perform all these tasks faster than younger children do. Presumably, all these tasks are carried out in working memory. When one task takes longer to carry out than another, it may reflect the expenditure of more "mental effort." If mental effort is limited, as information-processing theories typically assume, then tasks that require more mental effort will leave fewer cognitive resources available for other processing. This in turn could explain the generally poorer

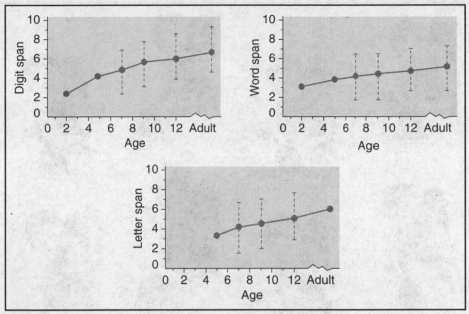

■ Figure 12.4: Developmental differences in digit span, word span, and letter span.

cognitive performance of younger children relative to older children and adults: The younger the processor, the more mental effort is required for a given task. How working-memory capacity and efficiency change with development is still a current research question (see Cowan et al., 2006, for a detailed example of research in this area).

ATTENTION AND PERCEPTUAL ENCODING

Ask any parent or teacher: Younger children have shorter attention spans than older ones. Because of this, they often spend less time exploring the information available to them from the environment. Preschoolers, in particular, often respond to complex cognitive tasks *impulsively*—that is, quickly and with many errors (Kogan, 1983). Perhaps related to this, younger children discriminate less between similar objects than do older children (E. J. Gibson & Spelke, 1983).

You can see a good example of this phenomenon if you look at the comics sections of many Sunday newspapers. Some run a puzzle activity that calls for the child to examine several very similar pictures and to find the two that are exactly the same. The pictures are usually visually complex, with a great number of objects and/or people and a great deal of detail and elaboration of each object. The differences tend to be in the details. For example, one picture might depict a girl with a spotted bow in her hair; another might show the same girl, in the same pose, with the same clothes except for a striped bow. Figure 12.5 gives an example of such a puzzle.

Preschoolers and children in early elementary school typically find these puzzles much more challenging than do older children or adolescents. In part, this has to do with the amount of time they spend looking back and forth between the pictures. Another part of the explanation, predicted by perceptual learning theory (Gibson, 1969), seems to be that younger children notice fewer differences in the first place.

Kemler (1983) has extended this idea, arguing that with development, children shift from a **holistic** approach to processing information to a more **analytic** one. By these terms, Kemler means that younger children approach information globally and pay attention to

■ Figure 12.5: Find the two pictures that match exactly.

the overall similarities between and among objects. For example, given a red triangle, an orange diamond, and a green triangle and asked to "put together the items that belong together," younger children tend to sort the red triangle and orange diamond together, because overall, these two objects are more similar to each other than either is to the green triangle. In contrast, older children and adults pay attention to particular parts or aspects of information. Given the same sorting task, adults would be likely to classify the red and the green triangles together, because they both share the dimension of shape.

Children have also been shown to have difficulty focusing their attention. In one study, Strutt, Anderson, and Well (1975) asked children and adults to sort as quickly as possible a deck of cards showing various geometric figures. Some cards showed figures that differed only in the relevant dimension—for example, only circles and squares when the child was asked to sort on the basis of shape. Other cards included figures that differed on both the relevant dimension and other, irrelevant dimensions—for example, the presence of a line or star either above or below the picture. The presence of irrelevant information did not affect the speed of sorting for adults. However, it did slow down sorting among 6-, 9-, and 12-year-olds; the younger the child, the greater the interference. This answer to the question "What develops?" implies that younger children approach cognitive tasks differently than do older children both perceptually and attentionally. Younger children encode and pay attention to different aspects of information than those aspects older children and adults emphasize. As a consequence, their information processing differs because it begins with different input. In addition, there are also quantitative improvements in the ability of older children and adults to focus their attention on a task (Couperus, 2011).

THE KNOWLEDGE BASE AND KNOWLEDGE STRUCTURES

Some developmental psychologists working in the information-processing tradition regard the acquisition of general knowledge and expertise as a crucial aspect of cognitive development. Studies of adults show that people differ in some cognitive processes as a function of level of expertise with the materials used in the task. For example, Chase and Simon (1973) showed a chess master (a certified "expert"), an experienced chess player, and a chess novice different chessboards with the pieces arranged in various ways. The task was to look at a particular board for

■ Photo 12.5: Chi's work suggests that in domains where children have expertise, such as knowledge of toys, children demonstrate better memorial ability.

5 seconds and then, after the board was removed from view, to reconstruct the placement of the pieces on a second, empty chessboard.

The investigators found that when the first chessboards depicted actual games (that is, the pieces were arranged in ways that might actually occur during a game), the master and experienced player performed much better than the novice in the number of pieces they could correctly place. However, when the pieces were displayed in random configurations, the chess master performed no better than the novice or the experienced player. Chase and Simon (1973) concluded that experts extract more information than do novices when the information being presented is of the type for which their expertise is relevant. Said another way, expertise helps a person acquire and organize information much more efficiently, thus leading to better overall performance when the information pertains to her area of expertise. Notice that this explanation fits well with the findings of Chi with child chess experts, discussed earlier.

Chi and Koeske (1983) carried out a related study with a single 4½-year-old fancier of dinosaurs. The investigators first queried the child about his familiarity with and knowledge about different kinds of dinosaurs and then drew up two lists: 20 dinosaurs that the child knew relatively more about and 20 that the child knew relatively less about. On three different occasions, the child was presented with each list, at the rate of 1 dinosaur name every 3 seconds, and was then asked to recall the list. The child recalled significantly more of the "familiar" dinosaurs (about 9 out of 20) than the "unfamiliar" ones (about 4 out of 20).

Chi and Koeske (1983) argued from these and other results that part of the reason why children typically perform so poorly on memory (and presumably other cognitive) tasks may be their relative lack of knowledge or expertise regarding the information used in the tasks. Given the opportunity to perform the same tasks with materials they know well, their performance improves dramatically. Presumably, familiar materials require less cognitive effort to encode, retrieve relevant information about, notice novel features of, and so on.

Other work, by Katherine Nelson and her colleagues, looked in a slightly different way at how children store and organize knowledge, particularly knowledge about events (Nelson,

1986). The primary method here is to ask children to describe their knowledge of familiar routines, such as "What happens when you go to day care?" or "Tell me what happens when you make cookies." In response to the latter request, Nelson and Gruendel (1981) obtained a variety of responses from children of different ages, ranging from

> Well, you bake them and eat them. (a 3-year-old)

to

> First you need a bowl, a bowl, and you need about two eggs and chocolate chips and an egg beater! And then you gotta crack the egg open and put it in a bowl and ya gotta get the chips and mix it together. And put it in a stove for about 5 or 10 minutes, and then you have cookies. Then ya eat them! (a child of 8 years, 8 months; p. 135)

First, clearly even 3-year-olds have some knowledge of this event. Nelson (1986) described the organization of this knowledge in terms of *scripts*, or *generalized event representations* (GERs). From Chapter 6, you may remember that scripts contain information organized temporally—that is, by the time in which each thing occurs in an event. Notice how the children use temporal links from one step to another—for example, "*First* you do X, *then* Y, and *after that* you do Z." One trend that appears with development is that the scripts become longer and more elaborate. Fivush and Slackman (1986) also showed that as children become more familiar with an event (for example, if the event is "going to kindergarten" and children are tested repeatedly as the school year goes on), their scripts also become more complex, specifying more conditional information, such as "If it's raining, we play indoors." Children's organization becomes more hierarchical as they specify more options or choices for different activities (for example, "I can play house, or I can draw, or I can read a book, until circle time"). Their organization also becomes more abstract; when describing their script, they mention fewer details specific to a certain day's activity.

Nelson (1986) argued that scripts help to support many cognitive activities, including comprehension, memory, and conversation. Scripts and GERs are said to provide the child with a "cognitive context" with which to interpret actions, events, and people in a situation. Especially because younger children appear to perform at their cognitive best only in certain contexts, it is important to learn which aspects of the context help or hinder them. Nelson believed that "the observed difference between situations where children perform well or poorly is that between those for which children have established a relevant GER and those for which they have not" (p. 16).

STRATEGIES

When confronted with a complex cognitive task, adults often develop certain systematic approaches to it that help them to manage the task requirements more efficiently. Such approaches are called **strategies**. For example, when studying for an upcoming examination, many college students review their lecture notes, develop outlines of each course reading, and consult with the instructor about material they find unclear. All of these activities are strategies.

The role of strategies in cognitive development has already been alluded to in the discussion of Flavell's classic work on rehearsal strategies (Flavell et al., 1966; Keeney et al., 1967). Recall that this work showed that younger children were less likely spontaneously to adopt a rehearsal strategy in a memory task but could be taught to use one. However, when not required to use the strategy, most younger children abandoned it. Keeney et al.

argued that nonrehearsers suffer from a *production deficiency*—that is, a tendency not to produce the appropriate strategy for a given task. Although the children were capable of using the rehearsal strategy, they did not do so spontaneously and did not use it when given the option not to.

Why? Some have answered that strategies require mental effort and younger children may simply find it much harder to use a strategy than older children (Howe & O'Sullivan, 1990). Perhaps with increasing cognitive development (for example, greater neurological maturation, more working-memory capacity, larger knowledge bases, or some other factor or combination of factors), the mental effort required to execute a strategy declines, making it a more useful addition to the cognitive repertoire.

This explanation is consistent with other research findings on strategy use, in which older children have been shown to be more flexible and better able to tailor their choice of which strategy to use on a task that allows for several different strategies (P. H. Miller, Haynes, DeMarie-Dreblow, & Woody-Ramsey, 1986). Siegler and Jenkins (1989), reviewing work on children's arithmetic strategies, also pointed out that although children and adults at almost any age usually have a variety of strategies they could use, with age and experience comes the likelihood of using more sophisticated strategies (that presumably demand more mental effort for execution). In any case, it is clear that strategies facilitate the processing of information and that people who use better strategies (for whatever reason) often have better cognitive performance. Younger children do not show the same use of strategies that older children and adults do and thus are at a disadvantage on many cognitive tasks.

METACOGNITION

Given the same cognitive task, older children are usually better than younger children at evaluating its complexity and monitoring their own performance. For example, in a memory study conducted by Flavell, Friedrichs, and Hoyt (1970), preschool and elementary school children were given a set of items to study until they were sure they could remember them. Older children were better able to judge when they had studied adequately and to predict how many items they would be able to recall.

Flavell (1985) described this as one aspect of **metacognition**, defined broadly as "any knowledge or cognitive activity that takes as its object, or regulates, any aspect of any cognitive enterprise" (p. 104). The general idea is that metacognition consists of "cognition about one's own cognition." It includes *metacognitive knowledge*—that is, knowledge about one's own cognitive abilities and limitations. You are probably pretty accurate, for example, at describing your memorial abilities, your attention span, and the relative depth and breadth of your knowledge of a particular domain (such as football, cognitive psychology, or trivia). You know your own areas of strength and weakness, you know what strategies work best for you, and you know when to use them. Younger children are less knowledgeable about their own abilities and are typically much too optimistic about how well, how easily, or how fast they can perform on most cognitive tasks.

Metacognition also includes *metacognitive experiences,* things that happen to you that pertain to your knowledge or understanding of your own cognitive processes. For example, experiences of uncertainty or doubt and periods of deep reflection over your performance, decision making, or values are all examples of metacognitive experiences. Flavell's (1985) idea is that older children and adults are better able to recognize, and realize the significance of, different metacognitive experiences.

Metacognitive knowledge and regulation are obviously important in many cognitive tasks. Part of the reason why younger children perform more poorly on cognitive tasks may be that they do not have the metacognitive knowledge about what the tasks demand. That is, they do not know how to judge the difficulty of the task and thus do not approach it with the necessary procedures or other tools. It may also be that younger children have less metacognitive control over their processing of information (A. L. Brown et al., 1983). Markman (1979), for instance, showed that third graders were less able than sixth graders to report inconsistencies or contradictions in passages they read, even when prompted to read the passages aloud. In a later study (Markman & Gorin, 1981), 8- and 10-year-old children who were explicitly told to look for inconsistencies in passages were able to do so. The general conclusion from these studies is that children do not spontaneously monitor their cognitive performance while reading but can be induced to do so. However, unless the conditions are optimal, children, especially younger children, may fail to notice when cognitive processing goes awry.

Cognitive developmental psychologists have more recently turned their attention to a related area of investigation: children's theories of mind (for example, Atance & O'Neill, 2004; Butterworth, Harris, Leslie, & Wellman, 1991; Flavell, 1999; Perner, Lang, & Kloo, 2002). The term *theory of mind* is meant to capture the intuition that adults treat one another as cognitive beings, making certain assumptions about each other's perceptual, attentional, memorial, language, and thinking skills, as well as their desires and intentions—in other words, their mental states. This set of assumptions is collectively referred to as a *theory of mind.*

One common task used to investigate children's (usually preschool children's) theory of mind is the so-called *false belief* task. For example, children might be told a story about a boy who puts a toy in a box and leaves the room. While he is away, his sister enters the room, takes the toy out of the box, plays with it, and puts it away in a different location. Children are then asked where the *boy* will think the toy is. In other words, can the children disentangle *their* own state of knowledge about the toy from the state of knowledge/belief of someone who lacks their information? Consistent with Piagetian theory, this ability develops slowly over the preschool period (Jenkins & Astington, 1996). Theory of mind appears related generally to language ability, although not to memory ability. Preschoolers apparently have much to learn about the mental states of others (for example, what others might be thinking, wanting, remembering) as well as their own mental states. Work by Flavell, Green, Flavell, and Grossman (1997) demonstrates that 4-year-olds even have difficulty knowing when they are engaging in inner speech to themselves!

We have reviewed a great deal of material on cognitive development. Yet given the number of active investigations in the field, we have barely scratched the surface of all the important available information.

Cognitive developmental psychologists are also challenged by the question "What causes development?" In particular, there is ongoing and lively debate over how much of cognitive development is caused by physical factors, such as genetics or maturation, and how much can be attributed to environmental forces, such as schooling or the opportunity for practice. A current focus within the field is to identify the factors that cause, hinder, or facilitate cognitive development.

Because this chapter focuses on infants, children, and adolescents, you might be left with the impression that cognition in adulthood does not change and/or is the same for all adults. This impression is false, as we will see in Chapter 13. Adults as well as children differ in their amount of expertise, as well as in the ways they characteristically carry out cognitive tasks. Moreover, recent work in cognition and aging (to be reviewed in the next chapter) suggests that changes in cognition as a function of age do not cease at puberty.

Summary

1. Cognitive performance varies for children of different ages. In other words, children do not perform in the same way as adults on many cognitive tasks, including tasks of perception, attention, memory, language, problem solving, and reasoning. Generally speaking, the younger the child, the greater the difference between his or her performance and that of a typical adult. Because children do differ from adults, it takes cleverness and care to design informative studies that can help explain how cognitive development occurs and can be facilitated.

2. The description of how children differ from adults or how younger and older children differ from one another is still a matter of debate. Some psychologists, especially those working in a Piagetian tradition, believe that the best description of cognitive development must emphasize qualitative differences among people of various developmental levels and underlying mental structures.

3. Piaget proposed a stage theory, which describes development as consisting of qualitatively different periods of development. Stage theories presume a fixed order to the progression of stages and typically assume that the proposed stages are universal across cultures.

4. Piaget divided cognitive development into four basic stages. The first, the sensorimotor period, is one in which infants gain new knowledge through their sensory and motor experiences and lack the capacity for mental representation. At around 18 months to 2 years, toddlers enter the preoperational stage of cognitive development, during which they acquire representational and symbolic abilities, language, and the capacity for imagination and fantasy play. At the same time, their cognitive abilities are constrained by their egocentrism, their centering on one dimension, and their irreversible thinking.

5. Piaget asserted that children of elementary school age (roughly 5 to 11 years) become concrete-operational thinkers; they can take account of more than one aspect of a situation, conserve quantity, think reversibly, and classify consistently. Finally, in adolescence, children acquire formal operations—the ability to think systematically, abstractly, and hypothetically.

6. Researchers working outside the Piagetian tradition focus on changes in the basic cognitive capacities (such as memory capacity, attention span, knowledge base) and in the ways in which information is organized. They consider the genetic and maturational underpinnings of cognitive functioning and the developmental changes that affect the approaches that children of different ages take toward cognitive tasks. Unlike Piagetian researchers, many non-Piagetian theorists reject the idea of different qualitative stages of cognitive development. Instead, they regard cognitive development as the gradual acquisition and organization of capacities, strategies, and knowledge that allow for more efficient cognitive performance.

Review Questions

1. What are the major assumptions of stage theories of development?

2. Explain how, in Piagetian theory, cognitive structures adapt during the course of development.

3. Piaget asserts that children at different stages of development differ from one another cognitively in qualitatively different ways. Illustrate this assertion with some specific examples.

4. Describe the major features of preoperational thought, according to Piaget.

5. Evaluate the implications of Baillargeon's research on perceptual development in infancy.

6. Why do most cognitive developmental psychologists distinguish between the terms *language learning* and *language acquisition*? What sorts of arguments are used in support of this distinction?

7. In what ways does research on the development of reasoning abilities in middle and late childhood support or run counter to Piagetian predictions?

8. Contrast two mechanisms that have been proposed to account for cognitive development.

Key Terms

analytic processing

concrete operations stage

formal operations stage

holistic processing

metacognition

nonstage theories of cognitive development

preoperational stage

sensorimotor stage

stage theories of cognitive development

stages

strategies

13

INDIVIDUAL DIFFERENCES IN COGNITION

CHAPTER OUTLINE

Individual Differences in Cognition

Ability Differences

Cognitive Styles

Learning Styles

Expert/Novice Differences

The Effects of Aging on Cognition

Gender Differences in Cognition

Gender Differences in Skills and Abilities

Verbal Abilities

Visuospatial Abilities

Quantitative and Reasoning Abilities

Gender Differences in Learning and Cognitive Styles

Motivation for Cognitive Tasks

Connected Learning

So far, we have been assuming that cognitive development proceeds in pretty much the same way for everyone. In the previous chapter, of course, we saw that children often don't approach cognitive tasks exactly the way adults do, but we made the assumption that with time, maturity, and perhaps education, they come to do so. In effect, we've been ignoring what psychologists call **individual differences**, stable patterns of performance that differ qualitatively and/or quantitatively across individuals.

In Chapter 14, we will consider differences in cognition as a function of one's culture. Here, we will consider some other sources of individual differences—differences in cognitive abilities, concentrating on intelligence, and differences in cognitive styles of approaching particular tasks. We will also consider gender differences in cognition: stable differences in cognition or cognitive processing of information that vary as a function of one's biological sex and psychological attitudes associated with one's sex.

Why are cognitive psychologists interested in individual or gender differences in cognition? Simply stated, if people vary systematically in the way they approach cognitive tasks, then psychologists cannot speak of "the" way cognition works. To present only one approach if in fact there are several is to ignore human diversity and to assume that only one way of carrying out a task exists. Researchers interested in individual and gender differences try to explain why some people seem to consistently outperform others on cognitive tasks and why some people feel more comfortable with certain cognitive tasks than with others.

INDIVIDUAL DIFFERENCES IN COGNITION _____

The term *individual difference* is meant to capture the intuition that different people may approach the same task in different ways. Psychologists who study personality traits are among those most likely to be interested in individual differences. The individual differences of interest to cognitive psychologists are generally of two distinct types: individual differences in abilities (that is, the capacities to carry out cognitive tasks) and individual differences in style (that is, the characteristic manner in which one approaches cognitive tasks).

ABILITY DIFFERENCES

Many psychologists equate **cognitive abilities with intelligence**. Hunt (1986), for example, has stated that "'intelligence' is solely a shorthand term for the variation in competence on cognitive tasks that is statistically associated with personal variables. . . . Intelligence is used as a collective term for 'demonstrated individual differences in mental competence'" (p. 102). Other psychologists do not equate the terms, but most agree that people vary in their intellectual (as well as several other important) abilities. Psychologists disagree over whether the best way to describe this variation is in terms of one general mental ability (called intelligence) or in terms of more numerous and varied intellectual abilities (Sternberg & Detterman, 1986).

Even psychologists who accept the idea of a general mental ability called intelligence debate just what the ability is. Some see it in terms of a capacity to learn efficiently; others, in terms of a capacity to adapt to the environment. Other conceptions of intelligence include viewing it as mental speed, mental energy, or mental organization (Gardner, 1983, 1999; Sternberg, 1986a). Many psychologists who study intelligence have looked at stable individual differences among various cognitive capacities to describe more general differences in people's performance on broader intellectual tasks. There are many lively and ongoing debates over what the set of cognitive capacities are; one representative list, described by Horn (1989), follows (note that the list below does not purport to represent totally independent skills or capacities):

- Verbal comprehension—Understand words, sentences, paragraphs.
- Sensitivity to problems—Suggest ways to solve problems.
- Syllogistic reasoning—Draw conclusions from premises.
- Number facility—Compute arithmetic operations.
- Induction—Indicate a principle of relations.
- General reasoning—Find solutions for algebraic problems.
- Associative memory—Recall associated element when given another element.
- Span memory—Immediately recall a set of elements after one presentation.
- Associational fluency—Produce words similar in meaning to a given word.

- Expressional fluency—Produce different ways of saying the same thing.
- Spontaneous flexibility—Produce diverse functions and classifications for an object.
- Perceptual speed—Find instances of a pattern under speeded conditions.
- Visualization—Mentally manipulate forms to visualize how they would look.
- Spatial orientation—Visually imagine parts out of place and put them in place.
- Length estimation—Estimate lengths or distances between points.

The point here is that people (both adults and children) can vary in many ways. Just as we all vary in athletic prowess, musical talent, or sense of humor, so too can we vary in intellectual or cognitive ways: in terms of memory capacity, attention span, concentration, and so on. These differences, in turn, can cause differences in how we approach and perform cognitive tasks.

A study by Keating and Bobbitt (1978) illustrates this point. These investigators conducted three experiments with both high-mental-ability (as assessed by a nonverbal intelligence test) and average-mental-ability 3rd, 7th, and 11th graders. The experiments were all based on cognitive tasks previously used with adults, including the memory-scanning experiments described in Chapter 5. The authors found that when they controlled for the effects of age (and presumably, therefore, for developmental level), ability differences were still apparent, especially on the more complicated

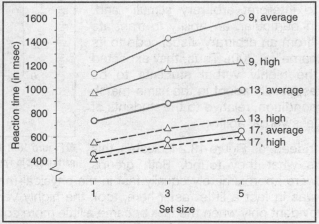

■ Figure 13.1: Mean reaction time (RT) in a memory-scanning task for children of different ages and abilities.

cognitive tasks. Figure 13.1, for instance, shows results of the memory-scanning task as a function of set size, age, and ability level. Note that older children had faster reaction times than younger children and that, within each age group, high-ability students were faster than average-ability students.

Keating and Bobbitt (1978) believed that both age and ability differences result from the efficiency with which basic cognitive processes (such as encoding and memory scanning) are carried out. They asserted that high-ability children (and adults) simply acquire, store, and manipulate basic information more rapidly and efficiently than do their same-age, normal-ability peers. The same kinds of speed and efficiency differences also occur between older and younger children.

A related, and classic, study by Hunt, Lunneborg, and Lewis (1975) examined a specific hypothesized component of intelligence, verbal ability. These authors examined two groups of undergraduate students: those with relatively high scores on a verbal subtest of a standardized test similar to the College Board's SAT and those with relatively low scores on the same test. (The authors pointed out that the latter group had scores that would be considered "average" in the general population.) The aim of the study was to investigate whether differences in verbal ability, as reflected in standardized scores, might be explained by differences in basic cognitive skills.

One of the many cognitive tasks they assigned to the participants was based on a perceptual matching task created by Posner, Boies, Eichelman, and Taylor (1969). In this task, participants are presented with two letters—for example, *A* and *B,* or *A* and *a,* or *A* and *A.* They are to decide, as quickly as possible, whether the two letters presented are the same. In one condition (called "physical match"), they are instructed to respond yes only when the two stimuli match exactly—"*A A*" or "*a a,*" for example, but not "*A a.*" In another condition (called "name match"), participants are instructed to respond yes if the two stimuli refer to the same letter, so that "*A A,*" "*a a,*" and "*A a*" should all receive yes responses.

Hunt et al. (1975) designed their experiment according to the following logic: A person's being highly verbal ought to imply "an ability to interpret arbitrary stimuli" and, in particular, an ability to translate "from an arbitrary visual code to its name"(p. 200). Thus, they expected the highly verbal students to be especially adept in the name-match condition, relative to the students of less verbal ability.

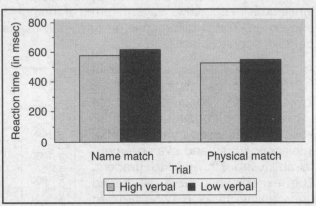

Indeed, as Figure 13.2 indicates, this is what they found. Both groups

■ Figure 13.2: Mean reaction time (RT) for high- and low-verbal participants in a perceptual matching task.

were approximately equally fast in the physical-match condition (the highly verbal group was in fact a little faster here, too); the highly verbal group's superiority really became evident only when the task became a little more complex. The authors explained that high verbal ability stems at least in part from an ability to make a conversion rapidly between a physical stimulus and a conceptual meaning—in this case, recognition of the particular letters.

Psychologists and educators debate fiercely the issue of whether intelligence is one thing or several. A controversial book aimed at the general public, *The Bell Curve* (Herrnstein & Murray, 1994), stirred a simmering pot of contention when it appeared, making (among others) the following strong assertions:

Here are six conclusions regarding tests of cognitive ability, drawn from the classical tradition, that are by now beyond significant technical dispute:

1. There is such a thing as a general factor of cognitive ability on which human beings differ.

2. All standardized tests of academic aptitude or achievement measure this general factor to some degree, but IQ tests expressly designed for that purpose measure it most accurately.

3. IQ scores match, to a first degree, whatever it is that people mean when they use the word *intelligent* or *smart* in ordinary language.

4. IQ scores are stable, although not perfectly so, over much of a person's life.

5. Properly administered IQ tests are not demonstrably biased against social, economic, ethnic, or racial groups.

6. Cognitive ability is substantially heritable, apparently no less than 40 percent and no more than 80 percent. (Herrnstein & Murray, 1994, pp. 22–23)

A large part of the reaction to this work stemmed from what critics took to be the authors' refusal to present other points of view in a balanced or responsible way (Gould, 1995; Kamin, 1995). Many critics in particular decried the idea that there is one basic cognitive ability, called intelligence, that is accurately measured by intelligence quotient (IQ) tests. Many others complained about the assumption that intelligence (whatever it is) is fixed and heritable. A recent review (Nisbett et al., 2012) reviews these and other issues.

One theorist, Howard Gardner (1983, 1993, 1999), had previously offered a theory directly contradicting the claims of Herrnstein and Murray. Gardner (1993) offered what he called a "pluralistic" theory of mind. He began by questioning what "an intelligence" is and offered this definition: "the ability to solve problems, or to fashion products, that are valued in one or more cultural or community settings" (p. 7). On the basis of a review of clinical data from brain-damaged individuals, studies of prodigies and gifted individuals, and experts in various domains from various cultures, Gardner (1983) proposed the existence of (at least) seven distinct, independent "human intellectual competences, abbreviated hereafter as 'human intelligences'" (p. 8). These intelligences, with two others added in Gardner's 1999 work, are listed in Table 13.1.

■ Table 13.1: Multiple Intelligences

Linguistic intelligence	The capacity to use language to communicate and to accomplish other goals; sensitivity to subtleties in both written and spoken language; the ability to learn foreign languages
Logical-mathematical intelligence	The ability to solve problems, design and conduct experiments, draw inferences; the capacity to analyze situations
Musical intelligence	The ability to analyze and respond to musical patterns; to compose or perform music
Bodily-kinesthetic intelligence	The ability to use one's body to perform artistically or athletically; to create physical products; to use either the whole body or parts of the body skillfully
Spatial intelligence	The ability to navigate skillfully through both wide and confined spaces; to visualize spatial scenes; to create products with spatial properties
Interpersonal intelligence	The capacity to understand other people's emotions, motivations, intentions, and desires; the ability to work effectively with others
Intrapersonal intelligence	The ability to understand one's own emotions, motivations, intentions, and desires and to use the information for self-regulation
Naturalist intelligence	The ability to recognize flora and fauna of one's environment; to skillfully classify organisms with respect to species and to chart the relationships among different species
Existential intelligence	The capacity to see one's place in the cosmos, especially in light of such issues as the nature of the human condition, the significance of life, the meaning of death, and the ultimate fate of the world both physical and psychological (Note: Gardner is still evaluating whether this capacity fully merits the label "intelligence.")

Gardner (1983, 1993, 1999) has argued that our Western culture places certain kinds of intelligence, specifically linguistic and logical-mathematical, on a pedestal. At the same time, our culture gives short shrift to the other intelligences, especially bodily-kinesthetic and interpersonal. We regard skilled athletes or politicians as people with talents but not as people who have a different sort of intelligence, like famous scientists or great poets. We make a distinction between talents and intelligence, Gardner believes, only so that we can hold on to the concept that there is only one mental ability. Gardner calls for a broader view of people's mental and cognitive abilities. He argues for a different kind of schooling that, instead of focusing only on linguistics and logic, also trains students as carefully in music, self-awareness, group processes, dance, and the performing arts.

Gardner's theory has captured the attention and enthusiasm of many psychologists and educators, some of whom are trying to implement the previously described **multiple intelligences (MI) theory** in their classes (see Gardner, 1993 and 1999, for some descriptions). There exist proposals for multiple creativities as well as intelligences, and educators have adopted these ideas enthusiastically (Han & Marvin, 2002). However, Gardner's theory awaits the development of assessment tools for each intelligence. Researchers and educators who hold to the concept of IQ as measuring the one true mental ability called intelligence have sophisticated tests that generally predict school performance adequately. Those interested in the idea of multiple intelligences have a great deal of work ahead of them to define the parameters of all the intelligences, to create valid measures of each, and to describe the interrelationships among different kinds of intelligences.

COGNITIVE STYLES

Gardner's theory of multiple intelligences points to the idea that people differ in their cognitive equipment. This idea comports well with another long-standing idea: that people differ not only in their abilities, capacities, and the efficiency with which they use each but also in terms of their **cognitive style**, that is, their habitual and preferred means of approaching cognitive tasks (Globerson & Zelnicker, 1989; Tyler, 1974). The term *cognitive style* is meant to imply certain personality and motivational factors that influence the way in which a person approaches a cognitive task (Kogan, 1983).

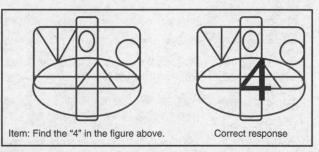

Item: Find the "4" in the figure above.   Correct response

■ Figure 13.3: Example of a field dependence/field independence (FD/FI) test item.

One example of a type of cognitive style is **field dependence/field independence (FD/FI)**, a term coined by psychologists who study perceptual processing (Witkin, Dyk, Faterson, Goodenough, & Karp, 1962; Witkin & Goodenough, 1981). The term refers to several phenomena, one of which is that some people find it much easier than other people to identify parts of a figure as being separate from a whole. An example of a task of field independence is shown in Figure 13.3. Field-dependent individuals would have a more difficult time finding the embedded picture in the larger picture (they are less able perceptually to divorce the embedded picture from its context), whereas field-independent people would find this task relatively easy.

Witkin and his associates see this style of cognition as being related to issues broader than perception of figures. According to the theory, this cognitive style refers to "the degree to which the person relies primarily on internal [field-independent, FI] or external [field-dependent, FD] referents in processing information from the self and the surrounding field" (Kogan, 1983, p. 663). Later conceptualizations broadened the definition of the style still more, associating the FI style with a generally autonomous manner in interpersonal relationships (a person who might be likely to form her own opinions, regardless of what her friends thought), whereas FD individuals are seen as more likely to rely on others, especially in ambiguous situations.

A second example of different types of cognitive styles has been called **cognitive tempo,** or the style of **reflectivity/impulsivity**. Kogan (1983) defined this style as "the extent to which a child delays response in the course of searching for the correct alternative in a context of response uncertainty" (p. 672). This can be illustrated with reference to Figure 13.4, which depicts an item from the Matching Familiar Figures Test (MFFT), developed by Kagan and his associates to assess cognitive tempo (Kagan, Rosman, Day, Albert, & Phillips, 1964).

The task posed to respondents is to find the item that exactly matches the item shown at the top. As you look at the other six pictures, notice that each is very similar to the top item. Thus, finding the exactly matching figure requires your careful attention.

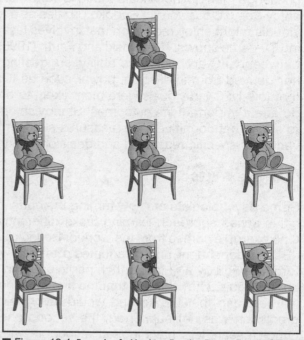

■ Figure 13.4: Example of a Matching Familiar Figures Test (MFFT) item.

Children vary in how they respond to MFFT items. Some respond very quickly; others, more slowly. Some make very few errors, even on difficult items; others make a number of errors, even on easy items. Many children fall into two categories: those who respond rapidly and make many errors (demonstrating an impulsive style) and those who respond slowly, with relatively few errors (demonstrating a reflective style; Tyler, 1974).

Originally, cognitive styles were thought of as optional, modifiable manners or problem-solving approaches that were independent of both intelligence and age. More recent research has challenged these assumptions. Cognitive styles do not appear to be easily modified through training. Moreover, cognitive styles show developmental differences; younger children are more likely to display impulsive and field-dependent styles, and older children tend to show more reflective and field-independent styles (Zelnicker, 1989).

Zelnicker (1989) also argued that reflectivity/impulsivity and FD/FI are not completely independent dimensions and that each relates to three underlying dimensions: selective attention, in particular the tendency to respond to whole stimuli or to their parts; attentional control, the focusing and shifting of attention; and stimulus organization, the mental transformation of stimulus input (for example, in mental rotation tasks as described in Chapter 8). Zelnicker asserted that an individual's cognitive style "determine[s] the quality of stimulus information accessible for further processing in solving . . . problems" (p. 187).

Another recent area of attention among cognitive style researchers concerns a concept called **need for cognition**, which roughly means a person's motivation to take on intellectual tasks and challenges (Cacioppo & Petty, 1982). Individuals with high need for cognition (NFC) seem to enjoy more those kinds of endeavors that involve thinking, problem solving, and reasoning and to derive more satisfaction from accomplishing an intellectual challenge than do individuals with a lower NFC. For example, high-NFC individuals might enjoy doing crossword or Sudoko puzzles as a form of recreation, whereas low-NFC individuals might enjoy recreation that involves less intellectual engagement, such as watching TV game shows. Klaczynski and Fauth (1996) demonstrated no significant relationship between NFC and cognitive ability, suggesting that NFC really is a stylistic dimension, not derived from intellectual power such as IQ. At the same time, the authors showed that low-NFC individuals were more likely to drop out of college, suggesting that styles do affect important life outcomes. Stanovich and West (1997, 1998, 2000) have gone on to show that cognitive style measures such as NFC do correlate with performance on a variety of specific reasoning and decision-making tasks.

LEARNING STYLES

Some psychologists are now turning their attention to whether people with different cognitive styles approach learning tasks differently, that is, have different **learning styles**. One example comes from the work of Rollock (1992), who gave 35 field-independent and 42 field-dependent undergraduates a task in which they listened to an audiotaped lecture followed by a quiz and then participated in an interactive demonstration followed by another quiz. They thought that the first learning condition would favor field-independent learners and that the second would favor field-dependent students. Although the first prediction was not supported, the second one received marginally significant support. Other researchers have looked at people with so-called visual versus verbal learning styles (e.g., Green & Schroeder, 1990), although again with mixed results in supporting the idea of distinct styles. The general idea here is that learners learn best when the mode of information presentation best suits their own individual learning style.

In a review of the literature on literature styles, Pashler, McDaniel, Roher, and Bjork (2009) looked for evidence of what they called the meshing hypothesis: the idea that instruction is most effective when it matches, or "meshes with," the learning style of the learner. They also looked for evidence for a weaker hypothesis, the "learning styles" hypothesis, which states that learning tailored to a learner's style can allow people to achieve "a better learning outcome" than they would achieve if this tailoring did not take place (Pashler et al., p. 108).

Pashler et al. (2009) talked in advance about what kind of evidence a study would have to provide in order to support either of these hypotheses:

First, on the basis of some measure or measures of learning style, learners must be divided into two or more groups (e.g., putative visual learners and auditory learners). Second, subjects within each learning-style group must be randomly assigned to one of at least two different learning methods (e.g., visual versus auditory presentation of some material). Third, all subjects must be given the same test of achievement (if the tests are different, no support can be provided for the learning-styles hypothesis). Fourth, the results need to show that the learning method that optimizes test performance of one learning-style group is different than the learning method that optimizes the test performance of a second learning-style group.

Thus, the learning-styles hypothesis (and particular instructional interventions based on learning styles) receives support if and only if an experiment reveals what is commonly known as a *crossover interaction* between learning style and method when learning style is plotted on the horizontal axis. Three such findings are illustrated in Figures 13.5A to 13.5C. For each of these types of findings, the method that proves more effective for Group A is not the same as the method that proves more effective for Group B. One important thing to notice about such a crossover interaction is that it can be obtained even if every subject within one learning-style group outscores every subject within the other learning-style group (see Figure 13.5B). Thus, it is possible to obtain strong evidence for the utility of learning-style assessments even if learning style is correlated with what might, for some purposes, be described as ability differences. Moreover, the necessary crossover interaction allows for the possibility that both learning-style groups could do equally well with one of the learning methods (see Figure 13.5C).

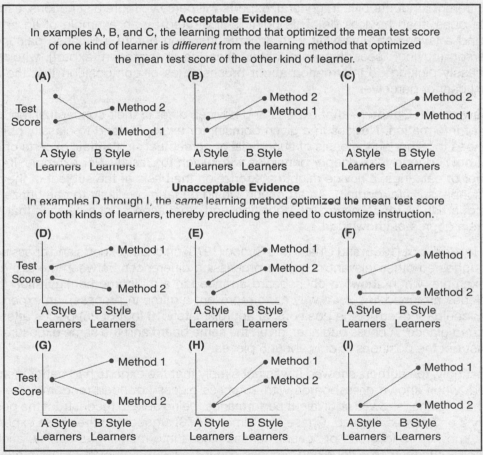

■ Figure 13.5: Acceptable and unacceptable evidence for the learning-styles hypothesis. In each of the hypothetical experiments, subjects were first classified as having Learning Style A or B and then were randomly assigned to Learning Method 1 or 2. Later, all subjects took the same test. The learning-styles hypothesis is supported if and only if the learning method that optimized the mean test score of one group is different from the learning method that optimized the mean test score of the other group, as in A, B, and C.

Figures 13.5D to 13.5I show some hypothetical interactions that would not provide support for the learning-styles hypothesis because, in each case, the same learning method provides optimal learning for every learner. Note that these findings are insufficient even though it is assumed that every interaction in Figure 13.5 is statistically significant. It is interesting to note that the data shown in Figures 13.5D and 13.5G do produce a cross-over interaction when the data are plotted sothat the horizontal axis represents learning method. . . . Thus, as noted earlier, a style-by-method crossover interaction constitutes sufficient evidence for the learning-styles hypothesis if and only if the horizontal axis represents learning style, as in Figures 13.5A to 13.5C. (p. 109)

EXPERT/NOVICE DIFFERENCES

Throughout earlier chapters, we have seen that people with expertise in a certain realm often approach a cognitive task differently from novices. We first encountered this topic in Chapter 3 when we discussed perceptual learning. If you recall, the point was made there that experts and novices, given equal exposure to information, acquire or "pick up on" different amounts of it. In general, experts will perceive more distinctions, especially subtle ones, than novices do. This point is illustrated by an example of an art historian and a layperson unfamiliar with art both standing before a Picasso painting. The layperson (novice) "sees" less information than the art historian (expert), who may be effortlessly picking up information about brushstrokes or composition that the novice simply cannot perceive.

We saw next in Chapter 7 that experts and novices differ in their conceptual representations of information. Novices in a given domain, for example, tend to classify objects or instances together on the basis of superficial or perceptual similarities; experts often use their knowledge to form deeper principles with which to classify. For example, if given a number of paintings, a novice might categorize on the basis of the subject of the picture (landscape, still life, portrait). An art expert would be far more likely to categorize on the basis of artist, historical period, composition, and other aspects of a painting that require a certain degree of knowledge.

Work by de Groot (1965) and Chase and Simon (1973) on chess experts and chess novices has suggested other relevant cognitive-processing differences between the two groups. For example, when shown a chessboard arranged in a midgame configuration (that is, the pieces arranged in such a way as to represent a game in process), an expert chess player could reconstruct the positions of approximately 16 (out of 25) pieces after only a 5-second glance. A chess beginner, given the same board and the same exposure, could reconstruct the positions of only about 5 pieces.

Interestingly, the authors showed it was not simply that the experts had better memories. Indeed, when shown chessboards with 25 chess pieces arranged randomly, the expert and the beginner showed equivalent performance, being able to reconstruct the positions of only 2 or 3 pieces. Instead, Chase and Simon (1973) argued that the chess expert used chess knowledge to group or "chunk" chess pieces into meaningful configurations. As Chapter 5 suggests, the chunking process can increase the amount of information held in working memory.

The findings on **expert/novice differences** just described sound a common theme: Your level of knowledge in a domain affects your cognition within that domain. Many cognitive processes—including perception and recognition; encoding; classification and categorization; and problem solving, reasoning, and decision making about information within the domain of expertise—appear affected.

THE EFFECTS OF AGING ON COGNITION

We saw in the previous chapter that cognitive skills and abilities develop, which means that children of different ages and levels of development may approach the same cognitive task in different ways. Age-related changes in cognitive processing do not cease in adolescence. In fact, researchers looking at adult development and aging have found a number of differences in cognitive processing between younger and older adults (Salthouse, 2012). Once again, this topic is a broad one, and we have space to mention only a few examples.

Relative to younger adults (those in their 20s and 30s), older adults (those in their 60s and older) show several differences in cognitive abilities and skills. For example,older adults perform less well on tasks of divided attention (such as those discussed in Chapter 4; McDowd & Craik, 1988); show age-related decrements in speech recognition and speech discrimination (Corso, 1981); and show declines in memory performance on a variety of memory tasks (Cavanaugh, 1993), as well as on a Tower of Hanoi problem-solving task (Davis & Klebe, 2001).

One example of these findings has to do with performance on working-memory tasks. Salthouse and Babcock (1991) studied the performance of adults aged 18 to 87 on various working-memory tasks, such as digit span, sentence comprehension, and mental arithmetic. The authors found, first, that older participants had shorter spans than younger participants. Salthouse and Babcock hypothesized, after extensive statistical analyses of their data, that the major factor accounting for this decline in span length was a decline in processing efficiency, or the speed with which various elementary cognitive operations (such as performing simple addition or comprehending a simple sentence) could be carried out.

Campbell and Charness (1990) found similar age-related declines in working memory. They gave three groups of adults (20-, 40-, and 60-year-olds) a task in which they learned an algorithm for squaring two-digit numbers. Participants worked for six sessions lasting 1 or 2 hours each. The authors report two significant findings. First, practice with the algorithm improved performance, in that errors declined over sessions. However, adults in the oldest group made more errors than the "middle-aged" adults, who in turn made more errors than the youngest adults. Even with practice, these age differences remained.

Baltes, Staudinger, and Lindenberger (1999), in a review of the literature, conclude that a general decline in the speed of processing of elementary cognitive operations occurs with age, perhaps accounting for the pattern of findings just reviewed. Paul Baltes and Margaret Baltes, well-known researchers on aging, have argued, however, that older adults often can strategically compensate for such declines by using selective optimization with compensation:

> When the concert pianist Arthur Rubinstein, as an 80-year-old, was asked in a television interview how he managed to maintain such a high level of expert piano playing, he hinted at the coordination of three strategies. First, he played fewer pieces (selection); he practiced these pieces more often (optimization); and to counteract his loss in mechanical speed he now used a kind of impression management, such as playing more slowly before fast segments to make the latter appear faster (compensation). (Baltes et al., 1999, pp. 483–484)

It is important to keep in mind, however, that differences in cognitive processing as a function of aging are still subject to individual differences from other sources. Such factors as intelligence, health, years of formal education, expertise, and cognitive style all continue to play important roles. The topic of the effects of aging on cognition, still in its relative scholarly infancy, will no doubt continue to support the idea that any individual's level of cognitive functioning depends on many factors, including factors specific to the individual such as those just described, as well as those of the task and the overall context (Lerner, 1990; Salthouse, 2012; Verhaeghen, 2011; Zöllig, Mattli, Sutter, Aurelio, & Martin, 2012).

This brief look at individual differences in cognitive abilities was intended to stress an important point: Not all people approach cognitive tasks in exactly the same way. Age, ability, expertise, and stylistic differences among people can affect their efficiency in acquiring or processing information, leading to differences in how much information is picked up or how thoroughly it is processed. These differences, in turn, could have great effects on how well a complicated cognitive task is performed.

In the last four decades, some psychologists have also wondered about gender as a source of individual differences in cognition. In the next section, we will examine whether men and women adopt different cognitive styles or strategies in their approaches to cognitive tasks.

GENDER DIFFERENCES IN COGNITION

The possible existence of gender differences can be fascinating. This fascination is especially pronounced in our culture, as psychologist Carol Nagy Jacklin (1989) noted:

> Specula tion about differences between females and males is a national preoccupation. In our culture, people care whether there are fundamental differences between girls and boys, and we place more emphasis on the possibility of such differences than on other kinds of distinctions that could be made. For example, we rarely wonder whether blue-eyed and brown-eyed or short and tall children differ from one another in intellectual abilities or personality. (p. 127)

Some cautions are in order before we examine the evidence regarding gender differences in cognition, especially because of the sensitive nature of the topic. One of the most important cautions regards the term *gender difference.*

To say there is a gender difference in performance on Task X can mean a number of very different things, as illustrated in Figure 13.6. One possible meaning is that the scores from members of one sex are higher than the scores from members of another sex, a possibility illustrated in Figure 13.6(A). Notice that the lowest-scoring member of one sex (the distribution to the right) still outperforms the very best member of the lower-scoring sex. Although many people interpret statements about gender (or other group) differences in these terms, reality is almost never this simple.

More realistic depictions of gender differences in performance are given in Figures 13.6(B), 13.6(C), and 13.6(D). The first of these illustrates no gender difference. The last two illustrate real gender differences in the mean level of performance, with different degrees of overlap in scores between people of different genders. In each case, although females on average score higher than males, some males score higher than some females. In both cases, then, it is impossible to predict how any individual (Sally Smith or Jack Jones) would score. All we can say is that, given large numbers of men and women, the average score for women will be higher than the average score for men.

A second caution concerns built-in biases in the research literature. Scientific journals are simply much more likely to publish research that reports significant differences between

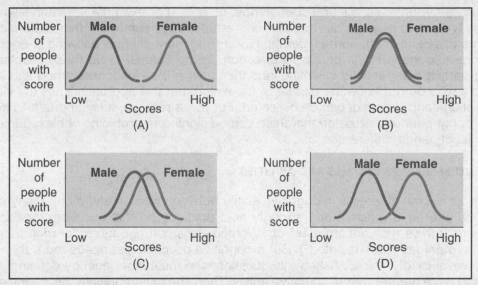

■ Figure 13.6: Examples of hypothetical gender distributions. Each curve depicts a hypothetical distribution of scores on some test for persons of one gender.

or among groups of people than to include research that does not find differences. (This is known as the "file drawer problem," because studies that do not obtain statistically significant results often languish in a researcher's file drawer.) In part, this is because journal space is limited and studies that find differences tend to be more interesting than those that don't (Tavris & Wade, 1984). In part, this is also because of difficulties in interpretation: Researchers who find no group differences cannot conclude there are no differences. Halpern (1992) explains why:

> Suppose you formulate the null hypothesis that no one has more than or less than one head. You could collect a large sample of people, count the number of heads per person, and presumably find that each has only one. However, you have not proved the null hypothesis, because only one exception, that is only one person with more or less than one head, can disprove it, and it is possible that you failed to include this person in your sample. Similarly, even large amounts of negative evidence cannot be used to prove that sex differences do not exist. (p. 33)

Another set of problems in interpreting research on gender differences concerns experimenter expectancy effects, the tendency for researchers unintentionally to influence the responses or behavior of research participants in the direction of the experimenter's hypothesis (Rosenthal & Rosnow, 1984). To remind you, we first discussed the influence of such effects in Chapter 8, when we reviewed imagery studies.

In many psychological studies, experimenters can avoid or minimize these effects by remaining "blind" to which condition a participant is in. For example, in a memory study, one experimenter could randomly assign participants to the experimental and control groups, and a second experimenter, who did not know which of them came from which groups, could administer the tests.

Gender differences research, however, is a different story. Whenever participants are observed or interviewed, it is almost impossible for the observer or interviewer to remain blind to the participant's gender. Thus, the observer or interviewer runs a risk of unintentionally and subtly "leading" the participant to behave in ways consistent with the study's hypotheses, cultural stereotypes, or both. For example, an interviewer who expects women to be more "verbal" or more "emotionally expressive" may unconsciously reinforce this behavior in women, perhaps by smiling more, thereby allowing or encouraging more responses in the predicted direction. Some studies avoid these problems by having participants respond in writing (and then having their responses typed and scored by raters who do not know the gender of the writer), but this approach limits the kinds of observations and data that can be collected. For these reasons, it is important to keep in mind throughout our discussion that there can be significant problems of bias, particularly in studies of gender differences.

GENDER DIFFERENCES IN SKILLS AND ABILITIES

Is there an overall difference in cognitive ability between women and men? Many people in our culture have different and strongly held opinions on this question (for example, "Everyone knows men are smarter," or "Women are smart enough to let men think that they [the men] are more talented"). But a cognitive psychologist needs more than opinion, however loudly voiced. Asked this question, she must first begin by defining what it means to have greater overall cognitive ability. Then she must translate this definition into specific behaviors or patterns of responses on specific tasks (this is called *operationalizing* the question—making it operational). Finally, she must recruit appropriate samples of men and women and administer the chosen tasks.

One kind of task the psychologist might choose is an intelligence test. However, a problem with this approach stems from the way in which intelligence tests are constructed. As Halpern (1992) points out, constructors of intelligence tests work hard to ensure that no overall differences exist between the scores of men and women. That is, many test constructors exclude from intelligence tests any items that show a reliable gender difference in responses.

However, this does not mean that men and women never show any differences in cognitive performance. In an early classic—but later heavily criticized—review of the sex differences literature, Maccoby and Jacklin (1974) identified three kinds of cognitive abilities that appeared to show reliable gender differences: verbal abilities, visuospatial abilities, and quantitative abilities. In this section, we will look at each of these in turn.

To do so, we will need first to consider methodological techniques used by psychologists when reviewing existing literature. Three major kinds of techniques have been used. The first, **narrative review**, involves locating and reading as many sources as one can and then writing up one's conclusions. Although such summaries can be useful, as Hyde and Linn (1988) pointed out, the narrative review has several shortcomings: "It is nonquantitative, unsystematic, and subjective, and the task of reviewing 100 or more studies simply exceeds the information-processing capacities of the human mind" (p. 54).

A second technique, used by Maccoby and Jacklin (1974), is called **vote counting**. As the name implies, this technique involves listing each study and counting the number of studies in the total that demonstrate a particular effect. In essence, each study then receives one "vote" in the final tally. Studies that do demonstrate a gender difference "vote" for the idea that gender differences really exist; studies that do not find a gender difference "vote" for the opposite proposition. Although an advance over the narrative review, vote counting still suffers from a number of problems. The most important is that each study is given equal weight, although many studies differ in overall quality, sample sizes, precision of the instruments used, and statistical power (Block, 1976; Hedges & Olkin, 1985; Hyde & Linn, 1988).

A more powerful technique for combining results from different studies is called **meta-analysis**. This involves the use of statistical methods to integrate the findings from different studies (Hedges & Olkin, 1985). Meta-analysis is gaining widespread popularity among psychologists. It allows the investigator to compare different studies quantitatively. A measure commonly used in meta-analysis is *d,* defined as the difference in mean scores between two groups, divided by the average standard deviation for the two groups. This measure is known as the **effect size**.

For a concrete example of effect size, suppose the following: Women outperform men on a specific verbal task. If the mean score for women is 100 and the mean score for men is 50 but if, on average, the standard deviation for the two groups is 75, the effect size of the study would be (100 – 50)/75, or .67. Essentially, an effect size tells us how much standardized difference lies between two (or more) means. Cohen (1969) provided rules of thumb for interpreting this value: Effect sizes of .20 are considered small; of .50, medium; and of .80, large. So our hypothesized value of .67 would count as a medium-to-large effect.

Verbal Abilities

What kinds of abilities count as "verbal abilities"? Different authors provide different definitions, of course, but a typical description includes breadth of vocabulary, speech fluency, grammar, spelling, reading comprehension, oral comprehension, and the ability to solve language puzzles such as verbal analogies or anagrams (Halpern, 1992; Williams, 1983). Maccoby and Jacklin (1974) concluded that the bulk of studies conducted up until 1974 suggested that although girls and boys showed approximately the same pattern of verbal abilities, after about age 11 and continuing through high school and beyond, females outperformed males on a variety of verbal tasks, including language comprehension and production, creative writing, verbal analogies, and verbal fluency.

A later review (Hyde & Linn, 1988) challenged Maccoby and Jacklin's conclusion. Using meta-analysis, the authors surveyed 165 studies (both published and unpublished) that met the following criteria: Participants were from the United States and Canada, were over 3 years old, and lacked language deficits (such as dyslexia); the studies reported original data; and the authors provided enough information for the calculation of effect sizes. The types of verbal abilities examined included vocabulary, analogies, reading comprehension, oral communication, essay writing, general ability (a mixture of other measures), SAT verbal scores, and anagrams.

Of the studies surveyed, roughly a quarter showed superior male performance, and three quarters showed superior female performance. However, when data were assessed in terms of statistical significance, only 27% of the studies found statistically significant higher female performance, 66% found no statistically significant gender differences, and 7% found statistically significant higher male performance. When the types of verbal tasks were taken into account, the only tasks to show reliable female superiority were those for anagrams, speech production, and general ability. The average *d* measures for these tasks were .22, .20, and .33, respectively, suggesting that even the significant gender differences were rather small. Analyzing gender differences as a function of age, the authors also found little variation in *d* measures according to whether the participants were preschoolers, children of elementary school age, adolescents, or adults.

Interestingly, studies published before 1973 showed a significantly larger gender difference (mean $d = .23$) than did more recent studies (those published after 1973; mean $d = .10$). Early work suggested that females had greater verbal abilities than males; more recent analyses, however, disputed this claim. Hyde and Linn (1988) concluded:

> We are prepared to assert that there are no gender differences in verbal ability, at least at this time, in American culture, in the standard ways that verbal ability has been measured. We feel that we can reach this conclusion with some confidence, having surveyed 165 studies that represent the testing of 1,418,899 subjects . . . and averaged 119 values of d to obtain a mean value of 10.11. A gender difference of one tenth of a standard deviation is scarcely one that deserves continued attention in theory, research, or textbooks. Surely we have larger effects to pursue. (p. 62)

Visuospatial Abilities

The term *visuospatial abilities* is awkward and hard to define, as previous authors have noted (Halpern, 1992; McGee, 1979; Williams, 1983). Typically, it refers to performance on tasks such as the mental rotation or mental transformation of different objects, shapes, or drawings, similar to those described in Chapter 8. Maccoby and Jacklin (1974) reported gender differences in visuospatial abilities as extremely reliable, asserting that boys "excel" in them once childhood is over. They reported a d measure of up to .40.

■ Photo 13.1: One task that appears to show reliable gender differences is that of mental rotation. On average, males perform better than females. However, many individual females can outperform many individual males, even on this task.

One task that appears to show reliable gender differences is mental rotation. On average, males perform better than females, although many individual females can outperform many individual males, even on this task. Over the past 25 years, researchers have reported consistently large ($d = .90$) gender effects on mental rotation tasks (Loring-Meier & Halpern, 1999).

Loring-Meier and Halpern (1999) performed a study to investigate which components of a mental rotation task showed gender differences. Was it the initial generation of an image? The maintenance of an image in working memory? The ability to scan a mental image? The ability to transform a mental image? The researchers had 24 males and 24 females complete four tasks originally designed by Dror and Kosslyn (1994). Two of the four tasks are described here.

The first, an image-generation task, asked participants to image a particular block letter, say *L*, by cueing it with a script lowercase version of the letter, say *l*. Following this, a set of four brackets would appear, with an *X* mark appearing somewhere within it. The participant had to decide whether the *X* appeared within the space where the uppercase block letter would be if it had been drawn inside the four brackets. Figure 13.7 provides an example.

The image-maintenance task presented participants with a pattern such as one of those shown in Figure 13.8. Participants were asked to memorize the pattern and press a key, causing the pattern to disappear. After an interval of 2,500 milliseconds, the screen presented an *X* and the participant had to decide if the pattern would have covered the *X*.

Results showed that, for all four tasks in the study, there was no difference in accuracy between males and females. However, on all four tasks, males were reliably faster than females, leading the authors to conclude that "males, in general, are more proficient in their use of visuo-spatial imagery" (Loring-Meier & Halpern, 1999, p. 470).

Linn and Petersen (1985), who conducted a meta-analysis of gender differences in spatial ability, concluded that the size of the gender difference in mental rotation differs

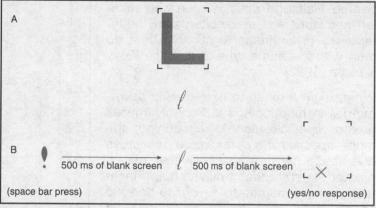

■ Figure 13.7: Examples of (A) a stimulus presented during the learning stage and (B) a trial sequence in the image-generation task.

SOURCE: Loring-Meier, S., & Halpern, D. F. Sex differences in visuospatial working memory: Components of cognitive processing. *Psychonomic Bulletin and Review*, *6*, p. 466. Copyright © 1999, Psychonomic Society, Inc. Reprinted with permission.

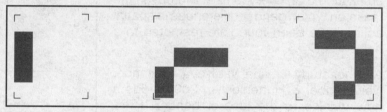

■ Figure 13.8: Examples of stimuli used for the image-maintenance task.

SOURCE: Loring-Meier, S., & Halpern, D. F. Sex differences in visuospatial working memory: Components of cognitive processing. *Psychonomic Bulletin and Review*, *6*, p. 468. Copyright © 1999, Psychonomic Society, Inc. Reprinted with permission.

as a function of the specific task. Generally speaking, the more rapid the processing of symbolic information required, the larger the gender difference. Mental rotation tasks that involved complex three-dimensional items generally showed larger gender differences than did mental rotation tasks with simpler, two-dimensional items. Linn and Petersen offered a number of possible reasons for the gender difference; for example, females may rotate items more slowly or may use different strategies in approaching the task.

Another reason may have to do with neurological findings on male and female brains. In a review, Levy and Heller (1992) note that, in general, females tend to have cerebral hemispheres that are less lateralized, or specialized in function, than are the cerebral hemispheres of males. It has long been known in psychology that the cerebral hemispheres have slightly different roles to play in our cognitive lives. For most of us (especially right-handed people), verbal fluency, verbal reasoning, and other types of analytical reasoning seem to be governed by left-hemisphere functioning. The right hemisphere, in contrast, seems specialized for understanding spatial relations as well as for interpreting emotional information.

To say that males are more lateralized than females is to say that males show greater asymmetries in the functioning of their two cerebral hemispheres. Females, for example, appear to have language functions represented in both hemispheres, at least to some degree. Related to this, women who suffer left-hemisphere damage often show better recovery of language functioning than do men with the same type of damage (Levy & Heller, 1992).

What might it mean to have greater asymmetries in functioning? It probably implies greater specialization in functioning; the more specialization, the more resources one has to perform a task. Overall, males' greater lateralization may equip them with more resources to devote to specific spatial tasks, such as mental rotation. Of course, this conclusion must be interpreted carefully. Although a gender difference in lateralization is well documented, this does not imply that every male shows greater lateralization than every female. Moreover, the tasks on which gender differences in spatial ability have been found are restricted to a narrow set.

Another study (Levine, Vasilyeva, Lourenco, Newcombe, & Huttenlocher, 2005) adds a new wrinkle to the idea of gender differences in spatial abilities. These authors gave two spatial and one nonspatial task to boys and girls over a 1-year period, beginning in the participants' second-grade year. The researchers found no gender differences in the nonspatial (syntax comprehension) task, as expected. Also as expected, there was an overall gender difference in performance on the two spatial tasks (mental rotation and making correspondences between photographs and maps). Surprisingly, however, this overall difference showed variation as a function of the children's socioeconomic status (SES), as shown in Figure 13.9. Specifically, lower-SES students did not show any gender difference on the tasks; only middle- and high-SES students exhibited the traditional male advantage on the spatial tasks. One possible explanation for the SES-related differences is as follows:

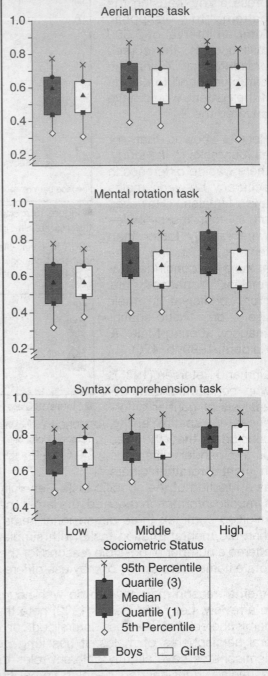

■ Figure 13.9: Box plots of score distributions (across time points) on the aerial maps task (top panel), mental rotation task (middle panel), and syntax comprehension task (bottom panel) as a function of sex and socioeconomic status.

An alternative explanation for the SES-related difference is that a differentially high level of engagement in the kinds of activities that promote the development of spatial skill is essential to the male spatial advantage. In lower-SES groups, these kinds of activities may be relatively unavailable to both boys and girls. Although little is known about what types of input can promote spatial skills, prior studies indicate that activities such as playing with Legos, putting puzzles together, and playing video games are correlated with spatial skill; further, boys spend more time on these activities than girls. . . . Although low-SES children certainly engage in sex-typed play, they may have less access than other children to toys and games that promote spatial skill, as some of these toys and games are relatively expensive. (Levine et al., 2005, p. 844)

Ultimately, the reasons for a gender difference in spatial ability may be found in biological factors, such as lateralization; socialization factors, such as access to puzzles and video games; or some combination. In any event, the differences have implications—for example, for the developers of important standardized tests such as the GRE and SAT:

> Many questions on these tests require the generation, maintenance, and transformation of visuospatial configurations. . . . On average, males score higher than females on these high-stakes tests. . . . These are speeded tests, which means that test takers who answer questions quickly are at an advantage compared with those who respond more slowly. (Loring-Meier & Halpern, 1999, p. 470)

Quantitative and Reasoning Abilities

The term *quantitative abilities* covers a variety of skills, including arithmetic knowledge and skill as well as an understanding of quantitative concepts (such as fractions, proportions, inverses). As with the terms *verbal abilities* and *visuospatial abilities,* the term *quantitative abilities* has meant slightly different things to different investigators.

Maccoby and Jacklin (1974) believed that boys and girls showed similar levels and patterns of mathematical ability through elementary school. Beginning at age 12 or 13, however, boys' achievement and skill began to increase faster than did girls'. Hyde (1981), conducting a meta-analysis of the studies originally cited by Maccoby and Jacklin, concluded that the median *d* score for all the studies was .43, showing that, on average, boys tend to outperform girls by about a half a standard deviation.

Studies by Benbow and Stanley (1980, 1983) provided more evidence in support of gender differences in mathematical ability. The investigators used data collected by the Study of Mathematically Precocious Youth (SMPY), a talent search used to identify extremely able junior high school students. The logic here is that until junior high, male and female students are exposed to the same math classes in school. Thus using junior high school students reduced the role of differential exposure to mathematics that might occur in high school, when males often enroll in more math classes than females.

In the SMPY studies, seventh and eighth graders took the College Board's SAT, a test familiar to high school juniors and seniors. Table 13.2 presents some of the results. Benbow and Stanley (1980) found that males' scores on the mathematical section of the SAT were approximately 30 points higher than females' scores, although both groups performed equally well on the verbal section. Moreover, the higher the score, the higher the ratio of men to women who had that score. For example, considering SAT scores of 700 and above (only 1 in 10,000 students scores this high), the ratio of men to women was 13 to 1 (Benbow & Stanley, 1983). There is some evidence, however, that gender differences occurred only on specific items, usually having to do with algebra rather than with geometry or arithmetic (Deaux, 1985).

■ Table 13.2: Mean SAT Scores of Mathematically Precocious Youths

Test Date	Grade	Number		SAT-V Score* (x̄ ± S.D.)		SAT-M Scores† x̄ ± S.D.		Highest Score		Percentage Scoring Above 600 on SAT-M	
		Boys	Girls	Boys	Girls	Boys	Girls	Boys	Girls	Boys	Girls
March 1972	7	90	77			460 ± 104	423 ± 75	740	590	7.8	0
	8†	133	96			528 ± 105	458 ± 88	790	600	27.1	0
February 1973	7	135	88	385 ± 71	374 ± 74	495 ± 85	440 ± 66	800	620	8.1	1.1
	8†	286	158	431 ± 89	442 ± 83	551 ± 85	511 ± 63	800	650	22.7	8.2
January 1974	7	372	222			473 ± 85	440 ± 68	760	630	6.5	1.8
	8†	556	369			540 ± 82	503 ± 72	750	700	21.6	7.9
December 1976	7	495	356	370 ± 73	368 ± 70	455 ± 84	421 ± 64	780	610	5.5	0.6
	8‡	12	10	487 ± 129	390 ± 61	598 ± 126	482 ± 83	750	600	58.3	0
January 1978	7 and 8‡	1549	1249	375 ± 80	372 ± 78	448 ± 87	413 ± 71	790	760	5.3	0.8
January 1979	7 and 8‡	2046	1628	370 ± 76	370 ± 77	436 ± 87	404 ± 77	790	760	3.2	0.9

N = 9,927.

*Mean score for a random sample of high school juniors and seniors was 368 for males and females (8).

†Mean for juniors and seniors: males, 416; females, 390.

‡These rare eighth-graders were accelerated at least 1 year in school grade placement.

SOURCE: Benbow, C. P., & Stanley, J. C. Sex differences in mathematical ability: Fact or artifact? Science, 210, 1263. Copyright © 1980, American Association for the Advancement of Science. Reprinted with permission.

Follow-up investigations of the SMPY students, conducted 20 years after they were first studied, revealed that gender differences did predict different outcomes in pursuit of educational degrees either in or related to mathematics (for example, engineering, computer science, physical sciences). Males were 5 to 7 times more likely than females, for example, to obtain a doctorate in one of these areas. In the surveys, males endorsed more highly than females the desire for achievement in their careers, whereas women endorsed more highly than men the desire for a balanced life (Benbow, Lubkinski, 2000; Lubkinski, Webb, Morelock, & Benbow, 2001).

Anita Meehan (1984) examined gender differences in other, related tasks, specifically Piagetian tasks of formal operations. Recall from Chapter 12 that formal-operational tasks include such things as logical reasoning, the ability to think systematically, and the ability to consider all possibilities. Meehan examined three kinds of formal-operational tasks: propositional logic tasks, combinatorial reasoning tasks, and proportional reasoning tasks. Performing meta-analyses on a total of 53 studies, Meehan discovered small and statistically nonsignificant values of d for the first two tasks, .22 and .10, respectively. The third task, a more explicitly quantitative task (having to do with ratios), showed an average d of .48.

We have seen so far that gender differences on some cognitive tasks—namely, some visuospatial and some quantitative tasks—seem established. However, Hyde (1981) made an important point: A statistically reliable effect (that is, with relatively low probability of occurring), if the null hypothesis is true, need not necessarily be a large effect. One way to measure the magnitude of an effect is to compute a quantity known to psychologists as the "percentage of variance accounted for." In lay terms, this measure reflects how much of the difference among scores is explained by a given variable. Hyde computed various measures of this magnitude and found that even for the highly reliable gender differences, the percentage of variance accounted for by gender was only between 1% and 5%. That is to say, knowing that a person is male or female can improve your guess about how well he or she might perform on a specific cognitive task (such as visuospatial or quantitative) by at most only 5%. Thus, generalizations such as "Women should avoid engineering" or "Men make more natural mathematicians" are wholly unwarranted by the existing data.

GENDER DIFFERENCES IN LEARNING AND COGNITIVE STYLES

So far, the evidence reviewed suggests that gender differences in cognition occur for only a few very specific tasks, and even then the gender differences are often small. This in turn suggests we have yet to find evidence that men and women have different basic cognitive capacities, skills, or abilities except perhaps for certain specific spatial and quantitative tasks.

However, women and men, as well as girls and boys, certainly often appear to teachers and instructors to have differential aptitudes or preferences. More women than men exhibit a "fear of mathematics" and avoid quantitative or analytical courses (such as those in mathematics, science, and logic) when given a choice, beginning in high school (Oakes, 1990). Certainly, it seems to teachers and others who work with students that cognitive gender differences abound. What accounts for the discrepancy between this anecdotal information and the studies reviewed earlier? One possibility is that gender differences arise not so much in basic cognitive resources (capacities, abilities, and the like) but rather in how these resources are used. Recall our earlier discussion of cognitive styles.

Perhaps it is in such approaches that women and men differ. In the next two sections, we will review two different but related proposals relevant to this idea.

Motivation for Cognitive Tasks

Research by psychologist Carol Dweck and her associates (Dweck, 1999; Dweck & Bush, 1976; Dweck, Davidson, Nelson, & Enna, 1978; Dweck, Goetz, & Strauss, 1980) has shown that even in elementary school, boys and girls show differential patterns of *achievement motivation.* This term refers to the ways in which people define and set goals, particularly the goals that are presumed to relate to their own competence (Dweck, 1986). Two major patterns of behavior that appear to affect the ways people approach a broad range of tasks have been identified: a mastery-oriented and a helpless pattern (Dweck, 1999; Dweck & Leggett, 1988).

Children and adults who adopt a **mastery orientation** set goals to challenge themselves and therefore to increase their competence, understanding, or mastery of something new. These individuals persist when they encounter obstacles or difficulty. Often they also appear to enjoy putting in more effort when it is called for. In contrast, individuals with a **helpless orientation** fail to set challenging goals and give up rather easily when "the going gets tough."

In a number of studies, Dweck and her colleagues have given older elementary school–age children a number of puzzles or similar problem-solving tasks.   Often the tasks are set up to be unsolvable, and children are given "failure feedback"—information that they have failed to complete a particular task correctly. In one study (Dweck & Bush, 1976), children received failure feedback from either a male or a female adult or peer. When the evaluator was an adult, and especially when the adult was female, girls tended to adopt a "helpless" strategy, attributing the cause of their failure to their own inability or lack of competence. Boys, in contrast, were likely in the same circumstances to attribute the failure to the evaluator's "fussiness." It is interesting that when peers administered the failure feedback, boys were much more likely to demonstrate a helpless strategy, and girls were much more likely to attribute problems to their own efforts.

Dweck et al. (1978) reported other findings that might explain why adults' feedback has such different effects on girls and boys. They examined the kind of feedback given to fourth- and fifth-grade girls and boys by classroom teachers. Every instance of feedback to children by the teacher was coded. The experimenters found that when looking at just the positive feedback given, for boys more than 90% of it related to the intellectual quality of their work, but for girls the corresponding figure was less than 80%. The discrepancy for negative feedback was even stronger: For boys, only about a third of the feedback concerned intellectual quality (the rest tended to be about conduct, effort, neatness, or other such things), but well over two thirds of the negative feedback girls received had to do with work-related aspects of their performance.

Dweck and Goetz (1978) concluded that girls, perhaps because of their greater compliance with adult demands, are seen by teachers as expending maximum effort and motivation. Therefore, teachers come to believe that girls' failure can be attributed only to lack of ability. Boys, in contrast, are more often seen by teachers as lacking in conduct or effort. Thus, when boys' performance falls short of expectation, teachers are more likely (in fact, 8 times more likely) to attribute the problem to a lack of motivation than to a lack of ability. As a consequence, boys may be inadvertently taught both to be less devastated by criticism (because they receive so much) and to take it less personally (because so much of it has to do with nonintellectual aspects of work and is instead directed to a perceived lack of motivation). Girls, receiving less criticism, have less opportunity to learn how to handle it. Further, adult criticism of girls' work tends to focus on a perceived lack of competence or ability. In short, girls get the message that failure signals lack of ability (something there is little remedy for); boys, that failure signals a lack of effort (for which the remedy is obvious).

Dweck et al. (1978) tested these ideas in a follow-up study. In it, they had children work on anagram puzzles, and a male experimenter provided failure feedback. Sometimes the feedback was of the sort given by teachers to boys ("You didn't do very well that time—it wasn't neat enough") and sometimes of the sort typically given by teachers to girls ("You didn't do very well that time—you didn't get the word right"). Following these experiences, all children were given another puzzle and were again given negative feedback; then they were asked the following question: "If the man told you that you did not do very well on this puzzle, why do you think that was?" The following choices were provided: "(a) I did not try hard enough. (b) The man was too fussy. (c) I am not very good at it." Children (both girls and boys) in the teacher–girl condition were more than 2 times as likely to attribute failure to choice (c), a perceived lack of ability. Children (again, both girls and boys) in the teacher–boy condition were far more likely to attribute failure to choice (a), a perceived lack of effort, or choice (b), the "fussiness" of the evaluator.

This research supports the idea that "evaluative feedback given to boys and girls . . . can result directly in girls' greater tendency to view failure feedback as indicative of their level of ability" (Dweck et al., 1978, p. 274). Whether and when these patterns of attribution become stable and generalized is an open question but may bode poorly for women's self-assessment, particularly for tasks perceived to be difficult.

Connected Learning

Feminist critiques of psychology (Belenky, Clinchy, Goldberger, & Tarule, 1986; Gilligan, 1982; Goldberger, Tarule, Clinchy, & Belenky, 1996) make even stronger claims about the different ways in which men and women approach cognitive tasks. Belenky and collaborators believe that today's predominant culture, historically dominated by males, has come to prize rationality and objectivity over other, equally legitimate, ways of understanding that may be more common among women:

> It is likely that the commonly accepted stereotype of women's thinking as emotional, intuitive, and personalized has contributed to the devaluation of women's minds and contributions, particularly in Western technologically oriented cultures, which value rationalism and objectivity. . . . It is generally assumed that intuitive knowledge is more primitive, therefore less valuable, than so-called objective modes of knowing. (p. 6)

Belenky et al. (1986) obtained their data from interviews of 135 women, some of whom were college students or alumnae, others of whom were members of what the authors called the "invisible colleges"—human service agencies supporting women while they parented their children. Women were described by the investigators as seeking **connected knowing,** in which one discovers "truth" through a conscious process of trying to understand. The kind of understanding sought involves discovery of a personal connection between the individual and the thing, event, person, or concept under consideration. It entails an acceptance and an appreciation for the thing, event, person, or concept on its own terms, within its own framework.

Another style of knowing these authors described, termed **separate knowing,** is perhaps more typical of males and also of women who are socialized in and successful in traditional male environments. This kind of knowing strives for objectivity and rigor—for the learner to "stand apart from" the thing, event, person, or concept being learned or understood. The orientation is toward impersonal rules or standards, and learning involves "mastery of" rather than "engagement with" the information to be learned. Separate knowing, according to Belenky et al. (1986), involves a different intellectual style in which one looks for flaws, loopholes, contradictions, or omissions of evidence in arguments or propositions. Connected knowing, in contrast, "builds on the [learner's] conviction that the most trustworthy knowledge comes from personal experience rather than the pronouncements of authorities. . . . At the heart of these procedures is the capacity for empathy" (Belenky, pp. 112–113).

If men and women do indeed have different styles of learning and understanding, then perhaps certain ways of processing information also differ in ease or familiarity. For example, mathematics or logic, each with an emphasis on rigor and proof, might seem more attractive to someone with a "separate" way of knowing; more interpretive cognitive tasks, such as understanding a poem or seeking out alternative perceptions, might come more easily to a "connected knower." If styles of knowing vary by gender, then this could influence the kinds of cognitive tasks men and women find easiest or most appealing.

Little has been done to assess the extent to which the different responses articulated by Belenky et al.'s (1986) female participants are a function of gender as opposed to socioeconomic status, level of education, or other factors. Some work has replicated the finding of gender differences in separate and connected knowing, even among college undergraduates at an elite liberal arts college (Galotti, Clinchy, Ainsworth, Lavin, & Mansfield, 1999; Galotti, Reimer, & Drebus, 2001; Marrs & Benton, 2009), but much more remains to be done. More recent work has suggested that a person's "way of knowing" shifts with the context in which the person is interacting, arguing against the idea that ways of knowing are stable tendencies (Ryan & David, 2003). Even if ways of knowing turn out to be largely stable, it is not yet clear whether different ways of knowing predict different kinds of cognitive performance on actual tasks. It remains for future research to examine these important issues.

Proposals from feminist research suggest that cognitive gender differences may not occur on specific tasks but rather on broad approaches to cognition itself. Future work must establish how different the "ways of knowing" are for people of different genders and must investigate how these differences in approach might translate into performance on specific cognitive tasks. It will also be important to assess the effect of gender independent of other demographic variables, such as socioeconomic status, level of education, or cultural heritage.

Summary

1. Cognition may not always operate the same way for all people. Potential sources of variation in the way people approach the cognitive tasks in their lives include individual differences in cognitive abilities, cognitive styles, and expertise, as well as age and gender.

2. Individuals apparently differ in their cognitive abilities, especially in such things as mental speed, storage capacity, and attention span. Some psychologists equate these cognitive abilities with intelligence. Other cognitive psychologists do not equate the two but see cognitive abilities as a part of intelligence. Still other psychologists reject the idea that there is one single thing called intelligence.

3. In addition, people can have different cognitive approaches to, or styles in regard to, different tasks. Two of the most investigated cognitive stylistic dimensions are field dependence/independence and reflectivity/impulsivity. Whether the two dimensions are unrelated and the degree to which cognitive styles are modifiable are two important questions for future research.

4. People's expertise can affect the ways in which they approach a cognitive task within their domain of expertise. Experts perceive more distinctions and categorize information differently than do novices. Experts can use their domain-related knowledge to chunk information so as to use their memories more effectively.

5. Age-related changes in cognitive processing do not disappear in adolescence; adults of different ages show some systematic differences in cognitive performance. Older adults perform slightly less well than younger adults on tasks of divided attention and working memory, for instance, perhaps because of a general decline in processing speed.

6. Research on gender differences in cognition is very active; therefore, any conclusions must of necessity be tentative. At present, it seems safe to say that with regard to ability, the overall patterns of performance of men and women, boys and girls, are far more similar than different, except on very specific tasks. Many descriptions of cognitive gender differences (for example, in verbal ability) have on close inspection proven either false or at best greatly exaggerated. Other, better established cognitive gender differences (for example, on mental rotation tasks or on certain mathematical tasks, especially algebraic ones) often depend on the age and educational background of the people surveyed and on the particular items used. Even for differences that are very well established, the magnitude of the difference between the average performance for males and the average performance for females is often quite small, accounting for up to only 5% of the total variance.

7. Another set of questions has to do with gender differences in cognitive style or approach. The issue here is whether females and males adopt different strategies in the ways in which they gather, process, or evaluate information. Carol Dweck's work suggests that boys and girls adopt different approaches to cognitive tasks, with girls tending to adopt a more "helpless" outlook, especially in the face of failure. It is not yet clear how girls and boys come to adopt different strategies, although Dweck's work implicates the typical patterns of feedback teachers give to boys and to girls. We can speculate that these kinds of feedback may also come from other agents of socialization—parents, siblings, peers, and others—but the evidence on this question remains to be gathered.

8. Proposals from feminist research suggest that cognitive gender differences may not occur on very specific tasks but rather on broad approaches to cognition itself. Future work must establish how different the "ways of knowing" are for people of different genders and must investigate how these differences in approach might translate into performance on specific cognitive tasks. It will also be important to assess the effect of gender independent of other demographic variables, such as socioeconomic status, level of education, or cultural heritage.

Review Questions

1. Discuss the reasons why cognitive psychologists need to know about stable individual and/or gender differences in cognition.

2. What does it mean to assert that stable individual differences in cognitive capacities exist? Is this assertion synonymous with the belief that stable individual differences in intelligence exist?

3. Contrast the classical view of intelligence with Gardner's view.

4. Discuss the idea of cognitive styles. How does this concept differ from the concepts of intelligence or cognitive abilities?

5. What cautions must be given in interpreting findings on gender differences (or for that matter, any group-related individual differences) in cognition?

6. Explain the logic of a meta-analysis. How is it performed? Why is it considered better than vote counting or narrative review?

7. Discuss the implications of the major findings regarding gender differences in cognitive abilities.

8. How might the work of Dweck and colleagues and Belenky and colleagues bear on the research on gender differences in cognition?

Key Terms

cognitive abilities

cognitive style

cognitive tempo

connected knowing

effect size (d)

expert/novice differences

field dependence/fieldinde-

pendence (FD/FI)

helpless orientation

individual differences

intelligence

learning style

mastery orientation

meta-analysis

multiple intelligences (MI) theory

narrative review

need for cognition

reflectivity/impulsivity

separate knowing

vote counting

CHAPTER 14

COGNITION IN CROSS-CULTURAL PERSPECTIVE

CHAPTER OUTLINE

Examples of Studies of Cross-Cultural Cognition
    Cross-Cultural Studies of Perception
      Picture Perception
      Visual Illusions
    Cross-Cultural Studies of Memory
      Free Recall
      Visuospatial Memory
    Cross-Cultural Studies of Categorization
    Cross-Cultural Studies of Reasoning
    Cross-Cultural Studies of Counting
Effects of Schooling and Literacy
Situated Cognition in Everyday Settings

Much of the literature covered so far has described the cognitive capacities and processes of people (usually adults, but in some cases children) in the United States or Europe. The implicit assumption has been that the models and theories of cognition developed from such samples are universal—that they apply to and can describe the performance and behavior of people throughout the world. However, research conducted with people from other cultures has often shown this assumption to be problematic, if not in error. In this chapter, we will examine some of this research and consider its implications for the study of cognition.

A number of issues must be discussed in order to consider cross-cultural research. First and foremost, we must come to terms with what makes a **culture**. Certainly, most would agree that people in rural India live in a different culture than people in downtown Baltimore. However, do people in rural New Hampshire experience a different culture than people living in Los Angeles?

Triandis (1996) makes a forceful argument that psychologists ignore culture at their intellectual peril:

> Almost all the theories and data of contemporary psychology come from Western populations (e.g., Europeans, North Americans, Australians, etc.). Yet about 70% of humans live in non-Western cultures. . . . If psychology is to become a universal discipline it will need both theories and data from the majority of humans. . . . Contemporary psychology is best conceived as a Western indigenous psychology that is a special case of the universal psychology we as contemporary psychologists would like to develop. When the indigenous psychologies are incorporated into a universal framework, we will have a universal psychology. (p. 407)

Psychologists, anthropologists, sociologists, and others have debated the issue of what defines a culture and have come to no widespread and clear-cut resolution to date. Cole and Scribner (1974) noted some of the ingredients of a culture: a distinct language; distinct customs, habits, and modes of dress; and distinct beliefs and philosophies. Other psychologists performing cross-cultural research have also examined factors such as ethnicity and social class in relation to performance on different types of tasks or to attitudes and beliefs (L. G. Conway, Schaller, Tweed, & Hallett, 2001; Kagitçibasi & Berry, 1989; Segall, 1986). In fact, Segall (1984) has made the argument that the concept of culture is nothing more than a collection of independent variables such as language, customs, and so on, although others (such as Rohner, 1984) disagree.

Triandis (1996) asserts that dimensions of cultural variation, which he calls cultural syndromes, can be used in the construction of psychological theories. A cultural syndrome is a "pattern of shared attitudes, beliefs, categorizations, self-definitions, norms, role

■ Table 14.1: Examples of Cultural Syndromes

Tightness	In some cultures, there are very many norms that apply across many situations. Minor deviations from the norms are criticized and punished; in other cultures, there are few norms, and only major deviations from norms are criticized.
Cultural Complexity	The number of different cultural elements, such as role definitions, can be large or small (e.g., about 20 jobs among hunters and gatherers versus 250,000 types of jobs in information societies).
Active-Passive	This syndrome . . . includes a number of active (e.g., competition, action, and self-fulfillment) and passive (e.g., reflective thought, leave the initiative to others, and cooperation) elements.
Honor	This pattern is a rather narrow syndrome, focused on the concept of honor. It emerges in environments in which property is mobile and to protect it individuals have to appear fierce so that outsiders will not dare to try to take it from them. It includes beliefs, attitudes, norms, values, and behaviors (e.g., hypersensitivity to affronts) that favor the use of aggression for self-protection, to defend one's honor, and to socialize children so that they will react when challenged.
Collectivism	In some cultures the self is defined as an aspect of a collective (e.g., family or tribe); personal goals are subordinated to the goals of this collective; norms, duties, and obligations regulate most social behavior; taking into account the needs of others in the regulation of social behavior is widely practiced.
Individualism	The self is defined as independent and autonomous from collectives. Personal goals are given priority over the goals of collectives. Social behavior is shaped by attitudes and perceived enjoyable consequences. The perceived profits and loss from a social behavior are computed, and when a relationship is too costly it is dropped.
Vertical and Horizontal Relationships	In some cultures hierarchy is very important, and in-group authorities determine most social behavior. In other cultures social behavior is more egalitarian.

definitions, and values that is organized around a theme that can be identified among those who speak a particular language, during a specific historical period, and in a definable geographic region" (p. 408). Table 14.1 gives examples of some cultural syndromes Triandis has identified.

The general issue is this: The term culture connotes so much that simply finding differences among individuals from one culture to another and attributing those differences to "culture" is a fairly empty statement (Atran, Medin, & Ross, 2005; Varnum, Grossman, Kitayama, & Nisbett, 2010). Instead, the goal is to "unpack" the term and to try to determine which aspects or dimensions of a culture contribute to the differences found. For example, might differences in counting skill be attributed to different uses of number within a culture? Might differences in perception have to do with the typical landscapes encountered by participants of different cultures? What, specifically, within the culture affects the ways in which people acquire, store, and process information?

Bovet's (1974) research addressed these questions by comparing the performance of children and adults from Algeria and Geneva, Switzerland, on Piagetian tasks of cognitive development. Bovet found some unusual patterns of results among her Algerian participants that she was able to relate to specific features of the Algerian culture. For example, Algerian children had a difficult time with the conservation of quantities. Bovet speculated that some of their difficulty reflected their everyday environment and customs:

> A further point to be mentioned is that eating and cooking utensils (bowls, glasses, plates) of the particular environment studied were of all shapes and sizes, which makes it somewhat difficult to make any comparisons of dimensions. Furthermore, the way of serving food at table was for each person to help from a communal dish, rather than for one person to share it out amongst those present; no comparison of the size of the portions takes place. Finally, the attitude of the mother who does not use any measuring instrument, but "knows" how much to use by means of intuitive approximations and estimations, may have some influence on the child's attitude. Thus, adult modes of thought can influence the development of notions of conservation of quantity in the child by means of familiar types of activities, in which the child participates, even if only as spectator. (p. 331)

■ Photo 14.1 and 14.2: (1) An American family eating dinner and (2) a family from another culture eating dinner. According to Bovet (1974), even an ordinary setting, such as the dinner table, can affect certain cognitive processing, such as concepts of measurement.

Bovet (1974) asserted that aspects of the culture, physical (the shapes and dimensions of eating utensils) as well as behavioral (the practices surrounding the serving of food), guide and constrain the assumptions and questions children naturally have about quantities. Contrast her description of Algerian culture with your impressions of middle-class North American culture: Dinner tables are set such that everyone has the same kind of glass, spoon, plate, and so on. A parent serves each child with roughly the same serving size (perhaps affected by the age or size of the child). Disputes about who "got more" (of, say, an appealing dessert) are common. All these factors might help, in subtle ways, to focus attention on quantities and how quantities relate to such things as container shape and perceptual appearance. This focus, in turn, might help performance on later tests of conservation. Of course, these assertions warrant more rigorous testing before we can accept them. Other aspects of the culture might produce the effect; without empirical testing, we can't be sure.

More recently, social psychologist Richard Nisbett and his colleagues have been investigating differences in cognitive processing by East Asian residents (for example, of Japan, China, Korea) and comparing this to cognitive processing of Western European and North American (primarily US) residents. These researchers hold that East Asians typically process information more holistically and more contextually, whereas Westerners process information more analytically (Ji, Peng, & Nisbett, 2000; Miyamoto, Nisbett, & Masuda, 2006; Nisbett & Norenzayan, 2002; Nisbett, Peng, Choi, & Norenzayan, 2001; Varnum et al., 2010).

A fundamental question raised by cross-cultural research is the degree to which practices, beliefs, competences, and capacities are culturally relative or culturally universal. To assert that a cognitive process is culturally relative is to assert that the process is specific to a particular culture or set of cultures (Poortinga & Malpass, 1986). For example, the ability to form hierarchically organized categories (e.g., poodles are dogs, which are mammals, which are animals, which are living things) may be much more relevant to people in some cultures than in others (Greenfield, 2005). Cultural universality, by contrast, refers to phenomena believed common to humankind, such as the use of language.

The answer to this question profoundly affects the way in which research questions are framed. If, for instance, a process, capacity, or strategy is assumed to be universal, then cross-cultural questions about it are likely to ask how cultural factors influence and shape it. The assumption here is that the process, capacity, or strategy exists in all cultures but that culture (or some aspect of culture) can facilitate, hinder, or otherwise alter the way it is expressed.

In contrast, people who hold a position of cultural relativism, especially radical cultural relativism (Berry, 1981, 1984), would *not* assume that the process, capacity, or strategy is necessarily present in all cultures. Moreover, they would be less likely to view culture as the sum of several independent factors. Instead, these researchers believe that culture is a kind of Gestalt that cannot be broken into pieces. Certain concepts, processes, capacities, and the like are thus relevant to, and therefore found in, only certain cultures. The kinds of theories and explanations of cognition offered are therefore necessarily different for all (or at least many) cultures.

Cross-cultural researchers face many methodological challenges that do not play as large a role in the research programs of researchers who operate strictly within one culture (such as most of the work described in Chapters 2 through 13). You may recall from introductory psychology that a true experiment involves (a) random assignment of participants to experimental conditions, (b) control over experimental treatments (that is, manipulation of independent variables), and (c) control over other confounding factors or events. Any experimenter has a difficult (if not impossible) task in achieving such control, but a cross-cultural researcher, in principle, can never achieve the first criterion (people cannot be randomly assigned to a culture either practically or ethically) and can probably never in reality achieve the second or third. After all, especially if certain tasks are more relevant to some cultures than others, it is nearly impossible to choose experimental tasks (such as memory tests and problem-solving tests) that are equally difficult and familiar, and equally a good measure of the aspect of behavior or ability under study, for people from different cultures (Malpass & Poortinga, 1986). For a variety of reasons unrelated to cognitive abilities, people from cultures in which the task is more familiar might outperform people from cultures in which the task is less familiar. Perhaps people from the former culture have had more practice with the task, or feel more comfortable with the task, or enjoy the task more. We will provide specific illustrations of this point.

By the way, you might have noticed that the inability to randomly assign people to cultures is a problem equivalent to the one faced by researchers studying gender, developmental, or other individual differences (L. G. Conway et al., 2001). So-called participant variables, such as age, gender, culture, and ethnic origin, are variables that a researcher cannot assign; this makes interpretation of experimental results all the more tricky.

Another problem in conducting cross-cultural research is that individuals within a culture may not take any note of or evaluate that culture (Kitayama, 2002). Cultural practices, such as daily routines, rituals, practices, styles of dress, and mannerisms, may be both tacit and implicit—widely shared within the culture and hence frequently unnoticed or regarded as unremarkable. As Kitayama puts it, "What culture is to humans, water is to fish" (p. 90).

In the last section of the chapter, we will examine research in the cross-cultural tradition carried out in the United States. Specifically, we will look at how people's performance works on everyday (that is, nonlaboratory, and often nonschool) cognitive tasks. One important question will serve as our focus: How well do theories and models of cognition, such as those described in earlier chapters, account for cognition "in the real world"? Much of the work reviewed in this chapter demonstrates that people's performance often displays context sensitivity; that is, it varies according to the task, the instructions, or other features of the environment.

EXAMPLES OF STUDIES OF CROSS-CULTURAL COGNITION _____

In this section, we will review a selection of cross-cultural cognition studies. As in the two previous chapters, it is impossible to examine each facet of human cognition cross-culturally. Instead, we will examine a very small sample of studies of cognitive capacities and processes from a cross-cultural point of view.

CROSS-CULTURAL STUDIES OF PERCEPTION

You may recall from Chapter 3 that the term *perception* refers to the interpretation of sensory stimuli—for example, using the information from your retinal image to see an object against a background or recognizing the furry creature meandering toward you as your cat. Because our perceptions typically occur quickly and effortlessly, it is tempting to conclude that perception is a built-in, hard-wired consequence of the way our sensory systems work. However, some landmark studies from cross-cultural psychology have directly challenged this assumption, showing that, quite literally, people from different cultures often "see things" quite differently. What follows below are good illustrations of the kind of top-down processing we talked about in Chapter 3.

Picture Perception

Studies by Hudson (1960, 1967) demonstrated that people from different cultures frequently do not see eye to eye. Hudson began with the intuition that Bantu workers in South African mines and factories seemed to have difficulty interpreting posters and films. To investigate why, he presented a variety of South Africans (both black and white, schooled and unschooled) with pictures such as those shown in Figure 14.1. Notice

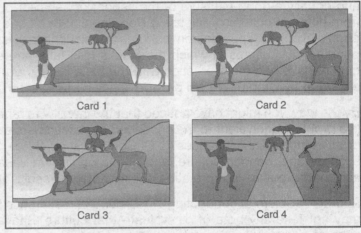

■ Figure 14.1: Stimuli from Hudson (1960).

that all the pictures depict an elephant, an antelope, a tree, and a man holding a spear. The cards differ in the depth cues presented. Card 1 uses object size (objects farther away are rendered smaller). Cards 2 and 3 also use superposition (nearer objects partially occlude farther objects). Card 4 uses all these cues and, in addition, some cues of linear perspective (lines that are parallel appear to meet in the distance; other outlines or contours are scaled to fit in this framework). Participants were asked to describe what they saw, what they thought the figures in the pictures were doing, and which pairs of figures were closest to each other.

Results showed that participants attending school typically came to a three-dimensional interpretation of the pictures (for example, seeing the man aiming the spear at the antelope, not the elephant; seeing the elephant as far away rather than very small). However, nonliterate workers, both black and white, typically "saw" the pictures two-dimensionally. Hudson (1960) argued that the cause of perceiving pictures three-dimensionally is not schooling per se but rather informal instruction and habitual exposure to pictures. He believed that such factors as exposure to pictures, photographs, and other illustrations in books and magazines available in the home provide a great deal of crucial, informal practice in "pictorial literacy." His speculation was based on the observation that schools provide little formal instruction in interpreting pictures, coupled with the observation that even the schooled black workers had greater difficulty than schooled white workers coming to three-dimensional pictorial interpretations.

Deregowski (1968), studying children and adult workers in Zambia, Central Africa, considered a different possibility. He wondered whether cross-cultural differences in pictorial perception really existed or whether some feature of Hudson's tasks caused participants to respond as if they couldn't interpret the pictures three-dimensionally. In one study, he gave participants two tasks: a version of the Hudson task and a task requiring them to make models from pictured depictions (such as those shown in Figure 14.2) out of sticks.

Deregowski (1980) found that although more than 80% of the participants failed to perceive the Hudson pictures three-dimensionally, more than half constructed three- rather than two-dimensional models. Deregowski argued, among other things, that perhaps his task and Hudson's differed in difficulty, with Hudson's requiring a more demanding response. For instance, perhaps the building task provides more guidance for the visual inspection of the picture, thus providing more cues to participants as to the "correct" interpretations.

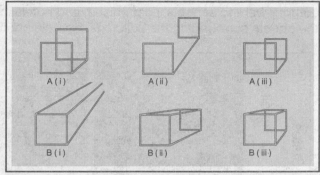

■ Figure 14.2: Stimuli from Deregowski (1968).

Cole and Scribner (1974) concluded from these and other studies that it is too simplistic to conclude that people either can or cannot perceive pictures three-dimensionally. The issue, they argued, is when and how people come to interpret a two-dimensional stimulus as having depth. Perhaps the content of the pictures (depictions of people and animals or depictions of abstract geometric forms) influences perception. Perhaps the mode of response (answering a question, building a model) influences the way people perceive pictures. Whatever the reasons, this work suggested that the ways in which people view and interpret two-dimensional pictures depicting three-dimensional scenes are not necessarily the same from culture to culture.

This point was amplified and extended in a study by Liddell (1997). She showed South African children in Grades 1, 2, and 3 various color pictures of people and scenes of African origin. Children were asked to examine pictures and to "tell [the tester] what you see in the picture." These commentaries, which were probed for completeness by familiar testers, were later coded for the number of labels a child provided (for example, "That's a flower," "That's a hat"), the number of links a child made between items in the picture (for example, "The table is in front of the lady"), and the number of narratives or interpretations of the picture the child made (such as "The mother is putting the child to bed").

In response to the total six-picture series given to each child, children averaged 65 labels, 23 links, and 3 narratives. In other words, rather than "interpreting" the pictures, these South African children tended instead to provide factual, even disembodied, pieces of information about them. Moreover, the tendency to provide interpretations decreased as a function of years of schooling, with Grade 3 children providing fewer than Grade 1 or 2 children. Liddell (1997) contrasted this finding with one obtained from a sample of British children, who showed increases in narratives as a function of years of schooling. She suggested that the explanation for the difference may lie in the South African system of elementary education, which emphasizes factual and descriptive lessons (as opposed to open-ended or creative ones). Alternatively (or additionally), maybe the paucity of picture books and early readers in most rural African homes precludes these children's complete acquisition of learning to decode or interpret pictures.

Another recent study of photograph perception also makes some very interesting points about cross-cultural differences in perception. Miyamoto et al. (2006) began by taking photographs in three US cities of various sizes (New York; Ann Arbor, Michigan; Chelsea, Michigan) along with three comparable cities in Japan (Tokyo, Hikone, Torahime). The authors went to schools, post offices, and hotels in each city and took photographs from the streets surrounding the buildings. Sample photos are presented in Figure 14.3.

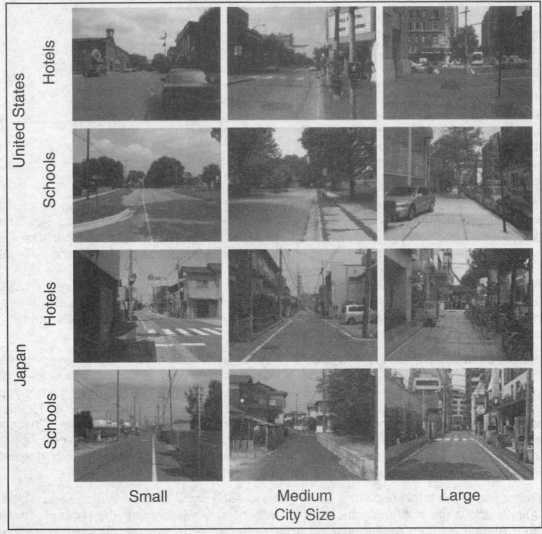

■ Figure 14.3: Examples of the pictures taken in front of US and Japanese schools and hotels used in Miyamoto et al. (2006).

The authors then had both Japanese and American participants (college students) rate each photograph on a number of dimensions, including the number of objects in each photograph, the degree to which the photograph seemed chaotic or organized, and how ambiguous or clear the boundaries between objects were. They also created objective measures of the scenes, using computerized image-recognition software. Their results showed that the photographs taken in Japan were more ambiguous and contained more elements (objects) than did American ones. They speculate that Japanese scenes may encourage more perception of context than do American scenes. This in turn could explain why, for example, in another of their studies, their American participants in a change blindness task (see Chapter 4) noticed more changes in the focal objects, whereas Japanese participants were more sensitive to changes in "background" or contextual objects (Masuda & Nisbett, 2006). Varnum et al. (2010) present arguments that these cognitive differences stem from differences in social orientation, with Americans being more likely to endorse the value of independence and Japanese tending to respect the social value of interdependence.

Visual Illusions

Other cross-cultural studies of perception have centered on visual illusions, such as those depicted in Figure 14.4. Rivers (1905) studied aspects of visual perception of people from the Torres Straits (Papuans from New Guinea) and people from southern India (the Todas).

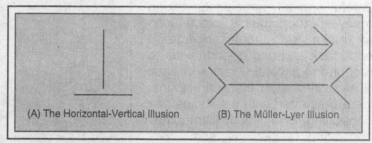

(A) The Horizontal-Vertical Illusion   (B) The Müller-Lyer Illusion

■ Figure 14.4: Some visual illusions studied cross-culturally.

Rivers reported that relative to Western samples, the people he worked with were more prone to the horizontal–vertical illusion, in which a vertical line appears longer than the horizontal line it bisects even though both are the same length. However, his participants were less prone than Westerners to the Müller-Lyer illusion, in which a line with an arrow "tail" on both ends is perceived as being longer than a line with an arrow "head" on both ends even though both lines are the same length.

Segall, Campbell, and Herskovits (1966) followed up on this observation, conducting a now classic study. In it, they used the Müller-Lyer and the horizontal–vertical illusions (refer to Figure 14.4) and worked with approximately 2,000 people from 14 African and Philippine locations and the United States. The investigators' hypothesis was that people's previous experience would affect their susceptibility to the illusions. In particular, Segall and colleagues believed that people who came from carpentered environments—characterized by wood or other materials arranged in straight lines, rectangular shapes, and other such geometric relationships—would be relatively more susceptible to the Müller-Lyer illusion. The idea here was that carpentered environments provide the people who live in them with a great deal of practice seeing rectangular shapes (boards, houses, windows) and therefore certain angles and junctions. The Müller-Lyer illusion taps into this experience as follows:

> Among persons raised in a carpentered world there would be a tendency to perceive the Müller-Lyer figure . . . as a representation of three-dimensional objects extended in space. In this instance the two main parts of the drawing represent two objects. On the [top of Figure 14.4(B)], for example, if the horizontal segment were perceived as the representation of the edge of a box, it would be a front edge; while on the [bottom], if the horizontal segment were perceived as the edge of another box, it would be the back edge along the inside of the box. Hence, the [top] horizontal would "have to be" shorter than the drawing makes it out, and the [bottom] horizontal would "have to be" longer. (Segall et al., 1966, pp. 85–86)

This argument is based on one offered by the psychologist Egon Brunswik (1956): People interpret cues in any situation according to the ways in which they have interpreted such cues in the past. People do this because in the past they have typically been correct in the way they have interpreted these cues. However, in certain situations, cues can be misleading and can cause people to make false interpretations.

Using analogous reasoning, Segall et al. (1966) predicted that people from cultures where the horizon is a part of the everyday landscape (such as desert or plains dwellers) would be more susceptible to the horizontal–vertical illusion than would people from cultures where the environment does not afford opportunities to view vast distances (such as jungle dwellers).

Segall et al. (1966) explained the task carefully to all participants, taking many methodological precautions to make sure they understood each task and had opportunities to respond to several versions of each illusion. On each trial, participants were presented with a stimulus pair containing two lines (sometimes consisting of illusions, sometimes consisting of other pairs of lines that produce no illusion) and had to indicate which line was longer. In general, the results confirmed the predictions just described, although both illusions were present in all cultures to a greater or a lesser degree. Despite some later disagreements

■ Photo 14.3: Segall and colleagues (1966) predicted that people from cultures in which the horizon figures prominently in the landscape will show increased susceptibility to the horizontal–vertical illusion.

over the findings by other investigators (see Deregowski, 1980, 1989, for reviews), Segall (1979) maintained that

> people perceive in ways that are shaped by the inferences they have learned to make in order to function most effectively in the particular ecological settings in which they live. The generalization that we can derive ... is that we learn to perceive in the ways that we need to perceive. In that sense, environment and culture shape our perceptual habits. (p. 93)

Notice that the issue being discussed has to do with perception, or how people interpret their sensory information, and not sensation, which is the acquisition of information. That is, no one claims there are cross-cultural differences in the way the visual (or auditory or olfactory) system works; rather they claim that differences may reside in the stages of cognitive processing that follow the initial acquisition of the information. To put it another way, the claim is made that culture affects the way people interpret sensory information to create meaningful interpretations of what they see.

CROSS-CULTURAL STUDIES OF MEMORY

Like perception, memory is widely regarded as a process central to almost every other form of cognition. Clearly, all people need a means of storing some of the information they encounter for possible later use. Thus, it seems reasonable to believe that memory should show many commonalities across cultures. In this section, we will examine some of the work on memory carried out with people of non-Western cultures.

Free Recall

Given the assumptions just stated, results from studies carried out with the Kpelle people of Liberia, Africa, were surprising (Cole, Gay, Glick, & Sharp, 1971). As one part of a long series of studies on Kpelle cognition, Cole et al. administered a free-recall task. They read participants a list of nouns (all having been demonstrated to refer to familiar objects). One set of lists (see Table 14.2) consisted of items that "clustered" into different categories (such as tools, articles of clothing); another set consisted of the same number and types of items but had no apparent clusters. Previous work using educated residents of the United States had shown that people's free-recall performance is enhanced when they are given clustered lists relative to nonclustered lists, especially when the items are presented in blocks, with all items from the same category presented together (Bousfield, 1953; Cofer, 1967).

Kpelle children (ranging in age from 6 to 14) and adults participated. Of the children, some were in school (first through fourth grades), and some were not; all the adults were schooled. The performance of the participants was compared with that of white, middle-class children from southern California.

■ Table 14.2: Stimuli Used by Cole et al. (1971)

Clusterable	Nonclusterable
Plate	Bottle
Calabash	Nickel
Pot	Chicken feather
Pan	Box
Cup	Battery
	Animal horn
Potato	Stone
Onion	Book
Banana	Candle
Orange	Cotton
Coconut	Hard mat
	Rope
Cutlass	Nail
Hoe	Cigarette
Knife	Stick
File	Grass
Hammer	Pot
	Knife
Trousers	Orange
Singlet	Shirt
Headtie	
Shirt	
Hat	

SOURCE: Cole and Scribner (1974, p. 127).

Cole and colleagues (1971) found large differences by age in their American sample, with older children recalling far more of the words on each list than younger children. Kpelle participants, however, showed only slight differences by age. Moreover, the schooled Kpelles did not outperform the nonschooled Kpelles by much of a margin. Although the clusterable lists were easier for all Kpelle and American samples, only the American participants displayed much clustering in their free recall. That is, regardless of how the items from the clusterable lists were presented, American children, especially those 10 years and older, were more likely to recall all the tools, then all the foods, and so on. The Kpelle participants, by contrast, were quite unlikely to do so.

It appeared, at first, as if the Kpelle had memory systems that worked differently than those of Americans. However, Cole et al. (1971) followed up this work by testing a number of rival hypotheses. Perhaps, for example, the Kpelle did not understand the task. Perhaps they were not very interested in the task and therefore did not try very hard. Perhaps the cues provided weren't clear enough. In a number of studies, the investigators gathered evidence against each of these.

In one series of studies, Cole et al. (1971) demonstrated that when the Kpelle were cued to recall items by category (for example, at the time of recall only, the experimenter said something like "Tell me all the clothing you remember. [S(ubject) responds.] Okay, now tell me all the tools you remember . . ."), their performance improved dramatically. This result (along with several others we don't have space here to review) suggested to Cole and Scribner (1974) that although the Kpelle may perform differently on a memory task, there is little evidence to support the view that memory systems function in qualitatively different ways than do American or Western European people's memory systems. In particular, Cole and Scribner argued:

> It appears that the cultural difference in memory performance tapped in the free-recall studies rests upon the fact that the more sophisticated (highly educated) subjects respond to the task by searching for and imposing a structure upon which to base their recall. Noneducated subjects are not likely to engage in such structure-imposing activity. When they do, or when the task itself gives structure to the material, cultural differences in performance are greatly reduced or eliminated. (p. 139)

We will return later to the effects of **schooling**, or years of formal education, particularly in Western-type schools, on cognition.

A more recent study (Gutchess et al., 2006) started from the premise that clustering is more common in Western cultures (e.g., in the United States) than Eastern ones (e.g., in China). The researchers gave free-recall tasks to both younger adults and elderly adults in both cultures, reasoning that clustering would be particularly difficult for elderly Eastern adults due to age-related cognitive limitations of the sort described in Chapter 13. Indeed, the authors found that while the groups from both cultures recalled about the same number of words, the extent of clustering was particularly different for Western versus Eastern elderly adults.

Visuospatial Memory

One criticism often raised about exporting traditional, laboratory-based experiments to other cultures is that the tasks themselves vary in familiarity, importance, and general level of interest to people from different cultures. If true, the charge raises serious problems for any cross-cultural research comparing the performance of people from different cultures on the same task. If experimental tasks are not closely derived from tasks that people normally engage in during their daily lives, people's performance will not be particularly informative with regard to their real abilities.

Many investigators, taking the criticism seriously, have tried to design studies that closely model real-life tasks. In one such study, Kearins (1981), studying visuospatial memory in desert Australian Aboriginal children and adolescents, presented participants with tasks in which they viewed arrays of objects for 30 seconds and then, after the objects were scrambled, reconstructed the arrays. Kearins's rationale was this: Traditional desert living requires a great deal of movement among widely spaced sites, many of which are "visually unremarkable." For various reasons having to do with unpredictable rainfall and the requirements of hunting and other food gathering, the routes between sites are rarely duplicated exactly. Presumably, this requires kinds of spatial knowledge other than route knowledge. One possibility is a greater ability to remember spatial relationships:

> Memory for a single environmental feature would be unlikely to have been a reliable identifier of any particular spot, both because outstanding features are rare in this region of many recurring features, and because of the need for approach from any direction. But particular spatial relationships between several features could uniquely specify a location, more or less regardless of orientation. Accurate memory for such relationships is thus likely to have been of considerable value both in movement between water sources and in daily foraging movements from a base camp. (p. 438)

Kearins (1981) presented both Aboriginal and white Australian children with four conditions. In each one, they saw a collection of 20 familiar objects. In two of the conditions, the objects were human-made artifacts (such as a knife or a thimble); in the other two, the objects were naturally occurring objects (such as a feather or a rock). In two of the conditions, all the objects were of the same type (such as all rocks or all bottles); in the other two, they were of

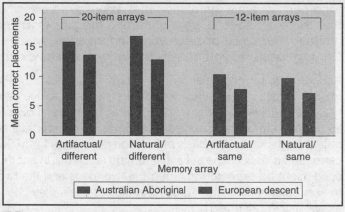

■ Figure 14.5: Results from Kearins (1981).

different types (such as a knife, an eraser, a thimble). Testing took place on benches in playgrounds or under trees, and care was taken to minimize the "testlike" nature of the task. Children viewed each array for 30 seconds, then closed their eyes while the objects were jumbled in a heap, and then were asked to reconstruct the array with no time limit.

Results, shown in Figure 14.5, revealed that Aboriginal adolescents outperformed their white age-mates in every condition. Kearins (1981) commented that the task seemed almost too easy for the Aboriginal children: A significant portion (ranging from 14% to 54% in different conditions, compared to an average of 4.5% for the white children) made no errors.

Observation of the Aboriginal participants revealed that they tended to sit very still while viewing arrays and did not show any evidence of rehearsal. White children and adolescents were much more likely to move around in their seats, to pick up objects, and to "mutter." In the reconstruction phase, Aboriginal children placed objects at a steady, deliberate pace and made few changes as they worked. White Australian children began the reconstruction phase "in great haste" and subsequently made many changes in where the objects were placed. Kearins (1981) believed the Aboriginal children were using a visual strategy; white children, a verbal strategy. When asked how they were performing the task, Aboriginal children tended to shrug or to say they remembered the "look" of the array; white Australians tended to describe verbal rehearsal strategies at length.

Kearins (1981) took the data from this and other experiments as supporting her idea that culture can impose "environmental pressure" selectively to enhance certain cognitive skills—in this case, visual rehearsal strategies. She further believed that once a certain skill is established, individuals are more likely to practice it, thus possibly enhancing the skill. Moreover, cognitive (and other) skills and habits useful within a culture are likely to be encouraged by parents and other adults from a child's early years. As a result, certain cognitive abilities become more prevalent and are better performed.

CROSS-CULTURAL STUDIES OF CATEGORIZATION

Imagine walking into a room and seeing a number of blocks of various sizes. On one side of each is painted a small, medium, or large circle, square, or triangle that is red or yellow or red-and-yellow striped. Imagine being asked to "put the ones together that go together," a vague instruction that asks you to classify. You can see immediately, I hope, that there are several ways of sorting the blocks: by painted shape, by block size, or by marking. We could observe your performance, and we could ask two questions about it: On what basis do you classify the blocks, and how consistent are you in using this basis?

According to psychologist Jerome Bruner (Bruner et al., 1966), the way we carry out classification tasks changes with development. At first, we tend to use perceptual bases for classification, especially color (Olver & Hornsby, 1966). Later, the basis of our sorting (when more meaningful objects, as opposed to blocks, are used) becomes less perceptual and more "deep," as we start to group objects together on the basis of function rather than form. So whereas a young child might group a carrot and a stick in one set and a tomato and a ball in another (paying attention to shape), an older child might be expected to group the two foods and the two artifacts. Moreover, children's ability to sort objects consistently, using whatever basis they choose, also increases with development, as we saw in Chapter 12.

Patricia Greenfield, a collaborator of Bruner's, carried out similar studies with unschooled Wolof children in rural Senegal, West Africa (Greenfield, Reich, & Olver, 1966). Children (ages 6 to 16) saw 10 familiar objects, 4 of which were red, 4 of which were items of clothing, and 4 of which were round (some objects had two or more of these properties). They were told to choose the objects that were "alike" and then to say how they were alike.

The question was "Did children use any of these bases in a systematic way, selecting all and only the red objects, all and only the round objects, or all and only the articles of clothing?" Most of the Wolof children (typically over 65%) selected items on the basis of color, but they showed great improvement with age in their ability to do so systematically. At age 6 or 7, only about 10% systematically selected all and only the four red objects; at age 9, about 30%; and by age 15, close to 100%.

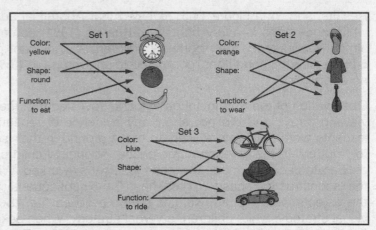

■ Figure 14.6: Stimuli used by Greenfield et al. (1966).

In a second study with schooled and unschooled Wolof children (ages 6 to 13) and unschooled adults, Greenfield et al. (1966) presented sets of three pictured objects. Within each set, two objects shared a color; two, a shape; and two, a function. Figure 14.6 provides some examples. Participants were asked to show which two of the three objects in each set were "most alike" and to explain why.

Greenfield et al. (1966) examined the bases on which children and adults grouped items. Schooling was found to have a very powerful effect. First, unschooled participants had more trouble interpreting the pictures and recognizing the depicted objects, a finding consistent with those reported by Hudson (1960), discussed earlier. Second, children who had attended school were much less likely to use color as a classification basis, and the decrease in preference for color was associated with years of schooling. Conversely, sorting on the basis of form and of function both rose with years of schooling. In fact, the use of either form or function as a basis for sorting was "virtually nonexistent" for unschooled participants (Greenfield et al., p. 295). In general, the authors concluded that "schooling appears to be the single most powerful factor we have found in the stimulation of abstraction" (p. 315).

Sharp and Cole, working with Mayan people in Yucatán, Mexico, wondered whether a preference for grouping by color necessarily precluded other bases for grouping (Cole & Scribner, 1974). They presented participants (children in the first, third, and sixth grades and adolescents with 3 or fewer years of school) with cards depicting various geometric figures that varied in color, shape, and number (such as one circle, two circles). After the participants had sorted the cards, the experimenters asked them to re-sort the cards on another dimension. The results showed, first, that the percentage of participants able to sort consistently on the basis of color, shape, or number rose dramatically with years of schooling. Second, the ability to reclassify also depended on schooling: First graders were almost completely unable to reclassify, and fewer than half of the third graders and adolescents (with 3 or fewer years of schooling) could reclassify. Of the sixth graders, 60% were able to re-sort, using a dimension different from that used in the first sorting.

Irwin and McLaughlin (1970) found another variable that affected performance on this task. They performed a similar experiment, using stimuli like those employed by Sharp and Cole as one condition and stimuli consisting of eight bowls of rice as another. Rice was a very familiar commodity to the study participants, Mano rice farmers in central Liberia. The bowls of rice differed in type of bowl (large or small) and type of rice (polished or not polished).

Results showed that although unschooled adults were not very able to re-sort either the cards or the bowls, all the participants, including the adults, were much more able to sort the rice than the cards quickly. In a later study, Irwin, Schafer, and Feiden (1974) worked with Mano farmers and American undergraduates. Both groups were given geometric shapes on cards (in one condition) and rice (in another condition) to sort. As expected, the Mano had trouble with the shapes but sorted the rice quite easily.

Conversely, the Americans did quite well sorting and re-sorting the shapes but were less adept at noticing all the possible bases for sorting the rice. Taken together with the earlier study, these results suggest that differential exposure to stimuli (presumably as a consequence of cultural setting) can have dramatic effects on even as supposedly basic a cognitive task as sorting.

Hatano et al. (1993) extended this line of investigation when they examined concepts of being biologically alive with children from Japan, Israel, and the United States. Although all three countries, in the authors' words, are "highly developed and scientifically advanced," they differ in the ways their dominant cultures regard the relationship of plants to animals.

> Japanese culture includes a belief that plants are much like human beings. This attitude is represented by the Buddhist idea that even a tree or blade of grass has a mind. Many Japanese adults . . . view plants as having feelings and emotions. Similarly, even inanimate entities are sometimes considered to have minds within Japanese folk psychology. (p. 50)

In contrast, "within Israeli traditions, plants are regarded as very different from humans and other animals in their life status" (p. 50).

Hatano et al. (1993) interviewed kindergartners and second and fourth graders in all three countries, asking them about whether people, other animals (a rabbit and a pigeon), plants (a tree and a tulip), and inanimate things (a stone and a chair) had various properties of animacy, such as whether they were alive; had things such as a heart, bones, or a brain; had sensory capacities to feel cold or pain; and could do things such as grow or die. The authors reported several interesting findings. One set concerned the "rules" that individual children seemed to be using. One rule, called the "people, animals, and plants" rule, meant that a child consistently judged these three things as being alive but inanimate things as not being alive. Another rule, the "people and animals" rule, involved judging only people and animals to be alive (not plants or inanimate things). The "all things" rule corresponded to consistent judgments that all things asked about, including the stone and chair, were alive.

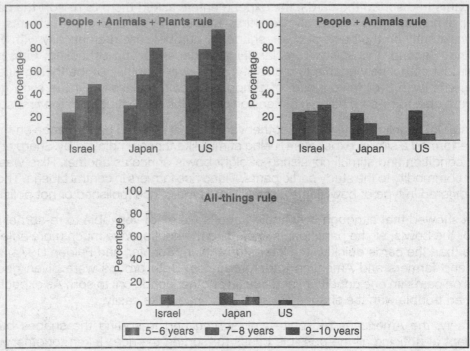

■ Figure 14.7: Percentage of children who adopted each rule regarding the classification of various entities as animate (Hatano, 1993).

Figure 14.7 presents some of the results. More children in the United States used the "people, animals, and plants" rule, and this pattern held for every age group tested. Children from Israel were more likely than children in either other country to deny that plants were alive (that is, to use the "people and animals" rule). The authors speculated that children's television programming in the United States may account for the apparent superiority of biological knowledge among children from the United States. They argued that various nature shows, magazines, and picture books are more common in the United States than in Japan or Israel and that these may be an influential determinant of children's conceptual knowledge, especially among kindergartners. Of course, this is not the only possible explanation, and it warrants further investigation.

Taken together, the studies reviewed in this section suggest that using familiar materials helps to uncover cognitive competence, a principle discussed originally in Chapter 12. Once again, the results described here provide reasons for caution in interpreting cognitive abilities, especially cross-culturally. People tend to believe there is only one (or only one correct) way of processing information in a cognitive task. The results of the several studies described in this chapter remind us that people may have considerably more flexibility in their cognitive processing and that the ways they approach a task depend on the context, the instructions, and even the stimulus materials.

CROSS-CULTURAL STUDIES OF REASONING

We saw in Chapter 11 that formal reasoning involves drawing conclusions based solely on the given information, or premises. Many psychologists and philosophers have assumed that such processing underlies the kinds of reasoning and thinking that occur frequently—that problems such as "All men are mortal; Socrates is a man; (therefore) Socrates is mortal," are basic and therefore rather easy to deal with.

A. R. Luria (1976), a student of the Soviet psychologist Lev Vygotsky, examined how farmers living in Central Asia, some literate and some not, approached such verbal syllogisms. Some of the syllogisms had familiar, practical content but required the participant to apply a familiar principle to a new environment. Here is an example: "Cotton grows where it is hot and humid. England is cold and damp. Can cotton grow there or not?" Another example: "In the Far North, where there is snow, all bears are white. Novaya Zemlya is in the Far North. What color are the bears there?"

The responses to these syllogisms depended on the background of the farmers. Those with no schooling simply refused to deal with the problem, typically responding something like "I don't know; I've seen a black bear, I've never seen any others. . . . Each locality has its own animals; if it's white, they will be white; if it's yellow, they will be yellow," or "How should I know?" (Luria, 1976, pp. 109–110). One respondent, a nonliterate 37-year-old resident of a remote village, summed up the problem: "We always speak only of what we see; we don't talk about what we haven't seen." When the experimenter asked, "But what do my words imply?" and repeated the syllogism, the villager responded,

> Well, it's like this: Our tsar isn't like yours, and yours isn't like ours. Your words can be answered only by someone who was there, and if a person wasn't there he can't say anything on the basis of your words. (p. 109)

Nonliterate villagers faced three limitations, according to Luria (1976). First, they had difficulty accepting (even for the sake of argument) initial premises that contradicted their own experience. Often such premises were dismissed and forgotten. Second, nonliterate villagers refused to treat general premises (such as "In the Far North, all bears are white") as truly general. Instead, they treated these statements as descriptions particular to one person's experience and again often ignored the premise in their reasoning. Third, those lacking literacy tended not to see the various premises as parts of a single problem but rather treated all the premises as independent pieces of information. The farmers who had participated in a literacy program, by contrast, accepted the fact that conclusions could be drawn not just from their own knowledge but from the problem (premises) itself and drew the correct conclusion.

However, looked at from another point of view, these villagers could be seen as reasoning logically, albeit with very different premises. In effect, their argument could be construed as follows: "If I had firsthand knowledge of a black bear, I could answer the question. I don't have firsthand knowledge; therefore, I cannot answer the question." Cole and Scribner (1974) reported similar results with reasoning tasks given to Kpelle tribespeople from Liberia. The following is an example:

EXPERIMENTER (LOCAL KPELLE MAN):	At one time spider went to a feast. He was told to answer this question before he could eat any of the food. The question is: Spider and black deer always eat together. Spider is eating. Is black deer eating?
SUBJECT (VILLAGE ELDER):	Were they in the bush?
EXPERIMENTER:	Yes
SUBJECT	Were they eating together?
EXPERIMENTER:	Spider and black deer always eat together. Spider is eating. Is black deer eating?
SUBJECT:	But I was not there. How can I answer such a question?
EXPERIMENTER:	Can't you answer it? Even if you were not there, you can answer it. (Repeats question)
SUBJECT:	Oh, oh, black deer is eating.
EXPERIMENTER:	What is your reason for saying that black deer is eating?
SUBJECT:	The reason is that black deer always walks about all day eating green leaves in the bush. Then he rests for a while and gets up again to eat. (p. 162)

Notice a few things here. First, the participant avoids answering the question, asserting that his lack of personal knowledge or experience prevents him from knowing the answer. His assumption is that questions can be answered based only on personal, firsthand knowledge. When pressed by the experimenter, the participant comes up with a response but again gives reasons that are based on his knowledge rather than on the premises of the syllogism itself. In Henle's (1962) terms, the participant has "failed to accept the logical task" (p. 370), refusing to draw conclusions based on (or based only on) the premises supplied by the experimenter.

Other participants in this study showed different ways of avoiding the task set for them by the experimenter. Some introduced new premises, usually ones that incorporated the participant's personal knowledge, so that a conclusion could be drawn and justified based on this knowledge. Research by Sylvia Scribner (Cole & Scribner, 1974) suggested that participants appeared to distort the syllogisms in memory, forgetting some premises and altering others, as this example shows:

PROBLEM:	The chief's brother either gave him a goat or he gave him a chicken. The chief's brother did not give him a goat. Did he give him a chicken?
SUBJECT:	Yes. I know he gave it to him.
(Subject is then asked recall the problem):	The chief's brother will give him a goat. If he does not **to** give him a goat, he will give him a chicken.
EXPERIMENTER:	What question did I ask?
SUBJECT:	You asked me, is the chief's brother going to give him a goat?

EXPERIMENTER:	(Reads problem again)
(Subject is asked to recall the problem):	Yes. That is what you told me. The chief's brother will give him a goat. If he does not give him a goat, he will give him a chicken.
EXPERIMENTER:	What question did I ask you?
SUBJECT:	You asked me, the chief's brother will give him a goat. If he does not give him a goat, will he give him a chicken? (p. 165)

Notice here that the participant does not reproduce all the premises in the problem. On each recall, he omits the second premise, that the chief's brother did not give him a goat. Without this premise, the question cannot be answered, perhaps accounting for the fact that the participant continually has difficulty keeping in mind the question asked.

Apparently, then, one difficulty with syllogistic reasoning with nonliterate people is their inability or unwillingness to "remain within problem boundaries" (Cole & Scribner, 1974, p. 168). Instead, people tend to omit, add, or alter premises so that conclusions can be drawn from personal knowledge. It is worth pointing out that such errors are not unique to people from nonliterate cultures. As we saw in Chapter 12, young children have difficulty staying "within bounds" when working on a reasoning task. In addition, the tendency to alter, omit, or add premises to a syllogism occurs with adults in the United States as well, especially on difficult problems, as Henle (1962) argued. This in turn suggests that the reasoning of people from other cultures does seem similar in terms of basic processes and that what is difficult for people in one culture also seems to be difficult for people in others. The data also suggest that schooling or literacy improves people's formal reasoning abilities, something we will explore in greater depth later.

However, recent work by Nisbett and his colleagues has suggested that not all cross-cultural differences in reasoning can be explained in terms of exposure to formal schooling. For example, content effects in formal reasoning tasks were found to be greater for Koreans than for Americans (Norenzayan, Choi, & Nisbett, 2002). Chinese and Korean university students used more intuitive strategies of reasoning compared with European American university students, who relied more on formal reasoning strategies (Norenzayan, Smith, Kim, & Nisbett, 2002). Norenazyan and Nisbett (2000) believe this cross-cultural difference in reasoning may be a consequence of a more general cultural difference in holistic (East Asian) versus analytical processing of information, discussed earlier. Nisbett and Norenzayan (2002) believe that part of the explanation for cross-cultural differences may be industrialization but part may also be the Western traditions of adversarial debate, contractual relationships, and formalization of knowledge.

CROSS-CULTURAL STUDIES OF COUNTING

One of the most fascinating lines of cross-cultural cognitive research centers on the development of mathematical (usually arithmetical) knowledge and problem solving. If you think about it, the development and use of an arithmetical system is critical for many kinds of everyday activities in almost all cultures: buying, selling, making change, keeping inventories, determining relative amounts, and the like. It is of great interest to note that not all cultures have developed the same systems and to examine the ways in which the systems that exist have evolved.

Let us first examine the arithmetic skill of counting. Work by Rochel Gelman and Randy Gallistel (1978) with preschoolers in the United States demonstrated that even very young children in the United States know a great deal about counting. With small numbers (that is, less than about 5), even 2- and 3-year-olds can count the number of items in a set. But what does it mean to count? Gelman and Gallistel offered this surprisingly complicated definition:

> [Counting] involves the coordinated use of several components: noticing the items in an array one after another; pairing each noticed item with a number name; using a conventional list of number names in the conventional order; and recognizing that the last name used represents the numerosity of the array. (p. 73)

Gelman and her colleagues observed the counting behavior of preschoolers and were able to identify several distinct "principles" of counting. These are described in the following list:

1. *The one-one principle.* Each item in a to-be-counted array is "ticked" in such a way that one and only one distinct "tick" is assigned to each item.
2. *The stable-order principle.* The tags (count words) assigned to each item must be chosen in a repeatable order.
3. *The cardinal principle.* When one is counting an array, the final tag represents the number of items in the set.
4. *The abstraction principle.* Any group of items, whether physical or not, whether of the same type or not, can be counted.
5. *The order-irrelevance principle.* The order of enumeration (that is, which item is tagged "1," which "2," and so on) of items in a set does not affect the number of items in the set or the counting procedure.

A child might have some but not all of these principles at any stage of development. Nonetheless, even if her "counting" behavior doesn't exactly match that of an adult, she can be properly described as "counting" if her behavior shows evidence of honoring at least some of the principles. For example, a child aged 2 years and 6 months counted a plate containing three toy mice as follows: "One, two, six!" Asked by the experimenter to count the mice once again, the child happily complied: "Ya, one, two, six!" (Gelman & Gallistel, 1978, p. 91). This child showed clear evidence of respecting the one-one and the stable-order principles and therefore really was counting, even though she used a different count-word sequence than adults do.

Cross-cultural work by Geoffrey Saxe (1981; Saxe & Posner, 1983) provides evidence that counting systems vary in different cultures. Saxe reported studies of children in a remote Oksapmin village in Papua New Guinea. Unlike the base-10 system of numbers used in our culture, Saxe found that the Oksapmin developed a body-part counting system with no base structure. Instead, the Oksapmin label 27 distinct body parts on the hands, arms, shoulders, neck, and head. Just as we count on our fingers, the Oksapmin count not only fingers but arm, shoulder, neck, and head locations, looping back and adding prefixes when they need a number larger than 27. Figure 14.8 illustrates the Oksapmin counting system.

One question that arose for Saxe and others was whether the existence of a "baseless" numeration system, as used by the Oksapmin, would change the understanding of certain numeric relations. For example, is a Piagetian number conservation task (see Chapter

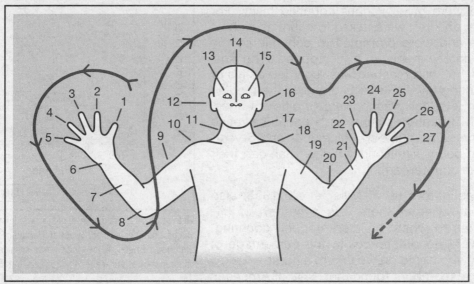

■ Figure 14.8: The Oksapmin counting system. The conventional sequence of body parts used by the Oksapmin, in order of occurrence: (1) tip^na, (2) tipnarip, (3) bumrip, (4) h^tdip, (5) h^th^ta, (6) dopa, (7) besa, (8) kir, (9) tow^t, (10) kata, (11) gwer, (12) nata, (13) kina, (14) aruma, (15) tan-kina, (16) tan-nata, (17) tan-gwer, (18) tan-kata, (19) tan-tow^t, (20) tan-bir, (21) tan-besa, (22) tan-dopa, (23) tan-tip^na, (24) tan-tipnarip, (25) tan-bumrip, (26) tan-h^tdip, (27) tan-h^th^ta.

12 if you need a review), which relies on understanding the concept of "more" or "less" than, much harder for Oksapmin children than for US children? Saxe (1981) found that although Oksapmin children generally develop counting and conservation concepts at later ages, their developmental pattern is quite similar to that of children in the United States. It is interesting that Oksapmin who participate frequently in a newly introduced money economy, which requires more arithmetic computation than does more traditional Oksapmin life, are changing and reorganizing their body-part numeration systems to make computation easier.

A more recent study bears on the issue of the base system and its relation to counting. K. F. Miller, Smith, Zhu, and Zhang (1995) asked preschool children from Champaign-Urbana, Illinois, and Beijing, China, to perform a variety of counting tasks. This comparison was interesting because Chinese and English differ in their naming conventions for numbers. Both have distinct and unpredictable names for the digits 1 through 10. That is, you cannot predict from knowing that the numeral 8 is named *eight* that the numeral 9 will be named *nine;* number names up through 10 are unordered.

However, for the second decade of numbers, the two languages diverge. Chinese uses a consistent base-10 system of naming: the name for 11 in Chinese translates literally to "ten one." In English, however, the names for 11 and 12 (*eleven* and *twelve*) do not make clear the relationship of these numbers to the numbers 1 and 2. After the number 20, the two languages name numbers in similar ways, although English throws in a few more twists than Chinese does (making 20 *twenty,* for instance). This led the investigators to predict that Chinese preschoolers would have an easier time learning to count, especially for numbers in the teens.

Children were given various counting tasks. For example, children were asked to count as high as possible and were prompted to continue by the experimenter whenever they stopped. The final number the child reached was regarded as his or her counting level. Figure 14.9 shows the median counting level for preschoolers of different ages. Although 3-year-olds from both countries reach about the same number, Chinese 4- and 5-year-olds can count significantly higher than can their American counterparts.

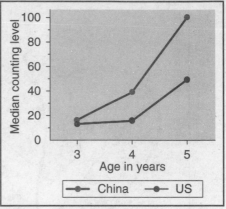

■ Figure 14.9: Median level of abstract counting (highest number reached) by age and language. Significant differences favoring Chinese-speaking children were found at ages 4 and 5 years, but not at age 3.

The investigators (K. F. Miller et al., 1995) also looked at whether there was a pattern of difference as to where children stopped counting. There were no differences in the percentage of children who could only count to a number below 10: The researchers found that 94% of American children and 92% of Chinese children all could count to this number. However, only 48% of American preschoolers could count to 20, in comparison with 74% of the Chinese preschoolers, a striking difference. This difference did not grow larger in succeeding decades, suggesting that counting breaks down for US children at the place where the languages differ in making clear the base-10 nature of the number system.

K. F. Miller et al. (1995) argues that such differences play a role in explaining why school-age children in China and Japan have been shown to outperform their same-age counterparts in the United States. Although many shortcomings in arithmetic instruction have been documented in the United States compared with that in some Asian countries (Stevenson et al., 1990), Miller et al. assert that some of the problem traces back, at least in part, to fundamental differences in understanding the base-10 nature of the number system at the time when children enter school.

Recent cross-cultural work on numerical cognition examines how people from different cultures map numbers onto a "mental number line"—an internal representation of the way in which different numbers relate to one another, where shorter distances between two numbers depict a closer numerical relationship. Debates are ongoing as to whether or not the specifics of the mental representation are culturally relative or universal (Bender, 2011; Nuñez, 2011).

Throughout this section, we have seen examples of the ways in which cognitive tasks and performance can differ across different cultures. We have also seen that one important variable affecting a number of different cognitive tasks is schooling. In the next section, we will examine the effects of this variable more closely, trying to isolate just what aspects of schooling produce the effect.

EFFECTS OF SCHOOLING AND LITERACY

What is it about schooling that apparently produces such widespread changes in cognition? Is it something about the curriculum specifically, or do the changes result from a more global aspect of the context of going to school? These questions are just beginning to be addressed in the cross-cultural study of cognition.

One candidate for the source of schooling effects is **literacy**, the ability to read and write. Many psychological, linguistic, and anthropological scholars believe that literacy has profound effects on society (Scribner & Cole, 1981). One assertion is that literacy changes thought in fundamental ways. Scholars dating back to Plato and Socrates have wondered whether written language promotes logical and abstract thinking in a way that oral language does not and cannot (Scribner & Cole). Goody and Watt (1968) argued, for instance, that disciplines such as history and logic are impossible without written language. Writing a text allows a permanency that oral language does not. This permanency allows people to carry on certain processes that might be impossible otherwise—for example, comparing two sentences to look for implications or inconsistencies, or examining the internal structure or syntax of a sentence.

Lev Vygotsky, a noted Marxist psychologist, argued, as Marx had, that a human being's "nature" was actually the product of his or her interaction with the environment (Vygotsky, 1986). Thus, cognitive processes and capabilities are not simply the result of our biological heritage but rather the result of human–environment interaction, which changes and shapes not only the environment but also the nature of our cognition (Scribner & Cole, 1981).

At any given time, the tools available for a task change the ways in which the task is carried out. For example, the invention and availability of word-processing software has changed the ways in which many professors and college students write papers. The World Wide Web has changed the way people acquire and search for information. Vygotsky thought the same principle applied to the existence of written language: It significantly transformed intellectual processes.

The Laboratory of Comparative Human Cognition (1983) described Vygotskian principles of how cultures affect cognition and cognitive development. First, cultures "arrange for the occurrence or non-occurrence" (p. 335) of particular problems and problem-solving environments. For example, whether one needs to learn to memorize prayers or pledges depends on whether the culture presents tasks or occasions for which they are recited from memory. If the culture does not require such memorization, then people within that culture have less need to develop strategies for and approaches to this task.

Second, the culture determines the frequency with which problems and practices occur. Does recitation take place daily? Weekly? Monthly? Frequency will no doubt affect how often practice with the tasks occurs.

Third, cultures determine which events go together. Does memorization occur with other tasks, such as reading or measuring? It seems likely that the co-occurrence of two tasks provides a different context for each and may therefore affect the way each is carried out.

Last, cultures "regulate the level of difficulty" of tasks within contexts (Laboratory of Comparative Human Cognition, 1983, p. 335). Cultures determine how younger members may approach a memorization task, for example. Cultures also figure out ways of establishing a graded series of tasks that culminate in final mastery. A 4-year-old, for example, may start out learning simple rhymes and gradually work up to long prayers or epic poems. The culture determines the path from first to final achievement.

Recall discussion of the work of Alexander Luria (a student of Vygotsky), who worked with farmers in Uzbekistan, a remote part of the former Soviet Union, during the 1930s (Luria,

1976). During that time, collectivization of farming and industrialization were being introduced, and the region experienced profound socioeconomic changes. As part of this social and economic revolution, some of the residents attended literacy programs. Luria compared, on a variety of perceptual, reasoning, and classification tasks, the performance of people who had and had not participated in a literacy program. He found consistent group differences: Nonliterate people were most likely to respond to tasks in a concrete, perceptual, and context-bound manner; the schooled group showed greater ability or propensity to deal with materials more abstractly and conceptually. The schooled group could reason from premises and draw inferences based on something other than their own experience.

One problem in interpreting Luria's (1976) findings is that two related but conceptually independent factors were confounded: literacy and schooling. As Scribner and Cole (1981) noted, schooling and literacy are often related but are not synonymous. In Luria's research, the participants who were literate were also those who had attended schools; the nonliterate participants were unschooled.

What effects might schooling have on cognition? First of all, it is worth noting the somewhat bizarre demands that school itself places on students. School is one of the few places where one person (the teacher) asks other people (the students) to answer questions that she or he already knows the answer to. Think how incongruous this situation would be in other contexts. Imagine someone walking up to you to ask directions to the library. Being a local resident, you know the way and provide a set of directions, such as "Go two blocks to the light, take a right, then take your first left, go halfway down the block, and you'll see it." Next, your conversation partner tells you your directions are faulty, that there is a simpler way to go. Would you consider this conversation "normal" or "typical"? Only in schoollike situations can a teacher pose questions to assess students' knowledge rather than to obtain information. This somewhat removes the school context from everyday life.

School differs from everyday contexts in a number of other respects. The subjects taught often make little contact with everyday life; students learning about, say, geography or history may never have the chance to experience the phenomena being discussed. Some of the subjects taught are abstract (such as arithmetic and geometry) and make few direct appearances in day-to-day living.

The motivation to complete a task in school—for example, learning a spelling list—is not intrinsic to the task itself in the way that motivation is for an everyday task—for example, learning to ride a bike. In the latter case, you learn because the task itself is important to you; in the former case, students often learn because the teacher or parent tells them to. Bruner (1966) has argued that schooling therefore provides practice in thinking about abstract topics in a decontextualized way—that is, removed from the present context of here and now.

Scribner and Cole (1981) carried out a series of studies to disentangle the effects of literacy from the effects of schooling. They worked with the Vai people in Liberia, West Africa, during the 1970s. The Vai are an interesting people to study because they invented their own writing system, called Vai script, that they use for many commercial and personal transactions. Vai script is taught not in school but in the home. Although only about 7% of the entire population was literate in Vai script at the time of the study, it was the most common written language known by adult males: 20% were literate in Vai script; 16% in Arabic (acquired mostly in the context of learning the Qur'an); and 6% in English, the official language of schools and government.

Interviews were held with 650 people, all aged 15 or older. In addition to completing a lengthy autobiographical questionnaire (regarding demographic information, schooling and literacy status, family schooling and literacy status, occupation, and the like), all respondents participated in an hour-long session in which various cognitive tasks were administered. Included in these were sorting tasks (stimuli used included both geometric figures and familiar objects), memory tasks (such as recalling the names of objects used in the sorting tasks), a logic task (presenting syllogisms, such as those described earlier), and a task of linguistic awareness (such as being asked whether the names of the objects "sun" and "moon" could be switched and what the consequences of such a switch would be). For some tasks, respondents were asked to provide verbal explanations, which were later scored.

The participants were divided into seven groups. The first six included only men 15 and older: nonliterate men; men who were literate in Vai script only; men literate in Arabic only; men literate in both Arabic and Vai; men who had attended some school and were literate in English, Arabic, and Vai; and men who had attended 10 years or more of school. The seventh group consisted of nonliterate women 15 and older (the data from 11 literate Vai women were not reported, presumably because the women were quite atypical in their literacy).

The general design called for comparisons of nonliterates, Vai script literates, and schooled groups. The results, some of which are summarized in Table 14.3, were surprising. For most of the cognitive tasks, there were only scattered and small effects of literacy per se. Scribner and Cole (1981) concluded that unschooled literacy (such as acquisition of Vai script literacy in the home) does not produce the general cognitive effects previously reported by Luria (1976) and others.

Schooling, in contrast, did produce a number of effects. The most evident effect was that schooling, especially with English instruction, increased the ability to provide verbal explanations and justifications. The participants who had attended school were much

■ Table 14.3: Results of Scribner and Cole (1981)

Tasks and Measures	Nonliterate Men	Vai Script Monoliterate	Arabic Monoliterate	Vai Arabic Biliterate	English Schooled	Grade 10+	Nonliterate Women
Geometric sorting (number dimensions sorted out of 3)	1.6	2.0	2.0	1.9	1.7	1.9	1.7
Verbal explanation (max score = 12)	5.3	5.1	5.8	5.6	5.6	9.3	4.9
Classification (max score = 6)	3.4	3.5	3.0	3.5	3.8	3.9	3.4
Verbal explanation (max score = 42)	31.5	31.2	29.0	29.5	32.5	34.6	30.5
Memory (number recalled, max = 24)	16.2	16.0	16.2	16.2	17.1	14.9	16.5
Logic (number correct, max = 6)	1.6	1.3	1.7	1.5	3.0	3.9	1.7
Theoretic explanations (max = 10)	6.1	5.7	6.2	5.7	7.6	7.9	6.2
Language objectivity (max = 3)	.7	.5	.9	1.2	1.3	1.3	.7

better able to provide coherent explanations of their answers than those who hadn't attended school. The group differences in explanations were sometimes evident even when the schooled and unschooled groups did not differ in performance. In other words, schooling affected not so much which responses were chosen but rather the skill with which respondents could explain and justify their choices.

Scribner and Cole (1981) did discover literacy effects on some specific tasks, however. Most had to do with knowledge of language in one form or another. For example, literate participants were more likely to give good explanations of what makes grammatical sentences in Vai. They also found it easier to learn to "read" other scripts, modeled after children's rebus puzzles (see Figure 14.10 for an example of a rebus puzzle). Scribner and Cole used these principles to invent Vai rebuses and taught these puzzles to both Vai-literate (unschooled) and nonliterate villagers. Literate villagers learned the task much more easily and significantly outperformed the nonliterate villagers.

■ Figure 14.10: Example of a rebus puzzle. Translation: In flower beds, watch out for bees.

What can we make of Scribner and Cole's (1981) findings? Contrary to some conventional wisdom, their studies do not support the idea that either literacy or schooling has profound effects on the ways in which cognitive processes operate. Although on some tasks, schooled and/or literate participants outperformed unschooled, nonliterate participants, the latter group often performed just as well, or only slightly worse, than the former groups. However, both literacy and schooling do apparently affect the ways in which some cognitive tasks are carried out, at least in some circumstances. So apparently both schooling and literacy make a difference to cognition, at least sometimes.

Reviewing all their findings, Scribner and Cole (1981) developed a "practice account of literacy" as a framework for understanding the experimental results. By *practice,* they refer to "a recurrent, goal-directed sequence of activities using a particular technology and particular systems of knowledge" (p. 236). These authors examined the knowledge and skills required for literacy and the knowledge and skills that the practice of literacy enables. What one does to become literate and what one does when one practices his or her literacy (say, by reading or writing a letter) strengthen some very specific skills. Scribner and Cole asserted that literacy does not promote broad, general cognitive changes but rather more localized and task-specific contextualized ones.

The same kind of argument might account for the effects of schooling. Recall that schooled Vai outperformed unschooled Vai only on tasks requiring verbal explanations. Scribner and Cole (1981) pointed to the "practice" of schooling, particularly English schooling, as a potent cause. Schools are places where a premium is placed on the ability to offer an articulate set of reasons for one's responses and to figure out ways to approach and master tasks removed from practical experience (Bruner, 1966). No wonder, then, that those with the most experience in this setting show the most ability to apply the specific skills this setting promotes in other circumstances.

To summarize, Scribner and Cole (1981) argued that cognitive skills are often context bound. From their perspective, it seemed unlikely that many broad cognitive abilities or skills, such as "thinking" or "categorization," exist that one or a few manipulations can affect or improve. Instead, these authors would argue that cognition is situated in, or intimately bound to, the conditions in which it naturally occurs. One's culture and one's everyday surroundings and tasks establish both boundaries and possibilities for the cognitive tasks that are practiced and therefore strengthened. Context and culture affect, and are affected by, cognition.

SITUATED COGNITION IN EVERYDAY SETTINGS

Situated cognition is not simply a phenomenon that occurs in foreign, distant cultures (B. G. Wilson & Myers, 2000). Cultural contexts affect cognition right here at home, as seen in some studies conducted in the workplace. Sylvia Scribner's work before her death included field studies in the United States at an industrial milk-processing plant (a "dairy") in which she investigated on-the-job cognition, or what she called "working intelligence" (Scribner, 1984, p. 9). In particular, she drew a distinction between practical and theoretical thought (Scribner, 1986). The latter is the kind of thinking demanded in many school activities: thinking divorced from a meaningful context, carried out on a task of perhaps limited interest, and performed for its own sake. Practical thought, by contrast, is more familiar and involves thinking "embedded in the larger purposive activities of daily life . . . [that] functions to achieve the goals of those activities" (p. 15). Examples include figuring out a supermarket "best buy" or diagnosing the cause of a machinery malfunction.

The site of Scribner's (1984) field studies employed 300 people in both white- and blue-collar positions. Certain blue-collar tasks were selected for study. These included product assembly (a warehouse job), inventory, and pricing delivery tickets. Scribner and associates began by observing people performing these jobs under normal working conditions, then constructed and presented workers with experimental simulations of these tasks.

From her earlier cross-cultural research, Scribner (1984) believed that cognitive skills are dependent on "socially organized experiences" (p. 10). In other words, the way in which a cognitive task is approached varies according to the environment and the context. She found the same sorts of patterns emerging in the dairy: Even a task as seemingly basic as mental calculation was accomplished in different ways by the same people in different circumstances.

The product assemblers (or preloaders, as they are sometimes called) provide a concrete example. Their job consists mainly of putting together specified quantities of various products and getting them ready to be loaded onto trucks. Scribner (1984) described the working conditions in more detail:

> Product assembly is a warehouse job. It is classified as unskilled manual labor and is one of the lowest paying jobs in the dairy. The perishable nature of dairy products requires that warehouse temperature be maintained at 38 degrees Fahrenheit; accordingly, the warehouse is, and is referred to as, an icebox.
>
> During the day, thousands of cases of milk products (e.g., skim milk, chocolate milk) and fruit drinks are moved on conveyor belts from the plant filling machines into the icebox, where they are stacked in

designated areas along with many other dairy products (e.g., yogurt, cottage cheese). Preloaders arrive at the icebox at 6 p.m. Awaiting them is a sheaf of route delivery orders, called load-out order forms. Each form lists the products and their amounts that a wholesale driver has ordered for his next day's delivery. The preloader's task is to locate each product. Using a long metal "hook," he pulls the required number of cases and partial cases of that product and transports them to a common assembly area near a moving track that circles the icebox.

    When all the items of a given truck order are assembled, they are pulled onto the track and carried past a checkpoint to the loading platform. (pp. 18–19)

Scribner (1984) noticed an interesting problem that preloaders faced in their jobs. Truck drivers wrote orders that expressed quantities of items in terms of one set of units (for example, quarts of milk, half-pints of chocolate milk), but fluid products in the warehouse were stored in cases, not in units. Cases of all products were the same size but contained a different number of units, depending on the product. So a full case could contain 4 gallon units, 9 half-gallon units, 16 quart units, 32 pint units, or 48 half-pint units.

Load-out forms were created by computer by converting drivers' orders into cases. So a particular driver's request for 4 gallons of fruit juice would be translated into one case. Often a driver's request did not divide evenly into number of cases. For example, if a driver requested 5 gallons of milk, that would translate into one case plus one unit. The load-out forms followed the following convention: If the number of "leftover" units was equal to half a case or less, the order was expressed as the number of cases plus the number of units (as in the 5-gallon example). If the number of "leftover" units was more than half a case, the number was expressed as the number of cases minus the number of units. So in the case of quarts (which come 16 to a case), if a driver ordered 30 quarts of chocolate milk, the load-out form would read 2 (cases = 32 quarts) – 2 (quarts)—that is, 32 – 2 = 30. (Warning: This system is not intuitive, so work through this example carefully yourself.)

Scribner's (1984) question was how preloaders dealt with mixed numbers, such as 3 + 1 or 7 – 5, in assembling orders. You might think such a question would be answered in a fairly obvious way: A preloader with an order for 1 – 6 would simply grab 1 case and remove 6 units from it. But this is not what happened.

In fact, the preloaders handled the very same problem (that is, 1 – 6) in several different ways. Sometimes they filled the order in the "obvious" way just described. Other times, they mentally "rewrote" the order and used nearby partially filled cases to reduce the actual number of units that had to be moved. For example, when a nearby partially filled case of quarts (remember, 16 quarts to the case) contained 14 quarts, the preloader simply removed 4 (1 case – 6 quarts = 10 quarts; 14 quarts – 4 quarts = 10 quarts). In another situation, a partially filled case contained 8 quarts, and the preloader simply added 2 more.

Scribner (1984, 1986) found that although the same problem was solved in different ways, the solution always honored the following rule: Satisfy the order with the least number of moves—that is, the least number of transfers of product units. Even when the "saving" of labor was small (for example, saving one transfer in an order totaling 500 units), experienced preloaders rapidly and almost automatically calculated and followed the most efficient solution. The mental calculations required are impressive because of both their rapidity and accuracy. Errors were rare. And most of the time, the workers were assembling a group of orders at the same time, thus most certainly increasing the cognitive demands of their job.

It also turned out that on-the-job training was necessary to develop this cognitive flexibility. "Novice" preloaders—that is, other workers in the dairy and a comparison group of ninth graders—were much less efficient and skilled, relative to the preloaders, at finding the optimal solution. Scribner (1984) constructed a simulation task with various orders and administered it to other dairy workers and to a group of ninth-grade students. When the optimal solution required some mental transformation of the order, preloaders found it about 72% of the time; inventory people (many of whom had some experience working as a preloader), 65%; clerks at the dairy (with little if any product assembly experience), 47%; and ninth graders, 25%. Students in particular tended to be very "algorithmic" and "literal" in their approaches to problems, solving each problem in the same way and in the way specified on the load-out form even when much easier strategies (that required some mental transformations) were available.

Scribner (1986) found similar examples of cognitive flexibility in other experienced workers working at other jobs. She concluded that although formal problem solving—such as that required in school, on tests, and in many cognitive psychology experiments—requires or encourages set approaches and fixed rules, practical thinking does not. Instead, practical thinking "frequently hinges on an apt formulation or redefinition of the initial problem" (p. 21). Practical problem solving is flexible and requires different approaches to the "same" problem, with each approach tailored to the immediate context. Note the difference between this kind of thinking and "academic" thinking, which typically requires or at least encourages all instances of a problem to be solved in the same way.

Similar findings were reported in another work setting, a grocery store (Lave et al., 1984). Although not generally part of a paying job, grocery shopping is an activity that must be completed frequently to maintain a family. Lave and associates used the grocery store as a setting for studies of cognitive processing in everyday life. These authors studied 25 grocery shoppers. Participants represented a range of socioeconomic statuses and had varying educational backgrounds. Researchers accompanied shoppers throughout shopping trips and recorded conversations they had with shoppers.

Typical supermarkets contain around 7,000 distinct items, and typical shoppers purchase about 50 weekly (Lave et al., 1984). Obviously, then, the number of potential decisions is quite large. How does the typical shopper manage to finish in about 1 hour? Again, the answer has to do with cognitive flexibility and adapting solutions to specific features of the problem.

One shopper, for example, found a package of cheese marked with a price that the shopper considered surprisingly high. To determine whether the price was correct, he found another package of cheese in the bin that weighed approximately the same amount. He then compared the prices on the two packages and indeed found them discrepant. Which one had the error? To find out, he compared these two packages to others in the bin, determining that the first one was, in fact, priced incorrectly. Notice here a "saving" in amount of mental effort: Although he could have calculated the price per ounce of each package, such calculations are mentally demanding and subject to error. Instead, he found an alternative way of solving the problem that was both more easily accomplished and less likely to be inaccurate.

Lave et al. (1984) were specifically interested in the arithmetic people used in grocery stores. The researchers found that people's in-store arithmetic was virtually flawless—accuracy was 98%, compared with an average accuracy of 59% that the same people had on school-like arithmetic tests. Why the discrepancy? In part, people often invented ways of circumventing traditional calculations, as in the example just given. Again, we see that the skills learned in school may be used outside the classroom in much more creative, flexible, and effective ways.

Ceci and Roazzi (1994) described similar findings reported by Carraher and associates with Brazilian children who worked as street vendors. When given problems embedded in real-life situations (for example, "If a large coconut costs 76 cruzeiros, and a small one costs 50, how much do the two cost together?"), children's performance averaged 98% correct. When the same problem was posed as a formal test question ("How much is 76 + 50?"), performance averaged only 37% correct.

Again, the point of much of the work described in this chapter is to show that much of what we take to be "the" way cognition works is really "a" way cognition works in a particular setting. Cognitive processes do not always work the same way, and some cognitive processes we may regard as fundamental (for example, processes involved in perception or memory or thinking) may change radically, even in adults. Nisbett and Norenzayan (2002) remind us that "cultural practices and cognitive processes constitute one another. Cultural practices encourage and sustain certain kinds of cognitive processes, which then perpetuate the cultural practices" (p. 562).

Summary

1. Cross-cultural cognitive research has shown that the ways in which a cognitive task is approached and executed need not be exactly the same for all people at all times. Some tasks, because they are familiar, are easier, at least in the way expected by a cognitive psychologist from mainstream US culture. As Wober (1969) put it, too often the use of cognitive tasks developed in one culture to study the cognition of people from another culture simply measures "How well can they do our tricks?" (p. 488). People from the second culture may perform poorly on the test but still have the cognitive capacities the test was designed to measure.

2. People from different cultures find ways of solving the cognitive (and other) challenges that confront them. A given environment, including a cultural one, strengthens certain skills, strategies, and approaches at the expense of others. This in turn makes certain tasks easier and seemingly more "natural" and others harder.

3. As noted earlier, cognition is often quite flexible. Practice with any task typically speeds execution and enables greater accuracy. This point raises another, however: Practice often affects the way a task is done. This suggests that researchers need to assess not only the familiarity of a task to a person from a given culture but also the person's specific level of practice with that (or a similar) task.

4. Formal schooling changes some, although certainly not all, important aspects of cognitive processing. In particular, schooling affects one's ability to deal with more "abstract" materials; to rely less heavily on contextual, immediate cues from the surrounding environment; and to explain one's responses and thinking more clearly. Schooling also helps people figure out how to approach novel tasks, especially in planning and structuring. All in all, schooling apparently helps

people "step back" from their everyday routine and promotes their thinking from different points of view. And, as the Laboratory of Comparative Human Cognition (1983) pointed out, school prepares people especially well to participate in cognitive psychology experiments!

5. Interestingly, basic academic skills turn out not to be entirely optimal for meeting everyday cognitive challenges. Practice with a specific task, whether grocery shopping or conducting inventory, apparently leads to the invention of clever shortcuts that reduce the effort (mental or physical) required and increase accuracy. Although schools may insist that students approach all calculation problems in similar ways, research is beginning to suggest that in the "real world," the approaches taken to a problem vary with the immediate context.

6. A general and important point is that models of a cognitive process often presume, implicitly, that the task in question is universally important and familiar, an assumption that researchers have recently questioned. Similarly, existing cognitive models often assume that the same cognitive procedures are used the same way for all versions of a problem, although new research challenges this belief. Dropping these assumptions will no doubt make the job of cognitive researchers much more difficult. In the long run, however, the new models will be more accurate and more complete.

Review Questions

1. What does it mean to assert that a particular cognitive capacity or skill is culturally relative or culturally universal? How do the assertions differ?

2. Describe Hudson's studies of pictorial perception and discuss their implications.

3. Kearins concluded that culture can impose "environmental pressure" on certain cognitive skills. Discuss this conclusion with respect to the empirical findings of Kearins or of others.

4. Schooling appears to help cognitive performance, especially on tasks such as formal reasoning. Explain why this might be so.

5. Schooling and literacy are distinct factors that appear to affect cognitive performance differently. Describe one or two of the differences and speculate on reasons for the difference(s).

6. How are Scribner's studies of dairy workers consistent with, and inconsistent with, cross-cultural studies of cognition?

Key Terms

cultural relativism	culture	schooling
cultural universality	literacy	situated cognition

GLOSSARY

ablation: Removal of cells or tissues, often through surgical means.

adaptive control of thought (ACT) model of memory: A theory of memory developed by John Anderson that specifies a networked memory comprised of working memory, declarative memory, and procedural memory.

affordance: A perceptual property of objects, places, and events that makes clear what actions or behaviors on the part of the perceiver are permitted in interaction with the object, place, or event.

amnesia: *See* **anterograde amnesia** and **retrograde amnesia**.

amygdala: An area of brain tissue with extensive connections to the olfactory system and hypothalamus, thought to be involved in mood, feeling, instinct, and short-term memory.

analogical reasoning: Drawing inductive inferences that specify a fourth (D) term that projects a relationship found between the first two (A and B) terms onto the third (C) term of the analogy, in problems of the form A is to B and C is to D.

analytic processing: A mode of processing information in which attention is paid to specific dimensions, features, or parts of stimuli rather than to their overall or global aspects.

anchoring: A decision-making heuristic in which final estimates are heavily influenced by initial value estimates.

anterograde amnesia: Lack of memory for events that occur after a brain injury. Contrast with **retrograde amnesia**.

aphasia: A disorder of language, thought to have neurological causes, in which either language production or language reception or both are disrupted.

artifact: *See* **artifact concept**.

artifact concept: Concept pertaining to manufactured or human-designed objects.

artificial intelligence: A branch of computer science concerned with creating computers that mimic human performance on cognitive tasks.

association: A connection or link between two units or elements.

attention: Cognitive resources, mental effort, or concentration devoted to a cognitive process.

attention hypothesis of automatization: The proposal that attention is needed during the learning phase of a new task.

attentional capture: A phenomenon in which certain stimuli seem to "pop out" and require a person to shift cognitive resources automatically to them.

attenuation theory: A model of attention in which unattended perceptual events are transmitted in weakened form but not blocked completely before being processed for meaning.

autobiographical memory: Memory for events and other information from one's own life.

automatic processing: The carrying out of a cognitive task with minimal resources. Typically, automatic processing occurs without intention, interferes minimally with other cognitive tasks, and may not involve conscious awareness.

availability heuristic: A strategy in which one estimates the frequency or probability of an event by the ease with which mental operations, such as retrieval of examples or construction of examples, can be carried out.

backtracking: A problem-solving technique that involves keeping track of where in the solving process assumptions are made so that they may later be changed.

basic level of categorization: A hypothesized type of concept thought to be at a psychologically fundamental level of abstraction.

behaviorism: A school of psychology that seeks to define psychological research in terms of observable measures, emphasizing the scientific study of behavior.

believability effect: The tendency to draw or accept conclusions from premises when the content of the conclusion makes intuitive sense, regardless of the logical necessity.

between-subjects design: A research paradigm in which different experimental participants participate in different experimental conditions.

bias: A tendency to think in a certain way or to follow certain procedures regardless of the facts of the matter.

bottom-up process: Cognitive (usually perceptual) process guided by environmental input. Also called *data-driven process.*

brain imaging: The construction of pictures of the anatomy and functioning of intact brains through such techniques as computerized axial tomography (CAT, or CT), positron emission tomography (PET), magnetic resonance imaging (MRI), or functional magnetic resonance imaging (fMRI).

Broca's aphasia: Also called *expressive* or *motor aphasia;* symptoms of this organic disorder include difficulty in speaking, using grammar, and finding appropriate words.

calibration curve: A plot of accuracy against confidence judgments. The more the curve approaches a 45-degree line, the better the "calibration" or "fit" between the two.

capacity: The sum total of cognitive resources available at any given time.

CAT scan: *See* **computerized axial tomography scan**.

categorical perception: The classification of sounds that vary on an acoustic dimension continuously into discrete categories.

categorical syllogism: *See* **syllogistic reasoning**.

categorization: The organization of information into coherent, meaningful groups.

category: A grouping of items sharing one or more similarities.

central executive (of WM): The proposed component of working memory (WM) responsible for directing the flow of information and selecting what information to work with.

cerebellum: Part of the brain that controls balance and muscular coordination.

cerebral cortex: The surface of the cerebrum, the largest structure of the brain, which contains both sensory and motor nerve cell bodies.

change blindness: The inability to detect changes to an object or scene, especially when given different views of that object or scene.

characteristic feature: A feature that is typically, though not always, a part of an object or concept.

chunking: The formation of individual units of information into larger units. This is often used as a means of overcoming short-term memory limitations.

classical view of concepts: The idea that all examples or instances of a concept share fundamental characteristics or features.

clinical interview: A research paradigm in which an investigator begins by asking participants a series of open-ended questions but follows up on the responses with specific questions that have been prepared in advance.

coding: The form in which information is mentally or internally represented.

cognitive abilities: Sources of individual differences in performance on cognitive tasks, including factors such as intelligence, memory capacities, attentional focus, knowledge base, strategies, and processing speed.

cognitive economy: A principle of hierarchical semantic networks such that properties and facts about a node are stored at the highest level possible. For example, the fact "is alive" would be stored with the node for "animal" rather than stored with each node under animal, such as "dog," "cat," and the like.

cognitive illusions: The systematic biases and errors in human decision making.

cognitive neuropsychology: A school of psychology that investigates the cognitive abilities and deficits of people with damaged or otherwise unusual brain structures.

cognitive overload: Breakdown of cognitive processing that occurs when the available information exceeds processing capacity.

cognitive revolution: A movement in psychology that culminated after World War II, characterized by a belief in the empirical accessibility of mental states and events.

cognitive science: An interdisciplinary field drawing on research from cognitive psychology, computer science, philosophy, linguistics, neuroscience, and anthropology. The central issues addressed involve the nature of mind and cognition and how information is acquired, stored, and represented.

cognitive style: A habitual and/or preferred means of approaching cognitive tasks.

cognitive tempo: A cognitive style dimension along which people differ in terms of their ability to respond slowly and carefully as opposed to quickly and with errors.

computer metaphor: The basis for the information-processing view of the brain. Different types of psychological processes are thought to be analogous to the workings of a computer processor.

computerized axial tomography (CAT, or CT) scan: An imaging technique in which a highly focused beam of X-rays is passed through the body from many different angles. Differing density of the organs of the body result in different deflections of the X-rays, which allows visualization of the organ. Also called *X-ray computed tomography scan.*

concept: A mental representation of a category.

conceptually driven process: *See* **top-down process**.

concrete operations stage: A Piagetian stage of middle childhood marked by the acquisition of certain mental operations such as conservation, classification, and seriation.

configural superiority effect (CSE): A perceptual phenomenon in which perception of an "odd stimulus out" is faster in a composite stimulus display than in a base stimulus display with fewer stimuli.

confirmation bias: A tendency to seek only information consistent with one's hypothesis.

connected knowing: An approach to knowledge and learning emphasizing the relevance of context and personal experience

connectionism: An approach to cognition emphasizing parallel processing of information through immense networks of interconnected nodes. Models developed in the connectionist tradition are sometimes declared to share certain similarities with the way collections of neurons operate in the brain; hence, some connectionist models are referred to as *neural networks.*

constructivist approach to perception: An understanding of perception as a process requiring the active construction of subjective mental representations not only from perceptual information but also from long-term memory.

content effect: Performance variability on reasoning tasks that require identical kinds of formal reasoning but are dissimilar in superficial content.

context effect: The effect on a cognitive process (for example, perception) of the information surrounding the target object or event. Sometimes called *expectation effect* because the context is thought to set up certain expectations in the mind of the cognitive processor.

contradiction: A statement that is false by definition of its form (for example, "A and not-A are both true").

controlled observation: A research paradigm in which an observer standardizes the conditions of observation for all participants, often introducing specific manipulations and recording responses.

controlled processing: The carrying out of a cognitive task with a deliberate allocation of cognitive resources. Typically, controlled processing occurs on difficult and/or unfamiliar tasks requiring attention and is under conscious control.

corpus callosum: The large neural structure containing fibers that connect the right and left cerebral hemispheres.

creativity: Cognitive processes that employ appropriate novelty; originality that suits some purpose.

critical thinking: A type of thinking that involves careful examination of assumptions and evidence and that is purposeful and deliberate.

cue overload: A principle of memory that states a retrieval cue will be most effective when it is highly distinctive and not related to any other target memories.

cultural relativism: A belief that cognitive practices, beliefs, competences, and capacities differ from culture to culture, depending on the tasks and contexts specific to a culture.

cultural universality: A belief that cognitive practices, beliefs, competences, and capacities do not differ from culture to culture but are common to humankind.

culture: The attitudes, traditions, artifacts, and behaviors that characterize a group of people.

data-driven process: *See* **bottom-up process**.

decay: A hypothesized process of forgetting in which material is thought to erode, break apart, or otherwise disintegrate or fade.

decision making: The process(es) by which an individual selects one course of action from among alternatives.

decision structuring: The process(es) by which an individual establishes the criteria and options for consideration.

declarative memory: A memory system thought to contain knowledge, facts, information, ideas, or anything that can be recalled and described in words, pictures, or symbols.

deductive reasoning: Drawing conclusions from only the given premises.

deductive validity: A property of some logical arguments such that it is impossible for the premises to be true and the conclusion(s) to be false.

defining feature: A feature that is necessarily a part of an object or concept. Also called a *necessary feature.*

demand characteristic: A property of certain tasks such that an experimental subject's behavior or responses are "cued" by the task itself.

descriptive models of thinking: Models that depict the processes people actually use in making decisions or solving problems.

dichotic listening task: A task in which a person hears two or more different, specially recorded messages over earphones and is asked to attend to one of them.

direct perception: A theory of perception, proposed by James J. Gibson, holding that information in the world is "picked up on" by the cognitive processor without much construction of internal representations or inferences. The emphasis is on direct acquisition of information.

distal stimulus: An object, event, or pattern as it exists in the world. Contrast with **proximal stimulus**.

divided attention: The ways in which a cognitive processor allocates cognitive resources to two or more tasks that are carried out simultaneously.

dual-coding hypothesis: The assertion that long-term memory can code information in two distinct ways, verbally and visually, and that items coded both ways (for example, pictures or concrete words) are more easily recalled than items coded in only one way (for example, abstract words).

dual-task performance: An experimental paradigm involving presentation of two tasks for a person to work on simultaneously.

echo: A sensory memory for auditory stimuli.

ecological approach: An approach to the study of cognition emphasizing the natural contexts or settings in which cognitive activities occur and the influences such settings have on the ways in which cognitive activities are acquired, practiced, and executed.

ecological validity: A property of research such that the focus of study is something that occurs naturally outside an experimental laboratory.

EEG: *See* **electroencephalography**.

effect size (d): A measure used in meta-analysis. Defined as the difference in mean scores between two groups, divided by the average standard deviation for the two groups.

electroencephalography (EEG): A technique to measure brain activity, specifically, to detect different states of consciousness. Metal electrodes are positioned all over the scalp. The waveforms that are recorded change in predictable ways when the person being recorded is awake and alert, drowsy, asleep, or in a coma.

elimination-by-aspects strategy: In decision making, the elimination of alternatives that exceed a threshold value on one or more dimensions.

emergence: A perceptual phenomenon in which qualitative differences appear as parts of a stimulus are added, such that whole stimuli take on properties that are novel and unpredictable.

empiricism: A philosophical doctrine emphasizing the role of experience in the acquisition of knowledge.

encoding: The cognitive process(es) by which information is translated into a mental or internal representation and stored.

encoding specificity: A principle of retrieval asserted by Tulving: At the time material is first put into long-term memory, it is encoded in a particular way, depending on the context present at the time; at the time of recall, the person is at a great advantage if the same contextually supplied information available at encoding is once again available.

encoding variability: The way the encoding of information varies as a function of context.

episodic buffer (of WM): The proposed component of working memory (WM) responsible for linking information across domains to form integrated units of visual, spatial, and verbal information with information in long-term memory.

episodic memory: A memory system proposed by Tulving that is thought to hold memories of specific events with which the cognitive processor has had direct experience.

ERP: *See* **event-related potential**.

event-related potential (ERP): An electrical recording technique used to measure the response of the brain to various stimulus events.

everyday reasoning: Mundane reasoning that differs from formal reasoning in its use of implicit premises, multiple solutions, personal relevance, and possible emotional involvement.

executive functioning: Cognitive processes that include planning, making decisions, implementing strategies, inhibiting inappropriate behaviors, and using working memory to process information.

exemplar view of concepts: The idea that a concept consists of mental representations of actual instances or examples.

exhaustive search: A search for information in which each item in a set is examined, even after the target is found.

expectation effect: *See* **context effect**.

expected utility theory: A normative model of decision making in which the decision maker weights the personal importance and the probabilities of different outcomes in choosing among alternatives in order to maximize overall satisfaction of personal goals.

experiment: A test of a scientific theory in which the researcher manipulates the independent variable.

experimental control: A property of research such that the causes of different behaviors or other phenomenon can be isolated and tested. Typically, this involves manipulating independent variables and holding constant all factors but the one(s) of interest.

experimenter expectancy effect: The influence on the performance of experimental participants generated by an experimenter's beliefs or hypotheses, which somehow get subtly transmitted to the participants.

expert/novice differences: A dimension of individual differences in which people's analytic approach in perception or problem solving increases as they gain familiarity with a domain.

expert system: A computer program designed to model the judgments of a human expert in a particular field.

explicit memory: Consciously recalled or recollected memory.

expressive aphasia: *See* **Broca's aphasia**.

eyewitness memory: A narrative memory of a personally witnessed event.

faculty psychology: The theory that different mental abilities, such as reading or computation, are independent and autonomous functions, carried out in different parts of the brain.

fallacy: An erroneous argument.

false memory: "Recollections" of "events" that never in fact occurred. *See also* **recovered memory** and **repressed memory**.

family resemblance structure of concepts: A structure of categories in which each member shares different features with different members. Few, if any, features are shared by every single member of the category.

fan effect: The phenomenon whereby retrieval time to retrieve a particular fact about a concept increases as more facts are known about that concept.

feature: A component, or part, of an object, event, or representation.

feature integration theory: A proposal that perception of familiar stimuli occurs in two stages. The first, automatic stage involves the perception of object features. The second, attentional stage involves the integration and unification of those features.

field dependence/field independence (FD/FI): A cognitive style dimension referring to the relative difficulty or ease individuals experience in ignoring background context to identify parts of a figure as separate from a whole.

figure-ground organization: A perceptual segregation of a stimulus into one or more objects of focal interest and background.

filter theory: A theory of attention proposing that information that exceeds the capacity of a processor to process at any given time is blocked from further processing.

flashbulb memory: A phenomenon in which people recall their personal circumstances (for example, where they were, whom they were with, what they were doing) at the time they heard of or witnessed an unexpected and very significant event (for example, an assassination, a natural disaster).

fMRI: *See* **functional magnetic resonance imaging**.

forebrain: The part of the brain containing the thalamus, hypothalamus, hippocampus, amygdala, and cerebral cortex.

forgetting: The processes that prevent information from being retrieved from a memory store.

form perception: The process by which the brain differentiates objects from their backgrounds.

formal operations stage: A Piagetian stage of adolescence marked by the acquisition of the ability to reason abstractly and hypothetically.

formal reasoning: Reasoning about problems with explicit premises, finite solutions, and well-defined operations.

framing effect: Decision-making bias caused by a propensity to evaluate outcomes as positive or negative changes from their current state.

frontal lobe: A division of the cerebral cortex located just beneath the forehead that contains the motor cortex, premotor cortex, and the prefrontal cortex.

functional fixedness: A problem-solving phenomenon in which people have difficulty seeing alternate uses for common objects.

functional magnetic resonance imaging (fMRI): An imaging technique that uses MRI equipment to examine blood flow in a noninvasive, nonradioactive manner.

functionalism: A school of psychology emphasizing questions such as why the mind or a particular cognitive process works the way(s) it does.

gambler's fallacy: An erroneous belief that a random process (for example, a coin flip or a spin of a roulette wheel) will automatically keep track of the outcomes in order to make the overall rate of an outcome in the short run equal to the overall rate of that outcome in the long run.

generate-and-test technique: A problem-solving strategy in which the solver enumerates (generates) possible solutions and then tries each to see if it constitutes a solution.

geon: A simple geometric component hypothesized to be used in the recognition of objects.

Gestalt principles of perceptual organization: Laws that explain the regularities in the way people come to the perceptual interpretations of stimuli. The emphasis is on the apprehension of whole structures rather on than the detection and assembly of parts of structures.

Gestalt psychology: A school of psychology emphasizing the study of whole entities rather than simple elements. Gestalt psychologists concentrate on problems of perception and problem solving and argue that people's cognitive experience is not reducible to their experience of simple elements (for example, sensations) but, rather, to the overall structure(s) of their experience.

GPS (General Problem Solver): A computer program developed by Allan Newell and Herbert Simon that solved problems in cryptarithmetic and logic using means–ends analysis.

grammar: A system of rules that produces well-formed, or "legal," entities, such as sentences of a language.

Gricean maxims of cooperative conversation: Pragmatic rules of conversation, including moderation of quantity, quality, relevance, and clarity.

helpless orientation: An approach to challenges in which the individual gives up easily and believes he or she will not succeed at the task at hand.

heuristic: A rule of thumb, or shortcut method, used in thinking, reasoning, and/or decision making.

hierarchical semantic network model of semantic memory: A model of semantic memory organized in terms of nodes and links that stores properties at the highest relevant node to conserve cognitive economy.

hindbrain: The part of the brain, containing some of the most evolutionarily primitive structures, that is responsible for transmitting information from the spinal cord to the brain, regulating life support functions, and helping to maintain balance.

hindsight bias: A tendency to exaggerate the certainty of what could have been anticipated ahead of time.

hippocampus: A structure of the brain in the medial temporal lobe; damage or removal can result in amnesia.

holistic processing: Attending to global aspects of a situation in processing information about it.

human factors engineering: An applied area of research that focuses on the design of equipment and technology that are well suited to people's cognitive capabilities.

hypothalamus: A structure in the forebrain that controls the pituitary gland and so-called homeostatic behaviors, such as eating, drinking, temperature control, sleeping, sexual behaviors, and emotional reactions.

hypothesis testing: An inductive reasoning strategy that involves testing a number of possible solutions to a problem and modifying them based on feedback.

icon: A sensory memory for visual stimuli.

ill-defined problem: A problem that does not have the goals, starting information, and/or legal steps stated explicitly.

illusory correlation: An association between factors that is not supported by data but seems plausible.

image theory: A descriptive theory of decision making that posits that the process consists of two stages: (1) a noncompensatory screening of options against the decision maker's image of values and future, in which the number of options is reduced to a very small set, and (2), if necessary, a compensatory choice process.

imaginal scanning: A task in which a participant is asked to form a mental image and to scan over it from one point to another.

implicit encoding: A principle of imagery that holds mental imagery is used in retrieving information about physical properties of objects, or of physical relationships among objects, that may not have been explicitly encoded.

implicit learning: Learning that occurs without explicit awareness of what has been learned.

implicit memory: Memory that is not deliberate or conscious but exhibits evidence of prior experience.

inattentional blindness: The phenomenon of not perceiving a stimulus that might be literally right in front of you, unless you are paying attention to it.

incidental learning: The retention of information even when it is not required of, or even intended by, the processor.

incubation: Unconscious processing that works on a specific problem while the mind is otherwise occupied.

individual differences: Stable patterns of performance that differ qualitatively and/or quantitatively across individuals.

inductive reasoning: Reasoning that involves drawing conclusions that are suggested but are not necessarily true.

inductive strength: A property of some logical arguments such that it is improbable (but not impossible) for the premises to be true and the conclusion false.

inference rule: Hypothesized special-purpose rule used in reasoning to draw conclusions.

information-processing approach: An approach to cognition that uses a computer metaphor in its explanations. Information processing equates cognition with the acquisition, storage, and manipulation of information (for example, what we see, hear, read about, think about) through a system consisting of various storage places and systems of exchange.

informationally encapsulated process: A process with the property of informational encapsulation, that is, isolation from other processes and data.

intelligence: Postulated by some psychologists to represent the sum total of a person's cognitive abilities and resources.

interference: A hypothesized process of forgetting in which material is thought to be buried or otherwise displaced by other information but still exists somewhere in a memory store.

introspection: A methodological technique in which trained observers are asked to reflect on, and report on, their conscious experience while performing cognitive tasks.

knowledge representation: The mental depiction, storage, and organization of information.

knowledge-based view of concepts: The idea that concepts function in relation to their instances as a scientific theory does to data supporting it.

language: A system of communication that is governed by a system of rules (a grammar) and can express an infinite number of propositions.

language acquisition: The process(es) by which a cognitive processor comes to develop linguistic competence and performance.

lateralization: Specialization of function of the two cerebral hemispheres.

learning style: An individual's habitual and preferred approach to learning tasks.

levels-of-processing theory of memory: An alternative to the modal view of memory, proposed by Craik and Lockhart, that postulates that memory depends not on a particular memory store but on the initial processing done to the information at the time of acquisition. "Shallow" or superficial levels of processing (for example, processing at the level of visual shape or acoustic sound) are thought to lead to less retention than "deeper" levels of processing (for example, processing done on the meaning of the information).

lexical ambiguity: The idea that some words have different meanings; for example, *bank* can refer to the side of a river or to a financial institution.

lexical decision task: A task in which an experimental subject is presented with letter strings and asked to judge, as quickly as possible, whether the strings form words.

lexicon: A mental store thought to hold a cognitive processor's knowledge of words, including their spelling, pronunciation, definition, part of speech, and so on.

limited-capacity processor: A system that acquires, stores, manipulates, and/or transmits information but has fixed limits on the amount or rate of processing that it can accomplish.

linguistic competence: Underlying knowledge that allows a cognitive processor to engage in a particular cognitive activity involving language, independent of behavior expressing that knowledge. Contrast with **linguistic performance**.

linguistic performance: The behavior or responses actually produced by a cognitive processor engaged in a particular cognitive activity involving language. Contrast with **linguistic competence**.

linguistics: A field of study focusing on the structure, use, and acquisition of language.

literacy: The ability to read and write.

localization of function: The "mapping" of brain areas to different cognitive or motor functions; identifying which neural regions control or are active when different activities take place.

logical connectives: Symbols used in logic arguments to form compound propositions. Examples: **&, V**.

long-term memory (LTM): A memory store thought to have a large, possibly infinite capacity that holds on to incoming information for long periods of time, perhaps permanently. Also called *secondary memory*.

long-term potentiation: A process, hypothesized to be a mechanism for long-term learning, in which neural circuits in the hippocampus are subjected to repeated and intense electrical stimulation, resulting in hippocampal cells that are more sensitive to stimuli than they were previously.

LTM: *See* **long-term memory**.

magnetic resonance imaging (MRI): A body-imaging technique in which a person is surrounded with a strong magnetic field. Radio waves are directed at a particular part of the body, causing the centers of hydrogen atoms in those structures to align themselves in predictable ways. Computers collate information about how the atoms are aligning and produce a composite three-dimensional image.

magnetoencephalography (MEG): A technique for mapping brain activity that measures changes in magnetic fields generated by electrical activities of neurons.

mastery orientation: An approach to challenges in which the individual sets challenging goals in order to increase competence, understanding, or mastery of something new.

means–ends analysis: A problem-solving strategy in which the solver compares the goal to the current state, then chooses a step to reduce maximally the difference between them.

medulla: A structure in the hindbrain that transmits information from the spinal cord to the brain and regulates life support functions such as respiration, blood pressure, coughing, sneezing, vomiting, and heart rate.

medulla oblongata: *See* **medulla**.

MEG: *See* **magnetoencephalography**.

memory: The cognitive processes underlying the storage, retention, and retrieval of information.

memory consolidation: The biochemical process(es) by which neural synaptic connections are strengthened or weakened.

memory system: A kind of memory (for example, episodic memory, semantic memory) that operates on distinct principles and stores a distinct kind of information.

memory trace: The mental representation of stored information.

mental representation: An internal depiction of information.

mental rotation: A type of visual imagery task in which subjects are asked to form an image of a stimulus and then to imagine how it would look as it rotates around a horizontal or vertical axis.

mental set: The tendency to adopt a certain framework, strategy, or procedure based on immediate experience or context.

meta-analysis: A technique to review findings in the literature involving the use of specific statistical methods in integrating the findings from different empirical studies.

metacognition: Awareness or knowledge of one's own cognitive processes and systems.

method of loci: A memorization method that requires the learner to visualize an ordered series of physical locations as mnemonic cues for a list of information.

midbrain: The part of the brain containing structures that are involved in relaying information between other brain regions and in regulating levels of alertness.

mnemonics: Strategies to facilitate retention and later retrieval of information.

modal model of memory: A theoretical approach to the study of memory that emphasizes the existence of different memory stores (for example, sensory memory, short-term memory, long-term memory).

modularity hypothesis: Fodor's proposal that some cognitive processes, in particular language and perception, operate on only certain kinds of inputs and operate independently of the beliefs and other information available to the cognitive processor or other cognitive processes.

mood-dependent memory effect: The empirical finding that people's ability to recall information is best when their mood at the time of recall matches their mood at the time of learning.

morpheme: The smallest meaningful unit of language.

motor aphasia: *See* **Broca's aphasia**.

motor cortex: A structure in the frontal lobe that controls fine motor movement in the body.

MRI: *See* **magnetic resonance imaging**.

multiattribute utility theory (MAUT): A normative model of decision making that provides a means of integrating different dimensions and goals of a complex decision. It involves six steps: (1) breaking a decision down into independent dimensions, (2) determining the relative weights of each of those dimensions, (3) listing all the alternatives, (4) ranking all the alternatives along the dimensions, (5) multiplying the rankings by the weightings to determine a final value for each alternative, and (6) choosing the alternative with the highest value.

multiple intelligences (MI) theory: Gardner's theory that intelligence can be divided into distinct types, including musical, bodily-kinesthetic, logical-mathematical, linguistic, spatial, interpersonal, and intrapersonal intelligences.

narrative review: A technique for literature reviews in which the author locates and reports on all the studies he or she can find, providing a qualitative summary.

nativism: A philosophical doctrine emphasizing the role of innate factors in the acquisition of knowledge.

naturalistic observation: A research paradigm in which an observer observes participants in familiar, everyday contexts while ideally remaining as unobtrusive as possible.

natural-kind concept: Concepts pertaining to naturally occurring substances.

necessary feature: *See* **defining feature**.

need for cognition: A dimension of individual differences in which people differ in their motivation to take on intellectual challenges or tasks.

neural network: *See* **connectionism**.

neuroscience: The scientific study of the nervous system.

nominal-kind concept: Concepts pertaining to ideas or objects that have well-delimited definitions.

nonanalytic concept formation: Cognitive processes that implicitly acquire knowledge of a complex structure during the memorization of examples.

nonstage theories of cognitive development: Theories of development that postulate only quantitative differences between individuals at different ages.

normative model of decision making: A model that defines ideal performance under ideal circumstances when making decisions or solving problems.

occipital lobe: A division of the cerebral cortex located at the back of the head that is involved in the processing of visual information.

overconfidence: An overly positive judgment of one's own decision-making abilities and performance.

paired associates learning: A memory task in which experimental subjects are first presented with a list of pairs of words (for example, *flag–spoon*) and later asked to recall the second word in a pair (for example, *spoon*) when presented with the first (for example, *flag*).

paradigm: A body of knowledge that selects and highlights certain issues for study. It includes assumptions about how a particular phenomenon ought to be studied and the kinds of experimental methods and measures that are appropriate to use.

parallel search: A search for information in which several stores or slots of information are simultaneously examined to match to the target.

parietal lobe: A division of the cerebral cortex located at the top rear part of the head that contains the primary somatosensory cortex.

pattern recognition: The classification of a stimulus into a category.

percept: The outcome of a perceptual process; the meaningful interpretation of incoming information.

perception: The interpretation of sensory information to yield a meaningful description or understanding.

perceptual learning: The changes in perception that occur as a function of practice or experience with the stimuli.

perceptual set: The tendency to perceive an object or pattern in a certain way, based on one's immediate perceptual experience.

person–machine system: The idea that machinery operated by a person must be designed to interact with the operator's physical, cognitive, and motivational capacities and limitations.

PET scan: *See* **positron emission tomography**.

phoneme: The smallest unit of sound that makes a meaningful difference between utterances in a given language.

phonetics: The study of speech sounds.

phonological loop (of WM): The proposed component of working memory (WM) responsible for subvocally rehearsing auditory information.

phonology: The study of the ways in which speech sounds are combined and altered in language.

phrenology: The idea (now discredited) that psychological strengths and weaknesses could be precisely correlated to the relative sizes of different brain areas.

plasticity: The ability of some brain regions to perform the functions of other, damaged regions.

pons: A structure in the hindbrain that acts as a neural relay center, facilitating the crossover of information between the left side of the body and the right side of the brain, and vice versa. It is also involved in balance and in the processing of both visual and auditory information.

positron emission tomography (PET): A brain-imaging technique that shows which areas of the brain are most active at a given point in time.

pragmatics: The rules governing the social aspects of language.

prefrontal cortex: A region in the frontal lobe that is involved with executive functioning.

premise: A statement, from which others are inferred, that helps establish what is already known about a problem.

preoperational stage: A Piagetian stage of early childhood marked by the acquisition of mental representation and symbolic functions.

prescriptive model of decision making: A model that tells us how we "ought" to make decisions or solve problems but that takes into account actual circumstances.

primacy effect: The improvement in retention of information learned at the beginning of a task.

primary memory: *See* **short-term memory**.

primary somatosensory cortex: A region in the parietal lobe involved in the processing of sensory information from the body—for example, sensations of pain, pressure, touch, or temperature.

priming: A phenomenon in which exposure to one stimulus facilitates response to another stimulus.

proactive interference: A phenomenon in which material learned earlier disrupts the learning of subsequent material.

probability: Measurement of a degree of uncertainty, expressed as a number between 0 and 1.

problem solving: The cognitive process(es) used in transforming starting information into a goal state, using specified means of solution.

problem space hypothesis: The idea that problem solving is isomorphic to a search through a mental graph, with nodes corresponding to every possible state of affairs of a problem and connections corresponding to legal moves.

procedural memory: A memory system thought to contain information concerning actions and sequences of actions—for example, one's knowledge of how to ride a bicycle or swing a golf club.

production rules: A hypothesized mental representation of procedural memory, which specifies a goal to be achieved, one or more conditions that must be true in order for the rule to be applied, and one or more actions that result from the application of the rule.

propositional complexity: The number of underlying distinct ideas in a sentence.

propositional reasoning: Drawing conclusions from premises that are in the form of true or false assertions.

prosopagnosia: A specific inability to recognize faces, even very familiar ones, with intact recognition of other objects.

prototype: An abstract representation of an idealized member of a class of objects or events.

prototype view of concepts: The idea that all concepts are organized around idealized mental representations of examples.

proximal stimulus: Reception of information and its registration by a sense organ—for example, retinal images in the case of vision. Contrast with **distal stimulus**.

psychological essentialism: The idea that people possess implicit theories about fundamental characteristics that all instances of a concept contain or embody.

quasi-experiment: An empirical study that appears to involve some, but incomplete, experimental control—for example, through nonrandom assignment of subjects to conditions.

rationality: A property of thinking or decision making such that the processes used are selected with the processor's overall goals and principles in mind.

reasoning: Cognitive process(es) used in transforming given information, called *premises*, into conclusions. Reasoning is often seen as a special kind of thinking.

reasoning by analogy: Problem solving that employs an analogy between the current problem and another problem that has already been solved.

recall: The retrieval of information in which the processor must generate most of the information without aids. *See also* **recognition**.

recency effect: The improvement in retention of information learned at the end of a task.

receptive aphasia: *See* **Wernicke's aphasia**.

recognition: The retrieval of information in which the processor must decide whether the information presented has been previously presented. *See also* **recall**.

recognition-primed decision making: A theory of expert decision making that holds that decision makers choose options based on analogy of a given situation with previously encountered situations.

recovered memory: Autobiographical memories, usually of traumatic events, that are not accessible for some period of time but later become able to be retrieved. *See also* **false memory** and **repressed memory**.

reflectivity/impulsivity: A cognitive style dimension referring to the way in which individuals trade off speed and accuracy of responding.

rehearsal: A mnemonic strategy of repeating information (either aloud or silently) to facilitate retention and later retrieval.

relational-organizational hypothesis: The idea that visual imagery aids memory by producing a greater number of associations.

repetition priming: Priming that facilitates the cognitive processing of information after a recent exposure to that same information.

representativeness heuristic: A belief that outcomes will always reflect characteristics of the process that generated them—for example, an expectation that the outcome of a series of coin flips will always look random.

repressed memory: A controversial explanation of amnesia for traumatic events. *See also* **false memory** and **recovered memory**.

retention duration: The amount of time a memory trace remains available for retrieval.

retina: A layer of visual receptor cells at the rear of the eyeball.

retinal image: A proximal stimulus for vision consisting of the projection of light waves reflected from stimuli and projected to a surface at the back of the eye.

retrieval: The processes by which stored information is brought back to conscious awareness.

retrieval cue: A stimulus that helps a person recall or recognize stored information.

retroactive interference: A phenomenon in which subsequently learned material lowers the probability of recalling earlier learned material.

retrograde amnesia: Amnesia concerning old events. Contrast with **anterograde amnesia**.

schema: An organized framework for representing knowledge that typically includes characters, plots, and settings and incorporates both general knowledge about the world and information about particular events. *See also* **script** and **story grammar**.

schema theory: A theory of attention that claims unattended information is never perceived.

schemata: Frameworks for organizing and representing knowledge that contain roles, variables, and fixed parts.

schemata/scripts view of concepts: The idea that all concepts are schemata.

schooling: The amount of time an individual spends in a formal academic setting.

script: A schema for routine events. *See also* **schema** and **story grammar**.

secondary memory: *See* **long-term memory**.

selective attention: The focusing of cognitive resources on one or a small number of tasks to the exclusion of others.

self-terminating search: A search for information that stops when a target is found.

semantic memory: A memory system proposed by Tulving that is thought to hold memories of general knowledge.

semantic network: A depiction of semantic memory consisting of nodes (which roughly correspond to words or concepts) and connections between nodes.

semantic priming: A phenomenon in which exposure to one word (e.g., *nurse*) facilitates the recognition of semantically related words (e.g., *doctor*).

semantics: The study of meaning.

sensorimotor stage: A Piagetian stage of infancy marked by the absence of the capacity for mental representation.

sensory aphasia: *See* **Wernicke's aphasia**.

sensory memory: A memory store thought to hold on to incoming sensory information for very brief periods. A different sensory memory store is hypothesized for each sensory system.

separate knowing: An approach to knowledge and learning emphasizing detachment, objectivity, rationality, rigor, and attempts to find flaws or loopholes in arguments or knowledge.

serial position effect: The phenomenon that items at the beginning or end of a list of items are more easily recalled than are items from the middle of the list.

serial search: A search for information in which several stores or slots of information are sequentially examined for match to the target.

short-term memory (STM): A memory store thought to hold on to incoming information for up to 20–30 seconds. Also called *primary memory.* It is thought to have a small capacity (up to 7 plus or minus 2 "slots").

situated cognition: A belief that one's culture and one's everyday surroundings and tasks set both boundaries and possibilities for the cognitive tasks that are practiced and therefore strengthened in the normal course of daily living.

size constancy: The phenomenon that one's perception of an object remains constant even as the retinal image of the object changes size (for example, because the object has moved closer or farther away from the perceiver).

space around the body: The area immediately around a person's body in which the person can easily perceive and act on objects.

space of navigation: Large spaces that people walk through, explore, or travel to and through.

space of the body: Awareness of where the different parts of one's body are located at any given moment and what other objects different body parts are interacting with; used, along with internal sensations, to direct different parts of the body spatially.

spacing effect: A phenomenon in which recall of material that is presented repeatedly is superior when the presentations are some time apart rather than immediately following one another.

spatial cognition: The knowledge and processes used to represent and navigate in and through space.

spatial updating: The processes by which individuals continually revise their mental representation of where things in the environment are with respect to their current location.

split-brained patient: An individual who has undergone surgery to sever the corpus callosum in the brain, usually to control the spread of seizures.

spreading activation: The excitation of one node in a semantic network by the excitation of another node to which it is connected; the excitation is said to flow across the connections.

stage theories of cognitive development: Theories of development that postulate qualitatively different periods (stages).

state-dependent learning: The phenomenon that recall is easier when the pharmacological state of the person at recall matches his or her pharmacological state during encoding.

state-dependent memory: The phenomenon that material is easier to retrieve when the learner is experiencing the same state or context (for example, physical location, physiological state) that she or he was experiencing at the time of encoding. *See also* **encoding specificity**.

STM: *See* **short-term memory**.

storage: The mental "holding on" to information between the time it is encoded and the time it is retrieved.

story grammar: A structure people are thought to use to comprehend large, integrated pieces of text. *See also* **schema** and **script**.

strategies: Deliberate plans or routines used to carry out particular cognitive tasks.

Stroop task: A task invented by J. R. Stroop in which a subject sees a list of words (color terms) printed in an ink color that differs from the word named (for example, *green* printed in blue ink). The subject is asked to name the ink colors of the words in the list and demonstrates great difficulty in doing so, relative to a condition in which non-color words form the stimuli.

structuralism: One of the earliest schools of cognitive psychology. It focused on the search for the simplest possible mental elements and the laws governing the ways in which they could be combined.

subjective contour: Illusory outline created by certain visual cues that lead to erroneous form perception. The existence of this phenomenon suggests that perception is an active constructive process.

subjective probability: An intuitive estimate of the likelihood of occurrence of an event.

subordinate level of categories: A level of categorization narrower than the basic level.

sunk cost effect: A bias in decision making in which already "spent" costs unduly influence decisions on whether to continue.

superordinate level of categories: A level of categorization broader than the basic level that includes exemplars that can be quite dissimilar from one another.

syllogistic reasoning: Reasoning with problems concerning relationships among categories; for example, "All A are B; some B are C; therefore, some A are C."

syntax: The arrangement of words within sentences; the structure of sentences.

tacit knowledge: People's underlying and implicit beliefs about a task or event.

tautology: A statement that is true by definition of its form (for example, "A is either true or it is false").

template: A stored pattern or model to which incoming information is matched in order to be recognized and classified.

temporal lobe: A division of the cerebral cortex located on the side of the head that is involved in the processing of auditory information and in some aspects of memory.

testing effect: The experimental finding that taking tests on material actually improves the learning of it, even when compared with simply repeatedly studying that material.

thalamus: A structure in the forebrain involved in relaying information, especially to the cerebral cortex.

theory-driven process: *See* **top-down process**.

thinking: A cognitive process used to transform or manipulate information that may be either focused (that is, solving problems with clear goals) or unfocused (that is, invoking loosely related ideas without a clear purpose).

TMS: *See* **transcranial magnetic stimulation**.

top-down process: Cognitive (usually perceptual) process directed by expectations (derived from context, past learning, or both) to form a larger percept, concept, or interpretation. Also called *conceptually driven* or *theory-driven process*.

transcranial magnetic stimulation (TMS): A noninvasive technique to study brain activity involving the use of a magnetic coil placed close to the scalp to induce electrical activity or inhibition in targeted brain circuits.

truth table: A method of showing when compound logical expressions are true and when they are false by considering every possible assignment of truth values to propositions.

typicality effect: The phenomenon whereby experimental subjects are faster to respond to typical instances of a concept (for example, *robin* for the concept "bird") than they are to atypical instances (for example, *penguin* for "bird").

unconscious processing: *See* **incubation**.

utility: A measure of a person's happiness, pleasure, or satisfaction with a particular outcome.

visual agnosia: An impairment in the ability to interpret (but not to see) visual information.

visual image: A mental representation of a stimulus thought to share at least some properties with a pictorial or spatial depiction of the stimulus.

visual search task: A task in which subjects are asked to detect the presence of a particular target against an array of similar stimuli.

visuospatial sketch pad: The proposed component of working memory that maintains visual or spatial information.

vote counting: A technique for literature reviews in which the author lists each study and counts the number of studies in the total that demonstrate a particular effect.

well-defined problem: A problem whose goals, starting information, and legal steps are stated explicitly.

Wernicke's aphasia: Also called *receptive* or *sensory aphasia;* symptoms of this organic disorder include difficulty in understanding speech and producing intelligible speech, although speech remains fluent and articulate.

Whorfian hypothesis of linguistic relativity: The idea that language constrains thought and perception such that cultural differences in cognition can be explained at least partially by differences in language.

within-subjects design: A research paradigm in which the same experimental participants participate in different experimental conditions.

word superiority effect: The phenomenon that single letters are more quickly identified in the context of words than they are when presented alone or in the context of random letters.

working backward: A problem-solving technique that identifies the final goal and the steps, in reverse order, that are necessary to reach the goal.

working memory (WM): A memory structure proposed by Baddeley, described as consisting of a limited-capacity work space that can be allocated, somewhat flexibly, into either storage space or control processing. It is thought to consist of three components: a central executive, a phonological loop, and a visuospatial sketch pad.

CREDITS AND SOURCES

Chapter 2

Figure 2.1: Adapted from Garrett, B. (2011). *Brain & behavior: An introduction to biological psychology,* p. 65.

Figure 2.2: Adapted from Garrett, B. (2011). *Brain & behavior: An introduction to biological psychology,* Fig. 8.4, p. 227.

Figure 2.3: Adapted from Garrett, B. (2011). *Brain & behavior: An introduction to biological psychology,* p. 58.

Figure 2.4: Adapted from Garrett, B. (2011). *Brain & behavior: An introduction to biological psychology,* p. 66.

Figure 2.5: Adapted from Petersen, S. E., Fox, P. T., Posner, M. I., Mintun, M., & Raichle, M. E. (1988). Positron emission tomographic studies of the cortical anatomy of single-word processing. *Nature, 333,* pp. 585–589.

Photo 2.1: ©Thinkstock/Stockbyte

Photo 2.2: ©Thinkstock/Hemera Technologies

Chapter 3

Figure 3.3: *Slave Market With Disappearing Bust of Voltaire.* (1940). Oil on canvas, 18-1/4 × 25-3/8 inches. Collection of the Salvador Dali Museum, St. Petersburg, Florida. © 2006 Salvador Dali Museum, Inc. © Kingdom of Spain, Gala-Salvador Dali Foundation, Figueres/Artist Rights Society [ARS] New York.

Figure 3.6: Pomerantz, J. R., & Portillo, M. C. (2011). Grouping and emergent features in vision: Toward a theory of basic Gestalts. *Journal of Experimental Psychology: Human Perception and Performance, 37,* p. 1332.

Figure 3.10: Biederman, I. (1987). Recognition-by-components: A theory of human image understanding. *Psychological Review, 94,* p. 122–123.

Figure 3.11: Biederman, I. (1987). Recognition-by-components: A theory of human image understanding. *Psychological Review, 94,* p. 116.

Figure 3.12: Biederman, I. (1987). Recognition-by-components: A theory of human image understanding. *Psychological Review, 94,* p. 119.

Figure 3.15: Posner, M. I., Goldsmith, R., & Welton, K. E., Jr. (1967). Perceived distance and the classification of distorted patterns. *Journal of Experimental Psychology, 73,* p. 30.

Figure 3.16: Cabeza, R., Bruce, V., Kato, T., & Oda, M. (1999). The prototype effect in face recognition: Extensions and limits. *Memory and Cognition, 27,* Fig. 1, p. 141. Copyright © 1999, Psychonomic Society, Inc. Reprinted with permission.

Figure 3.18: Gibson, J. J., & Gibson, E. J. (1955). Perceptual learning: Differentiation or enrichment? *Psychological Review, 62,* p. 36.

Figure 3.19: Reicher, G. M. (1969). Perceptual recognition as a function of meaningfulness of stimulus material. *Journal of Experimental Psychology, 81,* p. 277.

Figure 3.20: McClelland, J. L., & Rumelhart, D. E. (1981). An interactive activation model of context effects in letter perception: Part 1. An account of basic findings. *Psychological Review, 88,* p. 378.

Figure 3.21: McClelland, J. L., & Rumelhart, D. E. (1981). An interactive activation model of context effects in letter perception: Part 1. An account of basic findings. *Psychological Review, 88,* p. 380.

Figure 3.22: Johansson, G. (1973). Visual perception of biological motion and a model for its analysis. *Perception and Psychophysics, 14,* p. 202.

Figure 3.23: Gibson, J. J. (1950). *The perception of the visual world.* Boston, MA: Houghton Mifflin, p. 121.

Figure 3.24: Pepperell, R. (2011). Connecting art and the brain: An artist's perspective on visual indeterminacy. *Frontiers in Human Neuroscience, 5* (84), Fig. 10.

Photo 3.1: Nancy J. Ashmore

Photo 3.2: Nancy J. Ashmore

Chapter 4

Table 4.1: Simons, D. J., & Chabris, C. F. (1999). Gorillas in our midst: Sustained inattentional blindness for dynamic events. *Perception, 28,* Table 1, p. 1068.

Figure 4.2: Wood, N. L., & Cowan, N. (1995). The cocktail party phenomenon revisited: Attention and memory in the classic selective listening procedure of Cherry (1953). *Journal of Experimental Psychology: General, 124,* p. 253.

Figure 4.3: Neisser, U., & Becklen, R. (1975). Selective looking: Attending to visually specified events. *Cognitive Psychology, 7,* p. 485.

Figure 4.4: Simons, D. J., & Chabris, C. F. (1999). Gorillas in our midst: Sustained inattentional blindness for dynamic events. *Perception, 28,* Fig. 2, p. 1067.

Figure 4.5: Simons, D. J., & Levin, D. T. (1998). Failure to detect changes to people during a real-world interaction. *Psychonomic Bulletin and Review, 5,* Fig. 1, p. 646. Copyright ©1998, Psychonomic Society, Inc. Reprinted with permission.

Figure 4.6: Posner, M. I., & M. E. Raichie. *Images of mind.* Copyright ©1994, 1997 by Scientific American Library. Reprinted by permission of Henry Holt and Company, LLC, p. 158.

Figure 4.7: Banich, M. T. (1997). *Neuropsychology: The neural bases of mental function* (1st ed.), p. 239. Copyright ©1997 Wadsworth, a part of Cengage Learning, Inc. Reproduced by permission. http://www.cengage.com/permissions/.

Figure 4.10: Adapted from Schneider, W., & Shiffrin, R. M. (1977). Controlled and automatic human information processing: I. Detection, search, and attention. *Psychological Review, 84,* pp. 1–66.

Figure 4.11: Schneider, W., & Shiffrin, R. M. (1977). Controlled and automatic human information processing: I. Detection, search, and attention. *Psychological Review, 84,* p. 12.

Figure 4.13: Theeuwes, J., Kramer, A. F., Hahn, S., & Irwin, D. E. (1998). Our eyes do not always go where we want them to go: Capture of the eyes by new objects. *Psychological Science, 9,* 379–385, Fig. 1, p. 380.

Figure 4.14: Adapted from Spelke, E., Hirst, W., & Neisser, U. (1976). Skills of divided attention. *Cognition, 4,* p. 220.

Figure 4.15: Strayer, D. L., & Johnston, W. A. (2001). Driven to distraction: Dual-task studies of simulated driving and conversing on a cellular telephone. *Psychological Science, 12,* Fig. 1, p. 463.

Figure 4.16: Wilson, F. A., & Stimpson, J. P. (2010). Trends in fatalities from distracted driving in the United States, 1999–2008. *American Journal of Public Health, 100,* Fig. 3, p. 2216.

Chapter 5

Figure 5.2: Sperling, G. (1960). The information available in brief visual presentations. *Psychological Monographs, 74* (498), p. 3.

Figure 5.3: Waugh, N. C., & Norman, D. A. (1965). Primary memory. *Psychological Review, 72,* p. 91.

Figure 5.4: Adapted from Sternberg, S. (1966). High-speed scanning in human memory. *Science, 153,* pp. 652–654.

Figure 5.5: Adapted from Baddeley, A. D. (1990). *Human memory: Theory and practice.* Boston, MA: Allyn & Bacon.

Chapter 6

Box 6.1: Bartlett, F. C. (1995). *Remembering: A study in experimental and social psychology* (2nd ed.), p. 67. (Originally published 1932) Reprinted with the permission of Cambridge University Press.

Box 6.2: Bartlett, F. C. (1995). *Remembering: A study in experimental and social psychology* (2nd ed.), pp. 68–69. Reprinted with the permission of Cambridge University Press.

Figure 6.1: Ebbinghaus, H. (1913). *Memory: A contribution to experimental psychology* (H. A. Ruger & C. E. Bussenius, Trans.). New York, NY: Columbia University, Teacher's College, p. 75. (Original work published 1885)

Figure 6.2: Figure created by Roediger (1990). In Warrington, E. K., & Weiskrantz, L. (1970). Amnesic syndrome: Consolidation or retrieval? *Nature, 228,* p. 630. Copyright © 1970, Nature Publishing Group. Reprinted with permission.

Figure 6.3: Crowder, R. G. (1993). Short-term memory: Where do we stand? *Memory and Cognition, 21,* p. 143. Copyright © 1993, Psychonomic Society Inc. Reprinted with permission.

Figure 6.4: Banich, M. T. *Neuropsychology: The neural bases of mental function* (1st ed.), p. 337. Copyright © 1997 Wadsworth, a part of Cengage Learning, Inc. Reproduced by permission. http://www.cengage.com/permissions/.

Chapter 7

Box 7.1: Anderson, J. R. (1995). *Cognitive psychology and its implications* (4th ed.). New York, NY: W. H. Freeman, p. 282.

Table 7.2: Rosch, E., Mervis, C. B., Gray, W. D., Johnson, D. M., & Boyes-Braem, P. (1976). Basic objects in natural categories. *Cognitive Psychology, 8,* p. 388.

Figure 7.2: Collins, A. M., & Quillian, M. R. (1969). Retrieval time from semantic memory. *Journal of Verbal Learning and Verbal Behavior, 8,* p. 241.

Figure 7.4: Collins, A. M., & Loftus, E. F. (1975). A spreading activation theory of semantic processing. *Psychological Review, 82,* p. 412.

Figure 7.5: McClelland, J. L. (2000). Connectionist models of memory. In E. Tulving & F. I. M. Craik (Eds.), *The Oxford handbook of memory.* New York, NY: Oxford University Press, pp. 588–589; adapted from Rumelhart & Todd (1993).

Figure 7.6: Armstrong, S. L., Gleitman, L. R., & Gleitman, H. (1983). What some concepts might not be. *Cognition, 13,* p. 269.

Figure 7.7: Reber, A. S. (1967). Implicit learning of artificial grammars. *Journal of Verbal Learning and Verbal Behavior, 6,* p. 856.

Figure 7.8: Brooks, L. R. (1978). Nonanalytic concept formation and memory for instances. In E. Rosch & B. B. Lloyd (Eds.), *Cognition and categorization.* Hillsdale, NJ: Erlbaum, pp. 169–211.

Photo 7.1: Laurie J. Erickson

Photo 7.2: ©istock/Erik Lam

Chapter 8

Figure 8.1: Brooks, L. R. (1968). Spatial and verbal components of the act of recall. *Canadian Journal of Psychology, 22,* pp. 350–351.

Figure 8.2: Shepard, R. N., & Metzler, J. (1971). Mental rotation of three-dimensional objects. *Science, 171,* p. 701. Copyright © 1971, American Association for the Advancement of Science. Reprinted with permission.

Figure 8.3: Shepard, R. N., & Metzler, J. (1971). Mental rotation of three-dimensional objects. *Science, 171,* p. 701. Copyright © 1971, American Association for the Advancement of Science. Reprinted with permission.

Figure 8.4: Cooper, L. A., & Shepard, R. N. (1973). The time required to prepare for a rotated stimulus. *Memory and Cognition, 1,* p. 247. Copyright © 1973, Psychonomic Society, Inc. Reprinted with permission.

Figure 8.5: Cooper, L. A., & Shepard, R. N. (1973). The time required to prepare for a rotated stimulus. *Memory and Cognition, 1,* p. 248. Copyright © 1973, Psychonomic Society, Inc. Reprinted with permission.

Figure 8.6: Cooper, L. A. (1975). Mental rotation of random two-dimensional shapes. *Cognitive Psychology, 7,* p. 23.

Figure 8.7:   Biederman, I., & Gerhardstein, P. C. (1993). Recognizing depth-rotated objects: Evidence and conditions for three-dimensional viewpoint invariance. *Journal of Experimental Psychology: Human Perception and Performance, 19,* p. 1163.

Figure 8.8:   Kosslyn, S. M. (1973). Scanning visual images: Some structural implications. *Perception and Psychophysics, 14,* p. 91.

Figure 8.9:   Kosslyn, S. M., Ball, T. M., & Reiser, B. J. (1978). Visual images preserve metric spatial information: Evidence from studies of image scanning. *Journal of Experimental Psychology: Human Perception and Performance, 4,* p. 51.

Figure 8.10:   Tversky, B. (1981). Distortions in memory for maps. *Cognitive Psychology, 13,* p. 413.

Figure 8.11:   Chambers, D., & Reisberg, D. (1992). What an image depicts depends on what an image means. *Cognitive Psychology, 24,* p. 152.

Figure 8.12:   Kosslyn, S. M., Reiser, B. J., Farah, M. J., & Fliegel, S. L. (1983). Generating visual images: Units and relations. *Journal of Experimental Psychology: General, 112,* pp. 280, 287.

Figure 8.13:   Carmichael, L., Hogan, H. P., & Walter, A. A. (1932). An experimental study of the effect of language on the reproduction of visually perceived form. *Journal of Experimental Psychology, 15,* p. 80.

Figure 8.14:   Plotnick, R. R. (2012). *Context effect for identification of brand logos.* Unpublished manuscript, Carleton College, Northfield, MN.

Figure 8.15:   Reprinted by permission of Drew Dara-Abrams, PhD.

Figure 8.16:   Reprinted by permission of Drew Dara-Abrams, PhD.

Photo 8.1:   ©Thinkstock

Chapter 9

Box 9.1:   Garrett, M. F. (1990). Sentence processing. In D. N. Osherson & H. Lasnik (Eds.), *An invitation to cognitive science: Vol. 1. Language.* Cambridge, MA: MIT Press, pp. 133–175.

Box 9.2:   Just, M. A., & Carpenter, P. A. (1980). A theory of reading: From eye fixations to comprehension. *Psychological Review, 87,* p. 330.

Box 9.3:   Bransford, J. D., & Johnson, M. K. (1972). Contextual prerequisites for understanding: Some investigations of comprehension and recall. *Journal of Verbal Learning and Verbal Behavior, 11,* p. 718.

Box 9.4:   Thorndyke, P. W. (1977). Cognitive structures in comprehension and memory of narrative discourse. *Cognitive Psychology, 9,* pp. 80–82.

Table 9.1:   Adapted from Moates, D. R., & Schumacher, G. M. (1980). *An introduction to cognitive psychology.* Belmont, CA: Wadsworth.

Table 9.2:   Thorndyke, P. W. (1977). Cognitive structures in comprehension and memory of narrative discourse. *Cognitive Psychology, 9,* p. 79.

Table 9.3:   Berlin, B., & Kay, P. (1969). *Basic color terms: Their universality and evolution.* Berkeley: University of California Press.

Figure 9.4:   Reprinted by permission of Julia Strand, PhD, Visiting Assistant Professor of Psychology, Carleton College.

Figure 9.5: Reprinted by permission of Julia Strand, PhD, Visiting Assistant Professor of Psychology, Carleton College.

Figure 9.6: Kintsch, W., & Keenan, J. (1973). Reading rate and retention as a function of the number of propositions in the base structure of sentences. *Cognitive Psychology, 5,* p. 259.

Figure 9.7: Bransford, J. D., & Johnson, M. K. (1972). Contextual prerequisites for understanding: Some investigations of comprehension and recall. *Journal of Verbal Learning and Verbal Behavior, 11,* p. 717.

Chapter 10

Box 10.1: Perkins, D. N. (1981). *The mind's best work.* Cambridge, MA: Harvard University Press, p. 33.

Box 10.3: Duncker, K. (1945). On problem-solving. *Psychological Monographs, 58* (270), pp. 2–3.

Box 10.4: Gick, M. L., & Holyoak, K. J. (1980). Analogical problem solving. *Cognitive Psychology, 12,* pp. 351–353.

Table 10.1: Benfer, R. A., Brent, E. E., Jr., & Furbee, L. (1991). *Expert systems.* Newbury Park, CA: SAGE, p. 6.

Figure 10.4: Luchins, A. S. (1942). Mechanization in problem solving: The effect of *Einstellung. Psychological Monographs, 54* (248), p. 1.

Figure 10.5: Kellogg, R. T. (2012). *Fundamentals of Cognitive Psychology* (2nd ed.). Thousand Oaks, CA: Sage, p. 246, Fig. 9.2.

Figure 10.6: Kellogg, R. T. (2012). *Fundamentals of Cognitive Psychology* (2nd ed.). Thousand Oaks, CA: Sage, p. 267, Fig. 9.13.

Figure 10.12: Burns, B. D., & Vollmeyer, R. (2002). Goal specificity effects on hypothesis testing in problem solving. *Quarterly Journal of Experimental Psychology, 55A,* p. 245.

Photo 10.1: Timothy Komatsu and Kimberlynn Galotti

Chapter 11

Box 11.1: Reprinted from ALICE IN PUZZLE-LAND © 1982 by Raymond Smullyan, by permission of Collier Associates, P.O. Box 20149, West Palm Beach, FL 33416, USA.

Box 11.2: Reprinted from ALICE IN PUZZLE-LAND © 1982 by Raymond Smullyan, by permission of Collier Associates, P.O. Box 20149, West Palm Beach, FL 33416, USA.

Box 11.5: Adapted from Tversky, A., & Kahneman, D. (1973). Availability: A heuristic for judging frequency and probability. *Cognitive Psychology, 4,* pp. 212–214.

Box 11.6: Kahneman, D., & Tvyersky, A. (1973). On the psychology of prediction. *Psychological Review, 80,* p. 238.

Box 11.9: Klein, G. (1998). *Sources of power: How people make decisions.* Cambridge, MA: MIT Press, p. 32.

Table 11.1: Galotti, K. M. (1989). Approaches to studying formal and everyday reasoning. *Psychological Bulletin, 105,* p. 335.

Figure 11.6: Galotti, K. M. (2002). *Making decisions that matter: How people face important life choices.* Mahwah, NJ: Erlbaum, p. 97.

Chapter 12

Table 12.1: Data from Brown, R. (1973). *A first language: The early stages.* Cambridge, MA: Harvard University Press, as appears in Ingram (1989).

Figure 12.3: Baillargeon, R. (1994). How do infants learn about the physical world? *Current Directions in Psychological Science, 3,* pp. 134.

Figure 12.4: Dempster, F. N. (1981). Memory span: Sources of individual and developmental differences. *Psychological Bulletin, 89,* pp. 66–68.

Photo 12.1: Bill Anderson/Monkmeyer, Press Photo Service

Photo 12.2: Nancy J. Ashmore

Photo 12.3: Doug Goodman/Photo Researchers/Getty Images

Photo 12.4: Nancy J. Ashmore

Photo 12.5: Nancy J. Ashmore

Photo 12.7: ©Thinkstock

Chapter 13

Table 13.1: Adapted from Gardner, H. (1999). *Intelligence reframed: Multiple intelligences for the 21st century.* New York: Basic Books. (The first seven items were presented in Gardner, H. (1983). *Frames of mind: The theory of multiple intelligences.* New York: Basic Books.; the last two come from Gardner (1999).)

Table 13.2: Benbow & Stanley (1980). Copyright © 1980, American Association for the Advancement of Science.

Figure 13.1: Keating, D. P., & Bobbitt, B. L. (1978). Individual and developmental differences in cognitive-processing components of mental ability. *Child Development, 49,* 161.

Figure 13.2: Adapted from Hunt, E., Lunneborg, C., & Lewis, J. (1975). What does it mean to be highly verbal? *Cognitive Psychology, 7,* 194–227.

Figure 13.4: Kagan, J., Rosman, B. L., Day, D., Albert, J., & Phillips, W. (1964). Information processing in the child: Significance of analytic and reflective attitudes. *Psychological Monographs, 78* (1), p. 22.

Figure 13.5: Pashler, H., McDaniel, M., Rohrer, D., & Bjork, R. (2009). Learning styles: Concepts and evidence. *Psychological Science in the Public Interest, 9,* 110.

Figure 13.7: Loring-Meier, S., & Halpern, D. F. Sex differences in visuospatial working memory: Components of cognitive processing. *Psychonomic Bulletin and Review,* 6, p. 466. Copyright © 1999, Psychonomic Society, Inc. Reprinted with permission.

Figure 13.8: Loring-Meier, S., & Halpern, D. F. Sex differences in visuospatial working memory: Components of cognitive processing. *Psychonomic Bulletin and*

Review, 6, p. 468. Copyright © 1999, Psychonomic Society, Inc. Reprinted with permission.

Figure 13.9: Levine, S. C., Vasilyeva, M., Lourenco, S. F., Newcombe, N. S., & Huttenlocher, J. (2005). Socioeconomic status modifies the sex difference in spatial skill. *Psychological Science, 16,* 841–845.

Chapter 14

Table 14.1: Excerpted from Triandis, H. C. (1996). The psychological measurement of cultural syndromes. *American Psychologist, 51,* 408–409.

Table 14.2: Cole, M., & Scribner, S. (1974). *Culture and thought: A psychological introduction.* New York, NY: Wiley, p. 127.

Table 14.3: Adapted from Scribner, S., & Cole, M. (1981). *The psychology of literacy.* Cambridge, MA: Harvard University Press, p. 167.

Figure 14.1: Hudson, W. (1960). Pictorial depth perception in subcultural groups in Africa. *Journal of Social Psychology, 52,* p. 186.

Figure 14.2: Deregowski, J. B. (1968). Difficulties in pictorial depth perception in Africa. *British Journal of Psychology, 59,* p. 197.

Figure 14.3: Miyamoto, Y., Nisbett, R. E., & Matsuda, T. (2006). Culture and the physical environment: Holistic versus analytical perceptual affordances. *Psychological Science, 17,* 113–119.

Figure 14.5: Kearins, J. M. (1981). Visual spatial memory in Australian Aboriginal children of desert regions. *Cognitive Psychology, 13,* 441.

Figure 14.6: Greenfield, P. M., Reich, L. C., & Olver, R. R. (1966). On culture and equivalence: II. In J. S. Bruner et al. (Eds.), *Studies in cognitive growth* (pp. 270–318). New York, NY: Wiley, p. 290.

Figure 14.7: Hatano, G., Siegler, R. S., Richards, D. D., Inagaki, K., Stavy, R., & Wax, N. (1993). The development of biological knowledge: A multi-national study. *Cognitive Development, 8,* 58.

Figure 14.8: Saxe, G. B. (1981). Body parts as numerals: A developmental analysis of numeration among the Oksapmin in Papua New Guinea. *Child Development, 52,* 307.

Figure 14.9: Miller, K. F., Smith, C. M., Zhu, J., & Zhang, H. (1995). Preschool origins of cross-national differences in mathematical competence: The role of number-naming systems. *Psychological Science, 6,* 57.

Figure 14.10: Adapted from Scribner, S., & Cole, M. (1981). *The psychology of literacy.* Cambridge, MA: Harvard University Press, p. 167.

Photo 14.3: ©Thinkstock/Tom Brakefield

Adams, M. J. (1984). Aristotle's logic. In G. H. Bower (Ed.), *The psychology of learning and motivation* (Vol. 18, pp. 255–311). Orlando, FL: Academic Press.

Akshoomoff, N. A., & Courchesne, E. (1994). ERP evidence for a shifting attention deficit in patients with damage to the cerebellum. *Journal of Cognitive Neuroscience, 6,* 388–399.

Altmann, E. M., & Gray, W. D. (2002). Forgetting to remember: The functional relationship of decay and interference. *Psychological Science, 13,* 27–33.

Altmann, G. (1987). Modularity and interaction in sentence processing. In J. L. Garfield (Ed.), *Modularity in knowledge representation and natural language understanding* (pp. 249–257). Cambridge, MA: MIT Press.

Amsel, A. (1989). *Behaviorism, neobehaviorism, and cognitivism in learning theory: historical and contemporary perspectives.* Hillsdale, NJ: Erlbaum.

Anderson, J. R. (1974). Retrieval of propositional information from long-term memory. *Cognitive Psychology, 6,* 451–474.

Anderson, J. R. (1976). *Language, memory, and thought.* Hillsdale, NJ: Erlbaum.

Anderson, J. R. (1983). *The architecture of cognition.* Cambridge, MA: Harvard University Press.

Anderson, J. R. (1993). *Rules of the mind.* Hillsdale, NJ: Erlbaum.

Anderson, J. R. (1995). *Cognitive psychology and its implications* (4th ed.). New York, NY: W. H. Freeman.

Anderson, J. R. (2005). Human symbol manipulation within an integrated cognitive architecture. *Cognitive Science, 29,* 313–341.

Anderson, J. R., & Bower, G. H. (1973). *Human associative memory.* New York, NY: Wiley.

Anderson, J. R., Budiu, R., & Reder, L. M. (2001). A theory of sentence memory as part of a general theory of memory. *Journal of Memory & Language, 45,* 337–367.

Anderson, J. R., & Reder, L. M. (1999). The fan effect: New results and new theories. *Journal of Experimental Psychology: General, 128,* 186–197.

Anderson, M. C., & Neely, J. H. (1996). Interference and inhibition in memory retrieval. In E. L. Bjork & R. A. Bjork (Eds.), *Memory* (pp. 237–313). San Diego, CA: Academic Press.

Arkes, H. R., & Blumer, C. (1985). The psychology of sunk cost. *Organizational Behavior and Human Decision Processes, 35,* 124–140.

Arkes, H. R., & Hutzel, L. (2000). The role of probability of success estimates in the sunk cost effect. *Journal of Behavioral Decision Making, 13,* 295–306.

Armstrong, S. L., Gleitman, L. R., & Gleitman, H. (1983). What some concepts might not be. *Cognition, 13,* 263–308.

Ashcraft, M. H. (1978). Property norms for typical and atypical items from 17 categories: A description and discussion. *Memory and Cognition, 6,* 227–232.

Atance, C. M., & O'Neill, D. K. (2004). Acting and planning on the basis of a false belief: Its effects on 3-year-old children's reasoning about their own false beliefs. *Developmental Psychology, 40,* 953–964.

Atchley, P., Atwood, S., & Boulton, A. (2011). The choice to text and drive in younger drivers: Behavior may shape attitude. *Accident Analysis and Prevention, 43,* 134–142.

Atkinson, R. C., & Shiffrin, R. M. (1968). Human memory: A proposed system and its control processes. In K. W. Spence &J. T. Spence (Eds.), *The psychology of learning and motivation: Advances in research and theory* (Vol. 2, pp. 89–195). New York, NY: Academic Press.

Atran, S., Medin, D. L., & Ross, N. O. (2005). The cultural mind: Environmental decision making and cultural modeling within and across populations. *Psychological Review, 112,* 744–776.

Au, T. K. (1983). Chinese and English counterfactuals: The Sapir-Whorf hypothesis revisited. *Cognition, 15,* 155–187.

Au, T. K. (1984). Counterfactuals: In reply to Alfred Bloom. *Cognition, 17,* 289–302.

Averbach, E., & Coriell, A. S. (1961). Short-term memory in vision. *Bell System Technical Journal, 40,* 309–328.

Ayduk, O., Mischel, W., & Downey, G. (2002). Attentional mechanisms linking rejection to hostile reactivity: The role of "hot" versus "cool" focus. *Psychological Science, 13,* 443–448.

Baddeley, A. D. (1966a). The influence of acoustic and semantic similarity on long-term memory for word sequences. *Quarterly Journal of Experimental Psychology, 18,* 302–309.

Baddeley, A. D. (1966). Short-term memory for word sequences as a function of acoustic, semantic, and formal similarity. *Quarterly Journal of Experimental Psychology, 18,* 362–365.

Baddeley, A. D. (1976). *The psychology of memory.* New York, NY: Basic Books.

Baddeley, A. D. (1978). The trouble with levels: A reexamination of Craik and Lockhart's framework for memory research. *Psychological Review, 85,* 139–152.

Baddeley, A. D. (1981). The concept of working memory: A view of its current state and probable future development. *Cognition, 10,* 17–23.

Baddeley, A. D. (1984). Neuropsychological evidence and the semantic/episodic distinction. *Behavioral and Brain Sciences, 7,* 238–239.

Baddeley, A. D. (1986). *Working memory.* New York, NY: Oxford University Press.

Baddeley, A. D. (1990). *Human memory: Theory and practice.* Boston, MA: Allyn & Bacon.

Baddeley, A. [D.] (1992). Is working memory working? *Quarterly Journal of Experimental Psychology, 44A,* 1–31.

Baddeley, A. [D.] (1993a). Working memory and conscious awareness. In A. F. Collins, S. E. Gathercole, M. A. Conway, & P. E. Morris (Eds.), *Theories of memory* (pp. 11–28). Hove, UK: Erlbaum.

Baddeley, A. [D.] (1993b). *Your memory: A user's guide.* London, UK: Multimedia Books.

Baddeley, A. D. (2000). The episodic buffer: A new component of working memory? *Trends in Cognitive Sciences, 4,* 417–423.

Baddeley, A. [D.] (2007). *Working memory, thought, and action.* New York, NY: Oxford University Press.

Baddeley, A. D., & Andrade, J. (2000). Working memory and the vividness of imagery. *Journal of Experimental Psychology: General, 129,* 126–145.

Baddeley, A. D., & Hitch, G. J. (1974). Working memory. In G. A. Bower (Ed.), *The psychology of learning and motivation* (Vol. 8, pp. 47–90). New York, NY: Academic Press.

Bahrick, H. P. (1983). The cognitive map of a city: Fifty years of learning and memory. In G. H. Bower (Ed.), *The psychology of learning and motivation* (Vol. 17, pp. 125–163). New York, NY: Academic Press.

Bahrick, H. P. (1984). Semantic memory content in permastore: Fifty years of memory for Spanish learned in school. *Journal of Experimental Psychology: General, 113,* 1–29.

Baillargeon, R. (1994). How do infants learn about the physical world? *Current Directions in Psychological Science, 3,* 133–140.

Baillargeon, R., & Wang, S. (2002). Event categorization in infancy. *Trends in Cognitive Sciences, 6,* 85–93.

Baltes, P. B., Staudinger, U. M., & Lindenberger, U. (1999). Lifespan psychology: Theory and application to intellectual functioning. *Annual Review of Psychology, 50,* 471–507.

Bandura, A. (2001). Social cognitive theory: An agentic perspective. *Annual Review of Psychology, 52,* 1–26.

Banich, M. T. (1997). *Neuropsychology: The neural base of mental function.* New York, NY: Houghton Mifflin.

Banich, M. T. (2004). *Cognitive neuroscience and neuropsychology* (2nd ed.). Boston, MA: Houghton Mifflin.

Barkley, R. A. (1998). *Attention-deficit hyperactivity disorder: A handbook for diagnosis and treatment* (2nd ed.). New York, NY: Guilford Press.

Barnes, J. M., & Underwood, B. J. (1959). "Fate" of first-list associations in transfer theory. *Journal of Experimental Psychology, 58,* 97–105.

Baron, J. (1985). *Rationality and intelligence.* Cambridge, UK: Cambridge University Press.

Baron, J. (2000). *Thinking and deciding* (3rd ed.). Cambridge, UK: Cambridge University Press.

Baron, J. (2008). *Thinking and deciding* (4th ed.). Cambridge, UK: Cambridge University Press.

Barrett, L. F., Tugade, M. M., & Engle, R. W. (2004). Individual differences in working memory capacity and dual-process theories of the mind. *Psychological Bulletin, 130,* 553–573.

Barrouillet, P. (2011). Dual-process theories of reasoning: The test of development. *Developmental Review, 31,* 151–179.

Barsalou, L. W. (1983). Ad hoc categories. *Memory and Cognition, 11,* 211–227.

Barsalou, L. W. (1985). Ideals, central tendency, and frequency of instantiation as determinants of graded structure in categories. *Journal of Experimental Psychology: Learning, Memory, and Cognition, 11,* 629–654.

Barsalou, L. W. (1987). The instability of graded structure: Implications for the nature of concepts. In U. Neisser (Ed.), *Concepts and conceptual development* (pp. 101–140). New York, NY: Cambridge University Press.

Barsalou, L. W. (1988). The content and organization of autobiographical memories. In U. Neisser & E. Winograd (Eds.), *Remembering reconsidered: Ecological and traditional approaches to the study of memory* (pp. 193–243). New York, NY: Cambridge University Press.

Barsalou, L. W. (2008). Cognitive and neural contributions to understanding the conceptual system. *Current Directions in Psychological Science, 17,* 91–95.

Bartlett, F. C. (1932). *Remembering: A study in experimental and social psychology.* Cambridge, UK: Cambridge University Press.

Bartlett, F. [C.] (1958). *Thinking: An experimental and social study.* New York, NY: Basic Books.

Barton, M. E., & Komatsu, L. K. (1989). Defining features of natural kinds and artifacts. *Journal of Psycholinguistic Research, 18,* 433–447.

Bass, E., & Davis, L. (1988). *The courage to heal: A guide for women survivors of child sexual abuse.* New York, NY: Harper & Row.

Bates, E., Devescovi, A., & Wulfeck, B. (2001). Psycholinguistics: A cross-language perspective. *Annual Review of Psychology, 52,* 369–396.

Beach, L. R. (1993). Broadening the definition of decision making: The role of prechoice screening of options. *Psychological Science, 4,* 215–220.

Beach, L. R., & Mitchell, T. R. (1987). Image theory: Principles, goals, and plans in decision making. *Acta Psychologica, 66,* 201–220.

Bekoff, M., & Allen, C. (2002). The evolution of social play: Interdisciplinary analyses of cognitive processes. In M. Bekoff, C. Allen, & G. M. Burghardt (Eds.), *The cognitive animal: Empirical and theoretical perspectives on animal cognition* (pp. 429–435). Cambridge, MA: MIT Press.

Belenky, M. F., Clinchy, B. M., Goldberger, N. R., & Tarule, J. M. (1986). *Women's ways of knowing: The development of self, voice, and mind.* New York, NY: Basic Books.

Benbow, C. P., Lubinski, D., Shea, D. L., & Eftekhai-Sanjani, H. (2000). Sex differences in mathematical reasoning ability at age 13: Their status 20 years later. *Psychological Science, 11,* 474–480.

Benbow, C. P., & Stanley, J. C. (1980). Sex differences in mathematical ability: Fact or artifact? *Science, 210,* 1262–1264.

Benbow, C. P., & Stanley, J. C. (1983). Sex differences in mathematical reasoning ability: More facts. *Science, 222,* 1029–1031.

Bender, A. (2011). Cultural variation in numeration systems and their mapping onto the mental number line. *Journal of Cross-Cultural Psychology, 42,* 579–597.

Benfer, R. A., Brent, E. E., Jr., & Furbee, L. (1991). *Expert systems.* Newbury Park, CA: Sage.

Berlin, B., & Kay, P. (1969). *Basic color terms: Their universality and evolution.* Berkeley: University of California Press.

Berntsen, D., & Thomsen, D. K. (2005). Personal memories for remote historical events: Accuracy and clarity of flashbulb memories related to World War II. *Journal of Experimental Psychology: General, 134,* 242–257.

Berry, J. W. (1981). Cultural systems and cognitive styles. In M. P. Friedman, J. P. Das, & N. O'Connor (Eds.), *Intelligence and learning* (pp. 395–406). New York, NY: Plenum.

Berry, J. W. (1984). Towards a universal psychology of cognitive competence. *International Journal of Psychology, 19,* 335–361.

Bhatt, R. S., & Quinn, P. C. (2011). How does learning impact development in infancy? The case of perceptual organization. *Infancy, 16,* 2–38.

Biazak, J. E., Marley, S. C., & Levin, J. R. (2010). Does an activity-based learning strategy improve preschool children's memory for narrative passages? *Early Childhood Research Quarterly, 25,* 515–526.

Biederman, I. (1987). Recognition-by-components: A theory of human image understanding. *Psychological Review, 94,* 115–147.

Biederman, I., & Gerhardstein, P. C. (1993). Recognizing depth-rotated objects: Evidence and conditions for three-dimensional viewpoint invariance. *Journal of Experimental Psychology: Human Perception and Performance, 19,* 1162–1182.

Biederman, I., Glass, A. L., & Stacy, E. W., Jr. (1973). Searching for objects in real-world scenes. *Journal of Experimental Psychology, 97,* 22–27.

Bierwisch, M. (1970). Semantics. In J. Lyons (Ed.), *New horizons in linguistics* (pp. 166–184). Baltimore, MD: Penguin Books.

Bjorklund, D. F. (1997). In search of a metatheory for cognitive development (or, Piaget is dead and I don't feel so good myself). *Child Development, 68,* 144–148.

Bjorklund, D. F., & Green, B. L. (1992). The adaptive nature of cognitive immaturity. *American Psychologist, 47,* 46–54.

Black, I. B. (2004). Plasticity: Introduction. In M. S. Gazzaniga (Ed.), *The cognitive neurosciences* (3rd ed., pp. 107–109). Cambridge, MA: MIT Press.

Blake, R., & Shiffrar, M. (2007). Perception of human motion. *Annual Review of Psychology, 58,* 47–73.

Blanchette, I., & Richards, A. (2004). Reasoning about emotional and neutral materials is logic affected by emotion? *Psychological Science, 15,* 745–752.

Block, J. H. (1976). Issues, problems, and pitfalls in assessing sex differences: A critical review of *The Psychology of Sex Differences. Merrill-Palmer Quarterly, 22,* 283–308.

Bloom, A. H. (1981). *The linguistic shaping of thought: A study in the impact of language on thinking in China and the West.* Hillsdale, NJ: Erlbaum.

Bousfield, W. A. (1953). The occurrence of clustering in recall of randomly arranged associates. *Journal of General Psychology, 49,* 229–240.

Bovet, M. C. (1974). Cognitive processes among illiterate children and adults (S. Opper, Trans.). In J. W. Berry & P. R. Dasen (Eds.), *Culture and cognition: Readings in cross-cultural psychology* (pp. 311–334). London, UK: Methuen.

Bower, G. H. (1970). Imagery as a relational organizer in associative learning. *Journal of Verbal Learning and Verbal Behavior, 9,* 529–533.

Bower, G. H. (1981). Mood and memory. *American Psychologist, 36,* 129–148.

Bower, G. H., Black, J. B., & Turner, T. J. (1979). Scripts in memory for text. *Cognitive Psychology, 11,* 177–220.

Bower, G. H., & Karlin, M. B. (1974). Depth of processing pictures of faces and recognition memory. *Journal of Experimental Psychology, 103,* 751–757.

Bowerman, M. (1973). *Early syntactic development: A cross-linguistic study with special reference to Finnish.* Cambridge, UK: Cambridge University Press.

Braine, M. D. S. (1963). The ontogeny of English phrase structure: The first phase. *Language, 39,* 1–13.

Brainerd, C. J. (1978). The stage question in cognitive-developmental theory. *Behavioral and Brain Sciences, 2,* 173–213.

Bransford, J. D., Barclay, J. R., & Franks, J. J. (1971). Sentence memory: A constructive versus interpretive approach. *Cognitive Psychology, 3,* 193–209.

Bransford, J. D., & Johnson, M. K. (1972). Contextual prerequisites for understanding: Some investigations of comprehension and recall. *Journal of Verbal Learning and Verbal Behavior, 11,* 717–726.

Bressan, P., & Pizzighello, S. (2008). The attentional cost of inattentional blindness. *Cognition, 106,* 370–383.

Brewer, W. L. (1988). Memory for randomly sampled autobiographical events. In U. Neisser & E. Winograd (Eds.), *Remembering reconsidered: Ecological and traditional approaches to the study of memory* (pp. 21–90). New York, NY: Cambridge University Press.

Briand, K. A., & Klein, R. M. (1989). Has feature integration theory come unglued? A reply to Tsal. *Journal of Experimental Psychology: Human Perception and Performance, 15,* 401–406.

Briggs, G. E. (1954). Acquisition, extinction, and recovery functions in retroactive inhibition. *Journal of Experimental Psychology, 47,* 285–293.

Broadbent, D. E. (1958). *Perception and communication.* New York, NY: Pergamon Press.

Brooks, L. R. (1968). Spatial and verbal components of the act of recall. *Canadian Journal of Psychology, 22,* 349–368.

Brooks, L. R. (1978). Nonanalytic concept formation and memory for instances. In E. Rosch & B. B. Lloyd (Eds.), *Cognition and categorization* (pp. 169–211). Hillsdale, NJ: Erlbaum.

Brooks, L. R. (1987). Decentralized control of categorization: The role of prior processing episodes. In U. Neisser (Ed.), *Concepts and conceptual development: Ecological and intellectual factors in categorization* (pp. 141–174). Cambridge, UK: Cambridge University Press.

Brown, A. L., Bransford, J. D., Ferrara, R. A., & Campione, J. C. (1983). Learning, remembering, and understanding. In J. H. Flavell & E. M. Markman (Eds.), *Handbook of child psychology: Vol. 3. Cognitive development* (pp. 77–166). New York, NY: Wiley.

Brown, E. L., & Deffenbacher, K. (1979). *Perception and the senses.* New York, NY: Oxford University Press.

Brown, J. (1958). Some tests of the decay theory of immediate memory. *Quarterly Journal of Experimental Psychology, 10,* 12–21.

Brown, R. (1973). *A first language: The early stages.* Cambridge, MA: Harvard University Press.

Brown, R., & Hanlon, C. (1970). Derivational complexity and order of acquisition in child speech. In J. R. Hayes (Ed.), *Cognition and the development of language* (pp. 11–53). New York, NY: Wiley.

Brown, R., & Kulik, J. (1977). Flashbulb memories. *Cognition, 5,* 73–99.

Browne, B. A., & Cruse, D. F. (1988). The incubation effect: Illusion or illumination? *Human Performance, 1,* 177–185.

Bruner, J. S. (1957). Going beyond the information given. In Colorado University Psychology Department (Eds.), *Contemporary approaches to cognition* (pp. 41–69). Cambridge, MA: Harvard University Press.

Bruner, J. S. (1966). On cognitive growth: II. In J. S. Bruner et al. (Eds.), *Studies in cognitive growth: A collaboration at the Center for Cognitive Studies* (pp. 30–67). New York, NY: Wiley.

Bruner, J. S., Olver, R., Greenfield, P., Hornsby, J. R., Kenney, H. J., Maccoby, M., . . . Sonstroem, A. M. (Eds.). (1966). *Studies in cognitive growth: A collaboration at the Center for Cognitive Studies.* New York, NY: Wiley.

Brunswik, E. (1956). *Perception and the representative design of psychological experiments* (2nd ed.). Berkeley: University of California Press.

Bryan, W. L., & Harter, N. (1899). Studies on the telegraphic language: The acquisition of a hierarchy of habits. *Psychological Review, 6,* 345–375.

Bryant, F. B., & Guilbault, R. L. (2002). "I knew it all along" eventually: The development of hindsight bias in reaction to the Clinton impeachment verdict. *Basic and applied social psychology, 24,* 27–41.

Bugelski, B. R., Kidd, E., & Segmen, J. (1968). Image as a mediator in one-trial paired-associate learning. *Journal of Experimental Psychology, 76,* 69–73.

Burns, B. D., & Vollmeyer, R. (2002). Goal specificity effects on hypothesis testing in problem solving. *Quarterly Journal of Experimental Psychology, 55A,* 241–261.

Butler, A. C., & Roediger, H. L., III. (2008). Feedback enhances the positive effects and reduces the negative effects of multiple-choice testing. *Memory & Cognition, 36,* 604–616.

Butterworth, G. E., Harris, P. L., Leslie, A. M., & Wellman, H. M. (Eds.). (1991). *Perspectives on the child's theory of mind.* Oxford, UK: Oxford University Press.

Cabeza, R., Bruce, V., Kato, T., & Oda, M. (1999). The prototype effect in face recognition: Extensions and limits. *Memory & Cognition, 27,* 139–151.

Cabeza, R., & Nyberg, L. (2000). Imaging cognition II: An empirical review of 275 PET and fMRI studies. *Journal of Cognitive Neuroscience, 12,* 1–47.

Cabeza, R., Rao, S. M., Wagner, A. D., Mayer, A. M., & Schacter, D. L. (2001). Can medial temporal lobe regions distinguish true from false? An event related functional MRI study of veridical and illusory recognition memory. *Proceedings of the National Academy of Sciences, 98,* 4805–4810.

Cacioppo, J. T., & Petty, R. E. (1982). The need for cognition. *Journal of Personality and Social Psychology, 42,* 116–131.

Camaioni, L. (2001). Early language. In G. Bremner & A. Fogel (Eds.), *Blackwell handbook of infant development* (pp. 404–426). Malden, MA: Blackwell.

Campbell, D. T., & Stanley, J. C. (1963). *Experimental and quasi-experimental designs for research.* Chicago, IL: Rand McNally.

Campbell, J. I. D., & Charness, N. (1990). Age-related declines in working-memory skills: Evidence from a complex calculation task. *Developmental Psychology, 26,* 879–888.

Caplan, D. (1994). Language and the brain. In M. A. Gernsbacher (Ed.), *Handbook of psycholinguistics* (pp. 1023–1053). San Diego, CA: Academic Press.

Carlson, L., Zimmer, J. W., & Glover, J. A. (1981). First-letter mnemonics: DAM (Don't Aid Memory). *Journal of General Psychology, 104,* 287–292.

Carlson, N. R. (2013). *Physiology and behavior* (11th ed.). Boston, MA: Allyn & Bacon.

Carmichael, L., Hogan, H. P., & Walter, A. A. (1932). An experimental study of the effect of language on the reproduction of visually perceived form. *Journal of Experimental Psychology, 15,* 73–86.

Carpenter, P. A., & Just, M. A. (1983). What your eyes do while your mind is reading. In K. Rayner (Ed.), *Eye movements in reading: Perceptual and language processes* (pp. 275–307). New York, NY: Academic Press.

Casat, C. D., Pearson, D. A., & Casat, J. P. (2001). Attention-deficit/hyperactivity disorder. In H. B. Vance & A. Pumariega (Eds.), *Clinical assessment of child and adolescent behavior* (pp. 263–306). New York, NY: Wiley.

Case, R. (1978). Intellectual development from birth to adulthood: A neo-Piagetian interpretation. In R. S. Siegler (Ed.), *Children's thinking: What develops?* (pp. 37–72). Hillsdale, NJ: Erlbaum.

Casey, B. J., Giedd, J. N., & Thomas, K. M. (2000). Structural and functional brain development and its relation to cognitive development. *Biological Psychology, 54,* 241–257.

Casey, B. J., Tottenham. N., Listen, C., & Durston, S. (2005). Imaging the developing brain: What have we learned about cognitive development? *Trends in Cognitive Sciences, 9,* 104–110.

Catani, M., Jones, D. K., & Ffytche, D. H. (2005). Perisylvian language networks of the human brain. *Annuals of Neurology, 57,* 8–16.

Catrambone, R., & Holyoak, K. J. (1989). Overcoming contextual limitations on problem-solving transfer. *Journal of Experimental Psychology: Learning, Memory, and Cognition, 15,* 1147–1156.

Cavanaugh, J. C. (1993). *Adult development and aging* (2nd ed.). Pacific Grove, CA: Brooks/Cole.

Cave, K. R., & Bichot, N. P. (1999). Visuospatial attention: Beyond a spotlight model. *Psychonomic Bulletin & Review, 6,* 204–223.

Ceci, S. J., & Roazzi, A. (1994). The effects of context on cognition: Postcards from Brazil. In R. J. Sternberg & R. K. Wagner (Eds.), *Mind in context* (pp. 74–101). Cambridge, UK: Cambridge University Press.

Ceraso, J., & Provitera, A. (1971). Sources of error in syllogistic reasoning. *Cognitive Psychology, 2,* 400–410.

Chabris, C. & Simons, D. (2010). *The invisible gorilla and other ways our intuitions deceive us.* New York, NY: Crown.

Chabris, C. F., Weinberger, A., Fontaine, M., & Simons, D. J. (2011). You do not talk about Fight Club if you do not notice Fight Club: Inattentional blindness for a simulated real-world assault. *i-Perception, 2,* 150–153.

Chambers, D., & Reisberg, D. (1992). What an image depicts depends on what an image means. *Cognitive Psychology, 24,* 145–174.

Chambers, K. L., & Zaragoza, M. S. (2001). Intended and unintended effects of explicit warnings on eyewitness suggestibility: Evidence from source identification tests. *Memory & Cognition, 29,* 1120–1129.

Chapman, L. J., & Chapman, J. P. (1967a). Genesis of popular but erroneous psychodiagnostic observations. *Journal of Abnormal Psychology, 72,* 193–204.

Chapman, L. J., & Chapman, J. P. (1967b). Illusory correlation in observational report. *Journal of Verbal Learning and Verbal Behavior, 6,* 151–155.

Chapman, L. J., & Chapman, J. P. (1969). Illusory correlation as an obstacle to the use of valid psychodiagnostic signs. *Journal of Abnormal Psychology, 74,* 271–280.

Chase, W. G., & Simon, H. A. (1973). Perception in chess. *Cognitive Psychology, 4,* 55–81.

Cherry, E. C. (1953). Some experiments on the recognition of speech, with one and two ears. *Journal of the Acoustical Society of America, 25,* 975–979.

Chi, M. T. H. (1978). Knowledge structures and memory development. In R. S. Siegler (Ed.), *Children's thinking: What develops?* (pp. 73–96). Hillsdale, NJ: Erlbaum.

Chi, M. T. H., Feltovich, P. J., & Glaser, R. (1981). Categorization and representation of physics problems by experts and novices. *Cognitive Science, 5,* 121–125.

Chi, M. T. H., Glaser, R., & Farr, M. (Eds.). (1988). *The nature of expertise.* Hillsdale, NJ: Erlbaum.

Chi, M. T. H., & Koeske, R. D. (1983). Network representation of a child's dinosaur knowledge. *Developmental Psychology, 19,* 29–39.

Chomsky, N. (1957). *Syntactic structures.* The Hague, The Netherlands: Mouton.

Chomsky, N. (1959). A review of Skinner's *Verbal Behavior. Language, 35,* 26–58.

Chomsky, N. (1965). *Aspects of the theory of syntax.* Cambridge, MA: MIT Press.

Christiansen, M. H., & Chater, N. (Eds.). (2001). *Connectionist psycholinguistics.* Westport, CT: Ablex.

Clancy, S. A., Schacter, D. L., McNally, R. J., & Pitman, R. K. (2000). False recognition in women reporting recovered memories of sexual abuse. *Psychological Science, 11,* 26–31.

Clark, A. (2001). *Mindware: An introduction to the philosophy of cognitive science.* New York, NY: Oxford University Press.

Clark, E. V. (1993). *The lexicon in acquisition.* New York, NY: Cambridge University Press.

Clark, H. H., & Clark, E. V. (1977). *Psychology and language.* New York, NY: Harcourt Brace Jovanovich.

Clark, H. H., & Van Der Wege, M. M. (2002). Psycholinguistics. In H. Pashler (Series Ed.) & D. Medin (Vol. Ed.), *Stevens' handbook of experimental psychology: Vol. 2. Memory and cognitive processes* (3rd ed., pp. 209–259). New York, NY: Wiley.

Cofer, C. (1967). Does conceptual organization influence the amount retained in immediate free recall? In B. Kleinmuntz (Ed.), *Concepts and the structure of memory* (pp. 181–214). New York, NY: Wiley.

Cohen, J. (1969). *Statistical power analysis for the behavioral sciences.* New York, NY: Academic Press.

Cohen, N. J. (1997). Memory. In M. T. Banich (Ed.), *Neuropsychology: The neural base of mental function* (pp. 314–367). New York, NY: Houghton Mifflin.

Cohen, N. J., McCloskey, M., & Wible, C. G. (1990). Flashbulb memories and underlying cognitive mechanisms: Reply to Pillemer. *Journal of Experimental Psychology: General, 119,* 97–100.

Cohen, N. J., & Squire, L. R. (1980). Preserved learning and retention of pattern-analyzing skill in amnesia: Dissociation of knowing how and knowing that. *Science, 210,* 207–210.

Cole, M., Gay, J., Glick, J., & Sharp, D. W. (1971). *The cultural context of learning and thinking: An exploration in experimental anthropology.* New York, NY: Basic Books.

Cole, M., & Scribner, S. (1974). *Culture and thought: A psychological introduction.* New York, NY: Wiley.

Collins, A. M., & Loftus, E. F. (1975). A spreading activation theory of semantic processing. *Psychological Review, 82,* 407–428.

Collins, A. [M.], & Michalski, R. (1989). The logic of plausible reasoning: A core theory. *Cognitive Science, 13,* 1–49.

Collins, A. M., & Quillian, M. R. (1969). Retrieval time from semantic memory. *Journal of Verbal Learning and Verbal Behavior, 8,* 240–247.

Coltheart, M. (1980). Iconic memory and visible persistence. *Perception and Psychophysics, 27,* 183–228.

Conrad, C. (1972). Cognitive economy in semantic memory. *Journal of Experimental Psychology, 92,* 149–154.

Conrad, R. (1964). Acoustic confusion in immediate memory. *British Journal of Psychology, 55,* 75–84.

Conway, A. R. A., Cowan, N., & Bunting, M. F. (2001). The cocktail party phenomenon revisited: The importance of working memory capacity. *Psychonomic Bulletin and Review, 8,* 331–335.

Conway, L. G., III, Schaller, M., Tweed, R. G., & Hallett, D. (2001). The complexity of thinking across cultures: Interactions between culture and situational context. *Social Cognition, 19,* 228–250.

Cooper, L. A. (1975). Mental rotation of random two-dimensional shapes. *Cognitive Psychology, 7,* 20–43.

Cooper, L. A. (1976). Demonstration of a mental analog of an external rotation. *Perception and Psychophysics, 19,* 296–302.

Cooper, L. A., & Shepard, R. N. (1973). The time required to prepare for a rotated stimulus. *Memory and Cognition, 1,* 246–250.

Cooper, L. A., & Shepard, R. N. (1975). Mental transformations in the identification of left and right hands. *Journal of Experimental Psychology: Human Perception and Performance, 1,* 48–56.

Corso, J. F. (1981). *Aging sensory systems and perception.* New York, NY: Praeger.

Cosmides, L. (1989). The logic of social exchange: Has natural selection shaped how humans reason? Studies with the Wason selection task. *Cognition, 31,* 187–276.

Cosmides, L., & Tooby, J. (2000). The cognitive neuroscience of social reasoning. In M. S. Gazzaniga (Ed.), *The new cognitive neurosciences* (pp. 1259–1270). Cambridge, MA: MIT Press.

Cosmides, L., & Tooby, J. (2002). Unraveling the enigma of human intelligence: Evolutionary psychology and the multimodular mind. In R. J. Sternberg & J. C. Kaufman (Eds.), *The evolution of intelligence* (pp. 145–198). Mahwah, NJ: Erlbaum.

Couperus, J. W. (2011). Perceptual load influences selective attention across development. *Developmental Psychology, 47,* 1431–1439.

Cowan, N. (1995). *Attention and memory: An integrated framework.* New York, NY: Oxford University Press.

Cowan, N., Elliott, E. M., Saults, S., Nugent, L. D., Bomb. P., & Hismjatullina, A. (2006). Rethinking speed theories of cognitive development: Increasing the rate of recall. *Psychological Science, 17,* 67–73.

Cowper, E. A. (1992). *A concise introduction to syntactic theory: The government binding approach.* Chicago, IL: University of Chicago Press.

Craik, F. I. M., & Lockhart, R. S. (1972). Levels of processing: A framework for memory research. *Journal of Verbal Learning and Verbal Behavior, 11,* 671–684.

Craik, F. I. M., & Tulving, E. (1975). Depth of processing and retention of words in episodic memory. *Journal of Experimental Psychology: General, 104,* 268–294.

Crowder, R. G. (1972). Visual and auditory memory. In J. F. Kavanaugh & I. G. Mattingly (Eds.), *Language by ear and by eye: The relationships between speech and learning to read* (pp. 251–275). Cambridge, MA: MIT Press.

Crowder, R. G. (1976). *Principles of learning and memory.* Hillsdale, NJ: Erlbaum.

Crowder, R. G. (1993). Short-term memory: Where do we stand? *Memory and Cognition, 21,* 142–145.

Crundall, D., Underwood, G., & Chapman, P. (2002). Attending to the peripheral world while driving. *Applied Cognitive Psychology, 16,* 459–475.

Cuenod, C. A., Bookheimer, S. Y., Hertz-Pannier, L., Zeffiro, T. A., Theodore, W. H., & LeBihan, D. (1995). Functional MRI during word generation, using conventional equipment: A potential tool for language localization in the clinical environment. *Neurology, 45,* 1821–1827.

Damasio, A. R. (1994). *Descartes'error: Emotion, reason, and the human brain.* New York, NY: Avon Books.

Damer, T. E. (1980). *Attacking faulty reasoning* (2nd ed.). Belmont, CA: Wadsworth.

Damian, S. (2011). Spoken vs. sign languages: What's the difference? *Cognition, Brain, Behavior: An Interdisciplinary Journal, 15,* 251–265.

Daneman, M., & Carpenter, P. A. (1980). Individual differences in working memory and reading. *Journal of Verbal Learning and Verbal Behavior, 19,* 450–466.

Dara-Abrams, D. (2005). *Architecture of mind and world: How urban form influences spatial cognition.* Unpublished senior thesis, Carleton College, Northfield, MN.

Dartnall, T. (2002). (Ed.), *Creativity, cognition, and knowledge: An interaction.* Westport, CT: Praeger.

Darwin, C. T., Turvey, M. T., & Crowder, R. G. (1972). An auditory analogue of the Sperling partial report procedure: Evidence for brief auditory storage. *Cognitive Psychology, 3,* 255–267.

Davis, H. P., & Klebe, K. J. (2001). A longitudinal study of the performance of the elderly and young on the Tower of Hanoi puzzle and Rey recall. *Brain and Cognition, 46,* 95–99.

Dawson, M. R. W. (1998). *Understanding cognitive science.* Malden, MA: Blackwell.

de Groot, A. D. (1965). *Thought and choice in chess.* The Hague, The Netherlands: Mouton.

Deaux, K. (1985). Sex and gender. *Annual Review of Psychology, 36,* 49–81.

Del Missier, F., Mäntylä, T., & Bruine de Bruin, W. (2010). Executive function in decision making: An individual differences approach. *Thinking & Reasoning, 16,* 69–97.

Demakis, G. J. (2002). Hindsight bias and the Simpson trial: Use in introductory psychology. In R. A. Griggs (Ed.), *Handbook for teaching introductory psychology: Vol. 3: With an emphasis on assessment* (pp. 242–243). Mahwah, NJ: Erlbaum.

Demers, R. A. (1988). Linguistics and animal communication. In F. J. Newmeyer (Ed.), *Linguistics: The Cambridge survey: Vol. 3. Language: Psychological and biological aspects* (pp. 314–335). Cambridge, UK: Cambridge University Press.

Demetriou, A., Christou, C., Spanoudis, G., & Platsidou, M. (2002). The development of mental processing: Efficiency, working memory, and thinking. *Monographs of the Society for Research in Child Development, 67,* 1–169.

Dempster, F. N. (1981). Memory span: Sources of individual and developmental differences. *Psychological Bulletin, 89,* 63–100.

Deregowski, J. B. (1968). Difficulties in pictorial depth perception in Africa. *British Journal of Psychology, 59,* 195–204.

Deregowski, J. B. (1980). Perception. In H. C. Triandis & W. Lonner (Eds.), *Handbook of cross-cultural psychology: Vol. 3. Basic processes* (pp. 21–115). Boston, MA: Allyn & Bacon.

Deregowski, J. B. (1989). Real space and represented space: Cross-cultural perspectives. *Behavioral and Brain Sciences, 12,* 51–119.

DeRosa, D. V., & Tkacz, S. (1976). Memory scanning of organized visual material. *Journal of Experimental Psychology: Human Learning and Memory, 2,* 688–694.

Desimone, R. (1992). The physiology of memory: Recordings of things past. *Science, 258,* 245–246.

Dewey, J. (1933). *How we think.* Boston, MA: D. C. Heath.

Diamond, A. (1991). Frontal lobe involvement in cognitive changes during the first year of life. In K. R. Gibson & A. C. Petersen (Eds.), *Brain maturation and cognitive development: Comparative and cross-cultural perspectives* (pp. 127–180). New York, NY: Aldine de Gruyter.

Dror, I. E., & Kosslyn, S. M. (1994). Mental imagery and aging. *Psychology and Aging, 9,* 90–102.

Duncker, K. (1945). On problem-solving. *Psychological Monographs, 58*(270).

Dweck, C. S. (1986). Motivational processes affecting learning. *American Psychologist, 41,* 1040–1048.

Dweck, C. S. (1999). *Self theories: Their role in motivation, personality, and development.* Philadelphia, PA: Psychology Press.

Dweck, C. S., & Bush, E. S. (1976). Sex differences in learned helplessness: I. Differential debilitation with peer and adult evaluators. *Developmental Psychology, 12,* 147–156.

Dweck, C. S., Davidson, W., Nelson, S., & Enna, B. (1978). Sex differences in learned helplessness: II. The contingencies of evaluative feedback in the classroom; III. An experimental analysis. *Developmental Psychology, 14,* 268–276.

Dweck, C. S., & Goetz, T. E. (1978). Attributions and learned helplessness. In J. H. Harvey, W. J. Ickes, & R. F. Kidd (Eds.), *New directions in attribution research* (Vol. 2, pp. 157–179). Hillsdale, NJ: Erlbaum.

Dweck, C. S., Goetz, T. E., & Strauss, N. L. (1980). Sex differences in learned helplessness: IV. An experimental and naturalistic study of failure generalization and its mediators. *Journal of Personality and Social Psychology, 38,* 441–452.

Dweck, C. S., & Leggett, E. L. (1988). A social-cognitive approach to motivation and personality. *Psychological Review, 95,* 256–273.

Ebbinghaus, H. (1913). *Memory: A contribution to experimental psychology* (H. A. Ruger & C. E. Bussenius, Trans.). New York, NY: Columbia University, Teacher's College. (Original work published 1885)

Egan, D. E., & Greeno, J. G. (1974). Theory of rule induction: Knowledge acquired in concept learning, serial pattern learning, and problem solving. In L. W. Gregg (Ed.), *Knowledge and cognition* (pp. 43–103). Potomac, MD: Erlbaum.

Eich, E. (1995). Searching for mood dependent memory. *Psychological Science, 6,* 67–75.

Eich, J. E. (1980). The cue-dependent nature of state-dependent retrieval. *Memory and Cognition, 8,* 157–173.

Eimas, P. D. (1985). The perception of speech in early infancy. *Scientific American, 204,* 66–72.

Eimer, M., & Kiss, M. (2010). Top-down search strategies determine attentional capture in visual search: Behavioral and electrophysiological evidence. *Attention, Perception, & Psychophysics, 72,* 951–962.

Engle, R. W. (2002). Working memory capacity as executive attention. *Current Directions in Psychological Science, 11,* 19–23.

Ericsson, K. A., & Simon, H. A. (1984). *Protocol analysis: Verbal reports as data.* Cambridge, MA: MIT Press/Bradford.

Evans, J. St. B. T. (1972). Reasoning with negatives. *British Journal of Psychology, 63,* 213–219.

Evans, J. St. B. T., Barston, J., & Pollard, P. (1983). On the conflict between logic and belief in syllogistic reasoning. *Memory and Cognition, 11,* 295–306.

Fancher, R. E. (1979). *Pioneers of psychology.* New York, NY: Norton.

Farah, M. J. (1985). Psychophysical evidence for a shared representational medium for mental images and percepts. *Journal of Experimental Psychology: General, 114,* 91–103.

Farah, M. J. (1988). Is visual imagery really visual? Overlooked evidence from neuropsychology. *Psychological Review, 95,* 307–317.

Farah, M. J. (1990). *Visual agnosia: Disorders of object recognition and what they tell us about normal vision.* Cambridge, MA: MIT Press.

Farah, M. J., Péronnet, F., Gonon, M. A., & Giard, M. H. (1988). Electrophysiological evidence for a shared representational medium for visual images and visual percepts. *Journal of Experimental Psychology: General, 117,* 248–257.

Farber, D. A., & Beteleva, T. G. (2011). Development of the brain's organization of working memory in young schoolchildren. *Human Physiology, 37,* 1–13.

Feldman, J. A., & Ballard, D. H. (1982). Connectionist models and their properties. *Cognitive Science, 6,* 205–254.

Fiddick, L., Cosmides, L., & Tooby, J. (2000). No interpretation without representation: The role of domain-specific representations and inferences in the Wason selection task. *Cognition, 77,* 1–79.

Finke, R. A. (1989). *Principles of mental imagery.* Cambridge, MA: MIT Press.

Fischhoff, B. (1982). For those condemned to study the past: Heuristics and biases in hindsight. In D. Kahneman, P. Slovic, & A. Tversky (Eds.), *Judgment under uncertainty: Heuristics and biases* (pp. 335–351). Cambridge, UK: Cambridge University Press.

Fivush, R., & Slackman, E. A. (1986). The acquisition and development of scripts. In K. Nelson (Ed.), *Event knowledge: Structure and function in development* (pp. 71–96). Hillsdale, NJ: Erlbaum.

Flavell, J. H. (1985). *Cognitive development* (2nd ed.). Englewood Cliffs, NJ: Prentice Hall.

Flavell, J. H. (1999). Cognitive development: Children's knowledge about the mind. *Annual Review of Psychology, 50,* 21–45.

Flavell, J. H., Beach, D. R., & Chinsky, J. M. (1966). Spontaneous verbal rehearsal in memory task as a function of age. *Child Development, 37,* 283–299.

Flavell, J. H., Friedrichs, A. G., & Hoyt, J. D. (1970). Developmental changes in memorization processes. *Cognitive Psychology, 1,* 324–340.

Flavell, J. H., Green F. L., Flavell, E. R., & Grossman, J. B. (1997). The development of children's knowledge about inner speech. *Child Development, 68,* 39–47.

Fodor, J. A. (1983). *The modularity of mind: An essay on faulty psychology.* Cambridge, MA: MIT Press.

Fodor, J. A. (1985). Précis of *The modularity of mind. Behavioral and Brain Sciences, 8,* 1–42.

Fodor, J. A., & Pylyshyn, Z. W. (1981). How direct is visual perception? Some reflections on Gibson's "ecological approach." *Cognition, 9,* 139–196.

Fox, M. (2007). *Talking hands: What sign language reveals about the mind.* New York, NY: Simon & Schuster.

Frisch, D., & Clemen, R. T. (1994). Beyond expected utility: Rethinking behavioral decision research. *Psychological Bulletin, 116,* 46–54.

Frith, C. D., & Friston, K. J. (1997). Studying brain function with neuroimaging. In M. D. Rugg (Ed.), *Cognitive neuroscience* (pp. 169–195). Cambridge, MA: MIT Press.

Fromkin, V., & Rodman, R. (1974). *An introduction to language.* New York, NY: Holt, Rinehart & Winston.

Fukuda, K., & Vogel, E. K. (2011). Individual differences in recovery time from attentional capture. *Psychological Science, 22,* 361–368.

Galotti, K. M. (1989). Approaches to studying formal and everyday reasoning. *Psychological Bulletin, 105,* 331–351.

Galotti, K. M. (1999). Making a "major" real-life decision: College students choosing an academic major. *Journal of Educational Psychology, 91,* 379–387.

Galotti, K. M. (2002). *Making decisions that matter: How people face important life choices.* Mahwah, NJ: Erlbaum.

Galotti, K. M. (2005). Setting goals and making plans: How children and adolescents frame their decisions. In J. E. Jacobs & P. A. Klaczynski (Eds.), *The development of judgment and decision making in children and adolescents* (pp. 303–326). Mahwah, NJ: Erlbaum.

Galotti, K. M. (2011). *Cognitive development: Infancy through adolescence.* Thousand Oaks, CA: Sage.

Galotti, K. M., Baron, J., & Sabini, J. P. (1986). Individual differences in syllogistic reasoning: Deduction rules or mental models? *Journal of Experimental Psychology: General, 115,* 16–25.

Galotti, K. M., Ciner, E., Altenbaumer, H. E., Geerts, H. J., Rupp, A., & Woulfe, J. (2006). Decision-making styles in a real-life decision: Choosing a college major. *Personality and Individual Differences, 41,* 629–639.

Galotti, K. M., Clinchy, B. M., Ainsworth, K. H., Lavin, B., & Mansfield, A. F. (1999). A new way of assessing ways of knowing: The Attitudes Toward Thinking and Learning Survey (ATTLS). *Sex Roles, 40,* 745–766.

Galotti, K. M., & Ganong, W. F., III. (1985). What non-programmers know about programming: Natural language procedure specification. *International Journal of Man-Machine Studies, 22,* 1–10.

Galotti, K. M., & Komatsu, L. K. (1993). Why study deduction? *Behavioral and Brain Sciences, 16,* 350.

Galotti, K. M., Komatsu, L. K., & Voelz, S. (1997). Children's differential performance on deductive and inductive syllogisms. *Developmental Psychology, 33,* 70–78.

Galotti, K. M., & Kozberg, S. F. (1987). Older adolescents' thinking about academic/vocational and interpersonal commitments. *Journal of Youth and Adolescence, 16,* 313–330.

Galotti, K. M., Reimer, R. L., & Drebus, D. W. (2001). Ways of knowing as learning styles: Learning MAGIC with a partner. *Sex Roles, 44,* 419–436.

Galton, F. (1907). *Inquiries into human faculty and its development.* London, UK: J. M. Dent & Sons. (Original work published 1883)

Gardner, B. T., & Gardner, R. A. (1971). Two-way communication with an infant chimpanzee. In A. M. Schrier & F. Stollnitz (Eds.), *Behavior of nonhuman primates* (Vol. 4, pp. 117–184). New York, NY: Academic Press.

Gardner, H. (1983). *Frames of mind: The theory of multiple intelligences.* New York, NY: Basic Books.

Gardner, H. (1985). *The mind's new science: A history of the cognitive revolution.* New York, NY: Basic Books.

Gardner, H. (1993). *Multiple intelligences: The theory in practice.* New York, NY: Basic Books.

Gardner, H. (1999). *Intelligence reframed: Multiple intelligences for the 21st century.* New York, NY: Basic Books.

Garrett, B. (2011). *Brain & behavior: An introduction to biological psychology.* Thousand Oaks, CA: Sage.

Garrett, M. F. (1988). Processes in language production. In F. J. Newmeyer (Ed.), *Linguistics: The Cambridge survey: Vol. 3. Language: Psychological and biological aspects* (pp. 69–96). Cambridge, UK: Cambridge University Press.

Garrett, M. F. (1990). Sentence processing. In D. N. Osherson & H. Lasnik (Eds.), *An invitation to cognitive science: Vol. 1. Language* (pp. 133–175). Cambridge, MA: MIT Press.

Garry, M., & Wade, K. A. (2005). Actually, a picture is worth less than 45 words: Narratives produce more false memories than photographs do. *Psychological Bulletin and Review, 12,* 359–366.

Gathercole, S. E. (1994). Neuropsychology and working memory: A review. *Neuropsychology, 8,* 494–505.

Gathercole, S. E., & Pickering, S. J. (2000). Assessment of working memory in six- and seven-year-old children. *Journal of Educational Psychology, 92,* 377–390.

Gathercole, S. E., Pickering, S. J., Knight, C., & Stegmann, Z. (2004). Working memory skills and educational attainment: Evidence from national curriculum assessments at 7 and 14 years of age. *Applied Cognitive Psychology, 18,* 1–16.

Gauffroy, C., & Barrouillet, P. (2011). The primacy of thinking about possibilities in the development of reasoning. *Developmental Psychology, 47,* 1000–1011.

Gauthier, I., & Tarr, M. J. (1997a). Becoming a "greeble" expert: Exploring mechanisms for face recognition. *Vision Research, 37,* 1673–1682.

Gauthier, I., & Tarr, M. J. (1997b). Orientation priming of novel shapes in the context of viewpoint-dependent recognition. *Perception, 26,* 51–73.

Gauthier, I., Williams, P., Tarr, M. J., & Tanaka, J. (1998). Training "greeble" experts: A framework for studying expert object recognition processes. *Vision Research, 38,* 2401–2428.

Gazzaniga, M. S. (Ed.). (2009). *The cognitive neurosciences* (4th ed). Cambridge, MA: MIT Press.

Gazzaniga, M. S., & Sperry, R. W. (1967). Language after section of the cerebral commissures. *Brain, 90,* 131–148.

Gelman, R. (1979). Preschool thought. *American Psychologist, 34,* 900–905.

Gelman, R., & Baillargeon, R. (1983). A review of some Piagetian concepts. In J. H. Flavell & E. M. Markman (Eds.), *Handbook of child psychology: Vol. 3. Cognitive development* (pp. 167–230). New York, NY: Wiley.

Gelman, R., & Gallistel, C. R. (1978). *The child's understanding of number.* Cambridge, MA: Harvard University Press.

Gernsbacher, M. A. (1993). Less skilled readers have less efficient suppression mechanisms. *Psychological Science, 3,* 294–298.

Gernsbacher, M. A., & Kaschak, M. P. (2003). Neuroimaging studies of language production and comprehension. *Annual Review of Psychology, 54,* 91–114.

Gibbs, R. W., Jr. (1986). What makes some indirect speech acts conventional? *Journal of Memory and Language, 25,* 181–196.

Gibson, E. J. (1969). *Principles of perceptual learning and development.* New York, NY: Meredith.

Gibson, E. J., & Spelke, E. S. (1983). The development of perception. In J. H. Flavell & E. M. Markman (Eds.), *Handbook of child psychology: Vol. 3. Cognitive development* (pp. 1–76). New York, NY: Wiley.

Gibson, J. J. (1950). *The perception of the visual world.* Boston, MA: Houghton Mifflin.

Gibson, J. J. (1979). *The ecological approach to visual perception.* Boston, MA: Houghton Mifflin.

Gibson, J. J., & Gibson, E. J. (1955). Perceptual learning: Differentiation or enrichment? *Psychological Review, 62,* 32–41.

Gick, M. L., & Holyoak, K. J. (1980). Analogical problem solving. *Cognitive Psychology, 12,* 306–355.

Gick, M. L., & Holyoak, K. J. (1983). Schema induction and analogical transfer. *Cognitive Psychology, 15,* 1–38.

Gilhooly, K. J., & Floratou, E. (2009). Executive functions in insight versus non-insight problem solving: An individual differences approach. *Thinking & Reasoning, 15,* 355–376.

Gilligan, C. (1982). *In a different voice: Psychological theory and women's development.* Cambridge, MA: Harvard University Press.

Ginsburg, H. P., & Opper, S. (1988). *Piaget's theory of intellectual development* (3rd ed.). Englewood Cliffs, NJ: Prentice Hall.

Glaser, R., & Chi, M. T. H. (1988). Overview. In M. T. H. Chi, R. Glaser, & M. J. Farr (Eds.), *The nature of expertise* (pp. xv–xxviii). Hillsdale, NJ: Erlbaum.

Glenberg, A. M. (1977). Influences of retrieval process on the spacing effect in free recall. *Journal of Experimental Psychology: Human Learning and Memory, 3,* 282–294.

Globerson, T., & Zelnicker, T. (Eds.). (1989). *Human Development: Vol. 3. Cognitive style and cognitive development.* Norwood, NJ: Ablex.

Gobet, F., & Simon, H. A. (1996). The roles of recognition processes and look-ahead search in time-constrained expert problem solving: Evidence from grand-master-level chess. *Psychological Science, 7,* 52–55.

Godden, D. R., & Baddeley, A. D. (1975). Context dependent memory in two natural environments: On land and underwater. *British Journal of Psychology, 66,* 325–332.

Godden, D. R., & Baddeley, A. D. (1980). When does context influence recognition memory? *British Journal of Psychology, 71,* 99–104.

Goel, V., & Grafman, J. (2000). Role of the prefrontal cortex in ill-structured planning. *Cognitive Neuropsychology, 17,* 415–436.

Goldberger, N., Tarule, J., Clinchy, B., & Belenky, M. (Eds.). (1996). *Knowledge, difference, and power: Essays inspired by women's ways of knowing.* New York, NY: Basic Books.

Goldman, S. R., & Varnhagen, C. K. (1986). Memory for embedded and sequential story structures. *Journal of Memory and Language, 25,* 401–418.

Goldman-Rakic, P. S. (1987). Development of cortical circuitry and cognitive function. *Child Development, 58,* 601–622.

Goldstein, D. G., & Gigerenzer, G. (2011). Reasoning the fast and frugal way: Models of bounded rationality. In G. Gigerenzer & R. Hertwig (Eds.), *Heuristics: The foundations of adaptive behavior* (pp. 33–54). New York: Oxford University Press.

Goodman, N. (1972). *Problems and projects.* Indianapolis, IN: Bobbs-Merrill.

Goody, J., & Watt, I. (1968). The consequences of literacy. In J. Goody (Ed.), *Literacy in traditional societies* (pp. 27–68). Cambridge, UK: Cambridge University Press.

Gould, S. J. (1995). Mismeasure by any measure. In R. Jacoby & N. Glauberman (Eds.), *The bell curve debate: History, documents, opinions* (pp. 3–13). New York, NY: Times Books.

Graesser, A. C., & Clark, L. F. (1985). *The structures and procedures of implicit knowledge.* Norwood, NJ: Ablex.

Graham, E. R., & Burke, D. M. (2011). Aging increases inattentional blindness to the gorilla in our midst. *Psychology and Aging, 26,* 162–166.

Green, K. E., & Schroeder, D. H. (1990). Psychometric quality of the Verbalizer-Visualizer Questionnaire as a measure of cognitive style. *Psychological Reports, 66,* 939–945.

Greenberg, D. L. (2004). President Bush's false "flashbulb" memory of 9/11. *Applied Cognitive Psychology, 18,* 363–370.

Greenberg, S. N., Healy, A. F., Koriat, A., & Kreiner, H. (2004). The GO model: A reconsideration of the role of structural units in guiding and organizing text online. *Psychonomic Bulletin and Review, 11,* 428–433.

Greenfield, P. M. (2005). Paradigms of cultural thought. In K. J. Holyoak & R. G. Morrison (Eds.), *The Cambridge handbook of thinking and reasoning* (pp. 663–682). New York, NY: Cambridge University Press.

Greenfield, P. M., Reich, L. C., & Olver, R. R. (1966). On culture and equivalence: II. In J. S. Bruner et al. (Eds.), *Studies in cognitive growth* (pp. 270–318). New York, NY: Wiley.

Gregory, R. L. (1972). Cognitive contours. *Nature, 238,* 51–52.

Grice, H. P. (1975). Logic and conversation. In P. Cole & J. L. Morgan (Eds.), *Syntax and semantics: Vol. 3. Speech acts* (pp. 41–58). New York, NY: Seminar Press.

Griggs, R. A. (1983). The role of problem content in the selection task and in the THOG problem. In J. St. B. T. Evans (Ed.), *Thinking and reasoning: Psychological approaches* (pp. 16–43). London, UK: Routledge & Kegan Paul.

Griggs, R. A., & Cox, J. R. (1982). The elusive thematic-materials effect in Wason's selection task. *British Journal of Psychology, 73,* 407–420.

Gutchess, A. H., Yoon, C. Luo, T., Feinberg, F., Hedden, T., Jing, Q., . . . Park, D. C. (2006). Categorical organization in free recall across culture and age. *Gerontology, 52,* 314–323.

Haber, R. N. (1983). The impending demise of the icon: A critique of the concept of iconic storage in visual information processing. *Behavioral and Brain Sciences, 6,* 1–54.

Hahn, U., & Chater, N. (1997). Concepts and similarity. In K. Lamberts & D. Shanks (Eds.), *Knowledge, concepts, and categories* (pp. 43–92). Cambridge, MA: MIT Press.

Halford, G. S. (1989). Reflections on 25 years of Piagetian cognitive developmental psychology, 1963–1988. *Human Development, 32,* 325–357.

Halle, M. (1990). Phonology. In D. N. Osherson & H. Lasnik (Eds.), *An invitation to cognitive science: Vol. 1. Language* (pp. 43–68). Cambridge, MA: MIT Press.

Halpern, D. F. (1992). *Sex differences in cognitive abilities* (2nd ed.). Hillsdale, NJ: Erlbaum.

Hampton, J. A. (2007). Typicality, graded membership, and vagueness. *Cognitive Science, 31,* 355–384.

Han, K., & Marvin, C. (2002). Multiple creativities? Investigating domain-specificity of creativity in young children. *Gifted Child Quarterly, 46,* 98–109.

Hannon, E. M., & Richards, A. (2010). Is inattentional blindness related to individual differences in visual working memory capacity or executive control functioning? *Perception, 39,* 309–319.

Harley, T. A. (1995). *The psychology of language: From data to theory.* Hillsdale, NJ: Erlbaum.

Harnad, S. (Ed.). (1987). *Categorical perception.* Cambridge, UK: Cambridge University Press.

Harris, R. J. (1977). Comprehension of pragmatic implications in advertising. *Journal of Applied Psychology, 62,* 603–608.

Harrison, M. A. (2011). College students' prevalence and perceptions of text messaging while driving. *Accident Analysis and Prevention, 43,* 1516–1520.

Hasher, L., & Zacks, R. T. (1984). Automatic processing of fundamental information. *American Psychologist, 39,* 1372–1388.

Hatano, G., Siegler, R. S., Richards, D. D., Inagaki, K., Stavy, R., & Wax, N. (1993). The development of biological knowledge: A multi-national study. *Cognitive Development, 8,* 47–62.

Hauser, M. D. (2000). *Wild minds: What animals really think.* New York, NY: Henry Holt.

Haviland, S. E., & Clark, H. H. (1974). What's new? Acquiring new information as a process in comprehension. *Journal of Verbal Learning and Verbal Behavior, 13,* 512–521.

Hawkins, J., Pea, R. D., Glick, J., & Scribner, S. (1984). "Merds that laugh don't like mushrooms": Evidence for deductive reasoning by preschoolers. *Developmental Psychology, 20,* 584–594.

Healy, A. F., & McNamara, D. S. (1996). Verbal learning and memory: Does the modal model still work? *Annual Review of Psychology, 47,* 143–172.

Hebb, D. O. (1949). *The organization of behavior: A neuropsychological theory.* New York, NY: Wiley.

Hedges, L. V., & Olkin, I. (1985). *Statistical methods for meta-analysis.* New York, NY: Academic Press.

Heider, E. R. (1972). Universals in color naming and memory. *Journal of Experimental Psychology, 93,* 10–20.

Heil, E. (1997). Knowledge and concept learning. In K. Lamberts & D. Shanks (Eds.), *Knowledge, concepts, and categories* (pp. 7–41). Cambridge, MA: MIT Press.

Henle, M. (1962). On the relation between logic and thinking. *Psychological Review, 69,* 366–378.

Hennessey, B. A., & Amabile, T. M. (1988). The conditions of creativity. In R. J. Sternberg (Ed.), *The nature of creativity* (pp. 11–38). Cambridge, UK: Cambridge University Press.

Hergenhahn, B. R. (1986). *An introduction to the history of psychology.* Belmont, CA: Wadsworth.

Herrnstein, R. J., & Murray, C. (1994). *The bell curve: Intelligence and class structure in American life.* New York, NY: Free Press.

Hillner, K. P. (1984). *History and systems of modern psychology: A conceptual approach.* New York, NY: Gardner Press.

Hirst, W., Spelke, E. S., Reaves, C. C., Caharack, G., & Neisser, U. (1980). Dividing attention without alternation or automaticity. *Journal of Experimental Psychology: General, 109,* 98–117.

Hitch, G. J., Towse, J. N., & Hutton, U. (2001). What limits children's working memory span? Theoretical accounts and applications for scholastic development. *Journal of Experimental Psychology: General, 130,* 184–198.

Hochberg, J. E. (1978). *Perception* (2nd ed.). Englewood Cliffs, NJ: Prentice Hall.

Hockett, C. F. (1960). The origin of speech. *Scientific American, 203*(3), 88–96.

Hoelzl, E., Kirchler, E., & Rodler, C. (2002). Hindsight bias in economic expectations: I knew all along what I want to hear. *Journal of Applied Psychology, 87,* 437–443.

Hoffman, R. R., Bamberg, M., Bringmann, W., & Klein, R. (1987). Some historical observations on Ebbinghaus. In D. S. Gorfein & R. R. Hoffman (Eds.), *Memory and learning: The Ebbinghaus Centennial Conference* (pp. 57–76). Hillsdale, NJ: Erlbaum.

Holyoak, K. J., & Nisbett, R. E. (1988). Induction. In R. J. Sternberg & E. E. Smith (Eds.), *The psychology of human thought* (pp. 50–91). Cambridge, UK: Cambridge University Press.

Horn, J. L. (1989). Cognitive diversity: A framework of learning. In P. L. Ackerman, R. J. Sternberg, & R. Glaser (Eds.), *Learning and individual differences: Advances in theory and research* (pp. 61–116). New York, NY: W. H. Freeman.

Horton, D. L., & Mills, C. B. (1984). Human learning and memory. *Annual Review of Psychology, 35,* 361–394.

Howe, M. L., & O'Sullivan, J. T. (1990). The development of strategic memory: Coordinating knowledge, metamemory, and resources. In D. F. Bjorklund (Ed.), *Children's strategies: Contemporary views of cognitive development* (pp. 129–155). Hillsdale, NJ: Erlbaum.

Hubel D. H., & Wiesel T. N. (1959). Receptive fields of single neurons in the cat's striate cortex. *Journal of Physiology, 148,* 574–591.

Hubel, D. H., & Wiesel, T. N. (1962). Receptive fields, binocular interaction, and functional architecture in the cat's visual cortex. *Journal of Physiology, 160,* 106–154.

Hubel, D. H., & Wiesel, T. N. (1968). Receptive fields and functional architecture of monkey striate cortex. *Journal of Physiology, 195,* 215–243.

Hudson, W. (1960). Pictorial depth perception in sub-cultural groups in Africa. *Journal of Social Psychology, 52,* 183–208.

Hudson, W. (1967). The study of the problem of pictorial perception among unacculturated groups. *International Journal of Psychology, 2,* 89–107.

Hunt, E. (1978). Mechanics of verbal ability. *Psychological Review, 85,* 109–130.

Hunt, E. (1986). The heffalump of intelligence. In R. J. Sternberg & D. K. Detterman (Eds.), *What is intelligence? Contemporary viewpoints on its nature and definition* (pp. 101–107). Norwood, NJ: Ablex.

Hunt, E., & Agnoli, F. (1991). The Whorfian hypothesis: A cognitive psychology perspective. *Psychological Review, 98,* 377–389.

Hunt, E., Lunneborg, C., & Lewis, J. (1975). What does it mean to be highly verbal? *Cognitive Psychology, 7,* 194–227.

Hyde, J. S. (1981). How large are cognitive gender differences? *American Psychologist, 36,* 892–901.

Hyde, J. S., & Linn, M. C. (1988). Gender differences in verbal ability: A meta-analysis. *Psychological Bulletin, 104,* 53–69.

Hyman, I. E., Jr., Husband, T. H., & Billings, F. J. (1995). False memories of childhood experiences. *Applied Cognitive Psychology, 9,* 181–198.

Hyman, I. E., Jr., Boss, S. M., Wise, B. M., McKenzie, K. E., & Caggiano, J. M. (2010). Did you see the unicycling clown? Inattentional blindness while walking and talking on a cell phone. *Applied Cognitive Psychology, 24,* 597–607.

Ingram, D. (1989). *First language acquisition: Method, description, and explanation.* Cambridge, UK: Cambridge University Press.

Intons-Peterson, M. J. (1983). Imagery paradigms: How vulnerable are they to experimenters' expectations? *Journal of Experimental Psychology: Human Perception and Performance, 9,* 394–412.

Irwin, M. H., & McLaughlin, D. H. (1970). Ability and preference in category sorting by Mano schoolchildren and adults. *Journal of Social Psychology, 82,* 15–24.

Irwin, M. H., Schafer, G. N., & Feiden, C. P. (1974). Emic and unfamiliar category sorting of Mano farmers and U.S. undergraduates. *Journal of Cross-Cultural Psychology, 5,* 407–423.

Jacklin, C. N. (1989). Female and male: Issues of gender. *American Psychologist, 44,* 127–133.

James, W. (1983). *The principles of psychology.* Cambridge, MA: Harvard University Press. (Original work published 1890)

Jarvella, R. J. (1971). Syntactic processing of connected speech. *Journal of Verbal Learning and Verbal Behavior, 10,* 409–416.

Jaschinski, U., & Wentura, D. (2002). Misleading postevent information and working memory capacity: An individual differences approach to eyewitness memory. *Applied Cognitive Psychology, 16,* 223–231.

Jenkins, J. M., & Astington, J. W. (1996). Cognitive factors and family structure associated with theory of mind development in young children. *Developmental Psychology, 32,* 70–78.

Ji, L., Peng, K., & Nisbett, R. E. (2000). Culture, control, and perception of relationships in the environment. *Journal of Personality and Social Psychology, 78,* 943–955.

Johansson, G. (1973). Visual perception of biological motion and a model for its analysis. *Perception and Psychophysics, 14,* 201–211.

Johnson, M. K., & Hasher, L. (1987). Human learning and memory. *Annual Review of Psychology, 38,* 631–668.

Johnson, W. A., & Dark, V. J. (1986). Selective attention. *Annual Review of Psychology, 37,* 43–75.

Just, M. A., & Carpenter, P. A. (1980). A theory of reading: From eye fixations to comprehension. *Psychological Review, 87,* 329–354.

Just, M. A., & Carpenter, P. A. (1987). *The psychology of reading and language comprehension.* Boston, MA: Allyn & Bacon.

Kagan, J., Rosman, B. L., Day, D., Albert, J., & Phillips, W. (1964). Information processing in the child: Significance of analytic and reflective attitudes. *Psychological Monographs, 78*(1).

Kagitçibasi, C., & Berry, J. W. (1989). Cross-cultural psychology: Current research and trends. *Annual Review of Psychology, 40,* 493–531.

Kahneman, D. (1973). *Attention and effort.* Englewood Cliffs, NJ: Prentice Hall.

Kahneman, D., & Tversky, A. (1973). On the psychology of prediction. *Psychological Review, 80,* 237–251.

Kahneman, D., & Tversky, A. (1979). Prospect theory: An analysis of decisions under risk. *Econometrica, 47,* 263–291.

Kail, R. (1986). Sources of age differences in speed of processing. *Child Development, 57,* 969–987.

Kail, R. (1988). Developmental functions for speeds of cognitive processes. *Journal of Experimental Child Psychology, 45,* 339–364.

Kail, R., & Hall, L. K. (2001). Distinguishing short-term memory from working memory. *Memory & Cognition, 29,* 1–9.

Kamin, L. J. (1995). Lies, damned lies, and statistics. In R. Jacoby & N. Glauberman (Eds.), *The bell curve debate: History, documents, opinions* (pp. 81–105). New York, NY: Times Books.

Kane, M. J., Bleckley, M. K., Conway, A. R. A., & Engle, R. W. (2001). A controlled-attention view of working-memory capacity. *Journal of Experimental Psychology: General, 130,* 169–183.

Karnath, H-O. (2009). A right perisylvian neural network for human spatial orienting. In M. S. Gazzaniga (Ed.), *The cognitive neurosciences* (4th ed., pp. 259–268). Cambridge, MA: MIT Press.

Kastner, S., McMains, S. A., & Beck, D. M. (2009). Mechanisms of selective attention in the human visual system: Evidence from neuroimaging. In M. S. Gazzaniga (Ed.), *The cognitive neurosciences* (4th ed., pp. 205–218). Cambridge, MA: MIT Press.

Kearins, J. M. (1981). Visual spatial memory in Australian Aboriginal children of desert regions. *Cognitive Psychology, 13,* 434–460.

Keating, D. P., & Bobbitt, B. L. (1978). Individual and developmental differences in cognitive-processing components of mental ability. *Child Development, 49,* 155–167.

Keeney, T. J., Cannizzo, S. R., & Flavell, J. H. (1967). Spontaneous and induced verbal rehearsal in a recall task. *Child Development, 38,* 953–966.

Keil, F. C. (1989). *Concepts, kinds, and cognitive development.* Cambridge, MA: MIT Press.

Kellogg, R. T. (2012). *Fundamentals of Cognitive Psychology* (2nd ed.). Thousand Oaks, CA: Sage.

Kemler, D. G. (1983). Holistic and analytic modes in perceptual and cognitive development. In T. J. Tighe & B. E. Shepp (Eds.), *Perception, cognition, and development: Interactional analyses* (pp. 77–102). Hillsdale, NJ: Erlbaum.

Kempler, D., Metter, E. J., Riege, W. H., Jackson, C. A., Benson, D. F., & Hanson, W. R. (1990). Slowly progressive aphasia: Three cases with language, memory, CT and PET data. *Journal of Neurology, Neurosurgery, and Psychiatry, 53,* 987–993.

Keren, G. (2011). On the definition and possible underpinnings of framing effects: A brief review and critical evaluation. In G. Keren (Ed.), *Perspectives on framing* (pp. 3–33). New York, NY: Psychology Press.

Kerr, N. H. (1983). The role of vision in "visual imagery" experiments: Evidence from the congenitally blind. *Journal of Experimental Psychology: General, 112,* 265–277.

Kim, N. S., & Ahn, W. (2002). The influence of naïve causal theories on lay concepts of mental illness. *American Journal of Psychology, 115,* 33–65.

Kintsch, W., & Keenan, J. (1973). Reading rate and retention as a function of the number of propositions in the base structure of sentences. *Cognitive Psychology, 5,* 257–274.

Kirkpatrick, E. A. (1894). An experimental study of memory. *Psychological Review, 1,* 602–609.

Kitayama, S. (2002). Culture and basic psychological processes—toward a system view of culture: Comment on Oyserman et al. (2002). *Psychological Bulletin, 128,* 89–96.

Kitchin, R. M. (1994). Cognitive maps: What are they and why study them? *Journal of Environmental Psychology, 14,* 1–19.

Klaczynski, P. A., & Fauth, J. M. (1996). Intellectual ability, rationality, and intuitiveness as predictors of warranted and unwarranted optimism for future life events. *Journal of Youth and Adolescence, 25,* 755–773.

Klatzky, R. L. (1980). *Human memory: Structures and processes* (2nd ed.). San Francisco, CA: W. H. Freeman.

Klein, G. (1998). *Sources of power: How people make decisions.* Cambridge, MA: MIT Press.

Klein, G. (2009). *Streetlights and shadows: Searching for the keys to adaptive decision making.* Cambridge, MA: MIT Press.

Knauff, M., & Johnson-Laird, P. N. (2002). Visual imagery can impede reasoning. *Memory & Cognition, 30,* 363–371.

Koffka, K. (1935). *Principles of Gestalt psychology.* New York, NY: Harcourt Brace.

Kogan, N. (1983). Stylistic variation in childhood and adolescence: Creativity, metaphor, and cognitive styles. In J. H. Flavell & E. M. Markman (Eds.), *Handbook of child psychology: Vol. 3. Cognitive development* (pp. 630–706). New York, NY: Wiley.

Komatsu, L. K. (1992). Recent views of conceptual structure. *Psychological Bulletin, 112,* 500–526.

Kozlowski, L. T., & Cutting, J. E. (1977). Recognizing the sex of a walker from a dynamic point-light display. *Perception and Psychophysics, 21,* 575–580.

Kosslyn, S. M. (1973). Scanning visual images: Some structural implications. *Perception and Psychophysics, 14,* 90–94.

Kosslyn, S. M. (1976). Can imagery be distinguished from other forms of internal representation? Evidence from studies of information retrieval times. *Memory and Cognition, 4,* 291–297.

Kosslyn, S. M. (1980). *Image and mind.* Cambridge, MA: Harvard University Press.

Kosslyn, S. M., Ball, T. M., & Reiser, B. J. (1978). Visual images preserve metric spatial information: Evidence from studies of image scanning. *Journal of Experimental Psychology: Human Perception and Performance, 4,* 47–60.

Kosslyn, S. M., & Ochsner, K. N. (1994). In search of occipital activation during visual mental imagery. *Trends in Neuroscience, 17,* 290–292.

Kosslyn, S. M., Reiser, B. J., Farah, M. J., & Fliegel, S. L. (1983). Generating visual images: Units and relations. *Journal of Experimental Psychology: General, 112,* 278–303.

Kosslyn, S. M., Thompson, W. L., Kim, I. J., & Alpert, N. M. (1995). Topographical representations of mental images in primary visual cortex. *Nature, 378,* 496–498.

Kruglanski, A. W., & Gigerenzer, G. (2011). Intuitive and deliberate judgments are based on common principles. *Psychological Review, 118,* 97–109.

Kubilius, J., Wagemans, J., & Op de Beeck, H. P. (2011). Emergence of perceptual Gestalts in the human visual cortex: The case of the configural-superiority effect. *Psychological Science, 22,* 1296–1303.

Kuhn, D. (2006). Do cognitive changes accompany developments in the adolescent brain? *Perspectives on Psychological Science, 1,* 59–67.

Kung, H. F. (1993). SPECT and PET ligands for CNS imaging. *Neurotransmissions, 9*(4), 1–6.

LaBerge, D. (1995). *Attentional processing: The brain's art of mindfulness.* Cambridge, MA: Harvard University Press.

Laboratory of Comparative Human Cognition. (1983). Culture and cognitive development. In W. Kessen (Ed.), *Handbook of child psychology* (4th ed., Vol. 1, pp. 295–356). New York, NY: Wiley.

Lachman, R., Lachman, J. L., & Butterfield, E. C. (1979). *Cognitive psychology and information processing: An introduction.* Hillsdale, NJ: Erlbaum.

Lamberts, K., & Shanks, D. (Eds.). (1997). *Knowledge, concepts, and categories.* Cambridge, MA: MIT Press.

Landauer, T. K. (1986). How much do people remember? Some estimates of the quantity of learned information in long-term memory. *Cognitive Science, 10,* 477–493.

Lane, S. M., Mather, M., Villa, D., & Morita, S. K. (2001). How events are reviewed matters: Effects of varied focus on eyewitness suggestibility. *Memory & Cognition, 29,* 940–947.

Langley, P., & Jones, R. (1988). A computational model of scientific insight. In R. J. Sternberg (Ed.), *The nature of creativity: Contemporary psychological perspectives* (pp. 177–201). Cambridge, UK: Cambridge University Press.

Lashley, K. S. (1929). *Brain mechanisms and intelligence.* Chicago, IL: University of Chicago Press.

Lave, J. (1988). *Cognition in practice.* Cambridge, UK: Cambridge University Press.

Lave, J., Murtaugh, M., & de la Rocha, O. (1984). The dialectic of arithmetic in grocery shopping. In B. Rogoff & J. Lave (Eds.), *Everyday cognition: Its development in social context* (pp. 67–94). Cambridge, MA: Harvard University Press.

Lea, G. (1975). Chronometric analysis of the method of loci. *Journal of Experimental Psychology: Human Perception and Performance, 1,* 95–104.

Lerner, R. M. (1990). Plasticity, person–context relations, and cognitive training in the aged years: A developmental contextual perspective. *Developmental Psychology, 26,* 911–915.

Lesgold, A. (1988). Problem solving. In R. J. Sternberg & E. E. Smith (Eds.), *The psychology of human thought* (pp. 188–213). Cambridge, UK: Cambridge University Press.

Lesgold, A., Rubinson, H., Feltovich, P., Glaser, R., Klopfer, D., & Wang, Y. (1988). Expertise in a complex skill: Diagnosing x-ray pictures. In M. T. H. Chi, R. Glaser, & M. J. Farr (Eds.), *The nature of expertise* (pp. 311–342). Hillsdale, NJ: Erlbaum.

Lettvin, J. Y., Maturana, H. R., McCullogh, W. S., & Pitts, W. H. (1959). What the frog's eye tells the frog's brain. *Proceedings of the Institute of Radio Engineering, 47,* 1940–1941.

Levine, S. C., Vasilyeva, M., Lourenco, S. F., Newcombe, N. S., & Huttenlocher, J. (2005). Socioeconomic status modifies the sex difference in spatial skill. *Psychological Science, 16,* 841–845.

Levinson, S. C. (2000). *Presumptive meanings.* Cambridge, MA: MIT Press.

Levinson, S. C., Kita, S., Haun, D. B. M., & Rasch, B. H. (2002). Returning the tables: Language affects spatial reasoning. *Cognition, 84,* 265–294.

Levy, J., & Heller, W. (1992). Gender differences in human neuropsychological function. In A. A. Gerall, H. Moltz, & I. L. Ward (Eds.), *Handbook of behavioral neurobiology* (Vol. 11, pp. 245–274). New York, NY: Plenum Press.

Li, P., & Gleitman, L. (2002). Turning the tables: language and spatial reasoning. *Cognition, 83,* 265–294.

Liao, H., & Yeh, S. (2011). Interaction between stimulus-driven orienting and top-down modulation in attentional capture. *Acta Psychologica, 138,* 52–59.

Lichtenstein, S., Fischhoff, B., & Phillips, L.D. (1982). Calibration of probabilities: The state of the art to 1980. In D. Kahneman, P. Slovic, & A. Tversky (Eds.), *Judgment under uncertainty: Heuristics and biases* (pp. 306–334). Cambridge, UK: Cambridge University Press.

Liddell, C. (1997). Every picture tells a story—or does it? Young South African children interpreting pictures. *Journal of Cross-Cultural Psychology, 28,* 266–283.

Lin, E. L., & Murphy, G. L. (2001). Thematic relations in adults' concepts. *Journal of Experimental Psychology: General, 130,* 3–28.

Lindsay, D. S., & Read, J. D. (1994). Psychotherapy and memories of childhood sexual abuse: A cognitive perspective. *Applied Cognitive Psychology, 8,* 281–338.

Linn, M. C., & Petersen, A. C. (1985). Emergence and characterization of sex differences in spatial ability: A meta-analysis. *Child Development, 56,* 1479–1498.

Linton, M. (1975). Memory for real-world events. In D. A. Norman & D. E. Rumelhart (Eds.), *Explorations in cognition* (pp. 376–404). San Francisco, CA: W. H. Freeman.

Linton, M. (1982). Transformations of memory in everyday life. In U. Neisser (Ed.), *Memory observed: Remembering in natural contexts* (pp. 77–91). San Francisco, CA: W. H. Freeman.

Lipshitz, R., Klein, G., Orasanu, J., & Salas, E. (2001). Taking stock of naturalistic decision making. *Journal of Behavioral Decision Making, 14,* 331–352.

Lisker, L., & Abramson, A. S. (1970). The voicing dimension: Some experiments in comparative phonetics. In B. Hála, M. Romportl, & P. Janota (Eds.), *Proceedings of the Sixth International Congress of Phonetic Sciences: Held at Prague 7–13 September 1967* (pp. 563–567). Prague, Czechoslovakia: Academia Publishing House of the Czechoslovak Academy of Sciences.

Liu, L. G. (1985). Reasoning counterfactually in Chinese: Are there any obstacles? *Cognition, 21,* 239–270.

Locke, J. (1964). *An essay concerning human understanding* (A. D. Woozley, Ed.). New York, NY: New American Library. (Original work published 1690)

Loftus, E. F. (1975). Leading questions and the eyewitness report. *Cognitive Psychology, 7,* 560–572.

Loftus, E. F. (1979). *Eyewitness testimony.* Cambridge, MA: Harvard University Press.

Loftus, E. F. (1993). The reality of repressed memories. *American Psychologist, 48,* 518–537.

Loftus, E. F. (2000). Remembering what never happened. In E. Tulving (Ed.), *Memory, consciousness, and the brain* (pp. 106–118). Philadelphia, PA: Psychology Press.

Loftus, E. F., & Ketcham, K. (1994). *The myth of repressed memory.* New York, NY: St. Martin's Press.

Loftus, E. F., & Pickrell, J. E. (1995). The formation of false memories. *Psychiatric Annals, 25,* 720–725.

Logan, G. D., & Etherton, J. L. (1994). What is learned during automatization? The role of attention in constructing an instance. *Journal of Experimental Psychology: Learning, Memory, and Cognition, 20,* 1022–1050.

Logan, G. D., Schachar, R. J., & Tannock, R. (2000). Executive control problems in childhood psychopathology: Stop-signal studies of attention deficit hyperactivity disorder. In S. Monsell & J. Driver (Eds.), *Attention and performance XVIII: Control of mental processes* (pp. 653–677). Cambridge, MA: Bradford.

Logan, G. D., Taylor, S. E., & Etherton, J. L. (1996). Attention in the acquisition and expression of automaticity. *Journal of Experimental Psychology: Learning, Memory, and Cognition, 22,* 620–638.

Loring-Meier, S., & Halpern, D. F. (1999). Sex differences in visuospatial working memory: Components of cognitive processing. *Psychonomic Bulletin and Review, 6,* 464–471.

Lubinski, D., Webb, R. M., Morelock, M. J., & Benbow, C. P. (2001). Top 1 in 10,000: A 10-year follow-up of the profoundly gifted. *Journal of Applied Psychology, 86,* 718–729.

Luchins, A. S. (1942). Mechanization in problem solving: The effect of *Einstellung. Psychological Monographs, 54*(248).

Luck, S. J., & Mangun, G. R. (2009). Attention: Introduction. In M. Gazzaniga (Ed.), *The cognitive neurosciences* (pp. 185–187). Cambridge, MA: MIT Press.

Luger, G. F. (1994). *Cognitive science: The science of intelligent systems.* San Diego, CA: Academic Press.

Luria, A. R. (1976). *Cognitive development: Its cultural and social foundations* (M. Cole, Ed.; M. Lopez-Morillas & L. Solotaroff, Trans.). Cambridge, MA: Harvard University Press.

Maccoby, E. E., & Jacklin, C. N. (1974). *The psychology of sex differences.* Stanford, CA: Stanford University Press.

Maciej, J., Nitsch, M., & Vollrath, M. (2011). Conversing while driving: The importance of visual information for conversation modulation. *Transportation Research Part F, 14,* 512–524.

Mack, A. (2003). Inattentional blindness: Looking without seeing. *Current Directions in Psychological Science, 12,* 180–184.

MacLeod, C. M. (1991). Half a century of research on the Stroop effect: An integrative review. *Psychological Bulletin, 109,* 163–203.

Maier, N. R. F. (1930). Reasoning in humans: I. On direction. *Journal of Comparative Physiological Psychology, 10,* 115–143.

Maier, N. R. F. (1931). Reasoning in humans: II. The solution of a problem and its appearance in consciousness. *Journal of Comparative Physiological Psychology, 12,* 181–194.

Malpass, R. S., & Poortinga, Y. H. (1986). Strategies for design and analysis. In W. J. Lonner & J. W. Berry (Eds.), *Field methods in cross-cultural research* (pp. 47–83). Beverly Hills, CA: Sage.

Mandler, G. (1967). Organization and memory. In K. W. Spence & J. T. Spence (Eds.), *The psychology of learning and motivation* (Vol. 1, pp. 327–372). New York, NY: Academic Press.

Mandler, J. M., & Johnson, N. S. (1977). Remembrance of things parsed: Story structure and recall. *Cognitive Psychology, 9,* 111–151.

Markman, E. M. (1979). Realizing that you don't understand: Elementary school children's awareness of inconsistencies. *Child Development, 50,* 643–655.

Markman, E. M., & Gorin, L. (1981). Children's ability to adjust their standards for evaluating comprehension. *Journal of Educational Psychology, 73,* 320–325.

Markovits, H., Doyon, C., & Simoneau, M. (2002). Individual differences in working memory and conditional reasoning with concrete and abstract content. *Thinking & Reasoning, 8,* 97–107.

Marr, D. (1982). *Vision: A computational investigation into the human representation and processing of visual information.* San Francisco, CA: W. H. Freeman.

Marrs, H., & Benton, S. L. (2009). Relationships between separate and connected knowing and approaches to learning. *Sex Roles, 60,* 57–66.

Marslen-Wilson, W., & Welsh, A. (1978). Processing interactions and lexical access during word recognition in continuous speech. *Cognitive Psychology, 10,* 29–63.

Martin, K. A., Moritz, S. E., & Hall, C. R. (1999). Imagery use in sport: A literature review and applied model. *Sport Psychologist, 13,* 245–268.

Massaro, D. W. (1979). Letter information and orthographic context in word perception. *Journal of Experimental Psychology: Human Perception and Performance, 5,* 595–609.

Massaro, D. W., & Cohen, M. M. (1983). Evaluation and integration of visual and auditory information in speech perception. *Journal of Experimental Psychology: Human Perception and Performance, 9,* 753–771.

Massaro, D. W., & Loftus, G. R. (1996). Sensory and perceptual storage: Data and theory. In E. L. Bjork & R. A. Bjork (Eds.), *Memory* (pp. 67–99). San Diego, CA: Academic Press.

Masuda, T., & Nisbett, R. E. (2006). Culture and change blindness. *Cognitive Science, 30,* 381–399.

Matlin, M. W. (1988). *Sensation and perception* (2nd ed.). Boston, MA: Allyn & Bacon.

McClelland, J. L. (1988). Connectionist models and psychological evidence. *Journal of Memory and Language, 27,* 107–123.

McClelland, J. L. (2000). Connectionist models of memory. In E. Tulving & F. I. M. Craik (Eds.), *The Oxford handbook of memory* (pp. 583–596). New York, NY: Oxford University Press.

McClelland, J. L., & Rumelhart, D. E. (1981). An interactive activation model of context effects in letter perception: Part 1. An account of basic findings. *Psychological Review, 88,* 375–407.

McCloskey, M. E., & Glucksberg, S. (1978). Natural categories: Well defined or fuzzy sets? *Memory and Cognition, 6,* 462–472.

McCloskey, M. [E.], Wible, C. G., & Cohen, N. J. (1988). Is there a special flashbulb-memory mechanism? *Journal of Experimental Psychology: General, 117,* 171–181.

McCloy, R., Beaman, C. P., Frosch, C. A., & Goddard, K. (2010). Fast and frugal framing effects? *Journal of Experimental Psychology: Learning, Memory, and Cognition, 36,* 1043–1052.

McDowd, J. M., & Craik, F. I. M. (1988). Effects of aging and task difficulty on divided attention performance. *Journal of Experimental Psychology: Human Perception and Performance, 14,* 267–280.

McGaugh, J. L. (2000). Memory—A century of consolidation. *Science, 287,* 248–251.

McGee, M. G. (1979). Human spatial abilities: Psychometric studies and environmental, genetic, hormonal, and neurological influences. *Psychological Bulletin, 86,* 889–918.

McGeoch, J. A. (1932). Forgetting and the law of disuse. *Psychological Review, 39,* 352–370.

McKoon, G., Ratcliff, R., & Dell, G. S. (1986). A critical evaluation of the semantic-episodic distinction. *Journal of Experimental Psychology: Learning, Memory, and Cognition, 12,* 295–306.

McNeill, D. (1966). Developmental psycholinguistics. In F. Smith & G. A. Miller (Eds.), *The genesis of language: A psycholinguistic approach* (pp. 15–84). Cambridge, MA: MIT Press.

McRae, K. (2004). Semantic memory: Some insights from feature-based connectionist attractor networks. *Psychology of Learning and Motivation, 45,* 41–86.

Medin, D. L. (1989). Concepts and conceptual structure. *American Psychologist, 44,* 1469–1481.

Medin, D. L., Lynch, E. B., & Solomon, K. O. (2000). Are there kinds of concepts? *Annual Review of Psychology, 51,* 121–147.

Medin, D. L., & Smith, E. E. (1984). Concepts and concept formation. *Annual Review of Psychology, 35,* 113–138.

Meehan, A. M. (1984). A meta-analysis of sex differences in formal operational thought. *Child Development, 55,* 1110–1124.

Melton, A. W. (1963). Implications of short-term memory for a general theory of memory. *Journal of Verbal Learning and Verbal Behavior, 2,* 1–21.

Menon, V., Boyett-Anderson, J. M., Schatzberg, A. F., & Reiss, A. L. (2002). Relating semantic and episodic memory systems. *Cognitive Brain Research, 13,* 261–265.

Mervis, C. B. (1980). Category structure and the development of categorization. In R. Spiro, B. C. Bruce, & W. F. Brewer (Eds.), *Theoretical issues in reading comprehension* (pp. 279–307). Hillsdale, NJ: Erlbaum.

Mervis, C. B., Catlin, J., & Rosch, E. (1976). Relationships among goodness-of-example, category norms, and word frequency. *Bulletin of the Psychonomic Society, 7,* 283–284.

Meyer, D. E., & Schvaneveldt, R. W. (1971). Facilitation in recognizing pairs of words: Evidence of a dependence between retrieval operations. *Journal of Experimental Psychology, 90,* 227–234.

Michaels, C. F., & Carello, C. (1981). *Direct perception.* Englewood Cliffs, NJ: Prentice Hall.

Milham, M. P., Banich, M. T., Webb, A., Barad, V., Cohen, N. J., Wszalek, T., & Kramer, A. F. (2001). The relative involvement of anterior cingulate and prefrontal cortex in attentional control depends on nature of conflict. *Cognitive Brain Research, 12,* 467–473.

Miller, G. A. (1956). The magical number seven, plus or minus two: Some limits on our capacity for processing information. *Psychological Review, 63,* 81–97.

Miller, G. A., & Glucksberg, S. (1988). Psycholinguistic aspects of pragmatics and semantics. In R. C. Atkinson (Ed.), *Stevens' handbook of experimental psychology: Vol. 2. Learning and cognition* (2nd ed., pp. 417–472). New York, NY: Wiley.

Miller, G. A., & Johnson-Laird, P. N. (1976). *Language and perception.* Cambridge, MA: Harvard University Press.

Miller, G. A., & Nicely, P. (1955). An analysis of perceptual confusions among some English consonants. *Journal of the Acoustical Society of America, 27,* 338–352.

Miller, J. L. (1990). Speech perception. In D. N. Osherson & H. Lasnik (Eds.), *An invitation to cognitive science: Vol. 1. Language* (pp. 69–93). Cambridge, MA: MIT Press.

Miller, K. F., Smith, C. M., Zhu, J., & Zhang, H. (1995). Preschool origins of cross-national differences in mathematical competence: The role of number-naming systems. *Psychological Science, 6,* 56–60.

Miller, P. H. (2002). *Theories of developmental psychology* (4th ed.). New York, NY: Worth.

Miller, P. H. (2011). *Theories of developmental psychology* (5th ed.). New York, NY: Worth.

Miller, P. H., Haynes, V. F., DeMarie-Dreblow, D., & Woody-Ramsey, J. (1986). Children's strategies for gathering information in three tasks. *Child Development, 57,* 1429–1439.

Mitchell, T. R., & Beach, L. R. (1990). " . . . Do I love thee? Let me count . . .": Toward an understanding of intuitive and automatic decision making. *Organizational Behavior and Human Decision Processes, 47,* 1–20.

Miyake, A. (2001). Individual differences in working memory: Introduction to the special section. *Journal of Experimental Psychology: General, 130,* 163–168.

Miyamoto, Y., Nisbett, R. E., & Masuda, T. (2006). Culture and the physical environment: Holistic versus analytic perceptual affordances. *Psychological Science, 17,* 113–119.

Miyashita, Y. (1995). How the brain creates imagery: Projection to primary visual cortex. *Science, 268,* 1719–1720.

Moates, D. R., & Schumacher, G. M. (1980). *An introduction to cognitive psychology.* Belmont, CA: Wadsworth.

Montello, D. R. (2005). Navigation. In P. Shah & A. Miyake (Eds.), *The Cambridge handbook of visuospatial thinking* (pp. 257–294). New York, NY: Cambridge University Press.

Moray, N. (1959). Attention in dichotic listening: Affective cues and the influence of instructions. *Quarterly Journal of Experimental Psychology, 11,* 56–60.

Moray, N., Bates, A., & Barnett, T. (1965). Experiments on the four-eared man. *Journal of the Acoustical Society of America, 38,* 196–201.

Moshman, D. (2005). *Adolescent psychological development: Rationality, morality, and identity* (2nd ed.). Mahwah, NJ: Erlbaum.

Moshman, D., & Franks, B. A. (1986). Development of the concept of inferential validity. *Child Development, 57,* 153–165.

Moyer, R. S. (1973). Comparing objects in memory: Evidence suggesting an internal psychophysics. *Perception and Psychophysics, 13,* 180–184.

Mozer, M. C. (2002). Frames of reference in unilateral neglect and visual perception: A computational perspective. *Psychological Bulletin, 109,* 156–185.

Murdock, B. B. (1962). The serial position effect of free recall. *Journal of Experimental Psychology, 62,* 482–488.

Murphy, G. L. (2005). The study of concepts inside and outside the laboratory: Medin versus Medin. In W. Ahn, R. L. Goldstone, B. C. Love, A. B. Markman, & P. Wolff (Eds.), *Categorization inside and outside the laboratory: Essays in honor of Douglas L. Medin* (pp. 179–196). Washington, DC: American Psychological Association.

Murphy, G. L., & Medin, D. L. (1985). The role of theories in conceptual coherence. *Psychological Review, 92,* 289–316.

Murray, D. J. (1988). *A history of Western psychology* (2nd ed.). Englewood Cliffs, NJ: Prentice Hall.

Murtaugh, M. (1985). The practice of arithmetic by American grocery shoppers. *Anthropology and Education Quarterly, 16,* 186–192.

Nairne, J. S. (2002). Remembering over the short term: The case against the standard model. *Annual Review of Psychology, 53,* 53–81.

Neath, I., & Surprenant, A. (2003). *Human memory* (2nd ed.). Belmont, CA: Wadsworth.

Neely, J. H. (1990). Semantic priming effects in visual word recognition: A selective review of current findings and theories. In D. Besner & G. Humphreys (Eds.), *Basic processes in reading: Visual word recognition.* Hillsdale, NJ: Erlbaum.

Neimark, E. D., & Chapman, R. H. (1975). Development of the comprehension of logical quantifiers. In R. J. Falmagne (Ed.), *Reasoning: Representation and process* (pp. 135–151). Hillsdale, NJ: Erlbaum.

Neisser, U. (1963). Decision-time without reaction-time: Experiments in visual scanning. *American Journal of Psychology, 76,* 376–385.

Neisser, U. (1967). *Cognitive psychology.* New York, NY: Appleton-Century-Crofts.

Neisser, U. (1976). *Cognition and reality: Principles and implications of cognitive psychology.* San Francisco, CA: W. H. Freeman.

Neisser, U. (1982a). Memory: What are the important questions? In U. Neisser (Ed.), *Memory observed: Remembering in natural contexts* (pp. 3–19). San Francisco, CQ: W. H. Freeman.

Neisser, U. (1982b). Snapshots or benchmarks? In U. Neisser (Ed.), *Memory observed: Remembering in natural contexts* (pp. 43–48). San Francisco, CA: W. H. Freeman.

Neisser, U. (1983). The rise and fall of the sensory register. *Behavioral and Brain Sciences, 6,* 35.

Neisser, U. (1987). Introduction: The ecological and intellectual bases of categorization. In U. Neisser (Ed.), *Concepts and conceptual development: Ecological and intellectual factors in categorization* (pp. 1–10). Cambridge, UK: Cambridge University Press.

Neisser, U., & Becklen, R. (1975). Selective looking: Attending to visually specified events. *Cognitive Psychology, 7,* 480–494.

Nelson, K. (1986). Event knowledge and cognitive development. In K. Nelson (Ed.), *Event knowledge: Structure and function in development* (pp. 1–20). Hillsdale, NJ: Erlbaum.

Nelson, K., & Gruendel, J. M. (1981). Generalized event representation: Basic building blocks of cognitive development. In A. Brown & M. Lamb (Eds.), *Advances in developmental psychology* (Vol. 1, pp. 131–158). Hillsdale, NJ: Erlbaum.

Newcombe, N. S. (2002). The nativist-empiricist controversy in the context of recent research on spatial and quantitative development. *Psychological Science, 13,* 395–401.

Newell, A. (1980). Reasoning, problem solving, and decision processes: The problem space as a fundamental category. In R. S. Nickerson (Ed.), *Attention and performance VIII* (pp. 693–718). Hillsdale, NJ: Erlbaum.

Newell, A., & Simon, H. A. (1972). *Human problem-solving.* Englewood Cliffs, NJ: Prentice Hall.

Nickerson, R. S., & Adams, M. J. (1979). Long-term memory for a common object. *Cognitive Psychology, 11,* 287–307.

Nielsen, B. D., Pickett, C. L., & Simonton, D. K. (2008). Conceptual versus experimental creativity: Which works best on convergent and divergent thinking tasks. *Psychology of Aesthetics, Creativity and the Arts, 2,* 131–138.

Nilsson, N. J. (1998). *Artificial intelligence: A new synthesis.* San Francisco, CA: Morgan Kaufman.

Nisbett, R. E., & Norenzayan, A. (2002). Culture and cognition. In H. Pashler (Series Ed.) & D. Medin (Vol. Ed.), *Stevens' handbook of experimental psychology: Vol. 2. Memory and cognitive processes* (3rd ed., pp. 561–597). New York, NY: Wiley.

Nisbett, R. E., Peng, K., Choi, I., & Norenzayan, A. (2001). Culture and systems of thought: Holistic vs. analytic cognition. *Psychological Review, 108,* 291–310.

Norenzayan, A., Choi, I., & Nisbett, R. E. (2002). Cultural similarities and differences in social inference: Evidence from behavioral predictions and lay theories of behavior. *Personality and Social Psychology Bulletin, 28,* 109–120.

Norenzayan, A., & Nisbett, R. E. (2000). Culture and causal cognition. *Current Directions in Psychological Science, 9,* 132–135.

Norenzayan, A., Smith, E. E., Kim, B. J., & Nisbett, R. E. (2002). Cultural preferences for formal versus intuitive reasoning. *Cognitive Science, 26,* 653–684.

Norman, D. A., & Bobrow, D. G. (1975). On data-limited and resource-limited processes. *Cognitive Psychology, 7,* 44–64.

Nowakowski, R. S. (1987). Basic concepts of CNS development. *Child Development, 58,* 568–595.

Nowakowski, R. S., & Hayes, N. L. (2002). General principles of CNS development. In M. H. Johnson, Y. Munakata, & R. O. Gilmore (Eds.), *Brain development and cognition: A reader* (2nd ed.). Oxford, UK: Blackwell.

Nuñez, R. E. (2011). No innate number line in the human brain. *Journal of Cross-Cultural Psychology, 42,* 651–668.

Nyberg, L., & Cabeza, R. (2000). Brain imaging of memory. In E. Tulving & F. I. M. Craik (Eds.), *The Oxford handbook of memory* (pp. 501–519). Oxford, UK: Oxford University Press.

Nyberg, L., Forkstam, C., Petersson, K. M., Cabeza, R., & Ingvar, M. (2002). Brain imaging of human memory systems: Between-systems similarities and within-systems differences. *Cognitive Brain Research, 13,* 281–292.

Oakes, J. (1990). *Lost talent: The underparticipation of women, minorities, and disabled persons in science* (Rep. No. R-3774-NSF/RC). Santa Monica, CA: Rand. (ERIC Document Reproduction Service No. ED318640)

O'Craven, K. M., & Kanwisher, N. (2000). Mental imagery of faces and places activates corresponding stimulus-specific brain regions. *Journal of Cognitive Neuroscience, 12,* 1013–1023.

Olton, R. M. (1979). Experimental studies of incubation: Searching for the elusive. *Journal of Creative Behavior, 13,* 9–22.

Olver, R. R., & Hornsby, J. R. (1966). On equivalence. In J. S. Bruner et al. (Eds.), *Studies in cognitive growth: A collaboration at the Center for Cognitive Studies* (pp. 68–85). New York, NY: Wiley.

Orne, M. T. (1962). On the social psychology of the psychology experiment: With particular reference to demand characteristics and their implication. *American Psychologist, 17,* 776–783.

Ornstein, P. A., & Naus, M. J. (1978). Rehearsal processes in children's memory. In P. A. Ornstein (Ed.), *Memory development in children* (pp. 69–99). Hillsdale, NJ: Erlbaum.

Osherson, D. N., & Markman, E. (1975). Language and the ability to evaluate contradictions and tautologies. *Cognition, 3,* 213–226.

Owens, J., Bower, G. H., & Black, J. B. (1979). The "soap opera" effect in story recall. *Memory and Cognition, 7,* 185–191.

Paivio, A. (1965). Abstractness, imagery, and meaningfulness in paired-associate learning. *Journal of Verbal Learning and Verbal Behavior, 4,* 32–38.

Paivio, A. (1969). Mental imagery in associative learning and memory. *Psychological Review, 76,* 241–263.

Paivio, A. (1971). *Imagery and verbal processes.* New York, NY: Holt, Rinehart & Winston.

Paivio, A. (1975). Perceptual comparisons through the mind's eye. *Memory and Cognition, 3,* 635–647.

Paivio, A. (1983). The empirical case for dual coding. In J. C. Yuille (Ed.), *Imagery, memory and cognition* (pp. 307–332). Hillsdale, NJ: Erlbaum.

Palmer, S. E. (1975). The effects of contextual scenes on the identification of objects. *Memory and Cognition, 3,* 519–526.

Paap, K. R., Newsome, S. L., McDonald, J. E., & Schvaneveldt, R. W. (1982). An activation-verification model for letter and word recognition: The word-superiority effect. *Psychological Review, 89,* 573–594.

Pascual-Leone, J. (1970). A mathematical model for the transition rule in Piaget's developmental stages. *Acta Psychologica, 63,* 301–345.

Pashler, H. E. (1998). *The psychology of attention.* Cambridge, MA: MIT Press.

Pashler, H. [E.], Johnston, J. C., & Ruthruff, E. (2001). Attention and performance. *Annual Review of Psychology, 52,* 629–651.

Pashler, H. [E.], McDaniel, M., Rohrer, D., & Bjork, R. (2008). Learning styles: Concepts and evidence. *Psychological Science in the Public Interest, 9,* 105–119.

Patterson, R. D. (1990). Auditory warning sounds in the work environment. In D. E. Broadbent, J. T. Reason, & A. D. Baddeley (Eds.), *Human factors in hazardous situations* (pp. 37–44). Oxford, UK: Clarendon Press.

Payne, J. W. (1976). Task complexity and contingent processing in decision making: An information search and protocol analysis. *Organizational Behavior and Human Performance, 16,* 366–387.

Pellegrino, J. W., & Glaser, R. (1980). Components of inductive reasoning. In R. E. Snow, P. A. Federico, & W. E. Montague (Eds.), *Aptitude, learning, and instruction: Cognitive process analyses of aptitude* (pp. 177–217). Hillsdale, NJ: Erlbaum.

Perkins, D. N. (1981). *The mind's best work.* Cambridge, MA: Harvard University Press.

Perkins, D. N., Allen, R., & Hafner, J. (1983). Difficulties in everyday reasoning. In W. Maxwell (Ed.), *Thinking: The expanding frontier* (pp. 177–189). Philadelphia, PA: Franklin Institute.

Perky, C. W. (1910). An experimental study of imagination. *American Journal of Psychology, 21,* 422–452.

Perner, J., Lang, B., & Kloo, D. (2002). Theory of mind and self control: More than a common problem of inhibition. *Child Development, 73,* 752–767.

Petersen, S. E., Fox, P. T., Posner, M. I., Mintun, M. A., & Raichle, M. E. (1988). Positron emission tomographic studies of the cortical anatomy of single word processing. *Nature, 331,* 585–589.

Peterson, L. R., & Peterson, M. J. (1959). Short-term retention of individual items. *Journal of Experimental Psychology, 58,* 193–198.

Pezdek, K. (1994). The illusion of illusory memory. *Applied Cognitive Psychology, 8,* 339–350.

Piaget, J. (1968). *Six psychological studies* (D. Elkind & A. Tenzer, Trans.; D. Elkind, Ed.). New York, NY: Vintage Books. (Original work published 1964)

Piaget, J. (1972). Intellectual evolution from adolescence to adulthood. *Human Development, 15,* 1–12.

Piaget, J. (1988a). Piaget's theory. In P. H. Mussen (Ed.), *Manual of child psychology* (3rd ed., pp. 703–732). London, UK: Wiley. (Original work published 1970)

Piaget, J. (1988b). Piaget's theory [extract]. In K. Richardson & S. Sheldon (Eds.), *Cognitive development to adolescence* (pp. 3–18). Hillsdale, NJ: Erlbaum. (Original work published 1970)

Piaget, J., & Inhelder, B. (1967). *The child's conception of space* (F. J. Langdon & J. L. Lunzer, Trans.). New York, NY: Norton. (Original work published 1948)

Pillemer, D. (1984). Flashbulb memories of the assassination attempt on President Reagan. *Cognition, 16,* 63–80.

Pillemer, D. (1990). Clarifying the flashbulb memory concept: Comment on McCloskey, Wible, & Cohen (1988). *Journal of Experimental Psychology: General, 119,* 92–96.

Pinker, S. (1980). Mental imagery and the third dimension. *Journal of Experimental Psychology: General, 109,* 354–371.

Pinker, S. (2002). *The blank slate: The modern denial of human nature.* New York, NY: Viking Press.

Plotnick, R. R. (2012). *Context effect for identification of brand logos.* Unpublished manuscript, Carleton College, Northfield, MN.

Pomerantz, J. R., & Portillo, M. C. (2011). Grouping and emergent features in vision: Toward a theory of basic Gestalts. *Journal of Experimental Psychology: Human Perception and Performance, 37,* 1331–1349.

Poortinga, Y. H., & Malpass, R. S. (1986). Making inferences from cross-cultural data. In W. J. Lonner & J. W. Berry (Eds.), *Field methods in cross-cultural research* (pp. 17–46). Beverly Hills, CA: Sage.

Posner, M. I., Boies, S. J., Eichelman, W. H., & Taylor, R. L. (1969). Retention of visual and name codes of single letters [Monograph]. *Journal of Experimental Psychology, 79,* 1–16.

Posner, M. I., Goldsmith, R., & Welton, K. E., Jr. (1967). Perceived distance and the classification of distorted patterns. *Journal of Experimental Psychology, 73,* 28–38.

Posner, M. I., & Keele, S. W. (1968). On the genesis of abstract ideas. *Journal of Experimental Psychology, 77,* 353–363.

Posner, M. I., & Raichle, M. E. (1994). *Images of mind.* New York, NY: Scientific American Library.

Posner, M. I., & Snyder, C. R. R. (1975). Attention and cognitive control. In R. L. Solso (Ed.), *Information processing and cognition: The Loyola Symposium* (pp. 55–85). Hillsdale, NJ: Erlbaum.

Postman, L., & Phillips, L. W. (1965). Short-term temporal changes in free recall. *Quarterly Journal of Experimental Psychology, 17,* 132–138.

Postman, L., & Stark, K. (1969). Role of response availability in transfer and interference. *Journal of Experimental Psychology, 79,* 168–177.

Premack, D. (1976). *Language and intelligence in ape and man.* Hillsdale, NJ: Erlbaum.

Pritchard, T. C., & Alloway, K. D. (1999). *Medical neuroscience.* Madison, CT: Fence Creek.

Pullum, G. K. (1991). *The great Eskimo vocabulary hoax and other irreverent essays on the study of language.* Chicago, IL: University of Chicago Press.

Putnam, H. (1975). The meaning of "meaning." In H. Putnam (Ed.), *Philosophical papers: Vol. 2. Mind, language and reality* (pp. 215–271). New York, NY: Cambridge University Press.

Pylyshyn, Z. W. (1973). What the mind's eye tells the mind's brain: A critique of mental imagery. *Psychological Bulletin, 80,* 1–24.

Pylyshyn, Z. W. (1981). The imagery debate: Analogue media versus tacit knowledge. *Psychological Review, 88,* 16–45.

Quinlan, P. T. (2003). Visual feature integration theory: Past, present, and future. *Psychological Bulletin, 129,* 643–673.

Quinn, P. C., Bhatt, R. S., Brush, D., Grimes, A., & Sharpnack, H. (2002). Development of form similarity as a Gestalt grouping principle in infancy. *Psychological Science, 13,* 320–328.

Radford, A. (1988). *Transformational grammar.* Cambridge, UK: Cambridge University Press.

Rayner, K., & Sereno, S. C. (1994). Eye movements in reading. In M. A. Gernsbacher (Ed.), *Handbook of psycholinguistics* (pp. 57–81). San Diego, CA: Academic Press.

Reber, A. S. (1967). Implicit learning of artificial grammars. *Journal of Verbal Learning and Verbal Behavior, 6,* 855–863.

Reber, A. S. (1976). Implicit learning of synthetic languages: The role of instructional set. *Journal of Experimental Psychology: Human Learning and Memory, 2,* 88–94.

Reed, S. K., Ernst, G. W., & Banerji, R. (1974). The role of analogy in transfer between similar problem states. *Cognitive Psychology, 6,* 436–450.

Reicher, G. M. (1969). Perceptual recognition as a function of meaningfulness of stimulus material. *Journal of Experimental Psychology, 81,* 275–280.

Reitman, J. S. (1971). Mechanisms of forgetting in short-term memory. *Cognitive Psychology, 2,* 185–195.

Reitman, J. S. (1974). Without surreptitious rehearsal, information in short-term memory decays. *Journal of Verbal Learning and Verbal Behavior, 13,* 365–377.

Rensink, R. A. (2002). Change detection. *Annual Review of Psychology, 53,* 245–277.

Reuter-Lorenz, P. A., Baynes, K., Mangun, G. R., & Phelps, E. A. (Eds.). (2010). *The cognitive neuroscience of mind: A tribute to Michael Gazzaniga.* Cambridge, MA: MIT Press.

Revlis, R. (1975). Syllogistic reasoning: Logical decisions from a complex database. In R. J. Falmagne (Ed.), *Reasoning: Representation and process* (pp. 93–133). Hillsdale, NJ: Erlbaum.

Riby, L. M., Perfect, T. J., & Stollery, B. T. (2004). Evidence for disproportionate dual-task costs in older adults for episodic but not semantic memory. *Quarterly Journal of Experimental Psychology, 57A,* 241–267.

Richerson, P. J., & Boyd, R. (2000). Climate, culture, and the evolution of cognition. In C. Heyes & L. Huber (Eds.), *The evolution of cognition.* (pp. 329–346). Cambridge, MA: MIT Press.

Rips, L. J. (1989). The psychology of knights and knaves. *Cognition, 31,* 85–116.

Rips, L. J. (2001). Two kinds of reasoning. *Psychological Science, 12,* 129–134.

Rips, L. J., Shoben, E. J., & Smith, E. E. (1973). Semantic distance and the verification of semantic relations. *Journal of Verbal Learning and Verbal Behavior, 12,* 1–20.

Rivers, W. H. R. (1905). Observations on the senses of the Todas. *British Journal of Psychology, 1,* 321–396.

Rizzella, M. L., & O'Brien, E. J. (2002). Retrieval of concepts in script-based texts and narratives: The influence of general world knowledge. *Journal of Experimental Psychology: Learning, Memory, and Cognition, 28,* 780–790.

Robinson, J. A., & Swanson, K. L. (1990). Autobiographical memory: The next phase. *Applied Cognitive Psychology, 4,* 321–335.

Roediger, H. L., III. (1990). Implicit memory: Retention without remembering. *American Psychologist, 45,* 1043–1056.

Roediger, H. L., III, & Butler, A. C. (2010). The critical role of retrieval practice in long-term retention. *Trends in Cognitive Sciences, 15,* 20–27.

Roediger, H. L., III, & Guynn, M. J. (1996). Retrieval processes. In E. L. Bjork & R. A. Bjork (Eds.), *Memory* (pp. 197–236). San Diego, CA: Academic Press.

Roediger, H. L., III, & McDermott, K. B. (1995). Creating false memories: Remembering words not presented in lists. *Journal of Experimental Psychology: Learning, Memory, and Cognition, 21,* 803–814.

Roediger, H. L., III, Agarwal, P. K., McDaniel, M. A., & McDermott, K. B. (2011). Test-enhanced learning in the classroom: Long-term improvements from quizzing. *Journal of Experimental Psychology: Applied, 17,* 382–395.

Rogoff, B. (1990). *Apprenticeship in thinking: Cognitive development in social context.* New York, NY: Oxford University Press.

Rohner, R.P. (1984). Toward a conception of culture for cross-cultural psychology. *Journal of Cross-Cultural Psychology, 15,* 111–138.

Roland, P. E., & Friberg, L. (1985). Localization of cortical areas activated by thinking. *Journal of Neurophysiology, 53,* 1219–1243.

Rollock, D. (1992). Field dependence/independence and learning condition: An exploratory study of style vs. ability. *Perceptual and Motor Skills, 74,* 807–818.

Rosch, E. (1973). On the internal structure of perceptual and semantic categories. In T. E. Moore (Ed.), *Cognitive development and the acquisition of language* (pp. 111–144). New York, NY: Academic Press.

Rosch, E., & Mervis, C. B. (1975). Family resemblances: Studies in the internal structure of categories. *Cognitive Psychology, 7,* 573–605.

Rosch, E., Mervis, C. B., Gray, W. D., Johnson, D. M., & Boyes-Braem, P. (1976). Basic objects in natural categories. *Cognitive Psychology, 8,* 382–439.

Rosch, E., Simpson, C., & Miller, R. S. (1976). Structural bases of typicality effects. *Journal of Experimental Psychology: Human Perception and Performance, 2,* 491–502.

Rose, N. S., Myerson, J., Roediger, H. L., III, & Hale, S. (2010). Similarities and differences between working memory and long-term memory: Evidence from the levels-of-processing span task. *Journal of Experimental Psychology: Learning, Memory & Cognition, 36,* 471–483.

Rosenthal, R., & Rosnow, R. L. (1984). *Essentials of behavioral research: Methods and data analysis.* New York, NY: McGraw-Hill.

Ross, B. H., & Landauer, T. K. (1978). Memory for at least one of two items: Test and failure of several theories of spacing effects. *Journal of Verbal Learning and Verbal Behavior, 17,* 669–680.

Ross, M., & Sicoly, F. (1979). Egocentric biases in availability and attribution. *Journal of Personality and Social Psychology, 37,* 322–336.

Roth, D., Slone, M., & Dar, R. (2000). Which way cognitive development? An evaluation of the Piagetian and the domain specific research programs. *Theory & Psychology, 10,* 353–373.

Roth, E. M., & Shoben, E. J. (1983). The effect of context on the structure of categories. *Cognitive Psychology, 15,* 346–378.

Rubens, A. B., & Benson, D. F. (1971). Associative visual agnosia. *Archives of Neurology, 24,* 305–316.

Rubia, K., & Smith, A. (2001). Attention deficit-hyperactivity disorder: Current findings and treatment. *Current Opinion in Psychiatry, 14,* 309–316.

Rugg, M. D. (1997). Introduction. In M. D. Rugg (Ed.), *Cognitive neuroscience* (pp. 1–10). Cambridge, MA: MIT Press.

Rumelhart, D. E. (1989). The architecture of mind: A connectionist approach. In M. I. Posner (Ed.), *Foundations of cognitive science* (pp. 133–159). Cambridge, MA: Bradford Books.

Rumelhart, D. E., & McClelland, J. L. (1982). An interactive activation model of context effects in letter perception: Part 2. The contextual enhancement effect and some tests and extensions of the model. *Psychological Review, 89,* 60–94.

Rumelhart, D. E., & Norman, D. A. (1988). Representation in memory. In R. C. Atkinson (Ed.), *Stevens' handbook of experimental psychology: Vol. 2. Learning and cognition* (2nd ed., pp. 511–587). New York, NY: Wiley.

Rumelhart, D. E., & Ortony, A. (1977). The representation of knowledge in memory. In R. C. Anderson, R. J. Spiro, & W. E. Montague (Eds.), *Schooling and the acquisition of knowledge* (pp. 99–135). Hillsdale, NJ: Erlbaum.

Rumelhart, D. E., & Todd, P. M. (1993). Learning and connectionist representations. In D. E. Meyer & S. Kornblum (Eds.), *Attention and performance XIV* (pp. 3–30). Cambridge, MA: MIT Press/Bradford Books.

Runco, M. A. (2004). Creativity. *Annual Review of Psychology, 55,* 657–687.

Runco, M. A., & Sakamoto, S. O. (1999). Experimental studies of creativity. In R. J. Sternberg (Ed.), *Handbook of creativity* (pp. 62–92). Cambridge, UK: Cambridge University Press.

Ryan, M. K., & David, B. (2003). Gender differences in ways of knowing: The context dependence of the Attitudes Toward Thinking and Learning Survey. *Sex Roles, 49,* 693–699.

Sachs, J. S. (1967). Recognition memory for syntactic and semantic aspects of connected discourse. *Perception and Psychophysics, 2,* 437–442.

Sacks, O. (1985). *The man who mistook his wife for a hat, and other clinical tales.* New York, NY: Summit Books.

Salthouse, T. [A.]. (2012). Consequences of age-related cognitive declines. *Annual Review of Psychology, 63,* 201–226.

Salthouse, T. A., & Babcock, R. L. (1991). Decomposing adult age differences in working memory. *Developmental Psychology, 27,* 763–776.

Samuel, A. G. (2011). Speech perception. *Annual Review of Psychology, 62,* 49–72.

Sandler, W., & Lillo-Martin, D. C. (2006). *Sign language and linguistic universals.* Cambridge, UK: Cambridge University Press.

Sargent, J., Dopkins, S., Philbeck, J., & Chichka, D. (2010). Chunking in spatial memory. *Journal of Experimental Psychology: Learning, Memory, and Cognition, 36,* 576–589.

Savage-Rumbaugh, S., McDonald, K., Sevcik, R. A., Hopkins, W. D., & Rubert, E. (1986). Spontaneous symbol acquisition and communicative use by pygmy chimpanzees (*Pan paniscus*). *Journal of Experimental Psychology: General, 115,* 211–235.

Saxe, G. B. (1981). Body parts as numerals: A developmental analysis of numeration among the Oksapmin in Papua New Guinea. *Child Development, 52,* 306–316.

Saxe, G. B., & Posner, J. (1983). The development of numerical cognition: Cross-cultural perspectives. In H. P. Ginsburg (Ed.), *The development of mathematical thinking* (pp. 291–317). New York, NY: Academic Press.

Schacter, D. L. (1987). Implicit memory: History and current status. *Journal of Experimental Psychology: Learning, Memory and Cognition, 13,* 501–518.

Schacter, D. L. (1989). On the relation between memory and consciousness: Dissociable interactions and conscious experience. In H. L. Roediger III & F. I. M. Craik (Eds.), *Varieties of memory and consciousness* (pp. 355–389). Hillsdale, NJ: Erlbaum.

Schacter, D. L. (1996). *Searching for memory: The brain, the mind, and the past.* New York, NY: Basic Books.

Schank, R. C., & Abelson, R. P. (1977). *Scripts, plans, goals, and understanding: An inquiry into human knowledge structures.* Hillsdale, NJ: Erlbaum.

Schmidt, S. R. (2004). Autobiographical memories for the September 11th attacks: Reconstructive errors and emotional impairment of memory. *Memory & Cognition, 32,* 443–454.

Schneider, W., & Shiffrin, R. M. (1977). Controlled and automatic human information processing: I. Detection, search, and attention. *Psychological Review, 84,* 1–66.

Schraw, G., Dunkle, M. E., & Bendixen, L. D. (1995). Cognitive processes in well-defined and ill-defined problem solving. *Applied Cognitive Psychology, 9,* 523–538.

Schwartz, S. H. (1971). Modes of representation and problem solving: Well evolved is half solved. *Journal of Experimental Psychology, 91,* 347–350.

Schwartz, S. P. (1978). Putnam on artifacts. *Philosophical Review, 87,* 566–574.

Schwartz, S. P. (1979). Natural kind terms. *Cognition, 7,* 301–315.

Schwartz, S. P. (1980). Natural kinds and nominal kinds. *Mind, 89,* 182–195.

Scribner, S. (1984). Studying working intelligence. In B. Rogoff & J. Lave (Eds.), *Everyday cognition: Its development in social context* (pp. 9–40). Cambridge, MA: Harvard University Press.

Scribner, S. (1986). Thinking in action: Some characteristics of practical thought. In R. J. Sternberg & R. K. Wagner (Eds.), *Practical intelligence: Nature and origins of competence in the everyday world* (pp. 13–30). Cambridge, UK: Cambridge University Press.

Scribner, S., & Cole, M. (1981). *The psychology of literacy.* Cambridge, MA: Harvard University Press.

Searle, J. R. (1979). *Expression and meaning: Studies in the theory of speech acts.* Cambridge, UK: Cambridge University Press.

Sedlmeier, P., & Gigerenzer, G. (2000). Was Bernoulli wrong? On intuitions about sample size. *Journal of Behavioral Decision Making, 13,* 133–139.

Seegmiller, J. K., Watson, J. M., & Strayer, D. L. (2011). Individual differences in susceptibility to inattentional blindness. *Journal of Experimental Psychology: Learning, Memory, and Cognition, 37,* 785–791.

Segall, M. H. (1979). *Cross-cultural psychology: Human behavior in global perspective.* Pacific Grove, CA: Brooks/Cole.

Segall, M. H. (1984). More than we need to know about culture but are afraid not to ask. *Journal of Cross-Cultural Psychology, 15,* 153–162.

Segall, M. H. (1986). Culture and behavior: Psychology in global perspective. *Annual Review of Psychology, 37,* 523–564.

Segall, M. H., Campbell, D. T., & Herskovits, M. J. (1966). *The influence of culture on visual perception.* Indianapolis, IN: Bobbs-Merrill.

Shepard, R. N. (1966). Learning and recall as organization and search. *Journal of Verbal Learning and Verbal Behavior, 5,* 201–204.

Shepard, R. N. (1967). Recognition memory for words, sentences, and pictures. *Journal of Verbal Learning and Verbal Behavior, 6,* 156–163.

Shepard, R. N., & Metzler, J. (1971). Mental rotation of three-dimensional objects. *Science, 171,* 701–703.

Shiffrin, R. M. (1988). Attention. In R. C. Atkinson, R. J. Herrnstein, G. Lindzey, & R. D. Luce (Eds.), *Stevens' handbook of experimental psychology: Vol. 2. Learning and cognition* (2nd ed., pp. 739–811). New York, NY: Wiley.

Shiffrin, R. M. (1993). Short-term memory: A brief commentary. *Memory and Cognition, 21,* 193–197.

Shimamura, A. P. (1986). Priming effects in amnesia: Evidence for a dissociable memory function. *Quarterly Journal of Experimental Psychology, 38A,* 619–644.

Shimamura, A. P. (1995). Memory and frontal lobe function. In M. S. Gazzaniga (Ed.), *The cognitive neurosciences* (pp. 803–813). Cambridge, MA: Bradford.

Siegel, L. S., & Hodkin, B. (1982). The garden path to the understanding of cognitive development: Has Piaget led us into the poison ivy? In S. Modgil & C. Modgil (Eds.), *Jean Piaget: Consensus and controversy* (pp. 57–82). New York, NY: Praeger.

Siegler, R. S. (Ed.). (1978). *Children's thinking: What develops?* Hillsdale, NJ: Erlbaum.

Siegler, R. S., & Jenkins, E. (1989). *How children discover new strategies.* Hillsdale, NJ: Erlbaum.

Simmering, V. R. (2011). The development of visual working memory capacity during early childhood. *Journal of Experimental Child Psychology, 111,* 695–707.

Simons, D. J. (2010). Monkeying around with the gorillas in our midst: Familiarity with an inattentional-blindness task does not improve the detection of unexpected events. *i-Perception, 1,* 3–6.

Simons, D. J., & Ambinder, M. S. (2005). Change blindness: Theory and consequences. *Current Directions in Psychological Science, 14,* 44–48.

Simons, D. J., & Chabris, C. F. (1999). Gorillas in our midst: Sustained inattentional blindness for dynamic events. *Perception, 28,* 1059–1074.

Simons, D. J., & Jensen, M. S. (2009). The effects of individual differences and task difficulty on inattentional blindness. *Psychonomic Bulletin & Review, 16,* 398–403.

Simons, D. J., & Levin, D. T. (1997). Change blindness. *Trends in Cognitive Sciences, 1,* 261–267.

Simons, D. J., & Levin, D.T. (1998). Failure to detect changes to people during a real-world interaction. *Psychonomic Bulletin and Review, 5,* 644–649.

Simons, D. J., Nevarez, G., & Boot, W. R. (2005). Visual sensing *is* seeing: Why "mindsight" in hindsight, is blind. *Psychological Science, 16,* 520–524.

Simonton, D. K. (2011). Creativity and discovery as blind variation and selective retention: Multiple-variant definition and blind-sighted integration. *Psychology of Aesthetics, Creativity, and the Arts, 5,* 222–228.

Skinner, B. F. (1984). Behaviorism at fifty. *Behavioral and Brain Sciences, 7,* 615–667. (Original work published 1963)

Skyrms, B. (1975). *Choice and chance: An introduction to inductive logic* (2nd ed.). Encino, CA: Dickenson.

Smith, E. E., & Jonides, J. (1997). Working memory: A view from neuroimaging. *Cognitive Psychology, 33,* 5–42.

Smith, E. E., & Medin, D. L. (1981). *Categories and concepts.* Cambridge, MA: Harvard University Press.

Smith, E. E., Shoben, E. J., & Rips, L. J. (1974). Structure and process in semantic memory: A featural model for semantic decisions. *Psychological Review, 81,* 214–241.

Smith, S. M., & Blakenship, S. E. (1989). Incubation effects. *Bulletin of the Psychonomic Society, 27,* 311–314.

Smith, S. M., Brown, H. O., Toman, J. E. P., & Goodman, L. S. (1947). The lack of cerebral effects of d-tubercurarine. *Anesthesiology, 8,* 1–14.

Smullyan, R.M. (1982). *Alice in puzzle-land.* New York, NY: Penguin Books.

Spelke, E., Hirst, W., & Neisser, U. (1976). Skills of divided attention. *Cognition, 4,* 215–230.

Sperling, G. (1960). The information available in brief visual presentations. *Psychological Monographs, 74*(498), 1–29.

Springer, S. P., & Deutsch, G. (1998). *Left brain, right brain: Perspectives from cognitive neuroscience* (5th ed.). New York, NY: W. H. Freeman.

Stanovich, K. E., & West, R. F. (1997). Reasoning independently of prior belief and individual differences in actively open-minded thinking. *Journal of Educational Psychology, 89,* 342–357.

Stanovich, K. E., & West, R. F. (1998). Individual differences in rational thought. *Journal of Experimental Psychology: General, 127,* 161–188.

Stanovich, K. E., & West, R. F. (2000). Individual differences in reasoning: Implications for the rationality debate? *Behavioral and Brain Sciences, 23,* 645–726.

Stefik, M. (1995). *Introduction to knowledge systems.* San Francisco, CA: Morgan Kaufman.

Stein, B. S., & Bransford, J. D. (1979). Constraints on effective elaboration: Effects of precision and subject generation. *Journal of Verbal Learning and Verbal Behavior, 18,* 769–777.

Sternberg, R. J. (1977). Component processes in analogical reasoning. *Psychological Review, 84,* 353–378.

Sternberg, R. J. (1986). *Intelligence applied: Understanding and increasing your intellectual skills.* San Diego, CA: Harcourt Brace Jovanovich.

Sternberg, R. J. (1988). A three-facet model of creativity. In R. J. Sternberg (Ed.), *The nature of creativity: Contemporary psychological perspectives* (pp. 125–147). Cambridge, UK: Cambridge University Press.

Sternberg, R. J., & Detterman, D. K. (Eds.). (1986). *What is intelligence? Contemporary viewpoints on its nature and definition.* Norwood, NJ: Ablex.

Sternberg, R. J., & Gardner, M. K. (1983). Unities in inductive reasoning. *Journal of Experimental Psychology: General, 112,* 80–116.

Sternberg, S. (1966). High-speed scanning in human memory. *Science, 153,* 652–654.

Sternberg, S. (1969). Memory-scanning: Mental processes revealed by reaction-time experiments. *American Scientist, 57,* 421–457.

Stevenson, H. W., Lee, S., Chen, C., Lummis, M., Stigler, J., Fan, L., & Ge, F. (1990). Mathematics achievement of children in China and the United States. *Child Development, 61,* 1053–1066.

Strayer, D. L., & Johnston, W. A. (2001). Driven to distraction: Dual-task studies of simulated driving and conversing on a cellular telephone. *Psychological Science, 12,* 462–466.

Stroop, J. R. (1935). Studies of interferences in serial verbal reactions. *Journal of Experimental Psychology, 18,* 643–662.

Strutt, G. F., Anderson, D. R., & Well, A. D. (1975). A developmental study of the effects of irrelevant information on speeded classification. *Journal of Experimental Child Psychology, 20,* 127–135.

Sun, R., Merrill, E., & Peterson, T. (2001). From implicit skills to explicit knowledge: A bottom-up model of skill learning. *Cognitive Science, 25,* 203–244.

Suess, H. M., Oberauer, K., Wittmann, W. W., Wilhelm, O., & Schulze, R. (2002). Working-memory capacity explains reasoning ability—and a little bit more. *Intelligence, 30,* 261–288.

Suppes, P. (1957). *Introduction to logic.* Princeton, NJ: Van Nostrand.

Swinney, D. A. (1979). Lexical access during sentence comprehension: (Re)consideration of context effects. *Journal of Verbal Learning and Verbal Behavior, 18,* 645–659.

Tanenhaus, M. K., Magnuson, J. S., Dahan, D., & Chambers, C. (2000). Eye movements and lexical access in spoken-language comprehension: Evaluating a linking hypothesis between fixations and linguistic processing. *Journal of Psycholinguistic Research, 29,* 557–580.

Tarr, M. J. (2000). Visual pattern recognition. In A. E. Kazdin, (Ed.), *Encyclopedia of psychology* (pp. 1–4). Washington, DC: American Psychological Association.

Tarr, M. J., & Bülthoff, H. H. (1995). Is human object recognition better described by geon-structural-descriptions or by multiple-views? *Journal of Experimental Psychology: Human Perception and Performance, 21,* 1494–1505.

Tarr, M. J., & Pinker, S. (1989). Mental rotation and orientation-dependence in shape recognition. *Cognitive Psychology, 21,* 233–282.

Tavris, C., & Wade, C. (1984). *The longest war: Sex differences in perspective* (2nd ed.). San Diego, CA: Harcourt Brace Jovanovich.

Teasdale, J. D., Dritschel, B. H., Taylor, M. J., Proctor, L., Lloyd, C. A., Nimmo-Smith, I., & Baddeley, A. D. (1995). Stimulus-independent thought depends on central executive resources. *Memory and Cognition, 23,* 551–559.

Terrace, H. S. (1979). *Nim.* New York, NY: Knopf.

Thaler, R. H. (1980). Toward a positive theory of consumer choice. *Journal of Economic Behavior and Organization, 1,* 39–60.

Theeuwes, J., Atchley, P., & Kramer, A. F. (2000). On the time course of top-down and bottom-up control of visual attention. In S. Monsell & J. Driver (Eds), *Control of cognitive processes: Attention and performance XVIII* (pp. 105–124). Cambridge, MA: Bradford.

Theeuwes, J., Kramer, A. F., Hahn, S., & Irwin, D. E. (1998). Our eyes do not always go where we want them to go: Capture of the eyes by new objects. *Psychological Science, 9,* 379–385.

Thomson, D. M., & Tulving, E. (1970). Associative encoding and retrieval: Weak and strong cues. *Journal of Experimental Psychology, 86,* 255–262.

Thorndyke, P. W. (1977). Cognitive structures in comprehension and memory of narrative discourse. *Cognitive Psychology, 9,* 77–110.

Tomasello, M. (2006). Acquiring linguistic constructions. In D. Kuhn & R. S. Siegler (Vol. Eds.), *Handbook of Child Psychology: Vol. 2. Cognition, Perception, and Language* (6th ed., pp. 255–298). Hoboken, NJ: Wiley.

Trabasso, T., Secco, T., & van den Broek, P. W. (1984). Causal cohesion and story coherence. In H. Mandl, N. L. Stein, & T. Trabasso (Eds.), *Learning and comprehension of text* (pp. 83–111). Hillsdale, NJ: Erlbaum.

Trabasso, T., & van den Broek, P. W. (1985). Causal thinking and the representation of narrative events. *Journal of Memory and Language, 24,* 612–630.

Treisman, A. M. (1960). Contextual cues in selective listening. *Quarterly Journal of Experimental Psychology, 12,* 242–248.

Treisman, A. M. (1964). Verbal cues, language, and meaning in selective attention. *American Journal of Psychology, 77,* 206–219.

Treisman, A. M., & Gelade, G. (1980). A feature integration theory of attention. *Cognitive Psychology, 12,* 97–136.

Treisman, A. M., & Schmidt, H. (1982). Illusory conjunctions in the perception of objects. *Cognitive Psychology, 14,* 107–141.

Triandis, H. C. (1996). The psychological measurement of cultural syndromes. *American Psychologist, 51,* 407–415.

Tsal, Y. (1989a). Do illusory conjunctions support the feature integration theory? A critical review of theory and findings. *Journal of Experimental Psychology: Human Perception and Performance, 15,* 394–400.

Tsal, Y. (1989b). Further comments on feature integration: A reply to Briand and Klein. *Journal of Experimental Psychology: Human Perception and Performance, 15,* 407–410.

Tulving, E. (1972). Episodic and semantic memory. In E. Tulving & W. Donaldson (Eds.), *Organization of memory* (pp. 381–403). New York, NY: Academic Press.

Tulving, E. (1983). *Elements of episodic memory.* New York, NY: Oxford University Press.

Tulving, E. (1989). Remembering and knowing the past. *American Scientist, 77,* 361–367.

Tulving, E. (1995). Introduction to Section IV: Memory. In M. S. Gazzaniga (Ed.), *The cognitive neurosciences* (pp. 751–753). Cambridge, MA: Bradford.

Turing, A. M. (1936). "On computable numbers, with an application to the Entscheidungsproblem." *Proceedings of the London Mathematical Society 42,* 230–265.

Turvey, M. T., Shaw, R. E., Reed, E. S., & Mace, W. M. (1981). Ecological laws of perceiving and acting: In reply to Fodor and Pylyshyn (1981). *Cognition, 9,* 237–304.

Tversky, A. (1972). Elimination by aspects: A theory of choice. *Psychological Review, 79,* 281–299.

Tversky, A., & Kahneman, D. (1971). Belief in the law of small numbers. *Psychological Bulletin, 76,* 105–110.

Tversky, A., & Kahneman, D. (1973). Availability: A heuristic for judging frequency and probability. *Cognitive Psychology, 4,* 207–232.

Tversky, A., & Kahneman, D. (1981). The framing of decisions and the psychology of choice. *Science, 211,* 453–458.

Tversky, A., & Kahneman, D. (2000). Judgment under uncertainty: Heuristics and biases. In T. Connolly, H. R. Arkes, & K. R. Hammond (Eds.), *Judgment and decision making* (2nd ed., pp. 35–52). New York: Cambridge University Press.

Tversky, B. (1981). Distortions in memory for maps. *Cognitive Psychology, 13,* 407–433.

Tverksy, B. (1992). Distortions in cognitive maps. *Geoforum, 23,* 131–138.

Tverksy, B. (2005). Functional significance of visuospatial representations. In P. Shah & A. Miyake (Eds.), *The Cambridge handbook of visuospatial thinking* (pp. 1–34). New York, NY: Cambridge University Press.

Tyler, L. E. (1974). *Individual differences: Abilities and motivational directions.* Englewood Cliffs, NJ: Prentice Hall.

Unsworth, N., & Engle, R. W. (2005). Individual difference in working memory and capacity and learning: Evidence from the serial reaction time task. *Memory & Cognition, 33,* 213–220.

van den Berg, M., Kubovy, M., & Schirillo, J. A. (2011). Grouping by Regularity and the perception of illumination. *Vision Research, 51,* 1360–1371.

van den Broek, P., & Gustafson, M. (1999). Comprehension and memory for texts: Three generations of reading research. In S. R. Goldman, A. C. Graesser, & P. van den Broek (Eds.), *Narrative comprehension, causality, and coherence: Essays in honor of Tom Trabasso* (pp. 15–34). Mahwah, NJ: Erlbaum.

Varnum, M. E. W., Grossmann, I., Kitayama, S., & Nisbett, R. E. (2010). The origin of cultural differences in cognition: The social orientation hypothesis. *Current Directions in Psychological Science, 19,* 9–13.

Verhaeghen, P. (2011). Aging and executive control: Reports of a demise greatly exaggerated. *Current Directions in Psychological Science, 20,* 174–180.

von Winterfeldt, D., & Edwards, W. (1986a). *Decision analysis and behavioral research.* Cambridge, UK: Cambridge University Press.

von Winterfeldt, D., & Edwards, W. (1986b). On cognitive illusions and their implications. In H. R. Arkes & K. R. Hammond (Eds.), *Judgment and decision making: An interdisciplinary reader* (pp. 642–679). Cambridge, UK: Cambridge University Press.

Vygotsky, L. S. (1986). *Thought and language* (A. Kozulin, Trans.). Cambridge, MA: MIT Press.

Waltz, J. A., Knowlton, B. J., Holyoak, K. J., Boone, K. B., Mishkin, F. S., de Menezes Santos, M., Thomas, C. R., & Miller, B. L. (1999). A system for relational reasoning in human prefrontal cortex. *Psychological Science, 10,* 119–125.

Wang, R. F., Crowell, J. A., Simons, D. J., Irwin, D. E., Kramer, A. F., Ambinder, M. S., . . . & Hsieh, B. B. (2006). Spatial updating relies on an egocentric representation of space: Effects of the number of objects. *Psychonomic Bulletin & Review, 13,* 281–286.

Ward, T. B., Smith, S. M., & Finke, R. A. (1999). Creative cognition. In R. J. Sternberg (Ed.), *Handbook of creativity* (pp. 189–212). Cambridge, UK: Cambridge University Press.

Warren, R. M. (1970). Perceptual restoration of missing speech sounds. *Science, 167,* 392–393.

Warren, R. M., & Obusek, C. J. (1971). Speech perception and phonemic restorations. *Perception and Psychophysics, 9,* 358–362.

Warren, R. M., & Warren, R. P. (1970). Auditory illusions and confusions. *Scientific American, 223*, 30–36.

Warrington, E. K., & Weiskrantz, L. (1970). Amnesic syndrome: Consolidation or retrieval? *Nature, 228*, 628–630.

Wason, P. C. (1960). On the failure to eliminate hypotheses in a conceptual task. *Quarterly Journal of Experimental Psychology, 12*, 129–140.

Wason, P. C. (1968). Reasoning about a rule. *Quarterly Journal of Experimental Psychology, 20*, 273–281.

Wason, P. C. (1969). Regression in reasoning? *British Journal of Psychology, 60*, 471–480.

Wason, P. C. (1977). "On the failure to eliminate hypotheses . . ."—a second look. In P. N. Johnson-Laird & P. C. Wason (Eds.), *Thinking: Readings in cognitive science* (pp. 307–314). Cambridge, UK: Cambridge University Press.

Wason, P. C. (1983). Realism and rationality in the selection task. In J. St. B. T. Evans (Ed.), *Thinking and reasoning: Psychological approaches* (pp.44–75). Boston: Routledge & Kegan Paul.

Wason, P. C., & Johnson-Laird, P. N. (1970). A conflict between selecting and evaluating information in an inferential task. *British Journal of Psychology, 61*, 509–515.

Watkins, O. C., & Watkins, M. J. (1980). The modality effect and echoic persistence. *Journal of Experimental Psychology: General, 109*, 251–278.

Watson, J. B. (1913). Psychology as the behaviorist views it. *Psychological Review, 20*, 158–177.

Watson, J. B. (1930). *Behaviorism.* New York, NY: Norton.

Waugh, N. C., & Norman, D. A. (1965). Primary memory. *Psychological Review, 72*, 89–104.

Weaver, C. A., III. (1993). Do you need a "flash" to form a flashbulb memory? *Journal of Experimental Psychology: General, 122*, 39–46.

Weisberg, R. W. (1988). Problem solving and creativity. In R. J. Sternberg (Ed.), *The nature of creativity* (pp. 148–176). Cambridge, UK: Cambridge University Press.

Wells, G. L. (1993). What do we know about eyewitness identification? *American Psychologist, 48*, 553–571.

Wertheimer, M. (1945). *Productive thinking.* New York, NY: Harper & Brothers.

Whittlesea, B. W. A., & Price, J. R. (2001). Implicit/explicit memory versus analytic/nonanalytic processing: Rethinking the mere exposure effect. *Memory & Cognition, 29*, 234–246.

Whorf, B. L. (1956). *Language, thought, and reality.* Cambridge, MA: MIT Press.

Wickens, C. D. (1987). Attention. In P. A. Hancock (Ed.), *Human factors psychology* (pp. 29–80). Amsterdam, The Netherlands: North Holland.

Williams, J. H. (1983). *Psychology of women: Behavior in a biosocial context* (2nd ed.). New York, NY: Norton.

Wilson, B. G., & Myers, K. M. (2000). Situated cognition in theoretical and practical context. In D. H. Jonassen (Ed.), *Theoretical foundations of learning environments* (pp. 57–88). Mahwah, NJ: Erlbaum.

Wilson, F. A., & Stimpson, J. P. (2010). Trends in fatalities from distracted driving in the United States, 1999–2008. *American Journal of Public Health, 100*, 2213–2219.

Winston, P. H. (1992). *Artificial intelligence* (3rd ed.). Boston, MA: Addison-Wesley.

Witkin, H. A., Dyk, R. B., Faterson, H. F., Goodenough, D. R., & Karp, S. A. (1962). *Psychological differentiation: Studies of development.* New York, NY: Wiley.

Witkin, H. A., & Goodenough, D. R. (1981). *Cognitive styles: Essence and origins.* New York, NY: International Universities Press.

Wittgenstein, L. (1953). *Philosophical investigations.* New York, NY: Macmillan.

Wober, M. (1969). Distinguishing centri-cultural from cross-cultural tests and research. *Perceptual and Motor Skills, 28*, 488.

Wood, N. L., & Cowan, N. (1995). The cocktail party phenomenon revisited: Attention and memory in the classic selective listening procedure of Cherry (1953). *Journal of Experimental Psychology: General, 124,* 243–262.

Woods, S. K., & Ploof, W. H. (1997). *Understanding ADHD: Attention deficit hyperactivity disorder and the feeling brain.* Thousand Oaks, CA: Sage.

Woodworth, R. S., & Sells, S. B. (1935). An atmosphere effect in formal syllogistic reasoning. *Journal of Experimental Psychology, 18,* 451–460.

Wu, L., & Barsalou, L. W. (2009). Perceptual simulation in conceptual combination: Evidence from property generation. *Acta Psychologica, 132,* 173–189.

Xu, Y., & Corkin, S. (2001). H.M. revisits the Tower of Hanoi puzzle. *Neuropsychology, 15,* 69–79.

Yantis, S. (2000). Goal-directed and stimulus-driven determinants of attentional control. In S. Monsell & J. Driver (Eds)., *Control of cognitive processes: Attention and performance XVIII* (pp. 73–103). Cambridge, MA: Bradford.

Yantis, S., & Egeth, H. E. (1999). On the distinction between visual salience and stimulus-driven attentional capture. *Journal of Experimental Psychology: Human Perception and Performance, 25,* 661–676.

Yoshida, K. A., Iversen, J. R., Patel, A. D., Mazuka, R., Nito, H., Gervain, J., & Werker, J. F. (2010). The development of perceptual grouping biases in infancy: A Japanese-English cross-linguistic study. *Cognition, 115,* 356–361.

Yuille, J. C. (Ed.). (1983). *Imagery, memory and cognition.* Hillsdale, NJ: Erlbaum.

Yuille, J. C. (1993). We must study forensic eyewitnesses to know about them. *American Psychologist, 48,* 572–573.

Zatorre, R. J., Halpern, A. R., Perry, D. W., Meyer, E., & Evans, A. C. (1996). Hearing in the mind's ear: A PET investigation of musical imagery and perception. *Journal of Cognitive Neuroscience, 8,* 29–46.

Zelnicker, T. (1989). Cognitive style and dimensions of information processing. In T. Globerson & T. Zelnicker (Eds.), *Human development: Vol. 3. Cognitive style and cognitive development* (pp. 172–191). Norwood, NJ: Ablex.

Zhang, H., Mou, W., & McNamara, T. P. (2011). Spatial updating according to a fixed reference direction of a briefly viewed layout. *Cognition, 119,* 419–429.

Zillmer, E. A., & Spiers, M. V. (2001). *Principles of neuropsychology.* Belmont, CA: Wadsworth.

Zöllig, J. Mattli, F., Sutter, C., Aurelio, A., & Martin, M. (2012). Plasticity of prospective memory through a familiarization intervention in old adults. *Aging, Neuropsychology, and Cognition, 19,* 168–194.

INDEX

ability(ies)
  difference, 348–352
  gender difference in, 360–367
ablation, brain, 30
academic thinking, 401
acceptable evidence, 355
accuracy, 85
achievement motivation, 368
active-passive, 374
act models, 164–166
adaptive control of thought
  (ACT) model of memory,
  164–166
affordances, 60
aging effects on cognition,
  357–358
ambiguity, 223
amnesia, 149–153
amygdala, 27
analogical reasoning, 279,
  288–289
analytic approach to processing
  information, 339
anchoring, 301–302
anomaly, 223
anterograde amnesia, 150–151
antisaccade, 113
aphasia, 30–31, 244
apperceptive agnosia, 61
artifact concepts, 181
artificial intelligence, 12
assertives, 224
associational fluency, 348
associative
  agnosia, 62
  memory, 348
attention, 2, 66–67
  divided (see Divided attention)
  encoding, 339–340
  neural underpinnings of,
    79–81
  selective (see Selective
    attention)
attentional capture, 88–89
attentional (controlled) processing, 83–86
attention hypothesis of automatization, 91

attenuation theory, 73
auditory perception, 40
autobiographical memory,
  139–142
automatic
  encoding, 137
  processing, 83–86
availability, 296–299
  heuristic, 296

bachelor concept, 170
back propagation procedure,
  167
backtracking, 256–258
Baddeley model of working
  memory, 109–111
basic level of categorization, 172
behaviorism, 6–8, 22
believability effects, 286
Bell Curve, 350
between-subjects design, 14
bias(es), 292, 296
  confirmation (see Confirma-
    tion bias)
  hindsight (see Hindsight bias)
binaural presentation, 69
bodily-kinesthetic intelligence,
  351
bottom-up (data-driven) process, 45–53
brain
  imaging, 16
  -imaging techniques, 33–36
  interest in localizing language
    function in, 244
  lateralization of function,
    31–33
  localization of function, 29–31
  localizing memory in, 114
  recording techniques, 36–37
  structure of, 26–29
bridging inferences, 234
Broca aphasia, 244

calibration curve, 306
called to mind, 175. See also
  Exemplars

capacity, 103–104
  of LTM, 120–121
  of STM, 103
categorical constituent structure
  of sentence, 220
categorical perception, 50
categorical syllogisms, 285–286
category/categorization, 169
  classical view of, 169–170
  exemplar view of, 175–177
  knowledge-based view of,
    180–183
  prototype view of concepts,
    171–175
  schemata/scripts view of,
    177–180
central executive, 109–110
cerebellum, 27
cerebral cortex, 27, 80
childhood sexual abuse (CSA),
  149
chunking, 104
circular reactions, concept of,
  323
classical conditioning, 6
classical view of concepts and
  categorization, 169–170
classic problems, 253–260
clinical interviews, 15
cocktail party effect, 70–71
codes in long-term memory
  dual-coding hypothesis, 188
  relational-organizational
    hypothesis, 189
coding, 103–104
  of LTM, 121
cognition process, 3, 7, 12–13,
  16, 18–22, 376
  effects of aging on, 357–358
  gender differences in (see
    Gender differences in cog-
    nition)
  individual differences in (see
    Individual differences in
    cognition)
  influences on study of, 4
  language and (see Language
    and cognition)

cognitive abilities, 399
    with intelligence, 348
cognitive architecture theory,
    166
cognitive collage, 209
cognitive development, 319.
        See also Piagetian theory
    non-Piagetian approaches
        to, 329–337
cognitive economy, 160–161
cognitive illusions in decision
    making. See Decision
    making, cognitive illusions
    in
cognitive issues, 4
cognitive map, 209
cognitive neuropsychology, 68
cognitive overload, 293–294
cognitive processes, 2–3
cognitive psychology, 1, 7,
    99–100, 125, 145, 159
    beginning of, 25
    domain of, 2
    paradigms of, 17–22
    research methods in, 13–16
cognitive revolution, 10–13
cognitive science, 10–13
cognitive skills, 399
cognitive styles, 352–354
    gender differences in, 367–
        370
cognitive tempo, 353
collectivism, 374
commissives, 224
commonsense knowledge, 159
communication, 215–216
comprehending text passages,
    232–235
computerized axial tomogra-
    phy (CAT) scan, 33
computer metaphor, 12
concepts, 168–169
    classical view of, 169–170
    dimensions of, 182
    exemplar view of, 175–177
    knowledge-based view of,
        180–183
    prototype view of concepts,
        171–175
    schemata/scripts view of,
        177–180
conceptually driven process.
        See Top-down process
concrete operations stage in

Piagetian theory, 326–327
conditional reasoning, 284
configural superiority effect
    (CSE), 45
confirmation bias, 290, 304–
    305
connected
    knowing, 369
    learning, 369–370
connectionism, 18–19
connectionist approach, 18–19
connectionist model of word
    perception, 57–58
connectionist models, 166–168
consciousness, raw materials
    of, 5
consistent-mapping condition,
    84–85
consonants, 218–219
constructivist approach to per-
    ception, 58
content effect, 284
context effects, 53, 227
contradiction, 282
contrary recognition, 272
controlled
    observation, 15
    processing, 85
convergence schema, 260
corpus callosum, 31
counterfactual inference, 243
creative solutions, finding of,
    270–271
creative thinking, 251
creativity, 271
critical thinking, 273–274
cross-cultural cognition of per-
    ception, 377–382
cross-cultural research, 373,
    376–377
cross-cultural studies
    of categorization, 385–389
    of counting, 391–394
    of memory, 382–385
    of reasoning, 389–391
CT scan, 33
cue overload, 128
cultural
    complexity, 374
    relativism, 376
    stereotypes, 360
    syndromes, 374–375
    universality, 376
    variation, 374

culture, 373–374
    affect cognition and cogni-
        tive development, 395
    aspects of, 376
    cross-cultural research (see
        Cross-cultural research)
    meaning of, 375

decays, 105
decision board technique, 311
decision making, 2, 278
    cognitive illusions in, 295–
        306
    descriptive models of, 312–
        313
    meaning of, 292–293
    neuropsychological evidence
        on, 313–314
    phases of, 294–295
    rationality of, 293
    utility models of, 306–311
declarations, 224
declarative memory, 134, 165
deductive
    reasoning, 280–288
    validity, 280
deferred imitation, 324
demand characteristics,
    201–202
descriptive models of decision
    making, 307
dichotic listening task, 69
digit span, 339
dilemma, 293
directed remembering, 272
directives, 224
direct perception, 58–61
distal stimulus, 40
diverted attention, 87, 89–93
divided attention, 68, 89–93
domain-specific process, 240
dual-coding hypothesis, 188
dual-task performance, 89–91

ears, 69
echo, 101
echoic memory, 101–103
ecological approach, 20–21
ecological validity, 15
effect size, 361
effort, 75
electroencephalography (EEG),
    36–37
elimination by aspects, 311

emergence in perception, 45
empirical investigations of
    imagery, 189–191
empiricism, 4
encoding, 97
    specificity, 127
    variability, 128
English
    sentence, 217
    syntax, 217
enhancing-of-processing net-
    work, 80
entailment, 223
episodic buffer, 110
episodic memory, 129–131
epochs, 167
evaluation of decision, 295
even number concept, 170
event-related potentials (ERPs),
    36–37, 80–81, 207
everyday mechanisms, 272–
    273
everyday reasoning, 291–292
evolutionary approach, 19–20
executive functioning, 113–114
of brain, 27
exemplars, 175
exemplar view of concepts and
    categorization, 175–177
exhaustive search, 108
existential intelligence, 351
expectation effects, 53
expected utility (EU) theory,
    307–309
experimental control, 15
experimenter expectancy
    effects, 202
experiments, 3, 5, 13–14
expert difference, 356
expert–novice differences
    study, 265
expert systems, 269–270
explanation-based category,
    182
explicit memory, 131–133
expressional fluency, 349
expressive aphasia, 244
expressives, 224
extended event, 141
eyewitness memory, 144–146

faculty psychology, 29–30
failure feedback, 368
fallacies, 283

false belief task, 344
false memory, 146–149
family resemblance structure of
    concepts, 171
fan effect, 125
featural analysis, 48–51
feature integration theory,
    86–88
features, 48
field dependence (FD),
    352–353
field independence (FI),
    352–353
figure-ground organization, 42
filter theory of attention, 70, 73
final choice of decision, 295
flashbulb memory, 142–144
focused thinking, 251
forebrain, 27–29, 37
forgetting, 97, 104–106,
    121–125
formal operations stage in
    Piagetian theory, 327–328
formal reasoning, 291–292
formation of concepts, 168–169
frame
    size, 84
    time, 84
framing effects, 301
frontal lobe, 27
functional fixedness, 263
functionalism, 5–6, 8, 22
functional magnetic resonance
    imaging (fMRI), 35–37,
    149, 207, 246

gambler fallacy, 299
garden path sentences, 230
gathering of information,
    294–295
gaze durations of typical
    reader, 232
gender differences
    in cognition, 358–360
    in learning and cognitive
        styles, 367–370
    in skills and abilities,
        360–367
generalized event representa-
    tions (GERs), 342
general problem solver (GPS),
    255
general reasoning, 348
generate-and-test technique,

253–254
generative grammar, 11
geographic knowledge, 158
geons, 49
Gestalt principles of perceptual
    organization, 43
Gestalt psychology, 8
given–new strategy, 233
grammar, 215, 217
    proposed semantic relations
        for early, 333
    story (see Story grammars)
Gricean maxims of conversa-
    tion, 237–240
gustatory (taste) perception, 40

haptic (touch) perception, 40
helpless orientation, 368
heuristics, 196, 296
hierarchical semantic network
    model of semantic mem-
    ory, 161
hierarchy of color terms in dif-
    ferent languages, 243
hindbrain, 26–27, 37
hindsight bias, 304
hippocampus, 27
holistic approach to processing
    information, 339
honor, 374
horizontal relationship, 374
human cognition, 17
human–environment interac-
    tion, 395
human factors engineering, 10
human intelligences, 351
hypothalamus, 27
hypothesis testing, 288,
    290–291

iconic memory, 100–101
ill-defined problems, 252
illegal
    sentences, 219, 221
    stories, 235
illusory
    conjunctions, 87
    contours, 42–43
    correlation, 302–303
image theory, 312
imaginal scanning, 194
immediacy assumption, 232
implicit
    encoding/encoded, 198

knowledge, 159–160
learning, 176
memory, 131–133
impulsivity, 353
inattentional blindness, 76–79
incidental learning, 135
incoming messages, 73
incomplete representations, 263–264
incorrect representations, 263–264
incubation, 271–272
individual differences, 347
in cognition, 348–358
study of, 9
individualism, 374
induction, 288, 348
inductive
reasoning, 280, 288–291
strength, 280
inference rules, 269
informationally encapsulated process, 241
information overload, strategies for coping with, 294
information-processing approach, 17–19
instrumental conditioning, 6
intelligence, 348, 351
interacting images, 126
interactive processing, 271
interference, 105
interpersonal intelligence, 351
intrapersonal intelligence, 351
introspection, 5, 7, 16
instructions for, 252
investigations of neural underpinnings, 16
invisible colleges, 369

knowledge. See also Category/categorization; Concepts
base and structures, 341–342
-based view of concepts and categorization, 180–183
organizing, 159–168
representation, 2
Korsakoff syndrome, 132

language, 2
acquisition, 331
and cognition, 240–246
comprehension and production, 225–240
knowledge, 160
leaning, 331
production, 214
structure of, 216–225
use, 215
language acquisition device (LAD), 331
late childhood, reasoning abilities development in, 335–337
lateralization, 245
learning
connected (see Connected learning)
gender differences in (see Gender differences in learning)
styles, 354–356
legal sentences, 219
length estimation, 349
letter span, 339
levels-of-processing theory of memory, 134–137
lexical ambiguity, 230
lexical decision tasks, 162
lexicons, 160
limited-capacity processors of information, 10–11
linguistic(s), 11
competence, 218
intelligence, 351
performance, 218
literacy, 394–399. See also Schooling
localization of function, 12
logical connectives, 281
logical-mathematical intelligence, 351
long-term memory (LTM), 98–99, 103, 111, 113, 135, 139
aspects of, 120–129
codes in (see Codes in long-term memory)
subdivisions of, 129–134
long-term potentiation, 115
long-term storage (LTS), 98

magnetic resonance imaging (MRI), 33–34
magnetoencephalography (MEG), 36–37
masking, 101

mastery orientation, 368
matching familiar figures test (MFFT), 353
matrix completion problems, 289
means–ends analysis, 254–256
mechanically repetitive, 274
medulla, 26
memorable events, 141
memorial strategies, 334
memory(ies), 2
autobiographical (see Autobiographical memory)
consolidation, 153
eyewitness (see Eyewitness memory)
false (see False memory)
flashbulb (see Flashbulb memory)
levels-of-processing view, 134–137
long-term memory (LTM) (see Long-term memory (LTM))
malleability, 145
neurological studies of, 114–116
race, 97
reconstructive nature of, 137–153
recovered (see Recovered memory)
set, 84
set size, 107
short-term memory (STM) (see Short-term memory (STM))
span, 338
traditional approaches to study of, 98–108
working (see Working memory)
memory works, study by psychologists, 3
mental
association, 4
effort, 75
phenomena, 7
pictures, 187, 202
representations, 7–8, 159, 182
rotation of images, 191–194
set, 261
mental imagery
criticism of research and

theory, 201–206
nature of, 198
meta-analysis, 361
metacognition, 343–345
metacognitive
experiences, 343
knowledge, 343–344
regulation, 344
method of loci, 125
midbrain, 26–27, 37
middle childhood, reasoning
abilities development in,
335–337
mind hypothesis, 232
mind theory, 344
misremembering, 123
mnemonics, 125
modal model of memory, 98
modularity hypothesis, 240–
241
modus ponens rule, 282–283
modus tollens rule, 282–283,
291
mood-dependent memory
effect, 128
morphemes, 216–217
morphology, 216
motivation for cognitive tasks,
368–369
motor cortex, 27
multiattribute utility theory
(MAUT), 309–311
multiple intelligences (MI)
theory, 352
musical intelligence, 351

narrative review, 360
nativism, 4
naturalistic observation, 14–15
naturalist intelligence, 351
natural-kind concepts, 181
need for cognition (NFC), concept of, 354
network models, 160–164
networks of visual attention, 80
neural networks, 18
neurological maturation,
337–338
neuropsychological findings of
visual imagery, 206–208
neuropsychological views and
evidence, 244–246
neuroscience, 12
new instances, categorization

of, 168–169
Newsweek, 233
nominal-kind concepts, 181
nomination, 333
nonanalytic concept formation,
176
nonexistence, 333
nonsense syllables, 123
non-specific goal participants,
268
nonstage theories of cognitive
development, 319–320
normative models of decision
making, 306–307
noticing, 272
noun phrases (NP), 220–222
novice difference, 356
number facility, 348

object permanence, concept
of, 323
occipital lobe, 27
odd-quadrant discrimination
task, 44–45
olfactory perception, 40
operational network, 80
overconfidence, 305–306
overloaded attention, 87

paired associates learning, 123
paradigm, 17
parallel-distributed processing
(PDP), 18
parallel search, 107
parietal lobe, 27
pattern recognition, 2, 41
pay attention, 68
pegword method, 126
percept, 40
perception, 2, 63, 66, 99
bottom-up (data-driven)
process (*see* Bottom-up
(data-driven) process)
direct (*see* Direct perception)
disruptions of, 61–62
Gestalt approaches to,
41–45
meaning of, 39, 377–378
picture (*see* Picture perception)
top-down processes (*see*
Top-down processes)
types of, 40
perceptual
development in infancy,

330–331
encoding, 339–340
equivalence, 199
learning, 55–56
set, 261
speed, 349
person–machine system, 10
phoneme(s), 49, 216–217, 218
phoneme restoration effect,
227
phones, 218
phonetic(s), 218
ambiguity, 230
phonological
buffer, 111
loop, 110
rules, 219
phonology, 216, 218–219, 222
photograph perception, 380
phrase, 217
structure rules, 221
phrenology, 29–30
physical skills, 66
Piagetian theory
general principles, 320–322
post-Piagetian answers to
question what develops,
337–345
reactions to, 328
stages of development,
322–328
picture
metaphor, 202–205
perception, 378–381
pivot grammar, 332
plasticity of brain, 31
pluralistic theory of mind, 351
pons, 27
pop-out phenomena, 88
positron emission tomography
(PET), 34–36, 115, 207,
245–246
practice, 90
automaticity and effects of,
82–89
of schooling, 398
pragmatics, 217, 224–225
prefrontal cortex, 27, 337
preloaders, 399
premises, 278
preoperational stage in Piagetian theory, 324–326
preposing works, 221
preschoolers use of memorial

strategies, 334–335
prescriptive models of decision making, 307
prescriptive rules, 217
primacy effect, 98–99
primary circular reactions, 323
primary somatosensory cortex, 30
primed, 73
principle of closure, 43–44
principle of common fate, 43–44
principle of good continuation, 43–44
principle of proximity, 42–43
principle of similarity, 42–43
proactive interference (PI), 124
probe digit task, 105
problem, definition of, 260
problem solving, 2, 250, 278
  blocks to, 260–266
problem space hypothesis, 266–269
problem-specific knowledge or expertise, 264–266
procedural memory, 134
product assemblers, 399
production
  deficiency, 343
  rules, 165
proposition, 281
propositional complexity, 233
propositional reasoning, 281–285
propositional theory, 205–206
prosopagnosia, 62
prototype, 51
  matching, 51–53
prototype view of concepts, 171–175
proximal stimulus, 40–41
psychological essentialism, 180
pursuit rotor task, 112

quantifiers, 285
quantitative abilities, 365–367
quasi-experiments, 13–14

rationality of decision, 293
real-life expert decision making, 313
reasoning, 2, 278–280
  abilities, 365–367

by analogy, 258–260
deductive reasoning (see Deductive reasoning)
development of abilities in middle and late childhood for, 335–337
everyday reasoning (see Everyday reasoning)
inductive reasoning (see Inductive reasoning)
neuropsychological evidence on, 313–314
rebuses, 271
recall, 2, 131
  of events, 141
recency effect, 98–99
receptive aphasia, 244
recognition, 2
  by components, 49
  -primed decision making, 313
recovered memory, 146–149
recurrence, 333
reflective thinking, 273
reflectivity, 353
rehearsal, 99
relational-organizational hypothesis, 189
repetition priming, 132
representativeness heuristic, 299–300
repressed memories, 147
retention duration of memory, 104–106, 121–125
retina, 40
retinal image, 40
retrieval, 96
  cue, 124, 127
  of information, 107–108, 125–129
retroactive interference, 124
retrograde amnesia, 151–153
rewrite rules, 221

scanning images, 194–197
schemata, 137, 235–236
schemata/scripts view of concepts and categorization, 177–180
schema theory, 75–76, 177, 259
schooling, 394–399
science of mind, 5
scripts, 178–179, 342

Searle speech act theory, 224
secondary circular reactions, 323–324
secondary memory, 98
selective attention, 68–81
self-contradiction, 223
self-terminating search, 107
semantic(s), 216, 222–224
  functions, 333
  memory, 129–131, 140, 160, 169
  network, 160, 162
  priming, 168
sensitivity to problems, 348
sensorimotor stage in Piagetian theory, 322–324
sensory memory, 98. See also Perception
  meaning of, 99
  types of, 100–103
sentences, 217, 219
  comprehension, 229–232
  structure of, 220–221
separate
  knowing, 369–370
  network, 80
serial
  position effect, 98
  search, 107
series completion, 289
setting goals in decision, 294
shadow speech, 227
short-term memory (STM), 98–99, 103, 105–106, 112–113, 119, 134
  capacity and coding, 103–104
  retention duration and forgetting, 104–106
  retrieval of information, 106–108
silly sentences task, 112
simple propositions, 281
single-photon emission computed tomography (SPECT), 35, 37
situated cognition, 399–402
size constancy, 41
social exchange, 285
solution, general methods of, 253–260
space around the body, 208
space of navigation, 208–209
space of the body, 208

spacing effect, 128
span memory, 348
spatial
  cognition, 208–212
  equivalence, 199–200
  intelligence, 351
  orientation, 349
  updating, 209
specific goal participants, 268
speech
  errors in production, 228–229
  perception, 225–228
split-brained patients, 32–33
spontaneous flexibility, 349
sports psychologists, 187
spotlight approaches to attention, 74–75
spreading activation theory, 162–163
stages, 319
stage theories of cognitive development, 319
state-dependent learning, 128
state-dependent memory, 128
storage, 97
stored knowledge, 158–159
story grammars, 235–237
strategies, 342–343
stroop task, 82–83
structural equivalence, 200–201
structuralism, 5, 8, 22
structure score, 268
structuring decision, 295
study of mathematically precocious youth (SMPY), 365–367
subjective contours, 42–43
subordinate levels of categories, 172–173
suffix effect, 102
summarized events, 141
sunk cost effects, 302
superordinate levels of categories, 172–173
syllogistic reasoning, 285–288, 348
symbolic distance effect, 190

synonymy, 223
syntactic
  ambiguity, 230
  grammars, 235
syntactically ambiguous, 230
syntax, 216, 219–222

tacit knowledge, 201–202, 207
tautology, 282
template(s), 46–47
  matching, 46–48
temporal lobe, 27
tertiary circular reactions, 324
testing effect, 129
thalamus, 27
theory-driven process. See Top-down process
thinking, 250–251, 278, 401
three-term series problems, 197
tightness, 374
Time, 233
Toddlers' acquisition of syntax, 331–334
top-down process, 45, 53–58
trajectory image, 312
transcranial magnetic stimulation (TMS), 36–37
transformational
  equivalence, 200
  rule, 222
triangle concept, 170
true experiment, 13–14
truth table, 282
tumor problem, 258
typicality effect, 163

unattended
  ear, 71
  films, 76
unconscious processing, 271–272
underconfidence, 306
unfocused thinking, 251
ungrammatical
  sentences, 235
  stories, 235
unilateral neglect, 62
unrecalled items, 140

utility, 307

value image, 312
varied-mapping condition, 84–85
verbal
  abilities, 361–362, 365
  comprehension, 348
verb phrase (VP), 221–222
vertical relationship, 374
visual
  agnosias, 61–62
  illusions, 381–382
  images, 187, 202, 207
  memory, 101
  perception, 40, 187
  search task, 50, 83
visual imagery, 187
  principles of, 198–201
visualization, 349
visuospatial
  abilities, 362–365
  sketch pad, 110
vote counting, 360
vowels, 218–219

Wada test, 245
Wason selection task, 283, 285
well-defined problems, 252–253
Wernicke aphasia, 244
Wernicke area, 244
whole-report condition, 100–101
Whorfian hypothesis, 241–244
within-subjects design, 14
word, 217
  advantage, 56
  span, 339
  stem completion task, 132
  superiority effect, 56–57
working backward, 256
working memory (WM), 97, 99, 108–115
  capacity and processing speed, 338–339

X-ray CT, 33